Public Law after the Human Rights Act

Tom Hickman

·H A R T·
PUBLISHING

OXFORD AND PORTLAND, OREGON
2010

Published in the United Kingdom by Hart Publishing Ltd
16C Worcester Place, Oxford, OX1 2JW
Telephone: +44 (0)1865 517530
Fax: +44 (0)1865 510710
E-mail: mail@hartpub.co.uk
Website: http://www.hartpub.co.uk

Published in North America (US and Canada) by
Hart Publishing
c/o International Specialized Book Services
920 NE 58th Avenue, Suite 300
Portland, OR 97213-3786
USA
Tel: +1 503 287 3093 or toll-free: (1) 800 944 6190
Fax: +1 503 280 8832
E-mail: orders@isbs.com
Website: http://www.isbs.com

British Library Cataloguing in Publication Data
Data Available

ISBN: 978-1-84113-969-2

Typeset by Hope Services, Abingdon
Printed and bound in Great Britain by
TJ International Ltd, Padstow, Cornwall

FOREWORD

The Human Rights Act 1998 was a major watershed in UK public law. It is arguably the most important statute to impact on public law in the last century, and that is so notwithstanding continuing academic debate as to the precise extent of its effect in particular areas. The HRA has been of major significance in the reconfiguration of public law, and the shift towards a culture of justification that has been noted in the literature. The very profile of judicial review has altered such that there are far more cases raising rights-based claims in the context of judicial review than there were hitherto, and this is so notwithstanding the fact that prior to the HRA the courts had held that ECHR rights were embedded in the common law.

The HRA has posed new challenges for the judiciary at all levels, as the courts have grappled with the demands posed by the legislation. They have had to fashion the standard of review that is to apply under the HRA, the extent to which some deference or respect should be shown to the initial decision-maker and the factors that should be taken into account when making this determination. They have had to adjudicate on complex issues that were only partially resolved by the HRA itself, including matters as diverse as the approach to be taken to the interpretation of legislation under section 3 HRA, the meaning to be accorded to public authority for the purposes of the HRA, and the circumstances in which damages can be awarded when HRA rights are breached.

The judicial decisions on these and other matters have generated much public law scholarship, with articles and books analyzing such decisions from a variety of perspectives. There has, unsurprisingly, been debate and disagreement concerning the implications of such rulings in terms of positive law, and the desirability of the outcome in normative terms.

Tom Hickman's book on *Public Law after the Human Rights Act* constitutes a welcome and important addition to this literature. The author is well-placed to undertake this inquiry. He is an academic whose name is already well-known through a series of valuable and thought-provoking publications on a range of public law issues, including contributions that have tackled some of the central adjudicative issues that have arisen under the HRA. He is also a barrister in a leading set of public law chambers, and hence brings to this study the experience that comes from arguing such matters before the highest UK courts.

This book, as the title suggests, addresses central issues raised by the HRA and places them in the context of a broader inquiry as to their impact on public law. It is this very breadth of the study that makes it especially significant. Tom confronts foundational questions such as the relationship between the Human Rights Act and the common law, whether there is need to invent new public law doctrines to accommodate the Act, whether the HRA will lead to the demise of established doctrine, and the effect of the Act on the overall structure of public law. There are chapters dealing with the Common Law and the Human Rights Act, Constitutional Theory and Constitutional Dialogue, Standards and Rights in Public Law, Weight and Deference, Proportionality, Reasonableness, the Forbidden Process Element in Human Rights Review, the Substance and Structure of Public Law after the Human Rights Act, and the Right of Access to Court.

The inquiry is pursued vigorously through close analysis of case law and the academic literature. Tom has not been afraid to challenge those of all persuasions. Judicial decisions are criticized where it is felt that the courts have not reached the best result in relation to a central issue under the HRA. So too academics, when Tom believes that their approach to a particular doctrinal or conceptual issue is wanting. There will doubtless be those who disagree with Tom's own reasoning. It is a testimony to this valuable book that it will stimulate further debate on the central themes that pervade the Human Rights Act and its impact on public law. The book will be of interest to academics and practitioners alike.

Paul Craig
April 2010
Professor of English Law
University of Oxford

PREFACE

This book took shape over a number of years and at times there seemed little prospect of it ever being completed. Some of the material has already seen the light of day in articles in various law journals. For a time the idea was to publish a collection of lightly revised articles as studies on public law and human rights, with a little new material linking them all together. However, the linking material had something of the property of magic beans and it just kept on growing. The result is that six of the ten chapters in this book are entirely new (chapters 1, 2, 4, 5, 8 and 9). In addition, I have updated, corrected, added-to and generally fiddled-with the other material to such an extent that only chapters 6 and 11 remain essentially as previously published.[1] In some respects, the completed text still retains the character of a series of studies of central topics in public law. I make no claim to comprehensiveness. Whilst I hope that this book will be of interest to undergraduate students of public law it is not a textbook. Nor has it the unity of argument and comprehensive sweep of many legal monographs. A number of important issues relating to the interface of public law and human rights in the UK are not discussed here at any length and others are not discussed at all.

Two such issues merit mentioning. The first is the increasing resort to 'closed' hearings, based on 'closed' pleadings and evidence which is not disclosed to one of the parties. In place of disclosure a 'special advocate' is usually appointed to represent the interests of the disadvantaged party.[2] This process is an out-growth from immigration appeals in national security cases heard in the Special Immigration Appeals Commission. The propriety and proper boundaries of such an approach raises difficult questions which need urgently to be addressed by public lawyers, but it goes beyond the scope of this book to engage with them. The second subject I wish to mention is the relationship between public law principles and tort law and the blurring of the distinction between public and private law. This subject is discussed only partially in this book. I regret the omission of a chapter devoted to tort law and human rights as this was the subject which started me

---

[1] As 'The Substance and Structure of Proportionality' [2008] *PL* 694 and 'Between Human Rights and the Rule of Law: Indefinite Detention and the Derogation Model of Constitutionalism' (2005) 68 *MLR* 655. However these have been tweaked and a Postscript and lengthy footnote addressing an important article by John Finnis added to the latter. Other chapters have drawn on material published as, 'Constitutional Dialogue, Constitutional Theories and the Human Rights Act 1998' [2005] *PL* 306; 'Judges and Politicians after the Human Rights Act 1998: A Comment' [2008] *PL* 84; 'The Reasonableness Principle: Reassessing its place in the Public Sphere' (2004) 63 *CLJ* 166; 'The "Uncertain Shadow": Throwing Light on the Right to a Court under Article 6(1) ECHR' [2004] *PL* 122 some ideas are reflected in parts of J Beatson, S Grosz, T Hickman, R Singh *Human Rights: Judicial Protection in the UK* (Sweet & Maxwell, 2008).

[2] See the excellent report of Justice, 'Secret Evidence', June 2009 (Justice, London 2009).

down the road that led to this book, but the tort beans fell on fallow ground and since the beanstalk had grown quite tall enough, the chapter was never written.[3]

In working towards this book I have incurred many debts and any attempt to recall everyone who has generously given their time to answering questions, reading draft papers and providing support would fail to identify them all. Many have been acknowledged along the way, in journal articles and other projects. Over the past year, in which the book came together, I have benefitted greatly from the input and advice of David Dyzenhaus, Tom Poole, Raynor Thwaites, Adam Tomkins and Jeff King, all of whom have contributed to particular chapters through discussions or by commenting—in Jeff's case extensively—on drafts. Tim Owen QC kindly allowed me to quiz him about *Pierson's Case* and has provided me with a fascinating insight into the development of the case law on common law fundamental rights.

I am particularly grateful to David Dyzenhaus and the Faculty of Law at the University of Toronto for arranging for me to spend several weeks at the Faculty in the summer of 2009 as a visiting research fellow, without which the book could not have been completed. The University of Toronto Law Faculty is a fantastic institution and an unusually stimulating academic environment. I am proud to be one of its alumni and grateful that it continues to extend its hospitality. I must specifically thank the staff at the Bora Laskin Law Library for facilitating access to resources (including the invaluable but elusive late key) as well as fixing my laptop, which exploded at the worst moment.

I am also very grateful indeed to the Alexander Maxwell Scholarship Trust which granted me a scholarship to fund the research period in Toronto. Again, without the Trust's generous support the book would not have been completed. The Trust has an increasingly important role in assisting public law research in the UK to come to fruition. Details about the Trust can be found on the next page. Javan Herberg's support in my application to the Trust was greatly appreciated.

For agreeing to publish this book I have to thank Richard Hart, who has been amazingly attentive and accommodating since I first approached him with the idea. His team, in particular Rachel Turner, have been fantastic and have turned the manuscript around in an unbelievably short period of time. For agreeing to the re-publication of material, I am grateful to *Public Law*, the *Modern Law Review* and the *Cambridge Law Journal*. In the very final stages I benefitted from the assistance of Justin Lesley, a recent graduate and already a fine lawyer, who read, corrected and commented on many of the chapters. I would also like to thank Sir Jack Beatson, who has been a source of encouragement and inspiration since I first began researching and thinking seriously about these issues a decade ago. I am extremely grateful to him. Finally, I would like to thank Paul Craig for kindly agreeing to write a foreword to this book. Paul Craig's extraordinary contribution to public law scholarship has influenced my own thinking and writing about public law in countless ways and I am privileged that he has agreed to introduce the book.

---

[3] See eg, T R Hickman, 'Tort law, public authorities and the Human Rights Act 1998' in J Bell, D Fairgrieve and M Andenas, *Liability of Public Authorities in Comparative Perspective* (BIICL, London, 2002) ch 2.

LAW SCHOLARSHIP TRUST

CONTENTS

Contents

Contents

TABLE OF CASES

TABLE OF LEGISLATION

National Legislation

Australia

Canada

Israel

New Zealand

United States

1

Introduction

HUMAN RIGHTS PRINCIPLES have transformed public law in the United Kingdom. The transformation began well before the Human Rights Act 1998 (Human Rights Act) but the Human Rights Act represented a shift in gear. It accelerated the re-configuration of public law so that modern civil and political rights and freedoms, as set out in post-war international human rights instruments, are at its core and radiate even into areas seemingly distant from human rights concerns, such as planning disputes, taxation and hunting with hounds, to name but a very few. As the title suggests, this book is about how human rights principles have integrated with public law doctrines and, most importantly, how they *should* integrate. It is a book about the transformation of public law.[1] The book examines core public law principles and doctrines such as *Wednesbury* unreasonableness and process review, and it explains how these can and should be affected by human rights principles. It also critically examines principles which, rightly or wrongly, come bound-up with imported human rights jurisprudence, such as the doctrines of proportionality and due deference and the notion of derogation. It argues for organic change within the existing mechanics of public law, without the need for further radical doctrinal innovation. It rejects the idea that the reception of human rights principles should lead to public law becoming entirely rights-orientated or reduced to a single test of substantive justification. Human rights principles bring with them new complexities, new standards and new distinctions. These must integrate with the existing doctrines of public law and not supplant them.

The book also looks beyond the doctrines and the structure of public law to the underlying conception of constitutionalism that these reflect. The reception of human rights principles is part of an adjustment of not only the surface

---

[1] The term 'public law' is itself ambiguous and it is not used in a consistent way in this book. In part this is because of the ambiguity of the term itself, in part it is because it follows the usage of the courts (Lord Diplock, as we shall see, attributed a particular meaning to 'public law', which was a term that he himself introduced into domestic law), and in part this is because of the way the term has been used when material has been published previously. I prefer to use the term to mean the law relating to public bodies, whether this law relates to damages claims in tort, administrative law claims or claims under the Human Rights Act; but often the term is used in a more specific way to mean administrative law. I have reverted to more specific terminology where the context seems to require it.

architecture of public law but also of the constitution itself, and the relationship between law and politics. But again, the book argues that although courts have been given new powers and responsibilities their basic function and relationship to the other branches of the state should not be radically altered. The functions of judges and politicians remain distinct. It has always been the function of courts to determine what the law is and what rights people have. That remains the case, although the nature of those rights has changed. It also remains the case that courts interact with Government and Parliament in subtle and constructive ways. Their constitutional function in public law cases is not and never has been simply a matter of cutting-down political projects when they transgress legal rights and legal authority. Courts inculcate change, and they avoid determining the extent of our legal rights as often as they determine them. Furthermore, courts rightly have regard to the limitations of legal adjudication in determining whether our rights have been breached. But they ought never to renounce responsibility for determining what our rights are. They may have to give weight to assessments made by others as part of undertaking the task of determining whether there has been a violation of a protected right. They may even decide that the issue is one for another day. But they should never decide that the issue is for another person.

Given this, it is necessary for courts to define the scope of our rights in a way that balances the interests of the individual against those of the wider community. There must be sufficient scope, within the confines of what is unlawful, for the community to pursue its projects. But ultimately it falls to the courts to uphold the requirements of principle even where these conflict with a present expediency. For this reason, the constitutional system quite properly allows Parliament to have the last word. This is not so that Parliament can redefine the scope of fundamental principles, but to allow Parliament to depart from them. Under the Human Rights Act, Parliament retains the power to overrule judicial decisions. Rights-defying legislation also cannot be struck-down. This enables expediency to trump rights, but the politicians must face up to the injustice and must bear the political cost. The burden and the responsibility fall on society's representatives and not on the courts. The system under the Human Rights Act also allows the Government to derogate from human rights principles, which avoids adverse judicial determinations as to the justice of the measures in question. But it does not avoid the need for the Government and Parliament to face up to the fact that they are acting unjustly, since they must accept that they are disapplying human rights protections by the process of derogation.

In charting this path through public law doctrines and public law theory, this book seeks to steer a middle course between a functionalist, positivistic approach to public law, which views public law as a means of ensuring effective implementation of political projects, and a liberal legalist approach which views public law as a means of upholding inviolable rights and freedoms in the face of the majority's wishes. To invoke the well-known but still illuminating traffic light metaphor, the book seeks to rejuvenate an 'amber light' approach to public law and to take such an approach forward into the human rights era.[2] An 'amber light' approach recognises that part of the function of public law is to permit and enhance political projects, as well as curbing them. It thus emphasises the value of procedural as well as substantive norms, and the standard-setting as well as corrective (reviewing) function of administrative law. It seeks to reconcile the constitutional principle at the heart of the separation of powers that courts, and not Parliament or the executive, determine our rights, with the constitutional truth that Parliament and the executive have the primary role not only for promoting general welfare but also for protecting individual rights through principled projects and principled legislation (such as the Human Rights Act itself). In other words, it recognises the distinct constitutional function of courts and judges but also emphasises the courts' role in supporting and enhancing the 'political constitution'.[3]

This book therefore seeks to develop an account of how the courts should approach and decide human rights cases which is allied to politics, rather than divorced from politics. But it rejects the idea that judges are politicians in robes; just as it rejects the idea that the legal constitution must adopt a deferential posture towards politics and political mechanisms of accountability. The judges are responsible for determining whether our rights have been infringed, but that responsibility is tempered by the limits of their adjudicatory capacity and directed in part at promoting better and more principled governance.

The 'amber light' approach emerges in the discussion in each of the chapters in the following ways:

1. Chapter 2 surveys the changes brought about by the reception of human rights principles into domestic UK law and the way that political reform and legal renovation were interrelated. It outlines the manner in which the Human Rights Act interacts with the common law and uncertain relationship between the two.

2. Chapter 3 argues that the function of the courts is to determine legal rights and defend legal principle but that the relationship between the courts and the political branches at common law and under the Human Rights Act is,

---

[2] C Harlow and R Rawlings *Law and Administration* 2nd edn (London, Butterworths, 1997) ch 4. The amber light approach seems to have been squeezed out of public law thinking. It is true to say that the amber light approach was something of a pragmatic middle-ground between the idea of law as control and law as facilitator of politics, and it was never clearly developed. But amber light theory was regarded (wrongly in my view) as synonymous with liberal legalism by Adam Tomkins in his important article 'In Defence of the Political Constitution'(2002) 22 *OJLS* 157 and it finds no place in the 3rd edition of Harlow and Rawlings' book (Cambridge, Cambridge University Press, 2009). It is best, although incompletely, encapsulated in comments made by Martin Partington, who referred to those who, 'concede the desirability and need for the exercise of public power and thus reject the view that public law should be seen exclusively in terms of control of such power, but would argue that reliance on traditional political techniques for promoting accountability and control . . . is . . . inadequate, and forms of political control need to be buttressed by legal control': 'The Reform of Public Law in Britain: Theoretical Problems and Practical Considerations' in P McAuslan & JF McEldowney (eds), *Law, Legitimacy and the Constitution* (London, Sweet & Maxwell, 1985) 191, 193 (quoted by Michael Taggart in 'Reinvented Government, traffic lights and the convergence of public and private law' (1999) *PL* 124, 124).

[3] See further, T Hickman 'In Defence of the Legal Constitution' (2005) 55 *University of Toronto Law Journal* 981.

nonetheless, not merely the corrective, counterbalancing function of enforcing individual rights against political will but is also part of a constructive institutional dialogue. It describes this dialogue in a way which resists the idea that courts have been transformed into political actors.

3. Chapters 4 examines the transformation of the doctrinal structure of public law as it absorbed human rights principles and came to protect substantive standards and substantive rights. It explains that even human rights principles establish a range of standards that permit more or less scope for political action.

4. Chapter 5 rejects a model of human rights adjudication which requires judicial protection to be accompanied by a doctrine of deference which ascribes different degrees of judicial restraint and attributes primary responsibility for defining the scope of human rights in some contexts to the political branches. At the same time, the discussion accepts that the institutional limitations on courts mean that it is appropriate for courts to afford weight to assessments made by other persons where these are relevant to the court's judgments about whether a protected right has been infringed. It is argued that this is no more than the court performing its established adjudicatory role and is an extension of an ordinary judicial technique, in the field of human rights adjudication.

5. Chapter 6 sets out to show that the doctrine of proportionality has not been applied in a structured or principled manner by domestic courts. Domestic courts should develop a clear and rigorous test for examining the necessity of political projects, whilst at the same time allowing latitude to administrators so that the least intrusive measure does not necessarily have to be chosen in every case.

6. Chapter 7 explains that there remains an important role for a principle of reasonableness in public law after the Human Rights Act even in human rights cases, and examines the history and development of that principle in domestic law and in the case law of the European Court of Human Rights (ECtHR).

7. Chapter 8 emphasises the importance of process review as a means of promoting good decision-making which respects human rights. It demonstrates the importance of process review in human rights adjudication and rejects a blinkered focus on substantive judicial review. Such a focus is a product of the liberal legalist idea that human rights define the parameters of politics and that they do not impose norms aimed at enhancing political decision-making and ensuring that decisions are made properly by the responsible authority. This ignores a crucial dimension both of human rights jurisprudence and their protection through administrative law.

8. Chapter 9 considers substantive public law, and argues against the reduction of substantive public law to a single meta-principle, reflective of some underlying notion of justice or fairness. It defends a more complex architecture of public law principles on the basis of the need for legal certainty as to the standards governing the conduct and decision-making of public officials, and to maintain the normative distinctiveness of fundamental rights.

9. Chapter 10 examines case law on the right of access to court under Article 6 of the European Convention on Human Rights and Fundamental Freedoms

(European Convention) and suggests that it has two components: one procedural, a right of access, and one substantive, reflecting the principle of legal equality. It shows how these have often been collapsed in the case law, which obscures the distinct importance and normative scope of each principle. It is argued that the procedural right ought not to create new substantive rights; but the existence of a procedural right does not preclude the existence of any substantive protection. The substantive protection is reflected in a general constitutional safeguard against persons or groups of persons being elevated above the law's reach or placed beneath its protective embrace.

10. Finally, chapter 11 examines the provisions under the Human Rights Act for derogation from certain Articles. It is suggested that derogation should not be understood in the same way as limitations on rights, which define the scope of rights, but rather as a means of suspending human rights norms altogether to accommodate the political reality of emergency situations. This provides a theoretical basis from which to critically examine the decision of the House of Lords in *A v Secretary of State for the Home Office* (the Belmarsh Case) in which the UK's derogation from Article 5 of the European Convention was held to be invalid.[4]

The publication of this book comes at an interesting and uncertain time for public law. It coincides with the 10-year anniversary of the Human Rights Act coming into effect (on 2 October 2000). It also coincides with the first year of the new UK Supreme Court and a significant changing of the judicial guard.[5] These events might suggest a renewed willingness on the part of the judiciary to apply human rights principles robustly or to forge new paths. But the publication of the book also comes in a general election year, with all three major political parties seemingly committed to further constitutional reform. A change in government with the prospect of a change in the law of human rights in the UK introduces uncertainty that could inhibit judicial creativity and may ultimately curtail the role of courts in protecting human rights, depending on the nature and scope of such reform.

The Leader of the Conservative Party, David Cameron, has pledged to repeal the Human Rights Act if the party gains power at the next election. But he is also committed to enacting a Bill of Rights and this would apparently be designed in a way that continued to confer jurisdiction on domestic courts to enforce the European Convention. He has said that a Bill of Rights needs to, 'protect the fundamental rights set out in the European Convention on Human Rights in clearer and more precise terms'. He has also said that it must enshrine traditional British liberties, such as jury trial, whilst also setting out, 'the fundamental duties and responsibilities of people living in this country both as citizens and foreign nationals'.[6] It is

---

[4] [2005] 2 AC 68

[5] In particular, in the past year the two most senior Law Lords, Lord Bingham and Lord Hoffmann, both of whom have been instrumental in shaping the law under the Human Rights Act, retired.

[6] 'Balancing freedom and security—a modern British Bill of Rights' Centre for Policy Studies, speech 31 July 2006 www.cps.org.uk. This pledge was re-affirmed in *The Sun* newspaper, shortly after *The Sun* announced that it was supporting the Conservative Party in the 2010 General Election

presently unclear whether the 'Bill of Rights' that the Conservatives propose would subtract from the judicial protections under the Human Rights Act, such as by requiring an individual's breach of duty to the community to be balanced against the interference with his rights, or by some other device. It is also unclear whether the Conservative Party would seek to repeal the Human Rights Act before a Bill of Rights had been drawn-up and enacted to replace it.

The Liberal Democrats' policy is broadly similar although they have clearly expressed their desire for a Bill of Rights to build on and go further than the Human Rights Act in terms of protecting individual rights. They are also committed to a written constitutional document that would set out the separation of powers in terms:

> The Liberal Democrats will seek the public's approval to introduce a written constitution for Britain that defines and limits the power of government, with a Bill of Rights at its heart to protect individual rights—including, for the first time, the right to a clean environment. The Bill of Rights will strengthen and entrench the rights guaranteed in the Human Rights Act, which we have consistently supported. The constitution should also set out the powers of Parliament, Ministers, Judges, the Head of State and the national assemblies.[7]

The Labour Party's position is not far removed. In July 2007 the Labour Government published a 'route map' for further constitutional reform and stated that it would open up a 'dialogue within Parliament and with the people' about the potential for enacting a new written constitutional document.[8] In 2008 the Party indicated that it intended to 'move to the next stage in articulating the balance between rights to which we are entitled and obligations we owe each other'.[9] It seemed clear that the Labour Government would seek to introduce a Bill of Rights as part of a new written constitutional settlement. However, the much anticipated (and delayed) Green paper on Rights and Responsibilities, finally published in March 2009,[10] was long on words and short on proposals. It was conspicuously reticent about the Government's constitutional ambitions. On the one hand, and in common with the Conservative Party proposal, it expressed a firm desire for 'individual responsibility' to be 'given greater resonance' in the constitution, and, unlike the Conservatives, it also made clear that human rights would not be made contingent on the satisfaction of individual duties to society. But on the other hand, the Green Paper does not express any clear commitment to a Bill of Rights, at least one that is legally enforceable. It says that a new 'Bill of Rights and

campaign: 'My Blueprint for Britain' *The Sun*, 2 October 2009: 'We will replace the Human Rights Act with a new British Bill of Rights to strengthen Britain's traditional liberties'. *The Sun*, Britain's most read newspaper, has campaigned vociferously for the repeal of the Human Rights Act, and a *Sun* pledge is probably more likely to be kept than one made in an election manifesto.

[7] Liberal Democrats Policy Briefing, 'Civil Liberties' October 2009, p 1 www.libdems.org.uk.

[8] Green Paper 'The Governance of Britain' CM 7170, July 2007; the quotation is HC Debates vol 462 col 819, 3 July 2007 (The Prime Minister Gordon Brown MP).

[9] Justice Minister Michael Wills MP, speech on 'The Constitutional Reform Programme' Lincoln's Inn 14 February 2008.

[10] 'Rights and Responsibilities: developing our constitutional framework' Ministry of Justice, March 2009, Cm 7577.

'Responsibilities' could present an 'opportunity to bring together in one place a range of welfare and other entitlements currently scattered across the UK's legal and political landscape'. But it also expresses a preference for such rights and responsibilities not being, 'directly legally enforceable.'[11]

Whether or not the Human Rights Act is repealed, most of the issues considered in this book are likely to remain highly relevant, particularly if a broadly similar document is enacted in its place. Issues relating to proportionality, reasonableness, deference, and even substantive questions such as the scope of the right of access to the courts are likely to retain a central place in public law and are likely to arise in much the same way under a Bill of Rights. It is in any event desirable that public lawyers have fully considered and understood how the Human Rights Act interacts with public law to ensure that heresies and misconceptions are not to be carried forward with any further constitutional reform. The discussion in this book is also of some relevance to the debate about whether we should have a Bill of Rights and, more particularly, to the structural features that it would be desirable for any future Bill of Rights to have. The lessons that one can draw from the discussion of the Human Rights Act regime in this book include following:

1. Any domestic Bill of Rights that establishes fundamental domestic rights should not be subject to executive curtailment in circumstances where the Government enters into incompatible international obligations or where the United Nations Security Council requires measures to be taken that are incompatible with protected rights. Where new international obligations conflict with fundamental rights and liberties protected in the UK, Parliament should be required to approve a limitation on, or a derogation from, the protected rights (see chapter 2).

2. The Bill of Rights should specify that it does not inhibit common law development (see chapter 2).

3. There should be a power for courts to provide an effective remedy where primary legislation conflicts with Convention rights. This means that courts should be able to invalidate primary legislation enacted by the Westminster Parliament and provide an award of compensation where such legislation infringes protected rights. However, there should be provision for Parliament to have the final word and override any judicial determination, at least prospectively, if unprincipled legislation is considered to be absolutely required. This should require a positive responsive enactment by Parliament and not merely an ability, as under section 4 of the Human Rights Act, for Parliament and the Government to ignore a declaration of incompatibility. This would mean that it would clearly be Parliament's responsibility if a deviation from fundamental principle was considered to be politically necessary, since Parliament would ultimately have the power to effect such a deviation. As Lord Hoffmann stated in *Ex parte Simms*, our politicians would then have to

'squarely confront what it is doing and accept the political cost'.[12] There would be no exception in cases where legislation could not be read compatibly with protected rights. Amending legislation would not amend the right in question, it would only carve out a specific exception to it. In this way, a Bill of Rights would preserve Parliament's ultimate ability to make any law it wishes whilst bolstering the role of the courts in protecting individual rights. It would more completely reflect the model of strong form dialogic constitutionalism discussed in chapter 3.

4. There should not be a general qualification or limitation clause which applies to all rights (such as that contained in section 1 of the Canadian Charter of Fundamental Rights 1982[13]). This would remove the normative distinctiveness of different rights and impose a single test of justification for interferences with rights, which is not warranted. The Courts should be required to identify a standard of conduct required of each right contained in the Bill of Rights, which will vary from right to right (see especially chapters 4 and 9).

5. A domestic Bill of Rights should state explicitly that is the responsibility of the Courts to determine whether the rights have been infringed (see chapters 4 and 5).

6. A domestic Bill of Rights should include provision for public authorities to have due regard to the need to respect such fundamental rights when taking decisions that affect them such as that contained in section 38 of the Victoria Charter of Human Rights and Responsibilities Act 2006 (chapter 8).

7. There should be explicit and separate protection of legal equality and the right of access to Court (chapter 10).

8. There should be provision for derogation from certain articles. It should be made clear that the Court can determine whether such derogation is strictly necessary (chapter 11).

It is, however, possible for all of these reforms to be effected by means of amendment to the Human Rights Act (although the third arguably ought to have some special political imprimatur in order for the courts to recognise a further qualification to the principle of parliamentary sovereignty). The same could be said of adding to the range of protected rights, such as adding a protection of jury trial or explicit protection for legal equality. This could be done by amendment. Thus although it is not the purpose of this book to debate the desirability of a Bill of Rights, we must ask, if only for completeness, whether there are therefore any compelling reasons for the enactment of a Bill of Rights at all.

A Bill of Rights is legislation that sets out the core principles around which society agrees that it should be ordered. (The use of the word 'ordered' must be preferred to the word 'governed' to take account of the potential for a Bills of

---

[12] [2000] 2 AC 115

[13] Section 1 provides 'the Canadian Charter of Rights and Freedoms guarantees the rights and freedoms set out in it subject only to such reasonable limits prescribed by law as can be demonstrably justified in a free and democratic society.' This has been held to introduce a general qualification to rights to be judged by reference to a test of proportionality, see *R v Oakes* [1986] 1 SCR 103.

Rights to apply to non-governmental organisations and private persons as well as to Government.) To say that a Bill of Rights is legislation which is especially firmly entrenched or which confers higher-order power on the courts is to risk missing the key point. These are lawyers' definitions which put the cart before the horse. The reason why Bills of Rights characteristically prevail over majority will expressed from time-to-time in legislation is because of their special significance in society. Adherence to the protected rights is considered to be of overriding importance because they represent the long-held values and long-term commitments of society. The most significant argument for a Bill of Rights is therefore the social benefit that would come from setting out society's core values and long-term commitments. A Bill of Rights is justified, if at all, first and foremost as an exercise in state-building. Of course, this means that the principal reasons in favour of a Bill of Rights are sociological, political and cultural, rather than legal. And they are multifaceted. But such reasons resonate strongly with the political and social landscape of the UK at the present time. The following general and overlapping considerations seem to me to be of particular importance.

First, there is an extraordinary lack of awareness and understanding about the workings of the constitution in the UK. This is clear to anyone who has taught public law or constitutional law to law undergraduates. To most people, the workings of Parliament and the courts are a mystery glimpsed from time to time in the pages of newspapers or on the news. And yet the constitution is the bedrock of society. It is the basis on which power is exercised legitimately. A Bill of Rights has an important educative function, not only in making people aware of the importance of civil and human rights but also of the importance of the constitution and the separation of powers more generally. Secondly, and connectedly, the past 25 years has been one of the most significant periods of constitutional reform in history.[14] But these reforms have not been accompanied by any significant engagement with society generally on the part of politicians. The process of deciding upon and framing a Bill of Rights provides a unique opportunity for people to engage with the constitution through an exercise of state-building, including, importantly, the children and young people who will be the next generation of politicians, public officials and judges.

Thirdly, particularly since the terrorist attacks on New York and Washington DC on 11 September 2001, numerous statutes have been passed which have seriously encroached upon civil liberties, and there has been a concerning transfer of power to the executive. One only needs to refer to indefinite detention of foreign nationals; police powers to stop and search without reasonable suspicion; laws against public protest; and control orders. The Human Rights Act has had some successes in defending human rights in the face of such legislation. Even where legislation has not been declared incompatible with the European Convention the courts have blunted some of the worst excesses by robust interpretation. However,

---

[14] Professor Bogdanor has identified 15 separate reforms with constitutional significance since the Labour Government took office in May 1997: 'Our New Constitution'(2004) 120 *LQR* 242.

the Human Rights Act has not provided society with a set of rights and basic values against which government projects are held up to critical examination in the press, in Parliament and in society at large. On the contrary, the Human Rights Act has been portrayed as the enemy of the people rather than their guardian. Human rights principles are also too often viewed within government as obstacles to be circumvented rather than goals to be met. A Bill of Rights is needed if human rights are to be fully accepted by British society as the 'fundamental' and 'basic' standards to which all political projects must conform, and as establishing the baseline of legal *and political* legitimacy.

Fourth, and perhaps most importantly, the past few decades have witnessed the transformation of Britain into a multi-ethnic, pluralistic society. Traditional cultural and religious norms have been replaced by a huge diversity of different ways of life. The state has assumed a secular role. There is an obvious need for disparate ethnic and cultural groups in society to identify commonalities, and to do so in a way that affirms a mutual respect for individuals and groups making up society. A Bill of Rights is not only capable of expressing common values and principles that transcend cultural and religious differences but the exercise of drawing-up a Bill of Rights is in itself a way of engaging disparate groups in a common enterprise of state-building.

It is apparent from these reasons for enacting a Bill of Rights that the process by which we get there may be as important—and is possibly more important—than what the document ultimately says. It is only through an adequate process of engagement with society that politicians can hope to produce a document that will satisfy the needs set out above and that will command a sense of ownership throughout society as a whole, which the Human Rights Act itself lacks. A Bill of Rights should not be foisted on society by a political elite, still less by a single political party. It must be the product of engagement and consensus. It should not be rushed. Indeed, to rush the process without capitalising fully on the enormous potential that the process of discussing and framing a Bill of Rights itself has in educating and uniting members of society would be to waste a great opportunity, in addition to threatening the legitimacy of whatever legislation is eventually enacted.[15] However, it seems likely that this is what will happen. The politicians do not want a drawn-out process of consultation and civic engagement about a Bill of Rights.[16] If the Conservative Party regains office, the enactment of a Bill of Rights may appear to be a relatively straightforward and inexpensive reform, that can be

---

[15] See the excellent discussion in ' "Process", "A British Bill of Rights—Informing the Debate' JUSTICE (2007) ch 5.

[16] Although the Justice Secretary has made encouraging comments to the Joint Parliamentary Committee on Human Rights on this issue, and the Committee itself has endorsed the need for a deliberative process, there remains little detail or imaginative thinking about such a process. By contrast there is a disproportionate amount of thought about the *content* of a Bill of Rights. The Committee itself thought that six months would be sufficient time for public discussion. See 'A Bill of Rights for the UK?' Twenty-ninth report of session 2007–08, HL 165-I, HC 150-I, pp 85–92. It is notable that the bulk of the report is concerned with providing the answers to the questions that would be put to the public and that process is given little attention, at the end of the report.

implemented quickly. And the politicians are likely to want to have control over what the document says. This suggests that the opportunity will, indeed, be lost. Time will tell.

One final point ought to be made in relation to the possibility of future constitutional reform. This book documents the complex interrelationship between the common law and the Human Rights Act, and it makes manifest the difficulty and undesirability of seeking to disentangle human rights norms from public law. The point cannot be summed-up better than it has been expressed by Shivaji Felix who has described any attempt to repeal the Human Rights Act without an effective substitute as 'like trying to restore the egg from the omelette into which it has been beaten and cooked'.[17] The Act has required, prompted and underpinned common law development throughout public law as well as private law. The status of such developments would obviously be open to challenge if the Human Rights Act were to be repealed and nothing equivalent put in its place. There would be much litigation to determine which common law developments, and which precedents, survived the repeal. Furthermore, there are areas of the law, discussed in chapter 2, where the presence of the Human Rights Act has been held to hold-back common law development. Absent any equivalent statutory protection of human rights, such cases would also now be capable of being re-argued. These would be interesting times indeed, but the people most likely to benefit would be lawyers. It would certainly be a sad time for human rights.

---

[17] [2003] *PL* 829, Book Review of Adam Tomkins, *Public Law* (Oxford, OUP, 2003).

2

The Common Law and the
Human Rights Act

T HE HUMAN RIGHTS ACT and the common law are closely interwoven on a number of different levels. The way in which the Act gives effect to Convention rights in domestic law is modelled on the techniques employed by judges at common law. Rather than establishing a discrete legal regime for the enforcement of Convention rights, the Act requires the courts to interpret statutes and apply the common law consistently with such rights. Even the 'constitutional' status of the Act is itself a product of common law developments that preceded its enactment, in which the courts held that, notwithstanding the absence of a written constitution, the courts can recognise certain rights as having a 'constitutional' status. The chapters which follow examine specific topics in public law after the Human Rights Act, including the way in which the Human Rights Act has led to developments in the common law. The purpose of this chapter is to take a more general view of both the Act and its relationship with the common law. We begin with an examination of the shared roots of the Human Rights Act and common law constitutional rights, and the common law developments that influenced the enactment and the form of the Human Rights Act.

The Common Law Prelude to the Human Rights Act

Lawyers and legal historians argue about the accuracy of Dicey's claim, made as late as 1914, that there was no such thing as English administrative law,[1] but few

---

[1] AV Dicey, *Introduction to the Law of the Constitution*, 8th edn (London, Macmillan, 1915). In the same year as the 8th edition was published (the last edition by Dicey himself), a case note by Dicey on *Board of Education v Rice* [1911] AC 179 and *Local Government Board v Arlidge* [1915] AC 120 was published in the *Law Quarterly Review*. Dicey wrote: 'Modern legislation and that dominant legislative opinion which in reality controls the action of Parliament has undoubtedly conferred upon . . . servants of the Crown . . . a considerable amount of judicial or quasi-judicial authority. This is a considerable step towards the introduction among us of something like the *droit administratif* of France, but the fact that the ordinary law courts can deal with any actual and provable breach of the law committed by any servant of the Crown still preserves that rule of law which is fatal to the existence of true *droit*

dispute Lord Reid's statement in *Ridge v Baldwin* in 1963 that England did not then have a 'developed system of administrative law' capable of meeting modern needs,[2] and it is indisputable that in the course of the 1960s and 1970s the courts dusted off old doctrines and writs and developed a modern system of law for controlling the enormous post-war state apparatus.[3] The term 'public law' was first used in its modern form in a domestic reported case by Lord Diplock in *Home Office v Dorset Yacht Co*, decided in 1970, in which his Lordship stated that over the course of the preceding century the 'public law' concept of ultra vires had 'replaced' the civil law concept of negligence 'as the test of the legality' of acts done pursuant to a statutory discretion. It was only if a decision was first found to be ultra vires that the courts could determine if there had been 'an actionable infringement of the plaintiff's rights in civil law'.[4] Lord Diplock was among the vanguard of the judges who sought to develop a modern, discrete, administrative law,[5] but the fact that a judge of the highest court gave a speech in such terms reveals just how far public law had come.[6] Public law was developing as a jurisdiction that was separate from and prevailed over private law.[7] It is significant also that the idea of rights was associated by Lord Diplock with private law and not public law. The development of public law was not linked to the protection of rights. It was built on the supervisory jurisdiction of the courts to review the way decisions had been made; and, as Lord Diplock's reference to the ultra vires doctrine highlights, the justification was that the courts were holding public officials to the limits of the power that Parliament had conferred. Insofar as public law was viewed as establishing legal principles or standards applicable to government bodies, these were not equated with individual rights: public law, it has been said on

administratif.' 'The Development of Administrative Law in England' (1915) 31 *LQR* 148, 152. This passage makes clear that Dicey principally meant by 'administrative law' that which confers special advantages, not special controls, on the exercise of government power. But Dicey does seem to have been of the view that neither were to be found to any significant extent in the law of England at that time.

[2] *Ridge v Baldwin* [1964] AC 40, 72.
[3] In seminal cases such as *Ridge v Baldwin* (n 2); *R v Criminal Injuries Compensation Board, ex p Lain* [1967] 2 QB 864; *Anisminic Ltd v Foreign Compensation Commission* [1969] 2 AC 147; *Padfield v Minister of Agriculture, Fisheries and Food* [1968] AC 997; and *Gouriet v Union of Post Office Workers* [1978] AC 435. For a recent discussion of the contribution of the House of Lords to the development of administrative law in this period, see Paul Craig, ch 29 in L Blom-Cooper, B Dickson and G Drewry (eds) *The Judicial House of Lords: 1876–2009* (Oxford, Oxford University Press, 2009).
[4] *Home Office v Dorset Yacht Company* [1970] AC 1004, 1067–68. His Lordship also stated that the only limitations on public power that the 'courts of law have jurisdiction to enforce depends not on the civil law concept of negligence but on the public law concept of *ultra vires*'.
[5] See the discussion in ch 7, pp 201–204.
[6] In 1982 Lord Diplock stated that 'progress towards a comprehensive system of administrative law . . . I regard as having been the greatest achievement of the English courts in my judicial lifetime': *R v IRC, ex p National Federation of Self Employed and Small Businesses Ltd* [1982] AC 617, 641.
[7] An approach taken to a logical extreme in *O'Reilly v Mackman* [1983] 2 AC 237 and *Cocks v Thanet* [1983] 2 AC 286.

high authority, was concerned with enforcing 'public duties'[8] and correcting 'public wrongs',[9] rather than with protecting rights.[10]

The development of public law therefore represented a significant break with the Diceyan orthodoxy that the UK has no public law and that the law of the constitution—in so far as there is one—is simply the private law that has successfully adhered itself to the great edifice of politics. But it also continued to reflect the orthodoxy, which was central to Dicey's account of the English constitution, that private law is the means by which the unwritten constitution protects individual rights.[11] The implications, and the limits, of this way of thinking were demonstrated by a series of cases in which there was a clash between public power and private rights. The question raised by these cases was whether, if public power had been exercised reasonably and bona fide, public officials had a defence to claims in trespass and false imprisonment, even though private individuals would have no such defence. Perhaps the most important case was *Morris v Beardmore*, decided by the House of Lords in 1980.[12] Police officers had remained in the defendant's home despite being asked to leave, in order that they could obtain a breath test from the defendant. The defendant refused to supply one and was arrested. The Judicial Committee led by Lord Diplock held that express statutory words are required to authorise a trespass, and in their absence the demand and arrest were unlawful and the defendant had a good defence to a charge. Lord Diplock equated the protection offered by the tort of trespass with a 'common law right' of a person 'to keep his home free from unauthorised intruders'. Notably, he went out of his way to say that this result 'owes nothing to the European Convention for the Protection of Human Rights and Fundamental Freedoms.'[13] The reasoning was faithful to the idea that the common law protects rights through the law of tort and

---

[8] *M v Home Office* [1994] 1 AC 377, 389 (Lord Woolf). In his Hamlyn Lectures, 'Protection of the Public—a New Challenge', Lord Woolf spoke of the purpose of administrative law being concerned with enforcing public duties on behalf of the public as a whole, by contrast with private law which is concerned with enforcing individual rights. Lord Woolf, *Protection of the Public: A New Challenge* (London, Stevens, 1990) 33–34.

[9] In *R v Somerset CC, ex p Dixon* [1997] COD 323, 331 Sedley LJ stated that public law 'is not at base about rights, even though abuses of public power may and often do invade private rights; it is about wrongs—that is to say misuses of public power'.

[10] This corresponded with the liberal approach taken to *locus standi* by which all properly interested persons could apply to judicially review decisions of public bodies and not only those persons who were the subject of a decision or were directly affected. See *R v IRC, ex p National Federation of Self Employed and Small Businesses Ltd* [1982] AC 617, in which Lord Scarman spoke in terms of 'compelling the performance of public duty or in righting public wrongs' (648) and Lord Diplock framed the question as 'what was the public duty of the Board . . .?' (636). Contrast with *Gouriet* (n 3), in which it was held that an individual cannot sue for breach of public law wrongs unless he has suffered harm.

[11] For Dicey, the fact that all public officials were subjected to the ordinary law of the land and could be sued in tort (he conveniently sidelined Crown immunity from suit) was a cornerstone of the rule of law in England. He wrote that, 'With us every official, from the Prime Minister down to a constable or collector of taxes, is under the same responsibility for every act done without legal justification as any other citizen' (Dicey, *Law of the Constitution* (n 1) 189) and 'the principles of private law have with us been by the action of the Courts and Parliament so extended as to determine the position of the Crown and of its servants; thus the Constitution is the result of the ordinary law of the land' (ibid 199).

[12] *Morris v Beardmore* [1980] AC 446.

[13] ibid, 456.

not through public law, although it is not easy to reconcile with the view expressed in *Dorset Yacht* that private law does not mark the boundaries of public power, and it demonstrates the difficulties in seeking to establish a rigid distinction between public and private law in a system such as that in England where it has no historical pedigree.[14] Indeed, the logic of *Dorset Yacht* was taken to its logical conclusion in several later cases in which the opposite result was reached. These cases held that although public officers were acting without statutory authority, if they were acting reasonably and bona fide, they had a good defence to an action for trespass or false imprisonment. Perhaps the most infamous of these cases was *Percy v Hall*, in which police officers who repeatedly arrested and detained protesters at a military installation for contravention of a byelaw that was later held to be void for uncertainty were held to have a defence of 'lawful justification'.[15] The animating idea behind these cases was the idea of public duty. The courts preferred to protect public officials performing their public duties than to protect individual rights. It is cases such as these, in which public officials are provided with special 'public law' defences from the ordinary law, which demonstrate why Dicey was fearful of the development of administrative law, and again demonstrate just how far its development had progressed.

There was however a different way of thinking about the public law that began to emerge in the 1980s and which gained considerable ground in the 1990s. It was closely bound up with the campaign to incorporate the European Convention into domestic law. In 1965 the Government had granted individuals the right to petition the ECtHR directly. With this victory in the bag, a number of influential figures, perhaps most importantly Lord Scarman in his 1974 Hamlyn Lectures, began to call for the incorporation of the European Convention into domestic law.[16] After all, if individuals could sue the Government for breaching their human rights in Strasbourg, why could they not do so in London? The Conservative Government's election manifesto in 1979 included the promise that they would have all-party discussions on a Bill of Rights. But once in power, the Conservative

---

[14] See JFW Allison, *A Continental Distinction in the Common Law* (Oxford, Oxford University Press, 1996).

[15] *Percy v Hall* [1964] 4 All ER 523. See also *Wills v Bowley* [1983] 1 AC 57, in which the House of Lords held by a majority that where a policeman wrongly but reasonably believes that a person has committed an offence, the person cannot lawfully resist arrest, and *McLeod v Commissioner of Police for the Metropolis* [1994] 4 All ER 553, in which it was held that reasonable apprehension of a future breach of the peace constituted lawful justification for trespass (this was found to breach Art 8 in *McLeod v United Kingdom* (1999) 27 EHRR 493). For a powerful corrective, influenced by Art 5 of the European Convention, see *R v Governor of Brockhill Prison, ex p Evans (No2)* [2001] 2 AC 19 in which the House of Lords held that a prison governor had no defence to an action for false imprisonment although he had acted on a reasonable understanding of the law governing a prisoner's release date, and also *R (Laporte) v Chief Constable of Gloucestershire* [2007] 2 AC 105 holding that action taken to prevent a breach of the peace must be proportionate. For criticism, see T Weir, 'The Staggering March of Negligence', in J Stapleton and P Cane (eds) *The Law of Obligations: Essays in celebration of John Flemming* (Oxford, Clarendon Press, 1998) 110.

[16] Lord Scarman, *English Law—the New Dimension* (London, Stevens, 1974); A Lester, *Democracy and Individual Rights* (London, Fabian Society, 1969); M Zander, *A Bill of Rights?*, 3rd edn (London, Sweet and Maxwell, 1985) (1st edn 1975).

Party under Prime Minister Margaret Thatcher turned instead to making numerous inroads into civil liberties. The courts, despite their new-found powers of public law, were criticised for putting up little resistance and were perceived by many to be sympathetic to the Government.[17] Whilst calls for incorporation of the European Convention did not go away, it was clear that this would not be achieved under a Conservative Government.[18] Against this background, it is hardly surprising the same lawyers who were leading the campaign for incorporation of the European Convention by Parliament also turned to the possibility of giving effect to such rights through the common law, since the common law has historically evolved to meet the needs and values of the times. This, indeed, became a sustained long-term project for certain prominent practitioners, academics and even some judges, led by Lord Scarman. The ambition of that project is clear from the fact that, as has been seen, public law had not developed by reference to the need to protect individual rights at all.

It was significant that the legal project to incorporate human rights principles in domestic law progressed against the background of the renewed interest in and legitimacy of political liberalism, brought about by the publication of John Rawls' *A Theory of Justice*.[19] Rawls sought to identify a set of basic (liberal) entitlements to which he claimed everyone ought to subscribe in fairness to each other. This work was in turn translated into a theory of legal rights by work published in the late 1970s and throughout the 1980s by Ronald Dworkin.[20] Dworkin directly attacked the traditional positivistic account of common law adjudication as the implicit enforcement of parliamentary will (which he described as 'the ruling theory of law'),[21] on which the development of public law had been premised through

---

[17] Most sustainably by K Ewing and C Gearty, *Freedom under Thatcher* (Oxford, Oxford University Press, 1990) and see also JAG Griffths, *The Politics of the Judiciary* (Manchester, Manchester University Press, 1977).

[18] A high point of the political project to incorporate the European Convention was 'Charter 88' (1988), a campaign which started after the Conservative Party's success at the 1987 general election, in which leading public figures called for radical constitutional reform of the parliamentary system, including the enactment of a Bill of Rights. The campaign began with a special edition of the *New Statesman* magazine in 1988 and was continued by other published advertisements and petitions. Several organisations in this period proposed Bills of Rights for incorporation, the most influential being the Institute of Public Policy Research's draft Bill of Rights published in 1991, drawing heavily on the European Convention and UNCHR and International Covenant on Civil and Political Rights. It was published by the Constitution Project's Judiciary Working Group consisting mainly of lawyers: Anthony Lester QC (Chair), James Cornford (Director), Professor Ronald Dworkin, Sir William Goodhart QC, Patricia Hewitt, Professor Jeffrey Jowell, Nicola Lacey, Emeritus Professor of Law Keith Patchett and Sarah Spencer (formerly General Secretary of the National Council for Civil Liberties). A second edition was published in 1996 with a foreword by Francesca Klug.

[19] J Rawls, *A Theory of Justice* (Cambridge, Harvard University Press, 1971; revised 1979).

[20] *Taking Rights Seriously* (London, Duckworth, 1977; new impression 2000); *A Matter of Principle* (Cambridge, Harvard University Press, 1985) (both these books are collections of previously published articles); *Law's Empire* (London, Fontana Press, 1986); *Freedom's Law—The Moral Reading of the American Constitution* (Cambridge, Harvard University Press, 1996). Dworkin himself was probably more influenced by Dicey's rights-based approach to the common law constitution than he might admit: see eg TRS Allan, 'Dicey and Dworkin: the Rule of Law as Integrity' (1988) *OJLS* 266.

[21] Which he associated with the work of HLA Hart. See HLA Hart, *The Concept of Law*, 2nd edn (Oxford, Clarendon Press, 1997).

the medium of the ultra vires doctrine. Moreover, his work broke new ground in providing a developed theoretical account of legal rights that encompassed both written constitutional rights and traditional common law (private law) rights. He thus bridged private and public law, as well as the written and unwritten constitutional systems of the United States and the UK. His writing was thus particularly influential in the resurgence of common law constitutionalism and provided a powerful argument for the legitimacy of courts recognising liberal legal rights and not simply applying the will of Parliament.[22]

Dworkin's ideas were developed and applied in the context of domestic public law by academic lawyers such as TRS Allan and Jeffrey Jowell, as well as practitioners such as Anthony Lester.[23] Whilst Allan's work focused on uncovering and exploring principles of equality and justice which he claimed to be represented in Commonwealth case law, Jowell and Lester exploited the resurgence of liberalism by demonstrating how international human instruments provide lawyers with concrete reference points by which to argue for the reshaping of public law doctrines, and the reorientation of public law to protect modern civil and political rights. Add to this the fact that leading barristers (such as Anthony Lester himself) were prepared to argue before the higher courts that the courts should take into account international human rights law, and it is unsurprising that the common law gradually absorbed such principles, and a rights-based dimension to public law began to emerge.

The beginnings of this process can, in fact, be found in *Morris v Beardmore*. In his speech in that case, Lord Scarman referred to the 'fundamental' rights protected by the common law. In so doing, his Lordship was making a conscious effort to distinguish between ordinary private law rights and basic civil and political rights. He said that the adjective 'fundamental' is 'unfamiliar to common lawyers' (since they have no written constitutional rights), but was warranted both because of the importance attached by the common law to the privacy of the home and also because it is a right protected by the European Convention.[24] Lord Scarman's appeal to the idea of 'fundamental' rights and to the European Convention represented a deliberate attempt to set domestic law in a new direction and it stands in

---

[22] In this latter respect Dworkin's work remains novel, although see also P Craig, *Public Law and Democracy in the United Kingdom and the United States of America* (Oxford, Clarendon Press, 1991). Dworkin (who was a Professor of Law at Oxford and later University College London in addition to New York University) himself weighed in to the debate over the enactment of a British Bill of Rights in his influential 'Does Britain Need a Bill of Rights?' in R Gordon and R Wilmot-Smith (eds), *Human Rights in the United Kingdom* (Oxford, Oxford University Press,1997), and was one of the authors of the Institute for Public Policy Research's proposal (n 18).

[23] TRS Allan, 'Legislative Supremacy and the Rule of Law: Democracy and Constitutionalism' [1985] *CLJ* 111; 'Pragmatism and Theory in Public Law' [1988] 104 *LQR* 422; *Law, Liberty and Justice—the Legal Foundations of British Constitutionalism* (Oxford, Clarendon Press, 1993); J Jowell and A Lester, 'Beyond *Wednesbury*: substantive principles of administrative law' [1987] *PL* 368; A Lester, 'The Constitution: Decline and Renewal' in J Jowell in D Oliver (eds), *The Changing Constitution*, 2nd edn (Oxford, Clarendon Press, 1989); J Jowell, 'The Rule of Law Today' in ibid. For discussion of this strand of thought in domestic public law, see M. Loughlin, *Public Law and Political Theory* (Oxford, Clarendon Press, 1992) 206–29.

[24] *Morris v Beardmore* (n 12), 464.

marked contrast to the approach of Lord Diplock who not only, as we have seen, went out of his way to deprecate the significance of the European Convention but also to associate common law rights with ordinary private law rights. With hindsight it is notable that Lord Scarman commented in his Hamlyn Lectures that the European Convention and the Universal Declaration of Human Rights 'reflect a rising tide of opinion which, one way or another, will have to be accommodated in the English legal system.'[25] By 1980 his Lordship had evidently come to the view that another way had to be found.

The baton passed to other judges, in particular Lord Browne-Wilkinson. In the published version of his 1991 Harry Street Lecture (in which he relied on Lord Scarman's speech in *Morris v Beardmore*), his Lordship wrote:

> It has become so fashionable to urge constitutional reform by means of a Bill of Rights or by incorporation of the ECHR in domestic law that attention has been diverted from the principles of our indigenous common law. . . . It is now inconceivable that any court in this country would hold that, apart from statutory provision, the individual freedoms of private persons are any less extensive than the basic human rights protected by the ECHR.[26]

He went on to argue that the courts should recognise a presumption against interference with human rights. Unless a statute expressly or by necessary implication abrogates human rights, the courts should presume that no abrogation was intended to be authorised, in just the same way as they would strictly construe a taxing or penal statute.

The recognition of fundamental public law rights suffered a number of setbacks in the courts,[27] but they gradually found a foothold, first by the modulation of the standard of *Wednesbury* review, so that more anxious scrutiny was given to decisions where they affected important rights,[28] and secondly by the gradual recognition of free-standing rights recognised in public law.[29] It is this latter development which is the most remarkable. The protection afforded where such 'constitutional' or 'fundamental' rights were held to be engaged went beyond that afforded by the application of a modified *Wednesbury* test, in that breach of such rights rendered decisions and delegated legislation unlawful in the absence of clear authority in primary legislation. The courts followed the approach advocated by Lord Browne-Wilkinson, and before him Lord Scarman, by applying human rights principles through the medium of a presumption of parliamentary intention.[30] This gave the approach constitutional legitimacy and formally reconciled it with the ultra vires

---

[25] Lord Scarman, *English Law* (n 16) 14.

[26] 'The infiltration of a bill of rights' [1992] *PL* 397, 404–5.

[27] Especially *R v Secretary of State for the Home Department, ex p Brind* [1991] 1 AC 696 and *Wheeler v Leicester City Council* [1985] AC 1054.

[28] See *Bugdaycay v Secretary of State for the Home Department* [1987] AC 514 and *R v Ministry of Defence, ex p Smith* [1996] QB 517.

[29] The House of Lords confirmed that no claim in tort would lie for a breach of a constitutional right, in *Watkins v Secretary of State for the Home Department* [2006] 2 AC 395.

[30] See especially *R v Secretary of State for the Home Department, ex p Pierson* [1998] AC 539, discussed in ch 4, pp 105–108.

doctrine; although it barely disguised the magnitude of the constitutional development that it reflected. The very idea of 'constitutional' and 'fundamental' rights
was, as Lord Scarman suggested in *Morris v Beardmore*, antithical to what had
become orthodox thinking about UK law. The recognition of positive higher-
order rights as part of the domestic legal system broke the binary hierarchy of
common law and statute which had characterised the twentieth century domestic
legal system. Moreover, by recognising such rights at common law the courts
exploded the belief, which had come to dominate constitutional thinking, that if
higher-order positive rights were to be recognised in domestic law, they would
have to be enacted by Parliament and contained in a written Bill of Rights. The
absence of a written constitution in the UK was associated with a necessary
absence of positive rights. But since by the 1980s it had become clear that a written constitutional document might not be forthcoming, the courts, tentatively and
somewhat reluctantly, began to dismantle this constitutional orthodoxy.

The common law had historically protected physical integrity, liberty and property through private law rights, in particular trespass and false imprisonment, and
this provided an obvious analogy for the recognition of broader public law rights
that protected the same values. But more significantly there was one context in
which the courts had recognised a positive common law right which was not also
a right in tort.[31] This was the right of access to the courts. This right had been
asserted and applied by the courts from time to time throughout the twentieth
century, in cases in which judges had required clear parliamentary authority for
any action or delegated legislation restricting the right of access to the courts.[32]
These cases lent important legitimacy to the development of common law constitutional rights in the last decades of the twentieth century. However, the newly
recognised common law rights were not substantively neutral in the same way as
a right of access to the court, which was in essence a process right akin to a principle of natural justice. The new common law rights drew heavily on the substantive rights and freedoms set out in the European Convention, and the developing
case law of the ECtHR. Thus, by the time the Human Rights Act had come into
effect, domestic courts had already recognised common law constitutional rights
to freedom of expression, respect for reputation, liberty, and the right of access to

---

[31] There was also authority, which had some influence in the development of common law constitutional rights, for courts giving a strict construction to taxing statutes. This was influenced by art IV
of the Bill of Rights 1689 which prohibits the levying of taxation without statutory authority: see
Attorney-General v Wiltshire United Dairies Ltd (1921) 19 LGR 534; (1922) 127 LT 822. There is older
authority for the recognition of other common law rights, such as the right to vote (which was treated
as a property right); see in particular *Ashby v White* 92 ER 126; (1703) 2 Ld Raym 938.

[32] *R and W Paul v The Wheat Commission* [1937] AC 139; *Raymond v Honey* [1983] 1 AC 1 (both
referred to by Lord Browne-Wilkinson in his Harry Street Lecture (n 26)); *R v Deputy Governor of
Parkhurst Prison, ex p Leech* [1988] AC 533; *R v Lord Chancellor, ex p Witham* [1998] QB 575; *R v Lord
Chancellor, ex p Lightfoot* [2000] QB 597; building on *Chester v Bateson* [1920] 1 KB 829 and *Re Boaler*
[1915] 1 KB 21, and indirectly *Anisminic v Foreign Compensation Commission* [1969] 2 AC 147.
Particularly important were the two earlier cases of *Re Boaler* (primary legislation governing vexatious
litigants did not prevent an application to a magistrate for a summons) and *Chester v Bateson* (delegated legislation ultra vires where it restricted possession proceedings against munitions workers).

a court.[33] Although the reasoning in these cases harked back to historical cases in which judges had extolled the importance of protecting values of liberty, association and expression, the recognition of these new, modern, positive public law rights was influenced by the belief that the common law should keep pace with international human rights law.

We have already seen how extra-judicial speeches and publications by judges formed an important part of these developments. Indeed, as the legal developments gathered pace, so it seemed did the volume of extra-judicial publications. Almost all of this developed, in different ways, a liberal philosophy of common law constitutionalism. This emphasises just how direct and powerful the philosophical and jurisprudential developments were on the development of the law. Perhaps most prominent was the writing of Sir John Laws. He argued that ultimate sovereignty rests 'not with those who wield governmental power, but in the conditions under which they are permitted to do so'. He also claimed that the English constitution represents a 'framework of fundamental principles' and that judicial power 'in the last resort rests on the guarantee that this framework will be vindicated'.[34] As we shall see, Laws LJ's published writings, like those of Lord Scarman and Lord Browne-Wilkinson, have been reflected in his judicial pronouncements.[35]

The high point of the case law on common law constitutional rights in the pre-Human Rights Act period was the case of *Ex p Simms*.[36] Since we will return to this case at various points throughout this book, it is worth pausing to consider it here. In *Simms* the House of Lords unanimously held that a government policy, made pursuant to the Prison Rules 1964, denying prisoners access to investigatory journalists, was unlawful.[37] The policy was held to conflict with what Lord Steyn described as 'a fundamental or basic right'.[38] Lord Hoffmann explained that in so holding, the Court was appealing to 'principles of constitutionality little different from those that exist in countries where the power of the legislature is expressly

---

[33] *Reynolds v Times Newspapers* [2001] 2 AC 127 (freedom of expression and respect for reputation); *Khawaja v Secretary of State for the Home Department* [1984] 1 AC 74 and *Tan Te Lam v Superintendent of Tai A Chau Detention Centre* [1997] AC 97 (liberty); *R v Deputy Governor of Parkhurst Prison, ex p Leech* [1988] AC 533 (access to court); see also *McEldowney v Ford* [1971] AC 632 (requiring strict construction where a law interferes with freedom of association).

[34] Sir John Laws, 'Law and democracy' [1995] PL 72, 92. See also 'Is the High Court the guardian of fundamental rights?' [1993] *PL* 59, 'The constitution: morals and rights' [1996] *PL* 622, 'The Limitations of Human Rights' [1998] *PL* 254; also the influential papers by Sir Stephen Sedley, *The Making and Remaking of the British Constitution—The Radcliffe Lectures at the University of Warwick for 1996–97* (London, Blackstone Press, 1997), *Freedom, Law and Justice* (50th Hamlyn Lectures) (London, Sweet & Maxwell, 1999), 'The Sound of Silence: Constitutional Law without a Constitution' (1994) 110 *LQR* 270. A number of speeches by Lord Irvine, the former Lord Chancellor responsible for the passing of the HRA, are collected in *Human Rights, Constitutional Law and the Development of the English Legal System* (Oxford, Hart, 2004).

[35] See in particular ch 9, pp 271–72.

[36] *R v Secretary of State for the Home Department, ex p Simms* [2000] 2 AC 115.

[37] Moreover, despite the fact that they had subsequently become academic, it also declared unlawful two decisions of prison governors applying the policy to deny visits to journalists.

[38] *Ex p Simms* (n 36), 130.

limited by a constitutional document'.[39] The decision in *Simms*, and others like it, is undoubtedly open to the charge that authority for the legal right found to exist is to be found in the pages of *A Theory of Justice* rather than in the pages of the Law Reports. Although the Court invoked Article 10 of the European Convention, on freedom of expression, the specific right propounded—that is, the right of access to an investigatory journalist—was so 'basic' that it was without precedent both at common law and in the case law of the ECtHR. Nor could the House of Lords point to any international consensus: the only foreign jurisprudence cited to the court supported finding for the Government.[40]

However, closer attention to the particular circumstances at issue in *Simms* provides both the explanation and the justification for this apparently quite radical decision. Following prominent miscarriages of justice such as the case of the Birmingham Six, in 1995 Parliament had established the Criminal Cases Review Commission as an independent body responsible for reviewing convictions. The House of Lords in *Simms* put considerable emphasis on the fact that the Commission was at the time seriously under-resourced and ineffective. Moreover, it also emphasised the strong tradition in England of miscarriages of justice being exposed by investigative journalism. The appeal to the right to freedom of expression was therefore in fact closely tied to the right of access to justice[41] and that in fact, rather than reflecting the direct transplantation of abstract liberal theories into domestic law, it was a very practical response to the weaknesses of non-legal protections for human rights, albeit that it was one firmly on the liberal legal trajectory on which the law had been set by judges like Lord Scarman and Lord Browne-Wilkinson. It is also important to bear in mind that the effect of *Simms* was actually to *enhance* political as well as legal accountability. It did so by affording recognition and protection to the independent media as a crucial constitutional check on the conduct of state agencies. It also did so by requiring that any denial of access to investigatory journalists be explicitly addressed by primary legislation: the House of Lords took the ball out of the executive's hands and put it firmly in the hands of Parliament. As Lord Hoffmann explained in his speech, Parliament would have to 'squarely confront' the issue of whether an infringement of individual rights was necessary and would have to 'accept the political cost' if such an infringement was to be authorised.[42] *Simms* therefore demonstrates how the legal dimension to the unwritten constitution is responsive to its political aspect, and how the legal and political checks on public power are not necessarily in tension, but can work together in a mutually reinforcing way.

[39] ibid, 131.
[40] The closest Strasbourg case to the point was *Silver v United Kingdom* (1980) 3 EHRR 475 (Com), (1983) 5 EHRR 347, which only concerned restrictions on correspondence, and which was otherwise considerably limited. The United States Supreme Court has repeatedly held that the denial of prisoners' access to the media is compatible with freedom of expression: eg *Pell v Procunier*, 417 US 817 (1974).
[41] Counsel for the applicants only argued for a right to an oral interview with a journalist which was confined to the question of whether the prisoner had been wrongly convicted (see [2000] 2 AC 115, 124).
[42] [2000] 2 AC 115, 131 (Lord Hoffmann).

The Human Rights Act: Common law-plus

Despite the development of a common law jurisprudence on common law fundamental rights, which was still in its infancy throughout the 1990s, the legal and political checks on the Conservative Government since it came to power in 1979 had been shown to be remarkably few. It was in direct response to this that the Labour Party leadership in 1993 committed the party to the incorporation of the European Convention into domestic law, which became a manifesto pledge in 1997, the year the Party regained office.[43] The pledge was initially regarded as the first stage in a two-stage process of more thoroughgoing constitutional reform, which would include the enactment of a Bill of Rights; although once in power the Labour Government soon 'lost any appetite' for the enactment of a Bill of Rights.[44] By 1997 many of those lawyers who had been critical of the judiciary's newly acquired 'public law', and in particular its ineffectiveness in protecting individual rights, had become so disenchanted that they rallied to the call to incorporate the European Convention into domestic law. Of those who remained opposed to incorporation, many opponents and sceptics have subsequently been won over such that, whatever its support in the wider community, the Human Rights Act boasted and continues to boast a very considerable amount of support within the legal profession.[45]

The Human Rights Bill was introduced shortly after the Labour Party took office and was enacted in November 1998. The Human Rights Act came into force on 2 October 2000.[46] The Act enhances the common law protection of rights in the following ways:

---

[43] J Smith (Leader of the Labour Party), party conference speech 'A New Way Forward', Bournemouth 1993. See also J Smith and T Blair, *A New Agenda for Democracy: Labour's Proposals for Constitutional Reform* (London, Labour Party, 1993).

[44] For discussion and the quote see F Klug, 'A bill of rights: do we need one or do we already have one?' [2007] *PL* 701, 702–4. The issue of a domestic Bill of Rights has returned to the political agenda, see chapter 1 pp 5–7.

[45] For example, in the Preface to *Principles of Human Rights Adjudication* (Oxford: Oxford University Press, 2004) Professor Conor Gearty admits that he is 'largely enthusiastic' about the HRA, which 'may surprise those readers who are aware of my past record of opposition to proposals for a UK bill of rights'. Professor Keith Ewing's continued objections to the Human Rights Act are now significant for the apparent lack of any notable support for his views from the legal community, and his protestation that the Act has been 'futile' seem completely divorced from the reality of the transformation of public law and the huge number of political and legal changes that have been brought about by the Act (including in efforts by public bodies to avoid adverse court rulings). See K Ewing and J Tham, 'The continuing futility of the Human Rights Act' [2007] *PL* 668.

[46] The Home Secretary Jack Straw and Lord Chancellor Irvine of Lairg QC were responsible for the Bill in the Commons and Lords respectively. Both were former barristers: Lord Irvine had been Tony Blair's pupil-master (Blair also having been a barrister). Lord Irvine made his own contribution to the development of common law rights in *DPP v Jones* [1999] 2 AC 240, sitting in the Judicial Committee of the House of Lords. The Human Rights Act had had some effect in relation to devolved institutions through the Scotland Act 1998, the Government of Wales Act 1998 and the Northern Ireland Act 1998.

1. Section 2 establishes the concept of 'the Convention rights' which it defines by reference to the main articles of the European Convention. These go well beyond the narrow catalogue of common law constitutional rights.[47]
2. Section 3 requires that all legislation must be read, as far as possible to do so, consistently with Convention rights. This goes further than the strict construction given to legislation that conflicts with common law rights.
3. Section 4 permits courts to declare primary legislation incompatible with the Convention. The courts are therefore permitted to scrutinise the justification for primary legislation and declare legislation contrary to fundamental norms, which they could not previously do.
4. Section 6 makes it 'unlawful' for any public authority (excluding Parliament but including the courts) to act incompatibly with Convention rights. This gives all Convention rights at least an equivalent status in public law to common law constitutional rights. Furthermore, it extends not only to discretionary decisions made by public officials, but also to operational decisions. Unlike administrative law, the Convention rights and the Human Rights Act extend all the way down to 'on the ground' operational conduct. This challenges the normative and procedural distinction in domestic law between administrative law and tort.
5. Since all interferences with Convention rights must as a minimum be 'in accordance with law'[48] the Act, to the extent of its application, reverses the common law position that the Crown can do anything that a private individual could do and does not need positive legal authority for it.[49]
6. Section 8 provides a general remedial power which includes the possibility of awarding damages, which are not otherwise available for breach of public law norms unless the conduct in question constitutes an actionable tort.

Quite simply, the Human Rights Act reaches places that the common law cannot reach.

The Human Rights Act is, however, intended not only to bolster judicial supervision but also to inculcate a wider 'culture of human rights'.[50] By this it is meant a culture in public life in which 'fundamental principles are seen as central to the

---

[47] The most prominent non-inclusion is Art 13, the right to an effective remedy for breaches of Convention rights. The thinking behind this omission was that the Act itself is intended to provide an effective remedy and public authorities should not be required to fashion other remedies outside its scope. Art 1 was also omitted for essentially the same reason. Art 1 provides that the High Contracting Parties shall secure the Convention rights to everyone within their jurisdiction.

[48] See J Beatson, S Grosz, T Hickman, R Singh, *Human Rights: Judicial Protection in the United Kingdom* (London, Sweet & Maxwell, 2008) 3-11 to 3-27.

[49] See *Malone v Metropolitan Police Commissioner* [1979] Ch 344 (phone tapping); held to be a violation of Art 8 by the ECtHR in *Malone v United Kingdom* (1985) 7 EHRR 14.

[50] Introducing the Bill for its Second Reading in the House of Lords, Lord Irvine stated: 'This Bill will bring human rights home. People will be able to argue for their rights and claim their remedies under the Convention in any court or tribunal in the United Kingdom. Our courts will develop human rights throughout society. A culture of awareness of human rights will develop.' Hansard HL col 1228 (3 November 2007).

design and delivery of policy, legislation and public services'.[51] This culture is intended to permeate the decisions of central government, local authorities, schools, hospitals, police forces and other organs and agencies of the state, as well of course as Parliament and the legislatures in Wales, Scotland and Northern Ireland. The idea was well expressed by the Cabinet Secretary in evidence to the Joint Parliamentary Committee on Human Rights (itself established to ensure that the Westminster Parliament leads the way in inculcating a culture of human rights):

> Though it is clearly right that all public authorities should not act incompatibly with the Convention rights, the Act was intended to do more than merely avoid direct violations of human rights. As the senior judiciary have commented . . . this is a constitutional measure, legislating for basic values which can be shared by all people throughout the United Kingdom. It offers a framework for policy-making, for the resolution of problems across all branches of government and for improving the quality of public services. From this point of view it is not right to present the Human Rights Act as a matter for legal specialists. The culture of rights and responsibilities needs to be mainstreamed.[52]

The idea was that human rights values and human rights thinking would be integrated into the processes of public authorities and the mind-set of public officials, and that human rights would not just be audit principles against which decisions, policies and legislation have to measured, but would come to be seen as values and considerations that shaped government projects as they happened. Speaking on 9 December 1999, the Home Secretary Jack Straw stated that it would not only provide an 'ethical bottom line' for public authorities but would also give rise to a 'formal shared understanding of what is fundamentally right and fundamentally wrong'.[53] It is in this vein that the influential Joint Parliamentary Committee on Human Rights was established, to make reports to Parliament and scrutinise the human rights implications of Bills at Westminster. And in 2006, Parliament established the Commission for Equality and Human Rights which has statutory responsibility for promoting awareness of human rights and understanding of their importance.[54]

What is the Human Rights Act?

There continues to be debate about the 'status' of the Human Rights Act, in particular whether and to what degree it is a constitutional statute and whether it can

---

[51] See Joint Committee on Human Rights, 'The Case for a Human Rights Commission', Sixth Report 2002–2003 HC 489-I. Available at www.publications.parliament.uk/pa/jt200203/jtselect/jtrights/67/6702.htm.

[52] Evidence given to the JCHR on 21 March 2002, ibid.

[53] Jack Straw MP, 'Building on a Human Rights Culture', lecture at the Civil Service College.

[54] Equality Act 2006 s 9.

properly be described as 'a Bill of Rights'.[55] The Act it is very obviously not an ordinary statute, either in form or content. Two things are immediately obvious but nonetheless worth emphasising. First, there is no point in engaging in an argument over labels. Examination of the status of the Human Rights Act is only helpful if it either illuminates or has implications for the meaning of the Act and the way it is given effect. However, if the Human Rights Act is understood as a constitutional statute, that is to say, a statute with special constitutional significance, this has implications for how it is interpreted, because its interpretation will be guided by the form of constitutionalism that it embodies. Secondly, the status of any statute is not fixed. The New Zealand Bill of Rights 1990, for instance, was 'not greeted with any great interest or enthusiasm' and it 'perplexed both bench and bar', but as its legitimacy became accepted it came to be invested with greater significance and wider application as time passed.[56] It will be seen that even in its first 10 years, judicial attitudes towards the Human Rights Act have shifted.

Let us first consider the text of the Human Rights Act and the White Paper that preceded it, before considering what the courts have had to say about them.

The Preamble

If a non-lawyer looks at the Act, what they will see is a legal instruction manual about how certain specified articles of an international treaty signed in Rome in 1950, of which they will almost certainly have no familiarity, are to be given effect in domestic law. There is no Grand Preamble, no ringing affirmation of brotherhood, and the rights themselves are stuck at the back in a schedule. The Preamble is indeed decidedly ordinary. It describes the Act as:

An Act to give further effect to rights and freedoms guaranteed under the European Convention on Human Rights; to make provision with respect to holders of certain judicial offices who become judges of the European Court of Human Rights; and for connected purposes.

This is very far cry from 'We the People . . .'. Even New Zealand's Bill of Rights, a great deal more modest in its constitutional ambitions than most of its international predecessors,[57] states that it is an act to 'affirm, protect, and promote human rights and fundamental freedoms in New Zealand' and to affirm New Zealand's commitment to the International Covenant on Civil and Political

---

[55] For two arguments to the effect that the Human Rights Act is a Bill of Rights, see, F Klug, 'A bill of rights' (n 44) and A Kavanagh, *Constitutional Review under the UK Human Rights Act* (Cambridge, Cambridge University Press, 2009) ch 10. In a speech to the Institute of Public Policy Research on 13 January 2000, Jack Straw MP described the Human Rights Act as 'the first Bill of Rights this country has seen for three centuries'.

[56] G Huscroft and P Rishworth, ' "You Say You Want a Revolution": Bills of Rights in the Age of Human Rights', in D Dyzenhaus, M Hunt and G Huscroft (eds), *A Simple Common Lawyer—Essays in Honour of Michael Taggart* (Hart, Oxford, 2009) 126–27.

[57] The original government proposal was for a supreme law Bill of Rights, but the proposals were watered down. See Huscroft and Rishworth, ibid.

Rights. The Human Rights Act reads as if its enactment was just another day in the office for British parliamentarians.

The White Paper was little better. It referred to the Act saving litigants the 'inordinate delay and cost' of taking a case to the ECtHR. It even gave an estimate of the cost of taking a case to Strasbourg (£30,000), and referred to the effect of non-incorporation of the European Convention as 'a very practical one'. This was hardly a rousing call to rally 'round a new settlement of individual rights. But the White Paper did at least have a title that suggested something constitutionally significant—'Rights Brought Home'—and the Prime Minister's Preface located the legislation within the Labour Government's scheme of constitutional reform, which he said was aimed at modernising British politics and decentralising power. He also stated that the Act would 'enhance awareness of human rights in our society', which was an important reference to the desire to create a 'culture of human rights'. The White Paper also referred to another 'distinct benefit': that 'British judges will be enabled to make a distinctively British contribution to the development of the jurisprudence of human rights in Europe';[58] and it stated that, 'our judges will be able to contribute to this dynamic and evolving interpretation of the Convention'.[59] These aspects of the White Paper at least indicate that the purpose of the Act was not in fact simply that of saving litigants the cost of a trip to Strasbourg, but that it was envisaged that the Act would lead to a distinctive and domestic jurisprudence on human rights.

The Provisions of the Act

Reference to the Preamble and the White Paper therefore reveals a lack of clarity as to precisely what purpose the Human Rights Act was intended to fulfil, and whether it was intended as a constitutionally significant measure—a new Bill of Rights—or whether its purpose is a more modest, pragmatic one of providing a remedy in domestic law for breach of the UK's international obligations. The key provisions of the Act perpetuate this ambiguity.

Subsection 1(1) defines 'the Convention rights' by reference to certain specified articles of 'the Convention'. It has been suggested that since the identified articles are said in subsection 1(3) to be 'set out in Schedule 1', they therefore must be new domestic rights ('otherwise the Schedule would be redundant'[60]). But it is not as straightforward as this. Subsection 1(3) does not add to the definition of Convention rights, but simply sets out in long-form what is set out in short-form in subsection 1(1), ie it sets out the full text of the designated articles which could not sensibly have been set out in section 1 of the Act. Subsection 1(3) can be seen as a tidying-up provision. The Articles are defined not by reference to the

---

[58] Secretary of State for the Home Department, 'Rights Brought Home: The Human Rights Bill', (Cm 3782, 1997) [1.14].

[59] ibid [2.5].

[60] J Lewis, 'The European ceiling on human rights' [2007] *PL* 720, 724.

schedule but by reference to 'the Convention', and this is defined in the interpretation section of the Act as the European Convention agreed by the Council of Europe on 4 November 1950 'as it has effect for the time being in relation to the United Kingdom' (s 21(1)). On one view therefore, the Human Rights Act does not create new domestic rights but provides a remedy for breach of the UK's international obligations. There is, then, a tension at the very heart of the Act between the creation of new domestic rights and the provision of a remedy in domestic law for rights that exist on the international plane. As we shall see, the definition of Convention rights has given rise to considerable litigation.

Section 2 requires courts and tribunals to 'take into account' Strasbourg jurisprudence. Under the terms of the European Convention itself the ECtHR has jurisdiction to interpret the Convention and issue binding determinations against parties to cases before it (Articles 19, 32 and 46). If the purpose of the Human Rights Act was to enforce compliance with the United Kingdom's international obligations, then domestic courts should logically be required to follow the interpretation of the Convention pronounced by the Court. Section 2 therefore indicates that the Act was intended to create domestic rights and that domestic courts could develop a domestic constitutional rights jurisprudence.[61] This point can be put yet more forcefully with respect to section 6. This section creates a new type of illegality in domestic public law.[62] Any act or decision made by a public authority that is incompatible with Convention rights is rendered ultra vires by this provision. The Act did not have to establish a new and additional limit on the vires of public authorities. It could have simply provided that 'where a public authority acts incompatibly with the Convention a victim shall be entitled to just satisfaction'. The defendant to all Human Rights Act claims could have been United Kingdom Government (perhaps in the form of the Attorney-General), which is responsible for providing just satisfaction ordered by the ECtHR. Domestic courts could have been empowered to make declarations of infringements with the Convention and to order damages to be paid from central funds. That would have provided an individual with the same relief that they would have achieved in Strasbourg. If saving the costs and time of trips to Strasbourg was all that was intended, there was no need to go further and establish that Convention rights limit the power of public authorities. And yet Parliament chose to do so. A similar point can be made in respect of section 3, which provides that legislation must be read so far as possible compatibly with Convention rights. The effect of this is to establish rights and liabilities in domestic law not only against central government

---

[61] It is possible to suggest reasons, consistent with such a view, why domestic courts are not bound to the Strasbourg jurisprudence: in particular, that the Convention is a 'living instrument' so judgments of the ECtHR can become obsolete, and the ECtHR is not bound by its own judgments. But such explanations are incomplete. Obsolete judgments would have become irrelevant (or at least would not be determinative) and so would not be binding. The fact that the ECtHR is not bound by its former pronouncements says nothing about domestic institutions. It is inescapable that s 2 is not fully consistent with the idea that the Human Rights Act is simply a practical measure to allow remedies to be provided for breaches of the United Kingdom's international obligations.

[62] See PP Craig, *Administrative Law*, 6th edn (London, Sweet & Maxwell, 2008) 565–83.

and Parliament, but against all public bodies (if their actions are regulated by statute) and even private individuals seeking the benefit of statutory powers which are not compatible with Convention rights.[63]

The method used to incorporate the Convention in sections 6 and 3 is also significant for a second, related reason. With their focus on public law illegality and statutory interpretation, these provisions reflect an administrative law mind-set in the drafting of the Act. In order to appreciate the significance of this we need briefly to lift our gaze from the UK context. In other countries, bills of rights have been viewed as *constitutional* measures with no obvious or direct impact on *administrative* law. The distinction between constitutional and administrative law is not one that is recognised by UK (or at least English) lawyers, since in the absence of a written constitution and a power to strike down primary legislation, it is primarily in the foothills of administrative law that one has to look for constitutional rules and principles.[64] But in other countries the distinction is fundamental and the impact of constitutional rights on administrative law was not obvious. In Canada for instance, most claims brought under the Canadian Charter of Rights and Freedoms 1982 were challenges to Federal or Provincial legislation, and until recently it had little impact on administrative law. Although section 32(1) provides that the Charter applies to the governments of Canada and each province, as well as the various legislatures, the fact that an administrative decision impacted on a Charter right was simply viewed as a reason for applying a reasonableness standard of review to the decision, in preference to a test of patent unreasonableness.[65] It was only in *Singh Multani v Commissioner Scolaire Marguerite-Bourgeoysthe* that a majority of the Supreme Court of Canada decided that Charter standards must be directly applied to administrative decisions; the minority—reflecting the view that had hitherto dominated—considered that they could only be properly applied to legislation.[66] From the perspective of an English public lawyer, it is remarkable that

---

[63] eg *Ghaidon v Godin-Mendoza* [2004] 2 AC 557 (holding, in a claim between private individuals, that the Rent Act 1997 must be read as permitting right of same-sex spouse to succeed to statutory tenancy).

[64] Although such a power now exists in relation to EC law and under the devolution statutes.

[65] *Chamberlain v The Board of School District No 36 (Surrey)* [2002] 4 SCR 710 (decision of school board not to approve book showing same-sex couples as a teaching aid on family life curriculum held to be an unreasonable accommodation of religious opinions); see also *Slaight Communications Inc v Davidson* [1989] 1 SCR 1308 (Dickson CJ left open in that case the application of the Charter in administrative law; Lamer J would have applied s 1 of the Charter); *Ross v New Brunswick School District No 15* [1996] 1 SCR 825. The courts also intervened if a public authority misinterpreted a Charter right: *Nova Scotia (Workers' Compensation Board) v Martin* [2003] 2 SCR 504.

[66] [2006] 1 SCR 256, 2006 SCC 6. Charron J, giving the leading judgment, stated that the opinion of the minority judges, 'could well reduce the fundamental rights and freedoms guaranteed by the Canadian Charter to mere administrative law principles or, at the very least, cause confusion between the two' ([16]). The position in the United States is that the constitutional requirement that persons shall not be deprived of life, liberty or property 'without due process of law' (Fifth and Fourteenth Amendments) applies to administrative decision-making, but as one student textbook puts it: 'However much these issues interest the academics, it is entirely possible for an administrative law practitioner to spend thirty or forty years in practice without ever encountering a constitutional due process issue': WF Fox, *Understanding Administrative Law*, 5th edn (New York, LexisNexis, 2008) 109.

this issue had been unresolved in Canada for a quarter of a century and that it was, even then, so controversial. The New Zealand Bill of Rights also had no impact on administrative law until relatively recently. It was first applied to delegated legislation[67] before, in *Zaoui v Attorney-General*, the New Zealand Supreme Court finally held that the discretionary statutory power to deport persons on national security grounds was impliedly limited by the right to life and to be free from torture.[68] By contrast, sections 3 and 6 of the Human Rights Act have made the impact of the Act on administrative law direct and immediate.

Even the power in section 4 to issue declarations of incompatibility can be understood as a bolt-on to administrative law remedies and thus to administrative law. In *Simms*, Lord Hoffmann suggested that the declaration of incompatibility would serve an analogous function to the court requiring that legislative interferences with constitutional rights are express and unambiguous. He said, 'in the unusual case' where legislation will 'not to yield to the principle of legality' the courts will 'be able to draw this to the attention of Parliament' by making a declaration of incompatibility.[69] However, it is also possible to view the section 4 power as far more significant, with some even regarding it essentially as de facto judicial supremacy. One thing is clear. Section 4 is inconsistent with purpose of the Human Rights Act being solely that of providing a remedy in domestic courts for violations of international obligations. This is because section 4 does not provide such a remedy. It leaves primary legislation intact. It is not even possible for the court to award damages under section 8 when they make such a declaration.[70] It is much more consistent with the idea that the Act created new domestic constitutional rights against which primary legislation can be tested.

By contrast, section 7 of the Act points altogether in the opposite direction. Section 7 establishes a new cause of action under the Act but it limits it to situations where a person would be a victim 'for the purpose of Article 34 of the Convention': 'the Convention', we have seen, is defined by reference to the international treaty binding the United Kingdom. The remedial provision in section 8 is also expressly linked, albeit more loosely, to the Convention as an international instrument. It provides that damages should only be awarded where this is 'necessary to afford just satisfaction'. No express mention is made, but this is the criteria that governs the award of remedies in Strasbourg under Article 41. Then again, in relation to remedies other than damages, the Act uses language of 'just and appropriate'; language which is drawn directly from domestic law.

---

[67] *Drew v Attorney-General* [2002] NZLR 58 (CA); *Cropp v A Judicial Authority* [2008] NZSC 46. The thesis that the New Zealand Bill of Rights should have effect in administrative law was first advanced by J McLean, P Rishworth and M Taggart, 'The Impact of the New Zealand Bill of Rights Act 1990 on Administrative Law', in *Essays on the New Zealand Bill of Rights Act* (Auckland, Legal Research Foundation, 1992). The account here draws on Huscroft and Rishworth (n 56) 127–28.

[68] [2006] 1 NZLR 289 (SC).

[69] *R v Secretary of State for the Home Department, ex p Simms* [2000] 2 AC 115, 132.

[70] See *Burden & Burden v United Kingdom* (2008) 47 EHRR 38 in which the ECtHR held that the declaration of incompatibility does not provide an effective remedy under Art 13, contrary to the submissions of the UK Government.

Other provisions of the Act also point in these different directions. The special provisions guiding the court's interpretation of freedom of expression and freedom of thought, conscience and religion in sections 12 and 13 of the Act are far more consistent with an understanding of the Human Rights Act as a domestic constitutional measure creating domestic constitutional rights with a distinctively British meaning. Likewise, the additional domestic conditions for derogation from the Convention rights ('designation' (section 14) and a sunset clause (section 16)) also suggest that the Act is intended to establish a new domestic constitutional scheme.[71] But on the other hand, the provisions in section 18 governing the appointment of UK judges to the ECtHR emphasise the connection between the Act and the UK's international obligations under the Convention. All in all, the provisions of the Human Rights Act are riven with tensions. These tensions have been carried-through to the case law on the Act, have given rise to considerable uncertainty and have led directly to unsatisfactory consequences in terms of the protection of human rights.

The Case Law

This section seeks to elucidate how these tensions have played out in the case law under the Human Rights Act. There is as yet no settled approach, and different judges have expressed different views. However the first 10 years of the Act undoubtedly witnessed the dominance of the international/pragmatic/remedial over the domestic/constitutional perspectives, but the latter has exerted increasing influence.

In the early case of *Brown v Stott*, often relied upon as establishing the constitutional significance of the Human Rights Act, Lord Bingham described the European Convention as 'an important constitutional instrument', but he did not go as far as to say that the Human Rights Act had constitutional significance (indeed, the Convention was given relevant effect in that case through the Scotland Act 1998, and the Human Rights Act was not in issue).[72] Moreover, Lord Bingham in later cases consistently held that the purpose of the Human Rights Act was the relatively mundane one, not of giving 'victims better remedies at home than they could recover in Strasbourg but to give them the same remedies without the delay and expense of resort to Strasbourg'.[73] Lord Nicholls also championed this approach, if anything even more stridently than Lord Bingham.[74] For example in

[71] As to which see p 33 below. Likewise, the justification for reservations must be found in international law. Provision is also made in s 17 for periodic reviews of designated reservations.
[72] *Brown v Stott* [2003] 1 AC 681, 703.
[73] *R (Greenfield) v Secretary of State for the Home Department* [2005] 1 WLR 673 [19]; *R (Begum) v Governors of Denbigh High School* [2007] 1 AC 100 [29]; *Huang v Secretary of State for the Home Department* [2007] 2 AC 167 [8].
[74] *Aston Cantlow and Wilmcote with Billesley Parochial Church Council v Wallbank* [2004] 1 AC 546 [6]; *R (Quark Fishing Ltd) v Secretary of State for Foreign and Commonwealth Affairs* [2006] 1 AC 529 [33]–[34]. Lord Nicholls' speech in *Quark Fishing* was particularly influential to the majority in *Al-Skeini* (n 92 below).

Quark Fishing, relying on the Preamble to the Human Rights Act, Lord Nicholls asserted that it was intended to provide 'a means whereby persons whose rights under the Convention were infringed by the United Kingdom could, in future, have an appropriate remedy available to them in the courts of this country.' He drew support from the fact that only victims within the meaning of Article 34 can obtain a remedy under the Human Rights Act and said that the 'object' of sections 6 and 7 was to 'mirror' the rights and freedoms protected in international law. His Lordship also linked this to Article 13 of the European Convention, and suggested that the purpose of those provisions was simply to provide an effective remedy for breach of Convention rights to satisfy the UK's international obligations (a connection that has also been made by Lord Hope).[75] This approach thus viewed the Human Rights Act solely as a pragmatic, time and cost-saving measure that provided a remedy for breach of international law rights in domestic law. Of course, it was accepted that the Act creates domestic law rights in the sense of establishing a jurisdiction and providing a remedy in domestic courts, but on this view the rights themselves float somewhere in the stratosphere of international law and are not grounded in domestic constitutional law.

This understanding of the Human Rights Act crystallised into a powerful principle of purposive construction that has greatly influenced the Act's interpretation and effect. In one important example, *Greenfield*, the House of Lords, led by Lord Bingham, held that the courts should be guided by awards of damages made by the ECtHR under Article 41 in preference to the analogy with tort and discrimination claims, although these would provide a surer guide if the Act was thought to create new domestic rights. Such an approach ensures that claimants do not obtain larger compensation payments than they could obtain in Strasbourg.[76] That also means that the principle in tort law that 'unconstitutional conduct' by a public officer is capable of leading to an award of exemplary damages is not brought into play.[77] In line with *Greenfield*, the domestic courts have rejected the availability of punitive damages under the Human Rights Act, which is consistent with the idea that it is a measure to provide a Strasbourg remedy in domestic law and not to create new domestic human rights.[78]

Lord Bingham also led the House in *Quark Fishing*. In that case the House of Lords held that since the First Protocol of the European Convention had not been extended by the British Government to the South Georgia and South Sandwich

[75] *Quark Fishing*, ibid. On the connection with Art 13, see also *Re S* [2002] 2 AC 291 [68] (Lord Nicholls), *Quark Fishing* [34] (Lord Nicholls) applying *Aston Cantlow and Wilmcote* (n 74) [43] (Lord Hope).

[76] *Greenfield* (n 73). As we have seen, tort actions are historically the principal way of vindicating rights against the state. The level of Strasbourg awards is also influenced by political and economic considerations—such as the different value of money in, say, Sweden or Turkey—that have no relevance to a domestic cause of action.

[77] See *Kuddus v Chief Constable of Lancashire Constabulary* [2002] 2 AC 122, for a good recent example of such an award where the claimant was wrongly detained facing deportation: *Muuse v Secretary of State for the Home Department* [2009] EWHC 1886.

[78] See *Watkins v Secretary of State for the Home Department* [2006] 2 AC 395; *R (KB) v Mental Health Review Tribunal* [2004] QB 936.

Islands, a British Overseas Territory,[79] no action could be brought under the Human Rights Act for breach of that protocol by persons in the territory. Their Lordships relied on the fact that the claim would inevitably fail in Strasbourg.[80] There was less room for manoeuvre on this issue than the issue of damages, however, since as we have seen, 'the Convention' is defined in section 21(1) as the treaty agreed in Rome in 1950 'as it has effect for the time being in relation to the United Kingdom'. It would have been difficult to hold that the Convention rights included rights that had never been extended to a territory and had never bound the United Kingdom. The real significance of the case is the effect it had in *R (Al-Jedda) v Secretary of State for Defence*, a case of considerable importance in any consideration of the status of the Human Rights Act.[81]

The claimant in *Al-Jedda* was a British citizen who was at the time being detained indefinitely and without charge in a British military base in Iraq. He claimed that this breached Article 5 of the Convention. The question that the House of Lords was asked to consider (and the issue for which the case is well-known) was whether such detention was required by UN Security Council Resolution 1546 (2004) and subsequent resolutions, and if so, whether Article 5 of the European Convention was qualified by these resolutions. The House of Lords held that Article 5 was qualified, and rejected Mr Al-Jedda's claim. However the relevance of the arguments advanced in the House of Lords depended entirely on the correctness of a finding made by the Divisional Court, upheld in the Court of Appeal but not appealed to the House of Lords, that if Article 5 is qualified as a matter of international law, it is also qualified under the Human Rights Act.[82] The facts of *Al-Jedda* were, however, different from *Quark Fishing* in a very important respect. Whilst the Convention had not been extended to the South Georgia and South Sandwich Islands when the Human Rights Act was enacted, Security Council Resolution 1546 post-dated the Act. At the time of enactment, Article 5 was unqualified. The implication of the argument accepted by the Divisional Court and the Court of Appeal is that the rights protected by the Human Rights Act can be altered, limited and even repealed by the Government agreeing to inconsistent international obligations which have priority in international law over Article 5, and, most importantly, by any other superior and conflicting international obligations arising under Security Council Resolutions.

Both the Divisional Court and the Court of Appeal recognised that the definition of 'the Convention' in section 21(1) was not conclusive on this issue, and, relying heavily on *Quark Fishing*, they rested their judgments on the purposive principle of construction, to the effect that the Act should be interpreted in a

---

[79] Under Art 56 on territorial application of the treaty.
[80] *Quark Fishing* (n 74) concerning the allocation of fishing licences in South Georgia and South Sandwich Islands. A subsequent petition to the ECtHR was, indeed, held inadmissible: *Quark Fishing Ltd v United Kingdom* (2007) 44 EHRR SE4. *Quark Fishing* was applied to the British Indian Ocean Territory in *R (Bancoult) v Secretary of State for Foreign and Commonwealth Affairs* [2009] 1 AC 453.
[81] *R (Al-Jedda) v Secretary of State for Defence* [2008] 1 AC 332.
[82] Lord Rodger referred to the finding of the Court of Appeal without demur, ibid [53]–[54].

manner that provides individuals with a remedy for breach of the UK's international obligations that they could obtain in Strasbourg. The courts reasoned that if Article 5 is qualified as a matter of international law, no claim could succeed in Strasbourg, therefore a claim should not be capable of succeeding in the United Kingdom. They therefore reasoned that section 21(1) of the Act should be interpreted to mean 'the Convention' not only as it had effect at the date the Human Rights Act was enacted (as per *Quark Fishing*) but as it has effect *from time to time*.[83] However this extension of *Quark Fishing* is highly questionable. Sections 2 and 21(1) of the Human Rights Act define the Convention rights by reference to the treaty having effect 'for the time being'. Whilst this is admittedly a rather unusual and ambiguous statutory turn of phrase, the more natural meaning is surely that the Human Rights Act gave effect to the specified articles of the Convention subject to whatever qualifications or reservations may have affected their meaning *at the time of enactment*. Indeed, advancing just this argument, Keir Starmer QC, leading counsel for the claimant, contrasted the provision with section 2 of the European Communities Act 1972, which provides that all rights, powers, liabilities, responsibilities and restrictions 'from time to time created arising by or under' the European Treaties shall 'be given legal effect' in domestic law. If this submission had been accepted, the position would have been that 'the Convention rights' were cut loose from international law at the time of enactment of the Human Rights Act and entrenched there and then in domestic law as autonomous domestic rights. The umbilical cord with international law would have been cut. Such an interpretation sits more easily with the fact that domestic courts are not bound to apply Strasbourg judgments, despite the fact that the ECtHR pronounces authoritatively on the meaning of the Convention as a matter of international law. It also makes sense of sections 14 and 15 of the Human Rights Act, which require derogations and reservations, which qualify and suspend Convention rights as a matter of international law, to be 'designated' by an Order in Council. Indeed, the Court of Appeal's judgment seems to render the requirement of domestic designation otiose, since the effect of registering a derogation with the Council of Europe is to suspend the effect of the article derogated from, to the extent of the derogation, in international law. Following *Al-Jedda*, this would then have *automatic* effect under the Human Rights Act without the need for 'designation'.[84]

---

[83] [2007] QB 621 [96].

[84] The claimant appears to have deployed a slightly different argument relating to the provisions for derogation to the one advanced in the text. The argument was that the power to derogate under the Human Rights Act provides a means to give effect to UN Security Council Resolutions which conflict with Art 5: the Government can derogate from Art 5. The difficulty with this argument is that derogation is only permissible when the life of the nation is threatened, not when peacekeeping operations are carried out abroad. In responding to this submission the Divisional Court hinted at a response to the point made in the text, namely that a consequence of the reading contended for by the claimant would be that domestic courts could not scrutinise the validity of derogations because all that is required in the Act is 'designation' of a derogation to suspend a Convention right, which is a purely formal act: s 1(3) (see [62]): even an unsustainable derogation (eg one that was not strictly necessary or referred to a non-derogable right) would therefore be effective in domestic law if formally designated. However,

The approach that the Court of Appeal rejected in *Al-Jedda* is not only more consistent with the wording of the Human Rights Act, but it is also more principled. Since the UK's international obligations could not have automatically overridden the protections afforded by the Human Rights Act, qualification of Convention rights to meet conflicting international obligations would have required legislative qualification to the definition of the Convention rights in section 1 and the schedule to the Act, or in appropriate cases designated derogation from the Article in question. In either case, this would have required parliamentary approval for any limitation on Convention rights. Indeed, the absence of any such requirement, which is the effect of the Court of Appeal's judgment, as shown by the result reached by the House of Lords, is alarming if the Human Rights Act is thought to establish a constitutional guarantee of fundamental rights. In order to appreciate this, it is necessary to consider in more detail the issue that was considered by the House of Lords.

Security Council Resolution 1546 was adopted by the Security Council at the formal end of the occupation of Iraq. It recognised that notwithstanding the ending of the occupation, the situation in Iraq continued to constitute a threat to international peace and security. Acting under Chapter VII of the United Nations Charter the Resolution therefore welcomed the willingness of the Multi-National Force ('MNF') to continue its efforts to restore peace and security. It stated in the most general terms that the MNF should have 'authority to take all necessary measures' to this end. The Resolution also welcomed a letter written from US Secretary of State, General Colin Powell, to the President of the Security Council in which General Powell offered on behalf of the MNF to continue to provide forces to maintain security in Iraq. The letter said that the MNF 'stands ready' to undertake activities that were listed and included 'internment where this is necessary for imperative reasons of security'. The letter also referred to such matters as training the Iraqi army, providing humanitarian assistance and civil affairs support. The letter was annexed to the Resolution.

Given the perceived desire on the part of the Security Council to continue the powers and responsibilities of the MNF as an occupying power, the House of Lords held that the effect of the approval of the letter from General Powel was not only to *authorise* preventative detention in Iraq but to *require* it where it was deemed necessary to prevent threats to the security of Iraq. Since states have agreed under the UN Charter to 'accept and carry out' decisions of the Security Council, this created a prima facie conflict with the UK's obligations under Article

---

as argued in ch 11, s 14(1) can (and should) be read to so as to require that any designation order must relate to a *valid* derogation. There is therefore no need to read s 21(1) in the manner preferred by the Court of Appeal in order to permit the domestic courts to test the justification for derogation. A further point is that, taken to its logical conclusion, the approach adopted by the Court of Appeal in *Al-Jedda* would mean that the justification for any derogation should be judged by reference to the approach taken by the ECtHR: if the ECtHR would uphold the derogation so should domestic courts. But, as the House of Lords accepted in *A v Secretary of State for the Home Department (No 1)* [2005] 2 AC 68, the approach of the domestic court must be more robust than the Strasburg Court and the margin of appreciation doctrine should not be applied: eg [114] and [131] (Lord Hope).

5 of the Convention. This in turn brought into play Article 103 of the UN Charter, which was described by Lord Bingham as a 'miscellaneous provision' of the Charter, which provides that where there is a conflict between the obligations of states under the Charter and their obligations under any other international agreement, the Charter prevails.[85] This Article, their Lordships held, made clear that the obligations imposed under the Resolution must prevail over the UK's obligations under Article 5. As such, whatever it might say on its face, and notwithstanding the absence of derogation or reservation, it was held that Article 5 did not in fact preclude internment in Iraq.

On any view, the legal authority for the detention of the claimant was highly circuitous. The combined effect of the Court of Appeal and House of Lords' judgments was this: indefinite detention of a British citizen without charge or trial—described by Lord Carswell as 'so antithetical to the rule of law . . . that recourse to it requires to be carefully scrutinised'[86]—was found to be justified by reference to the terms of a letter annexed to the back of a Security Council Resolution (which was itself an executive measure couched in most general terms) which not only failed to establish a requirement to take measures infringing liberty in terms, but had to be interpreted broadly and contrary to liberty in order to achieve this result, and which, so interpreted, was then held via a 'miscellaneous' provision of the UN Charter, to qualify a core protection in a human rights treaty that had previously been described by Lord Bingham in *Brown v Stott* as having 'constitutional' significance for European States.[87] All of this was underpinned by an unnecessary interpretation of section 21(1) of the Human Rights Act, interpreted against individual rights and informed by an unnecessarily narrow and unitary view of the purpose of the Act. In the Divisional Court, Moses and Richards JJ did at least express unease with such a result:

> The notion that so fundamental a right as that which is enshrined and protected in Art.5, namely the right to liberty, can, in an area within the jurisdictional scope of the 1998 Act, be removed, is startling; not least because it has been achieved without any express warning in the resolution itself and without any announcement by the Executive, still less the opportunity for scrutiny by Parliament.[88]

Despite these comments, when it came to the interpretation of the meaning of section 21(1), Parliament was not, as one might have expected, *presumed* to have intended that its approval is required for rights guaranteed by the Human Rights Act to be taken away. Nor was it presumed, as it might well have been, that Parliament would not have intended the domestic courts to be drawn 'deep inside the realm of international law—indeed inside the very chamber of the UN Security Council itself'.[89]

---

[85] *Al-Jedda* (n 81) [30].
[86] ibid [130].
[87] *Brown v Stott* [2003] 1 AC 681, 703.
[88] [2005] HRLR 39 [34].
[89] *Al-Jedda* (n 81) [55] (Lord Rodger).

Had the Human Rights Act been recognised as establishing domestic rights in the full sense, and not simply being a pragmatic measure to provide a remedy for breach of international obligations, these undesirable implications would have been avoided.[90] Indeed, had the possibility been admitted that the purpose of the Human Rights Act is not unitary—and that it displays a tension between different objectives—the attractions of a contrary interpretation would have carried greater force. The implications, and the possibilities, are well illustrated by *Kadi v United Kingdom*, in which the European Court of Justice rejected an analogous submission that Security Counsel Resolutions requiring the freezing of assets of certain named persons associated with Al Qaeda overrode the protections of fundamental rights implied into the EC Treaty. The Court held that the EC was a discreet legal order and an international agreement not amending the EC Treaty could not have the effect of prejudicing the constitutional principles derived from it.[91] *Kadi* highlights the fact that the Human Rights Act does not establish fully domestic constitutional rights. In the light of *Kadi*, as well as developments to which we will come on to refer, it is possible that the decision of the Court of Appeal in *Al-Jedda* will not be the last word on this issue, although given the weight of case law that now rests on that judgment, it may be too late to roll back the law on this issue.

Reference to the practical, remedial purpose of the Human Rights Act had the opposite effect in *Al-Skeini*, in that it led to the wider protection of rights.[92] But as in *Al-Jedda*, this drew the courts deep into areas previously governed by international law. The claim was brought by relatives of a number of Iraqi nationals who had allegedly been killed by British Forces operating in Iraq. The Human Rights Act is silent as to its extra-territorial effect. The House of Lords held that a claim can be maintained under the Human Rights Act for the actions of United Kingdom public authorities operating abroad if individual complainants are within the 'jurisdiction' of the United Kingdom as defined by Article 1 of the European Convention (which is not given effect by section 1 of the Human Rights Act). Thus the jurisdiction of the Human Rights Act was held to be co-extensive with that under the Convention. This ensured that extra-territorial claims could be remedied under the Act if they would succeed in Strasbourg. The Committee further held that, as a matter of international law, the extra-territorial jurisdiction of contracting states under Article 1 of the European Convention does not extend to persons abused or killed by military operations abroad, but it was accepted by the Government by the time that the case reached the House of Lords that there was an exception in cases where an individual was detained abroad in a British

---

[90] The Court of Appeal's judgment in *Al-Jedda* has given the executive enormous powers to restrict the liberty of the individual. Consider for example *A v HM Treasury* [2009] 3 WLR 25 involving executive measures taken pursuant to Security Council Resolutions targeted at specific individuals believed to be international terrorists, to freeze their assets without due process. The case was appealed to the House of Lords but the *Al-Jedda* point was not taken.

[91] *Kadi (Spain and Others, interveners) v Council of the European Union (France and Another, interveners)* (Joined Cases C-402/05 P and C-415/05 P).

[92] *R (Al-Skeini) v Secretary of State for Defence* [2008] 1 AC 153.

detention facility. In such cases the individual in question would be within the jurisdiction of the United Kingdom.[93]

Interestingly, Lord Bingham dissented in *Al-Skeini*, on the basis that even the purposive construction of the Human Rights Act could not without more displace the presumption against extra-territorial application of United Kingdom legislation. He also thought it fair to presume that Parliament would not have intended the Act to apply to the conduct of British troops abroad without explicitly saying so. He thought that comments made by Lord Nicholls in *Quark Fishing* (in which his Lordship said that the extra-territorial scope of the Act is to be determined, following the purposive approach, by looking at the extra-territorial jurisdiction of the Convention recognised by the ECtHR) were rather too unconditional and had not been endorsed by the other judges in the case. But Lord Rodger (with whom Baroness Hale and Lord Carswell agreed) applied Lord Nicholls' comments with undiluted force. Lord Brown also determined the case by reference to the remedial, pragmatic purpose of the Act and, although recognising that they were not directly in point, also placed weight on Lord Nicholls' comments.[94]

The purposive approach also underpins the decision of the House of Lords in *Ullah*, relating to section 2 of the Act. Lord Bingham held that although domestic courts are not bound to follow judgments of the ECtHR, they should follow any clear and constant jurisprudence because the ECtHR has authority in international law for interpreting the Convention. The courts should not give Convention rights a more generous interpretation than the Strasbourg Court has done. It was said that only in 'special circumstances' would domestic courts be entitled to depart from Strasbourg case law.[95]

The fact that there are several circumstances which have been regarded as 'special' does not lessen the grip that *Ullah*, and thus the purposive principle, have had on the law. It is worth briefly considering these exceptional classes of case. One circumstance that was always going to be regarded as special is where the ECtHR has failed to understand domestic law or where the ECtHR is not as well informed of all the material facts, and in such cases domestic courts have felt able to depart from

---

[93] This was the case in relation to one of the claimants in *Al-Skeini*, Baha Mousa, who had been killed by British troops. Given this concession, a public inquiry was subsequently established to investigate the death: www.bahamousainquiry.org/

[94] See *Al-Skeini* (n 92) [20] and [24] (Lord Bingham), [58] (Lord Rodger), [86]–[88] (Baroness Hale), [96] (Lord Carswell). Lord Brown stated: 'its very purpose being to ensure that, from the date it took effect, it would no longer be necessary for victims to complain about alleged violations of the Convention internationally in Strasbourg instead of domestically in the UK. It is less than obvious that Parliament would have wanted to confine its effect rigidly within the borders of the UK rather than allow it to extend also to the handful of cases where Strasbourg recognises an extraterritorial reach for the Convention itself' ([138]); he noted Lord Nicholl's comments at [143].

[95] *R (Ullah) v Special Adjudicator* [2004] 2 AC 323 [20]. Whilst Lord Bingham did not expressly link this approach to the purpose of the Act, he applied the words of Lord Slynn in *Alconbury* in which his Lordship had reasoned that if domestic courts do not follow the ECtHR jurisprudence, 'there is at least a possibility that the case will go to that court, which is likely in the ordinary case to follow its own constant jurisprudence': *R (Alconbury Developments Ltd) v Secretary of State for the Environment, Transport and the Regions* [2003] 2 AC 295 [26] The justification for the *Ullah* principle was thus intensely pragmatic.

a Strasbourg judgment and engage in a constructive (ie remedial) 'dialogue' with the ECtHR.[96] On the other hand, where the ECtHR has had all the arguments canvassed before it and has a firm grasp of domestic law, the jurisprudence will be followed.[97] Another context in which domestic courts have a freer hand is in relation to categories of case that have not been considered by the ECtHR. In some cases the absence of Strasbourg case law on a particular issue has meant that the domestic courts have had to determine issues of principle, which in some cases has led to considerable developments in the protections afforded. Thus a body of domestic law has developed which precludes deportation of non-nationals where this would lead to a 'flagrant breach' of Articles 5, 6 and 8 in their home country, although the ECtHR had gone no further than contemplating that deportation might infringe Articles 5 and 6.[98] The House of Lords has also held that Article 3 guarantees a right to asylum-seekers not to be left destitute[99] and extended the operational duty to take reasonable steps to prevent detained persons from committing suicide to the context of mental health law.[100] There are also cases where the Strasbourg law is beyond its use-by date. In such cases it it is possible to argue that if the ECtHR were to consider the matter again, it would take a different view of the position than that contained in its established judgments, since the Convention is a 'living instrument'. In *JJ v Secretary of State for the Home Department* Lord Carswell relied on the fact that in the particular context of Article 5, the ECtHR had envisaged that developing legal standards and attitudes will further increase the variety of forms of deprivation of liberty, in concluding that an 18-hour curfew imposed by a control

---

[96] Thus in *R v Spear* [2003] 1 AC 734 concerning courts martial the House of Lords declined to follow *Morris v United Kingdom* (2002) 34 EHRR 52 on the basis that the ECtHR had been given 'rather less information' about courts martial procedure than it had. In *Cooper v United Kingdom* (2004) 39 EHRR 8 the ECtHR back-tracked. Similarly, in *Z v United Kingdom* (2002) 34 EHRR 3 the ECtHR corrected a misunderstanding of English tort law, following criticism in *Barret v Enfield LBC* [2001] 2 AC 550. See generally *Kay v Lambeth LBC* [2006] 2 AC 465 [28], where Lord Bingham said that 'there are isolated occasions . . . when a domestic court may challenge the application by the Strasbourg court of the principles it has expounded to the detailed facts of a particular class of case peculiarly within the knowledge [for which also read *understanding*] of national authorities'. *Kay* is itself part of an on-going tug-of-war between the House of Lords and the ECtHR: see *Connors v United Kingdom* (2004) 40 EHRR 189 and *Doherty v Birmingham City Council* [2009] 1 AC 637. Also see on the relationship with the ECtHR, *R v Lyons (Isidore Jack) (No 3)* [2003] 1 AC 976 [46] (Lord Hoffmann); *Al-Skeini* (n 93) [90] (Baroness Hale), [105]–[106] (Lord Brown); *Re G (Adoption: Unmarried Couple)* [2009] 1 AC 173 [35] (Lord Hoffmann). Most recently, in the case of *R v Horncastle* [2009] UKSC 14 the Supreme Court has refused to apply Strasbourg case law on the use of hearsay evidence in criminal trials on the basis that the Court has not sufficiently appreciated particular aspects of domestic rules of procedure and evidence.

[97] *R (Anderson) v Secretary of State for the Home Department* [2003] 1 AC 837. In *AF v Secretary of State for the Home Department* [2009] 3 WLR 74, the Secretary of State sought to argue that the Grand Chamber in *A v United Kingdom* (2009) 49 EHRR 29, which was almost directly on point, had not had 'the full picture'. This submission was rejected on the basis that Strasbourg was not only fully appraised of the relevant law and arguments, but had been invited to rule definitively on the issue (see [53] (Lord Phillips), [82] (Lord Hope) and [111] and [119] (Lord Brown)).

[98] *Ullah* (n 95); *EM (Lebanon) v Secretary of State for the Home Department* [2009] 1 AC 1198, [2008] 3 WLR 931; *RB (Algeria) v Secretary of State for the Home Department* [2009] 2 WLR 512 (Art 5, also developing the law under Art 8).

[99] *R (Limbuela) v Secretary of State for the Home Department* [2006] 1 AC 396.

[100] *Savage v South Essex Partnership NHS Foundation Trust* [2009] 1 AC 681. The ECtHR had only recognised a less exacting duty in this context: *Powell v United Kingdom* (2000) 30 EHRR CD 362.

order was unlawful. He reasoned, 'I think that nowadays a longer curfew regime than 16 hours a day (with the additional restraints imposed in these cases) would surely be classified in Strasbourg as a deprivation of liberty.'[101]

Cases such as these, in which the domestic courts have to some degree parted company with the Strasbourg jurisprudence, cannot truly be regarded as establishing a domestic jurisprudence of constitutional rights because such departures are necessary incidents of the domestic courts having a jurisdiction to remedy violations of the European Convention. They are consistent with the domestic courts seeking to provide a remedy which would be provided if the claimant were to go all the way to Strasbourg. They are therefore consistent with the pragmatic, remedial approach to the Human Rights Act reflected in *Ullah*.

These cases point us to another consequence of the purposive approach taken by the domestic courts. If the purpose of the Act is simply to provide a remedy that could be obtained in Strasbourg and to save litigants the cost of a trip across the channel, then the function of the courts in cases where no Strasbourg case is on point should be to attempt to predict what the Strasbourg court would decide if it were seized of the matter. Whilst it is often the case that lawyers attempt to predict what courts will decide, the function of the courts is to interpret the law for themselves and decide what they think the right answer is. The slip into predictive reasoning is indicative of the courts treating Strasbourg jurisprudence, and Convention rights under the Human Rights Act, as if it is foreign law which is to be applied in domestic courts as a question of fact. Indeed, when the cases are examined, numerous examples of predictive rather than normative reasoning can be found. A clear example is provided by Lord Rodger's speech in *Al-Jedda* in which he stated:

> The House . . . is called upon to assess how a claim by the appellant, that his international law rights under article 5(1) of the Convention had been violated by the United Kingdom, would fare before the European court in Strasbourg.

Lord Roger then formulated the issues in the case as three questions, each of which asked how the ECtHR would resolve the issues if they arose in a case before it.[102] His Lordship proceeded to analyse the Strasbourg jurisprudence in an attempt to form an opinion on how the claimant's case would fare in Strasbourg. He concluded that it would fail.[103]

---

[101] *JJ v Secretary of State for the Home Department* [2008] 1 AC 385 [106].

[102] *Al-Jedda* (n 81) [55]: 'How would that court resolve the two issues of international law? Would the European court hold that the appellant's complaint was incompatible *ratione personae* with the provisions of the Convention? If not, would it hold that, by reason of articles 25 and 103 of the Charter, in so far as there was a conflict, the obligations of the British forces under Security Council Resolution 1546 prevailed over the United Kingdom's obligations under article 5(1) of the European Convention?'

[103] ibid [105], [111] and [117]. By contrast, Baroness Hale expressed the main issue in explicitly normative terms: 'some way has to be found of reconciling our competing commitments under the United Nations Charter and the European Convention' ([125]). Even so, predictions as to the approach that would be taken by the ECtHR were still influential. For example, Lord Bingham stated: 'I do not think that the European court, if the appellant's article 5(1) claim were before it as an application, would ignore the significance of article 103 of the Charter in international law' ([36]).

The *Al-Jedda* case did not relate to the substantive meaning of Convention rights, a question that might receive a different answer depending on one's cultural and moral perspective, but rather to a more formal question about the hierarchy of norms in international law.[104] This however is not the explanation for the resort to predictive reasoning in Lord Rodger's speech. A similar approach can be found in many other cases under the Human Rights Act, including cases squarely relating to the substantive interpretation of the scope of Convention rights, as the above quotation from *JJ* shows.[105] Sometimes it is at the forefront of judgments and sometimes it is a component of a more normative analysis. But where this resort to predictive reasoning occurs, it is a reflection of thinking about the Human Rights Act in terms of it being a pragmatic measure intended to provide a remedy for breaches of international law, and not as a statute establishing domestic constitutional rights. But this point can be taken further. Upon reflection, what is in fact more surprising and significant than the frequency with which judges lapse into predictive reasoning when applying the Human Rights Act is the extent to which they do *not* do so, given the prominence of the remedial view of the purpose of the Human Rights Act in the case law under the Act. It is often the case that what courts say they are doing distracts attention from what they are actually doing. In this context it might be suggested that whilst the courts say that they are simply providing a Strasbourg remedy in domestic courts, they are in fact developing a domestic jurisprudence on the interpretation of the European Convention. There are cases which provide support to such a view more explicitly, and it is to these that we now turn.

Constitutional Understandings of the Human Rights Act

The international/remedial/practical understanding of the Human Rights Act has never been perfectly reflected in the case law, and we have already identified some tensions in the cases. Some judges have set out their stall clearly against such an

---

[104] Essentially the same point was made by Lord Brown in *JJ* (n 101) [106] about the issue of interpretation of the Convention that arose in *Al-Skeini*: 'whereas the issue in *Al-Skeini* was as to the reach of article 1 itself—an issue to which the European Court of Human Rights in *Bankovic v Belgium* (2001) 11 BHRC 435, paras 64 and 65, had made plain that the "living instrument" approach does not apply— here by contrast the court recognised in Guzzardi . . . that developing legal standards and attitudes will further increase the variety of forms of deprivation of liberty.'

[105] See also *EM (Lebanon)* (n 98) [15] (Lord Hope), *Countryside Alliance* [2008] 1 AC 719 [127] (Baroness Hale). Where a predictive approach is taken, it follows logically that courts should place weight on the views of persons and bodies which are well-informed about the ECtHR and the likely outcome of any consideration by it. In *Re G* (n 96) Lord Hoffmann thought it 'not at all unlikely that if the issue in this case were to go to Strasbourg, the court would hold that discrimination against a couple who wish to adopt a child on the ground that they are not married would violate article 14.' He then supported his view by reference to the opinion of the Joint Parliamentary Committee on Human Rights and a respected academic who had been commissioned by the Northern Ireland Government to consider the issue ([27]–[28]). For reasons explained below, Lord Hoffmann's consideration of what the likely outcome would be in Strasbourg was expressly subsidiary in this case, because on the facts he felt free to interpret the Convention for himself.

approach. The most explicit has been Laws LJ. His Lordship has described the Human Rights Act as a 'constitutional statute',[106] and in *Begum* his Lordship stated:[107]

> I think it important to have in mind that the court's task under the Human Rights Act 1998, in this context as in many others, is not simply to add on the Strasbourg learning to the corpus of English law, as if it were a compulsory adjunct taken from an alien source, but to develop a municipal law of human rights by the incremental method of the common law, case by case, taking account of the Strasbourg jurisprudence as section 2 of the 1998 Act enjoins us to do.

However, judges are rarely quite so forthright, and close scrutiny is required if we are to tease out the influence of this way of thinking in other cases. Let us consider four particular examples that evidence the influence of this alternative understanding of the Act.

The first example is provided by *Re McKerr*.[108] The issue was whether the obligation arising under Article 2 of the Convention to investigate a death in certain circumstances can be enforced under the Human Rights Act in relation to deaths occurring before it came into effect. Since a claim could have been brought in Strasbourg it was argued that domestic law should be given retrospective effect, since this would ensure that the claimant was not forced to petition the ECtHR. The House of Lords rejected the submission, holding that the Human Rights Act had created new domestic law rights, and could not provide a remedy, such as ordering an investigation, in relation to conduct occurring prior to its enactment. Lord Nicholls stated that rights under the Convention and those under the Human Rights Act 'now exist side by side', and since the Act had created new, distinct, domestic law rights, they could not be extended backwards in time.[109] Lord Nicholls' comments about the Human Rights Act and the Convention standing side by side are often relied upon as showing that the Human Rights Act has created domestic constitutional rights. But it is, of course, incontrovertible that the Human Rights Act has created domestic law rights in the sense of having provided a *cause of action* in domestic courts for breaches of Convention rights. The interesting question is whether the substantive rights themselves are of the nature and status of domestic constitutional rights or whether they are in reality international law rights given effect in domestic law. Lord Nicholls' speech does not address this point, because he was simply making the obvious point that the Human Rights Act is a creature of domestic law which has created a cause of action in the domestic courts that did not previously exist. It would be surprising if his Lordship intended to go further than this, given his comments in *Quark Fishing*. However, Lord

---

[106] *Thoburn v Sunderland City Council* [2002] 3 WLR 247 [62].
[107] *Begum v Tower Hamlets LBC* [2002] 1 WLR 2491 [17]. Lord Steyn possibly hinted at a similar view in *Brown v Stott* [2003] 1 AC 681, 798 where he described the European Convention on Human Rights as 'our Bill of Rights' and said this was the matrix in which the Human Rights Act should be considered.
[108] *Re McKerr* [2004] 1 WLR 807.
[109] ibid [25].

Hoffmann made comments that did go further than this, and which clearly suggested that the Convention rights are substantively domestic in nature. His Lordship stated:

> What the Act has done is to create domestic rights expressed in the same terms as those contained in the Convention. But they are domestic rights, not international rights. Their source is the statute, not the Convention. They are available against specific public authorities, not the United Kingdom as a state. And their meaning and application is a matter for domestic courts, not the court in Strasbourg.[110]

More ambiguously, Lord Rodger stated that the Human Rights Act 'reproduces' Convention rights in domestic law and that the domestic rights are set out in schedule 1 of the Act.[111] Although these comments can be reconciled with the approach taken in *Quark Fishing* by reference to the particular wording of section 21(1) of the Human Rights Act,[112] they are undoubtedly in tension with *Al-Jedda*, which depended on the reasoning that section 2 of the Act merely identified international obligations binding the United Kingdom from time to time, the breach of which can be remedied in domestic courts.[113]

The second example is *YL v Birmingham City Council* in which a majority of the House of Lords gave a restrictive interpretation to the meaning of 'public authority' under section 6 of the Act.[114] Pursuant to its duty under section 21 of the National Assistance Act 1948 to provide accommodation to the claimant, the local authority contracted with a company running private care homes. The company subsequently sought to remove the claimant from her home, and an action was brought under the Human Rights Act against the company. The majority held that the care home provider was not a public authority within the meaning of section 6 of the Act. Notably, Lord Neuberger placed particular reliance on the principle in *Quark Fishing Ltd* and on his Lordship's assessment that the claimant would not be able to maintain an action in Strasbourg against the United Kingdom for its conduct. Most interesting however are the dissenting speeches of Lord Bingham and Baroness Hale. Lord Bingham reasoned that section 6 is a 'provision in a domestic statute, to be construed as such' and its meaning 'is not to be found in the Convention'. He thought it should be given a 'generously wide scope'.[115] But

---

[110] ibid [63].

[111] ibid [75].

[112] Lord Hoffmann rested his judgment in that case on those words without reference to *McKerr*. He would have held that even if the Convention had been extended to South Georgia and the South Sandwich Islands, an action under the Act would still not have been possible because s 21(1) refers to the Convention as it has effect in relation to the United Kingdom, and the Secretary of State had acted on behalf of Her Majesty as sovereign of the South Georgia and South Sandwich Islands (*Quark Fishing* (n 74) [56]).

[113] Lord Hoffmann was not part of the Committee in *Al-Jedda* or *Al-Skeini*, but Lord Rodger referred without demur to the Court of Appeal in his speech in *Al-Jedda* (n 81 [53]) and gave the leading speech on the extra-territorial scope of the Human Rights Act in *Al-Skeini*. However in *Al-Jedda* Lord Rodger also stated that Convention rights are 'distinct obligations' in domestic law and the Convention is not incorporated as such (ibid [51]).

[114] *YL v Birmingham City Council* [2008] 1 AC 95 .

[115] ibid [4].

of course the scope of the European Convention had previously been regarded as determinative of the scope of the Act in *Quark Fishing, Al-Jedda, Al-Skeini* and *Ullah*. When read alongside his speech in *Al-Skeini*, Lord Bingham's remarks indicate that he held a more nuanced and less one-dimensional understanding of the purpose of the Human Rights Act than his reasoning in cases such as *Ullah* suggests. Baroness Hale gave a speech to similar effect. Whilst she noted that the United Kingdom Government is often held responsible in Strasbourg for acts or omissions of private bodies, and referred to the purposive principle of interpretation, it is notable that her Ladyship did not consider whether an action by the claimant would actually have succeeded in Strasbourg. Instead, she emphasised that the Human Rights Act was also intended to promote Convention values in society, and referred to a statement by Jack Straw MP who promoted the Bill in Parliament, that it was intended to go 'at least' as wide as the United Kingdom's responsibilities under the European Convention.[116] This was a significant break with the purposive approach, and suggested a constitutional dimension to the Human Rights Act.

The third example is *Animal Defenders*, in which House of Lords rejected a challenge to a blanket statutory prohibition on political advertising contained in section 321(2) of the Communications Act 2003 by an animal rights organisation who had fallen foul of it.[117] The Committee held that a judgment of the ECtHR pointing the other way was confined to its facts and did not establish a determinative principle.[118] Importantly, Lord Scott contemplated the possibility that domestic courts might give a different interpretation to Convention rights under the Human Rights Act to those given by the ECtHR. He said that a 'divergence' was at least implicitly contemplated by section 2 of the Human Rights Act. He then went on to ask whether a declaration of incompatibility is intended to draw the Government and Parliament's attention to a breach of international law or to a breach of the Human Rights Act. His Lordship reasoned:

> An important purpose of a declaration of incompatibility is, as I see it, to draw the attention of the Government, Parliament and the United Kingdom public to an inconsistency between the provision of domestic legislation in question and the rights under domestic law conferred on the applicant . . .[119]

But Lord Scott also reasoned that a declaration has also the former purpose of drawing attention to the fact that the United Kingdom is in breach of its international obligations. His Lordship left open what is the 'prime purpose'. Although Lord Scott did not refer to it, these comments are supported by the House of Lords' decision in *Bellinger v Bellinger*, in which the House of Lords rejected the

[116] ibid [54]. Interestingly, relying on comments made by Lord Nicholls in *Aston Cantlow and Wilmcote with Billesley Parochial Church Council v Wallbank* [2004] 1 AC 546 [11]. For Jack Straw's statement (Second Reading): Hansard HC col 773 (16 February 1998).
[117] *R (Animal Defenders International) v Secretary of State for Culture, Media and Sport* [2008] 1 AC 1312.
[118] The case was *VgT Verein gegen Tierfabriken v Switzerland* (2001) 34 EHRR 159.
[119] *Animal Defenders* (n 117) [46].

submission that since the United Kingdom had already been found to be in breach of its international obligations by the ECtHR in respect of the recognition of trans-sexual persons, there was no need for the Court to make a declaration of incompatibility.[120] His comments make explicit the tensions inherent in the Human Rights Act. Nonetheless, Lord Bingham and Baroness Hale went out of their way to disprove the remarks made by Lord Scott on the basis that the courts should follow the Strasbourg case law and there is therefore no scope for the divergence that he contemplated.

The final case, *Re G (Adoption: Unmarried Couple)*, however, amply vindicates Lord Scott's remarks.[121] The Adoption (Northern Ireland) Order 1987 imposed a blanket ban on two unmarried people being approved jointly as adoptive parents. The ECtHR had previously held that even express discrimination against homosexuals, precluding them from adopting children, was within States' margin of appreciation.[122] The claim in *G*, which was brought by a heterosexual couple, therefore seemed doomed. The House of Lords squarely faced the issue of whether it could legitimately condemn the order if it thought that the ECtHR would not do so. The Committee held unanimously that it could. Echoing his speech in *McKerr*, Lord Hoffmann, leading the Committee, reasoned that Convention rights are domestic law rights set out in the schedule to the Human Rights Act which simply 'reproduc[e] *the language* of the international Convention' (emphasis supplied). He held that, the 'first duty' of domestic courts, 'is to give effect to the domestic statute according to what they consider to be its proper meaning'.[123] Lord Mance stated that the schedule to the Human Rights Act included new domestic rights that fall to be interpreted as a matter of domestic law.[124]

An important feature of *Re G* was undoubtedly that there was no question of the House of Lords, by its interpretation of Article 14, putting the United Kingdom in breach of its international obligations, as it would have done if it had given a more restrictive, rather than a more liberal, interpretation to a Convention right than the ECtHR had done. Moreover, the favoured interpretation of Article 14 did not go beyond what Strasbourg had held the Convention could be interpreted to require: it was an interpretation that was within the margin of appreciation of national authorities. This latter point was emphasised by the majority. It allowed them to claim that their approach was consistent with *Ullah*.[125] However, that the majority speeches were reflective of a more constitutional way of thinking about the Human Rights Act can hardly be denied. It is highlighted by the terms of Lord Walker's dissent. Lord Walker reasoned that it could not confidently be predicted that the ECtHR would condemn the Order, if asked to do so, and therefore the Committee was going further than it was required to go by the Human Rights Act,

---

120 *Bellinger v Bellinger* [2003] 2 AC 467.
121 *Re G (sub nom Re P) (Adoption: Unmarried Couple)* [2009] 1 AC 173.
122 *Frette v France* (2002) 38 EHRR 438.
123 *Re G* (n 121) [33]–[34].
124 ibid [129].
125 ibid [30]–[38] (Lord Hoffmann), [50] (Lord Hope), [120] (Baroness Hale).

and such a step could only properly be taken by Parliament or by the Strasbourg Court itself.

Moreover, Baroness Hale expressly recognised the tension within the Human Rights Act that was exposed by the case. She said that the case raised a question as to whether the Convention rights under the Human Rights Act are rights defined by the ECtHR but given effect in United Kingdom law, or rights defined by United Kingdom courts within the parameters prescribed by the ECtHR. Baroness Hale might have added a further alternative: that the Human Rights Act creates rights defined by United Kingdom courts guided by the approach taken by the ECtHR. She nonetheless rightly described this as a 'dilemma' and admitted that it was one that she did not find easy to resolve. She referred to statements made in Parliament during the passing of the Bill to the effect that, 'the courts must be free to develop human rights jurisprudence and to move out in new directions', and she concluded that where a domestic court applying the Human Rights Act forms the view that there is no objective justification for different treatment, the domestic court should afford the individual a remedy, because it is their duty to act compatibly with Convention rights (as public authorities under section 6).[126] However the dilemma cannot be reconciled so easily. The failure to afford a remedy is generally only a breach of Article 13 of the Convention and this article is not given effect by the Human Rights Act. The dilemma is more deep-rooted. We have seen that Lord Hoffmann found the answer in the domestic nature of 'Convention rights'. This, it is respectfully submitted, is indeed where the answer lies. But Lord Hoffmann's view is in tension with the numerous cases in which the international nature of Convention rights has been influential and indeed determinative. The emphasis given by Lord Hoffmann and Lord Mance to the fact that the Human Rights Act sets out domestic rights in the schedule is, as we have seen, contrary to the idea that the rights given effect by the Act are actually those which inhabit the realm of international law.[127]

The approach taken in *G* is also difficult if not impossible to reconcile with other cases.[128] In *M v Secretary of State for Work and Pensions*, the House of Lords held that regulations for the calculation of child support contributions which were less

---

[126] ibid [118]–[119] and [122]. For the parliamentary comments, see Jack Straw MP, Hansard HC col 768 (16 February 1998) and Lord Irvine LC, Hansard HL cols 514–15 (18 November 1997).

[127] Jonathan Lewis has also contended that this case represents an erosion of the 'mirror principle' and suggests that the approach of Lord Hoffmann and Baroness Hale departs from that of Lord Bingham and Lord Brown. The reference to Lord Brown is to his Lordship's suggestion in *Al-Skeini* that the *Ullah* principle could be rephrased to mean 'no less, but certainly no more': (n 95) [106]. See J Lewis '*In re P and others*: an exception to the "no more, certainly no less" rule' [2009] *PL* 43, 46. Whilst in broad agreement with Lewis's analysis, the discussion here, which has ranged wider than the courts' approach to s 2 which is Lewis's concern, has suggested that Baroness Hale's position has differed significantly from Lord Hoffmann's (indeed she endorsed Lord Brown's comments in *Al-Skeini* at (n 95) [90]).

[128] In *R (Clift) v Secretary of State for the Home Department* [2007] 1 AC 484 the House of Lords refused to recognise that the nature and length of a prison sentence constitutes a 'status' under Art 14 and therefore that different treatment by reference to a prisoner's status requires justification. They did so because the ECtHR had not gone so far. But, following the logic of *G*, the House of Lords should have decided whether as a matter of principle it considered that Art 14 was applicable.

[handwritten note: Q, is it the role of the UK cause to follow the ECtHR or to go their own way / direction]

favourable to mothers whose partners contributed to her mortgage if her partner was another woman, did not constitute unlawful discrimination on grounds of sexual orientation contrary to Arts 8 and 14 of the Convention.[129] The majority reasoned that the ECtHR would have held that discrimination on grounds of sexual orientation was still within the United Kingdom's margin of appreciation. But in *G* the House of Lords held that on the assumption that discrimination against unmarried couples was within the United Kingdom's margin of appreciation, it was nonetheless unjustified. Now recall Lord Scott's maligned remarks in *Animal Defenders*. It can now be seen that his Lordship identified an aspect of the tension that came to the fore in *G*. Imagine for example if the legislation in issue in *G* had been primary legislation rather than delegated legislation. The House of Lords would surely have declared it incompatible with the Convention rights given their reasoning in that case. But, at least on the assumption postulated by the Committee that the ECtHR would have held that the matter fell within the United Kingdom's margin of appreciation, in so doing they would not have been declaring a breach of the United Kingdom's international obligations but rather declaring the legislation incompatible with the rights protected by the Human Rights Act.

Is the Human Rights Act a Constitutional Statute?

Those who argue that the Human Rights Act is a 'constitutional statute' tend to point principally to the fact that the courts have not applied the doctrine of implied repeal to its provisions and therefore that it is afforded some special status by the courts. The argument is that legislation enacted by Parliament since 2 October 2000 which impliedly limits Convention rights is qualified by section 3 of the Human Rights Act, rather than the Human Rights Act being limited insofar as it conflicts with the latter statute.[130] This argument is rather a strange one. As Professor David Feldman has explained, section 3 operates like the Interpretation Act 1978 in 'shaping the interpretation and implementation of other legislation.'[131] Legislation that is inconsistent with Convention rights does not impliedly repeal the Convention rights because the meaning of the latter statute, properly understood, does not limit Convention rights insofar as it can be interpreted compatibly with them. It only limits Convention rights if it cannot be given a compatible meaning, and in such a case the latter statute will prevail. The point is that Convention rights, given effect through section 3 of the Human Rights Act,[132] are *interpretive* norms. They are just as much part of the actual meaning of the subsequent legislation enacted by Parliament as the provisions of the interpretation Act

---

[129] *M v Secretary of State for Work and Pensions* [2006] 2 AC 91.

[130] See AL Young, *Parliamentary Sovereignty and the Human Rights Act* (Oxford, Hart, 2009) 54–63.

[131] D Feldman, 'The Human Rights Act 1998 and Constitutional Principles' (1999) 19 *Legal Studies* 165.

[132] For present purposes we can leave to one side ss 6 and 4.

or the principles of construction at common law. By contrast the provisions of a latter statute which appear to limit a Convention right are not interpretative norms, and their meaning is subject to rules and principles of interpretation. Section 3 of the Human Rights Act would only be tested against the doctrine of implied repeal if Parliament enacted a rule of interpretation which in a particular instance led to a competing interpretation of a statutory provision. In such a scenario the court would have to decide whether the status of the Human Rights Act is such that the interpretive norm contained in section 3 should prevail over that contained in the later statute.[133]

It must also be doubted whether any other provisions of the Human Rights Act have any resistance to repeal. It would seem to operate like a normal statute in relation to express amendment of its provision.[134] In *A v B*, the Supreme Court held that section 65(2)(a) of the Regulation of Investigatory Powers Act 2000, which provides that the Investigatory Powers Tribunal is the 'only appropriate tribunal' for considering claims under section 7(1)(a) of the Human Rights Act brought against the intelligence services prevents claims also being commenced in the courts, although section 7(2) of the Human Rights Act provides that claims can be brought under section 7(1)(a) in such court of tribunal 'as may be determined by rules'. The relevant rules provided that claims could be brought in the courts. Therefore if section 65(2)(a) was read so as to exclude claims against the intelligence services under the Human Rights Act in the ordinary courts, it would have the effect of impliedly repealing section 7(2).[135] The Supreme Court nonetheless held that section 65(2)(a) did prevent actions proceeding in the ordinary courts and prevailed over section 7(2).[136] Although their Lordships reasoned that that the 2000 Act, the Human Rights Act and the rules are all part of a single legislative scheme, they did not do so in order to rebut an argument that the Human Rights Act was being impliedly repealed by the 2000 Act, but in order to rebut the submission that the right of access to the ordinary courts was ousted by section 65(2)(a) of that Act. No point was in fact taken as to the resistance of the Human Rights Act to implied repeal before Supreme Court or before the courts below, no doubt reflecting the fact that such a submission would have received short shrift.

---

[133] For a much more detailed analysis of this point, reaching the same conclusion, see Young, *Parliamentary Sovereignty*, ch 2, n 130. In particular, Young states: 'section 3(1) itself can be impliedly repealed, but . . . this would only be the case where a future legislative provision imposed a contradictory duty of interpretation on the judiciary' (53).

[134] The Act has been amended by primary legislation on several occasions, albeit to make relatively minor changes relating to the establishment of the Supreme Court and alterations to the devolution arrangements for Wales. Section 145 of the Health and Social Care Act 2008 essentially amends s 6 of the Human Rights Act so as to overrule the effect of *YL* in relation to care homes. It has the effect of extending rather than restricting s 6. Although this provision does not formally amend s 6 it in effect does so, and the change could have been affected by amendment.

[135] CPR 7.11 states: '(1) A claim under section 7(1) of the 1998 Act in respect of a judicial act may be brought only in the High Court, (2) Any other claim under section 7(1)(a) of that Act may be brought in any court.'

[136] [2010] 2 WLR 1.

The reason why the Human Rights Act is properly regarded as having a special status in domestic law is therefore not because of any special resistance to repeal. It is because, however mundane the drafters made it sound, it is an Act that purports to protect fundamental rights and freedoms and, moreover, it does so not only by providing a remedy for breaches of human rights and fundamental freedoms, but (and this is crucial) by establishing such rights and freedoms as general norms, that apply to all legislation and all conduct of public authorities. Of course the rights and freedoms *could* have been given *greater* protection (such as by prevailing over primary legislation), and the norms *could* have been even more generally framed (such as by applying to private parties as well as public authorities), but despite its limits, the Human Rights Act has a central controlling role in the legal system as a whole, and in public law especially, where it operates by establishing general criteria of legality.[137] As such, the Human Rights Act is a core component of the rule of law as it operates in the United Kingdom today. Indeed, as we have seen, it goes considerably further than the doctrine of common law fundamental rights which are themselves described as 'constitutional' because of their general nature and effect in controlling both the meaning of legislation and public authority decision-making. If the litmus test of constitutionality is satisfied in respect of common law public law rights, then the position is a fortiori in relation to the Human Rights Act.

As the discussion in the previous section has shown, it is nonetheless an unfortunate fact that the rights protected by the Human Rights Act are worryingly fragile in important respects. The most significant of these is the vulnerability of Convention rights to repeal or amendment by executive action in international law. But the degree to which domestic courts feel bound to follow, and attempt to predict, Strasbourg court judgments is also concerning and a powerful contrary indication that the Act does not establish domestic constitutional rights.

A further consideration in this respect is the degree of public and political disenchantment with the Act. There can be little doubt that the Human Rights Act has failed to capture the public imagination and has been much maligned in the English and Scottish newspapers. Britain's best-selling newspaper, *The Sun*, has an on-going campaign calling for the 'scrapping' of what it describes as a 'disgraceful' piece of legislation.[138] In 2005 the Department of Constitutional Affairs sought to

---

[137] It is also of importance that the Northern Ireland Act 1998, the Scotland Act 1998 and the Government of Wales Act 1998, each define 'the Convention rights' by reference to the meaning given in the Human Rights Act. This is a point of much wider significance, not least because it raises questions about the form of constitutionalism in those regions given that the scope of devolved power is limited by reference to the Convention rights: are these domestic constitutional rights established by the Human Rights Act, or are they international obligations binding on the United Kingdom? For some discussion on the constitutional relationship between the Human Rights Act and the devolution legislation, which regrettably goes beyond the scope of this book, see Beatson, Grosz, Hickman and Singh, *Human Rights*, (n 48) ch 8.

[138] 'Time to Act' *The Sun* (London, 15 May 2006). A characteristic example is in an article published in 2006 in which the paper claimed that, 'The HRA has been to blame for a string of barmy court rulings. It also prevents Britain from deporting known foreign criminals': 'Terror Laws "Abuse Rights"' (London, 29 June 2006). The Scottish press has been particularly incensed by the finding that the

correct what it described as 'myths and misconceptions' about the Act. The Lord Chancellor in his introduction to this Review stated that, 'The purpose and effect of the Human Rights Act has been widely misrepresented and misunderstood.' Misapprehensions, he said, 'abound' not only among the general public, but also among public servants.[139] Even so, Labour ministers, particularly since the terrorist attacks in September 2001, have been highly critical of judicial decisions under the Act and related pieces of legislation.[140] The Conservative Party has stated that if they take power at the 2010 general election they will repeal the Act and replace it with a Bill of Rights. These counter-considerations do not however detract from the legal significance of the Human Rights Act and its centrality to the current constitutional order.[141] What they do is make clear that it would be wrong to speak of the Human Rights Act as a 'Bill of Rights', which requires legislation to have a degree of popular and political importance[142]—both in fact and by design—as a criterion of constitutional legitimacy, which the Human Rights Act does not have. Whilst it might be a controlling influence on the entire legal system, it does not have the same centrality and degree of gravitational force in politics and general society.[143] It is hard to think of a single instance of a politician or public official being censured by a non-lawyer for breaching a Convention right; on the contrary, the Human Rights Act is usually portrayed as the villain of the piece.

Effect on the Common Law

The early indications were that the Human Rights Act would accelerate the common law's fledgling protections of human rights. However, as time has gone on, a

system of slopping-out and associated prison conditions is not Convention compatible: eg 'Convicts' £50m "human rights" pay-out facing the axe' *Scotsman* (Edinburgh, 12 March 2009) and editorial 'Time to clear the lingering stink of slopping-out court challenges'.

[139] Department of Constitutional Affairs, *Review of the Implementation of the Human Rights Act* (July 2005) 5 (Introduction by the Lord Chancellor).

[140] See 'Terror Laws "Abuse Rights"'' (n 137) on the Home Secretary's reaction to Mr Justice Sullivan's judgment in *MB v Secretary of State for the Home Department* [2006] HRLR 29. "Human Rights Rule will Cripple Troops" *The Sun* (London, 19 May 2009) reporting the Secretary of State for Defence's comments that the Court of Appeal's judgment in *Smith* [2009] EWCA Civ 441 (holding that the military must take appropriate measures to protect the life of soldiers inside military bases) will have serious detrimental effect on the ability of the armed forces to operate, and the Shadow Home Secretary's comments, which were less guarded, 'to apply the Human Rights Act in a War Zone flies in the face of common sense'. See also 'Human Rights Act will hamper soldiers in action, warns MOD' *Independent* (London, 17 May 2009).

[141] On which see V Bogdanor, *The New British Constitution* (Oxford, Hart, 2009).

[142] Contrast P Alston, *Promoting Human Rights Through Bills of Rights* (New York, Clarendon, 1999) 10 and A Kavanagh, *Constitutional Review under the UK Human Rights Act* (Cambridge, Cambridge University Press, 2009) 308 who define a Bill of Rights by reference to its legal status and effect.

[143] Shortly after *The Sun* publicly transferred its support from Labour to the Conservative Party, David Cameron, the Conservative Party leader, made a number of pledges in the newspaper which included that the Conservatives would, 'replace the Human Rights Act with a new British Bill of Rights to strengthen Britain's traditional liberties': 'My Blueprint for Britain' *Sun* (London, 2 October 2009).

far more complex picture has developed, of which a dominant feature has been the inhibiting effect that the Human Rights Act has had on common law development. Much of this book is concerned with the effect of the Human Rights Act on the common law in the context of public law. This section serves to introduce the issue by a general survey.

There are two ways that the Human Rights Act can lead to development of the common law.[144] The first is where the Human Rights Act requires a development of the common law in order to ensure that the law is compatible with Convention rights. This occurs because the court is a public authority under section 6 of the Human Rights Act, and therefore when a judicial decision would constitute a breach of Convention rights the courts are required not to reach such a decision and ensure that the law is compatible with the Convention. This is subject to three caveats. The first caveat is that since the Human Rights Act does not give effect to Article 13 of the European Convention, the courts are not required to fashion remedies for breaches of Convention rights committed by other state agencies. Thus in *Re S*, the House of Lords held that the courts were not required to fashion a system of 'starred care plans' to ensure that children taken into care had an effective remedy for any failings by the local authority.[145] The second caveat is that the courts do not act unlawfully when they are required or entitled to reach a decision by the terms of primary legislation (s 6(2)). The source of the incompatibility is the legislation and not the courts. If appropriate, the courts can declare such legislation to be incompatibility with Convention rights (s 4), but they must first consider whether it would be possible to read the legislation consistently with Convention rights (s 3). The third caveat is that the courts cannot be required to develop the law to ensure that there is no incompatibility with articles of the Convention where to do so would take them outside their constitutional responsibility, most obviously where it would require them to step across the Rubicon between interpreting the law and legislating. Again, the defective state of the law that gives rise to a breach of Convention rights is not properly attributable to the courts but to Parliament.[146]

The second way that the Human Rights Act leads to the development of the common law relates to those cases where its influence is indirect: where it does not *require* common law change but it does *support* such change. The common law is always sensitive to statute and is influenced by principled legislation.[147] The Human Rights Act will therefore signal to judges the values that the general law should reflect in a modern democracy.[148] Many of these are already found in the

---

[144] These points are developed at length in Beatson, Grosz, Hickman and Singh, *Human Rights* (n 48) 4-159 to 4-235, and 6-128 to 6-155.

[145] *Re S (Minors) (Care Order: Implementation of Care Plan)* [2002] 2 AC 291.

[146] Parliament cannot be held liable for a failure to legislate (Human Rights Act s 6(3)), but the Government will be responsible for the defective state of the law in Strasbourg.

[147] See J Beatson, 'The Role of Statute in the Development of Common Law Doctrine' (2001) 117 LQR 247; see also the discussion of Dicey in ch 3 pp 76–81.

[148] In 2000 Anthony Lester QC and David Pannick QC wrote, in comments later approved by Lord Walker, that 'Convention rights must be woven into the fabric of domestic law. In the absence of a British Constitution, it is especially important to weave the Convention rights into the principle of the common law and equity so that they strengthen rather than undermine those principles . . .': 'The

common law, but the existence of the Human Rights Act is capable of giving them added force. The Human Rights Act also alters the legal relationship between individuals and public authorities, and this has implications for the application of common law doctrines such as 'proximity' in tort law, and 'relevant considerations' in public law, which are reflective of that relationship and the particular context in which individuals are affected by decisions of public bodies.

As mentioned above, the early indications suggested that the common law would be invigorated by the Human Rights Act. It also appeared that the common law would remain the primary source of human rights protection. In a judgment delivered in October 1999 in *Reynolds v Times Newspapers Ltd*, the House of Lords interpreted the defence of qualified privilege consistently with Articles 8 and 10 of the Convention, although the Human Rights Act was not then in effect.[149] The House of Lords referred to the 'fundamental' common law rights of freedom of expression and protection of reputation in emphasising that the common law was a sufficient source of fundamental rights and human rights values, albeit that the common law was to be developed in the light of the enactment of the Human Rights Act.[150] Lord Nicholls said that these common law rights would be 'buttressed' by the Human Rights Act, and that henceforth, '[t]he common law is to be developed and applied in a manner consistent' with Article 10 of the Convention.[151] Lord Steyn stated that the 'constitutional dimension' of freedom of expression would be 'reinforced'.[152] Lord Cooke stated that the European Convention, in particular amongst international human rights instruments, 'should have an important part to play in developments of the common law.'[153] All of this was in tune with previous cases in which the domestic courts had emphasised that the common law provides no less protection for human rights than the European Convention and in which the common law had been influential in the development of common law standards.[154]

In a similar vein, in May 2001, the House of Lords decided in *Daly* that a prison policy requiring inspection of privileged correspondence in the absence of the prisoner was unlawful, on the basis that it infringed a common law constitutional right to privileged legal advice. Lord Cooke stated that it was 'of great importance

---

Impact of the Human Rights Act on Private Law: the Knight's Move' (2000) 116 *LQR* 380, 383; cited in *Doherty v Birmingham City Council* [2009] 1 AC 367 [109].

[149] *Reynolds v Times Newspapers Ltd* [2001] 2 AC 127.

[150] ibid 190 (Lord Nicholls).

[151] ibid 200.

[152] ibid 207. In *R v Shayler* [2003] 1 AC 247 [22] Lord Bingham stated that the Human Rights Act has 'underpinned' the fundamental right to freedom of expression recognised by the common law.

[153] *Reynolds* (n 149) 223

[154] *Attorney General v Guardian Newspapers Ltd* [1987] 1 WLR 1248, 1296–97 (Lord Templeman); *Attorney-General v Guardian Newspapers (No 2)* [1990] 1 AC 109, 283–84 (Lord Goff); *Derbyshire County Council v Times Newspapers Ltd* [1993] AC 534, 551 (Lord Keith); *R v Lord Chancellor, ex p Witham* [1997] QB 575, 585 (Laws LJ); *R v Home Secretary, ex p Leech* [1994] QB 198, 210 (CA); *Director of Public Prosecutions v Jones* [1999] 2 AC 240; and *R v Governor of Brockhill Prison, ex p Evans* [2001] 2 AC 19; although cp *Hunter v Canary Wharf Ltd* [1997] AC 655 in which the law of nuisance was not developed (contrary to the views of Lord Cooke (714–15) who dissented) in a way that would have protected the plaintiffs' Art 8 rights.

that the common law by itself is being recognised as a sufficient source of the fundamental right to confidential communication with a legal adviser . . .', not least because the decision on the common law would have persuasive influence in other common law jurisdictions.[155] Lord Bingham, who gave the leading speech, adopted these comments expressly and simply noted that the same result would have been reached applying the Convention rights directly.[156] Alongside *Reynolds*, *Daly* signalled that the common law would continue to be developed and applied where possible in preference to the Human Rights Act. Strasbourg principles would be deployed to influence common law development and the Human Rights Act would act as a safety net for cases where the common law did not apply. The fact that it rapidly became clear that damages would rarely be awarded under the Human Rights Act, and then only of modest amounts, seemed to emphasise that the common law would remain the default position.[157]

However, the limitations of the common law were gradually being exposed, and a clear divergence between common law rights and the jurisprudence emanating from the ECtHR was developing. In part this was a result in the dramatic increase in the number of cases decided by the ECtHR and the rapid expansion of the scope of the Convention rights, such as by the ECtHR's development of its positive obligations jurisprudence in seminal cases such as *Osman v United Kingdom*[158] and *Hatton v United Kingdom*.[159] The pace and extent of these developments could not be matched by the common law. This can be illustrated by returning to the case of *Re McKerr*. The case concerned the shooting of three men, including the applicant's father, by the Royal Ulster Constabulary in 1982. A police investigation had produced a lengthy report but an inquest had been abandoned. The applicant and his mother raised a complaint in Strasbourg. In May 2001 the ECtHR ruled that there had been shortcomings in relation to the investigation of the deaths, in breach of Article 2.[160] This finding required a development of the Court's case law under Article 2. The text of that article says nothing about any investigatory obligation. The ECtHR first mentioned the need for 'some form of effective official investigation' in its judgment in *McCann v United Kingdom*, delivered in 1995, but in that case it had said that it was unnecessary to decide what form such an investigation should take, and the principle was neither developed nor applied.[161] A breach of the investigatory obligation was found on facts even

---

[155] *R (Daly) v Secretary of State for the Home Department* [2001] 2 AC 532 [23] (Lord Bingham) and [30] (Lord Cooke of Thorndon).

[156] Lord Scott also stated agreement with Lord Cooke. Lord Steyn and Lord Hutton agreed with Lord Bingham. Had it not been for Lord Steyn's celebrated, albeit entirely obiter, exegesis on the doctrine of proportionality applicable in relation to qualified Convention rights, the case would have had nothing much do with the Human Rights Act at all. Their Lordships also held that proportionality would in any event be applicable when applying common law rights: see the discussion in ch 9, pp 266–67.

[157] *Greenfield* (n 73); *Anufrijeva v Southwark LBC*, [2004] QB 1124.

[158] *Osman v United Kingdom* (2000) 29 EHRR 245.

[159] *Hatton v United Kingdom* (2003) 37 EHRR 28.

[160] *Re McKerr* (2002) 34 EHRR 20.

[161] *McCann v United Kingdom* (1996) 21 EHRR 97 [161]–[162]. See further the discussion in ch 10, p 313.

more extreme than those in *McCann* in *Kaya v Turkey* in 1999,[162] where an investigation of a shooting by Turkish security services had proceeded on the assumption that the victim had been fighting for the PKK. But it was only in *McKerr v United Kingdom* and the linked case *Jordan v United Kingdom*[163] that the full breadth of the investigatory obligation was articulated and its potential implications for the UK became clear. It was following this judgment that the domestic proceedings were brought in the High Court in Northern Ireland, seeking an order requiring the establishment of an adequate investigation and damages.[164] It was argued that the common law imposed a procedural obligation on the Government to hold an investigation into a death which mirrored that under Article 2.[165] Counsel relied on a statement by Lord Bingham to the effect that 'the sanctity of human life underpins the common law' and that a state must take 'appropriate legislative and administrative measures' to protect life.[166] However, notwithstanding the developments in the common law protection of human rights in this period, it was too large a step for the courts to establish a requirement to hold an investigation on the back of this dicta. Lord Nicholls considered that such a development would be 'far removed from the normal way the common law proceeds'.[167] In other words, the common law could not keep pace with the development of Convention jurisprudence by the Strasbourg court. His Lordship also referred to the existence of the Human Rights Act as a reason for the courts being slow to re-enter the field by developing the common law.[168] This line of reasoning was to assume greater prominence in later cases even where the step that the courts were being asked to take was not so great.

A second case that exposed the increasing divergence between the common law and Strasbourg was *JD v East Berkshire Community Health NHS Trust*. In a judgment delivered in July 2003, the Court of Appeal departed from the House of Lords' judgment in *X (Minors) v Bedfordshire County Council* in holding that health care professionals and social workers owe a duty of care to children when making child care decisions. This ruling was premised on the fact that since a claim could be brought under the Human Rights Act and Article 8 for essentially the same conduct, the policy reasons for refusing to recognise such a duty of care that had been found persuasive in *X (Minors)* had evaporated. This was held to be the case even in respect of negligence occurring before the Human Rights Act came in to effect. In reasoning that is contrary to that in *McKerr*, the Court held that:

---

[162] *Kaya v Turkey* (1999) 28 EHRR 1.
[163] *Jordan v United Kingdom* (2003) 37 EHRR 2.
[164] *Re McKerr* [2003] NICA 1.
[165] *McKerr v United Kingdom* (2001) 34 EHRR 20.
[166] *R (Amin) v Secretary of State for the Home Department* [2003] 3 WLR 1169 [30].
[167] *Re McKerr* [2004] 1 WLR 807 [30].
[168] ibid [30]–[32]. Lord Steyn also asked: 'why is there now a need to create a parallel right under the common law?' ([51]). Lord Hoffmann held that it was impossible to find such a broad common law principle as the claimant was asserting ([71], in accord Lord Brown [91] and [96]).

the absence of an alternative remedy for children who were victims of abuse before October 2000 militates in favour of the recognition of a common law duty of care once the public policy reasons against this have lost their force.[169]

However, as in *McKerr*, the common law was ultimately found to be insufficiently elastic to cover all the same ground as is covered by Article 8 of the Convention. The Court maintained the rule that no duty of care is owed to parents (although their rights are recognised by Article 8), on the ground that recognising such a duty would conflict with the overriding best interests of the child. In this respect, it was held, the policy considerations underpinning *X (Minors)* had not lost their force. An appeal from this ruling failed in the House of Lords. Lord Bingham, dissenting, would have extended the common law to apply also to parents in order to reflect the principle that 'wrongs should be remedied':

> . . . the question [arises] whether the law of tort should evolve, analogically and incrementally, so as to fashion appropriate remedies to contemporary problems or whether it should remain essentially static, making only such changes as are forced upon it, leaving difficult and, in human terms, very important problems to be swept up by the Convention. I prefer evolution.[170]

But even Lord Bingham had to recognise limits on the degree to which the common law can develop to protect Convention rights. In *Watkins v Home Secretary* he led the Judicial Committee in rejecting a claim in tort for a breach of the common law constitutional right to legal professional privilege when prison officers had, as had been found by the judge at trial, in bad faith opened the privileged correspondence sent to the claimant.[171] Lord Bingham said that in the absence of actionable harm, no action could be maintained in tort, although there was a breach of a public law constitutional 'right'. He distinguished *JD v East Berkshire Community Health NHS Trust* because, he said, in that case there was no 'settled principle' pointing against liability. But his Lordship also invoked the existence of a remedy under the Human Rights Act as an additional reason for not developing the law of

---

[169] *JD v East Berkshire Community Health NHS Trust* [2004] QB 558 [83] (judgment of the Court); departing from *X (Minors) v Bedfordshire County Council* [1995] 2 AC 633.

[170] Lord Bingham had given a powerful dissent in *X (Minors)* in the Court of Appeal to similar effect: [1994] 2 WLR 554. See also the two joined cases of *Smith v Chief Constable of Sussex Police* [2009] 1 AC 225, concerning police failure to protect a person who complained of persistent threats from his former partner. A majority of the Committee held that the scope of the common law duty of care is more restrictive than the positive duty under *Osman v United Kingdom*, which arises where the police ought to know of an imminent risk to life. Lord Hope stated that the common law must 'stand on its own feet' and any 'short-fall' will be dealt with under the Human Rights Act ([82]). Lord Brown stated likewise: 'I see no sound reason, however, for matching this with a common law claim also. That to my mind would neither add to the vindication of the right nor be likely to deter the police from the action or inaction which risks violating it in the first place' ([139]). Differing materially, Lord Bingham stated that whilst there will always be differences between common law and Convention rights, so far as practicable the law should develop in harmony but, having held (in dissent) that the common law applied to the claimant, he refused to consider whether Art 2 would also have applied ([58]).

[171] *Watkins v Home Secretary* [2006] 2 AC 395 [26].

tort.[172] More significantly still, Lord Rodger stated that there is no longer any need for judges to resort to the 'heroic efforts' of developing a jurisprudence on common law constitutional rights. He said that claimants can be expected to invoke the Human Rights Act rather than seek to fashion a new common law right.[173] The contrast between this reasoning and that in *Daly* is marked. Rather than the Human Rights Act being regarded as a safety-net for a reinvigorated common law, which itself provides a sufficient source of human rights protection, the common law has increasingly been put to one side, and its development postponed, in favour of the Human Rights Act.

However, if the Human Rights Act has in many cases stunted the development of the common law in the public law context, the opposite is true in claims against private parties in which the Human Rights Act cannot be directly invoked. In this context the courts have developed a hitherto unknown tort of misuse of private information (encompassing the publication of photographs) which partially fills the void created by the absence of a tort of privacy in UK law. This cause of action precisely mirrors Article 8 in relation to the protection of personal information. In practice, the courts apply the case law under that article directly, as if the defendant were a public authority, and balance any intrusion into a person's privacy against freedom of expression where this right is in conflict with it.[174] It is not entirely clear whether the courts have developed the law by reference to the values of the Convention or because they consider that they are compelled to do so in order to ensure that the UK does not breach its international obligations to protect Article 8.[175] Lord Hoffmann's speech in the leading case was certainly premised on the former approach. He held that, 'The time has come to recognise that the values enshrined in articles 8 and 10 are now part of the cause of action for breach of confidence' and he stated that it was unnecessary to consider whether this was required under section 6 of the Human Rights Act.[176]

---

[172] In accord: Lord Hope [32], Lord Walker [73(4)], Lord Carswell [77]. It is unclear why the claimant did not claim for a trespass to his chattels: possibly because the letters had not been written by him (although he had a right to possess them), or possibly because exemplary damages were sought and so misfeasance was preferred; the circumstances in which the non-consensual opening of mail without statutory authority might constitute a tort on conventional principles appears not to have been argued or properly considered. See also *Wainwright v Home Office* [2004] 2 AC 406 in which the House of Lords held that an intrusive and unlawful strip-search, although actionable in damages under the Human Rights Act, is not actionable in tort in the absence of trespass. In *Smith* (n 170) Lord Bingham distinguished *Wainwright*, saying that it stood for the proposition that the fact that a cause of action exists under the Human Rights Act does not call for the 'instant manufacture of a corresponding common law right where none exists' ([58]).

[173] *Watkins* (n 171) [64].

[174] *Campbell v Mirror Group Newspapers Ltd* [2005] 1 WLR 3394 (concerning publication of photographs and information relating to counselling the model Naomi Campbell was receiving for a drug habit). See also, *McKennitt v Ash* [2008] QB 73 and *Murray v Express Newspapers* [2008] 3 WLR 1360.

[175] The former is more consistent with the approach of the House of Lords in *Campbell*. The latter is more consistent with the reasoning of the Court of Appeal in *A v B plc* [2003] QB 195. See the discussion in Beatson, Grosz, Hickman and Singh, *Human Rights* (n 48) 4–193 to 4–244.

[176] *Campbell* (n 174) [17] and [18].

In conclusion, there is no consistent judicial approach to the relationship between the Human Rights Act and the common law, just as there is no consistent approach to the status and nature of the Human Rights Act. To some extent this is a natural reflection of the common law system, in which the law is an amalgam of different opinions by judges who have different perspectives. But the discussion has shown that the tensions in the cases reflect tensions in the terms and purposes of the Human Rights Act itself. It is clear, however, that the Act has had, and will continue to have, a powerful influence on the development of the common law. It may be that the tensions are so pervasive, and the effect on the common law is so context-specific, that no general principles governing the relationship will emerge. It does seem however, that the common law has been unable to keep pace with developments in the Convention jurisprudence made by the Strasbourg Court and domestic courts. Domestic courts have increasingly preferred to resort to the Human Rights Act at the expense of the common law. Human rights principles have, in a sense, become the new common law. It is human rights jurisprudence that is now developed to reflect changing attitudes and requirements, in accordance with liberal values which they reflect; whereas the common law has looked sluggish and off the pace. Whilst this may itself be an indication of judges increasingly regarding the Human Rights Act as a constitutional statute, it is an approach that does not come without risks. If the Human Rights Act is repealed, the common law might yet be called into service once again, either in the absence of some alternative to the Human Rights Act or as a supplement to a Bill of Rights. If so, there will be areas where the common law protections will be exposed to challenge in Strasbourg and the inhibiting effect that the Human Rights Act has been held to have on common law development will be particularly regrettable. The common law will be left playing catch-up.

3

Constitutional Theory and Constitutional Dialogue

WHENEVER JUDGES INTERPRET a statute or interpret the common law, they do so by implicit reference to an underlying set of values and principles that guide their task. In most cases, after the facts have been found, the case before a judge can be resolved by reference to the words of a statute or the text of some previous judicial decision. But often cases are more difficult, and the law often is not altogether clear. In such cases the precise nature of the background understanding to which judges refer is of more importance, and differences in the principles and values to which judges appeal, as well as their hierarchy in the judicial mind, can profoundly affect the outcome of the case. Whilst the text of the Human Rights Act provides an important limit on the need for judges to refer to deeper, background, principles, it nonetheless leaves considerable scope for interpretation, and many difficult cases arise.[1] In such cases judges have to appeal to guiding principles and values. One of the most important is the doctrine of purposive interpretation. The courts will interpret an act to achieve the purpose that was intended by Parliament to be achieved, so far as the text permits this. But the purpose of the Human Rights Act is not, as we have seen, either unitary or free of difficulty. Moreover, in the case of the Human Rights Act, the task of purposive interpretation has an added dimension. Since the Act has constitutional significance it is legitimate, indeed necessary, to ask what form of constitutionalism it best reflects. The answer to that question will itself inform the interpretation of its terms by the courts in cases of doubt, and so determine the outcome of cases that arise before them.

The answer to that question, as well as the nature of the debate about what the answer is, is also important for other, less immediately practical, reasons. It helps us to address more general questions about the nature of the constitution in the United Kingdom after the Human Rights Act and it informs our consideration of future constitutional reforms, such as the potential for the enactment of a Bill of Rights. This chapter considers the form of constitutionalism that the Human

---

[1] 'Skilfully drawn though these provisions are, they leave a great deal of open ground. There is room for doubt and for argument. It has been left to the courts to resolve these issues when they arise': *Aston Cantlow and Wilmcote with Billesley Parochial Church Council v Wallbank* [2004] 1 AC 546 [36] (Lord Hope).

Rights Act expresses and the debate between commentators on this subject. Since that debate is not free-floating, but is itself just one recent hydra-head of a vast literature on constitutional theory, this chapter locates the debate in the wider field of constitutional theory as a way of exploring the nature of modern constitutionalism in the United Kingdom.

Two Schools of Thought

Broadly speaking, it is possible to identify two schools of thought on the form of constitutionalism exhibited by the Human Rights Act.[2] First, there are those who have been called the 'incorporationists' and the 'true blue human rights lawyers'.[3] These lawyers consider that human rights must be put beyond the reach of parliamentary majorities, and that the idiosyncrasies of the Human Rights Act should, by a combination of benevolent interpretation and judicial fortitude, form no barrier to the establishment of a form of higher order Convention law. This view reflects the liberal constitutional project which we encountered in chapter 2.[4] According to this view, human rights should be rendered immune from political interference by transforming them into a form of higher law protected by judges. Legality and right is thus conceived as setting the immovable parameters within which politics may legitimately operate. Professor Jeffrey Jowell has thus argued that under the Human Rights Act, the courts are 'charged by Parliament with delineating the boundaries of a rights-based democracy'.[5]

Secondly, there are those who argue that questions about the scope of rights are far too controversial and important to be removed from the people and entrusted to judges. They point to the tension between attributing to persons the autonomy and responsibility to be rights-bearers whilst at the same time denying them the ability to decide amongst themselves what limits on their conduct this status entails.[6] Behind this approach lies the overlapping political traditions of civic republicanism, participatory democracy and civil libertarianism. From this perspective the Human Rights Act is not viewed as an institutional platform for removing certain issues *from* political debate, but rather as enabling courts to participate *in* that debate. It is argued that such participation will bring added value to political controversy by clarifying and solidifying certain arguments and by giving a particularly powerful voice to minorities, interest groups and others

---

[2] See D Nicol, 'Are Convention rights a no-go zone for Parliament?' [2002] *PL* 438.

[3] C Gearty, 'Revisiting Section 3(1) of the Human Rights Act' (2003) 119 *LQR* 551. See also C Gearty, 'Civil Liberties and Human Rights' in N Bamforth and P Leyland (eds), *Public Law in a Multi-Layered Constitution* (Oxford, Hart Publishing, 2003) 380–81.

[4] See ch 2, pp 15–17.

[5] J Jowell, 'Judicial deference: servility, civility or institutional capacity?' [2003] *PL* 592, 597.

[6] This is an argument put sustainedly in J Waldron, *Law and Disagreement* (Oxford, Clarendon Press, 1999).

who manage to enlist the support of the courts as a means to reform. This second approach to the Human Rights Act has invoked the concept of 'constitutional dialogue'. Professor Francesca Klug, for example, considers that the Human Rights Act's great innovation is enabling the courts to participate in and generate debate about where the line should be drawn where rights collide.[7] She suggests that the Human Rights Act is a 'third wave' Bill of Rights which is not premised on the assumption that the judiciary is the exclusive protector of human rights. Instead, she argues that it is intended to establish a dialogue between the courts, Parliament and the executive about the meaning and effect of Convention rights.[8]

The idea that modern constitutionalism should be understood in terms of a constitutional dialogue between courts, legislatures and executives has become common currency in public law scholarship across the common law world.[9] It has particular resonance in countries that have adopted Bills of Rights under which courts do not purport to have the last word on matters of fundamental rights and in which settled legal positions frequently display contributions from each of the branches. Given its prominence in the literature on the Human Rights Act, this chapter will address this constitutional concept in some detail.

[7] F Klug, 'The Human Rights Act—a "third way" or a "third wave" Bill of Rights' [2001] *EHRLR* 361.

[8] Klug, 'The Human Rights Act' ibid at, 370. In 'Judicial Deference Under the Human Rights Act 1998' [2003] EHRLR 125, 130–32, Klug states: 'Behind the construction of ss.3 and 4 was a carefully thought-out constitutional arrangement that sought to inject principles of parliamentary accountability and transparency into judicial proceedings without removing whole policy areas to judicial determination. In other words it sought to create a new dynamic between the two branches of the State . . . In the academic literature it could be called a "dialogue approach" . . . [The Human Rights Act] was not enacted so that the courts could have the final say in areas where there is no settled human rights answer . . . Parliament would be entitled to choose to protect its democratic mandate on an issue where the human rights case law is far from settled. Encouraging this kind of "dialogue" was one of the purposes of the Human Rights Act'. See also F Klug, 'A Bill of Rights: do we need one or do we already have one?' [2007] *PL* 701. For variants on this dialogic approach see also RA Edwards, 'Judicial Deference under the Human Rights Act' (2002) 65 *Modern Law Review* 859; K Starmer, 'Two Years of the Human Rights Act' [2003] EHRLR 14; C Gearty, 'Reconciling Parliamentary Democracy and Human Rights' (2002) 118 *LQR* 248, 250 and 'Civil Liberties' (n 3); R Clayton, 'Judicial Deference and "Democratic Dialogue": the legitimacy of judicial intervention under the Human Rights Act 1998' [2004] *PL* 33; D Nicol, 'Statutory interpretation and human rights after *Anderson*' [2004] *PL* 274 and 'Gender Reassignment and the Transformation of the Human Rights Act' (2004) 120 *LQR* 194; AL Young, *Parliamentary Sovereignty and the Human Rights Act* (Oxford, Hart, 2009) especially ch 5.

[9] For discussions of the voluminous American literature see G Calabresi's important and influential 'Foreword: Antidiscrimination and Constitutional Accountability (What the Bork-Brennan Debate Ignores)' (1991) 105 *Harvard Law Revue* 80; also TJ Peretti, *In Defense of a Political Court* (Princeton, Princeton University Press, 1999) 55–74. The seminal Canadian article is PW Hogg and AA Bushell, 'The Charter Dialogue Between Courts and Legislatures (or Perhaps the *Charter of Rights* Isn't Such a Bad Thing after All)' (1997) 35 *Osgood Hall Law Journal* 75, and for a sustained and sensitive discussion which addresses much of the literature, see K Roach, *The Supreme Court on Trial—Judicial Activism or Democratic Dialogue* (Toronto, Irwin Law, 2001) and also 'Dialogue or Defiance: Legislative Reversal of Supreme Court Decisions in Canada and the United States' (2006) 4 *International Journal of Constitutional Law* 347 and 'A Dialogue of Principle and a Principled Dialogue: Justice Iacobucci's Substantive Approach to Dialogue' (2007) 57 *University of Toronto Law Journal* 449. Israeli and Australian perspectives can be found respectively in A Barak, 'Foreword: A Judge on Judging—The Role of a Supreme Court in a Democracy' (2002) 116 Harv LRev 16 and L McDonald, 'New directions in the Australian Bill of Rights debate' [2004] *PL* 22.

Undoubtedly, with its varied array of innovative oratorical devices, the Human Rights Act certainly presents itself as a particularly promising candidate for understanding in dialogic terms. Instead of being able to strike down legislation, section 4 enables a court to *declare* its view that legislation is incompatible with Convention rights. Where a court is considering making such a pronouncement, section 5 requires both that it *notify* the relevant government minister and that it *hear* the Government's considered view on the parliamentary legislation in question. Even ministers themselves are required to make statements either of compatibility (s 19(1)(a)) or incompatibility (s 19(1)(b)) as Bills proceed through Parliament. Thus, on the face of the Human Rights Act section 4 presents itself as an engine for dialogue between the branches of government. It provides the courts with a voice to inform the executive that despite having considered its arguments to the contrary, they consider primary legislation to be incompatible with the Convention. Parliament can consider and debate the declaration, if it wishes, and can respond by enacting primary legislation. Alternatively, a declaration of incompatibility triggers a power to amend the legislation by a fast-track executive process under section 10 of the Human Rights Act. The amending legislation requires parliamentary approval but not enactment. There is, then, a process that involves input form each body at different junctures and which appears to take a conversational form. For this reason section 4 is at the centre of the views of those who present the Human Rights Act in dialogic terms. The point is put particularly clearly by Professor Tom Campbell:

> . . . it would be best if declarations of incompatibility were to be seen as routine and unproblematic. If moral disagreement over what the provisions of the ECHR should be taken to mean is accepted as commonplace, because of the inherently controversial nature of the issues which call to be determined in making such interpretations, then the courts should be regarded as having the right to make only provisional determinations of what it is that human rights asserted in the ECHR require us to do. These determinations may, with perfect propriety, be challenged and overturned by elected governments after public debate.[10]

This approach hinges upon the possibility and desirability of substantive disagreement about the scope and content of Convention rights being played-out through the use of section 4 declarations, political debate and response. Those who praise the Human Rights Act's dialogic character believe that the role of the courts under the Human Rights Act is to *propose* to the other branches answers to substantive questions of justice. It envisages courts proposing arguments of principle to the political branches, and so will here be termed 'principle-proposing dialogue'. It is said that, in this way, the Human Rights Act provides for an effective synthesis of parliamentary democracy and human rights by forging a partnership between legislature, executive and judiciary. Importantly it is implicit in this view that the Government can legitimately deviate from declarations on competing grounds of principle as well as of expediency.

[10] T Campbell, 'Incorporation through Interpretation' in T Campbell, KD Ewing and A Tomkins (eds), *Sceptical Essays on Human Rights* (Oxford, OUP, 2001).

This reveals a deeper feature of arguments that rely on section 4 to 'reconcile parliamentary democracy and human rights'. Behind such arguments lies a radical reconceptualisation of the separation of powers, according to which the courts are transformed from arbiters of rights, albeit subject to legislative overrule, to a form of privileged pressure group whose function it is to raise good reasons why a litigant's interests should be respected. It abandons the idea that the courts should hold government to fundamental principle and the law, and repositions the courts within the forum of ordinary politics, providing not a check or balance, but counsel. Professor Danny Nicol has developed this line of thinking furthest, in a paper in which he has argued that the Human Rights Act requires a profound shift in our very conception of the judicial role. Judicial output needs to be reconceptualised as a 'contestable entity, wherein courts present their thoughtful opinions on rights, which Parliament can substitute with its own favoured interpretation.' He says that elucidating the meaning of Convention rights should therefore be seen as a shared responsibility between the judiciary and the legislature.[11]

Now let us return to the first school of thought: the liberal legalists, or incorporationists. Those who view the Human Rights Act from this perspective consider that declarations of incompatibility should be exceptional, and they deny that the importance of the Human Rights Act lies in any dialogic character. Section 4 should not be viewed a means for generating debate over substantive questions of justice, but rather that it works with section 10 merely to provide a safeguard against the administrative disruption that might be caused by striking down primary legislation. On this latter view, the dialogic contribution of section 4 relates merely to questions of legal aesthetics and not questions of constitutional justice.

This school of thought emphasises section 3's injunction to read legislation so far as it is possible to do so compatibly with Convention rights. This provision bolsters the common law doctrine of legality which provides that legislation must be read according to the presumption that Parliament intends to conform to fundamental rights. In *Ex p Simms*, Lord Hoffmann stated that this doctrine is the means by which courts at common law can 'apply principles of constitutionality little different from those which exist in countries where the power of the legislature is expressly limited by constitutional document'.[12] However the range of common law constitutional rights is much slimmer and is less clearly structured than those under the Convention, and at common law Convention rights themselves could only be appealed to where the law was ambiguous. Section 3 now requires that courts take a strong interpretive approach to ensure compatibility with Convention rights whenever they interpret legislation. For this reason it has been suggested that section 3 might be used to elevate Convention rights to 'the supreme law of the land'.[13]

[11] D Nicol, 'Law and politics after the Human Rights Act' [2006] *PL* 722, 743.
[12] *R v Secretary of State for the Home Department, ex p Simms* [2000] 2 AC 115, 131.
[13] Nicol, 'Statutory Interpretation and Human Rights' (n 8) at 274; Gearty, 'Revisiting Section 3(1) of the Human Rights Act' (n 3) and Gearty, 'Reconciling Parliamentary Democracy and Human Rights' (n 8), and Campbell, 'Incorporation through Interpretation' (n 10).

However, the strength of the section 3 injunction remains uncertain and ultimately depends upon what Gearty has termed 'the limits of the possible'. He points out that theoretically, and reading section 3 as a whole, the interpretive power can either be read so narrowly that it is 'reduced to an empty shell', in which case a section 4 declaration would have to be issued in almost every case of prima facie incompatibility, or it can be read so widely that all legislation should be read to be Convention compatible, unless it is expressly stated not to be.[14] The importance of this to our present discussion lies in the fact that like section 4, section 3 leaves a great deal open (on Gearty's view, almost everything) and thus any interpretation of section 3's scope must be informed by an appeal to a theoretical account of the appropriate relationship between the courts and Parliament.

The foregoing discussion now allows us to see that those who view the Human Rights Act as a constitutional mechanism for courts to raise fundamental questions of rights with the other branches of government will argue for a minimal use of section 3. By contrast, viewing the Human Rights Act from the perspective of rights absolutism and judicial supremacy leads to the view that section 3 should be read as expansively as possible, since it is the most potent mechanism for insulating fundamental rights from ordinary politics. Thus, Gavin Phillipson argues that section 3 should be given the maximum possible scope, 'so that it virtually always achieves Convention compliance', and consequently there would be almost no call to resort to section 4 at all.[15]

The prevailing interpenetrations of the Human Rights Act are therefore set in a markedly polarised frame: either it is to be understood from the perspective of judicial supremacy, inviolable incorporated rights, and of law-bounding politics, or it is to be understood in dialogic terms, as collapsing any distinction between law and politics, departing from the separation of powers, and providing minori-

---

[14] Gearty. 'Reconciling Parliamentary Deocracy and Human Rights' (n 8).

[15] G Phillipson, '(Mis)-reading section 3 of the Human Rights Act' (2003) 119 *LQR* 183, 187. Phillipson supports this view by unhelpful and unconvincing textual gymnastics. He suggests that s 3 can, in effect, pull itself up by its own bootstraps because it must also apply to itself. The result, he says, is that courts must take a Convention-friendly approach, ie they must invariably read statutes compatibly with it. However the Convention articles do not mandate any particular degree or method of incorporation and thus a more limited reading of s 3 would *not* be *incompatible* with Convention rights, giving the interpretive obligation no purchase. Phillipson's equivocation between what is *required* and what might be *desirable* is a lacunae filled by his preference for rights supremacy. Phillipson has subsequently sought to fill this lacunae by looking outside the Human Rights Act to the common law: G Phillipson, 'Deference, Discretion, and Democracy in the Human Rights Act Era' (2007) 60 *Current Legal Problems* 40, 62–63. He points to the obligation under Art 1 of the European Convention to 'secure' to everyone the protected rights and freedoms. Since Art 1 is not one of the 'Convention rights' given effect by s 1 of the Human Rights Act, Phillipson is compelled to appeal to the common law presumption that ambiguous law will be interpreted consistently with the UK's international obligations (Phillipson may do better in fact to rely on Art 13, the right to an effective remedy, which is not satisfied by the grant of a declaration of incompatibility, but which also is not given effect by the Human Rights Act: see *Burden & Burden v United Kingdom* (2007) 47 EHRR 48, 41, and there is some good authority to suggest it can be resorted to to interpret the Act: *R (Al-Skeini) v Secretary of State for Defence* [2008] 1 AC 153 [149] (Lord Brown) and [57] (Lord Rodger)). However, Phillipson's new weave does not meet, and indeed implicitly concedes, the point that s 3 cannot pull itself up by its own bootstraps, and makes clear that his preferred interpretation of s 3 rests on an underlying belief in the form of constitutionalism expressed by the Human Rights Act.

ties with little more than judicial signatures on their petitions to Parliament. But since the cardinal, and uncontroversial, features of the Human Rights Act are that (1) it has bolstered the court's ability to protect human rights, and (2) it has ultimately preserved parliamentary sovereignty, both perspectives provide impoverished accounts of the form of constitutionalism underpinning the Human Rights Act. The rights supremacy perspective fails to explain or emphasise the dialogic features of the Human Rights Act or the relationship between the protection of human rights and the preservation of parliamentary sovereignty, while the dialogic perspective, as it is currently conceived, insists that the Human Rights Act should be understood as providing individuals with a means of political participation rather than a method of protection. In fact, a much more fruitful position lies between these polarities, and it provides a far more convincing understanding of the form of constitutionalism embodied in the Human Rights Act. But in order to understand the nature of this middle position we must first establish the polarities on the wider theoretical field.

This chapter therefore takes the following course. The following two sections survey the general field of constitutional theory. They do so from a novel perspective. The discussion focuses on the degree to which constitutional theories allow for or require constructive collaboration between the courts, executive and Parliament. That is to say, from the perspective of 'constitutional dialogue'. Analysing constitutional theories in this way, and from this perspective, allows us to see important commonalities between theorists who are generally considered quite dissimilar. And in this way we are able to locate the polarities of view that currently dominate thinking on the Human Rights Act within the field of constitutional theory. The ultimate purpose of the survey is to identify a variety of constitutional theory that lies between the two extremes. This middle position, it is argued, is reflected in commonalities in the theories of two influential theorists: Professors Alexander Bickel and Albert Venn Dicey. Of course, the constitutional models developed by these theorist cannot be applied directly to the Human Rights Act. The point is that it is the insights of these theorists, and the constitutional orientation of their constitutional thinking, that best illuminates, or at least helps to explain, the form of constitutionalism underpinning the Human Rights Act.

Non-Dialogic Constitutional Theories

The notion of 'dialogue' reflects the insight that courts do not always, and do not simply, resolve questions of principle that litigants bring before them and that they interact with legislatures and governments in ways that are both subtle and constructive. Broadly speaking, constitutional theories can be described as 'dialogic' when they emphasise the legitimacy and desirability of courts not resolving questions of principle but instead allowing those issues to be considered and resolved by others. Other theories either leave out of account this aspect of judicial function, or contend that it is an exceptional and undesirable trait that is to be tolerated rather than admired. The place to commence our survey, both logically and chronologically, is with such theories, which can conveniently be divided between theories of formal legality and theories of substantive legality.

Theories of Formal Legality

Let us first consider theories of formal legality. These theories are closely associated with a pure form of legal positivism. They conceive of law in a manner that excludes space for the courts to operate as independent constitutional actors with a distinct normative role in the constitutional order and view them instead as tasked with applying the wishes of those who are responsible for making the law. The approach is reflected in Austin's insistence that all law is traceable to a single source, and therefore that every positive law is a direct or circuitous command of a sovereign.[16] On this view, constitutional arrangements are necessarily understood in terms of agency and subordination to the sovereign, which has an ultimate monopoly on making law.[17] In turn this means that when courts are faced with a direct expression of sovereign will in the form of an Act of Parliament, it is their job as parliamentary agents—akin, in fact, to administrative officials—to apply that will undiluted and unchallenged; where the intentions of the legislature are ambiguous, the courts must do not more than work out as best they can what it would have intended to be the result in the case before them.[18]

On this analysis, the rule of law must be understood in purely formal terms: the only rights that courts are able to identify flow not from moral values or moral consensus, but from the sovereign itself. Writing in this vein, Jeffrey Goldsworthy explains that courts must act as 'an agent striving to interpret and apply statutes equitably, so as better to serve the legislature's values, intentions and purposes'.[19] This approach excludes scope for normative dialogue between the courts and the other branches, since the courts to not make law and cannot challenge sovereign will in any form.[20] The role of the courts is a subservient and formal one and the

---

[16] J Austin, *The Province of Jurisprudence Determined*, 2nd edn (1861) 121. See also HLA Hart, *The Concept of Law* (Oxford, Clarendon Press, 1961), chs II–IV.

[17] J Austin, *Lectures on Jurisprudence*, vol. II, 2nd edn (1863) 351.

[18] See generally J Bentham, *An Introduction to the Principles of Morals and Legislation* (reprinted, 1996). Intention here has to be understood in authorial terms. Theories that are based on broader notions of intention that absorb values or normative principles taken from constitutional history or moral consensus build in room for dialogue between this history and consensus and bald parliamentary will. See TRS Allan, 'Constitutional Dialogue and the Justification of Judicial Review' (2003) 4 *OJLS* 563 and 'Legislative Supremacy and Legislative Intent: A reply to Professor Craig' (2004) 24 *OJLS* 563.

[19] J Goldsworthy, 'Legislative Intentions, Legislative Supremacy, and Legal Positivism' in J Goldsworthy and T Campbell (eds), *Legal Interpretation in Democratic States* (Aldershot, Ashgate, 2002) 66.

[20] However, even a relatively pure positivistic theory may not entirely exclude space for courts to 'talk back' to legislatures in the form of administrative feedback, particularly where the application of legislation appears to lead to somewhat absurd or disadvantageous results. Bentham proposed a very

form of constitutionalism rests, to borrow a phrase from Lon Fuller, on a one-way projection of authority (downward).[21]

Whilst this view can fairly be attributed to Austin, it is often also unfairly attributed to Dicey.[22] We shall see that Dicey's constitutional exposition was in fact very different from this positivistic theory. The association with Dicey may nonetheless in part explain the long shadow that this view has cast over the development of English public law. Thus, this view is responsible for the prevalence of the idea that the legitimacy of judicial review is derived from the will of Parliament and that the function of the courts is simply to enforce the boundaries of statutory power demarcated in an Act of Parliament. It is also responsible for the dominant but erroneous idea that there is a rigid distinction between the constitutionally assigned function of each branch of state, with the function of the courts being simply to apply the law, not to develop or protect principles in collaboration with the other branches of the state. This was articulated by Lord Mustill in the *Fire Brigades Union* case in the following terms:[23]

> It is a feature of the peculiarly British conception of the separation of powers that Parliament, the executive and the courts have each their distinct and largely exclusive domain. Parliament has a legally unchallengeable right to make whatever laws it thinks right. The executive carries on the administration of the country in accordance with the powers conferred on it by law. The courts interpret the laws, and see that they are obeyed. This requires the courts on occasion to step into the territory which belongs to the executive, to verify not only that the powers asserted accord with the substantive law created by Parliament but also that the manner in which they are exercised conforms with the standards of fairness which Parliament must have intended.

Importantly, the idea of formal legality is paralleled in American constitutional theory and appears with particular prominence in Learned Hand's theory of judicial review. In a famous series of lectures, Hand argued that the constitutional function of the Supreme Court is simply to act as ultimate arbiter of the Constitution.[24] This reflected an inherited way of thinking about the constitutional arrangements, according to which the Supreme Court essentially operates as sovereign agent. After the American revolution had cut the cord of British sovereignty, existing institutions 'were construed by translating the name and style of

---

limited non-adjudicatory function for the courts in pointing to failings of utility in the operation of legislation and even suggested the suspension of some legislation pending legislative reconsideration: see GJ Postema, *Bentham and the Common Law Tradition* (Oxford, Clarendon Press 1986) 434–39.

[21] L Fuller, *The Morality of Law*, New Haven, Yale University Press, rev 2nd edn (1969) 207.

[22] For a recent example, see P Cane, in L Pearson, C Harlow and M Taggart (eds), *Administrative Law in a Changing State, essays in Honour of Mark Arondon* (Oxford, Hart, 2008). For subtleties in Austin's positivism, see the discussion in WE Rumble, *The Thoughts of John Austin: Jurisprudence, Colonial Reform and the British Constitution* (London, Athlone Press, 1985), especially ch 4.

[23] *R v Secretary of State for the Home Department, ex p Fire Brigades Union* [1995] 2 AC 513, 567. See also Lord Templeman in *M v Home Office* [1994] 1 AC 377, who began his speech thus: 'My Lords, Parliament makes the law, the executive carry the law into effect and the judiciary enforce the law' (395).

[24] L Hand, *The Bill of Rights* (Cambridge, Harvard University Press, 1958).

the English sovereign into that of our new ruler,—ourselves, the People'.[25] The Constitution thus took the place of the People or Parliament as the definitive embodiment of the sovereign will; and the courts took up their seat enforcing it. Hand thus argued that the Supreme Court is charged merely with keeping legislatures within their accredited authority and should intervene only to prune those legislative forays that are so clearly unconstitutional that they threaten the enterprise of governance itself. For Hand, it was inappropriate for the Court to second-guess legislatures on inherently contestable questions of morality and it had no place engaging in the sort of compromises between clashing demands and values that he considered to be the hallmark of politics.

In this way Hand sought rigidly to compartmentalise the legal and political realms and excluded scope for interaction between them. This is well illustrated by Hand's dismissal of the idea that there is scope for the judiciary to act as a 'suspensive veto', enabling courts to delay the more hasty and ill-considered acts of government.[26] Likewise he rejected the idea that the Supreme Court should 'point the way' to a resolution of social conflicts, because for a judge to 'serve as communal mentor' would be, he considered, 'a very dubious addition to his duties and one apt to interfere with their proper discharge'.[27] Hand's vision of constitutionalism was one of 'frontiers' and 'invasions', of constitutional 'authorisations' and 'grants'. One finds no sense of collaboration; no notion that the Supreme Court has any legitimate bearing on political controversy.[28] Not only should courts not have the last word on matters of fundamental principle, but they should have no say at all.

Theories of Substantive Legality

Certain theories of substantive legality are premised on the idea that some issues are so fundamental as to warrant their complete removal from ordinary politics and legislative competence. Rights are thus conceived in absolute terms and protected by being accorded the status of higher law. Such theories reflect the incorporationist or rights supremacy approach to the Human Rights Act.

However, as with theories of formal legality, such theories are also of very different types. Consider first the views of Robert Bork. He argues that only the original framers of constitutions and elected legislatures have any legitimate role in the political process. Like Hand's theory, Bork's approach marginalises any dialogue

---

[25] JB Thayer, 'The Origin and Scope of the American Doctrine of Constitutional Law' (1893) 7 Harv Law Rev 129, 131.

[26] A judicial holding, he said, does not 'send back the challenged measure for renewed deliberation', rather 'it forbids it by making a different appraisal of the values . . .': Hand (n 24) at 70.

[27] Hand (n 24) at 71; also L Hand, *The Spirit of Liberty* (New York, Alfred A Knopf, 1952) 181.

[28] By collaboration is meant an independent judicial function conceived as part of a joint project of achieving a just and stable society, to which courts, executives and legislatures contribute and necessarily interact. See further B McLachlin, 'Charter Myths' (1999) 33 *University of British Columbia Law Revue* 23.

between courts and legislatures because their modes of reasoning should, in his view, be wholly different. But unlike Hand, Bork argues that the Supreme Court should subject legislatures to fundamental rights. For Bork, the Court should engage in the backward-looking exercise of examining the pedigree of fundamental principles, applying only those that were part of the Constitution as originally understood. By contrast, forward-looking compromises are properly forged only in legislatures or governments.[29]

The anti-dialogic nature of Bork's theory is well illustrated by his criticism of the Canadian Supreme Court decision in *Vriend v Alberta*. In that case the Supreme Court held that Alberta's Individual's Rights Protection Act was unconstitutional insofar as it excluded sexual orientation as a ground of unlawful discrimination (the Supreme Court had itself read sexual orientation into section 15 of the Charter in *Egan and Nesbitt v Canada*[30]). The decision was justified by reference to a dialogic conception of the Supreme Court's function. Iacobucci J. stated:[31]

> [T]he *Charter* has given rise to a more dynamic interaction among the branches of governance. This interaction has been aptly described as "dialogue" by some. In reviewing legislative enactments and executive decisions to ensure constitutional validity, the courts speak to the legislative and executive branches.

He stressed that the Court was promoting democratic values and not necessarily foreclosing different political responses to controversial issues. Following the case, L'Heureux-Dubé J. expressed the matter in more explicit terms, noting the 'general failure of the political process to recognise the rights of lesbians and gays without the pressure of court decisions behind them'.[32] Bork dismisses these views as 'a dramatic invasion of the legislature's domain'.[33] If the principled approach preferred by the judges could be demonstrated by appealing to contemporary cultural values then they should, Bork says, 'go instead into the political arena' and there ensure that it is enacted.[34] For Bork, the actions of judges reading such principles into the Constitution themselves are no less than 'moral imperialism', 'invasions of turf' and 'judicial *coup d'etat*'.[35] As with Hand, the metaphors disclose the rigidity of Bork's conception of the separation of powers.

Ronald Dworkin's very different constitutional theory exhibits a similar rigidity. He argues that the very essence of constitutionalism is the restriction that absolute substantive rights place on the actions of majorities and the need for courts to remove these issues altogether from the legislative domain. That Bork and Dworkin can be considered side-by-side when their theories are looked at

---

[29] R Bork, *The Tempting of America—The Political Seduction of the Law* (1990); *Coercing Virtue—The Worldwide Rule of Judges* (Toronto, Vintage Canada, 2002).
[30] *Egan and Nesbitt v Canada* [1995] 2 SCR 513.
[31] *Vriend v Alberta* [1998] 1 SCR 493 [137].
[32] The remarks, cited in Bork, *Coercing Virtue* (n 29) at 99, were her opening remarks to a panel discussion on 'The Legal Recognition of Same-Sex Partnerships' (London, 1 July 1999).
[33] Bork, *Coercing Virtue* (n 29) at 97.
[34] Bork, *Tempting of America* (n 29) at 192.
[35] Bork, *Coercing Virtue* (n 29) 141.

from the perspective of constitutional dialogue emphasises just how varied theories sharing a similar dialogic approach can be. In other respects their theories are radically at odds: whereas Bork considers that constitutional rights should be identified by reference to their pedigree, Dworkin insists that judges have a licence to interpret the constitution in its best contemporary moral light and that the 'constitutional sail' is, he says, 'a broad one'.[36]

Dworkin argues that individual rights are derived from abstract notions of justice and their development and application is heavily dependent on judicial ideology independent of social consensus. Thus it is not the Supreme Court's function to engage in a 'dialogue between the judges and the nation, in which the Supreme Court is to present and defend its reflective view of what citizen's rights are . . . in the hope that people will in the end agree'.[37] There is therefore no reason for a Dworkinian judge to avoid capturing moral rights in the hope that deferring the matter will ripen the issue for resolution at a latter date, or to prompt legislatures into adopting a more principled stance. The assigned judicial role is to call fundamental issues 'from the battle ground of power politics to the forum of principle'.[38] As Dworkin argued in his introduction to 'The Philosopher's Brief' to the Supreme Court when it decided the issue of assisted suicide, for the Supreme Court to avoid the issue of principle would 'be the most statesmanlike way in which the Court could make the wrong decision'; and this was despite the fact that it would give the public 'an opportunity to participate more fully in the argument about principle'.[39] In sum, the Dworkinian judge seeks to remove certain issues of fundamental justice from ordinary politics, not promote discussion about them.[40]

[36] R Dworkin, *Freedom's Law—The Moral Reading of the American Constitution* (Cambridge, Harvard University Press, 1996) 12. See generally *Taking Rights Seriously* (London, Duckworth, 2000); *A Matter of Principle* (Cambridge, Harvard University Press, 1985); *Law's Empire* (London, Fontana, 1986).

[37] Dworkin, *Taking Rights Seriously* (n 36) 146.

[38] Dworkin, *A Matter of Principle* (n 36) 71. In his 'Does Britain Need a Bill of Rights?' in R Gordon and R Wilmot-Smith (eds), *Human Rights in the United Kingdom* (Oxford, Clarendon Press, 1996), Dworkin expressed his dislike of qualified rights models of constitutionalism. However, he also proposed a dialogic form of bill of rights, which would preserve parliamentary sovereignty, as a second-best solution. But for his objections to parliamentary sovereignty, see 'Interpretation, Politics and Law', Sir David Williams Lecture (Cambridge University Faculty of Law, 23 April 2004).

[39] R Dworkin 'The Philosopher's Brief' (1997) 44 *New York Review of Books* 5 in the case of *Washington v Glucksberg* 117 S Ct 1781 (1997). The Court did leave the issue open for another day with indications that such a right existed: see CR Sunstein, *One Case at a Time—Judicial Minimalism on the Supreme Court* (Cambridge, Harvard University Press, 1999) 75–116.

[40] Dworkin is critical of the passive virtues and suggests that they should only be employed in the most extreme situations: 'Rawls and the Law' (2004) 72 *Fordham Law Revue* 1387. Dworkin has suggested that his approach would generate debate on issues such as abortion, but the suggestion is tentative and portrayed as merely a potentially beneficial side-effect of his constitutional theory: see *Freedom's Law* 7, 29–31, 344–46, also 71 and *cf A Matter of Principle* 70, (both n 36).

Dialogic Theories I: Principle-Proposing Dialogue or Weak Form Dialogue

Dworkin developed his constitutional theory out of a critique of the pure form of positivism, described above, which he considered to be the ruling theory of law.[41] By approaching constitutional theory from the perspective of constitutional dialogue we can now see that the effect is to substitute one non-dialogic theory for another, and for rights supremacists and incorporationists this substitution has been given concrete endorsement by the Human Rights Act. But we have seen that others view the Human Rights Act in dialogic terms: as a means for judges to propose arguments of principle to other branches. This view has a somewhat mixed constitutional lineage. It is an approach perhaps most famously displayed by Abraham Lincoln's stance after the Supreme Court's disastrous decision in *Dred Scott v Sandford*,[42] which held that the chattel status of blacks enjoyed constitutional protection, and that a Congressional prohibition of slavery was therefore unconstitutional. Lincoln's response was to say that although the decision was entitled to 'a very high respect', it was only binding on the parties to it and did not have to be followed by the political branches. In his First Inaugural Address, Lincoln stated that the people will have 'ceased to be their own rulers' if 'the policy of the government, upon vital questions affecting the whole people, is to be irrevocably fixed by the Supreme Court ...'.[43] The idea was that the courts did not have a monopoly on interpreting the law and the correct interpretation of the Constitution was a matter that could not be settled by the Supreme Court.

It is important to bear in mind that such an approach can work both ways. It formed the basis of southern opposition to the Supreme Court decision in *Brown v Board of Education*[44] holding that school segregation violated the Fourteenth Amendment. In particular, it underpinned the stance of the governor of Arkansas who refused to follow the injunction to implement the decision with 'all deliberate speed'. This led to the case of *Cooper v Aaron* in which the Supreme Court articulated the requirement for state officials and legislatures to follow its orders. Justice Frankfurter stated in a concurring Opinion:[45]

> Criticism need not be stilled. Active obstruction or defiance is barred. Our kind of society cannot endure if the controlling authority of the Law as derived from the

---

[41] Dworkin, *Taking Rights Seriously* (n 36); also Dworkin, 'Rawls and the Law' (n 40).

[42] *Dred Scott v Sandford* 60 US (19 How) 393 (1857).

[43] See M Tushnet, *Taking the Constitution Away from the Courts* (Princeton, Princeton University Press, 1999) 8–9 and AM Bickel, *The Least Dangerous Branch—The Supreme Court at the Bar of Politics* (New Haven, Yale University Press, 1962) 260–61.

[44] *Brown v Board of Education* 347 US 483 (1954) and *Brown II* 349 US 294 (1955).

[45] *Cooper v Aaron* 358 US 1 (1958), 24–25. The quotation reference is President Andrew Jackson's Message to Congress of 16 January 1833, II Richardson, *Messages and Papers of the Presidents* (1896 edn) 610, 623.

Constitution is not to be the tribunal specially charged with the duty of ascertaining and declaring what is 'the supreme Law of the Land.' . . . The Constitution is not the formulation of the merely personal views of the members of this Court, nor can its authority be reduced to the claim that state officials are its controlling interpreters.

Notwithstanding the lesson of *Brown*, Mark Tushnet has developed a constitutional theory that, he says, attempts to take Lincoln's beliefs to heart.[46] Tushnet argues that no special weight should attach to pronouncements of the Supreme Court merely in virtue of the fact that they derive from a supreme judicial office. If decisions have any special weight it must derive purely from expertise in formulating arguments of principle. However, once the value of judicial determination of rights is denied, Tushnet finds that there is no justification for maintaining judicial input into moral debate at all. He considers that if anything judicialisation distorts moral dilemmas with overtures of legality.[47] His 'popular constitutional law' therefore ends up stripping courts of their constitutional duties altogether in preference to an approach that he expressly associates with the type of common law constitutionalism that we will discuss later on.[48] His analysis reveals that the value of the judiciary and its contribution to the collaborative enterprise of governance lies in determining rights. Once the determination of certain questions of justice is removed from the judicial competence there is little reason to retain a judicial contribution to such questions whatsoever.

It is nonetheless in this tradition that those who have opposed the liberal legalist account of the Human Rights Act have written. They have argued that judicial interpretations of the European Convention should be merely 'provisional' and should have a 'contested not absolute status', because both courts and Parliament have 'interpretive legitimacy'.[49] The courts should use section 4 declarations where it is reasonable for people to disagree about the rights in issue.[50] The idea is that the courts should not be regarded as resolving questions of principle even when they address such issues head-on (and purport to have resolved them). The function of the courts is to propose principled arguments for resolution by the political branches. On this view, the courts are denied the function of finally resolving questions of legal principle and are assigned instead the role of participant in a debate about their scope and content. Professor Nicol has argued that since the courts will thus share responsibility for interpreting Convention rights with politicians, they should not be inhibited by considerations of prudence and should speak 'uncompromisingly' as 'honest orators' and 'ideological partisans'.[51]

---

[46] Tushnet (n 43) 181. See further M Tushnet, *Red, White and Blue—A Critical Analysis of Constitutional Law* (Cambridge, Harvard University Press, 1988). For another example of such a theory see CP Manfredi, *Judicial Power and the Charter—Canada and the Paradox of Liberal Constitutionalism*, 2nd edn (Oxford, Oxford University Press, 2001).

[47] See also Waldron, *Law and Disagreement* (n 6).

[48] ibid 163–65.

[49] See especially Campbell, 'Incorporation through Interpretation' (n 10), Nicol, 'Law and Politics After the Human Rights Act' (n 11) 744; the articles by Klug (n 8).

[50] Young, *Parliamentary Sovereignty* (n 8) 140.

[51] Nicol, 'Law and Politics After the Human Rights Act' (n 11) 744–45, 750.

Similar views have been expressed in the Canadian context by Professor Kent Roach, who has argued that the function and legitimacy of the Canadian Supreme Court is conceived in terms of its ability to remind legislatures and society about anti-majoritarian and often unpopular principles and to 'enrich democratic debate'. Roach advocates 'over-enforcement' of the Canadian Charter of Rights and Freedoms 1982, because 'it will result in spirited and self-critical dialogue in which Parliament considers and responds to Charter decisions'. He therefore considers that judges should interpret rights 'generously, perhaps too generously' and should 'run the risk of being overly active'.[52]

Dialogic Theories II: Strong Form Dialogue

Up to this point we have covered the ground underlying contemporary thinking on the Human Rights Act. This section argues that there is a middle position between these polarities. It expounds a theoretical perspective that accepts the distinct and valuable judicial role in determining substantive questions of rights, while emphasising the relationship between courts and other branches. To be sure, even this remains a broad field—encompassing the theories of Dicey and Bickel—and it is clearly capable of much refinement. But the task here is simply to expound its central characteristics.

It is worth outlining these characteristics at the outset. Theories occupying this middle position reflect a belief that the courts have a vital constitutional role in protecting fundamental principles from the sway of popular sentiment. They do not simply have a subordinate or formal task, but must capture and insulate the enduring long-term values and principles of the community. Furthermore it is the courts, and not Parliament or the executive, which determine the meaning of fundamental principles.

Nonetheless, the courts recognise in the first place that such principles evolve and ripen over time. This is a process that is influenced, today at least, as much by principled legislation, such as legislation on discrimination or children's rights, as by the steady case-by-case progression of the common law. The function of the courts is to work in collaboration with the other branches in evolving and fostering the acceptance of such principles. However this is not accomplished by treating judicial determinations as provisional, but by well-established judicial techniques of prudence and restraint, such as by the courts leaving things undecided, by deciding cases on narrow or formal grounds, by supplying multiple overlapping reasons, or by numerous other adjudicatory techniques. In advancing towards principled goals, the courts, like the political branches, must exhibit the capacity to compromise and to accommodate the needs of expediency, but the courts ought to do so as far as possible by preserving the integrity of principle

---

[52] Roach, *The Supreme Court on Trial* (n 9) 238 and 284.

wherever possible. This is in stark contrast to the principle-proposing dialogue we have previously considered, by which the courts are encouraged to robustly set out their principled view but at the risk that the political branches will reject it for some passing reason and in so doing cut down or redefine the principle, so setting back the progression towards a more just society. By recognising the need for courts to accommodate the needs of expediency, as well as their role in developing principle and curbing unprincipled legislation, the middle position rejects a rigid separation of powers. Instead, it emphasises a degree of overlap and exchange. This represents an understanding of constitutionalism that focuses as much on the manner that courts manage their relationship with the other branches as on elucidating the scope of fundamental rights as a check on politics. Now let us turn to consider constitutional theories that reflect such an approach. The discussion is divided between Bickel's writing in the context of constitutional and judicial supremacy, and Dicey's writing on the common law tradition.

Constitutional Supremacy

The idea of constitutional dialogue can be traced to Alexander Bickel's writings on US constitutional law. Bickel drew attention to, and praised, the various ways that even in a system of judicial supremacy the Supreme Court can force legislatures to take a second look at their political projects, without absolutely prohibiting them. However, this dialogic aspect of Bickel's theory is usually divorced from the context of the strong judicial role that he approved.[53] Quite why this is so is unclear.[54] It might be because of the apparent inconsistency between according the judiciary a strong role in developing and protecting fundamental principles from popular opinion, whilst at the same time advocating that courts prompt legislatures to willingly observe and protect principle without their being compelled to do so. But it is the way that Bickel married the two positions that points us towards the middle position between rights supremacy and a form of dialogue between the branches in which courts are able only to propose arguments of principle.

Bickel's book *The Least Dangerous Branch* is today associated with two ideas encapsulated in two phrases that he coined to describe them. The first is the idea of 'the counter-majoritarian difficulty', which refers to the fact that the decisions of the US Supreme Court are immune from ordinary political reversal. Bickel provided various arguments as to how this state of affairs could achieve 'a measure of

---

[53] See Calabresi 'Foreword: Antidiscrimination and Constitutional Accountability' (n 9).

[54] It might be due to the conservative turn Bickel's views displayed in his later work, which undoubtedly advocated a more circumscribed judicial function: He shifted away from the idea of the court having a role in shifting society along a trajectory of principle, leaving it to look only to tradition. Contrast eg Bickel, *The Least Dangerous Branch* (n 43) 236–37 with *The Supreme Court and the Idea of Progress* (New Haven, Yale University Press, 1978) and *The Morality of Consent* (New Haven, Yale University Press, 1975). See JH Ely, *Democracy and Distrust—A Theory of Judicial Review* (Cambridge, Harvard University Press, 1980) 71–72; A Kronman, 'Alexander Bickel's Philosophy of Prudence' (1985) *Yale Law Journal* 1567; Bork, *Tempting of America* (n 29) 188.

consonance' with the principle of self-rule.[55] In particular, he stressed the Court's creative ability to establish and renew a coherent body of principled rules independent of majority will, according to the constraints of reason. He placed considerable value on the Court's position 'altogether aside from the current clash of interests' and its evolutionary process of law-making that 'tests as it creates', which he saw as an important tonic to the prospective, general and abstract nature of the legislative enterprise.[56] Thus, for Bickel the Supreme Court fulfilled the important task of evolving and defending from the majority the enduring values and aspirations of society (*cf* Hand),[57] which is neither a search for moral right answers (*cf* Dworkin) nor for the original meaning of the constitutional text (*cf* Bork).

The second idea for which Bickel's book is famous is the idea that it is a legitimate part of the Supreme Court's armoury to exercise 'the passive virtues'. Doctrines such as standing and ripeness enable the Court to avoid constitutional adjudication on the merits of particularly controversial questions. Taking this aspect of Bickel's theory in isolation tempts commentators to portray Bickel as advocating judicial deference and the judicial ducking of difficult questions wherever possible. Moreover, it seems that if the Court is to withdraw from the political fray, it will be in pursuit of a clearer separation of powers and a circumscribed legal domain. But in fact Bickel explicitly conceived of constitutional adjudication—that is, the evolution and defence of fundamental principle—as a political function and, what is more, one that is part of a collaborative political venture with the other branches of government. He appreciated only a 'partial' separation of the legislative and judicial functions which 'cannot and need not be rigidly compartmentalised'.[58] Far from being the means for keeping law and politics separate, or for deferring to other branches, the passive devices should be understood as the primary medium by which the Court manages its political function and the fertile and crucially important interface with legislatures.

It follows that the value of the passive devices is not in their scope for deference as such. Their value lies in the fact that they enable the Court to engage other branches in 'Socratic colloquies', to prompt legislatures down more principled paths and allow principle to be 'evolved conversationally not perfected unilaterally'.[59] The relationship between this conversational aspect to constitutional adjudication and the peculiarly valuable counter-majoritarian role that the Court fulfils is subtle. The passive devices are not only necessary for the evolution, protection and promotion of principle, that is, they do not simply flow *from* this

---

[55] Bickel, *The Least Dangerous Branch* (n 43) 23–33.
[56] See also ibid 70, 236–37 and Bickel, *Idea of Progress* (n 54) 82–88, 112–13.
[57] Bickel, *The Least Dangerous Branch* (n 43) 25–26, 115, 237.
[58] ibid 25, also see p 261: 'The functions cannot and need not be rigidly compartmentalised. The Court often provokes consideration of the most intricate issues of principle by the other branches, engaging them in dialogues and "responsive readings"; and there are times also when the conversation starts at the other end and is perhaps less polite. Our government consists of discrete institutions, but the effectiveness of the whole depends on their involvement with one another, on their intimacy, even if it often is the sweaty intimacy of creatures locked in combat.'
[59] ibid 244.

counter-majoritarion function—that would be to put the cart somewhat before the horse—rather, the devices indicate what the Court's peculiar function is, and to a significant degree actually define it. It is therefore mistaken to associate the passive devices with deference to the political branches: on the contrary, they permit and legitimise the Court's counter-majoritarian function.

Take the doctrines of vagueness, statutory construction and non-delegation. These allow the Court to avoid the merits of a moral dispute and ask instead 'for a legislative affirmation of just what it is that necessity demands'.[60] Like common law presumptions, they undeniably check or frustrate legislative projects, and so are passive only comparatively, but they 'leave the other institutions, particularly the legislature, free—and generally invite them—to make or remake their own decisions for prospective application to everyone in like cases, and often in some fashion even to the litigant immediately concerned'.[61] In other words, they draw the concrete application of general laws to the attention of the legislature, while allowing them room for the pursuit of their political goals in accordance with the requirements principle. Yet even here the dialogue may be still more robust, since the remittance will often be accompanied by a more or less firm indication of the principled response that is appropriate, even constitutionally acceptable.[62] Unlike the intimations of a sovereign agent, the rhetoric of a Supreme Court, while never immovable or absolute, has great weight and influence on the reshaping of political programmes. Such intimations might also accompany uses of the truly passive doctrines of standing and ripeness. Although such doctrines might be thought to work against litigants in the short term, they allow principle to prevail at a later date, where deciding the case on a principled basis at the first opportunity would likely legitimise legislative projects.

Indeed, this legitimising potential was Bickel's central concern and the ability to avoid it, by resort to the passive devices, a primary indication of the Court's ability to pursue society's principled trajectory. Ordinary politics, Bickel recognised, was a matter of constantly compromising principled goals. The passive devices, in allowing courts to manage the scope and, to some extent, the timing of its substantive adjudications, reveal the Court's ability to shield fundamental principles and maintain its principled trajectory in the face of the ever present need for compromises of expediency. As he said, they cushion 'the clash between the Court and any given legislative majority and strengthens the Court's hand in gaining acceptance for its principles'.[63]

Thus Bickel appreciated that the Court's counter-majoritarian role is only sustainable if it can allow for compromises without jeopardising the integrity of fundamental principles. Without such an ability, constitutional law would be forced down one of two paths. It would either be forever bending to the needs of the moment and legitimising legislative projects, in which case it would provide no

---

[60] ibid 188.
[61] ibid 201–2.
[62] See ibid 188.
[63] ibid 116.

added value to ordinary politics and might actually obstruct principled government, or alternatively constitutional law would become so pervasive as to increasingly paralyse politics altogether. Neither route is acceptable. As Bickel eloquently put it, 'No good society can be unprincipled; and no viable society can be principle-ridden.'[64]

Lincoln's view on the slavery issue provides a concrete illustration. Bickel described Lincoln's position before the civil war as graphically illustrating the sort of compromises that characterise ordinary politics. Lincoln held firmly to the principle that all men are created equal, but the hard fact was that conformity with the principle was a long way off and required myriad compromises, not only in terms of practicability but also to maintain consent in the face of widespread prejudices.[65] Bickel recognised that the Court's principled function required that the principle of equality be not compromised, but unlike Dworkin, Hand and Bork he accepted that a vital component in the Court's constitutional role is to allow for such compromises, by exercising the passive virtues. Hence, the Court's infamous attempt in *Dred Scott* to resolve the slavery issue by deciding the case on the broadest grounds that it would possibly bear represented the very opposite of Court's role in prompting the movement towards principle.[66] It cut down the principled goal of abolition and renounced any future role in moving society towards a more just position. The case forced Lincoln, as we have seen, to deny that the Court had any role in expounding generally binding constitutional principles. But the position was forced upon him not because *Dred Scott* was wrong in principle—although it was—but because it failed to allow for the compromises that remained necessary. It should have been decided on narrower grounds; instead it demonstrated the most egregious constitutional mismanagement.[67]

An illuminating contrast can be drawn with *Brown*, in which the Supreme Court finally upheld the principle of substantive racial equality. *Brown* itself pushed American society further along the constitutional trajectory in pursuit of an 'emergent' principle than the people, left to themselves, were yet prepared to go.[68] It was a decision that encountered the counter-majoritarian difficulty head-on, since the principle affirmed ran counter to the views and lifestyles of the majority of people to whom it was chiefly applicable. It was also a decision that had far-reaching reverberations and would obviously encounter serious practical problems of implementation.[69] Despite this, the Court determined that the compromising of principle on grounds of expediency had been and could be

---

[64] ibid 64.

[65] ibid 65–72.

[66] See also Sunstein, *One Case at a Time* (n 39) 36–38.

[67] Similarly, Jackson J dissenting in *Korematsu v United States* (1944) 323 US 214, 245–46: '. . . a judicial construction of the due process clause that will sustain this order is a far more subtle blow to liberty than the promulgation of the order itself. . . . the Court for all time has validated the principle of racial discrimination in criminal procedure and of transplanting American citizens. The principle then lies about like a loaded weapon ready for the hand of any authority that can bring forward a plausible claim of urgent need . . .'.

[68] Bickel, *The Least Dangerous Branch* (n 43) 194.

[69] ibid 248–50.

sufficiently defeated to permit principle to prevail. But it was a step that still neces-sitated the most careful management and that required a delicate exchange with other branches. As Bickel explained, the 'all deliberate speed' order enabled the Court to assume a passive posture, allowing the political institutions to work out their compromises without jeopardising the principle of non-segregation itself.[70]

Importantly, the conversation with the other branches was not simply a matter of mechanics, but of fostering assent and acceptance of the principle propounded, and the Court's decision exerted an educating influence on the course of events.[71] Here is a profound difference with theories of absolute rights. Dworkin, for exam-ple, rejects the notion that the Court has any role in allowing space for compro-mising the principled goal in the short term so as to ease the passage to its general acceptance. To borrow words from Hand, Dworkin would have had the Court hitch its wagons to a star;[72] whereas Bickel would not. By contrast, Hand himself was critical of *Brown* because he considered that the issue was one requiring com-promise and political settlement and the Court had therefore stepped outside its assigned sphere. Any benign effects from the 'moral radiation' of the decision, for Hand, were beside the point: it was quite inappropriate for the Court to pursue social justice goals in the mould of a third legislative chamber.[73]

Common Law Constitutionalism

Bickel distinguished his theory from common law adjudication on the grounds that at common law, judges are something like administrative officials working underneath a sovereign.[74] This harks back to the pure form of positivism that we discussed earlier. It is however rather a crude understanding of common law con-stitutionalism. In fact, Bickel's hasty dismissal of common law adjudication ignored important commonalities. Even in the face of parliamentary supremacy, theorists have long appreciated the ability of courts to bring principle to bear on legislative projects and advance principled goals in collaboration with Parliament. Furthermore, they have recognised that the common law courts have a key role in insulating principles from Parliament and majority opinion.

Properly understood, Dicey's vision of constitutional law is of this character. Dicey claimed that the constitution is 'pervaded by the rule of law' because its general principles (such as the right to personal freedom or the right to public meeting) have been identified and protected by *the ordinary courts*.[75] In other

---

[70] ibid 254.

[71] See ibid ch 6; and also Bickel, *Idea of Progress* (n 54) 4–7, 91–95, 117–51.

[72] Dworkin, *Law's Empire* (n 36), on *Brown* 390–91. Speaking of politics, Hand said: '. . . we shall not succeed by hitching our wagons to a star, but by a prayerful attempt in each case to make some compromise that will, for a substantial time if possible, effect a settlement' (*Spirit of Liberty* (n 27) 228).

[73] Hand, *Spirit of Liberty* (n 27) 54 and 70.

[74] Bickel, *The Least Dangerous Branch* (n 43) 40.

[75] AV Dicey, *Introduction to the Study of the Law of the Constitution*, 8th edn (London, Macmillan, 1959) 189 ('the universal subjection of all classes to one law administered by the ordinary Courts . . .'

words, Dicey considered it to be the independent protection of fundamental principles—independent, that is, of Parliament and the executive or any special jurisdiction or tribunal dependent on them—which is a central component in the rule of law. According to Dicey, the principal manner by which courts protect rights is the provision of remedies to individuals wronged by the conduct of public officials. Indeed, for Dicey the soundest way to identify the principles of the constitution is to draw generalisations from the circumstances in which courts provide remedies. To start from the other end risks identifying as rights those declarations that exist as merely moral or political aspirations. The objection to Dicey's approach, however, is that his faith in the positive law renders his account purely formal: talk of rights, remedies, and the rule of law is constitutional camouflage that barely conceals the dependency of individual rights on the acquiescence of Parliament. It seems to follow, as many commentators have argued, that Dicey is unable to marry his vision of the courts with this gunman writ large, for it would be a union of subservience and agency.

Trevor Allan has mounted a strong defence of Dicey against such charges by pointing out that, in the face of parliamentary supremacy, Dicey identified a substantive and independent role for the courts which provides a check on parliamentary projects. In particular, Dicey wrote that, 'from the moment Parliament has uttered its will as lawgiver, that will becomes subject to the interpretation put upon it by the judges of the land'. In turn, judicial interpretation will be dictated by the 'spirit of the common law' which embodies a commitment to the rule of law and civil liberties. These will, in effect, be accorded a degree of weight against apparently conflicting parliamentary intentions, thus allowing for an interpretation that, in Dicey's much forgotten words, 'would not commend itself either to a body of officials, or to the Houses of Parliament, if the Houses were called upon to interpret their own enactments'.[76] Allan thus argues that Dicey viewed the common law as an elaborate scheme of justice which operates to restrain and curtail ill-considered or unprincipled legislative measures.[77] In this way, the provision of remedies by the courts is shown to have substantive teeth.

In fact Dicey went further than even Allan has allowed. In his *Law and Public Opinion*, Dicey expounded in more detail the relationship between courts and Parliament and therein makes plain the degree of freedom he considered that common law judges have in interpreting statutes. Thus, he states that judges may 'indirectly limit or possibly extend, the operation of a statute' in what 'in truth' amounts to 'judicial legislation'.[78] Indeed, the common suggestion that Dicey's

[76] Dicey, *The Law of the Constitution* (n 75) at 409.

[77] TRS Allan, 'The Rule of Law as the Rule of Reason: Consent and Constitutionalism' (1999) 115 *LQR* 221, 243; also see TRS Allan, *Law, Liberty and Justice* (Oxford, Clarendon Press, 1993) 10 and TRS Allan, *Constitutional Justice—a Liberal Theory of the Rule of Law* (Oxford, OUP, 2001) 14, 214–15.

[78] AV Dicey, *Lectures on the Relation between Law and Public Opinion in England during the Nineteenth Century*, 2nd edn (London, Macmillan, 1914) 488 and 490. Dicey also states in *The Law of the Constitution* that 'Such principles, moreover, as you can discover in the English constitution are, like all maxims established by judicial legislation, mere generalisations drawn from the decisions or dicta of judges' (n 75) 192).

model of the rule of law rests on a distinction between making law (Parliament) and interpreting and applying the law (courts), with the courts acting as faithful parliamentary agent, is simply wrong and misleading. Dicey himself was emphatic in rejecting the notion that judges only interpret the law, even when they construe statutes, unless, he says, by that it is meant 'only that the very elastic term "interpretation" may be so extended as to cover everything which is done by an English judge when performing his judicial duty' (including making law and applying principle).[79] Prefiguring Bickel, Dicey urged that the essence of the rule of law lies in the *different forms* of law-making that inhere in legislatures and the courts. Far from being passive constitutional arbiters, applying the express or perceived wishes of a sovereign Parliament, he emphasised the courts' special role in developing principle as society evolves. It is built up gradually, in the context of concrete cases, always seeking to maintain consistency.[80] In making law in this way the courts base their decisions on the deposited values and principles to which society strives to conform. Dicey was also clear that the protection of principle is not a function exclusive to the courts. He appreciated the value of legislation in bolstering the rule of law and protecting individual rights. Moreover, he considered that certain particularly principled statutes, such as the Habeas Corpus Acts and the Petition of Right, had an affinity for common law precedents and he even ventured that those that are sufficiently sound in principle should be applied, like precedents, according to their spirit, in preference to their words.[81]

It is now possible to see how Dicey viewed the law as applied as representing the outcome of *both* legislative and judicial contributions. The courts, he stated, inject into the law a 'peculiar cross-current of opinion'. He admits that this opinion will be affected by the political biases of judges—and may occasionally be archly conservative[82]—however, this cross-current of opinion is generally, and in itself, beneficial. Allan has developed a similar idea that he describes as an 'imaginary dialogue' between courts and Parliament. Since statute is enacted into, and has legal significance only in respect of, a settled constitutional legal order marshalled by the courts, common law reason and legislative will are 'combined' and 'interdependent'.[83] This sense of imaginary dialogue points to more explicit ways that

---

[79] Dicey, *Law and Public Opinion* (n 78) 491.

[80] ibid 364–67. Cardozo, who was influenced by Dicey, set out a similar, but much more developed, view of common law adjudication in BN Cardozo, *The Nature of the Judicial Process* (New Haven, Yale University Press, 1921).

[81] Dicey, *Law and Public Opinion* (n 78) 370 and 489. In his *The Law of the Constitution*, Dicey mentions that both the Bill of Rights and the Petition of Right 'have a certain affinity to judicial decisions' and 'bear a close resemblance to judicial decisions' (n 75) 191 and 192. In advocating that some statutes may be treated more like precedents, Dicey not only prefigured Cardozo (n 80) but also writers such as Roscoe Pound, Rupert Cross, Guido Calabresi, Ronald Dworkin and Jack Beatson. This is an aspect of Dicey's theory not appreciated by Allan, see: TRS Allan, 'Dworkin and Dicey: The Rule of Law and Integrity' (1988) OJLS 266, 272.

[82] Dicey, *Law and Public Opinion* (n 78) 363–64, 369.

[83] Allan, 'Constitutional Dialogue' (n 18) 565; also see TRS Allan, 'Legislative Supremacy and Legislative Intention: Interpretation, Meaning and Authority' (2004) 63 *CLJ* 685. Allan paints a picture of the rule of law in which law is required to have the agreement of both courts and legislatures, but in which the will of both is inevitably moulded to some degree. He accepts that

Allan and Dicey's theories are dialogic.[84] By bringing common law reason to bear on legislative projects, the courts demand more or less explicit wording on the part of those exercising legislative functions where their actions would abrogate fundamental rights. Parliament is thereby required, as a general matter, to face squarely the prospect of infringing rights. Furthermore, following particular instances of judicial firmness, Parliament may be presented with the concrete implications of its actions for reconsideration. In this way the 'peculiar cross-current of opinion' directly influences legislative projects.[85]

This is analogous to Bickel's idea that deciding cases on grounds that avoid determining fundamental principles for all time permits the issue of principle to be cast back into the political realm to ripen and develop until such time as the Court cannot avoid having to determine it or considers it prudent to do so. Moreover Dicey, like Bickel, believed that the courts have an educative role in making clear the degree to which the law or legislation departs from principle or society's values. This in turn can prompt more enlightened governance. As Dicey said in his *Introduction to the Law of the Constitution*, 'In England judicial notions have modified the actions and modified the ideas of the executive government.'[86]

Dicey illustrated the way that courts can stimulate enlightened legislation by a lengthy discussion of the Court of Chancery's inroads into the rule denying married women the right to hold property. The Chancery Court's equitable jurisdiction meant that its incursions into the inequitable rule were inevitably limited. Nonetheless, by successive acts of judicial legislation the court 'told upon the whole public opinion of England as to the property rights which a married woman ought to possess'.[87] The effect was that England had legislation aimed at giving property rights to all married women well before France or Scotland. Dicey's lesson is that in studying the development of the law, 'we must allow at every turn for the effect exercised by the cross-current of judicial opinion which may sometimes stimulate, which may often retard, and which constantly moulds or affects, the action of that general legislative opinion which tells immediately on the course of parliamentary legislation'.[88]

It remains to be explained how Dicey reconciled his strong conception of the judicial protection of principle with the ultimate ability of Parliament to disregard

---

when statute apparently conflicts with fundamental principles, principled interpretation can take courts beyond anything that can be conventionally termed 'interpretation'. Allan, 'Constitutional Dialogue' (n 18) 571–72 and 574.

[84] In none of his writings does Allan advert to Dicey's views in *Law and Public Opinion*, although it indicates more in common between their respective approaches than even Allan allows for, particularly in Allan's more recent work.

[85] See Dicey, *Law and Public Opinion* (n 78) 369–70.

[86] Dicey, *The Law of the Constitution* (n 75) 409

[87] Dicey, *Law and Public Opinion* (n 75) 394. Prompting the piecemeal but fundamentally important reforms of the Married Women's Property Acts of 1870, 1874, 1882 and 1893.

[88] Dicey, *Law and Public Opinion* (n 78) 398. Putting a similar point he also stated: 'In England judicial notions have modified the action and influenced the ideas of the executive government' and this leads parliamentary sovereignty to be exercised in the spirit of legality (*The Law of the Constitution* (n 75) 414).

it. The tension between the supremacy of Parliament and the rule of law has often been thought to be an incoherent aspect to Dicey's articulation of the constitution. But on the contrary, Dicey not only reconciled these different ideas but the nature of this reconciliation is central to his account of constitutionalism. The fact that Parliament can ultimately overrule a judicial decision permits Parliament to give effect to the needs of the moment even where these require basic principles to be compromised or set aside. But in so doing, Parliament does not delete or destroy for all time the principle protected and affirmed by the common law. On the contrary, the principle endures as part of the more general scheme of values and principles that make up the common law. Thus, Dicey explained how unprincipled legislative incursions would be viewed as 'exceptions to common law principles'. This ultimately preserves the integrity of the (common law) principle itself since, as Dicey said, such principles 'can hardly be destroyed without a thorough revolution in the institutions and manners of the nation'.[89] Since it is not possible to legislate such a revolution into being, rights protected at common law were resistant to, if not actually immune from, legislative repeal.[90] This idea can be illustrated by reference to *Anisminic v Foreign Compensation Commission*. The actual result of that case, providing a right of judicial review from decisions of the Foreign Compensation Commission, was overruled by Parliament. But the parliamentary intervention did not affect the *principle* that the decision gave effect to, that legislation purporting to oust the supervisory jurisdiction of the High Court must be very strictly construed.[91]

It can thus be seen that the ultimate ability for Parliament to overrule the courts was regarded by Dicey as the way that the constitution allowed for political compromises to be made and given effect to, whilst at the same time limiting the effect of such compromises and ensuring that the courts' protection of those fundamental principles to which society is committed is not undermined. Dicey appreciated that parliamentary supremacy does not set up a direct challenge to the fundamental principles protected by the courts. Rather, it is a safety valve for demands of expediency, while preserving the integrity and endurance of fundamental principle.[92]

---

[89] Dicey, *The Law of the Constitution* (n 75) 201.

[90] Although this feature of the common law protection of principle persists today, it is obscured by the pervasiveness of modern legislation. By contrast, the constitution expounded by Dicey referred largely to a different state of affairs. As Austin put it: 'The statute law is not of itself an edifice, but is merely stuck from time to time upon the edifice reared by judges'. Austin (n 16) 368.

[91] *Anisminic v Foreign Compensation Commission* [1969] 2 AC 147 was overruled by the Foreign Compensation Act 1969. By contrast, a very rare example of Parliament attempting not only to overrule the application of a common law principle in a particular case, but to overrule the principle itself, is provided by the War Damage Act 1965, which purports to abolish the principle established in *Burmah Oil* that there is a right to compensation for destruction of property in wartime to prevent it falling into the hands of the enemy: *Burmah Oil Co (Burmah Trading) Ltd v Lord Advocate* [1965] AC 75. Even that, however, has not excluded the effect of *Burmah Oil* in analogous cases.

[92] Allan advances similar arguments: Allan, 'Constitutional Dialogue' (n 18) 575–77. Dicey, of course, witnessed the dawn of the new age of social welfare legislation and appreciated the threat posed to the constitutional equilibrium that underpinned his interpretation of the rule of law. In particular, he was concerned by the placing of individual rights in the hands of quasi-judicial officers connected

Dicey thus explained how to reconcile the apparently irreconcilable: a strong judicial function in protecting society's long-term values with a supreme legislature mostly pursuing society's shorter-term needs. But the subtle and important core of his exposition, and the aspect that exhibits the true nature of the continuum between it and the form of constitutionalism underpinning the Human Rights Act, lies in the way that the branches *interact* and each accommodate *both* these aspects of an effective and just constitutional order. The key to understanding Dicey's conception of constitutionalism lies not in which branch has the last word, but in the form of collaboration between them. In this he foreshadowed Bickel's reconciliation of judicial supremacy and majoritarian democracy.[93] Although Bickel and Dicey were concerned with constitutions that appear to give the last word to different branches, their approaches meet on middle ground. For both Bickel and Dicey it is the essential function of the courts to identify, incubate and protect principle and most particularly fundamental rights. These are not pulled from the air, but are deduced from precedent, changing public opinion, and principled legislation. They are crystallised over time. And where political compromise is necessary, the courts will seek to avoid or limit damage to established or emergent principles and thus to retain their integrity for the future.

Constitutional Theory and the Human Rights Act

From Common Law Constitutionalism to the Human Rights Act

There is, then, a rich and important dialogic middle ground that is obscured by the polarities of, on the one hand, rights supremacy and on the other, principle-proposing dialogue. This middle ground has been described as exhibiting a strong form of constitutional dialogue. It allows for a judicial function that both insulates principle from majorities and engages on a wider dialogic enterprise with society that involves a certain degree of give and take, prudential management and persuasion in the evolution and protection of principle.

It is important to emphasise that the connection between the Human Rights Act and this form of constitutional dialogue is both theoretical and historical. There is, of course, rather a large time gap between Dicey's dialogic exposition of constitutionalism and the Human Rights Act, but the continuity can been seen if we look again at the case of *Simms*. It will be recalled that in *Simms*, the House of Lords explicitly endorsed constitutional review at common law and Lord Hoffmann

---

with the executive. In modern conditions in which statute dominates the legal terrain, those working from the Diceyian tradition have argued for the toughening of constitutional rights and tighter constraints on the ability for Parliament to override settled fundamental principles. Without doubt, the success of this project is evidenced by the Human Rights Act.

[93] See also Dicey's footnote on the US Supreme Court cited above (n 81) 172–73 in which he discusses the various ways that the Court is responsive to society and the other branches and vice versa.

indicated that the common law was thus able to operate in a manner that mirrored constitutional review in systems in which legislative competence is explicitly curtailed by constitutional document. However, Lord Hoffmann also stated that the common law principle of legality means only 'that Parliament must squarely confront what it is doing and accept the political cost'.[94] In other words, common law constitutional principles can be exerted against legislation to force Parliament to appreciate the unprincipled implications of its projects, while ultimately allowing for the rights to be compromised by sufficiently clear and unambiguous legislative replies. Lord Hoffmann's two statements can therefore be rendered consistent by locating them within the context of strong form dialogic constitutionalism.[95]

We have seen that section 3 of the Human Rights Act represents a continuation of this common law approach. We can now draw an important conclusion: it is a mischaracterisation to view section 3 in terms of incorporationalism and section 4 in terms of dialogue. The difference between the provisions lies in the *different forms of dialogue* that they embody and in the different relationship between the courts, executive and legislature that they suggest. We should therefore look in a little more detail at the two provisions.

Section 3 and Section 4 of the Human Rights Act

It is possible to identify several differences between the dialogic operation of section 3 and section 4. Section 3 is faithful to a conception of the judicial function of determining individual rights. It complements the process by which courts determine whether, taking the governing legal materials, the applicant is entitled to judgment against the defendant. By contrast, section 4 invites the courts to make a determination of whether a provision of legislation is incompatible with a Convention right, notwithstanding that it governs the case. This places the courts in an unfamiliar advisory position—one that both Bickel and Dicey viewed as a departure from the proper judicial role. Viewed in another way, section 4, unlike section 3, decouples right from remedy. Whilst section 3 allows relief to the applicant and those similarly situated, section 4 leaves the legislative provision in place, with its pernicious effects continuing to apply to those subject to it.

Section 3 is a stronger provision also because it ensures that judicial determinations cannot be passively ignored, as declarations of incompatibility can be. Instead, they must be actively overridden and in sufficiently clear and precise terms (a point that we return to below). Moreover, such override must be achieved by primary legislation. This ensures that, unlike section 10 procedure, deviations from principle are explicit and have a full democratic stamp.[96] Alternatively, if

---

[94] *R v Secretary of State for the Home Department, ex p Simms* [2000] 2 AC 115, 131.

[95] However, Lord Hoffmannn in *Simms* hinted that he might accept only a process-based foundation to the common law approach, ie that judicial input is limited to drawing matters to Parliament's attention. Following through his reasoning may suggest that on his view, constitutional principle might not be resistant to legislative replies (*Simms* (n 94) 131).

[96] An opposing interpretation is offered by Roach, *The Supreme Court on Trial* (n 9) 279–80, especially n 62.

Parliament wishes to give principled guidance to courts on the interpretation of Convention rights, rather than merely overruling a particular interpretation of a specific provision of primary legislation under section 3, it can always build it in to the Human Rights Act itself by amendment: an example is already contained in section 13 which guides the courts' interpretation of the Convention in the context of freedom of thought, conscience and religion.

To be sure, the manner in which section 4 and section 10 operate to preserve parliamentary sovereignty is not an ideal solution, from the perspective of a model strong form dialogue.[97] But there is an attractive interpretation of these provisions that is consistent with such a constitutional model. First, the declaration of incompatibility can be viewed as a device that allows courts to vent their scorn on a piece of rights-defying legislation, thus excluding it from the integrity of the law. It follows that courts should make declarations as a matter of course where legislation is incompatible with a Convention right and where such legislation cannot be interpreted consistently with it.[98] Secondly, far from being an engine for dialogue, section 4 can be understood simply as a concession to the difficulties inherent in judicial law-making. Although as a matter of fact, all the political responses to declarations of incompatibility have been by way of primary legislation, we have seen that this is equally possible in response to a section 3 interpretation. The difference between section 4 and section 3 is that the former triggers a power for a minister to order such amendments to the legislation as he or she considers necessary. This suggests that the purpose of declarations of incompatibility is not to parley with Parliament, but simply to provide a mechanism for the law to be brought into line where legislation, rather than interpretation, is needed. The appropriate governmental response under section 10 is merely an administrative one of re-drafting the provisions so that the right is respected.

Thirdly, section 3 should not be read minimally in order to favour the use of section 4 declarations, but equally should not be read maximally so as *always* to find Convention compliance. Following the middle course leads to the rejection of such extremes. It indicates that the line cannot be drawn in abstraction, but depends on context, the proper limits of judicial law-making and the dictates of prudence.

Status of Judicial Decisions

We have seen that those who consider that the Human Rights Act should be understood from the perspective of dialogue (that is, the principle-proposing variety) consider that legal determinations should be provisional and contestable.

---

[97] A preferable device would have been something like s 33 of the Canadian Charter, which allows legislation to be enacted contrary to the Charter but only where it 'expressly' declares that it is to have such effect and, moreover, it is limited to five years' duration so that it cannot be outlasted by the life of a parliament and its renewal therefore requires electoral mandate. Contrast Manfredi, *Judicial Power and the Charter* (n 46) 181–99.

[98] As Lord Nicholls has stated in rejecting a submission that a declaration should not be issued in the exercise of the court's discretion, it is desirable that the House as court of final appeal 'should formally record that the present state of statute law is incompatible with the Convention': *Bellinger v Bellinger* [2003] 2 AC 467 [55].

A question that arises from such a focus is whether the courts' dialogic function is supposed to be limited to cases decided under the Human Rights Act. To the extent that commentators do take this view, their claim is that the courts put on a different hat when they decide cases under the Human Rights Act from the hat they wear when they decide all other cases in public law and private law. Such a view would be odd, to say the least, since it would require the courts to adopt a schizophrenic attitude to their own function. This is well illustrated by *Daly* because the finding of a breach of the European Convention (and so section 6) was coextensive with a finding of a breach of the common law. The House of Lords held that a policy requiring the absence of prisoners during examination of privileged correspondence breached the common law right to confidentiality of privileged communications as well as the right to respect for correspondence under Article 8 of the Convention. Lord Bingham stated that, 'the common law and the convention yield the same result'.[99] In so stating, his Lordship was not declaring a conclusion of principle on the common law claim, and a mere opinion as to the correct interpretation of the Convention (to be resolved by some other branch of the state) on the Human Rights Act claim. Moreover, it would not be sensible to treat the status of their Lordships' conclusions on the Convention and the common law any differently. Apart from anything else, if the decision was thought be questionable from a moral or political point of view, such questions would be equally applicable to the right found to exist under the Convention as that found to be part of the common law. Furthermore, the court approaches both issues in precisely the same way. Any distinction between the court's two conclusions would therefore be arbitrary. Proponents of this form of constitutional dialogue might seek to take refuge from such criticism in the distinction between section 4 of the Human Rights Act and sections 6 and 3, and argue that the court should only be treated as functioning dialogically (in the principle-proposing sense) when a declaration of incompatibility is made under section 4. Essentially, the argument would be that the courts wear a different hat only when they grant a declaration of incompatibility (and *Daly* was not a section 4 case, because it concerned a policy, not an Act of Parliament). The problem is that such an argument would replace one arbitrary distinction with another. Whether or not a Convention right is interfered with by primary legislation as opposed to secondary legislation, or policy, may simply be a matter of chance or expediency. It bears no necessary connection to, for example, how controversial or complex the question in issue is.[100] There is therefore no good reason for thinking that the nature of a court's decision that there has been a violation of the European Convention is different just because the infringement is attributable to an Act of Parliament.[101]

---

[99] *R (Daly) v Secretary of State for the Home Department* [2001] 2 AC 532 [23].

[100] This is well illustrated by the case of *Re G (Adoption: unmarried couples)* [2009] 1 AC 173; see the discussion in ch 2 pp 44–45 and ch 5 p 160.

[101] To say that the *nature* of the adjudication is the same is not the same as saying the *substance* of the adjudication is the same. As a matter of substance, there is authority for the proposition that additional latitude should be given to primary legislation, at least on some issues: see ch 5, pp 156–68.

The point is reinforced when one considers that under the Human Rights Act, primary legislation includes certain Orders in Council as well as measures of the general synod of the Church of England;[102] whilst under the Scotland Act 1998 and the Northern Ireland Act 1998 the courts can strike down primary legislation made by the Scottish Parliament and the Northern Ireland Assembly.[103] Properly understood, section 4 relates only to the remedy that the court grants when it finds a violation of the Convention: it cannot change the nature of its adjudication.

A yet further distinction that has been suggested is between cases in which it is reasonable to disagree about the interpretation of the Convention right, and those cases where it is not. It has been suggested that when there is reasonable disagreement over the meaning of a particular Convention right in a particular context, the courts should be regarded as having only proposed the legally required result, leaving the legislature to 'definitively resolve' the issue.[104] But this would be the most slippery point of distinction of all. On one view, all decisions in the appellate courts reflect cases on which two views of the result can reasonably be held. Moreover, even if the idea is understood in a more limited way to include only difficult cases involving moral or socio-political controversy, it would still apply to an enormous number of issues arising before the courts, and since they also arise in cases not brought under the Human Rights Act, there is no good reason for drawing the line there. Highly controversial decisions with massive political consequences arise in all sorts of areas. Consider by way of example recent judicial decisions in such diverse areas as the medical care available to failed asylum-seekers, the legality of the imposition of bank charges and the enforceability of pre-nuptial agreements, all of which raise considerable moral and political issues, and the courts' judgments in these cases are highly controversial.[105] Whilst judges should of course take account of the fact that issues that arise before them are morally and politically controversial, and this may lead them to interpret the law in a way that provides considerable latitude to the political branches (or to duck the issue altogether), it would be the thin edge of a very large wedge to argue that where the courts have determined what Convention rights require, the status of such judgments should be regarded as provisional.

Judicial Decision-Making

It has also been argued by those who have advanced a dialogic understanding of the Human Rights Act that judges should shrug off any concerns about prudence

---

[102] s 21(1).

[103] Scotland Act 1998 s 29(2)(d); Northern Ireland Act 1998 s 6(2)(c).

[104] Young, *Parliamentary Sovereignty* (n 8) 140. See also Klug 'Deference' and 'Bill of Rights' (n 8). In the former, Klug maintains that the purpose of the Human Rights Act is to give Parliament the final say where there is 'no settled human rights answer' (132).

[105] *R (A) v Secretary of State for Health* [2009] EWCA Civ 225; *Office of Fair Trading v Abbey National plc* [2009] 2 WLR 1286; *Radmacher v Granatino* [2009] 2 FLR 1181. For a recent controversial case arising under the Race Relations Act 1976, see *R (E) v JFS Governing Body* [2010] 2 WLR 153 (whether school admission policy requiring children to have Jewish mothers was racially discriminatory).

and restraint, and decide cases robustly and as 'partisans' for rights. It is not altogether clear what is meant by this,[106] but a possible example is provided by *A v Secretary of State for the Home Department* (*A (No 1)*), in which the House of Lords held that that there was a state of emergency threatening the life of the nation which justified derogation from the Convention. In the face of a robust dissent on this point from Lord Hoffmann, three members of the Committee admitted to having doubts about the correctness of their conclusion.[107] This may be a good example of when, according to scholars such as Nicol and Roach, they should have acted as partisans for rights. They should have shrugged-off such doubts and decided the case robustly against the Government and thereby presented the principled view for consideration by Parliament. But one only has to spell out such an approach to see that it would be deeply unappealing and wrong. It would be irresponsible for judges to act as ideological partisans in this way. There can be no justification for judges being institutionally or ideologically predisposed to one party to a case, whether that is a detained individual or the Government. It would also be irresponsible for judges to ignore their doubts about whether they have reached the right result on the basis that it is open to Parliament to come back and change the decision if it does not agree with it. Judges must strive to reach the right result irrespective of what Parliament or the Government could or might do. Moreover, as a matter of practicalities there will rarely be parliamentary or governmental time available to debate, still less correct, judicial decisions. The suggestion that courts should be prepared to risk being wrong on the basis that it might enrich political debate is therefore not only unprincipled but also dangerous.

A (No 1) in fact provides a very good example of where an exercise of the passive virtues would have been preferable. Those Lordships who had doubts about whether there was a national emergency would have been better off leaving the question undecided since it was entirely unnecessary to decide the issue. A majority of their Lordships (including all of the doubters) concluded that even if there was a public emergency, the legislation in question which permitted detention without charge of non-nationals suspected of involvement in terrorism, was discriminatory and disproportionate. Instead, their Lordships established for all time that the evidence presented to them was sufficient to establish a national emergency threatening the life of the nation, if only just, and they have provided government with a get out of jail free card to be used in the future. In the words of Justice Jackson, already cited, the judgment will lie around in the law reports, 'like

---

[106] See eg Nicol, 'Law and Politics After the Human Rights Act' (n 11) and Roach, *The Supreme Court on Trial* (n 9). For further discussion, T Hickman, 'Courts and politics after the Human Rights Act: a comment' [2008] *PL* 84, 90–91. We must leave aside the difficulty that arises where the case raises competing rights between private parties, as it frequently does particularly where primarily legislation is said to be incompatible with Convention rights.

[107] Lord Bingham said he had 'misgivings' (*A v Secretary of State for the Home Department* [2005] 2 AC 68 [26]), Lord Scott expressed 'very great doubt' ([154]), Lord Rodger acknowledged 'hesitation' ([165]). Contrast Lord Hope, 'ample evidence' ([118]), and Baroness Hale, 'not . . . qualified or even inclined' to hold otherwise ([226]).

a loaded weapon' ready for the hand of another government which wishes to 'bring forward a plausible claim of urgent need'.[108]

The arguments for understanding the form of constitutionalism under the Human Rights Act as exhibiting a form of principle-proposing dialogue are therefore unattractive and not particularly coherent. At the risk of over-simplification, the short point is this: it is not the function of courts to advance argument but to hear it. The Human Rights Act does not transform them into a form of privileged pressure group and does not affect any radical alteration to the judicial function.

Legislative Replies

In the following section we see how strong form dialogue also provides concrete solutions to the breadth of the interpretative duty under section 3 in particular cases. At this juncture, however, we must consider another aspect of section 3 that is open to interpretation and that has not yet been the subject of judicial consideration: namely, the nature of the obligation in respect of parliamentary replies to judicial interpretations. Consider three possible responses to a strained construction of a statute under section 3: (1) Parliament repeals the provision but enacts a new provision in the same terms; (2) Parliament enacts a provision that seeks expressly to reverse the judicial decision; (3) Parliament repeals the provision and re-enacts it in modified form. It is suggested that in each of situations (1), (2) and (3) adherents of principle-proposing dialogue should argue for the provision to stand. Their argument would be that Parliament had considered the judicial proposal and had rejected it. In terms of situations (1) and (2) they may say that it is not 'possible' to interpret the provision in any other way. But to be perfectly consistent they would view Parliament's response as putting forward a different, considered, and equally reasonable interpretation of Convention rights in each of the situations (1), (2) and (3), and on this basis the question of resorting again to either section 3 or section 4 does not arise because there is no presumptive incompatibility on which it can bite.

However, adopting a strong conception of constitutional dialogue, this would be the wrong judicial response. In situation (1) a court should hold that nothing has changed and that it is still possible to read the legislation compatibly with the Convention.[109] The exception to this would be where the Government could show that the provision had become necessary and could therefore be justified. Unless the court had deemed the original provision offensive per se, or because of the objective that it was intended to meet was itself offensive, courts should always consider changing their stance on the basis that, as circumstances change,

---

[108] Above n 67.

[109] On this analysis, legislative intent is judged on an objective basis and not by reference to any particular author. On which see Dworkin, *Law's Empire* (n 36), Theories that are based on broader notions of intention that absorb values or normative principles taken from constitutional history or moral consensus build in room for dialogue between this history and consensus and bald parliamentary will. See TRS Allan, 'Constitutional Dialogue' (n 18) and 'Legislative Supremacy and Legislative Intent' (n 18).

positions that once were unjustifiable have become justified.[110] In terms of situation (2), the court's approach should largely depend on how clear the provision is. If its meaning is clearly to override Convention rights then the court should issue a section 4 declaration. If not, it should interpret the provision under section 3, pushing Parliament to use ever more explicit wording that would ultimately require the Government to issue a declarations under section 19(b) of the Human Rights Act, to the effect that the provision is not compatible with Convention rights.

Situation (3) is a little more complicated and is dependent on the precise nature of the initial judicial decision. It may be that the court's interpretation of the legislative provision was not the only position that would be Convention-compatible. On this basis the court should identify a 'core' Convention requirement and insist that the legislative reply meet this threshold. Beyond this core requirement the court could accept a range of different legislative schemes even if they struck the balance between rights slightly differently to the initial court decision. The question might, however, not just be one of balance between rights but it might, like the position considered above in relation to situation (2), be one of justification. The original statutory provision might well have been considered too broad and although the legislative reply reigned-in the court's interpretation it may well be that it is sufficiently nuanced to be a justified legislative response.

These points can be illustrated by reference to an exchange between the courts and Parliament in Canada. In *R v O'Connor* the Supreme Court held that restriction on disclosure of the therapeutic records of alleged victims in sexual assault and rape cases violated the rights of the accused to a fair trial.[111] In an effort to protect the privacy rights of victims, Parliament quickly responded, enacting legislation severely restricting the situations in which disclosure should be made. The legislation was subsequently upheld by the Supreme Court in *R v Mills*.[112] From the perspective of principle-proposing dialogue, the Court should have simply

---

[110] Canadian scholars have developed the idea that s 1 of the Charter, which allows violations of rights to be justified, is the 'engine of dialogue' because it allows legislatures to pursue the same ends by other means more mindful of the principle defended by the Court. The point applies in much the same way under the Human Rights Act, since interference with most Convention rights admits of justification. Although further exploration of this point would take the discussion here too far afield, it raises the question whether the nature of qualified rights means that principle itself is compromised in a manner that Bickel and Dicey resisted. A negative answer to this question is, however, warranted for several connected reasons: (1) unlike rights under the US Constitution or at common law, Convention rights have clear textual grounding that separates (and thereby protects) the fundamental principle from the grounds for justification; (2) grounds for justifications are carefully circumscribed and do not open up holes in the principle that can threaten to engulf it; (3) justified interferences do not 'lie around' in the precedents book like a 'loaded weapon', but rather are liable to be swept up by the requirements that states have limited time to put their houses in order and are subject to evolving standards: *Chapman v UK* (2001) 33 EHRR 18; *Goodwin v UK* (2002) 35 EHRR 447.

[111] *R v O'Connor* [1995] 4 SCR 411.

[112] *R v Mills* [1999] 3 SCR 668. For one of several American examples, see *Planned Parenthood v Casey* 505 US 833 (1992) which modified *Roe v Wade* 410 US 113 (1973) whilst holding firm to the core principle propounded.

accepted these provisions.[113] In fact, although the Court did not strike down new provisions, it read them in a way that preserved a broad discretion to the trial judge protecting the 'right of the accused to make full answer and defence [that] is a core principle of fundamental justice'.[114] In so deciding, the majority held that 'Parliament may build on the Court's decision, and establish a different scheme as long as it remains constitutional'.[115] The resulting scheme therefore reflected the result of both legislative and judicial input. Although the Court ultimately protected principle, it also promoted a principled vision that was subject to some give and take.

From Theory to Practice: *Bellinger v Bellinger* and *Re S*

The important case of *Bellinger v Bellinger* illustrates how the theoretical perspective of strong form dialogue provides a platform for analysis of the developing case law on the Human Rights Act. According to section 11(c) of the Matrimonial Causes Act 1973, a marriage shall be void if the parties to it are not respectively male and female. Whilst the terms male and female are not defined by Parliament, the High Court held in *Corbett v Corbett* that this was to be determined by reference to chromosomal, gonadal and genital tests as at birth, thus excluding post-operative transsexuals.[116] Mrs Bellinger is a male-to-female post-operative transsexual who petitioned for a declaration that notwithstanding this case law, her marriage was valid. The case followed the decision of the ECtHR in *Goodwin v UK*, not in the context of marriage, that the failure to ensure legal parity for transsexual persons violated their Article 8 rights. The Strasbourg decision led to the commencement of a new process of consultation in the UK and the Government proposed to make amendments to primary legislation allowing, amongst other legal changes, for transsexuals living permanently in their acquired gender to marry in that gender. Against this background the House of Lords in *Bellinger* refused to give section 11(c) the 'novel, extended meaning' that would either have recognised Mrs Bellinger's marriage or permitted her to marry again. It held that *Corbett v Corbett* should continue to be applied.[117]

---

[113] Relying on the court's statement that it does 'not hold a monopoly on the protection and promotion of rights and freedoms; Parliament also plays a role in this regard . . .' (*Mills* (n 112) [58]) some Canadian commentators have indeed characterised the decision in this way: see J Cameron, 'Dialogue and Hierarchy in *Charter* Interpretation: A Comment on *R. v. Mills*' (2000) 38(4) *Alberta Law Review* 1051.

[114] *Mills* (n 112) [93]. For discussion, see Roach, *The Supreme Court on Trial* (n 9) at 277–81 and Cameron (n 113). In *Doucet-Boudreau v A-G of Nova Scotia* (2003) 232 DLR (4th) 577, Iacobucci and Arbour JJ stated: 'Deference ends . . . where constitutional rights that the courts are charged with protecting begin' [36].

[115] *Doucet-Boudreau* (n 114) [55]. The court will not always recognise room for give and take: compare *Sauvé v Canada* [2002] 3 SCR 519.

[116] *Corbett v Corbett* [1971] P 83; followed by the Nullity of Marriage Act 1971 s 1, subsequently re-enacted in s 11(c) of the 1973 Act.

[117] *Bellinger v Bellinger* [2003] 2 AC 467 [36] (Lord Nicholls); *Goodwin* (n 110).

However, the interpretation argued for was perfectly semantically feasible, indeed straightforward, as is shown by the fact that for the purposes of the proceedings the petitioner was treated as a female (as well as married).[118] The House preferred to issue a declaration that section 11(c) was incompatible with Article 8 of the Convention. In so doing it relied on a number of substantive arguments reflecting the preference of leaving the 'deep waters' of transsexual status to Parliament.[119] Lord Nicholls, whose speech had the unanimous consent of the Committee, argued that reading section 11(c) so as to validate Mrs Bellinger's marriage would have far-reaching ramifications and that it raised issues of social policy and of administrative feasibility that the courts could not determine.[120] Most significantly, although it was accepted by the Government before the House of Lords that Mrs Bellinger herself was entitled to have her acquired female gender recognised, their Lordships were generally concerned that drawing the line between male and female was a task with complexities that the court was ill-suited to grapple with. It raised complex medical, ethical and political issues, not only in the context of marriage but in other contexts, where the full recognition of acquired gender would throw up difficult legal and policy issues. Moreover the evidence and argument had been directed only to Mrs Bellinger's case. The whole issue of the legal rights of transsexual persons, their Lordships considered, was one better dealt with by Parliament.[121] Importantly, Lord Nicholls' assessment was that this was 'the more especially' the case, given that the Government had 'announced its intention to introduce comprehensive primary legislation on this difficult and sensitive topic'.[122]

The essential holding in *Bellinger*, only partially obscured by the fact it was legalistically addressed in terms of what was 'possible' under section 3, was that the whole issue of transsexual status is a matter of 'social policy' for Parliament and not for the courts. In so holding, the Committee appeared to indicate that it preferred to view its role, at least in relation to the case before it, in terms of principle-proposing dialogue. It lent its weight to the process of reform, but did not feel able to determine for itself the question of fundamental rights that was raised.[123] In the event this approach worked relatively well. In 2004 Parliament enacted legislation

---

[118] ibid [62] (Lord Hope).

[119] ibid [42] (Lord Nicholls).

[120] ibid [38].

[121] ibid [39]–[43] (Lord Nicholls), [61] (Lord Hope), [76] (Lord Hobhouse).

[122] *Bellinger* (n 117) [37].

[123] In response to the statement in the text (when previously published), Aileen Kavanagh has remarked that the court 'felt well able to determine the question of fundamental rights at issue' because it decided that the claimant's rights had been violated (although in fact this was conceded) and made a declaration accordingly (A Kavanagh, *Constitutional Review Under the Human Rights Act* (Cambridge, CUP, 2009) 137). This is true, and it supports a view expressed below that the case can be understood as an exercise of the passive virtues. But it remains the case that, (1) the court refused to protect Mrs Bellinger's rights by granting a remedy that was effective—a remedy under s 3 being superior, from the perspective of strong-form dialogue, and (2) it declined to make a principled determination setting out the circumstances in which a male-to-female transsexual is entitled to be regarded as a 'female'. In the text that follows, I have sought to clarify my view on *Bellinger v Bellinger* in response to Kavanagh's pertinent criticisms.

conferring legal rights, prospectively, on all transsexual persons who are able to demonstrate to a panel that they have, or have had, gender dysphoria and that they live permanently in their acquired gender.[124]

However, it is important to appreciate the weakness of the House of Lords' approach. In the first place, it was far from clear that the House of Lords had avoided judging the contours of the line between male and female because it was quite possible that the primary legislation would be the subject of a future challenge or challenges to determine whether the line had been drawn by Parliament in a manner compatible with the Convention.[125] Individuals who fell on the wrong side of the line would still be able to say that their rights had not been respected by Parliament and such claims could easily be envisaged. Whilst it must be acknowledged that the courts faced with such a claim would be entitled to give weight to the view of Parliament following its detailed consultation and consideration process, the courts would still have had to judge each case on its merits (and may yet have to do so if a claim is brought). Making a declaration of incompatibility did not therefore necessarily avoid the courts having to determine borderline cases.

It may be that their Lordships thought that since this was a matter that had to be left to Parliament, a court faced with a future challenge to the primary legislation would have to simply accept the legislative reply as a considered response in the light of pronouncements of both the Strasbourg Court and the House of Lords. That would at least be consistent with the principle-proposing stance their Lordships adopted, but it would be a dereliction of the Court's function under the Human Rights Act to ensure that even primarily legislation in social policy areas is compatible with Convention rights. Faced with such a challenge, the courts ought to at least decide whether the claimant in question is entitled to have their acquired gender recognised.

It is unsurprising that the Committee declined to stray into the deep waters of deciding upon the legal entitlements of transsexual persons generally. But it did not have to do so in order to overrule *Corbett v Corbett* and interpret the word 'female' under section 11(c) of the Matrimonial Causes Act 1973 as including Mrs Bellinger. Before the House of Lords, the Government accepted that the interpretation given to section 11(c) in *Corbett v Corbett* was a violation of Mrs Bellinger's rights as from the date of the decision in *Goodwin v United Kingdom*. The Committee did not need to go any further than the circumstances of her case, and certainly did not need to go beyond the issue of marriage into other areas where the rights of transsexual persons to recognition of their acquired gender was not recognised. There was no substance to Lord Nicholls' fear that the Court had to settle government policy on the legal entitlements of transsexuals across the board, or do nothing at all. It did not need to decide where the line should be drawn in general, or whether other people in different circumstances should also be recognised as 'female'. Whilst it is true, of course, that excluding Mrs Bellinger's

---

[124] Gender Recognition Act 2004, finally effective in 2005.

[125] In the event, the line has been tailored to comply with the principle propounded by the Strasbourg Court. However, it was not retrospective.

marriage from section 11(c) would have established a principle and set a precedent for other cases,[126] the courts could then have progressed case-by-case after hearing full argument on other difficult factual situations. As noted above, they had not obviously avoided doing so in any event. Nor would this approach have precluded legislative intervention to draw the line, and no doubt if Parliament had chosen not to intervene, a relatively clear line would have emerged in the courts. Indeed, in the Court of Appeal, Thorpe LJ had stated, after a careful review of the expert evidence:

> Whilst conceding that any line can be said to be arbitrarily drawn and to lack logic, I would contend that spectral difficulties are manageable and acceptable if the right is confined by a construction of section 11(c) of the 1973 Act to cases of fully achieved post-operative transsexuals such as the present petitioner.[127]

The House of Lords did not consider the suggestion and was not inclined to engage with the facts.

Moreover, although Lord Nicholls mentioned the 'far reaching ramifications' of the courts recognising Mrs Bellinger's marriage as not falling foul of section 11(c) of the 1973 Act, he did not specify what these were and the only evidence before the Court appears to have related to difficulties that arose from *Goodwin v United Kingdom*, from changes required to the law in contexts other than marriage.[128] Thorpe LJ stated in a dissenting judgment in the Court of Appeal that since the issue was limited to marriage, and not the various other contexts that were in issue in *Goodwin v United Kingdom*, any potential difficulties arising from recognising Mrs Bellinger's right to marry would be much reduced.[129] Any difficulties would have been further reduced by the fact that, as Lord Hope noted in his speech, section 3 cannot alter the meaning of legislation prior to the enactment of the Human Rights Act, which would mean that the effect of a section 3 interpretation would

---

[126] A point made by Kavanagh, *Constitutional Review* (n 123) 138.

[127] *Bellinger v Bellinger*, [2002] Fam 150 [152] (Thorpe LJ).

[128] See the Court of Appeal's judgment at [99]–[104] and [150]–[152] discussing the Interdepartmental Working Group on Transsexual People Report (2000) which followed the judgment of the ECtHR. Lord Nicholls did later mention the fact that marriage has legal consequences in many areas, such as contract, pensions, social security and even the criminal law, he did so to make the point that there was a need for certainty as to where the line was to be drawn.

[129] *Bellinger* (n 127) [152]. Thorpe LJ made clear that the Court needed only to resolve a narrow issue under the Matrimonial Causes Act and it remained open to Parliament to address the wider issues raised by the recognition of acquired gender in other contexts: '[It was contended that] any relaxation of the present clear-cut boundary would produce enormous practical and legal difficulties. I grant at once that to give full legal recognition to the transsexual's right to acquire (perhaps not irreversibly) his or her psychological gender gives rise to many wide-ranging problems, some profoundly difficult. . . . Indeed such a development would almost certainly throw up additional problems as yet unforeseen. But we are not contemplating or empowered to contemplate such a fundamental development. That indeed can only be for parliament. All we consider is whether the recognition of marriage should be denied to a postoperative male-to-female transsexual applying the decision in *Corbett v Corbett (orse Ashley)* [1971] P 83. In that context difficulties are much reduced. We need concern ourselves only with those that arise from recognising marriages already celebrated and permitting the future celebration of marriages between parties one of whom is a transsexual seeking to satisfy the requirements of section 11(c) of the 1973 Act in his or her postoperative gender.'

probably have been prospective only.[130] Aileen Kavanagh has defended the judgment on the basis that had the Matrimonial Causes Act been read in the way contended for by Mrs Bellinger, this would have 'run the risk' of 'untold and potential negative consequences'. But they were just that, *untold* and *potential*.[131] No doubt a clear and coherent legislative scheme, reforming all the areas in which a breach of Article 8 arose, would have been *preferable*, but the test under section 3 is whether the interpretation contended for is *possible*. And any unforeseen consequences could have been rectified by legislation in any event. The policy considerations in *Bellinger v Bellinger* were not sufficiently established to make it impossible for the courts to interpret section 11(c) compatibly with Article 8, on the contrary, as Bickel teaches, a narrow holding would here have been the prudent course: it would have invited prompt parliamentary action; it would have provided a remedy to Mrs Bellinger—even if possibly only prospective; and it would have reserved the ultimate ability of the courts to assess the principled issue.

Thus, consider the possibility that *Bellinger* had been followed by a change of government with a different policy and different priorities. This hypothetical government limited the reform or abandoned it altogether.[132] Courts in future litigation would have been helpless, discovering that the House of Lords had renounced the ability to assist transsexuals by denying the ability to embrace them within section 11(c).[133] Instead, the House of Lords rather conspicuously took the opportunity of passing the buck on the controversial issue of transsexual status to the Government. Surely the Human Rights Act requires a more robust judicial role in the protection of principle? By invoking section 3, the House of Lords would not have cut down legislative projects, or usurped Parliament by removing an issue from the political forum; instead it would have set in motion a more powerful principle protecting form of dialogue between courts, executive and Parliament. Like the Canadian Supreme Court in *O'Connor*, the House of Lords would have preserved its ability to read-down the legislation to protect the core right in future situations and, as *Mills* shows, this would have allowed some future give and take between the courts and Parliament in determining precisely where the protection of transsexual status should begin and end, should that prove necessary. Instead, the House of Lords disclaimed any future input into the question.

It is suggested, however, that the explanation of *Bellinger* is not that the House was accepting generally that it should adopt a principle-proposing stance on

[130] *Bellinger* (n 117) [65]. His Lordship was not content to rest his judgment on this point because it would have been possible for Mrs Bellinger to 'try again some other day'.
[131] Kavanagh, *Constitutional Review* (n 123) 139.
[132] As it was, the Court of Appeal strongly criticised the slow progress of the reforms: [2002] Fam 150 [96] and [109]. Even in the House of Lords the Government was unable to give any assurance about the introduction of compliant legislation. Government counsel even submitted that no declaration should be issued because of the difficulty of deciding on new policies and of drafting new legislation. Lord Hobhouse's response was that 'The argument for further time is now itself incompatible with the rights conferred by the Convention' (*Bellinger* (n 117) [78]–[79]).
[133] Indeed, this second hypothetical scenario suggests a second course, that it would have been preferable to dismiss the claim on the ground that the relief sought would have required s 3 to have retrospective effect, than to grant a declaration of incompatibility which might be ignored.

matters of fundamental rights. The weak and deferential posture adopted by the House of Lords can only be understood on the basis that it followed a decision of the Strasbourg Court binding on the Government, and that statutory reform was well progressed (albeit that it was still proceeding slowly[134]). It is perhaps doubtful that their Lordships would have thought the issue so much more suitable for Parliament if the indications had been that the Government supported the law as it stood. From this perspective then, it is possible to understand the judgment as an exercise in judicial prudence. Indeed, although a narrow holding would have been one way that the Court could have displayed a passive virtue, the refusal to invoke section 3 can also be regarded as an exercise of a passive virtue of sorts. The real question then, and perhaps where my disagreement with the judgment lies, does not relate to the form of constitutionalism animating the speeches, but whether or not the particular exercise of judicial prudence was a wise one.

Indeed the approach to the Human Rights Act advocated here certainly recognises limits on judicial law-making even in the context of pressing human rights concerns.[135] We should remember that context and prudence are crucially important to an approach based on a strong form of dialogic constitutionalism and are crucial to understanding the case law on section 3.[136] This is well illustrated by the case of *Re S*.[137] The case concerned the Children Act 1989, which established a detailed legislative scheme for the protection of vulnerable children. The House of Lords recognised that a 'cardinal feature' of this scheme is the division of responsibility between courts and local authorities: after a care order has been made, it is local authorities and not the courts that have parental responsibilities for the child. However, all too frequently, local authorities failed to meet the objectives of the care plans governing their relations with the children in their care. Such failings, even if perfectly innocent, could violate family rights under Article 8 of the Convention. The problem was widely recognised and was the subject of numerous studies, conferences and reports.

The Court of Appeal considered that it could remedy the situation by reading into the 1989 Act a scheme by which the courts would retain supervisory jurisdiction over children by starring certain key milestones in care plans, which if not met would re-trigger the judicial process. This scheme had not been canvassed before the Court and was derived from suggestions made at a conference held in 1997. Indeed, it was not considered wholly acceptable even to the claimants. It was made clear by counsel in one of the joined cases before the House of Lords that the

---

[134] In the Court of Appeal, Butler-Sloss P and Robert Walker LJ described the lack of progress as 'profoundly unsatisfactory': *Bellinger* (n 117) [109].

[135] See further Dicey, *Law and Public Opinion* (n 78) at 396, 489.

[136] In particular, it is no coincidence that the House of Lords adopted a much more intrusive approach to s 3 where legislation sought to limit the jurisdiction of the courts to ensure that defendants in criminal cases receive a fair trial (*R v A (No 2)* [2002] 1 AC 45), since it mirrors the approach taken at common law with respect to attempts to oust the jurisdiction of the courts more generally. See further A Kavanagh, 'Statutory interpretation and human rights after *Anderson*: a more contextual approach' [2004] *PL* 537 and 'The Elusive Divide between Interpretation and Legislation under the Human Rights Act, 1998' (2004) 24 *OJLS* 259.

[137] *Re S (Minors) (Care Order: Implementation of Care Plan)* [2002] 2 AC 291.

claimants sought the affirmation of the Court of Appeal's judgment only as an interim measure, and that it was still necessary for Parliament to revisit the area.[138]

The claimants' case therefore sought to exploit a view of the courts as a forum to pressure Parliament and promote principled arguments. In truth, they were not arguing for a determination of their rights. As the House of Lords rightly held, the Act itself did not violate Convention rights, it simply meant that the only remedy for the violation of Convention rights by local authorities was an application to the courts under the Human Rights Act, and this was not an effective way to protect family rights, especially those of children who would find it difficult to mount a legal claim in the event of serious failings (a problem, it should be noted, that even the Court of Appeal's innovations would not have alleviated). But it is central feature of the Human Rights Act that courts do not have to develop effective remedies for violations of Convention rights, reflected in the deliberate omission of Article 13 of the Convention from the Human Rights Act. This properly limits the scope for judicial law-making and appreciates the crucial role for Parliament in protecting principle. As Dicey said, the 'duty of a Court, in short, is not to remedy a particular grievance, but to determine whether the grievance is for which the law provides a remedy'.[139] Yet it was the absence of an effective remedial system that formed the nub of the claimants' case in *Re S*, not a legislative interference with their Convention rights.

The House of Lords held that establishing a new system of judicial supervision was a step in the pursuit of the protection of principle that was too large for the courts to take, and might disrupt local authority activities and resource allocations in unforeseeable ways.[140]

Furthermore, it was open to the House of Lords to issue a section 4 declaration in respect of incompatibility between the general scheme of the 1989 Act and Article 6 of the Convention, on the basis that it did not provide sufficient procedural safeguards for parents and children in respect of childcare decisions. Insofar as this related simply to a failure to provide, Lord Nicholls stated that a section 4 declaration had nothing to bite upon—no specific statutory incompatibility. Moreover, although his Lordship acknowledged that a declaration might be issued with respect to the basic principle of the 1989 Act denying parents and children an ability to challenge in court decisions of local authorities following care orders, the issue, he decided, should be reserved, since it had caused no injustice to the claimants.[141] The sum of this reasoning is that there was a clear rejection of the use of section 4 to converse with the Government and to advise it on questions of principle, as well as a refusal to exert exclusive dominium over questions of fundamental principle. The issue was avoided and cast back in to the political arena.

---

[138] 'Although Parliament should address the matter as soon as possible, the Court of Appeal decision should stand in the interim' (*Re S* (n 138) 301).

[139] Dicey, *Law and Public Opinion* (n 78) 365.

[140] Crucial to understanding the case is that by striking out a care order in one of the two cases, the Court of Appeal unintentionally created uncertainty about who was responsible for the children (*Re S* (n 137) [21] (Lord Nicholls)).

[141] ibid [83]–[88].

It might well be concluded that the Human Rights Act therefore had nothing to add in *Re S*, but that would overlook perhaps the most important feature of the case. Notwithstanding that the House of Lords rightly adhered to the role of determining rights, it still prompted further legislation. Their Lordships underlined the problems that had been highlighted in earlier litigation by stating in strong terms that legislation was now urgently required.[142] At the same time, the Court reserved its position and added bite to its words by making clear that where local authorities went seriously awry in future—a position that was almost inevitable under the existing scheme—the courts would be able to find specific violations of Article 8, as well, of course, as the indication of incompatibility with Article 6.

We should also note that resort to section 4 would have been particularly unwelcome, since it would have empowered the Government to depart from the 'cardinal feature' of the scheme that Parliament had approved and enacted without recourse to primary legislation by means of section 10 procedure. The effect of not issuing a declaration of incompatibility was therefore to prompt the Government into action and to ensure that the matter was debated and legislation enacted by Parliament. The somewhat paradoxical result is that by not using section 4 to converse with Parliament, the courts engaged in a far more robust form of constructive dialogue with Parliament.

Much to its credit, Parliament responded quickly. Within the year, amendments had been made to the 1989 Act providing, amongst other things, for local authority review of care plans, the appointment of a reviewing officer to monitor the local authority's performance and the ability to refer matters to the Children and Family Court Advisory and Support Service.[143] Quite clearly, legal changes of this nature are well beyond the capacities of even the most ingenious of courts.

Re S therefore reveals that dialogue is at the heart of the Human Rights Act, but that it does not centre round declarations of incompatibility or require a realignment of the separation of powers by transforming the courts into mere advocates before the other branches. It affirms that the distinctive judicial function under the Human Rights Act is the determination of questions of rights. It illustrates how the courts are engaged in a collaborative endeavour with the Government and Parliament in protecting individual rights.

---

[142] 'I cannot stress too strongly that the rejection of this innovation on legal grounds must not obscure the pressing need for the Government to attend to the serious practical and legal problems identified by the Court of Appeal or mentioned by me' (*Re S* (n 137) [106] (Lord Nicholls)); '. . . I would strongly urge that the Government and Parliament give urgent attention to the problems clearly described by the Court of Appeal and by my noble and learned friend so that we do not continue failing some of our most vulnerable children' (ibid (n 137) [112] (Lord Mackay)).

[143] Adoption and Children Act 2002 ss 118 and 121. See Hansard HC col. 51 (20 May 2002) (Jacqui Smith MP).

Conclusion

The discussion in this chapter has located the Human Rights Act, and the form of constitutionalism that it embodies, within the wider field of constitutional theory. It has shown how it occupies the middle ground between (non-dialogic) theories of formal and substantive legality and the (dialogic) idea that judges are politicians in robes, whose role in human rights cases is to put forward principled arguments for consideration by the political branches. Neither analysis is satisfactory. Non-dialogic theories fail to account for the way that the courts interact with the political branches and the fact that they do accommodate the needs of expediency. The idea of principle proposing dialogue affords courts a weak role in the constitutional system according to which their determinations by the courts as to what the law requires are to be regarded as provisional determinations, offered for acceptance or rejection by the political branches. On this account, section 4 of the Human Rights Act is a key provision which enables the courts to contribute to such debates. But this view lacks coherence: the line between when court determinations are to be regarded as provisional proposals and when they are not is impossible to draw. It is also highly undesirable as it reduces the role of the courts to that of a privileged political pressure group and renounces their constitutional responsibility to determine whether legal rights have been violated. The form of constitutionalism underpinning the Human Rights Act is to be found in the fertile dialogic middle ground between these two extremes. It is the courts' function to determine questions of principle, but the various branches of the state do not merely *counteract protectively* but they also *interact productively*, such as when the courts recognise a degree of latitude for the political branches to make decisions that interfere with protected rights or where they avoid purporting to determine questions of principle and allow matters to remain within the realm of politics.

4

Standards and Rights in Public Law

THIS CHAPTER AND the next chapter explain the relationship between the legal *standards* applicable to an executive decision or legislation, the *latitude* permitted by those standards, and the *weight* afforded by the court to the person or persons responsible in determining whether those standards have been breached and the permitted latitude exceeded. This relationship is central to understanding how modern public law works. Whilst much of the discussion, particularly in the next chapter, is directed to the Human Rights Act, the relationship between the concepts of standards, latitude and weight is applicable to public law as a whole.

Efforts to encapsulate aspects of this relationship under the Human Rights Act have led commentators and courts to employ a range of different concepts, including, 'discretionary area of judgment', 'relative institutional competence' and 'margin of discretion'. This has created a great deal of confusion, not least because these terms are often used differently by different people. Moreover these are not just labels: the courts have been urged to adopt a new doctrine—'due deference'—to demarcate the relative institutional functions of the courts, the executive and Parliament under the Human Rights Act, notwithstanding that no such doctrine is to be found in traditional domestic public law, the text of the Human Rights Act or in the jurisprudence on the European Convention. This chapter and the following chapter seek to explain the law in a way that makes clear that no supplementary concepts or doctrines are either necessary or desirable. The building blocks for a coherent application of public law principles are already in place and, properly understood, provide all that is necessary to construct a coherent approach to public law after the Human Rights Act.

The topics are divided between the chapters as follows. Standards are dealt with in this chapter, which necessarily includes a discussion of the latitude afforded to the state by such standards. The next chapter deals with how the courts go about determining whether such standards have been breached, which is an exercise that often requires the courts to afford weight to the assessments of others. It is in this context that the concept of deference is considered.

The approach that is developed here is in accordance with the Joint Opinion of the Committee of the House of Lords in *Huang*. In that Opinion the Committee referred to the considerable amount of argument that it had heard, and the considerable amount of authority that had been cited to it, on 'due deference, discretionary areas of judgment, the margin of appreciation, democratic accountability, relative institutional competence, a distinction drawn by the Court of Appeal between decisions based on policy and decisions not so based, and so on.'[1] The Committee stated that 'that there has been a tendency, both in the arguments addressed to the courts and in the judgments of the courts, to complicate and mystify what is not, in principle, a hard task to define, however difficult the task is, in practice, to perform.'[2] In *Huang* and in subsequent appeals, the House of Lords has eschewed such concepts, doctrines and terminology. This book has done likewise. It attempts to elucidate and clarify how public law after the Human Rights Act fits together by reference to established principles and adjudicatory methods.

Standards of Review and Standards of Legality

As a starting point, it is helpful to draw a distinction between two senses in which legal standards are applied by the courts in public law. On the one hand, public law standards demarcate the boundaries of the High Court's supervisory jurisdiction. They are the rules and principles that dictate the degree of scrutiny, or lack thereof, that the courts will give to decisions made by the executive and inferior tribunals. Public law standards are in this sense avowedly directed to *the courts*, and not to inferior tribunals or public officials. On the other hand, some public law standards are directed not to the courts but at public officials. They are rules and principles that set the legal standards that apply to public officials and inferior tribunals when making their decisions. Public law essentially does both of these things: it establishes standards for courts when making their decisions, and it establishes standards for tribunals and public officials to apply when they make theirs. Many of the rules and principles that have been developed by the courts can be seen to be predominantly rules of either the first sort or of the second sort. Recognising this helps to shed light on the developments and tensions within public law. This chapter will therefore utilise this distinction in seeking to elucidate such developments, and we will also need to refer back to it in later chapters.

In order to clarify the discussion of public law standards here, we will employ the following terminology. Where public law rules or principles are principally directed at the courts themselves we will call these, consistently with common usage, 'standards of review'. Where public law rules or principles are principally directed not at the courts but at the primary decision-makers, we will call these 'standards of legality', because they set standards directed to the decision-maker that supplement those conditions on the exercise of power which are expressly set out in the empowering legislative provision (they are, in other words, rules and principles which 'supply the omission of the legislature'[3]).

---

[1] *Huang v Secretary of State for the Home Department* [2007] 2 AC 167 [14].
[2] ibid.
[3] *Cooper v Wandsworth Board of Works* (1863) 14 CB (NS) 180, 194 (Byles J).

It is worth emphasising that the distinction between standards of review and standards of legality is not one that is formally drawn in the law. Nor is it any part of the thesis of this book that it should be. It is simply a helpful and often overlooked distinction, and one that is particularly pertinent when considering the emergence of human rights standards in public law, not least because, as will be explained, the recognition, development and application of substantive human rights standards has been and continues to be held back by the traditional fixation on public law's function in setting standards of review. Now let us also concede that this distinction is not always helpful and that some rules and principles resist classification as either standards of review or standards of legality. The duty to take into account relevant considerations, for example, seems principally to be a standard of legality since it is a duty directed at the public official. But it is often referred to by courts when articulating the degree of scrutiny that they will give to decisions of inferior courts and tribunals ('the court should only intervene if the decision-maker has failed to take into account something relevant to his decision'). However, the fact that the distinction is not always illuminating does not mean that it has no utility, any more than it could be said that a Hohfeldian analysis of legal concepts has no utility because it will often, if not usually, be entirely unilluminating. The difference between a standard of review and a standard of legality can, in fact, be very clear. This can be illustrated by the following example. Consider the fictional example of the State of Georgania. Georgania has a Bill of Rights which stipulates that 'everyone has a right to communicate on a privileged and confidential basis with their legal advisers' and makes clear that no public authority is entitled to violate that right. But the Georganian Parliament has also enacted legislation which states that in an action for judicial review of a decision of a public authority the Georganian courts can only quash a decision if it is shown that the decision was patently unreasonable. Under this scheme, the Bill of Rights establishes a clear standard of legality but the court is restrained to review compliance with that standard, at least in a judicial review action, on a patent unreasonableness basis. The Georganian courts therefore hold that a decision by a public official that an inspection of a person's correspondence would violate the Bill of Rights will not be quashed unless no public official could have concluded that the inspection would not violate the Bill of Rights.[4] It applies the standard of review to the standard of legality. This shows how standards of review differ from standards of legality, and how they both can operate at the same time. Indeed, had the

---

[4] The Supreme Court of Canada, in *Minister of Citizenship and Immigration v Khosa* 2009 SCC 12 drew a related, but not identical, distinction between a ground of review established by the Federal Courts Act RSC 1985 c F-7, which creates grounds for upholding a judicial review claim against decisions made under nominated Federal statutes, including grounds such as error of law, excess of jurisdiction and breach of natural justice, and a standard of review, such as reasonableness, patent unreasonableness or correctness standard. A further distinction is between a standard of review and a standard of proof, a distinction articulated by the United States Supreme Court in *Concrete Pipe & Products of California Inc v Construction Laborers Trust* 508 US 602 (1993). These two other distinctions are mentioned in order to clarify the distinction drawn in the text, as well as to underscore the one-dimensional view of public law that has taken root in the United Kingdom.

Georganian legislation not been enacted, and had the courts decided for them-selves whether or not inspection of correspondence breached the bill of rights, the Georganian courts would still have been applying a standard of review: they would have been applying a *correctness* standard of review. Whenever the law imposes a standard by way of a rule or a principle on a public body, a standard of review must always be applied to determine whether it has been breached.

In the example just given, both the standard of legality and the standard of review were established by the Georganian Parliament. This makes the distinction between the two particularly clear. In domestic public law the position is not as clear-cut. The courts, as we shall see, have themselves recognised common law principles that operate as standards of legality in the same way as the right to legal privilege under the Georganian bill of rights operated as a standard of legality, and they have also recognised common law principles that operate as standards of review in the same way as the legislation enacted by the Georganian Parliament. But since this has been the product of pragmatic and incremental common law development, rather than by legislative intervention, the two different roles that are being performed have not been cleanly distinguished, or even explicitly addressed, in the case law. The Human Rights Act has added a range of statutory standards to this public law mix, and it calls for some attention to this distinction. Therefore, with the distinction between standards of review and standards of legality in mind, let us turn to consider the development of modern public law. In so doing we need to return to the subject of the development of common law con-stitutional rights, which was introduced in chapter 2.[5]

The Common Law

Administrative law has always recognised standards of legality in the form of prin-ciples of natural justice. Thus the courts have, amongst other things, established duties on public officials to notify persons of pending decisions, to allow affected persons to make representations and in some cases a duty on public officials to give reasons for the decisions that they make. In *Ridge v Baldwin* for instance, Lord Reid accepted the submission made on behalf of the plaintiff that a watch com-mittee had been 'bound to observe what are commonly called the principles of natural justice'.[6] These principles conditioned the power to dismiss a borough constable, which 'could not then have been exercised and cannot now be exercised until the watch committee have informed the constable of the grounds on which they propose to proceed and have given him a proper opportunity to present his case in defence'.[7] The focus was firmly on the duty applicable to the watch com-mittee, and not on the power of the courts to scrutinise its decision. In a series of

---

[5] See pp 17–21.
[6] *Ridge v Baldwin* [1964] AC 40, 64.
[7] ibid, 79.

decisions following *Ridge v Baldwin*, these principles were extended more generally to administrative decision-making.[8]

However, by contrast, the common law did not impose any *substantive*
standards on public officials to which their decisions had to conform. The substantive standards of legality were the terms of the empowering statute, which
were not supplemented by any substantive common law principles. The courts
would require the statutory conditions to be observed. This is what Lord Diplock
described as 'illegality' in the *GCHQ* case. His Lordship said, 'the decision-maker
must understand correctly the law that regulates his decision-making power and
must give effect to it.'[9] As Lord Diplock's remark makes clear, insofar as a standard
of review was applied to determine whether the substantive legal standards had
been observed, it was a correctness standard.[10] The question of whether the
conditions of the statute had been fulfilled was a matter for the courts, just as the
question of whether the rules of natural justice had been observed was a matter for
the courts.

How does the *Wednesbury* case fit into this scheme? As is well known, Lord
Greene MR held that the courts can quash decisions taken in the exercise of a statutory discretion where they are, 'so unreasonable that no reasonable authority could
ever have come to it'.[11] In so stating, he was obviously describing a standard of
review, rather than a standard of legality. He was describing how the courts should
exercise their supervisory jurisdiction over the administration: he was not describing a substantive principle to which government decisions must conform. Indeed,
the question to which Lord Greene expressly directed his judgment was this: 'What,
then, is the power of the courts?'[12] It is significant that his Lordship did not frame
the question in terms of identifying the duties on the local authority. Having posed
this question, Lord Greene then rifled through the doctrines of relevant and irrelevant considerations, bad faith, and so on, none of which had been relied upon by
the plaintiff. Having done so, his Lordship held that the only basis on which a court
could otherwise interfere was, 'if a decision on a competent matter is so unreasonable that no reasonable authority could ever have come to it, *then the courts can
interfere*'.[13] Note again, the terms of the answer given by Lord Greene were directed
to the circumstances in which the courts can interfere. The focus was therefore

[8] See *Lloyd v McMahon* [1987] 1 AC 625; *R v Civil Service Appeal Board, ex p Cunningham* [1991]
4 All ER 310; *R v Higher Education Funding Council, ex p Institute of Dental Surgery* [1994] 1 WLR 242;
R v Secretary of State for the Home Department, ex p Doody [1994] 1 AC 531; *R (Bibi) v Newham LBC
(No1)* [2002] 1 WLR 237; *Secretary of State for the Home Department v AF (No 3)* [2009] 3 WLR 74.
There is, however, no 'general' duty to give reasons—see *R (Hasan) v Secretary of State for Trade and
Industry* [2009] 3 All ER 539.
[9] *Council of Civil Service Unions v Minister for the Civil Service* [1985] AC 374, 410 (*GCHQ* case).
[10] Lord Diplock could have stated (eg) that the courts should only interfere if public officer's understanding of the statutory requirements was unreasonable. For a case in which such an approach was
taken, see *R v Monopolies and Mergers Commission, ex p South Yorkshire Transport Ltd* [1993] 1 WLR
23, discussed in Craig, *Administrative Law*, 6th edn (London, Sweet & Maxwell, 2009) 14-034,
pp 460–61.
[11] *Associated Provincial Picture Houses Ltd v Wednesbury Corporation* [1948] 1 KB 223, 230.
[12] ibid, 228.
[13] ibid, 230 (emphasis supplied).

firmly on articulating the power of the courts—the standard of the court's review. It was not a case about the duties imposed on public authorities.[14]

Traditionally, administrative law has limited its recognition of common law standards of legality to procedural standards. In relation to the substance of the decision, the courts have applied a standard of review analysis and have focused on the restricted power of the court to intervene to quash an administrative decision. The imposition of *substantive* principles that would condition the exercise of general powers was associated in the minds of lawyers with a written constitutional document or Bill of Rights, which the United Kingdom did not have. Politicians were trusted not to interfere with our cherished liberties and it was felt that the responsibility that they owed to local and national electorates was a sufficient guarantee that they would not exercise their powers in ways that interfered with such liberties. This constitutional orthodoxy was challenged in *Wheeler v Leicester City Council*. The case concerned a judicial review brought by six members of Leicester Rugby Club against a decision by the City Council to ban the club and its members from using its recreation ground on the grounds that the club had refused to object to a proposed rugby tour of South Africa by some of its members (to which councillors were opposed). The Court of Appeal held that the ban was not unlawful. Browne-Wilkinson LJ (as he then was) dissented. His dissenting judgment challenged the constitutional orthodoxy head-on, and it became an important staging post towards the recognition of human rights principles in domestic public law. Browne-Wilkinson LJ stated:[15]

> Until comparatively recent times this sort of question did not arise in practice. Without any written constitution ensuring individual human rights, constitutional conventions were observed whereby the majority exercised their powers so as to give effect to their own policies but not so as to discriminate against individuals who did not agree with them. However with the present polarisation of political attitudes the observance of such conventions has diminished. There is no written constitution which delimits what is within the ambit of the powers of the elected majority by declaring certain individual rights which cannot be overridden by the views of the majority.

---

[14] It is even possible to suggest that the distinction between standards of review and standards of legality was implicitly recognised by Lord Greene in his judgment. Counsel for the plaintiff had submitted that there was a duty on the authority to act reasonably and that the court should interfere where it considered that a decision was unreasonable. Lord Greene MR accepted that 'the discretion must be exercised reasonably'—a standard of legality—but went on to reject the submission that the court could interfere simply because this standard had not been met (*Associated Provincial Picture Houses Ltd v Wednesbury Corporation* (n 11), 229). He explained that, given the matter was assigned to the local authority and was within its 'knowledge and expertise', the courts would only intervene if the decision was unsupportable or the unreasonableness 'overwhelming'. The same point could be made about *Kruse v Johnson* [1898] 2 QB 91. Lord Russell CJ stated that courts should jealously guard against unreasonable exercise of statutory powers by private corporations; but when it comes to legislation made by 'public representative bodies', courts could only find it to be unreasonable where 'they were found to be partial and unequal . . .; if they were manifestly unjust; if they disclosed bad faith; if they involved such oppressive or gratuitous interference with the rights of those subject to them as could find no justification in the minds of reasonable men'. He continued to state that it is only in this sense 'that the question of unreasonableness can properly be regarded [by the courts]' (99–100).

[15] *Wheeler v Leicester City Council* [1985] AC 1054, 1063.

In this passage, Browne-Wilkinson LJ articulated the constitutional orthodoxy reflected in cases such as *Wednesbury*, that in the absence of any constitutional Bill of Rights the substantive checks on government are political and not legal, only to go on to reject it as outdated. For Browne-Wilkinson LJ, the failure, or at least the fragility, of the political checks meant that, in the absence of written constitutional protections, there was a deficit in the protection afforded to individual rights within the UK constitution.

None of the judges in the Court of Appeal (or Forbes J at first instance) felt able to hold that the attitude of the council was so unreasonable that no reasonable council could would have banned the club from using the recreation ground. Browne-Wilkinson LJ therefore thought that the time had come to recognise that it would be unlawful for public officials to infringe 'the fundamental freedoms of speech and conscience' in the absence of clear statutory authority to do so. Importantly, Browne-Wilkinson LJ did not seek to build such protections out of (or into) the *Wednesbury* standard: his approach was not one based on standards of review, but on standards of legality. As his judgment explicitly recognised, he was advocating the use of the common law to do that which a statutory Bill of Rights would do, he was not seeking to apply an enhanced standard of scrutiny to the council's decision.

However, Browne-Wilkinson LJ's approach appeared to come out of the blue, was contrary to the orthodoxy that he himself recognised and articulated, and was not grounded in authority. Whilst his Lordship referred to judicial statements emphasising the importance of freedom of speech, he referred to only one case[16] by analogy, and then somewhat limply, to justify the idea that such a freedom should qualify general discretionary power. The case, decided in 1921 and never subsequently applied in a reported judgment, held that a public authority cannot impose a charge on an individual without express authority of Parliament, a principle that is in fact squarely based on article 4 of the Bill of Rights 1689.[17]

Browne-Wilkinson LJ's idea was in any event scotched in the House of Lords[18] and the courts reverted to the position where, in the absence of a written constitution, substantive standards of legality are not applied at common law. Instead, in subsequent cases the courts set about modifying the *Wednesbury* standard of review, applying it with greater intensity and rigour.[19]

---

[16] ibid 1064–65. Whilst Browne-Wilkinson LJ preferred to describe this approach as giving effect to common law 'immunities' from government intrusion, rather than 'positive rights', this distinction is not material to the present discussion. The case is discussed further in 265–66.

[17] The case referred to was *Attorney-General v Wiltshire United Dairies Ltd* (1921) 19 LGR 534, (1922) 127 LT 822. On Art 4 of the Bill of Rights see, *Customs and Excise Commissioners v Total Network SL* [2008] 1 AC 1174.

[18] *Wheeler* (n 15). Their Lordships found rather imaginative and unconvincing justifications for quashing the decision, namely that it had been taken unfairly and for an improper purpose. See ch 9, pp 265–66.

[19] See eg *Bugdaycay v Secretary of State for the Home Department* [1987] AC 514, 531 (Lord Bridge): 'The most fundamental of all human rights is the individual's right to life and when an administrative decision under challenge is said to be one which may put the applicant's life at risk, the basis of the decision must surely call for the most anxious scrutiny.' Also *R v Ministry of Defence, ex p Smith* [1996] QB 517, discussed below, pp 111.

We have seen in chapter 2 how this position gradually altered in the 1990s, and that the courts began to recognise 'fundamental' and 'constitutional' common law rights. Let us now consider in a little more detail the genealogy of this line of case law. It was noted in chapter 2 that the doctrine of constitutional rights has its origin in cases protecting access to the courts. The doctrine first crystallised in the case of *Leech* in 1993, in which the Court of Appeal held that general words in the Prison Act 1952 could not authorise the making of prison rules permitting unrestricted examination of prisoners' legal correspondence. Lord Steyn delivered the judgment of the Court. Drawing on previous cases that had referred to the right of prisoners to have unimpeded access to court, Lord Steyn reasoned that the right of access to court is of 'fundamental importance' and said that 'Even in our unwritten constitution it must rank as a constitutional right.' Not only did Lord Steyn recognise that this right has a higher-order status from other legal rights, he also made the connection with the idea of 'civil rights' and the presumption of statutory interpretation against statutory interference with vested rights, which provided the bedrock justificatory principle for the development and application of other 'fundamental' common law 'civil rights'.[20] This was precisely what Lord Browne-Wilkinson had anticipated in *Wheeler* and advocated in his speech on the 'Infiltration of a Bill of Rights' in 1991 and it was, less directly, the approach signposted by Lord Scarman in *Morris v Beardmore*. Whilst none of these views were cited by Lord Steyn, they appear to have been highly influential in the Court of Appeal's judgment.

In 1997 the House of Lords decided *R v Secretary of State for the Home Department, ex p Pierson*,[21] another prison case. Both Browne-Wilkisnon and Steyn LJJ were now sitting as Lords of Appeal in Ordinary. Both judges took the opportunity to set out, in separate speeches but in remarkably similar terms, a carefully crafted legal justification for the recognition and application of fundamental rights in public law. This justification had been conspicuously absent from Lord Browne-Wilkinson's judgment in *Wheeler* and remained underdeveloped in Lord Steyn's judgment in *Leech*. That the speeches in *Pierson* were reflective of a wider agenda on the part of these judges cannot be doubted against the background of these cases. Most remarkably, the invocation of fundamental rights and the accompanying legal justification was produced by Lord Steyn and Lord Browne-Wilkinson of their own motion. Counsel's submissions in *Pierson* had not invoked the idea of fundamental rights, let alone proposed the detailed and sophisticated intellectual justification by reference to judicial and academic authorities which subsequently appeared in the speeches of Lord Browne-Wilkinson and Lord Steyn. Counsel did not even rely on *Leech*.

---

[20] *R v Home Secretary, ex p Leech* [1994] QB 198, 210, applying *Raymond v Honey* [1983] 1 AC 1 (holding that a prisoner has a right to the court to seek to commit the prison governor for contempt) and *R v Secretary of State for the Home Department, ex p Anderson* [1984] QB 778 (holding that a prisoner has a right of unimpeded access to a solicitor). The other members of the Court were Neill and Rose LJJ.

[21] *R v Secretary of State for the Home Department, ex p Pierson* [1998] AC 539, 573.

The case concerned a challenge by a prisoner to a decision by the Home Secretary that had effectively increased the penal element of his sentence retrospectively. The prisoner's counsel argued that the decision infringed a principle of non-aggravation of penalties; but he did not leave this modest terrain and did not locate such a principle within any broader idea of constitutional rights. It nonetheless evidently presented the opportunity that Lord Browne-Wilkinson and Lord Steyn had been waiting for. On this occasion, they appear to have had the intellectual and constitutional justification for the doctrine of constitutional rights ready up their sleeves. Lord Browne-Wilkinson began by setting out the general principle that Parliament does not legislate in a vacuum, and that statutes are drafted on the assumption that the ordinary common law will apply to them, for which he found authority in *Cross*, *Bennion*, and *Maxwell*, the most authoritative sources on statutory interpretation.[22] He then said that where wide powers are conferred on a public official, 'Parliament implicitly requires the decision to be made in accordance with the rules of natural justice'. His authority for this proposition was the judgment of the House of Lords in *Ex p Doody*.[23] Next, he identified the closest thing that the common law had recognised to a substantive legal right, namely the right of access to a court, and said that general words also could not alter such a 'basic "constitutional right" as the right of access to the courts'.[24] Lord Steyn's judgment in *Leech* here played its part.[25] This permitted Lord Browne-Wilkinson to draw the following conclusion:

> I think the following proposition is established. A power conferred by Parliament in general terms is not to be taken to authorise the doing of acts by the donee of the power which adversely affect the legal rights of the citizen or the basic principles on which the law of the United Kingdom is based unless the statute conferring the power makes it clear that such was the intention of Parliament.[26]

Lord Steyn reasoned in almost precisely the same way. Relying on *Cross* and *Maxwell*, his Lordship invoked the principle of statutory interpretation that statutes are presumed not to alter 'fundamental principles governing civil liberties'. This presumption is, he said, the same as the 'intellectual justification' for Byles J's statement in *Cooper v Wandsworth Board of Works* (applied, as his Lordship noted, by Lord Reid in *Ridge v Baldwin*) that 'the justice of the common law' will supply the omission of the legislature in requiring public officials to abide

[22] Sir Rupert Cross, *Cross on Statutory Interpretation*, 3rd edn (London, LexisNexis, 1995) 165–66; FA Bennion, *Bennion, Statutory Interpretation*, 2nd edn (London, LexisNexis, 1992) 727; and P St J Langan (ed), *Maxwell on the Interpretation of Statutes*, 12th edn (London, Sweet & Maxwell, 1969) 116, for the proposition that, 'Parliament does not legislate in a vacuum: statutes are drafted on the basis that the ordinary rules and principles of the common law will apply to the express statutory provisions' (573).
[23] *R v Secretary of State for the Home Department, ex p Doody* [1994] 1 AC 531.
[24] Referring to *R v Lord Chancellor, ex p Witham* [1998] QB 575.
[25] As did the judgment of Laws LJ in *Ex p Witham* (n 24), holding that rules prescribing court fees which prevented poor litigants from gaining access to court constituted an interference with the constitutional right of access to court, and were not justified by express words of statute.
[26] *Ex p Pierson* (n 21), 573.

by principles of natural justice.[27] Lord Steyn concluded that the decision of the Home Secretary was unlawful because it conflicted with the 'fundamental principle' that 'a sentence lawfully passed should not retrospectively be increased'.[28] By contrast, Lord Browne-Wilkinson, despite laying the foundations for the application of substantive common law rights, was unable to find such a principle to place on them, his comments were therefore obiter.

The effect of these seminal speeches was that Lord Browne-Wilkinson and Lord Steyn had recognised that substantive civil rights—going beyond procedural rights to natural justice and the right of access to the court—could exist at common law independently of the law of tort, and can be applied, consistently with constitutional principle, to restrain government action. Their speeches are in this respect contrary to the House of Lords' judgment in *Wheeler*. Perhaps the most brilliant thing about the speeches of Lord Browne-Wilkinson and Lord Steyn is the way they camouflaged their radical innovation in the trappings of uncontroversial and respected doctrine. In a classic common law trick, they suggested that they were simply propounding the law as it always had been. It would be fascinating to know what went on behind the scenes in *Pierson*, not only because Lord Browne-Wilkinson and Lord Steyn departed so radically from counsel's submissions and then set out the doctrine of constitutional rights in such remarkably similar terms, but also because the other members of the Judicial Committee did not at this time expressly sign up to their views. That did not happen until the case of *Simms*.

In *Simms*[29] the House of Lords held that a prison policy prohibiting prisoners from meeting with investigative journalists was unlawful. Lord Browne-Wilkinson was the senior Law Lord on the Judicial Committee but on this occasion he did no more than agree with a speech given by Lord Steyn. Lord Steyn reasoned that the policy interfered with freedom of expression which was a 'basic' and 'fundamental' common law right. He applied the speeches given by Lord Browne-Wilkinson and himself in *Pierson* and argued that the principle of statutory interpretation operates 'as a constitutional principle'. Lord Millett and Lord Hoffmann agreed with Lord Steyn, thus confirming the authority of constitutional rights jurisprudence in English law and the authority of Lord Browne-Wilkinson and Lord Steyn's speeches in *Pierson*. In a short concurring speech Lord Hoffmann made explicit the connection between the approach developed by the common law and the approach taken under a written constitution. He stated:

> In the absence of express language or necessary implication to the contrary, the courts therefore presume that even the most general words were intended to be subject to the basic rights of the individual. In this way the courts of the United Kingdom, though acknowledging the sovereignty of Parliament, apply principles of constitutionality little different from those which exist in countries where the power of the legislature is expressly limited by a constitutional document.[30]

---

[27] *Cooper v Wandsworth Board of Works* (1863) 14 CB(NS) 180.
[28] *Ex p Pierson* (n 21), 591.
[29] *R v Secretary of State for the Home Department, ex p Simms* [2000] 2 AC 115.
[30] ibid 131.

With these insightful words, Lord Hoffmann almost made the doctrine of constitutional rights his own. His Lordship completed the exercise of joining the dots left unjoined by Browne-Wilkinson LJ's judgment in *Wheeler*. It had been explicitly accepted that the common law could make up for the absence of substantive rights set out in a written constitutional document by enforcing modern civil and political rights as part of a common law constitution, and that these common law rights have a degree of resistance to statutory restriction. The House of Lords' judgment in *Wheeler* was reversed *sub silentio*.

Before leaving this topic it is relevant to our theme that Lord Steyn connected his reasoning in *Pierson's* case with Dicey's idea that even under a system of Parliamentary sovereignty, the law is exercised in what he called the 'spirit of legality'.[31] Adopting this language, Lord Steyn described the courts' recognition and application of common law fundamental rights as the 'principle of legality'. The reasoning is apt, not only in giving renewed life to Dicey's idea that the common law controls the meaning of statutes and thereby protects individual rights against Parliamentary intrusion, but also in distinguishing the idea of principles of *legality* from the idea of standards of *review*.[32] *Pierson* and *Simms* represented a tectonic shift in the orientation of substantive public law from its focus on standards of review to a recognition of substantive standards of legality to accompany the principles of natural justice.

The Human Rights Act

The Human Rights Act has established in domestic law standards of legality that apply to all decisions of public officials and to all inferior courts and tribunals. These standards are both substantive and, particularly but not exclusively in relation to Article 6, also procedural. Section 6(1) of the Act states that it is 'unlawful for a public authority to act in a way which is incompatible with a Convention right'. The Convention rights themselves are not standards of review, they are norms of general application and not principles directed to the courts. This was made clear in *Simms* by Lord Hoffmann. His Lordship stated that the Human Rights Act has 'expressly enacted' the principle of legality and 'supplements' the rights that are recognised at common law.[33] Article 3, for example, prohibits in absolute terms torture and inhuman and degrading treatment or punishment. This is a standard of legality: it is a norm directed at public authorities and not at the courts. If a public authority commits an act of inhuman treatment it will have acted unlawfully. Article 3 says absolutely nothing about what standard the courts should apply in determining whether Article 3 has been breached.

Other rights have some qualification, not all of the same type. But they are no less standards of legality. Article 2 prohibits intentional deprivation of life save

---

[31] *Ex p Pierson* (n 21), 587–91.
[32] See ch 3 p 78.
[33] *Ex p Simms* (n 29), 131–32.

insofar as it is 'absolutely necessary' for certain specified purposes, such as in defence of any person from unlawful violence. Article 8 is less restrictively qualified. It states:

1. Everyone has the right to respect for his private and family life, his home and his correspondence.
2. There shall be no interference by a public authority with the exercise of this right except such as in accordance with the law and is necessary in a democratic society [for specified purposes] . . .

Articles 9, 10 and 11 have a similar structure. But they remain standards of legality: if a public authority acts in manner which represents an unnecessary interference with an individual's right to respect for his private life, the public authority has acted unlawfully.

It is important to emphasise that the second paragraph of these articles is just as much a component of the rights and freedoms they protect as the first paragraph. If conduct is necessary then it is not in breach of the right; if it is unnecessary then it is in breach of the right. The concept of necessity, together with the specified legitimate aims and the 'accordance with the law' requirement, together establish the boundaries of the right in question.[34] Furthermore, even so-called 'absolute' rights are often defined by reference to a balancing of interests and in some cases have even absorbed a proportionality analysis. This is the case for example with respect to Article 6. Many of the protections under Article 6, whether express (such as public pronouncement of judgment) or implied (such as the right to a court), are only breached by conduct that is unnecessary and disproportionate despite the fact that the text of Article 6 itself includes no such qualification.[35]

It may seem trite to say that the Human Rights Act has established standards of legality, but the implications are frequently overlooked because of the tendency to approach the Human Rights Act from the perspective of administrative, rather than constitutional, law. In other jurisdictions such implications have been treated as anything but trite. It was explained in chapter 2 that it took many years for the Canadian and New Zealand Courts to recognise that the Canadian Charter of Rights and Freedoms 1982 and the New Zealand Bill of Rights 1990 establish standards of legality in administrative law, and for them to move away from a standard of review approach even where decisions affected protected rights.[36] Thus, in the Canadian context, Professor David Mullan (arguing that the majority judgment in *Multani* conveniently ignored much contrary case law) has stated that, though 'not consistently',

---

[34] Simon Atrill has made this point more forcefully still: 'The confusion arises because Arts 8–11 look different. However, they still result in the definition of a right, as with all the other Articles: what is important is that, in the end, all rights emerge as being "unqualified" in the sense that they cannot be overridden. Indeed, it is this quality that makes them rights. The language of "qualified" and "unqualified" rights, therefore, is misleading': S Atrill, 'Keeping the executive in the picture: a reply to Professor Leigh' [2003] *PL* 41, 44. This is in keeping with Ronald Dworkin's definition of rights: see R Dworkin, *Taking Rights Seriously* (London, Duckworth, 1977, new impression 2000) 294–311.
[35] *B v United Kingdom* (2002) 34 EHRR 19; *Ashingdane v United Kingdom* (1997) 7 EHRR 528.
[36] Ch 2, pp 28–29.

the Supreme Court is perfectly content to let [the] enhanced common law do its work even when Charter rights and freedoms are implicated in the decision under attack. It is also evident that the Supreme Court continues to have difficulty integrating the protections that the Charter provides to the rights and freedoms of Canadians into a coherent methodology of judicial review.[37]

In the United Kingdom context, the distinction between standards of review and standards of legality has been easily understood in relation to rights that are not expressly qualified. But the expressly qualified nature of Articles 8, 9, 10 and 11 has led to confusion and it is suggested that this confusion has arisen for two connected reasons. First, the apparent structural difference between qualified rights and 'absolute' rights suggests that whereas absolute rights have clear limits, breach of a qualified right depends on the cogency of particular and localised reasons supplied for the measure in question. This in turn suggests that the courts are engaged in reviewing the reasons given at the expense of determining whether the outcome of the decision is substantively compatible with the Convention right.[38] Secondly, the ECtHR applies a proportionality test to determine whether an interference with qualified rights is necessary and, since at least the *GCHQ* case, when Lord Diplock mentioned the possible reception of the principle of proportionality into administrative law, proportionality has been thought of as a standard of review that can sit alongside or develop out of *Wednesbury* review.[39] Proportionality has therefore been thought of as a doctrine that primarily modulates the intensity of the court's review of administrative action, and it has thus been contrasted with *Wednesbury* review.[40] Indeed, in *Daly* Lord Steyn's discussion of the proportionality test to be applied under the Human Rights Act, which expressly followed academic commentators, identified several differences between *Wednesbury* review and proportionality review, all of which related to the different approach that the court should take in reviewing the decision, rather than the different substantive standard of legality that is applied: proportionality may 'require the reviewing court to assess the balance'; it may 'require attention to be directed to . . . relative weight'; and it may require more than 'heightened scrutiny'.[41] In viewing proportionality through the lens of administrative law and treating it as a standard of review, Lord Steyn missed a crucial dimension of the application of the proportionality test under the Human Rights Act which is that proportionality is not a heightened standard of review but

[37] D Mullan, 'The Canadian Charter of Rights and Freedoms: A 'Direct Driver; of Judicial Review of Administrative Action in Canada?' in L Pearson, C Harlow and M Taggart (eds), *Administrative Law in a Changing State, essays in Honour of Mark Aronson* (Oxford, Hart, 2009) 144.
[38] The House of Lords sought to scotch such confusion in *Denbigh High School* and *Miss Behavin' Ltd*, in which they held that the courts should only be concerned with the outcome of a decision and not the way it was reached. In so holding, their Lordships extinguished any process element from Human Rights Act review. These cases are subject to critical consideration in ch 8.
[39] *GCHQ* (n 9), 410, discussed in ch 9, p 263.
[40] There were also tactical reasons for portraying proportionality as a standard of review rather than a standard of legality, because it was in this way that lawyers sought to persuade the courts in the years following the *GCHQ* case, in cases such as *Ex p Brind* [1991] AC 696, that a proportionality test could be developed out of *Wednesbury* review.
[41] *R (Daly) v Secretary of State for the Home Department* [2001] 2 AC 532 [27].

part of the definition of qualified rights. Professor Ian Leigh has previously made much the same point. He has explained that section 6(1) of the Human Rights Act creates a species of illegality review (using Lord Diplock's terminology) and does not purport to introduce a standard of review or modify the *Wednesbury* standard. As he says, '[t]his would, doubtless, appear much clearer had the debate about incorporation never become entangled with the common law grounds for review of discretion from *Brind* onwards.'[42]

The Standard of Review under the Human Rights Act

Given that the Human Rights Act establishes new standards of legality it is necessary to ask what standard of review should be applied to determine whether they have been breached. Should a court intervene whenever there has been, in its view, a breach of Convention rights, or only when there is a *manifest* departure from a Convention right? Should it apply a patent unreasonableness test to the judgment of a public official that a decision is compatible with Convention rights, a merits review, or some other standard of review? The question is answered by reference to the purpose of the Human Rights Act, which is (at least in part) intended to provide the remedy for breaches of Convention rights and to avoid the need for individuals to seek a remedy in Strasbourg. The courts must therefore determine whether there has been a breach of Convention rights. The standard is a correctness standard.

This point is illustrated by reference to the pre-Human Rights Act case of *Ex p Smith*, in which the Ministry of Defence policy of preventing homosexuals from serving in the armed forces was said to be a breach of the right to respect for private life, and unlawful at common law. In accordance with established case law, the court recognised that the *Wednesbury* test had to be applied with heightened intensity. It formulated a test, which came to be known as the 'super-*Wednesbury*' test, which is formulated in terms that a decision of a public official will be unlawful if a reasonable public official could not consider the measure to be justified.[43] In addressing the issue, the court gave anxious scrutiny to the reasons advanced by the Secretary of State, but nonetheless held that the Secretary of State could reasonably justify the policy. One way of understanding the super-*Wednesbury* test (although not necessarily the way the courts have understood it) is that a *Wednesbury* standard of review is applied to determine whether there is a breach of the standard of proportionality reflected in Article 8(2). The two tests are hitched together.

---

[42] I Leigh, 'Taking rights proportionately: judicial review, the Human Rights Act and Strasbourg' [2002] *PL* 265, 283. Paul Craig also treats breach of Convention rights as a ground of illegality in his textbook *Administrative Law*, 6th edn (London, Sweet & Maxwell, 2009) 565–84, although he discusses proportionality alongside *Wednesbury* (635–39).

[43] *R v Ministry of Defence, ex p Smith* [1996] QB 517 (DC) 538 (Simon Brown LJ), 554 (Sir Thomas Bingham MR).

The effect of applying the super-*Wednesbury* standard, in any event, was that the domestic courts in *Ex p Smith* were unable to provide a remedy for a disproportionate interference with Article 8 unless the decision was so disproportionate that no reasonable public official could regard it as proportionate. In a subsequent application to Strasbourg, the ECtHR found that the UK was in breach of Article 13 because domestic courts had failed to provide a remedy for disproportionate conduct simpliciter. It stated that applying a *Wednesbury* standard of review to the question of necessity, 'effectively excluded' consideration of whether the measure satisfied a pressing social need and was proportionate.[44] Since a central purpose of the Human Rights Act is to provide an Article 13-compliant remedy in domestic law, the decision in *Smith & Grady v United Kingdom* precludes the application of a reasonableness standard of review when judging whether a an interference with Convention rights is necessary and proportionate: it effectively requires the application of a correctness standard of review to that issue, and when applying section 6 of the Human Rights Act generally.

Moreover, the ECtHR has itself rejected the submission, advanced by the UK Government in the early cases of *Handyside v United Kingdom*, that *its* role is limited to reviewing decisions made by domestic authorities on grounds of reasonableness. The Court held that although it does recognise that national authorities have a certain margin of appreciation, this does not mean that 'the Court's supervision is limited to ascertaining whether a respondent State exercised its discretion reasonably, carefully and in good faith'.[45] It must ask whether the exercise of discretion is in breach of the Convention, and that requires it to determine whether it is disproportionate. Since the Human Rights Act is intended to provide at least as good a remedy in domestic law as that provided by the Strasbourg Court, it must follow that courts should not apply a standard of review that is limited to determining whether domestic authorities made reasonable, careful and good faith attempts to act compatibly with Convention rights, including reasonable, careful and good faith attempts to act proportionately.

Domestic courts seem to have accepted that this is what is required, both in cases such as *Huang v Secretary of State for the Home Department*,[46] where the House of Lords held that the Immigration Appeal Tribunal is required to make a *de novo* determination as to whether deportation would, at the time of determination, breach Convention rights, and also in judicial review cases, where the question is whether a decision of the executive that has already been taken has

[44] *Smith & Grady v United Kingdom* (2000) 29 EHRR 493 [138].
[45] In *Handyside v United Kingdom* (1976) 1 EHRR 737 [47]–[52]. See also *Sunday Times v United Kingdom* (1979–80) 2 EHRR 245 [59]. In *Handyside*, the Court recorded ([47]) that, 'According to the Government and the majority of the Commission, the Court has only to ensure that the English courts acted reasonably, in good faith and within the limits of the margin of appreciation left to the Contracting States by Article 10(2). On the other hand, the minority of the Commission sees the Court's task as being not to review the Inner London Quarter Sessions' judgment but to examine the Schoolbook directly in the light of the Convention and of nothing but the Convention.' The Court accepted that it had to examine the Schoolbook directly and test the deicision against the standard of necessity, but this was subject to the Court affording national authorities a 'margin of appreciation' (on which see below).
[46] *Huang* (n 1).

breached a person's Convention rights. Baroness Hale more recently described it as 'straightforward' that it is the court before which a complaint of a breach of Convention rights is raised 'who decides whether or not a claimant's Convention rights have been infringed.' She said that the role of the court in human rights cases is 'quite different' from its function in an ordinary judicial review case, because it is not necessarily reviewing a decision that a measure taken by a public authority was compliant with Convention right, but deciding for itself whether such a measure is incompatible with the Convention.[47] All this is welcome, but the proposition that the Human Rights Act establishes standards of legality to which a correctness standard of review is applied is often lost sight of.

Substitution of Judgment

The fact that the courts rightly apply a correctness standard to determine whether conduct is in breach of a Convention right brings us an old chestnut of administrative law: the distinction between review and substitution of judgment. It is vital to the legitimacy of judicial review that this distinction does not collapse. The development of administrative law in the United Kingdom has always been the subject of an implicit agreement between the courts and the executive that the courts are not seeking to usurp the role of the executive and are not trying to run the country. The case law in the second half of the twentieth century is littered with reassuring statements by judges who are advancing the law in some new direction, to the effect that the development will not result in courts substituting their judgment for accountable politicians, or will not result in courts sitting in appeal from administrative decisions. But the question can be asked: does it not follow that by requiring the administration to conform to *substantive* standards, the courts can substitute their judgment for that of an elected or accountable decision-maker? After all, if the watch committee whose flagrant denial of natural justice was the subject of *Ridge v Baldwin*, had, rather than not adverting to the matter, actually concluded that it was not necessary to inform the constable of the case against him, their decision on this issue *would* have been reversed by the House of Lords.

The answer to this question is 'yes, but . . .'. There undoubtedly is and must be a substitution of judgment by a court if a public authority has concluded that its

---

[47] *Miss Behavin' Ltd v Belfast City Council* [2007] 1 WLR 1420 [31]; also see [13] (Lord Hoffmann), [44] (Lord Mance), [88] (Lord Neuberger); and *Huang* (n 1) [8] and [20]. See also *R (Countryside Alliance) v Attorney General* [2008] 1 AC 719 [125]. The same is true of legislation: 'For better or worse, Parliament has entrusted us with the task of deciding whether its legislation is compatible with the Convention rights.' (Baroness Hale); *Wilson v First County Trust (No 2)* [2004] 1 AC 816 [141] (Lord Hobhouse). The point made here does not affect the criticism levelled at the judgment of the House of Lords in *Miss Behavin' Ltd* in ch 8, in holding that no defects in the process by which a public authority reaches a decision (unless a breach of a discreet procedural right) is actionable under the Human Rights Act.

conduct is consistent with Convention rights and the court decides that it is not. But the substitution of judgment relates to only this aspect of the decision made, namely, whether the decision results in a breach of a Convention right. It does not relate to the question of whether or not the decision is desirable in the public interest. This is precisely the same approach that public law takes in relation to substantive conditions on the exercise of power that are set out in the governing statute. Consider again Lord Diplock's statement that the decision-maker, 'must understand correctly the law that regulates his decision-making power and must give effect to it.'[48] This means that if the power to do Y requires that X be present, the courts can and will determine whether X is present and will substitute their view on that question for the view of the primary decision-maker. In any Human Rights Act challenge there will be a re-determination of the question of whether the decision has breached a Convention right (assuming that the decision-maker addressed the issue in the first place), and both sides will usually have the opportunity to contend that the decision did or did not breach a Convention right by reference to arguments and evidence that were not considered at the time the decision was made.[49] In many cases, of course, the public official will not have considered whether their decision breaches a Convention right. Doctors, teachers, social workers and other public servants do not, as Lord Hoffmann has put it, 'have text books on human rights law at their elbows'.[50] This indicates that the courts, in applying standards of legality, are not exercising a reviewing role properly so called, but are simply enforcing norms against the state. In *Ridge v Baldwin*, it was immaterial whether the watch committee had or had not addressed its mind to what the Chief Constable ought to be told.

The courts therefore do engage in merits review of the issue of whether there has been a breach of a Convention right, but that does not mean that the courts substitute their judgment for the executive in relation to the decision as a whole. The requirement in *Ridge v Baldwin* that the watch had to permit the plaintiff to make representations in no way stipulated whether or not the plaintiff should be dismissed. So correctness review under the Human Rights Act requires substitution on only one, usually narrow, aspect of the decision, and then only if the matter has been considered by the public official.

Consider, for example, the case of a school that decides that it needs to improve discipline. It has a large number of options open to it and it can choose any course of conduct so long as its decision is reasonable and it does not violate a Convention right. The courts will determine whether or not the chosen measure breaches a Convention right (or is reasonable if a conventional judicial review challenge is brought) but it will not tell the school how to improve discipline. Indeed, in the context of school discipline the Convention standards leave considerable latitude to domestic authorities. As Lord Nicholls explained in *R (Williamson) v Secretary*

---

[48] *GCHC* case (n 9), 410.

[49] As long as it relates to the circumstances at the time the alleged interference with Convention rights occurred.

[50] *R (SB) v Governors of Denbigh High School* [2007] 1 AC 100 [68].

of State for Education and Employment, not even all corporal punishment is prohibited under the Convention.[51] The example is particularly illuminating because in this context Parliament has gone further than the European Convention requires and has prohibited all corporal punishment in schools.[52] It has thus established standards of substantive legality that go beyond those imposed by the Human Rights Act. The point is that when courts determine whether or not a public authority has breached a Convention right, they decide that issue on the merits, but they do not tell public authorities what decisions they should make, or whether to make a decision at all. They address only the question of whether the course of action that has been taken or which the authority wishes to take is compatible with the Convention. Precisely the same analysis applies to common law rights.

Since we are considering the degree to which the Convention requires judges to stand in the shoes of politicians and public officials, it is worth also making the somewhat obvious but nonetheless much ignored point that although the ECtHR has given Convention rights a broad and liberal interpretation, the Convention touches on only a fraction of decisions made by public authorities. The vast majority of decisions made by public authorities are not within the ambit of any Convention right. Human rights cases are represented disproportionately in the law reports, in part because the principles in play are in a state of development and in part because legal aid is more readily available to fund judicial review claims where there is a serious infringement of human rights. One way to get a flavour of the vast majority of decisions that are made by reviewable public authorities every day which do not touch on human rights considerations is to look at schedule 2 to the Parliamentary Commissioner Act 1967. This sets out a list of quangos and public bodies that are associated with a central government department such that a minister is accountable to Parliament for their actions, albeit indirectly. Even this list does not include local government agencies and public bodies for which central government is not responsible. Just under 'A' we find alongside the Ministry of Agriculture, Fisheries and Food (most of the activities of which do not engage the Convention), the Accounts Commission for Scotland, the Arts Council, the Authorised Conveyancing Practitioners Board, the Agriculture Wages Board, and the Apple and Pear Research Council; the list under 'B' includes the British Museum, the Boundary Commission, the British Tourist Authority and the British Potato Council (etc), the list goes on (and on). Assuming these authorities are making decisions, however menial and mundane, on a day-to-day basis, and even accepting that some of the decisions of such bodies will interfere with Convention rights, it seems likely that the vast majority of decisions made by

---

[51] '. . . not every act of corporal punishment of a child at school violates article 3 or article 8, even though to some extent it may adversely affect a child's physical and moral integrity.' *R (Williamson) v Secretary of State for Education and Employment* [2005] 2 AC 246 [27], referring to *Costello-Roberts v United Kingdom* (1995) 19 EHRR 112.

[52] Section 548(1) of the Education Act 1996 as amended states: 'Corporal punishment given by, or on the authority of, a member of staff to a child—(a) for whom education is provided at any school . . . cannot be justified in any proceedings on the ground that it was given in pursuance of a right exercisable by the member of staff by virtue of his position as such.'

public authorities are made without the European Convention coming into play at all.[53]

Standards under the European Convention

Even where a public authority wishes to adopt a measure that does interfere with a Convention right, the Convention does not generally prescribe the course that the executive must take. Usually, and even in the case of some rights expressed to be unqualified such as Article 6, the Convention permits some latitude to decision-makers. Contrary to suggestions sometimes found in the case law and in law journals, this latitude is not afforded because the Convention *does* prescribe a single outcome, but the courts defer or give *weight* to the executive (concepts that will be discussed in due course). Likewise, one often sees it suggested that it is only deference that prevents human rights adjudication becoming 'merits review'.[54] But on the contrary, the Convention usually recognises a range of different courses of action are permissible. Even in relation to absolute rights, the ECtHR has some-times conditioned the scope of such rights in ways that permit decision-makers a degree of latitude even when they are prima facie infringed; this is the case with respect to the prohibition on forced labour, as we shall see. This is not a question of weight or deference, but simply a reflection of the scope of the right in question. The scope of different rights varies. They impose different standards. Let us now consider the range of standards applicable in human rights cases in more detail.

When it comes to determining whether States have exceeded the permissible degree of latitude afforded by the Convention, there is a tendency to view propor-tionality as the only game in town. This is perhaps understandable, given that pro-portionality is undoubtedly the central and most pervasive standard in the case law of the ECtHR, as well as being reflected in the constitutional jurisprudence of countries such as Canada, Israel, Ireland, Germany, New Zealand and India. But it is not the only game in town. It is worth recalling that Lord Steyn in *Daly* pref-aced his comments on the distinction between *Wednesbury* review and propor-tionality by stating that he was offering only a few generalisations and it would be necessary to make due allowance 'for important structural differences between various Convention rights'.[55] This section elucidates those differences. Moreover, it is contended here that not only is it important to take *account* of the structural differences between Convention rights, but it is also only by reference to such

---

[53] When the Convention is not in play, the decisions of all public bodies must comply with the ordi-nary principles of judicial review. Although there is no empirical evidence to back this up, my guess is that these principles still restrain public bodies from undertaking activities that they would like to take (and absent the availability of judicial review, would take) more than does the European Convention.

[54] See eg *Tweed v Parades Commission* [2007] 1 AC 650 [55] (Lord Brown) and p 170.

[55] *Daly* (n 41).

differences that the principle of proportionality under the Convention can itself be fully understood.

In its first and still its most important consideration of the concept of 'necessity' in the early case of *Handyside v United Kingdom*, the ECtHR defined that concept by contrasting it with other standards contained in the ECtHR regime. In the course of explaining the need for recognising that domestic authorities have a 'margin of appreciation' in taking action interfering with Convention rights, the Court made clear that, irrespective of such a margin of appreciation, there is a degree of latitude in the concept of necessity itself. It said: 'The Court notes at this juncture that . . . the adjective "necessary", within the meaning of Article 10(2), is not synonymous with "indispensable", neither has it the flexibility of such expressions as "admissible", "ordinary", "useful", "reasonable" or "desirable".'[56] The Court approved and invoked this statement in subsequent judgments, including when articulating the principle of proportionality in *Sunday Times v United Kingdom* and *Silver v United Kingdom*.[57] In itself this statement illuminates our understanding of what is meant by necessity and proportionality, but the real importance of the statement is apparent only from the footnotes that correspond to each of the expressions put in quotation marks by the Court in *Handyside* (omitted in subsequent cases). This shows that the expressions were not plucked from the air, or from the public law of any contracting state. They are taken from the text of the Convention itself: they are standards contained in other Convention rights.

Thus, the Court drew a parallel between the term 'indispensable' and the requirement that lethal force be used only where 'absolutely necessary' (Article 2(2)), that public and press be excluded from court only where this is 'strictly necessary' (Article 6(1)) and the requirement that any derogation from the European Convention be 'strictly required by the exigencies of the situation' (Article 15(1)). On the other hand, the terms 'normal' and 'ordinary' were equated to the exceptions on the right to be free from slavery and forced labour contained in Article 4, which includes work required during the 'ordinary course of detention' and work forming part of a 'normal civic obligation'. The term 'useful' is taken from the French text of Article 1, Protocol 1 which refers to deprivations of property, 'pour cause d'utilité publique'. The term 'reasonable' is identified as the standard adopted by Article 6(1) and Article 5(3) in respect of the right to a trial within a 'reasonable time'. Each of these standards is intended to represent a fair balance between the general interests of the community and those of the individual in the context in which they apply.[58] The fact that several of these standards are contained in rights that are not often litigated should not obscure their importance to

---

[56] *Handyside* (n 45) [48]. Approved by Lord Bingham in *R v Shayler* [2003] 1 AC 247.
[57] *Sunday Times v United Kingdom* (n 45); *Silver v United Kingdom* (1983) 5 EHRR 439 [97].
[58] See *Soering v United Kingdom* (1989) 11 EHRR 439 [89]: 'inherent in the whole of the Convention is a search for a fair balance between the demands of the general interest of the community and the requirement to protect fundamental individual rights'.

the Convention scheme as a whole. It is this range of standards which represents the Convention scheme.

Normal and Ordinary

Article 4(2) of the European Convention establishes an absolute prohibition on forced labour. However Article 4(3) sets out a number of situations that are not regarded as forced labour. Article 4(3) is drafted in terms of defining the scope of the prohibition contained in Article 4(2), and not in terms of a limitation on the right not to be subjected to forced labour. But in one sense Article 4(3) operates like a limitation clause (such as that set out in Article 8(2)), because like a limitation clause it sets out circumstances that will not breach the right in question. Work required in the 'ordinary course of detention' and work which 'forms part of normal civic obligations' is said not to constitute a breach of the prohibition. There is, notably, no requirement that such work is *necessary*. In *Van der Mussele v Belgium*, the Court held that these situations are illustrative of situations that do not amount to forced labour which are 'grounded on the governing ideas of the general interest, social solidarity and what is in the normal or ordinary course of affairs.'[59] The court recognised a wide variety of situations in which states might legitimately require their citizens to work against their will. Where such work is customarily required, as long as it is not imposed on discriminatory grounds or in a way that places an excessive burden on particular individuals, it will not be regarded as forced labour. On the facts of *Van der Mussele v Belgium*, the ECtHR held that obligations on pupil avocats to work pro bono and to bear their own costs did not constitute forced labour. The Court's analysis contrasts markedly with its approach where it applies a standard of necessity, not only structurally but also substantively. Thus, successive Chairmen of the Belgian Ordre des Avocats had regarded the regime as intolerable, and the Belgian Government conceded before the Court that it was 'outmoded' and, far from pursuing any pressing social need, was 'inspired by "paternalism"'.[60] The Court nonetheless found no violation of Article 4. Such a result would have been inconceivable, given these facts, had the Court been applying a test of necessity.

In the Public Interest

Article 1 of the First Protocol requires that any deprivation of a person's possessions is in the 'public interest' and that controls imposed on the use of possessions are in the 'general interest'. This is not the language of necessity, and it is well

---

[59] *Van der Mussele v Belgium* (1983) 6 EHRR 163 [39]. In determining what constitutes work done in the ordinary course of detention under Art 4(3)(a), the Court requires that the work must be for the ordinary purpose of such work, namely, for the rehabilitation of the prisoner, and that it has its basis in a general legal standard which has equivalents in other contracting states: *De Wilde, Ooms and Versyp v Belgium (No 1)* (1971) 1 EHRR 373 [90] (Vagrancy cases); *Van Droogenbroeck v Belgium* (1982) 4 EHRR 443 [59].

[60] *Van der Mussele* (n 59) [40].

established that contracting states have greater latitude under this article than other substantive rights such as Article 8 and Article 10. The ECtHR has said that the notion of general interest is 'necessarily extensive'.[61] Even in deprivation of property cases, by contrast with control of use cases, the ECtHR has said that it will not disturb a legislature's judgment as to what is in the public interest unless it is 'manifestly without reasonable foundation'.[62] In the leading case of *James v United Kingdom* the ECtHR upheld legislation on leasehold reform on the basis that there was evidence to support the Government's belief that there was 'social injustice' that needed to be corrected and it could not therefore be said to have been 'manifestly unreasonable'.[63]

In addition to the public interest test, which determines whether a control of use or deprivation of possessions is permissible at all, the ECtHR has read an implied proportionality requirement into Article 1 of the First Protocol in relation to the terms on which the control of use or deprivation is given effect. It is not applied with the same rigour as in other contexts in which a proportionality test is applied, and the ECtHR has expressly rejected the contention that it requires the least drastic solution to the social problem to be taken, saying that this would amount to a test of strict necessary.[64] In *James v United Kingdom* the ECtHR held that the means used to effect the leasehold reforms were 'reasonable' and 'suited', and the Government's reasons for certain of the conditions 'could not be regarded as irrational'. This was sufficient for the Court to dismiss the application.[65] The difference between the standards applied under Article 1 of the First Protocol and under other qualified Convention rights was recognised by the House of Lords in the *Countryside Alliance* case, in which it was held that the standard of justification imposed by Article 1 of the First Protocol is different from the requirement of necessity under Article 8(2). Baroness Hale said in respect of the public interest requirement: 'this is not a taxing standard to meet'.[66]

Reasonable

As the ECtHR noted in *Handyside v United Kingdom*, there is an obligation on states to ensure that individuals in both civil and criminal matters have a trial within a reasonable time (Article 5(4) and Article 6(1)). This is not a peripheral right: it is in fact the most breached article of the European Convention.[67] Despite this, states are given considerable latitude in complying with the obligation. The ECtHR held in *Brogan v United Kingdom* that the notion of 'reasonable time' is a 'less strict requirement' which is 'clearly distinguishable' from the right to have a

---

[61] *James v United Kingdom* (1986) 8 EHRR 123 [46].
[62] ibid; *Jahn v Germany*, App Nos 46720/99, 72203/01 and 72552/01.
[63] *James v United Kingdom* (n 61) [49].
[64] ibid [51].
[65] ibid [51], [52].
[66] *Countryside Alliance* (n 47) [47] (Lord Bingham), [121] and [129] (Baroness Hale), [155]–[156] (Lord Brown).
[67] See the discussion in *Cocchiarella v Italy*, App No 64886/01, 29 March 2006.

determination of the lawfulness of detention dealt with 'speedily' (Article 5(4)) and the right to be brought 'promptly' (in the French text, 'ausitôt') before a judge following arrest (Article 5(3)).[68]

The obligation is also focused on the conduct of the state authorities, rather than the right of the individual. The Privy Council in *Spiers v Ruddy* held that a breach comes to an end once proceedings are expedited, which is consistent with the focus being on the conduct of the authority, rather than establishing an individual right to trial within a certain time.[69] Even very extreme delays will be tolerated if these are reasonable and are not attributable to fault or tardiness on the part of domestic authorities. Thus, in one case the ECtHR held that there had been no violation despite a delay of almost five years in determining an unjust dismissal claim because of a sudden increase in cases before the courts, stressing that the state had made reasonable efforts to alleviate the temporary backlog.[70]

Even so, it is still incumbent on the relevant authorities to take into account the nature of what is 'at stake' for the applicant. The Court has emphasised that greater solicitude or a 'special duty to act expeditiously' or a 'duty to exercise exceptional diligence'[71] is required in relation to 'important personal interests' such as in relation to proceedings concerning mental health,[72] family relations,[73] title to land,[74] employment[75] and criminal responsibility.[76] A reasonableness standard has also been applied in relation to the implied duty on state authorities to take positive measures to protect individuals from real and immediate risks to their life, physical integrity and property, which we will consider in detail in chapter 7.[77]

Necessity/Proportionality

In *Handyside v United Kingdom*, the ECtHR explained the degree of latitude inherent in the concept of necessity by reference to the greater degree of latitude found in concepts such as reasonableness and usefulness, and the lesser degree of latitude

---

[68] *Brogan v United Kingdom* (1988) 11 EHRR 117 [59]. The right to a trial within a 'reasonable' time under the Convention must therefore be distinguished from its more famous cousin in the Sixth Amendment of the United States Constitution, which guarantees the more absolute 'right to a speedy trial'.

[69] *Spiers (Procurator Fiscal) v Ruddy* [2008] 1 AC 873.

[70] *Buchholz v Germany* (1981) 3 EHRR 597 [52].

[71] *Poiss v Austria* (1988) 10 EHRR 231 [60]; *H v France* (1989) 12 EHRR 74 [85].

[72] *Bock v Federal Republic of Germany* (1989) 12 EHRR 247 [48].

[73] 'Moreover, this case concerned matters central to the enjoyment of private and family life, namely relations between spouses, as well as between the parents and their children. Finally, the Court cannot disregard the personal situation of the applicant who, for some nine years, suffered by reason of the doubts cast on the state of his mental health which subsequently proved unfounded. This represented a serious encroachment on human dignity' (*Bock v FRG* (n 72) [48]).

[74] *Poiss v Austria* (n 71) [60]; *Hentrich v France* (1994) 18 EHRR 440 [61].

[75] *Obermeier v FRG* (1991) 13 EHRR 290 [72]: '[the Court] stresses that an employee who considers that he has been wrongly suspended by his employer has an important personal interest in securing a judicial decision on the lawfulness of that measure promptly.'

[76] *Baggetta v Italy* (1988) 10 EHRR 325 [24].

[77] See *Osman v United Kingdom* (2000) 29 EHRR 245 (Arts 1 and 8); *E v United Kingdom* (2003) 36 EHRR 31 (Art 3).

reflected in the idea of indispensability. This makes plain that the concept of necessity does by its nature give some latitude to states irrespective of any 'margin of appreciation' that is afforded, but that latitude is considerably more restricted than that afforded to states under the reasonable time guarantees, for example.

The ECtHR has formulated the test of necessity in various ways but it most commonly describes it as requiring that a measure pursues a 'pressing social need' and is proportionate to the 'legitimate aim' pursued.[78] There are a couple of references to the notion of 'minimal impairment', imported from the case law of the Supreme Court of Canada's jurisdiction under the Canadian Charter of Rights and Freedoms 1982, to be found in the case law, but the court has not articulated a test of least restrictive means.[79] That is not to say that the possibility of the state authority adopting a less restrictive alternative course of conduct is not highly relevant to the proportionality analysis: where there is no explanation for why less restrictive measures have not been considered or taken, findings of disproportionality have been made.[80] In other cases, however, the ECtHR is less concerned, and looks at whether an overall fair balance has been struck.[81]

The concept of proportionality as applied in domestic law is the subject of chapter 6. It will be seen that the domestic courts have articulated a domestic approach to proportionality based on the test set out by the Privy Council in *de Freitas.*[82] This is to be welcomed, as there are several difficulties in applying the ECtHR proportionality jurisprudence directly to domestic law. In the first place the Court has not developed any clearly structured approach to necessity and proportionality, and has frequently fallen back on the notion of fair balance. Secondly, its application of those principles that it has articulated is obscured by the overlay of the margin of appreciation doctrine, which is not applicable in the domestic context.[83] And, thirdly, befitting its role as an international court which is scrutinising the conduct of contracting States, the Court also takes a rather holistic view of proportionality. In particular it does not distinguish between the conduct of different agencies of the contracting States, including between the executive, courts and Parliament.[84] In the domestic context, the Human Rights Act requires that claimants focus their complaints against a particular provision in an Act of Parliament or against particular acts or legal provisions for which the defendant is

---

[78] *Silver v United Kingdom* (n 57) [97]; *Dudgeon v United Kingdom* (1981) 4 EHRR 149 [53].
[79] See *Ahmed v United Kingdom* (2000) 29 EHRR 1 [63] and *Foxley v United Kingdom* (2001) 31 EHRR 25 [43]. The Court cited the Canadian case law but adopted a different analysis when considering the disenfranchisement of prisoners in *Hirst v United Kingdom (No 2)* (2006) 42 EHRR 41.
[80] For example, *Bartik v Russia*, App No 55565/00, 16 September 2004.
[81] In *Silver v United Kingdom* (n 57) the ECtHR was prepared to assume that the applicant prisoner whose letters had been censored had been given an opportunity to re-draft them ([102]).
[82] *de Freitas v Permanent Secretary of Ministry of Agriculture, Fisheries, Lands and Housing* [1999] 1 AC 69.
[83] See below pp 123–25.
[84] For example, in *Camenzind v Switzerland* (1999) 28 EHRR 458 in considering the proportionality of a search of property the court considered not only the manner in which the search was conducted but also the legal provisions under which it was conducted and procedural safeguards in Swiss law.

responsible. That provides the opportunity to apply a more focused proportionality analysis.[85]

Strict Necessity/Strict Proportionality

We have seen that in its statement of principle in *Handyside v United Kingdom*, the ECtHR equated the standards of absolute necessity (Article 2(2)), strict necessity (Article 6(1)) and strictly required (Article 15(1)). It equated them with the idea of indispensability. The court has also implied a strict necessity standard in certain other limited contexts, such as restrictions on the right of defence[86] and the use of force against persons deprived of their liberty.[87]

The Court explained what is meant by strict necessity in *McCann v United Kingdom* in the context of the deliberate shooting of IRA members in Gibraltar by the British SAS:

> In this respect the use of the term 'absolutely necessary' in Article 2(2) indicates that a stricter and more compelling test of necessity must be employed from that normally applicable when determining whether State action is 'necessary in a democratic society' under paragraph 2 of Articles 8 to 11 of the Convention. In particular, the force used must be strictly proportionate to the achievement of the aims set out in sub-paragraphs 2(a), (b) and (c) of Article 2.[88]

The Court then said that in keeping with the importance of the right to life in a democratic society, the Court must, in making its assessment, subject deprivations of life to the most careful scrutiny, particularly where deliberate lethal force is used, taking into consideration not only the actions of the agents of the state who actually administer the force but also all the surrounding circumstances, including such matters as the planning and control of the actions under examination.

The Court has suggested that strict necessity requires the least drastic solution to be taken.[89] In *Van Mechelen v The Netherlands* the test was nonetheless applied

---

[85] See for example *R (G) v Nottinghamshire Healthcare NHS Trust* [2009] EWCA Civ 795 in which a majority of the Court of Appeal held that a smoking ban in a high security psychiatric hospital did not violate Art 8. Lord Clarke MR and Moses LJ endorsed the Divisional Court's view that the margin of appreciation in relation to social policy should be a wide one. In mirroring the ECtHR's approach to proportionality, the analysis lacks structure and is unsuited to the domestic context. Keene LJ (dissenting) took a more structured approach to proportionality applying the *de Freitas* test, without reference to the margin of appreciation. His Lordship held that the ban was 'more than necessary' and therefore disproportionate.

[86] *Van Mechelen v The Netherlands* (1997) 25 EHRR 647 [58].

[87] *Menesheva v Russia* (2007) 44 EHRR 56 [56]; *Selmouni v France* (2000) 29 EHRR 403 [99]. The jurisprudence under Art 14 has also distinguished between cases where very weighty reasons will be required to justify discrimination (eg on grounds of sex, serial orientation, nationality, eg *Petrovic v Austria* (1998) 33 EHRR 307 [37]) and in the context of race where no justification is permitted, and other cases where a more relaxed standard of 'reasonable and objective justification' is applied: *Belgian Linguistics Case* (1979) 1 EHRR 252 [10].

[88] *McCann v United Kingdom* (1996) 21 EHRR 97 [149]; although the Court was divided on the application of this test to the facts, there was no dissent from this as a statement of principle.

[89] *James v United Kingdom* (n 61) [51]; *Van Mechelen v Netherlands* (1997) 25 EHRR 647 [58].

in a more nuanced way. The issue was whether evidence in a criminal trial could be given by anonymous police officers in a separate room from the defence. The court did not rule out such a procedure, but said that it had not been explained to its satisfaction why less drastic measures could not have been taken, such as preventing the accused from seeing the faces of the officers, and there had been no rigorous examination about whether the claimed justification—fear of reprisals—was justified.[90] Therefore, the Court did not say that the measure taken could never be justified, but that the Government of the Netherlands had failed to satisfy the burden of showing that the measures were strictly necessary.

In *Van Mechelen* the postulated less-restrictive alternatives would not have been unduly onerous on the courts or the prosecution. However, where the alternatives will be extremely burdensome, the Court will not necessarily require them to be taken. In this way, even the strict proportionality requirement builds in some latitude to decision-makers. Thus, in *Campbell and Fell v United Kingdom*, concerning the requirement of a public hearing, the Court accepted that disciplinary proceedings against prisoners could be held in private because to allow the public to attend or to hold them outside prison precincts would 'undoubtedly occasion difficulties of greater magnitude than those that arise in ordinary criminal proceedings' and would impose a disproportionate burden on the prison authorities.[91]

The Margin of Appreciation Doctrine and the Discretionary Area of Judgment

The articulation of this scheme of standards by the ECtHR in *Handyside v United Kingdom* was by way of digression in the course of articulating what became known as the margin of appreciation doctrine. After pointing out that the notion of necessity has an in-built degree of latitude, it then said: 'Nevertheless, it is for the national authorities to make the initial assessment of the reality of the pressing social need implied by the notion of "necessity" in this context.' This was because, as it had already explained, the context—public decency and censorship—was one in which the 'requirements of morals varies from time to time and from place to place' and that:

> By reason of their direct and continuous contact with the vital forces of their countries, State authorities are in principle in a better position than the international judge *to give an opinion* on the exact content of these requirements as well as on the 'necessity of a "restriction" or "penalty" intended to meet them.'[92]

It is clear from this statement, and in particular the emphasised words, that the ECtHR conceived the margin of appreciation doctrine, at least initially, not as

---

[90] *Van Mechelen* (n 89) [60]–[61].
[91] (1984) 7 EHRR 165 [87].
[92] (1979–80) 1 EHRR 737 [48] (emphasis supplied).

building in an added degree of latitude permitted to the various rights, or as loosening the requirements of those rights, but as recognising that national authorities were better placed to judge whether the Convention rights had been breached and whether the degree of latitude permitted by those rights had been exceeded. In establishing the margin of appreciation doctrine, the Court was not modifying, glossing or interpreting the standards set out in the Convention. It was recognising that national authorities would be in a superior position to judge what those standards required in the given circumstances.[93]

Of course, the Court chose to adopt a spatial metaphor which makes it appear as if it is narrowing the scope of rights and correspondingly broadening the permitted area (margin) of freedom that the rights permit states to enjoy; but that is not in fact the way the doctrine was initially understood.[94] The scope and content of the rights and freedoms was unchanged by the doctrine. The Court simply recognised that it would sometimes fall to domestic authorities to determine whether their conduct violated those rights. In this, the margin of appreciation doctrine can be contrasted with the 'living instrument' doctrine, which recognises that the content of Convention rights evolves over time. This manifestly does alter the content of the standards of legality established by the Convention.[95]

The *Handyside v United Kingdom* approach to the margin of appreciation doctrine represents by far the dominant approach in the Court's case law on margin of appreciation,[96] but there are cases in which the court has appeared to apply the margin of appreciation doctrine as a way of determining that Convention rights have not been infringed because the state has not 'overstepped' the discretion that was afforded to it (or vice versa).[97] The ECHR's judgments in such cases is generally perfunctory and conclusory, with almost no reasoning. It has been criticised by commentators and in one strongly worded opinion by Judge Rozakis.[98]

---

[93] George Letsas makes the same point in 'Two Concepts of the Margin of Appreciation' (2006) 4 *OJLS* 705, 721: 'Under the structural concept of the doctrine, we may say that state authorities enjoy a margin of appreciation, in that the Court will not substantively scrutinize their decision. Their margin has to do with the relationship between the European Court of Human Rights and national authorities, rather than with the relationship between human rights and public interest.'

[94] On 'spatial metaphors' in United Kingdom and Strasbourg law, see M Hunt, 'Sovereignty's Blight: Why Contemporary Public Law Needs the Concept of "Due Deference"', in N Bamforth and P Leyland (eds), *Public Law in a Multi-Layered Constitution* (Oxford, Hart, 2003).

[95] *Tyrer v United Kingdom* (1978) 2 EHRR 1 [16]. In *R v DPP, ex p Kebilene* [2000] 2 AC 326, 380 Lord Hope treated the margin of appreciation doctrine as bound-up with the living instrument approach and stated that by 'conceding a margin of appreciation to each national system, the court has recognised that the Convention, as a living system, does not need to be applied uniformly by all States but may vary in its application according to local needs and conditions.' Lord Hope referred to this statement in *Re G (Adoption: Unmarried Couple)* [2009] 1 AC 169 [47].

[96] For example, *Frette v France* (2004) 38 EHRR 438; *Goodwin v United Kingdom* (2002) 35 EHRR 447; *Wingrove v United Kingdom* (1997) 24 EHRR 1.

[97] For example, *Van Kuck v Germany* (2003) 37 EHRR 51 [84]–[85] and *Janowski v Poland* (2000) 29 EHRR 705 [35], discussed in Letsas, 'Two Concepts of the Margin of Appreciation' (n 93) 712.

[98] R Singh, 'Is there a role for the "Margin of Appreciation" in national law after the Human Rights Act?' (1999) 1 EHRR 4; Letsas, 'Two Concepts of the Margin of Appreciation' (n 93) 709–15. Judge Rozakis' opinion is in *Odievre v France* (2004) 38 EHRR 43.

It is clear from *Handyside v United Kingdom* that the considerations that influence the ECtHR in granting a margin of appreciation to domestic authorities do not all apply to domestic courts. Indeed, in *Handyside v United Kingdom* the ECtHR included 'judicial' authorities amongst those domestic authorities that are better placed to judge what the Convention requires, thereby recognising that domestic courts are better placed to interpret the requirements of the Convention in certain contexts than the ECtHR itself is. This is because the margin of appreciation reflects the ECtHR's appreciation of its limitations not only as a court but also, and more importantly, as an international institution.[99]

Domestic courts have recognised that the application of the margin of appreciation doctrine is, for this reason, not apt in the domestic setting; but they have also recognised that some of the reasons underpinning the margin of appreciation doctrine are pertinent to domestic courts in determining whether the executive and Parliament has breached Convention rights; such as where the executive or legislature has superior knowledge and expertise, or in cases where its democratic credentials are particularly important.[100] It was to reflect such factors that in *Kebilene*, Lord Hope stated that domestic courts should recognise that public authorities have a 'discretionary area of judgment' under the Human Rights Act. Although the application of the margin of appreciation doctrine was rightly rejected, Lord Hope unfortunately chose to adopt a different spatial metaphor, which suggested that the Human Rights Act builds in additional leeway to decision-makers, in addition to that which Convention standards already recognise.[101] The use of the discretionary area of judgment doctrine as well as other metaphors and doctrines has now been disapproved by the House of Lords in *Huang*, as we saw at the outset of this chapter.

The next chapter seeks to articulate how domestic law can and does accommodate the considerations which led to the adoption of the 'discretionary area of judgment' doctrine without the need to employ it, or any similar doctrine, in modern public law.

Conclusion

This chapter has examined the nature and effect of standards in modern public law. It has laid some basic building blocks for the more elaborate and detained building work carried out in later chapters. It has explored how substantive standards of legality came to be accepted at common law, how these grew out of the procedural standards of legality that the common law previously recognised, and

---

[99] The ECtHR's procedures are also far more limited than domestic courts, for instance most cases are decided on the papers and the Court rarely engages in fact-finding and does not hear witnesses.
[100] *Ex P Kebilene* (n 95) 380.
[101] For analogous and more sustained criticism on this point, see Hunt, 'Sovereignty's Blight', (n 94).

it has explained the way that standards of legality (whether procedural or substantive) differ in nature from standards of review. The discussion then went on to examine the nature and range of different standards that are applicable under the Human Rights Act, and explained how enforcing these does require a merits review and substitution of judgment in relation to the question of whether such standards have been breached, but this is not the same as the courts standing in the shoes of the administrator or sitting on appeal from him or her. Public officials very often do not give any thought at all to whether their decisions are compatible with Convention rights; insofar as they do, this is only one, subsidiary, aspect of the decisions that they take. Public officials do not get up in the morning and decide to make a proportionate interference with a protected right. They pursue policy objectives. They act according to their assessment of what the general interest requires. The courts do not tell them what objectives to pursue or how best to pursue them. But if the decision maker has turned his or her mind to whether the decision that they are minded to take would breach the Convention the courts must substitute their judgment for that of the decision-maker if they disagree with it. But it is this aspect of the decision, and this aspect alone, on which the judges can substitute their judgment. This is very far from turning judges into politicians or civil servants.

Furthermore, this chapter has explained that all the Convention standards build in latitude to decision-makers which allows them to reach a range of decisions all of which can be compatible with the Convention right. The degree of latitude afforded to public officials varies depending on the standard that is applicable, which is dependent on the right in issue. We will examine in more detail in later chapters particular standards, such as reasonableness and proportionality, and in doing so we will examine the degree of latitude that they leave to decision makers. But the first important point to make clear is that Convention rights do leave a hole in Dworkin's doughnut and recognise in principle that the executive and Parliament can make a range of permissible decisions within the bounds of what is lawful under the Convention scheme.[102]

The enforcement of standards of legality does not therefore require judges to sit in appeal on the decisions that have been made, because so long as the decision is compatible with the right in issue they have no jurisdiction to intervene. They do not have to ask themselves whether the decision is one that they would have taken had they been charged with the job of making the decision. Consider again the decision of a school that needs to improve discipline. In any action against the school by a disciplined pupil, whether at common law or under the Human Rights Act, it will not be open to the court to decide whether enhanced disciplinary measures are needed, nor will it decide what the different options are, nor will it choose between them. If and to the extent that the measure that is eventually chosen interferes with the right to respect for private and family life, the court will

---

[102] For his doughnut, see Dworkin, *Taking Rights Seriously* (n 34) 31: 'Discretion, like the hole in a doughnut, does not exist except as an area left open by a surrounding belt of restriction'.

prevent any disciplinary measures from being taken that are disproportionate. But that is very far from putting the court in the shoes of the school. It will simply demarcate certain measures as off-limits. The unspoken pact between judges and politicians that judges will not take over the administration of the country has not and will not be broken by the proper application of human rights standards after the Human Rights Act.[103]

---

[103] This point is developed further in the context of the domestic law on proportionality in ch 6, and particularly in the context of the requirement that measures are the 'least restrictive' of the affected right. The discussion also considers a partial exception to the points made here: the situation where there are only two possible courses of conduct, one of which is disproportionate (see p 178).

5

Weight and Deference

THE PREVIOUS CHAPTER described the way that standards of substantive legality protecting rights have been introduced into domestic public law, via the common law and the Human Rights Act, and the way that these differ from the traditional way that administrative law addressed substantive issues, by applying a standard of review: the *Wednesbury* test. It has also been explained that the Convention introduces a range of standards, and through these ensures that there is scope for public officials and legislatures to make a range of different decisions, even where a proposed measure engages Convention rights, without transgressing what is permitted and lawful. This chapter considers how standards of legality fall to be applied by the courts. It is in particular concerned with the circumstances where a court is not as well placed to evaluate one or more of the considerations that led to the decision (or the legislative measure) as some other person, usually, but not always, the primary decision-maker himself. There are three options for how this issue should be addressed by public law. One option would be for the courts to apply a reasonableness or patent unreasonableness standard of review to the question of whether the standard in question has been breached. On this approach the relevant legal question would be: could a reasonable decision-maker have concluded that this decision did not violate fundamental rights? But we have already concluded in chapter 4 that this is an impermissible approach. When applying Convention rights and constitutional common law rights, as well as procedural standards of fairness and natural justice, the court must decide for itself whether the decision taken by the public official breaches the requisite standards. The second option is for the courts to import or invent a new doctrine with a set of prescriptive principles that structure the judicial approach to determining whether rights have been breached, and which overlay and supplement the substantive human rights norms and public law standards themselves. The principles would identify the circumstances or categories of case in which it is appropriate for the court to defer to the judgment made by the person or body with superior capacity or credentials. The third option is for the courts to take account of the various considerations that require it to give weight to the views of another person on a case-by-case basis, without needing to go through a process of categorisation and without needing to apply prescriptive principles to structure whether and how much weight to afford to them. Following other commentators, we can call this a non-doctrinal approach, since the task of the courts is not regulated by any doctrine, but is simply part of the ordinary business of judging.[1] In contrast, the first and second possible approaches are different types of doctrinal approach.

This chapter argues that the third approach is preferable, and it attempts to justify and develop that approach by a sustained examination of what it entails and how it works. A non-doctrinal approach, such as the one developed in this chapter, does not, contrary to the suggestion of Jeff King,[2] leave judges with a general discretion about whether or not to give weight to the views of others and how much weight to afford their views. Just as a judge has to justify rejecting the testimony of a witness by reference to a good reason, such as their lack of credibility, so a judge would have to justify affording weight to the views expressed by the primary decision-maker or another person with a good reason, such as the superior expertise of the person or body concerned in relation to a particular issue. The good reasons for affording weight to the views of others are extremely fact-specific, but it is possible to make some generalisations about what sort of things count as good reasons and what sort of things count as bad ones. This chapter thus examines what counts as good and bad reasons for judges affording weight to the views of another person or body; but it does not go further and seek to distil these into prescriptive, and thus confining, categories; nor will it seek to articulate different degrees or amounts of weight to be associated with any particular categories of case or any particular reason for affording weight to others.

The issue addressed in this chapter was directly considered by the House of Lords in *Huang v Secretary of State for the Home Department*. *Huang* is a particularly important case because not only was this important issue directly addressed as part of the ratio of the judgment, but the judgment itself was expressed in a joint opinion of all five members of the Judicial Committee that heard the case, led by Lord Bingham. The opinion of the judges expressly rejected a doctrinal approach to deference and the Committee criticised the introduction of concepts such as the 'discretionary area of judgment', 'deference', 'relative institutional competence' and distinctions between 'policy' and 'principle'.[3] Despite this, some commentators have continued to argue that the law needs to develop a doctrinal approach

---

[1] See in particular the discussion of J King, 'Institutional Approaches to Judicial Restraint' (2008) 28 *OJLS* 409.

[2] King, 'Institutional Approaches' ibid. In his important theoretical survey of the issue of deference, King argues that the courts should take an intermediate path between a 'fully-non doctrinal approach' to judicial restraint that requires us to 'trust either judges or the existing legal standards to meet this need if and when it arises' (ibid 411) and a formalist, doctrinal, approach by which the way in which judges approach the issue of weight is structured by formal doctrinal categories. One might think, therefore, that this chapter develops in concrete terms a judicial approach that is fully in line with that advocated by King. In my view, this is very close to being the case. However, the approach developed in this chapter is developed by reference to the House of Lords' opinion in *Huang v Secretary of State for the Home Department* [2007] 2 AC 167, which King deprecates. He regards *Huang* as muddled in rejecting a doctrinal approach, whilst also going on to explain that there are good and bad reasons for affording weight to the views of others. It is argued here that the approach taken in *Huang* was not only coherent but right, and it does not drive one back onto the rocks of formal categorisation.

[3] *Huang* (n 2).

based on 'deference'.[4] The approach taken in this chapter follows the approach endorsed by the House of Lords. It seeks to explicate that approach in greater depth and detail. Contrary to the views of some commentators,[5] it is respectfully submitted that the judgment of the House of Lords was both welcome and right.

Huang: A Non-Doctrinal Approach

The Judgment in *Huang*

The appeal in *Huang* concerned two immigration appeals to the Immigration Appeals Tribunal (IAT) by non-citizens who claimed that, although they had been refused asylum, their deportation would breach Article 8 of the Convention. The legislative provisions then in force provided for an appeal from decisions of immigration officers or the Secretary of State firstly to an adjudicator, and then upward to the IAT. Both an adjudicator and the IAT were expressly empowered to determine whether the conduct proposed by the Government would breach the person's Convention rights by virtue of section 6(1) of the Human Rights Act.[6] We need to consider the reasoning of the House of Lords in some detail.

The House of Lords began by noting that the IAT is charged by Parliament with determining whether deportation would breach a Convention right. First, it does not have a 'secondary, reviewing function' such as would be the case if it applied a test of irrationality to the original decision. The Committee was emphatic on this point: 'The appellate immigration authority must decide for itself whether the impugned decision is lawful and, if not, but only if not, reverse it.' It rejected previous case law in which it had been held that a reasonableness test should be bolted on to the test of proportionality, so that an appeal should only be allowed where the decision to deport, 'could [not] reasonably be regarded as proportionate'. It made

---

[4] Aileen Kavanagh argues that the idea of deference has 'attracted much judicial support' and believes that 'a reconciliation between the twin demands of respecting the authority of Parliament as the primary law-maker and protecting Convention rights, is partly realised through a doctrine of deference': A Kavanagh, *Constitutional Review under the Human Rights Act* (Cambridge, CUP, 2009) 167–68; Mike Taggart has argued that 'it is precisely the articulation and application of deference in the particular context that should be encouraged': M Taggart, 'Proportionality, Deference, *Wednesbury*' (2008) *New Zealand Law Review* 423, 460; Murray Hunt has argued that there is a 'need to redouble our efforts to explain why public law needs a concept of due deference': M Hunt, 'Against Bifurcation' in D Dyzenhaus, M Hunt and G Huscroft (eds), *A Simple Common Lawyer—Essays in Honour of Michael Taggart* (Oxford, Hart, 2009) 121; most recently, Alison Young has argued that the doctrine of deference permeates human rights review, A Young, 'In Defence of Due Deference' (2009) 72 *MLR* 554.

[5] Mike Taggart has argued that *Huang* 'provides no guidance whatsoever' (Taggart, 'Proportionality' (n 4); Hunt agrees (Hunt, 'Against Bifurcation' (n 4) 117). Neither make any attempt to unpack the opinion and implications of *Huang*; Kavanagh has articulated a scheme of deference which is straightforwardly inconsistent with the view of the Committee, without engaging with it directly.

[6] The provisions are set out and discussed in *Huang* (n 2) [10]–[11]. They have since been amended to provide one tier of appeal, but this is not material here.

clear that the IAT must apply a correctness standard to the question whether deportation would constitute a disproportionate interference with a person's family life.[7]

Secondly, the Committee reasoned that the IAT must determine whether deportation would breach Convention rights at the time that it considers the matter and on the evidence as it stands then (and not as it stood when the initial decision was communicated). In other words, the nature of the IAT's statutory function is not a reviewing function, or even an appeal function in the orthodox sense;[8] the IAT provides a *de novo* appeal. It makes the decision as if it were the first authority to do so on the basis of a fuller and up-to-date picture.[9]

Of course, even in making a *de novo* determination of the Convention rights in issue, the IAT is still not making the same decision as the Home Office. It is still not determining whether it would be desirable to deport the individual in question: that is a matter for the Home Office. It is simply identifying whether, on the facts, the individual cannot be deported because it would be unlawful to do so. If it found that deportation would not be unlawful, that would leave open the question of whether the individual *should* be deported. (We will need to consider later the relevance of the fact that *Huang* concerned an immigration appeal and not a judicial review case.)

The House of Lords was invited by counsel for the Secretary of State to defer to the Secretary of State's assessment that the removal of the applicants from the United Kingdom would not breach Article 8, and also to defer to Parliament's approval of the Immigration Rules on which the Secretary of State had relied in seeking to deport them. The Committee was referred to a large number of cases in which the terminology of 'due deference', 'discretionary area of judgment' and 'relative institutional competence' had been used by domestic courts. It was also referred to a number of leading articles on the idea of deference, including articles contending that a doctrine of deference ought to be recognised as a free-standing doctrine in public law.[10] Lord Bingham said that both in the submissions made to the Committee and in the previous judgments of courts, the invocation of these

---

[7] *Huang* (n 2) [11] and [12].

[8] Appeals to statutory tribunals are often of a very different nature than appeals from first instance courts because witness statements and other evidence are often able to be adduced which will not have been previously considered. Particularly where the appeal is on human rights grounds, often the tribunal will be required to assess whether there would be a breach at the time of the hearing, and not (or as well as) when the decision was first made. The same is true of appeals and reviews by the High Court of control order decisions made under the Prevention of Terrorism Act 2005: see *MB v Secretary of State for the Home Department* [2007] QB 415.

[9] *Huang* (n 2) [11] and [13]. These two points are not identical (although they are run together by the Committee at [13]) because the court can apply (and it was argued in ch 4 should apply) a correctness standard under s 6 of the Human Rights Act in every case, including when it is reviewing a decision already made, rather than conducting a de novo hearing.

[10] In addition to a huge number of authorities on this point, the House of Lords was referred to at least the following academic works: D Dyzenhaus, 'Law as Justification: Etienne Mureinik's Conception of Legal Culture' (1998) 14 *South African Journal on Human Rights* 11, 37 and M Hunt, 'Sovereignty's Blight: Why Contemporary Public Law Needs the Concept of "Due Deference"', in N Bamforth and P Leyland (eds), *Public Law in a Multi-Layered Constitution* (Oxford, Hart, 2003) 337–70; J Jowell, 'Judicial deference: servility, civility or institutional capacity' [2003] *PL* 592.

phrases and principles had a 'tendency to . . . complicate and mystify'. The Committee rejected the submission that it should recognise a doctrine of deference in terms.[11] The Committee was very obviously frustrated, even annoyed, with the importation of such terminology (with its associated academic baggage). It considered the introduction of a novel doctrine of 'deference' to be not only unnecessary but also positively unhelpful. In this they followed comments that had been made by several judges in previous cases who had deprecated the attempt to introduce the terminology of deference into domestic public law after the Human Rights Act.[12]

Instead, the Committee set out to describe the approach that the IAT should take in determining whether there has been a breach of a Convention right. For present purposes the key point is this. The Committee accepted that the IAT—despite having to determine for itself, to a correctness standard, whether deportation would breach a Convention right—would nevertheless have to afford 'weight' where 'appropriate' to the decision of those, such as immigration officials and the Secretary of State, who have 'responsibility for a given subject matter and access to special sources of knowledge and advice'. The Committee saw nothing exceptional in this. In its view it is simply how any 'rational judicial decision-maker is likely to proceed', and the Committee explained that it was no more than the performance of the 'ordinary judicial task'.[13] These comments are essentially the nub of the judgment in *Huang* in relation to this issue. Precisely what is meant by a person having responsibility for a given subject matter and access to special knowledge and advice is something that we will need to consider in detail. But the opinion in *Huang* needs to be unpicked bit-by-bit, and we should first turn to the question of weight.

The Adjudicative Method Explained: Two Senses of 'Weight'

Their Lordships stated that when determining whether deportation of an individual would breach their Article 8 rights, the IAT must first establish the facts of the individual's case. No 'weight' is to be afforded at this stage. The impact on the individual will be the subject of witness statements and live evidence that was not before the initial decision-maker. The IAT will therefore be better informed:

> These [facts] may well have changed since the original decision was made. In any event, particularly where the applicant has not been interviewed, the authority will be much better placed to investigate the facts, test the evidence, assess the sincerity of the

---

[11] *Huang* (n 2) [14] and [16].

[12] Lord Hoffmann criticised the term 'deference' because the allocation of decision making responsibility is a matter of law, not 'courtesy or deference': *R (Pro Life Alliance) v BBC* [2004] 1 AC 185 [75]–[76], Lord Walker agreed [144]. See also *R (Gillan) v Commissioner of Police for the Metropolis* [2005] QB 338 (CA) [35] (Lord Woolf CJ), [2006] 2 AC 307 (HL) [17] (Lord Bingham).

[13] *Huang* (n 2) [16].

applicant's evidence and the genuineness of his or her concerns and evaluate the nature and strength of the family bond in the particular case.[14]

Therefore at this first stage there is no good reason for the IAT to confer *any* weight on the decision or opinion of the primary decision-maker as to the impact of deportation on the individual concerned.

Having established the facts, the IAT must then 'weigh' these against 'all that tells in favour' of the refusal of leave to remain in the United Kingdom. The Secretary of State, as he did in *Huang*, will inevitably advance a number of different reasons why deportation of the individual is in the public interest. The Committee said that some of these factors will be general: the need to have clear and predictable rules, and the need to ensure the immigration system is not perceived to be unduly porous, the need to avoid a perception that asylum-seekers can get away with committing fraud or crime if they have a family life in the United Kingdom and cannot be deported. Other matters relied upon by the Secretary of State will be more specific to the individual's case, such as where the individual had been involved in drug-trafficking and there is thought to be a particular need to deter non-nationals from engaging in drug-trafficking, or where the individual poses a threat to good community relations. Their Lordships then stated:

> The giving of weight to factors such as these is not, in our opinion, aptly described as deference: it is performance of the ordinary judicial task of weighing up the competing considerations on each side and according appropriate weight to the judgment of a person with responsibility for a given subject matter and access to special sources of knowledge and advice.[15]

It will be seen that this statement runs together two senses in which 'weight' is to be afforded by the IAT to the view of the Secretary of State in relation to public interest considerations. On the one hand, 'weight' is being used to describe how the considerations pointing towards removal and the impact on the individual's private life are to be reconciled. These competing considerations must be 'weighed', which is to say 'balanced'. On the other hand, the term 'weight' is being used to describe the degree to which the court accepts the assessment of the Secretary of State as to the importance of the policy considerations, both general and specific, on which he relies in maintaining that deportation is necessary. Importantly, the court must ultimately reach its own view as to how important the policy considerations are, and it must ultimately weigh these against the facts that it has found relating to the impact of deportation on the individual and his or her family.

Whenever the Convention standards require a balance to be struck between competing interests, the courts will have to 'give weight' to relevant factors in the first sense, but they do not necessarily have to afford any weight in the second sense. Thus, the House of Lords explained in *Huang* that no weight should be afforded to the judgment of the immigration officer or the Secretary of State's view

14 *Huang* (n 2) [15].
15 ibid [16].

as to the degree of impact on family life. This is because the IAT was in a much better position to assess the impact on the individual and his family, having heard and read more evidence about the appellant's circumstances than the relevant immigration officer will have done, and because the initial decision-maker had no special expertise in making such an assessment (if anything, the IAT has more expertise in assessing the veracity and cogency of the relevant evidence). Indeed, most of this evidence will have been adduced after the initial decision has been made. Of course, as we have seen, the facts of an individual's case before the IAT must be weighed against the countervailing policy considerations, in relation to which weight had to be accorded to the views of the Secretary of State. But there will be cases, possibly rare, when the court is not required to afford any weight in the second sense on *either* side of the scales. This will occur where the court is as well or better placed than the public official to determine all matters relevant to the question of whether Convention rights have been breached.[16]

This can be illustrated with an example from a completely different context: the grant of injunctions to maintain anonymity for the protection of children. In such cases the courts will have to 'weigh' the risks to the child of not granting anonymity to the child or her patents against considerations of open justice and freedom of expression of the media.[17] Although giving weight to each relevant consideration in the first sense, no weight will be afforded in the second sense (although issues of medical evidence or conferring weight on media experts might potentially arise). Of course, in the example just given, the court is not reviewing the decision of a public official, but it shows how the courts can and indeed must engage in balancing exercises without affording weight to anyone in the second sense in which that term was used in *Huang*.

It is also clear that weight can be afforded in the second sense but not the first. This occurs, for example, where an 'absolute' right has allegedly been infringed and where no balancing of interests is permissible. Thus, in deportation cases the court will have to determine whether there is a 'real risk' of ill-treatment where a person is returned to their home country. In many cases expert evidence is adduced, sometimes by the Home Office as well as by the claimants. The court will have to give weight to the views of those who are better informed than it is, although the risk of harm is not balanced against any public interest.[18] The point can also be illustrated by the case of *Bloggs 61*, in which a prisoner challenged a decision to transfer him out of a protected witness unit and back into the general prison population, on the basis that it endangered his life. In considering whether there was a risk to life sufficient to engage Article 2 of the Convention—a question that does not involve giving weight to anything in the first sense because no bal-

---

[16] It is perhaps worth emphasising at this point that the court is of course only concerned with whether a Convention right (or other right) has been breached and not with the same question as the primary decision-maker, such as whether and if so what decision should preferably be taken (see chs 4 and 6 which develop this point).

[17] See *S (A Child) (Identification: Restrictions on Publication)* [2004] Fam 43.

[18] See *Saadi v Italy* (App no 37201/06) (Grand Chamber), 28 February 2008.

ancing of interests is permissible—the Court of Appeal decided that weight had to be given to the assessments made by the police and prison service. Auld LJ stated that the prison service, with its experience of prison conditions and its experience of the relative efficacy of different protective regimes and measures, and the police, with their expert and close knowledge of the level of risk, are 'better placed than the court to assess the risk to life in such a context'.[19]

Identifying these two senses in which the term 'weight' is used is important, because courts and commentators often refer lazily to weight being afforded to *the balance struck* by the executive, whereas often, if not more usually, it is only appropriate to afford weight, if at all, to an assessment of one or more factor, and often, as in *Huang*, even where a balancing exercise is required, on only one side of the scales. Sometimes, of course, it is difficult to unpick the different assessments that form part of an overall decision. This is particularly so when legislation is in issue. But it is important that so far as possible, the different component parts of a decision are distinguished because courts may be justified in affording weight to assessments forming one part of a decision and they are not justified in affording weight to other assessments forming part of a decision. This was indeed the case in *Huang*, as we have seen, and it is particularly instructive in making clear that courts must be as precise as possible in identifying the particular issue on which they are affording weight to the views of the decision-maker and justify it with a good reason for doing so.

But What is Weight?

Up to this point we have been using the language of 'weight' without having paused to consider what it means. The House of Lords in *Huang* stated that affording weight to a person with responsibility and special sources of knowledge and advice is an ordinary judicial task. It is, in other words, something that courts do instinctively as part of the exercise of judging. It will be suggested that affording weight to the assessments and views of others, in the sense meant in *Huang*, is actually part of any rational decision-making process where other people, whose opinions are known to the decision-maker, have relevant knowledge or experience that the decision-maker lacks. This can be illustrated with an example. In many barristers' chambers in England it remains the practice that once a year, members of chambers meet to decide whether to offer a tenancy to one or more 'pupils', trainee barristers who have been training in chambers over the course of the previous year. Each member of chambers who attends the meeting has to decide whether a pupil should be offered tenancy.[20] For the purposes of this example let us imagine a meeting to discuss a pupil barrister called Phillip.

---

[19] *R (Bloggs 61) v Secretary of State for the Home Department* [2003] EWCA Civ 686 [65] (Auld LJ, approving Ousely J) and [81] (Keene LJ).

[20] In some sets of chambers decisions are made by committee, but the same point could be made. The account given here is generalised and fictional, and if it precisely reflects the approach of any particular chambers, it is coincidental.

Over the course of his year in chambers, Phillip has rotated through four 'pupil supervisors', with whom he has worked closely. He has undertaken a number of pieces of work for other members of chambers and advocacy training with yet more members of chambers. Phillip has had other contact with members of chambers in numerous other ways, over the course of what has been a hectic and challenging year. The point is that lots of members of chambers will have acquired relevant knowledge about Phillip's attributes and attainments, and some people will have a great deal of knowledge. But no one person will know everything. How then do members of chambers who attend the meeting each decide on Phillip's fate? Practices in different chambers of course vary. But in many cases, members of chambers will read written reports produced by pupil supervisors and assessors (if written assessments have been set), they will hear oral presentations by members of chambers at the meeting and there will be discussion, often brief, sometimes prolonged. The process is generally extremely rigorous and no member of chambers takes their responsibility lightly. In cases where all the opinions and evidence point the same way, the decision will of course be an easy one for all of them to make. But sometimes there will be disagreements between people with relevant knowledge. Phillip's is such a case. Two of his pupil supervisors speak very strongly for him, but two others say his work with them was poor. His advocacy is reportedly below-par.

The only rational and fair way to decide such a case is for the decision-makers carefully to evaluate each piece of evidence that they have, both written and oral, to determine how cogent it is and how significant it is overall. The views of Phillip's pupil supervisors will be vastly more important than the views of other members of chambers. The views of Phillip's most recent pupil supervisor will inevitably count for more than those of his first one. The views of a pupil supervisor with many years of experience will count for more than those of a pupil supervisor who has little experience, and so on. In Phillip's case one of the supervisors who gives a very good report is his most recent pupil supervisor, who is also known to have extremely exacting standards. One person provides an account of mitigating circumstances for his advocacy that was not known to the person who delivered the advocacy report. And of the other people who have relevant experience of Phillip, those who have most recent experience give the most encouraging reports. On balance, enough voting members therefore think he has met the standards, and he is offered a tenancy.

The idea of *weight* precisely encapsulates this process (in fact it has been a struggle to avoid the term to this point). The views of the pupil supervisors are given very considerable weight because they are in the best position to judge the candidate and have spent most time with them. Extra weight is given to the views of those who have more recent (and therefore more relevant) experience of Phillip. Less weight is given to the advocacy report once it is clear that it had not been fully informed, and so on. It is also worth observing that nobody's opinion is given additional weight just because they are more important people within chambers, or simply because they have a particular role or rank. Such considerations would be irrelevant to the question that each person had to decide, which was whether Phillip was up to the job. The only considerations that affect the weight given to the opinions of others relate to the other person's knowledge of Phillip and expertise in making judgments about the performance of pupils.

In much the same way, judges routinely give weight to the views of professionals in many areas of law, such as family law or mental health law, and not only in public law. This is why the Committee in *Huang* thought it was not difficult to describe this aspect of judicial decision-making, and that giving weight to the decisions of those with special knowledge and expertise was something that 'any rational judicial decision-maker' would do. Judges are not qualified social workers, or doctors, or teachers, or economists, and they generally do not have the benefit of advice from other individuals with expertise or experience in a particular field.[21] When they recognise their lack of knowledge or competence relative to another person, they understandably give weight to their views.

The point can also be made that the terminology of deference is not apposite to describe this process. In the example given above, it would obscure the fact that each member of chambers has the responsibility of making up their own mind and not relinquishing that responsibility, in substance if not in form, by accepting the opinion of another after deciding that that person is in a better position to judge. Moreover, the terminology of deference, as opposed to the terminology of weight, fails to capture the way that the amount of significance afforded to the views of others will *vary*. Weight is, by its very nature, variable. Deference, used in a substantive sense to mean something other than 'courteous regard', seems naturally to mean submission or yielding to the will of another.[22]

The Importance of a Non-Doctrinal Approach

It is the pervasive and inherently fact-sensitive nature of this feature of decision-making which makes it unsuitable for crystallisation into a formal doctrine or set of prescriptive categories.[23] That would create only confusion and distortion. There are at least three particular reasons why the exercise should not be embarked upon.[24] First, a doctrinal approach would require the reasons for affording weight to the assessments made by primary decision-makers to be crystallised into rules

---

[21] Save in respect of judges sitting on specialist tribunals with experienced lay members.

[22] See *The Oxford English Dictionary*, vol IV, 2nd edn (Oxford, Clarendon, 1989) 380; BA Garner (ed), *Black's Law Dictionary*, 7th edn (Minnesota, St Paul, 1999) 432 defines 'defer' as: 'To show deference to [another]; to yield to the opinion of [because it was a political question, the courts deferred to the legislature]'.

[23] As Laws LJ attempted, in *International Transport Roth GmbH v Secretary of State for the Home Department* [2003] QB 728 [79]–[87].

[24] See also TRS Allan, 'Human Rights and Judicial Review: A critique of "Due Deference"' (2006) 65 *CLJ* 671, who argues that a doctrinal approach leads to short-circuiting of the relevant substantive questions and, by overlaying standards that permit latitude to decision-makers with an additional concept of deference, leads to double-counting; in accord King, 'Institutional Approaches' (n 1). It does not always, in fact, lead to double-counting, for reasons explained below.

or principles which then prescribe a certain test or judicial approach (if A, then B). But the reasons can only be given at a high level of abstraction, notably: better expertise, greater knowledge and, perhaps (see below) relevant democratic credentials. Once the reasons descend from these heights they become no more than examples—albeit often informative and illuminating examples—of where on the particular facts and in the particular circumstances and given the particular procedures, such superiority has been found to exist in a relevant respect, given the particular legal issue to be determined by the court. It is unsafe to reason from more specific generalisations or categories of case, such as that the case concerns matters of policy, or raises an issue of public morals, or concerns a ministerial decision (A1, A2, A3 etc), to the conclusion that weight should be afforded, because such generalisations will very often not be true.

Secondly, even if one could generalise in a suitably specific way about the circumstances in which weight should be afforded by a court to the decision of another, these circumstances would only stipulate a highly generalised and abstracted legal result (i.e. B), namely, that the court should afford weight to the decision in question. This would in truth be legally meaningless, since weight can range from a gram to a tonne. Moreover, experience suggests that in practice it would create an inference that significant or substantial weight should be afforded, that is to say, something closer to a tonne than a gram, which will very often not be warranted and so again will lead to distortion and wrong results. Any attempt to establish a genuinely meaningful doctrinal approach would have to refine the notion of weight into identifiable degrees or measures (if not of weight, then of area, space or force). This process of categorisation would itself result in distortions and serious imperfections in the model; but when combined with a process of principle-distillation at the other end (i.e. A1 = B1, A2 = B2, etc), as any doctrinal approach worth its salt must seek to do, the whole exercise begins to look dangerously unstable and, as the House of Lords appreciated in *Huang*, hopelessly and unnecessarily complicated. The reason why this is so is that the reasons for affording weight to the views of another person and the amount of weight to afford to their views are two sides of the same coin. Affording weight to a decision of another, judged perfectly, is no more than an expression and acknowledgment of the limitations of one's own knowledge and expertise. That will, moreover, be inherently fact- and issue-specific.

Overlaying these reasons is a third. The institutional capacity of courts is not a constant. It is closely entwined with the procedures that have been adopted in the case, the degree to which evidence has been adduced and tested, and the form that the proceedings have taken. We will discuss this further below, it is sufficient at this juncture to make the general point that where there has been disclosure in a case, or cross-examination of witnesses, or expert evidence adduced, the court will be much better placed to determine relevant issues. In another case (eg a claim commenced under CPR Part 54 rather than CPR Part 7), an analogous issue might fall to be determined without the court having the same advantages. Greater weight will therefore have to be afforded by the second court to the views of other persons with relevant knowledge. The expertise of judicial tribunals in the United Kingdom also varies. If a claim is determined by a tribunal with special expertise, such as the Special Immigration Appeals Commission on national security matters, or the Competition Commission in relation to competition matters, the tribunal will be less inhibited in reaching all relevant conclusions without having to draw heavily on the assessments made by others. Even within the High Court itself, divisions and judges have developed special expertise that will affect the degree of weight that they feel compelled to confer on the views of others.[25]

Thus, the House of Lords in *Huang* was, with respect, right to reject the invitation to recognise a doctrine of deference or articulate categories of circumstances where weight or a discretionary area of judgment should be afforded: that would only distort what judges routinely and instinctively do anyway, and would not be sustainable in the long term.[26]

The Relationship between Weight and Standards

Of course, it might be worth making the attempt at formulating a doctrinal approach if this were necessary to improve the justice or coherence of the law. But in developing the approach taken in *Huang*, this chapter (together with the last chapter) seek to make good the expectation of the House of Lords that it is not necessary. The approach also seeks to develop methods that are already immanent in the common law, rather than importing from outside, or inventing from scratch. How then does the idea of weight fit with the discussion of standards of legality and standards of review, considered in chapter 4? That is to say, how in practice does the idea of affording weight fit into the scheme of public law norms? That question has already been partially answered,[27] but it is worth addressing the point more fully at this juncture.

The answer is straightforward, and it can be explained in four steps.

Step 1:   Standards of legality, save insofar as they are developed incrementally as part of the development of the law such as by the 'living instrument' interpretation of the European Convention, are fixed. The meaning of 'torture' does not change from case to case; the meaning of 'family' does not change; and the standards such as reasonableness, proportionality and strict proportionality, which apply in many cases, but not all, also do not, or should not, merge into one another: they have a meaning that is relatively well understood, and that meaning is in part discerned by reference to the contradistinction between themselves within the Convention scheme.

[25] This is the case in relation to judges sitting in the Family Division and it is also recognised that certain judges in the Administrative Court (several of whom have chaired the Special Immigration Appeals Commission) have developed particular expertise in national security matters. Numerous other examples could be given.
[26] *cf* the views of Professor Mike Taggart, who has criticised the House of Lords in *Huang* for not taking this course: Taggart, 'Proportionality' (n 4) 460.
[27] See ch 4, pp 123–25 (margin of appreciation and respective competence).

Step 2:   It is impermissible under the Human Rights Act for domestic courts to apply any standard of review to determine whether these standards have been breached, other than a correctness standard. To take an extreme example by way of illustration: they may not ask whether a reasonable decision-maker would regard the interrogation of a person with electric shocks as constituting torture (still less whether no reasonable authority could so regard it). To take a thankfully more common example: the courts ought not to ask whether a reasonable decision-maker would regard a person's place of work as their home, and they may not ask whether a reasonable decision-maker would regard the interference as proportionate. They must decide all of these things for themselves.

Step 3:   It is nonetheless the case that when applying these principles and norms (in the examples: torture, home, proportionality), the courts will often lack perfect knowledge about whether there has *in fact* been a breach in a particular case. There will be other people or bodies, notably the primary decision-maker, who are better placed to determine at least some sub-issues that are relevant to the general issue of whether the norm has been contravened. The court will therefore give weight to their view in relation to that issue. This is inevitable. This is not the same as applying a standard of reasonableness or patent unreasonableness review to the decision (although there will be cases when it might look similar), any more than the members of chambers in our example were asking whether the views of the pupil supervisors that Phillip had or had not met the requisite standard for tenancy were rational. That was not what they were doing: they were affording weight to such views in determining for themselves whether the requisite standard had been met by Phillip.

Step 4:   This approach is not novel or unique to adjudication under the Human Rights Act or other cases (such as immigration appeals) raising human rights issues. This can be seen by reference to the principles of natural justice. When the courts apply these principles they apply a correctness standard of review. It is for the courts themselves to decide whether a person ought to have been given a hearing, or whether a person ought to have been told the case against them. The courts do not ask whether a reasonable decision-maker would have afforded a hearing to the claimant, or whether the decision-maker made a rational decision in refusing a hearing. There is no room for such latitude. The courts decide for themselves whether a hearing ought to have been afforded, or whether further particulars ought to have been given about the case against them. Even so, there will be circumstances when the question whether the principles of natural justice have been breached will involve the court affording weight to the views of the public authority whose conduct is said to be unfair. A recent illustration is provided by a judicial review claim brought against the National Institute for Health and Clinical Excellence ('NICE'), the body responsible for appraising the clinical and cost effectiveness of pharmaceutical products in England and Wales. The claimant pharmaceutical company challenged guidance recommending a more limited use for one of their products. The company claimed that there had been a failure to respect natural justice because it had not been provided with a fully executable version of NICE's computerised economic model. One of the objections to disclosure of the model was that it would adversely affect NICE's appraisal process for pharmaceutical products. Richards LJ, giving the only reasoned judgment in the Court of Appeal, thought this concern was a serious one, to which weight should be given.[28] He concluded: 'The view I have come to is that, notwithstanding NICE's considered position to the contrary (to which in itself I am prepared to give some weight), procedural fairness does require release of the fully executable version of the model.' The NICE case illustrates several things. It demonstrates how courts afford weight to primary decision-makers even when it falls to the court itself to determine whether the public law standard has been breached; it makes clear that this is not the same as applying a reasonableness or irrationality standard of review; and it shows how affording weight in this way is, as the House of Lords pointed out in *Huang*, an ordinary part of the judicial process which is not special or limited to the human rights context.

TRS Allan's Non-Doctrinal Approach

Before moving on to consider the circumstances in which weight can properly be afforded in public law adjudication, it is necessary to consider a powerful critique of the idea of a doctrine of deference by Professor TRS Allan. It is not Allan's critique of a *doctrinal* approach to deference that is our concern, because for the reasons already given, the inappositeness of a doctrinal approach can be readily accepted. However, one of the reasons why Allan rejects a doctrine of deference is because he considers that the considerations which would underpin the principles of judicial restraint that such a doctrine would seek to articulate are 'external' to the determination of rights, and that, 'The only proper question for the court is simply whether or not the decision falls within the sphere of decision-making autonomy that the claimant's right, on its correct interpretation, allows.'[29] On this view, it is not legitimate for the court to afford weight to the views of others, because the result of so doing is that the outcome of the determination as to whether a Convention right has been breached will be influenced, if not determined, by considerations that are not relevant (ie external) to that question, namely, the expertise, experience and democratic credentials of the alleged rights-infringer. Allan's view seems to be that insofar as deference factors should have any role to play, they should influence the judicial interpretation of the right in question. Thus he says, for instance, that the 'scope for reasonable judgment, and

---

[28] *R (Eisai Ltd) v National Institute for Health and Clinical Excellence* [2008] EWCA Civ 438 [66]. See also in a different context, for example, the general principle applicable in both appeals and in judicial review claims that, 'It is . . . self-evidently right that national courts must give great weight to the views of the executive on matters of national security.' *Secretary of State for the Home Deprtment v Rehman* [2003] 1 AC 153 [31] (Lord Steyn).

[29] Allan, 'Human Rights and Judicial Review' (n 24) 689.

the legitimacy of the pertinent legislative and administrative choices, depend on analysis of the rights in question . . .'.[30]

We have accepted that a doctrinal approach should be foresworn. We can also accept the first step in Allan's argument: that considerations leading to the conferral of weight (ie 'responsibility for a given subject matter and access to special sources of knowledge and advice') are external to the question of whether a right has in fact been breached. They are, precisely, factors exposing the *inability* of the court fully to determine that issue, and the superior ability of another person or body to assess at least one aspect of that determination. In this sense they are external to the question of whether a right has been infringed. For example, depending on the manner and forum by which the human rights issue falls to be determined, factors requiring weight to be afforded to the views of the government may or may not be present, or may not be present to such an extent. Thus, if the issue falls to be determined by the Special Immigrations Appeals Commission, the procedures and expertise of that Commission may permit it to decide for itself whether there has been a breach of a human right without affording any substantial weight to the views of the Secretary of State or his advisers. But the same issue arising before the High Court in a judicial review might require the judge to afford substantial weight to such views because of the different procedures and expertise of the tribunal. The alleged rights infringement would be the same in both cases, but the tribunal's ability to determine whether that right had been infringed would necessarily be influenced by factors external to that question relating to the nature and process of the forum. So we can also accept Allan's view that deference factors are external to the question of whether a right has in fact been breached.

But from here, Allan's reasoning becomes untenable. If Allan's view is that such factors should simply be ignored by judges, then Allan's theory is unreal: such factors are pervasive in judicial adjudication.[31] Moreover, where a person with superior knowledge or expertise has made a relevant assessment, this will be highly relevant to the judge's determination, and to ask him or her to ignore it is to ask the judge to ignore something which has obvious relevance to their ability to arrive at the right answer. The judge does not have to accept it. If, on the other hand, Allan's view is that such factors should lead to judges relaxing the scope of the right in question—and this is probably the best interpretation of Allan's argument— then his argument is inconsistent. Having claimed, rightly, that such matters are external to the question of whether a right has in fact been breached, it is inconsistent for him then to build the considerations into the interpretation of the right in question. They are either external or they are not. But such case-specific considerations cannot in any event be properly built in to the right in question. It would have the effect that rights would mean something different depending on the credentials and capacity of the person or body breaching them, and on the capacity and experience of the tribunal determining whether rights have been

---

[30] ibid 694.
[31] This view is suggested by Allan, ibid 676. See also the criticism of Allan's views in Craig, *Administrative Law*, 6th edn (London, Sweet & Maxwell, 2008) 604–6.

breached. There is nothing in the text of the European Convention or in the jurisprudence of the Strasbourg Court to support such a radical proposition.

This point can be illustrated by reference to the case law on Articles 2 and 3 of the Convention in respect of risk on return. Let us assume that the United Kingdom Government enters a diplomatic agreement with another state that if a person is returned they will not be mistreated or subjected to the death penalty. A very senior diplomat gives evidence of the basis for the deportation decision, to the effect that for various reasons it is the view of the Foreign Office that the undertaking will be complied with. Assuming that Allan's position is that the court should not ignore the superior position of the diplomat and the Secretary of State, then he is committed to saying that the tests under Article 2 and 3 must be altered. But how so? The standard—ie the requisite level and immediacy of risk—in these cases is not altered to reflect the court's lack of knowledge and expertise: it remains constant. Nor should it be altered. The question is whether the requisite threshold level of risk exists. It falls to the court or tribunal to determine this issue, but courts and tribunals (including the Strasbourg Court) are handicapped in doing so, and if they are to strive to arrive at the correct conclusion they must give appropriate weight to the views of those who have superior knowledge and expertise.

Of course, in engaging in this exercise the courts will be alive to the fact that the person with special knowledge and expertise is not independent and that there will be something for the government to gain politically in deporting the person in question which may have had an influence, consciously or unconsciously, on the government's factual and predictive assessment. These considerations will have to be taken into account when assessing the degree of weight to be afforded to the assessments that have been made by the government.

If the correct analysis, as has been submitted here, is that the 'external' considerations relate to the weight given to each relevant opinion, then the same must also be true in cases where the test being applied is not whether there is a 'real risk' of death or ill-treatment on return, but 'proportionality' or some other Convention standard. Thus, when the court is faced with deciding whether it is disproportionate for a prison governor to impose restrictions on a prisoner's private meetings, it will have to give weight to the governor's assessment of the risks that arise and other possibilities that there might be to mitigate them.[32] The court must nonetheless decide whether the measures go too far and, in doing so, the test that it applies should be an unadorned proportionality test.

Whilst it must be admitted that the proportionality standard is sometimes relaxed by courts to take account of such external considerations, this in part driven by the confusion in the law that *Huang*, and the discussion here, is an attempt to remedy.[33] It may be that public law will never attain the purity and coherence that the discussion here aspires to, and it may possibly not be able to do so. But we are still working on the foundations, and these must be as sturdy as possible.

---

[32] By analogy, see *Bloggs 61* (n 19).

[33] Moreover, the unstructured application of the proportionality standard is the subject of a sustained critique in ch 6.

Non-IAT Cases

As we have noted, *Huang* concerned an immigration appeal, and not a judicial review claim. In an immigration appeal the IAT has to find the primary facts relevant to the appellant's case, and determine the impact on the appellant's rights for itself. The relevant time for addressing the balance of respective interests is at the time of the hearing and not when the initial decision to deport is made. By contrast, in judicial review cases (and to some extent even other statutory appeals), the situation is usually different for a number of reasons and modifications need to be made to the approach set out by the House of Lords accordingly. Let us consider a few differences that impact on the attribution of weight.

First, unlike IAT hearings, most judicial review claims and statutory appeals will be backward-looking to the time the impugned decision was taken. This will remove the advantage that the court has in IAT cases in being in a position to consider new material and circumstances that have not been considered by the primary decision-maker.[34] Secondly, unlike in IAT cases, where the tribunal is best placed to determine the impact of deportation on the individual and their family, there are cases in other contexts where the court will be justified in affording weight to the assessment of the public official or public body, not only on need for the measure in question, but also in relation to the degree of impact on individual rights. Consider for example a decision of the broadcasting and communications regulator, the Office of Communications (Ofcom), to introduce new regulations on television advertising that interfere with freedom of commercial expression of broadcasters and companies who advertise on television. Ofcom is under a statutory duty to carry out an impact assessment before introducing any regulation.[35] It will also carry out a consultation exercise. The degree that proposed regulation interferes with commercial expression will itself involve complex and highly technical judgments about the effect of the measure on industry participants which Ofcom will in most cases be better placed to make than the courts, not only because of its expertise but also because of the knowledge that it has obtained in conducting the impact assessment and consultation exercise. The court will therefore be prepared to give weight to Ofcom's judgment on both impact and public interest. Such a scenario, where weight is to be attributed to a public authority's assessments on both sides of the scales, as in the example just given, is one where the court will inevitably also give weight to the *balance struck* by the decision-maker.

Thirdly, in judicial review cases there *may* be scope for affording weight to the balance struck by the public official because the public official is the person who has been designated by Parliament with striking the balance or because the public

---

[34] In national security cases, such as under the Prevention of Terrorism Act 2005 and in immigration cases in SIAC, where the court is required to assess the balance of interests at the time it considers the matter, the practice has developed whereby the Security Service will submit updated statements taking account of new evidence or developments in order to ensure that the court is able to give weight to its views.

[35] Communications Act 2003 s 7(3).

official (or legislature) has superior democratic credentials. The same cannot be said when Parliament has provided for a *de novo* hearing by an appeal tribunal. That tribunal is essentially a primary decision-maker with responsibility for making the decision. This brings us to a very difficult problem: the problem of constitutional restraint. In *Huang*, the House of Lords dismissed the Secretary of State's reliance on two Court of Appeal cases in which particular weight had been afforded to the Secretary of State's decisions in the context of immigration control on the basis that these were 'not merely challenges by way of judicial review rather than appeals but cases where Parliament had specifically excluded any right of appeal.'[36] The point appears to be (and it was not made explicit) that it might have been appropriate in those cases to afford weight to the views of the Secretary of State because, unlike when the IAT exercises its statutory jurisdiction, the court has not been designated by Parliament as the authority with responsibility for making the decision.[37] To return to our example involving Phillip, this is like saying that the members of chambers should afford weight to the views of Phillip's pupil supervisors simply because of their position and status, *irrespective* of their superior knowledge of Phillip, or that weight should be given to the views of some other person simply because they have been designated under chambers rules with making a recommendation or initial decision. Later we will have to consider whether the Committee in *Huang* can properly be regarded as having endorsed such an approach.

Reasons for Affording Weight: Good and Bad

Experience and Expertise

In *Huang* the House of Lords explicitly recognised that where the public official has access to superior knowledge and advice on a particular subject matter, this is a good reason for affording weight to their views on that subject. The Committee therefore held that the Secretary of State's opinion about the importance of robust immigration control, in deterring immigrants from committing crimes and in disrupting drug trafficking (which is a topic on which the Home Office would have particular knowledge and expertise) should be given weight. This can be contrasted with the Committee's finding that no weight should be afforded to immigration officials in relation to the facts of the individual case and the 'nature and

---

[36] *Huang* (n 2) [16]. The cases were *Samaroo v Secretary of State for the Home Department* [2001] EWCA Civ 1139 and *R (Farrakhan) v Secretary of State for the Home Department* [2002] QB 1391. The cases are considered below.

[37] It is worth flagging here a point that will be developed later, namely, that there is a difference between affording weight based on separation of powers grounds and affording weight on the basis of electoral accountability. The latter consideration applies equally to the question of whether weight should be given to judgments made by the Secretary of State in immigration appeals.

strength of the family bond'. Since the IAT would have seen and heard much fuller evidence than the immigration officials, including the testing of that evidence by cross-examination, the Committee said that the IAT was 'much better placed' to assess that evidence.[38] This makes clear that it is not sufficient for a body to have particular expertise (as immigration officials do in assessing the veracity of claims made by immigrants) but that expertise and knowledge must be *relevant* and *superior* in relation to a particular aspect of the decision before it will be appropriate to confer any weight on views of a public official.

The Committee then went on to say that, having taken full account of the views of the Secretary of State as to the importance of, inter alia, maintaining robust immigration rules, it was for the IAT to determine the overall question, whether the interference with family life was sufficiently serious to amount to a disproportionate interference with Article 8 of the Convention.[39] At this juncture we must note an important, and possibly intentional, ambiguity in the House of Lords' reference to a person having 'responsibility for a certain subject matter'. On the one hand this may be read in the context of the reference to the body having superior knowledge and advice, as a reference to the person's expertise. Where a body has responsibility for a certain matter, it is fair to assume it has expertise in that context and/or access to special knowledge and advice. As Lord Bingham stated in *R (SB) v Governors of Denbigh High School*, in respect of the decision of a school and its governors to determine a uniform policy, 'the power of decision has been given to them for the compelling reason that they are best placed to exercise it'.[40] This seems to be the natural meaning of the sentence, and no more should be read in to it.

However, it could be argued that the House of Lords was indicating that weight should be afforded to a public body (the Home Office, or Ofcom, or whichever public authority) purely because they have responsibility (in the sense of having a designated jurisdiction) for a particular field of activity, irrespective of whether the body has any superior knowledge or expertise on a particular issue that is relevant to the decision in question. It seems unlikely that this is what the Committee meant, not least because the task of immigration officials is not only to enforce immigration controls, but also to apply human rights principles in that context. They have a dual responsibility. And yet, as we have seen, the House of Lords was clear that no weight should be placed on the assessment of the immigration authorities on this aspect of the decision. Furthermore, it has been mentioned above that their Lordships distinguished two judicial review cases in which no appeal lay to the IAT, and in which particular weight had been afforded to the views of the Secretary of State as to the reasons for deportation and exclusion of individuals from the United Kingdom. If the Committee was intimating that added weight should be afforded in judicial review cases because the court does *not* have principal responsibility for making the decision, it must have been accepting

[38] *Huang* (n 2) [25].
[39] ibid [20].
[40] *R (SB) v Governors of Denbigh High School* [2007] 1 AC 100 [34].

that the IAT *does* have primary decision-making responsibility for determining if a person should be deported. We will have to consider later whether the Committee was right to draw this distinction, but for present purposes the fact that it did sheds light on what it meant when it referred to a person having responsibility for a given subject matter. It confirms that this was being used as shorthand for the body having particular expertise.

In the public law context, the law reports are littered with examples of the courts affording weight to the views of public officials based on their superior experience or expertise. The courts have nonetheless acknowledged that the overall question of Convention compliance is theirs to determine. Let us consider three initial examples.

In *R (Szuluk) v The Governor of HMP Full Sutton*, Sedley LJ stated that, 'the court will ordinarily accept from the executive the evaluation of risk of serious abuse of outside mail because the prison service knows far more about it than the court does . . .'.[41] He then said that the court's task is to determine whether this risk constitutes a pressing social need and the measure taken is proportionate. In *R (Laporte) v Chief Constable of Gloucester Constabulary*, in which the police turned back a coach travelling to an anti-war protest, Lord Carswell said that he was conscious of the difficulty facing police officers when managing protests, and he would 'pay considerable respect to the judgment of the officer making the decision on the ground'. Nonetheless he went on to emphasise that the burden was on the police to establish that their conduct was proportionate, and in his opinion, and that of the Committee, this had not been established.[42] In *R (SB) v Governors of Denbigh High School*, the House of Lords refused to require a school to permit a female student to wear a jilbab in contravention of its uniform policy, in part because the court lacked the 'experience, background and detailed knowledge of the head teacher, staff and governors' about the contribution of the uniform policy to the harmony and success that the school enjoyed.[43] Lord Scott also placed weight on the fact that Muslims were represented on the governing body, and the head teacher had grown up in India to a Bengali Muslim family.[44]

This brings us to a case which is of more general importance, and to which we will need to return: *R (ProLife Alliance) v British Broadcasting Corporation*.[45] In that case, the House of Lords had to consider a decision taken by the chief political adviser to the BBC to refuse to broadcast a party election broadcast (PEB) by the claimant on the basis that the graphic depiction of an abortion offended taste

[41] *R (Szuluk) v The Governor of HMP Full Sutton* [2004] EWCA Civ 1426 [26].
[42] *R (Laporte) v Chief Constable of Gloucester Constabulary* [2007] 2 AC 105 [106]. Lord Bingham was to the same effect at [55]. In *Quayle*, the Court of Appeal did not consider itself to be qualified to hold that legislation criminalising the possession of cannabis breached Art 8 of the Convention because this 'would involve an evaluation of the medical and scientific evidence, a weighing of the competing arguments for and against the immediate change recommended by the Select Committee and the Runciman Committee, a greater understanding of the nature and progress of the tests of cannabis which have taken and are taking place': *R v Quayle* [2006] 1 WLR 3642 [68].
[43] *SB* (n 40) [34] (Lord Bingham).
[44] ibid [74].
[45] *R (ProLife Alliance) v British Broadcasting Corporation* [2004] 1 AC 185.

and decency or was likely to be offensive to public feeling. Before taking the decision, the BBC had convened a panel including Channel 4's Head of News, Current Affairs and Business, and executives in the legal and compliance departments from the other broadcasters, to consider the programme. The panel was unanimously of the view that the programme would 'be offensive to a very large number of viewers'. Subsequently two edited versions of the programme were submitted for broadcast in Wales, which was the only region where the claimant had satisfied the conditions for showing a party election broadcast. The BBC's Senior Political Adviser consulted colleagues in Wales, including the BBC's Controller of BBC Wales. Again, the programme was unanimously refused. A fourth version was eventually accepted and broadcast showing only the word 'CENSORED' on the screen. There was evidence that terrestrial broadcasters undertake surveys and research projects into public opinion and decency and, of course, regularly receive complaints from the public which they are required to consider and assess.

On the question of whether the broadcast would have offended taste and decency, as opposed to the question whether such a standard was capable of overcoming the right of freedom of expression,[46] weight was afforded to the decision of the BBC and the views of the broadcasters that had contributed to it. Lord Walker focused on the *advantages* that the broadcasters had over the courts:

> They are, by their training and experience, well qualified (so far as anybody, elected or unelected, could claim to be well qualified) to assess the Alliance's PEB as against other more or less shocking material which might have been included in news or current affairs programmes, and to form a view about its likely impact on viewers in Wales (the only country where the 'CENSORED' version was eventually shown).[47]

For Lord Walker it was important that the panel could draw on their experience of other previous broadcasts which might have proved to be offensive. They would have a much clearer idea than the court about what the public can generally tolerate in terms of television broadcasts, as well as fully understanding the relevance of the nature of different types of broadcast (news, documentary, entertainment, etc). Lord Hoffmann, by contrast, focused his comments on the *disadvantages* that the courts were labouring under in attempting to deduce what would cause offence to the ordinary person. His Lordship said that public opinion on matters of taste and decency is 'diverse, sometimes unexpected and in constant flux' and that generally accepted standards on these questions are 'not a matter of intuition on the part of elderly male judges'. He pointed out that broadcasters spend considerable amounts of time and money researching public opinion, which would be

---

[46] The claimant did not challenge the requirement that programmes that offend taste and decency should not be shown. Lord Hoffmann did consider whether the condition could be justified but held that the only right protected by Art 10 in the circumstances was to a 'right to fair consideration for being afforded the opportunity to [express one's opinions on television]; a right not to have one's access to public media denied on discriminatory, arbitrary or unreasonable grounds' (*Prolife Alliance* [58]), which conferred sufficient latitude on Parliament to permit the imposition of a prohibition on broadcast of offensive material ([77]). Lord Walker took a similar approach (eg [140]).

[47] ibid [124].

superfluous if it is something which is capable being deducted by a single person.[48] Lord Hoffmann went on to say that he also attached 'some importance' to the fact that several of the people involved in making the decision, including both the BBC's Senior Political Adviser and the BBC's Controller for Wales, were women. It is welcome that Lord Hoffmann openly expressed the unease that he, and possibly all members of the Committee, felt in being asked to judge the reaction that women in particular would have to the election broadcast. Lord Hoffmann was keenly aware that approximately 200,000 women each year have an abortion in the United Kingdom, many of whom will no doubt be teenagers. One obvious issue was how these women would react to seeing a programme that depicted real life images of an abortion being carried out, and the results of others. Since the images were truly disturbing, even to the elderly male judges who had viewed them,[49] it is obvious that the reaction of women who have had, or who might be planning to have, an abortion would be a matter of particular sensitivity, and an elderly male judge might properly consider that he was not well-suited to judge it.

It is worth emphasising at this juncture that the purpose of this section of the discussion has been to identify examples where the court has afforded weight to the primary decision-maker on some aspect of a more general issue that is before the court for determination. It is not contended that judges should accept such judgments without scrutiny. Moreover, we are only here concerned with 'weight' in the second sense in which it was used in *Huang*, and not weighing competing interests. For instance, in the *ProLife Alliance* case, if a proportionality analysis had been applicable the views of the BBC ought still to have been tested against that criterion.

The Process of Reaching a Decision[50]

In some cases a primary decision-maker does not have any particular expertise or experience, but nonetheless has carried out a rigorous decision-making process which affords him or her knowledge superior to that of the court. In one sense the decision-maker has acquired an expertise during the course of making the decision, and in this sense this ground for affording weight to the decision-maker overlaps with the previous discussion.

---

[48] The comments of Lord Walker and Lord Hoffmann discussed here are in *Prolife Alliance* (n 45) [124] and [80] respectively.

[49] The programme was described by Laws LJ in the following terms: 'It shows the products of a suction abortion: tiny limbs, bloodied and dismembered, a separated head, their human shape and form plainly recognisable. There are some pictures showing the results of the procedures undertaken to procure an abortion at later stages. There is no sound on the video. . . . They are, I think, certainly disturbing to any person of ordinary sensibilities.' (*R (Prolife Alliance) v BBC* [2002] 3 WLR 1080 [13]).

[50] Challenges to primary and secondary legislation raise special problems because reasons are not generally supplied, and documents produced prior to enactment are not generally of any relevance to determining whether the legislation substantively is justified. For consideration, see J Beatson, S Grosz, T Hickman and R Singh, *Human Rights: Judicial Protection in the United Kingdom* (London, Sweet & Maxwell, 2008) 3-229.

It has been noted that in *R (SB) v Governors of Denbigh High School* the House of Lords gave weight to the experience and expertise of the school in upholding its decision not to permit a Muslim student to wear a jilbab to school. As well as having undoubted experience in relation to the value of the uniform policy, the teaching body and the school's governors had some expertise in assessing the requirements of the claimant's religion.[51] But the House of Lords also attributed weight to its assessment in this latter respect on the basis that the school officials had acquired considerable amount of knowledge over a number of years by the 'immense pains' it had taken in ensuring its uniform policy took adequate account of Muslim beliefs.[52] In setting the uniform policy the school had consulted parents, students and the imams of the three local mosques. When, several years later, the claimant refused to attend school unless she was permitted to wear a jilbab, the school consulted two local mosques, the London Central Mosque Trust and the Islamic Cultural Centre, all of which approved of the uniform policy as it stood. Following further representations, additional inquiries were made and consideration was given to the matter and additional advice sought, with the same effect. The process of identifying and considering relevant information, and balancing respective interests, was extremely thorough, lengthy, inclusive and complex. The courts could not hope to replicate such an excise within the parameters of a judicial hearing. Lord Bingham accordingly held that the court had to respect the 'detailed knowledge', as well as the expertise, of the school authorities. Baroness Hale gave weight to the fact that the school's approach had been 'thoughtful'.[53]

The Reasons Given for a Decision

It is sometimes suggested that the fact that a decision made by a public official is well-reasoned is a good reason for affording it weight and respect. This was suggested in *Belfast City Council v Miss Behavin' Limited*,[54] in which it was also suggested that particular weight will be afforded to decisions where the decision-maker has expressly taken into account the impact of the decision on Convention rights. Lord Rodger, for instance, stated that where a public authority has carefully weighed the various competing considerations and concluded that interference with a Convention right is justified, a court will attribute due weight to that conclusion in deciding whether the action in question was proportionate and lawful.[55] Baroness Hale stated that although public authorities do not need to address Convention rights that are affected by their decisions specifically, their views will carry less weight where they have not done so. And Lord Mance added that where a decision-maker has not addressed the balance between competing rights, the court is

[51] Mention was made of the fact that the head teacher, a woman, had grown up in India to a Bengali Muslim family.
[52] *SB* (n 40) [33] (Lord Bingham). In accord [44] (Lord Hoffmann).
[53] ibid [34] and [98]
[54] *Belfast City Council v Miss Behavin' Ltd* [2007] 1 WLR 1420.
[55] ibid [26].

deprived of the assistance and reassurance provided by the primary decision-maker's 'considered opinion' on Convention issues. He stated that the court's scrutiny is bound to be closer, giving due weight to such judgments as were made by the primary decision-maker on such matters as he or it considered.[56] Thus, broadly speaking, the more carefully reasoned a decision is, and the more carefully and exactly the competing interests have been balanced, the greater the weight that will be given to the assessment of the primary decision-maker.

At first sight this seems to be common sense, but in fact the underlying justification for this approach is actually far from self-evident. There is a circularity in conferring weight on the reasons given for an interference with a Convention right when the sufficiency of the reasons advanced in the litigation in defence of the decision is itself the matter in issue. The court cannot know whether the reasons supplied at the time are worthy of respect until it has first determined what reasons are sufficient to justify the decision. To take an extreme example, imagine a case where a public authority revokes a licence and gives a very full reasoned decision that addresses in detail the effect on freedom of expression. Despite the density and sophistication of the reasons given, they are spurious and sophistic. There can be no good reason in such a case for the court to afford weight to the views of the authority just because it has engaged in an elaborate process of justification. The authority might get an 'A for effort' but that should not affect the assessment of whether its views were correct.

It is no answer to say that if the content of the reasons turns out, on analysis, to be spurious or sophistic, the court will reject them, because the idea that weight will be afforded where the effect on Convention rights has been explicitly addressed is content independent: the justification for affording weight arises from the mere fact that such reasons have been advanced. Insofar as it is not content independent, there is an obvious problem of circularity. The question of whether to reject the reasons is the very question on which they are given weight.

The danger is twofold. In the first place there is a danger that only those reasons that are obviously insubstantial or wrong will be rejected. Secondly, the mere fact that an authority has provided detailed reasons, even if they are actually misguided, will in most cases lead to a reluctance to disturb their decision, and the courts' supposedly independent function in determining for themselves whether fundamental rights have been infringed will be significantly diluted. There is also an important policy consideration here. If public authorities can anticipate that weight will be given to their views when their decisions are impeccably clothed with reasons addressing every possible impact on human rights, no matter how insubstantial the logic or evidential foundation, they will inevitably be encouraged to make even greater use of lawyers at the decision-making stage.[57] The upshot is

---

[56] *Miss Behavin'* ibid [46] and [47]. Lord Neuberger agreed with Baroness Hale and Lord Mance ([90]) and went on to state that a council faced with an application for a sex establishment licence would be well advised to consider expressly the applicant's right to freedom of expression.

[57] There would be little detriment in doing so because, as discussed further in ch 8, the effect of the decision in *Miss Behavin'* (n 54) is that the public authority can advance more substantial justifications ex post facto if necessary.

that the approach of the House of Lords in *Miss Behavin' Limited* potentially corrodes judicial review under the Human Rights Act and creates perverse incentives for public bodies to legalise their administrative processes.

The approach of the House of Lords can, however, be justified if the comments made by their Lordships are restrictively understood as limited to the following situation. The situation is where the decision-maker is in a better position than the court to weigh the respective interest involved. Where this is the case, the fact that the decision-maker can demonstrate that it has addressed explicitly all relevant issues will allow the court to have confidence in giving weight to its assessment, or the balance struck. Clearly, if the decision-maker had never considered the relevant issues or considerations, it would be dangerous to afford weight to its decision, no matter how much special knowledge and expertise it possessed. But in this scenario, the presence, content and comprehensiveness of the reasons supplied are not themselves the basis on which weight is afforded. Weight is afforded because the decision-maker is in a superior position to the court and has demonstrated that it has applied its superior knowledge and expertise to the issues in question.

Let us return to an example that has been used previously: the decision of Ofcom to impose regulation on a certain aspect of television advertising. If Ofcom gave cursory reasons for imposing such regulation, an issue would arise as to whether, despite its undoubted expertise, it had properly considered and weighed the respective interests. Doubt on that score would reduce the weight that could be afforded to the decision. But if the decision was very carefully reasoned there would be greater certainty that it had applied its expertise fully to the decision in question, and the court could be more confident in conferring weight on the decision.

The example of Ofcom has been chosen because, for reasons already explained, Ofcom's expertise will often relate to the considerations on both sides of the balance. The way it strikes the balance will itself therefore be deserving of respect and the reasons that it gives for its decision will be given weight. But there are cases, such as *Huang*, where the court is better placed to assess the impact on Convention rights. The courts need to be very careful not to defer to the reasons given by a public authority for interfering with a Convention right in circumstances where its expertise or superior knowledge does not embrace all the considerations relevant to the decision. In such a case there is no justification for confering any weight on the balance actually struck by the public authority between Convention rights and the public interest considerations, since one of the main issues will be whether the public authority has placed sufficient weight on the impacted Convention right, on which it has no claim to special expertise. The fact that the authority has given detailed and careful reasons will not improve the situation.[58]

---

[58] An implication of this argument must be acknowledged. In *Miss Behavin'* (n 54) their Lordships held that weight could be afforded to the balance struck by the public authority where it was fully reasoned. It has been suggested that this can only be justified where there is some other reason for affording weight to the public authority's assessment. The implication of this is that where the court is justified in affording weight to one aspect of the decision made by a public authority, but not the balance struck by it, the more carefully reasoned and explained its consideration, the more weight the court is likely to give to this consideration. Thus, where the court is entitled to give weight to the

The approach of the House of Lords in *Belfast City Council v Miss Behavin' Limited*, although not accepting a doctrine of deference, undoubtedly has something in common with the approach advocated by Professor David Dyzenhaus and Murray Hunt, who have articulated the idea of 'due deference' as requiring a 'respectful attention to the reasons offered or which could be offered in support of a decision'.[59] The argument potentially suffers from the same problems as the approach taken by the House of Lords, and can only be cured from fatal problems of circularity in the same way. The very exercise that the court is engaged in is judging whether the reasons are sufficient. It cannot at the same time defer to their cogency, and it would be inappropriate to give weight to the mere fact that reasons have been provided or appear on their face to be well done. But if so, then it must be acknowledged that it is experience, knowledge and expertise that are the touchstones for deference, and not reasons. Indeed, where the issue is whether conduct has in fact breached a protected right, or where the court or tribunal is considering human rights compliance *de novo*, the public authority will often have the opportunity to file evidence justifying the decision on more complete grounds. It will be appropriate in many cases for courts to afford weight to assessments expressed in such evidence, although it goes well beyond the reasons initially given for the decision. The connection between deference and reasons is therefore misguided. The giving of reasons is neither a necessary nor sufficient condition for affording weight.

Limits of Adjudication and the Relevance of Court Procedure

We have considered situations where a primary decision–maker is in a better position than the court to make assessments that form part of the decision or legislation under review, and we have concluded that there is a good reason for the courts giving weight to such assessments in considering whether some public law standard has been infringed. Part, but by no means all, of the reason for the handicap under which the courts labour is the form that adversarial hearings, and particularly judicial review proceedings, take. Let us consider three aspects of these limitations.

First, the court will not necessarily have all the material before it that the decision-maker has relied upon directly or indirectly. Indeed, where the decision-maker relies on accumulated knowledge or experience, this will inevitably be the case. In judicial review proceedings it is usual for the defendant public authority to justify its decision in a witness statement explaining the basis on which the decision was taken, but there will not have to be disclosure of every document relevant

Secretary of State's assessment of the deterrent effect of deporting non-nationals who have engaged in criminal activity, the court is likely to give this added weight, the more fully the point is explained and justified.

[59] D Dyzenhaus, 'The Politics of Deference: Judicial Review and Democracy' in M Taggart (ed), *The Province of Administrative Law* (Oxford, Hart Publishing, 1997) 286; Hunt, 'Against Bifurcation' (n 4) and 'Soverignty's Blight' (n 10).

to the decision and the key advisers or decision-maker will not be subject to cross-examination. In appropriate cases the court can mitigate the effect of these limitations on its own knowledge of the relevant issues by modifying its procedure.[60] In *Tweed* the House of Lords recognised that particularly in human rights claims, it is sometimes appropriate for underlying documents to be disclosed in order for the primary facts to be carefully examined.[61] In *Gillan* the Commissioner of Police of the Metropolis relied on two witness statements, by a senior Home Office civil servant and the Assistant Commissioner, setting out the utility of stop and search powers in combating the terrorist threat to London. It was apparent that both individuals had been influenced by advice from the Security Service. Lord Bingham in his speech observed that an offer to explore the Security Service intelligence by using special advocate procedure had been declined and the evidence therefore had to be accepted.[62] In *R (Wilkinson) v Broadmoor Special Hospital Authority* the Court of Appeal held that where in exceptional cases issues about the necessity of forced medical treatment arise in a judicial review claim, the court should permit medial expert witnesses to be cross-examined.[63]

The fact that the court can mitigate certain disadvantages that it faces also tells us something about the notion of affording 'weight' to a public authority's assessment. It shows that reasons for affording weight on grounds of limited competence are not reasons of justiciablity or of constitutional principle. They are essentially pragmatic reasons, closely bound up with the court's fact-finding function. *Gillan* well illustrates that even in the context of national security, an assertion that expert judgment should not be second-guessed is a generalisation that is not always warranted because it may be possible and appropriate for the underlying material to be tested

Secondly, the court will often not have the same time and resources to devote to weighing the relevant factors as a public authority may often employ in reaching its decision. A clear example would be the assessment made by a public authority after a major consultation exercise, which may involve the consideration of a large number of consultation responses, other studies and impact assessments, over many months. This limitation is inherent in the judicial function: courts cannot reconstitute themselves as public inquires.

Thirdly, the nature of an adversarial trial means that there are limitations on the courts' ability to assess the *effects* of decisions taken by public authorities, which may have myriad implications and ripple-effects throughout government

---

[60] The court in *R v Quayle* [2005] 1 WLR 3642 in several joined criminal appeals in which defendants sought to raise defences of necessity to prosecutions for cultivation, possession and supply of cannabis, stated that it had 'not been put in a position procedurally' to judge the compatibility of drug legislation with the European Convention ([66])

[61] *Tweed v Parades Commission for Northern Ireland* [2007] 1 AC 650.

[62] *R (Gillan) v Commissioner of Police of the Metropolis* [2006] 2 AC 307 [17]

[63] [2002] 1 WLR 419. The court took the view that it would have to consider for itself whether the patient was competent as part of this assessment (essentially as a precedent fact to the legality of the administration of the treatment). Normally such issues will be determined by the Mental Health Tribunal: see *R (B) v S* [2006] 1 WLR 810.

or society. There are also limitations on the degree to which courts are able to assess the potential effectiveness of alternative courses of conduct. These are what Professor Lon Fuller described as 'polycentric' issues. Fuller illustrated what this means with the example of a regime that establishes a tribunal for setting prices of goods. That task raises significant polycentric problems, because any rise in the price of product A is likely to affect in varying degrees demand for and therefore the price of products B, C, and D. And each of these separate effects may have their own complex repercussions for the economy. The court cannot easily evaluate these effects, not least because not all of the affected parties (which will be different depending on the price alteration that the tribunal is minded to make) will have the opportunity to present evidence and argument.[64]

However, it is important to bear in mind that what is relevant is not the limits on the courts' ability to determine certain issues, but their *relative* lack of competence. Polycentric issues are also extremely difficult for politicians and public authorities to judge. The extent to which such issues have been examined will often be apparent from the evidence before the court. It is only when the primary decision-maker is better placed than the court to consider such issues, and has done so, that the court will need to afford weight to the decision-maker's views. The court should only do so to the extent required to reflect the *relative* disparity in competence. It is also important to recall that, however difficult polycentric issues are, courts have to grapple with polycentric issues all of the time. Indeed, they may be said to be pervasive in litigation, raising general issues of law and policy.[65] For instance, in assessing whether it is unlawful for a public authority to ban swimming in a shallow lake on its land, an assessment must be made of the likelihood and likely seriousness of an accident, the social value of the activity and the cost of precautions, including the costs and effects for public authorities and others in similar situations. This includes consideration of the knock-on effect on other projects if finite resources were used on preventative measures.[66] The courts have also taken into account the potentially inhibiting effect on public services of a finding of liability, which is a matter that requires assumptions to be made about the knock-on effects of a decision on the performance of public services.[67] There is therefore nothing intrinsically unsuitable or exceptional about polycentric issues being subject to legal adjudication, and the courts should not too readily accept the assessment of the primary decision-maker simply because they perceive there to be significant issues of policy or polycentricity.

---

[64] LL Fuller, 'The Forms and Limits of Adjudication' (1978) 92 *Harvard Law Review* 353, 394–405.

[65] JA King, 'The pervasiveness of polycentricity' [2008] *PL* 101.

[66] See eg *Tomlinson v Congleton Borough Council* [2004] 1 AC 46 [34], [40]–[43] (Lord Hoffmann); see also *Miller v Jackson* [1977] QB 966 (balancing the value of cricket and the likely effect on the sport of granting an injunction against the importance of property rights).

[67] See eg *X (Minors) v Bedfordshire CC* [1995] 2 AC 633; *Gorringe v Calderdale MBC* [2004] 1 WLR 1057; the Compensation Act 2006 s 1, which requires a court considering a claim in negligence or breach of statutory duty whether finding liability would prevent a desirable activity from being undertaken at all, to a particular extent or in a particular way, or discourage persons from undertaking functions in connection with a desirable activity. A similar point is made by A Kavanagh, *Constitutional Review under the UK Human Rights Act* (Cambridge, CUP, 2009) 184–85.

Constitutional Reasons for Affording Weight

Finally, we turn to the most difficult and disputed issue in this context: whether the court should give weight to a decision made by a public authority because it, and not the court, is the authority with responsibility to make the decision. This is often referred to as a 'constitutional' reason for affording weight or deference to the public authority or legislature to distinguish it from the 'practical' or 'institutional' limitations that we have so far discussed. Judges and commentators are divided on whether this is a good reason for conferring weight on the decision of the primary decision-maker.[68]

It is however possible to unpack this idea further. On the one hand, the fact that the primary decision-maker is *elected* might be a reason for affording his or her decision weight. This was the approach taken by the Court of Appeal in *Farrakhan*, in which the Court refused to overturn a decision to exclude the leader of the Nation of Islam from the United Kingdom, partly on the basis that the Secretary of State is 'democratically accountable for this decision'.[69] Lord Hoffmann put this most clearly in *Rehman*, when he said that certain decisions 'require a legitimacy which can only be afforded by entrusting them to persons responsible to the community through the democratic process.' He said that certain decisions must be made by persons 'whom the people have elected, and whom they can remove.'[70] We can term this the 'ballot box' argument for affording weight to decisions of public officials.

On the other hand, the emphasis might be placed on the fact that Parliament has conferred primary responsibility for making the decision on the public official or public authority in question. Again, this point was also relied upon in *Farrakhan*, the court emphasising that the Secretary of State was responsible for making the decision and, moreover, that Parliament had not provided for any right of appeal.[71] But this is not the ballot box argument in different clothes, although they are very often run together by courts and commentators. Consider Ofcom again. Ofcom and its board are not directly accountable to the electorate—the chief executive is not required to be a member of the House of Commons, for example. Whilst it makes a report to Parliament every year, its electoral accountability is indirect at best, and it consciously operates independently of any department of

---

[68] For: Sir David Keene, 'Principles of deference under the Human Rights Act' in H Fenwick, G Phillipson and R Masterman, *Judicial Reasoning under the UK Human Rights Act* (Cambridge, CUP, 2007); Lord Hoffmann, 'Separation of Powers' [2002] 7 *JR* 137; Lord Hoffmann, 'Bentham and Human Rights' (2001) 54 *Current Legal Problems* 61; Hunt, 'Sovereignty's Blight' (n 10); Hunt 'Against Bifurcation' (n 4); King (n 1); Kavanagh (n 67). Against: Lord Steyn, 'Deference: a tangled story' [2005] *PL* 346; and Jowell, 'Judicial deference' (n 10); Allan, 'Human Rights and Judicial Review' (n 24); Beatson, Grosz, Hickman and Singh, *Human Rights* (n 50) [3-199] to [3-210].

[69] *R (Farrakhan) v Secretary of State for the Home Department* [2002] QB 1391 [74].

[70] *Secretary of State for the Home Department v Rehman* [2003] 1 AC 153 [62].

[71] *Farrakhan* (n 69).

government.[72] However the Court of Appeal's comments just cited would plainly apply to Ofcom, because it is the body that Parliament has designated as responsible for regulating communications and broadcasting in the UK. We can term this second type of reason for affording weight to a primary decision-maker the 'allocation of functions' argument.

(a) *Huang* and the Ballot Box Argument

Let us now return to *Huang*. There is no doubt that on this issue the opinion in *Huang* is highly ambiguous, and offers some support to both supporters and opponents of both the ballot box argument and the allocation of function argument. Those who support the ballot box argument can point to the Committee's discussion of *Kay v Lambeth London Borough Council*, in which the House of Lords held that housing legislation strikes a fair balance between the right to respect for the homes of lessors and the property rights of their landlords.[73] It was held in *Kay* that courts should implement that legislation, and any human rights challenge would have to be a direct challenge to the legislation itself, for a declaration of incompatibility.[74] Counsel for the Secretary of State had relied on *Kay* in support of a submission that the Immigration Rules are also intended to strike the balance and that they had an 'imprimatur of democratic approval'. The House of Lords said that the analogy was unpersuasive. Domestic housing policy, it explained, had been a continuing subject of discussion and debate in Parliament over very many years, with the competing interests of landlords and tenants fully represented, as also the public interest in securing accommodation for the indigent, averting homelessness and making the best use of finite public resources. The outcome, which changes from time to time, 'may truly be said to represent a considered democratic compromise'. The Committee said that the same cannot be said of the Immigration Rules, 'which are not the product of active debate in Parliament, where non-nationals seeking leave to enter or remain are not in any event represented.'[75]

The Committee's statement that housing legislation represents a 'democratic compromise' is what has attracted commentators who claim *Huang* approved democratic deference.[76] But the comment distracts attention from the fact that the House of Lords unanimously held that no weight should be afforded to the

---

[72] Certain of Ofcom's functions are required to be pursued by boards that have appointed members from the various regions of the United Kingdom (see s 12(5) of the Communications Act 2003 (Contents Board)). Section 12(6) states that in appointing an English representative, Ofcom 'must have regard to the desirability of ensuring that the person appointed is able to represent the interests and opinions of persons living in all the different regions of England'.

[73] *Huang* (n 2) [17]; *Kay v Lambeth LBC* [2006] 2 AC 465. Murray Hunt for example, seeks to rely on the Committee's discussion of *Kay* for this purpose: Hunt 'Against Bifurcation' (n 4) 119.

[74] This issue has been the subject of continuing litigation (eg *Doherty v Birmingham City Council* [2009] 1 AC 367 and *Manchester City Council v Pinnock* [2009] EWCA Civ 852, the content of which is not relevant to the present discussion.)

[75] *Huang* (n 2) [17].

[76] See eg Hunt, 'Agianst Bifurcation' (n 4) 118–19.

Immigration Rules on democratic grounds. This finding has significant implications, because the Secretary of State is directly accountable to Parliament for the content of the rules, which are made under a discretion conferred by section 3 of the Immigration Act 1971, and they are laid before Parliament and subject to a resolution of disapproval by Parliament. Despite this, the House of Lords rejected the submission that the rules have the 'imprimatur of democratic approval' or that there is a presumption that they comply with Article 8 because they 'represent the view of the Secretary of State and of Parliament as to the proper balance between respect for family life and the public interest in immigration control.'[77] In addition to this, 'democratic accountability' was one of the terms that was explicitly disapproved by the Committee in *Huang*, alongside 'deference', 'policy' and 'relative institutional competence' as an inappropriate concept to employ to structure judicial decision-making. Therefore if there is any role for the ballot box argument after *Huang*, it must be confined to primary legislation, and then only in very unusual cases where there has been a lengthy and detailed democratic consideration. But this points to the answer to this little conundrum. The House of Lords' comments in *Huang* about *Kay* are best understood as not endorsing the ballot box argument, but rather reflecting the fact that Parliament was far better placed than the courts to consider all the relevant considerations when it came to the particular issue of housing policy. Before we examine this point in more detail, let us consider the support that *Huang* gives to the allocation of functions argument.

(b) *Huang* and the Allocation of Functions Argument

It will be recalled that in *Huang* the Secretary of State also relied on *Farrakhan* and *Samaroo* in support of an argument for deferring to the decision of the Secretary of State, and that the House of Lords refused to accede to this submission on the basis that these were judicial review cases, not statutory appeals, and indeed Parliament had excluded an appeal from those decisions.[78] Arguably, this provides some support for the allocation of functions ground for affording weight to a decision of a public authority, whether it is an electorally accountable minister or a largely unaccountable regulator or quango. Furthermore, the Committee also made some ambiguous comments about Lord Steyn's judgment in *Daly*. It said: 'The point which, as we understand, Lord Steyn wished to make was that, although the Convention calls for a more exacting standard of review, it remains the case that the judge is not the primary decision-maker.'[79] It then distinguished the position of the IAT as a primary-decision-maker. On one reading, this suggests that weight should be afforded to the views of a primary decision-maker *merely*

---

[77] The submission is recorded in *Huang* (n 2) 173.
[78] See above p 145.
[79] *Huang* (n 2) [13].

because that person is responsible for the decision.[80] A yet further point is that, as we have seen, the House of Lords referred to a decision-maker having 'responsibility for a given subject matter' possibly as a reason for affording weight to their view which was intended to be separate from the presence of superior knowledge and expertise.

However these comments can be understood in a different way. The Committee emphasised that the IAT must decide the issue of compatibility with Convention rights on the facts and evidence as they stood at the time of its determination. This undoubtedly sets it apart from a court hearing a judicial review claim. Moreover, the fact that a public body and not a tribunal has been given the power to make the principal decision is an *indicator* of its superior expertise to determine at least some aspect of it. It will be recalled that Lord Bingham in *R (SB) v Governors of Denbigh High School* reasoned that the power of decision had been given to the governors and the senior teachers for the compelling reason that they were 'best placed to exercise it'.[81] Indeed, the task of immigration officials is not only to enforce immigration controls but also to apply human rights principles in that context. They have a dual responsibility. And yet, as we have seen, the House of Lords was clear that no weight should be placed on the assessment of the immigration authorities on this aspect of the decision.

Nonetheless it is certainly the case that the House of Lords left open the question of whether weight should be afforded on the basis of the allocation of functions argument. It did not overrule the decisions of the Court of Appeal in *Farrakhan* and *Samaroo*, and identified a potential basis on which the deference afforded in those cases on allocation of functions grounds might be justifiable.[82] However, the House of Lords did not have to consider whether affording weight on allocation of functions grounds is legitimate in judicial review cases because the point was not in issue, and it gave no reasoned attention to that point. Indeed, it dismissed the potential relevance of *Farrakhan* and *Samaroo* with something of a waft of a judicial hand. We must therefore address that issue, together with the legitimacy of the ballot-box argument, at the level of principle.

(c) Arguments Against Conferring Weight on Constitutional Grounds

The arguments against the legitimacy of courts appealing to the allocation of functions argument and the ballot box argument as reasons for affording weight to the

---

[80] It might even be taken to suggest that a reasonableness standard of review (or at least something other than a correctness standard of review) should be applied to test compatibility with Convention rights in a judicial claim relying on s 6(1) of the Human Rights Act. This would by contrary to what seems now to be the established opinion: see ch 4 pp 111–13.

[81] *SB* (n 40) [34].

[82] This is an example of how thinking about the Human Rights Act from an administrative law perspective, and the perspective of standards of review rather than standards of legality, is deeply ingrained in English law.

decision of the primary decision-maker are compelling, and can be summarised as follows. First, the Human Rights Act applies equally to all decisions of public authorities and all legislation, primary and secondary. There is nothing in the Human Rights Act that suggests that individual rights should be any less secure against interferences for which the public officials responsible are accountable to the electorate. Indeed, whether an interference with a protected right is attributable to an executive decision, a decision of a quango or regulator, or to secondary legislation or primary legislation, is often a matter of administrative convenience or history. In *Re G (Adoption: Unmarried Couple)*, for instance, the House of Lords held that Northern Ireland law prohibiting unmarried opposite-sex partners from adopting was contrary to Article 14 read with Article 8. Since the provision in question had been enacted under the Northern Ireland Act 1974 by the Adoption (Northern Ireland) Order 1987, during a period of direct rule from Westminster, it fell to be disapplied by the court. But had the law not been changed in England and Wales in 2002 to permit adoption by unmarried couples, a legal challenge against the law there would have been a challenge to primary legislation.[83] Therefore the fact that the challenge was a challenge to secondary legislation was a matter of history and chance, and no more. And there is no good reason why the right of individuals to adopt should have meant anything different in England and Wales, because the law in question happened to have been made by primary legislation. Convention rights do not have a different meaning, or confer different levels of protection, depending on what branch of government is responsible for the interference.[84]

Secondly, the Human Rights Act, as the courts have accepted, has expressly made it the duty of the courts to determine whether decisions and acts of the political branches of the state are compatible with Convention rights. The argument that Parliament has conferred responsibility on a particular public official or body to make a particular decision does not meet the point that Parliament has also conferred a duty on the court to determine one aspect of that decision, namely whether it is compatible with Convention rights (as we saw in chapter 4, that is not the same question as determining what decision the authority should take or what is in the public interest, generally speaking).

Thirdly, the argument that the courts are not 'democratic' begs the question of the meaning of 'democracy'. If the Human Rights Act is understood as recognising that there must be restrictions on what an elected government (which may not itself represent a majority of the population in respect of any particular decision or generally) may do, then the relevance of the court's lack of electoral accountability falls away. This was the view of Lord Bingham in *A (No 1)*:[85]

[83] Adoption and Children Act 2002 s 50 (which came into effect in 2005).
[84] The Human Rights Act makes only one exception: proceedings of Parliament itself are expressly stated not to be subject to the obligation in s 6(1) to be compatible with Convention rights: HRA s 6(3) excludes Parliament from the definition of 'public authority'.
[85] See *A v Secretary of State for the Home Department* [2005] 2 AC 68 [42].

It is of course true that the judges in this country are not elected and are not answerable to Parliament. It is also of course true . . . that Parliament, the executive and the courts have different functions. But the function of independent judges charged to interpret and apply the law is universally recognised as a cardinal feature of the modern democratic state, a cornerstone of the rule of law itself.

Lord Bingham, citing Professor Jeffrey Jowell, stated that the courts under the Human Rights Act are concerned with delimiting the scope of rights-based democracy, and said that this role could not be described as undemocratic.[86] One does not have to be a die-hard legal liberalist to accept the essential point of this argument, which is that the constitutional function of the courts under the Human Rights Act, however precisely it is defined, is not undemocratic but is intended to bolster the constitution and democratic values. The courts would therefore be swimming against the tide brought in by the Human Rights Act itself, if they attributed normative force to the views of Parliament and the executive as to whether there has been a breach of a Convention right simply on the basis that they, and not the courts, are answerable to the electorate.

(d) Moves Away From Constitutional Deference

There is, however, undoubtedly support in the case law for affording weight to the decisions of public officials on what are usually described rather vaguely as 'democratic' grounds, either in relation to matters of 'policy'[87] or more generally. In *ex p Kebilene*, in comments that have been much cited, Lord Hope said that the courts will defer 'on democratic grounds' to the decision of an elected person or body whose acts are said to be incompatible with Convention rights.[88] Lord Bingham himself said in *R v Lichniak*, 'The fact that section 1(1) represents the settled will of a democratic assembly is not a conclusive reason for upholding it, but a degree of deference is due to judgment of a democratic assembly on how a particular social problem is best tackled.'[89] How are these comment to be reconciled with Lord Bingham's comments in *A (No 1)*? And what are we to make of the remarks of the House of Lords about *Kay* in *Huang*? It is suggested that many of the important cases which appear to endorse constitutional deference can be explained on the basis that the weight afforded by the court was due to the superior knowledge and capacity of Parliament (or devolved legislature) to make

---

[86] See Jowell, 'Judicial deference' (n 10), 597. In accord, Steyn, 'Deference' (n 68), 355.

[87] eg *R (ProLife Alliance) v BBC* [2004] 1 AC 185 [76] (Lord Hoffmann); *Huang v Secretary of State for the Home Department* [2005] 3 All ER 435 [53] (Laws LJ).

[88] *R v DPP, ex p Kebilene* [2000] 2 AC 326, 380: 'In some circumstances it will be appropriate for the courts to recognise that there is an area of judgment within which the judiciary will defer, on democratic grounds, to the considered opinion of the elected body or person' (Lord Hope); *R v Lambert* [2002] QB 1112 [16] (Lord Woolf CJ). These statements have been approved in a number of subsequent cases.

[89] *R v Lichniak* [2003] 1 AC 903, 912.

assessments, and not because it is 'democratic' as such.[90] It is also suggested that in recent cases we can detect a move away from constitutional deference to a recognition that weight should only be afforded to Parliament and the executive on the basis of considerations of relative institutional capacity, where Parliament or the executive is actually better placed to make relevant judgements.

It will be recalled that in *Huang* the House of Lords explained that the difficult problems posed in the context of housing policy had been a matter of on-going consideration by Parliament over many years. The Committee expressly adverted to the fact that the views of landlords had been 'fully represented', as had the social policy needs relating to the indigent and homeless. Although the Committee used the word 'democratic', the reasons that they identified were not democratic reasons as such, but reasons relating to the fact that Parliament was far better placed to judge the considerations on both sides of the scales and to strike the balance between them. The fact that the different groups affected were represented in the process is not itself a democratic consideration. We have seen that in the *ProLife Alliance* case the House of Lords relied on an analogous consideration in affording weight to a decision of the BBC. This factor will also apply to some extent to Ofcom, in relation to which the ballot box argument does not apply. Ofcom is obliged by statute to ensure that interests of different regions of the country are represented when exercising certain functions.[91] It is also required to carry out consultation exercises to ensure that the views of industry participants and others affected by its decisions are directly represented. This will obviously give it an expertise that the courts do not possess, which will be reflected in the weight afforded to its assessments. But it is not a 'democratic' reason for affording weight to its views. The process of formulating the housing legislation considered in *Kay* was more detailed, inclusive, and wide-ranging than decisions made by regulators or the BBC, but part of the reason for giving weight to the balance struck by Parliament was the same, and it is not, properly analysed, anything to do with its superior democratic credentials. We need to give further consideration to the advantages that Parliament has over courts in determining certain issues.

Parliament has a number of related advantages over courts because of the extent of its deliberative and consultative mechanisms. These make it well-suited to determining complex issues. Controversial matters can be debated, reports can be produced, committees can scrutinise bills and ad hoc committees and commissions can be set up. The courts cannot do these things. Therefore in a number of unsuccessful challenges to primary legislation, the courts have placed weight on such considerations in affording weight to the choices made by Parliament.[92] But

[90] Lord Steyn has said that the 'true justification' for restraint is relative 'institutional competence' and 'capacity': 'Deference' (n 68), 352.

[91] See n 72.

[92] See eg *R (Williamson) v Secretary of State for Education and Employment* [2005] 2 AC 246 [51]: 'The subject has been investigated and considered by several committees, including the Plowden Report: *Children and their Primary Schools* (1967) (Central Advisory Council for Education (England)), the Elton Report: *Discipline in Schools* (1989) and the Williams Report: *Childhood Matters* (1996) (the National Commission of Inquiry into the Prevention of Child Abuse). The issue was fully

these advantages are not directly related to Parliament's democratic character (and, indeed, much value is provided by the contribution of the unelected House of Lords).

Parliament's *representative* character can also be a good reason for the courts affording weight to its assessments, because it provides a cross-section of opinion which is particularly relevant and important to certain issue. This is most obvious in relation to questions of public opinion and what is required to maintain public confidence.[93] Public opinion and public confidence are not matters that are often relevant in judging the compatibility of legislation with Convention rights. One of the core purposes of recognising certain rights as fundamental is that they cannot be overridden by public clamour. But there are contexts in which a judgment about public confidence or about public opinion will be relevant, and in such cases Parliament is undoubtedly better placed to judge it. It has also been held that Parliament is better suited to judge matters of 'broad social policy'. In *Wilson*, Lord Nicholls said this is because Parliament is 'charged' with 'primary responsibility' for social policy. This can be taken as a reference to a constitutional ground for deference, reflecting a background understanding of the separation of powers. But such comments can equally be regarded as reflecting the same idea that we saw at work in *Huang*, namely that Parliament is simply better able to judge the need for social policy measures and the impact of those measures and the possible alternatives. Indeed, Lord Nicholls went on to say in *Wilson* that the court's readiness to intervene will depend 'on the circumstances', and that the more 'broad' the issue, the greater weight would be afforded to the legislative judgment.[94]

Lord Hope's remarks in *ex p Kebilene* about constitutional deference were considered by the House of Lords in *Re G (Adoption: Unmarried Couple)*. The comments were qualified both implicitly and explicitly by their Lordships. The Court of Appeal in Northern Ireland had upheld the Adoption (Northern Ireland) Order 1987 on the basis that it was a question of social policy, relying explicitly on *ex p Kebilene*. The House of Lords, as we have seen, took a different approach, scrutinising the legislation and holding it inapplicable because it prevented unmarried opposite-sex partners, in an enduring relationship, who had the personal aptitude and qualities for being good parents from adopting children (Lord Walker dissented). Lord Hope said that although the matter involved social policy, his comments in *ex p Kebilene* were not in point because the issue of discrimination on grounds of status would always be suitable for judicial scrutiny.[95] Moreover, Lord Hope indicated, albeit slightly equivocally, that the fact that the

---

debated in Parliament' (Lord Nicholls). Although conferring a 'considerable degree of latitude' to Parliament on this issue, Lord Nicholls did not refer to any 'democratic' reason. See also *Wilson v First County Trust (No 2) Ltd* [2004] 1 AC 816 [70].

[93] On Parliament being better suited to address what is necessary to restore public confidence, see *R v A (No 2)* [2002] 1 AC 45 [84] (Lord Hope); and on Parliament being better suited to determine what restrictions on political advertising are necessary to protect democracy, see *R (Animal Defenders) v Secretary of State for Culture, Media and Sport* [2008] 1 AC 1312 [33] (Lord Bingham).

[94] *Wilson v First Country Trust Ltd (No 2)* [2004] 1 AC 816 [70]. Also see *Williamson* (n 92).

[95] *Re G (Adoption: Unmarried Couple)* [2009] 1 AC 173 [48].

question was a 'political' and 'contentious' issue in Northern Ireland made it more, rather than less, important that the court ensure that the discrimination was justified because of the greater risk of individual rights, including in this case the rights of children, being breached without adequate objective justification.[96]

These comments represent an important step away from the idea of constitutional deference for two reasons. First, Lord Hope viewed his comments in *ex p Kebilene* as subject-matter specific. In principle they applied to an executive order as much as to primary legislation. This suggests that Lord Hope's comments in *ex p Kebilene* were directed at suitability, rather than any lack of electoral accountability. Secondly, Lord Hope explicitly qualified his comments in *ex p Kebilene* in recognising that even in the context of legal provisions underpinned by considerations of broad social policy, particular issues within that context are suitable for close judicial scrutiny. Lord Mance also applied an important gloss to Lord Hope's remarks in *ex p Kebilene*. He cited them for the proposition that the courts would give 'appropriate weight to considerations of relative institutional competence' and that the precise weight will depend on whether the decision falls within an area in which the legislature 'can claim particular experience'.[97] Neither Lord Hoffmann nor Baroness Hale referred to Lord Hope's comments in *ex p Kebilene* at all.[98]

Another welcome decision is *Baiai*, in which the House of Lords held that a policy that required the Secretary of State to refuse consent for non-nationals to marry when they had not been granted leave to enter for at least six months with three months unexpired was contrary to Article 12 of the European Convention. Lord Bingham, giving the leading speech, rebuffed the submission made on behalf of the Secretary of State that the matter fell within an area of social policy, saying that it was 'too sweeping' a submission and the court could not 'abdicate its function' of deciding whether the policy was lawful, which on the facts required no more than 'an accurate analysis of the scheme and the law'.[99] The case confirmed that a decision made in an area of broad social or economic policy does not automatically qualify for weight. It will depend on the precise issues and grounds on which a measure is challenged.

The waters get deeper in the context of public morality and ethics. Where Parliament interferes with Convention rights in order to protect public morals or ethical considerations, the courts will inevitably have to confer considerable weight on Parliament's decision, not only because of the procedural advantages

---

[96] The text extrapolates, it is hoped fairly, from Lord Hope's remark that, 'The more contentious the issue is, the greater the risk is that some people will be discriminated against in ways that engage their Convention rights' (*Re G* (n 95) [48]).

[97] ibid [130].

[98] Lord Hoffmann said that courts will generally respect the choices made by Parliament between rational alternatives in an area of social policy (*Re G* ibid [20]). Lord Hoffmann eschewed a 'weight' approach and preferred to apply a wide latitude or 'rationality' approach to such questions. (In the context of national security, see *Secretary of State for the Home Department v Rehman* [2003] 1 AC 153 [49]–[54], [62]). In *Re G* (n 95) his Lordship did not refer to any constitutional reasons for taking this approach, although he had previously stated: 'majority approval is necessary for a proper decision on policy or allocation of resources': *ProLife Alliance* (n 87) [76].

[99] *Baiai and Trzcinska v Secretary of State for the Home Department* [2009] 1 AC 287 [25].

that Parliament has for debating and scrutinising such issues, but also because of the representative character of the institution. A particularly good example is provided by the legal challenges in Scotland and England to legislation banning hunting with hounds. The Inner House of the Court of Session held that judging what is necessary to prevent cruelty to animals had a long legislative pedigree. It identified a number of respects in which Parliament was better placed to judge what was required. MSPs had the 'means at hand' to inform themselves of the relevant views and evidence, including considering representations from interest groups, the formal reception of evidence and debate. It also stated: 'MSPs are elected on their policies on matters such as this.'[100]

Difficulties of course arise because at the core of the idea of human rights is the acceptance that unpopular minorities must be protected from the prejudice and caprice of majorities. And as Allan has written, a consensus of opinion that 'embodies a widespread misunderstanding of the requirements of respect [for protected rights]' is of little value in determining whether rights have been respected.[101] Moreover, courts frequently determine matters of the most ethically difficult and controversial kind. For instance, in *Re A (Children) (Conjoined Twins: Surgical Separation)*, the court was asked to decide whether it was in the best interests of conjoined twins for one to be saved in circumstances where the other would die, and where the view of medical professionals was at odds with those of the parents. Ward LJ stated that the 'only arbiter of [the] sincerely held difference of opinion is the court. Deciding disputed matters of life and death is surely and preeminently a matter for a court of law to judge. That is what courts are here for.'[102]

Identifying the circumstances in which *particular* weight should be afforded to legislatures in matters of ethics and popular morality would require us to travel well beyond the confines of this chapter. It suffices here to make the point that there are cases in which legislatures are better placed to determine the importance of such considerations in relation to particular issues in part because of their representative character. It is hard to deny that the question of whether hunting with hounds is cruel is one such issue. As Lord Hoffmann pertinently remarked in the *ProLife Alliance* case: 'Independence makes the courts more suited to deciding some kinds of questions and being elected makes the legislature or executive more suited to deciding others.'[103]

(e) Is Parliamentary Suitability the Ballot Box Argument in Disguise?

Some readers of the previous section of this chapter might wonder whether the judicial recognition that Parliament is better suited to determining certain questions,

---

[100] *Adams v Scottish Ministers* [2004] SCC 665 [48]. Much the same reasoning is found in the judgment of the House of Lords in the English proceedings: *R (Countryside Alliance) v Attorney-General* [2008] 1 AC 719, in which the decision of the Inner House was cited approvingly.
[101] Allan, 'Human Rights' (n 24) at 691.
[102] *Re A (Children) (Conjoined Twins: Surgical Separation)* [2001] Fam 147, 174.
[103] *Prolife Alliance* (n 87) [76].

particularly where this is in part due to its representative character, and affording weight to Parliament's assessments on this basis collapses back into the ballot box argument. This is not the case. The ballot box argument, even if it applies with particular force in certain contexts, in principle requires weight to be afforded to all legislation (and all decisions made by ministers), no matter what its subject matter and no matter how little scrutiny it received prior to enactment, simply by dint of its 'democratic' credentials.[104] As Lord Steyn has stated extra-judicially in response to Lord Hoffmann's support for the ballot box argument in *Rehman*:

> If valid, this reason is self sufficient and controlling. If this reasoning were to be extended to Convention rights [*Rehman* was not a Convention rights case], courts would be required automatically to defer, on constitutional grounds, on any occasion on which a qualified Convention right was claimed to be defeated by a particular public interest.[105]

The argument would, for example, apply to the Immigration Rules which are drawn up by a minister and laid before Parliament, yet we have seen that the House of Lords in *Huang* refused to afford *any* weight to the democratic credentials of the Immigration Rules. On the other hand, as shown by the *ProLife Alliance* case and the Ofcom example, weight can be afforded to public authorities on the basis that they better represent the views of sections of society without such bodies having any claim to be democratically accountable through the ballot box, save in a very indirect way. We can therefore be confident that affording weight to Parliament or public officials because they are *better suited* to determining certain issues is not the same as the ballot box argument.

(g) Conclusion on Democratic Reasons

There are plenty of dicta in the case law with which one could seek to support a doctrine of restraint on the basis of a lack of accountability simpliciter. But taking a step back and taking a more general view of the case law, the existence of such a doctrine seems to conflict with the efforts made by the courts in cases such as *Huang*, *Williamson* and *Adams* to identify the reasons why the legislature is in a superior position to the court to form a judgment on certain, clearly identified, issues. Moreover, applying the label 'democratic' to reasons for affording weight to the legislature does not add anything to them. In truth the absence of the court's 'democratic' credentials is not a ground in itself for deferring to the legislative judgment. In many cases, reference to the democratic nature of the decision-maker seems to be used as a shorthand when the court does not wish to unpick the various reasons why the decision-maker is better placed to make a particular assessment. (This is the way it was used in *Huang* in the short discussion of *Kay*.) Whilst such an approach is understandable, there are dangers in using the term

---

104 This was recognised by Laws LJ in his judgment in *International Transport Roth Gmbh v Secretary of State for the Home Department* [2003] QB 728, in which he said that greater deference is due to an Act of Parliament (376–78).

105 Steyn, 'Deference' (n 68), 358.

'democratic' in such a way. In the first place, it is highly misleading in terms of the idea of constitutionalism and democracy that underpins adjudication under the Human Rights Act. It fails to recognise the crucial democratic role in the courts upholding fundamental rights. Secondly, there is a danger in it being applied over-liberally and lazily to justify deference to legislatures that is undeserved. Even when the legislation can be said to concern public morals or social policy, particular issues that arise in litigation may not have been given much, if any, consideration, or might not be central to the legislative scheme. If courts clearly identify, as they did in the hunting cases, the reasons why relevant assessments are better made by legislatures, this will help to ensure that undue weight is not afforded and that categories of case are not rendered resistant to judicial scrutiny. This is, indeed, the lesson of *Re G (Adoption: Unmarried Couple)*.

The Importance of the Right

Most discussions of deference assume that where a right is more important, this provides a reason for affording less weight, or deference, to the decision of the primary official.[106] But it is not clear why this is so. Consider again the example given of the chambers meeting. Why should a person at the meeting give less weight to those better placed to make assessments than him or her, just because the decision has an important effect on people's lives? If in an individual case the decision would have particularly severe effects for them, why should a person at the meeting confer less weight on the judgment of others? If the weight afforded is perfectly reflective of the relative knowledge and capacity of the individuals at the meeting, then the impact of the decision ought to make no difference to the degree of reliance placed on the judgment of others. What might be legitimate and appropriate, if a decision has a particularly grave impact, is for the individuals on whose shoulders the decision falls to be made to make additional efforts to acquaint themselves with the relevant facts. But in so doing they would be seeking to *increase* their knowledge and expertise. This in turn would alter the balance of relevant knowledge of expertise between themselves and others. With their enhanced decision-making capacities they would be entitled *on that ground* to confer less weight on the decisions of others: there would be greater parity between each individual decision-maker.

Thus, properly understood, the fact that an administrative decision has a particularly severe impact on an individual is not itself a reason for the courts affording less weight to the assessments made by the responsible public officer, and requires less weight to be afforded only indirectly. In reality it enjoins the courts to modify their scrutiny and adapt their procedures so that they can enhance their own knowledge of the relevant facts. This is precisely what they do. In *Tweed* for example, the House of Lords recognised that where an important human rights

---

[106] eg Kavanagh, *Constitutional Review under the Human Rights Act* (n 4) 175.

issue was in play, the Administrative Court is more likely to require underlying documents to be disclosed, and it is also more likely that cross-examination will be permitted.[107] The point has already been made that the degree of weight that courts should afford to others is not absolute, but is influenced by the form that the proceedings have taken.

Often the concern to give 'enhanced scrutiny' to decisions with particularly severe implications (and correspondingly the more relaxed scrutiny afforded where the impact is not so severe) is given effect in another, conceptually different, but in practice closely linked, way. Courts will often in practice be adjusting the standard that they are applying, in substance if not in form. The judges may be edging further from a rationality standard towards a reasonableness or yet more intrusive standard, or they may be moving in the other direction. Sometimes courts do modify their language to reflect this. There are a number of examples of the courts lapsing into the language of rationality when applying a proportionality test in the context of housing and social security benefits.[108] It is probably inevitable that public law will give effect to the same considerations in different ways. A perfectly coherent doctrinal and analytical methodology in public law might well be desirable, but that is probably crying for the moon.

The Doctrine of Deference Reconsidered

The non-doctrinal approach of TRS Allan has already been considered. In this section we seek to apply the reasoning in this chapter to a recent and sustained articulation of a fully doctrinal approach to these issues. In an important book on the Human Rights Act, Kavanagh has argued that the courts need to adopt a doctrine of deference and has articulated what she says that this means. But when Kavanagh's argument is closely examined, the fragility of attempts to classify situations in which weight should be afforded to the views of primary decision-makers and to categorise different degrees of weight, becomes apparent. Furthermore, the analysis, for all its sophistication, demonstrates how the adoption of a doctrine of deference would threaten to water-down protections for human rights.

Kavanagh argues that 'inter-institutional comity' and 'respect' between the braches of state justifies the courts in deferring to their assessments. She suggests, moreover, that courts put this deference into practice by 'attaching appropriate weight' to their decisions.[109] She then draws a distinction between 'minimal deference' and 'substantial deference'. The former she describes as the 'judicial attribution of some presumptive weight' to a decision or legislation. It requires that they 'should be treated seriously as a *bona fide* attempt to solve whatever social

[107] *Tweed v Parades Commission for Northern Ireland* [2007] 1 AC 650; *R (Wilkinson) v Broadmoor Hospital* [2002] 1 WLR 419; and *R (Al Sweady) v Secretary of State* [2009] EWHC 2387 (Admin) [29].
[108] See ch 6, p 168.
[109] Kavanagh (n 4), ch 7, especially p 169.

problem they set out to tackle'. She says, 'judges (acting in their judicial capacity) cannot make light of, or be sceptical about' legislation.[110] Substantial deference by contrast 'has to be earned' and can be afforded where the executive or a legislature (1) is more competent to decide the matter, (2) has more expertise, or (3) has more legitimacy to decide the issue.[111] On top of this, Kavanagh draws an additional distinction between 'partial' or 'persuasive' deference, and a further one between 'absolute' or 'complete' deference.[112] In order to create a meaningful doctrinal approach, Kavanagh has not only to identify principles justifying deference, but also has to draw distinctions between degrees, types or amounts of deference (ie she attempts to articulate the equations, $A1 = B1$, $A2 = B2$, etc).

In considering Kavanagh's suggested doctrinal approach, the first point that we should record is that it appears to be entirely unnecessary. Kavanagh accepts that what (on her analysis) deference and comity mean in practice is the affording of weight to primary decision-makers. She even uses the terminology of weight herself. Terms such as 'comity' and 'deference' are not necessary to describe, still less to structure, the judicial attribution of weight to the views of other persons and bodies, as this chapter has attempted to show.[113] Of course, this would be justifiable (as an explanatory tool but not as a doctrine) if the approach had significant explanatory force. But the second criticism is that it is unclear what minimal and substantial deference are in fact intended to describe.

Kavanagh says that minimal deference requires that decisions should be treated as serious attempts to resolve social problems. But it is well-established in public law that judges will not and must not approach decisions taken by those seeking to act in the public interest in a sceptical way, or in a way that presumes incompetence or bad faith on the part of a public official. In the *Wednesbury* case Lord Greene MR said that, 'It is not to be assumed *prima facie* that responsible bodies like the local authority in this case will exceed their powers'.[114] This is essentially an attitude; a recognition of general competence and good faith on the part of public bodies—as Kavanagh puts it, 'showing or manifesting respect'.[115] But Kavanagh goes further and contends that there is a 'presumptive weight' in favour of decisions and legislation made by public authorities.[116] Whilst acknowledging that there are different

---

[110] ibid 181.

[111] ibid 181–82.

[112] ibid 172.

[113] Indeed, Kavanagh states that 'Given the enormous constitutional importance of these issues (as well as their complexity), we need to separate out the various elements, and clarify their nature and their interrelationship, using the most accurate and helpful terminology we can' (ibid 207). This observation is fully in accordance with the approach taken in this chapter which has resisted any attempt to 'complicate and mystify' the law in this area by the introduction of terminology or doctrinal categorisation.

[114] *Associated Provincial Picture Houses Ltd v Wednesbury Corp* [1948] 1 KB 223, 228. In fact, the traditional standard of review, in placing the burden on the claimant to show the decision is unreasonable, goes further and effectively establishes a presumption that a public official has not exceeded his or her powers. For analogous comments in the context of delegated legislation see *Kruse v Johnson* [1898] 2 QB 91.

[115] Kavanagh (n 4) 198.

[116] For example, ibid 170, .

degrees of presumptive weight, Kavanagh suggests that in any case where presumptive weight is afforded (which is in every case of minimal deference), the 'alleged violation of Convention rights must be *substantial* and/or *clearly demonstrated* in order to outweigh the presumptive weight in its favour' (emphasis in original). Kavanagh later refers back to this comment in describing minimal deference and adds, 'the error of the legislation must be sufficiently grave to override the presumptive weight in its favour'.[117] Although in these comments Kavanagh refers to legislation, both remarks are also explicitly associated with executive decisions because of the democratic credentials of the decision-maker.[118] Minimal deference therefore seems to range from the uncontroversial proposition that the government and legislatures should be treated with respect, which is already reflected in public law, to the far more substantive and controversial proposition that a significant burden is and should be placed on claimants to establish a sufficiently grave, substantial or clearly demonstrated Convention breach.

Moreover, Kavanagh also states:

> The duty of *minimal deference* accounts for the fact that judges ought not to invalidate an Executive decision, or declare an Act of Parliament to be incompatible with the HRA, *merely* on the basis that they disagree with it or because they might have come up with a different solution if they had had the power to make the primary decision.[119]

This perpetuates the expansive sense in which minimal deference is used. As we have seen (see chapter 4), there is a very different and important explanation for why the courts ought not to hold a decision or legislation to be contrary to Convention rights because they disagree with it, namely, that this is not the test for breach of a protected right. This is not the standard the law requires them to apply. The example we considered was that of a school which decides to impose new disciplinary measures. Judges might not agree with the disciplinary measure introduced by the school, but that does not establish a breach of the European Convention. It must be inhumane or degrading, or a disproportionate interference with respect for private or family life (etc). This is why judges ought not to invalidate decisions on the basis that they do not agree with them. It is very different from the attribution of weight or deference.[120]

---

[117] ibid, 172, 181–82.

[118] Kavanagh argues that minimal deference is owed to both executive and legislative decisions: ibid 190–96, and in making the former comment Kavanagh relies on dicta of Lord Bingham in *A (No 1)* (n 85) [26] in which he was reviewing the decision of the Home Secretary that there was a public emergency permitting derogation from Art 5 of the European Convention and the making of a designation order under s 14 of the Human Rights Act, and not, at least directly, a decision of Parliament. In fact, different considerations do apply in relation to primary legislation because Parliament cannot justify its legislation before the courts and it must therefore stand as Parliament's case. The Government's justification of it may be rather different from what Parliamentarians had in mind: see ch 6, pp 183–84.

[119] Kavanagh (n 4) 181.

[120] The same can be said for standards of legality at common law: eg in respect of fairness, 'But the question is not what I would have done if I had been a member of the panel, but whether the panel's refusal of a short adjournment was fair. After much hesitation I have come to the conclusion that it was. Wise it was not. But fair it was . . .' *R v Panel for Takeovers and Mergers, ex p Guinness* [1990] 1 QB 146, 187 (Lloyd LJ).

In addition, Kavanagh also discusses decisions of courts not to determine certain issues, and exercise other 'prudential' techniques, as well as the courts' choice between remedying a rights violation through sections 3 and 4 of the Human Rights Act as examples of deference.[121] However, the sense in which courts, in making such decisions, are affording weight to legislation or the decision made by the primary decision-maker is not explained and is impossible to understand. In these instances courts are undoubtedly influenced by their own limited competence but they are not conferring weight on assessments or decisions that have been made by others (on the contrary, the point is that the judges are leaving it to others to take decisions they have not taken and want to avoid (see chapter 3)). Kavanagh's notion of deference is therefore too inclusive and too slippery: it obscures more than it reveals.[122]

This brings us to a final concern with Kavanagh's attempt to construct a doctrine of deference. This concern is that her construction is not only novel but dangerous.[123] To be fair to Kavanagh, she argues that *substantial* deference on constitutional grounds should be exceptional, and that substantial deference is not automatically due because a case concerns national security, or policy or any other subject matter, which resemble arguments advanced in this chapter.[124] With all of this we can agree. But the idea that the courts should recognise *presumptions* against rights and/or in favour of the government—which is what Kavanagh's thesis boils down to in practical doctrinal terms—would be dangerous if ever it were to be implanted into human rights law. It is a fundamental proposition that 'an authority which seeks to justify a restriction on a fundamental right on the ground of a pressing social need has a burden to discharge'.[125] Moreover, in many areas of human rights law, there is specific jurisprudence on the respective burdens of argument and evidence of government and individuals. These are carefully tailored to the contexts of the nature of the interference with the right in question.[126] For example, where a person claims that his deportation will expose him or her to a real risk of ill-treatment or torture on return, the ECtHR has developed the

---

[121] Kavanagh (n 4) 176–78, 229–30.

[122] It must also be noted that Kavanagh's discussion consistently assumes that weight (deference) should be afforded to a decision or legislation *as a whole*. This seems to underpin the idea that the courts are entitled to presume that the correct balance has been struck by the decision-maker or the legislature. We have seen however that in many if not most cases the court will only be justified in affording weight to one or more of the assessments that have formed part of the overall decision, or which lie behind legislation. If this is the case, why should any presumptive weight be afforded in relation to the decision or legislation's (overall) compatibility with Convention rights?

[123] *cf* the discussion of proportionality by J Jowell and A Lester, 'Proportionality: Neither Novel Nor Dangerous' in JL Jowell and D Oliver (eds), *New Directions in Judicial Review* (London, Stevens & Sons, 1988).

[124] For example, Kavanagh (n 4) 190–93, 209. It has been suggested that the representative character of institutions may make them better placed to determine certain questions. Kavanagh suggests that in exceptional cases their democratic legitimacy might be an 'advantage' (196): on this point Kavanagh's views may not differ greatly from those set out in this chapter.

[125] *R v Shayler* [2003] 1 AC 247 [59] (Lord Hope).

[126] *Saadi v Italy* (n 18) [129]. For another example, see the rule that a tribunal is presumed to have acted impartially under Art 6 until the contrary is proven: *Piersack v Belgium* (1982) 5 EHRR 169 [30].

following approach which strikes a fair balance between the interests of the general community and those of individuals threatened with deportation:

> ... in principle [it is] for the applicant to adduce evidence capable of proving that there are substantial grounds for believing that, if the measure complained of were to be implemented, he would be exposed to a real risk of being subjected to treatment contrary to Article 3. Where such evidence is adduced, it is for the Government to dispel any doubts about it.

The idea that, through the medium of a doctrine of deference, the courts should recognise presumptions, or afford presumptive weight, to the decision of the government based on such factors as democratic legitimacy would at best unnecessarily complicate human rights litigation, and at worst would undermine human rights protection.

Conclusion

This chapter has explained how public law already contains the components necessary for a coherent and workable approach to determining human rights cases and in public law more generally. It has argued against a doctrine of deference and in favour of the non-doctrinal approach approved by the House of Lords in *Huang*: the courts apply Convention rights as standards of legality (in the same way that principles of natural justice and common law constitutional rights are applied) without an overlay of reasonableness review, subject only to the ordinary judicial technique of affording weight to relevant assessments made by those with superior knowledge and expertise. The chapter has explored the various reasons, good and bad, which have been suggested for affording weight to decisions of public officials. The primary purpose of that exercise was to illustrate the general argument that a doctrinal approach is unnecessary, and to explore the approach taken in *Huang* in more detail, and not to reach definite conclusions on such points. It has nonetheless been suggested that constitutional arguments for judicial restraint are contrary to the scheme of the Human Rights Act and that there has been a discernible shift away from the acceptance of such arguments emerging in the case law.

6

Proportionality

AFTER YEARS OF teasing excitable public lawyers and nervous public servants, the House of Lords in *Daly* finally accepted that the principle of proportionality is a principle of public law.[1] Although UK courts had previously applied a principle of proportionality in the context of EC law before *Daly*, they were required to do so under EC law. By contrast, the courts are not bound by the Human Rights Act 1998 to apply a test of proportionality when applying the European Convention, let alone when applying the common law.[2] In *Daly* a proportionality analysis was applied in holding that there had been a violation of the claimant's fundamental common law right to the confidentiality of his correspondence with his legal advisers[3] and, in a much cited but entirely obiter speech, Lord Steyn took the opportunity of stating emphatically that the principle of proportionality, as opposed to the *Wednesbury* principle or any derivative of it, should also be applied in appropriate cases when assessing the justification of interferences with Convention rights.[4] The speech was expressly approved by the

---

[1] *R (Daly) v Secretary of State for the Home Department*, [2001] 2 AC 532. In *Council of Civil Service Unions v Minister for the Civil Service* [1985] 1 AC 374, 410, Lord Diplock, in his seminal exposition of the grounds of modern public law, referred to the 'possible adoption' of the principle of proportionality; then, in *R v Secretary of State for the Home Department, ex p Brind* [1991] 1 AC 696, one member of the Committee applied proportionality (Lord Templeman), two said it was unconstitutional (Lord Ackner and Lord Lowry) and two (Lord Bridge and Lord Roskill) refused to apply it, despite the fact that there was a clear interference with freedom of expression, but then said they were not excluding its application as part of the 'future development of the law'. When presented with a further opportunity in *R v Chief Constable of Sussex, ex p International Trader's Ferry Ltd* [1999] 2 AC 418, their Lordships performed another feint by suggesting that there might not be a great deal of difference between *Wednesbury* and proportionality after all. Meanwhile, they had developed and applied the novel principle called the 'principle of legality', which did much of the work of a proportionality principle where common law rights were at stake: see, eg *R v Secretary of State for the Home Department, ex p Simms* [2000] 2 AC 115, see further ch 4 pp 105–108.

[2] Proportionality is not a term found in the Convention, it is a concept which has been adopted and applied by the Strasbourg Court when applying the Convention. Domestic courts are not bound to follow the Strasbourg Court: HRA s 2(1).

[3] Lord Bingham stated: 'the policy provides for a degree of intrusion into the privileged legal correspondence of prisoners which is greater than is justified by the objectives the policy is intended to serve, and so violates the common law rights of prisoners' (*Daly* (n 1) [21]). The First Division of the Inner Court of Session did not demur from a concession by the Counsel for the Scottish Ministers in *Somerville v Scottish Ministers* [2006] CSIH 52, 2007 SC 140 that a test which is at least 'akin' to proportionality is to be applied where there is an interference with a 'fundamental' common law right ([125]).

[4] *Daly* (n 1) [24]. Lord Steyn's speech has been approved and applied in, amongst other cases: *R (Begum) v Governors of Denbigh High School* [2006] UKHL 15, [2007] 1 AC 100 [30] (Lord Bingham);

---

other members of the Committee and was later described by a Joint Opinion of the House of Lords in *Huang v Secretary of State for the Home Department* as 'justly celebrated'.[5]

Having received the principle of proportionality into domestic law, it is incumbent on the courts to develop a clear and principled conception of proportionality and to locate it within the wider field of public law standards. To this end, a number of cases, including several judgments of the House of Lords, have sought to articulate how the test of proportionality should be applied by domestic courts. This chapter suggests that these cases are problematic and that a clear and principled approach to the principle of proportionality is yet to emerge. It goes on to suggest a principled approach to proportionality, drawing on lessons from other jurisdictions.[6]

The focus of this chapter is on the internal structure of proportionality rather than its relationship to other standards, such as the principle of reasonableness, which is the subject of other chapters.[7] One cannot sensibly address this more general issue without first having a clear idea of the concept of proportionality itself. The House of Lords has rightly postponed dealing with the wider aspect of the recognition of the proportionality principle.[8]

The Distinct Roles of Public Officials and Judges

Lord Steyn explained in his speech in *Daly* that the benefit of the doctrine of proportionality as a legal test is that it is capable of being more precise and sophisticated than a reasonableness test, as well as requiring a more intrusive review of a decision made by a public official which requires the courts to 'assess the balance' struck by the primary decision-maker. Lord Steyn was careful to state that this did not entail a shift to 'merits review' because, he said, the roles of judge and decision-maker are 'fundamentally distinct and will remain so'.[9] These remarks can be distilled into three propositions: (1) proportionality provides a structured and precise approach to judicial review, (2) proportionality permits an engagement with the substance of a decision, and (3) proportionality is not merits review: the

A v Secretary of State for the Home Department [2005] 2 AC 68 [40] (Lord Bingham); *Shayler* (n 4) [33] (Lord Bingham), [75] (Lord Hope).

[5] *Huang v Secretary of State for the Home Department* [2007] 2 AC 167 [13].

[6] The discussion draws on the case law of the Supreme Courts of Canada and Israel. The Canadian case law has been particularly important and influential following the seminal judgment of Dickson CJ in *R v Oakes* [1986] 1 SCR 103. The Israeli case law builds on this jurisprudence whilst considering the issue of proportionality afresh. The discussion here draws on T Hickman, 'Proportionality: Comparative Law Lessons' [2007] *JR* 31.

[7] See chs 7 and 9.

[8] *Somerville v Scottish Ministers* [2007] UKHL 44, [2007] 1 WLR 2734.

[9] *Daly* (n 1) [27]–[28]. Citing J Jowell, 'Beyond the rule of law: towards a constitutional judicial review' [2000] *PL* 671, 681.

roles of judges and administrators remain fundamentally distinct. The second and third propositions are in tension: they pull in opposite directions. On the one hand, proportionality review requires courts to roll up their sleeves and examine the substance of a decision, but on the other hand they must not engage in merits review. It is hardly surprising that this has left judges and commentators alike scratching their heads. The difficulty of reconciling these two propositions is at the heart of the problems that have beset the courts in identifying and applying the principle of proportionality in a structured and principled way. The structure of proportionality must reflect these propositions: it must require engagement with the substance without substituting the judge for the administrator. Before we turn to examine the content and structure of the proportionality test, it is therefore necessary to make some preliminary remarks about the relationship between these two propositions. In doing so we need to drawn on the general analysis of public standards and of courts affording weight to the assessments of primary decision makers which was the subject of chapters 4 and 5.

Lord Steyn was clear that when assessing the balance that has been struck by a public official between competing interests, the court is required to address the 'relative weight accorded to interests and considerations'.[10] This represents a review of the substance of the decision in the sense that it requires an appraisal of the cogency, including the relative cogency, of the reasons for and against the decision which has been made. The courts have also made clear that, since it is for them to determine whether a public authority has breached a Convention right, it must also be for them to determine whether a decision is proportionate.[11] It follows that the courts *must substitute* their decision as to whether a decision is proportionate for any assessment of proportionality made by the primary decision-maker. To this extent, then, the courts do engage in a merits review.

Of course, as we saw in chapter 5, it is well established that in many cases the courts will afford weight to the assessment of the primary decision-maker. And we have also seen that this does not alter the nature of the decision that the courts have to make, only the manner in which they make it. As the House of Lords explained in *Huang*, the exercise of affording weight to a primary decision-maker is simply the performance of the ordinary judicial task of according appropriate weight to the judgment or evaluation of a person with responsibility for a given subject-matter where they have 'access to special sources of knowledge and advice'.[12] In other words, where the capability and credentials of a person or body are better suited to evaluating a matter in issue, the courts will give weight to the views of that person or body. But this is a common feature of adjudication. The courts routinely afford weight to assessments made by expert witnesses, specialist tribunals, lower courts' evaluation of facts, and decisions of professionals in respect of matters

---

[10] *Daly* (n 1) [27].

[11] eg *Belfast City Council v Miss Behavin' Ltd* [2007] 1 WLR 1420 [31] (Baroness Hale); also *Shayler* (n 4) [79] (Lord Hope).

[12] *Huang* (n 5) [16] (Lord Bingham, giving the joint opinion of the Committee).

within their expertise, for example in professional negligence and employment cases, to name but a few examples. In all these contexts and others, courts give weight to the competence and capability of another person or body that is better able than the court itself to make an assessment, such as an assessment of risk, or of value, or of harm, on a matter in issue in proceedings. This does not necessarily mean that the court is performing a distinct exercise from the other body, or not evaluating the merits of its decision. On the contrary, their tasks are usually closely analogous and overlapping, it is just that the court is less well able to carry out at least some aspects of a requisite assessment than the other person or body and is quite rightly influenced by its superior capacity and expertise.

An illustration from the public law context shows how affording weight to a primary decision-maker does not mean that the court is avoiding merits review (or engaging in a distinct exercise). The example is provided by those cases where a primary decision-maker has superior capabilities and credentials to the court in relation to matters relevant to a proportionality analysis but the primary decision-maker has not, for whatever reason, carried out a relevant assessment. It has simply failed to address the issue. If it had done so (for example, by carrying out a risk assessment, where risk is relevant to whether the decision made is proportionate), the court would have afforded it weight. But absent such an assessment, the court must make a substantive decision for itself, as best it can, on the evidence available. This makes clear that affording weight to the superior capabilities and credentials of another person or body *assists* the courts in undertaking a merits review of aspects of a decision, but it does not mean that the court is not carrying out a merits review.

It is suggested that the key to unlocking this issue lies not in the notion of 'merits review', because as we have seen, courts do engage in a merits review of any assessment by the decision-maker of the proportionality of their decision, but in the notion that the roles of judges and administrators remain 'fundamentally distinct'. This reflects the fact that decisions of public officials are made on the basis of what they consider to be in the public interest and not on the basis of what is proportionate; and there may be a difference between what is proportionate and what is in the public interest.[13] As Lord Hoffmann has stated, '[i]n a democratic society, decisions as to what the general interest requires are made by democratically elected bodies or persons accountable to them'.[14] The merits review undertaken by the court therefore relates to only one aspect of the decision made, namely, whether it is proportionate.

Generally speaking, the courts have no jurisdiction to pronounce on whether or not a decision best advances the public interest, or to substitute their view of

---

[13] The term 'public interest' is being used here as shorthand and includes fulfilling the political objective or purpose of the statutory power. For the different questions that are addressed by courts and administrators, see ch 4.

[14] *R (Alconbury Developments Ltd) v Secretary of State for the Environment, Transport and the Regions* [2003] 2 AC 295 [69], also [74]–[75] (Lord Hoffmann), [139] (Lord Clyde), [176] (Lord Hutton).

whether a decision is desirable for that of the public authority. It is in this sense that the roles of courts and administrators are distinct, even when the courts are charged with assessing whether a decision is proportionate. Put simply, courts and public officials address different questions. In so far as public officials do consider, in the course of making their decisions, whether the decision that they are minded to make will be proportionate (and they do not generally have to do so[15]), this is only one, subsidiary, aspect of their determination. This aspect of their determination *is* open to merits review and the courts can substitute their own view. But if a court finds that a decision is proportionate, it cannot interfere with the course taken by the public official; and if it finds that a decision is disproportionate this does not entail the courts finding that the decision is not desirable in the general interest.[16]

It follows that if the tension between the propositions underpinning the proportionality principle in domestic law is to be resolved, a distinction must be maintained between what is in the public interest and what is proportionate. They cannot always point to the same result. The structure of the proportionality principle must therefore allow for a range of decisions to be made to advance the public interest within the parameters of what is proportionate. If what is proportionate and what is in the public interest are always one and the same, then judges and decision-makers will not be performing distinct constitutional roles. If they are not, as they should not be, then any challenge to a decision within the range of proportionate decisions will have to be made on the basis that it amounts to an incorrect assessment of what is best in the public interest, and such a challenge can only be made through political channels. This point has been well expressed by the Supreme Court of Israel in its leading judgment on proportionality under the Basic Law, which stated:

> Not infrequently, there are a number of ways that the requirement of proportionality can be satisfied. In these situations a 'zone of proportionality' must be recognized . . .[17]

It is, then, in this way that the function of the court and that of public officials are truly distinct, providing the explanation for why proportionality review does not amount to a merits review, or something akin to an appeal of the decision in question.[18] There is a merits review, but on only one dimension of the decision

---

[15] See *R (SB) v Denbigh High School* [2007] 1 AC 100 and the discussion in ch 8.

[16] Jeffrey Jowell states: 'Judges are not being set free to second-guess administrators on the merits of their policies . . . the courts will look to the process of justification of the decision and to the inherent qualities of a democratic society. This kind of review of the constitutional co-ordinates of the decision is a far cry from review on the basis of the desirability of the decision in abstract terms.': Jowell, 'Beyond the rule of law' (n 9), 681–82.

[17] HCJ 2056/04 *Beit Sourik Village Council v Government of Israel* [42].

[18] Julian Rivers makes a similar point in distinguishing between 'deference' and 'restraint'. He claims that deference is based on 'institutional competence' and represents 'what the courts can accept is a sound judgment of fact' on the part of the public authority; but this is not 'freedom of choice', because the court has to determine what is proportionate. By contrast, restraint represents recognition that there are a 'set of options which are legally acceptable because all are proportionate . . . There is no intrinsic reason why a judge could not make a choice as well, but such a choice would be illegitimate. Their role is to secure legality, not correctness.': J Rivers, 'Proportionality and Variable Intensity of Review' (2006) 65 *CLJ* 174, 193.

made; namely, whether it is proportionate. There is not a merits review of all aspects of the decision: it is not a 'full' merits review.

It may be putting the matter a little high to say that the roles of judges and decision-makers are 'fundamentally' distinct, even so. There are, for instance, situations where the issues of proportionality and best interests will be collapsed. This is the case, for example, where the essence of the decision that a public official has to make is whether a particular course of conduct is disproportionate. This is seen most clearly where there is a straight choice between two courses of action, one of which interferes with a protected right.[19] Consider for instance a decision to evict travellers from land that they do not own. The essential question is one of proportionality: would eviction constitute a disproportionate interference with private and family life or the enjoyment of possessions? Another example is deportation decisions. Since there are only two courses of action open to the public authority, the decision of the court will address the same issue as the public authority must address when making its decision. Even so, it is important to bear in mind that if the court finds that eviction of the travellers would be proportionate, this does not amount to a finding that eviction should take place or is the best or right course of action in terms of the public interest. That is a political question that the court remains barred from considering. Therefore even in such a case the roles of politician and judge are seen to be distinct.

Less commonly, cases also arise where there are a number of different options open to a public authority but where only one would be proportionate. Again, the distinction between the decision that the public official has to make and that which the courts make is collapsed. The only question is one of proportionality because the application of that test identifies only one course of action as legitimate. But these instances where proportionality and the merits are collapsed are neither alarming nor novel. There have always been rare cases in which the courts have stipulated that there is only one rational or reasonable decision open to a public authority and this determines what course of action the authority must take. Indeed, in such cases the courts have been prepared to make a mandatory order requiring the public authority to act in that way.[20] The existence of such cases does not mean that the roles of judges and decision-makers are not distinct, which is shown by the vast majority of cases where the issue of proportionality and the question of what is in the public interest are separate and can lead to different answers.

---

[19] This explains the case of *R (Wilkinson) v Broadmoor Hospital Authority*, [2002] 1 WLR 419. The Court of Appeal held that the court must inevitably reach its own view on whether or not the claimant was capable of refusing consent to medical treatment and whether it was necessary under Art 8 or in breach of Arts 2 or 3 ECHR. Since the courts now have jurisdiction to determine what is in a patient's best interests at common law and the only other criterion is whether treatment would breach a Convention right, the question whether treatment should be administered is subject to full merits review by the Family Division, subject to weight being afforded to the opinions of medical professionals.

[20] *R v Ealing LBC, ex p Parkinson* (1996) 8 Admin LR 281, 287 (Laws J).

These preliminary remarks indicate that the structure of proportionality, if it is to remain faithful to the third proposition derived from Lord Steyn's speech in *Daly,* must prevent collapse into 'full' merits review, in terms of stipulating in every case what course of action a public authority must take whilst at the same time involving the court in balancing the competing interests, in order to determine whether the balance struck is proportionate. The following section considers how the courts in this country and in other jurisdictions have sought to do this. Drawing on the lessons learnt from examining these cases, a more principled approach is then proposed.

Least Injurious Means and Fair Balance

The closest that domestic courts have come to establishing a structured approach to proportionality is in their adoption of the three-stage test of proportionality approved by the Privy Council in *de Freitas v Permanent Secretary of Ministry of Agriculture.*[21] This test was particularly influenced by the approach taken by the Supreme Court of Canada.[22] The *de Freitas* test was referred to by Lord Steyn in *Daly* and approved in the joint opinion of the Committee in *Huang,* as well as by the House of Lords in other cases.[23] It must therefore be taken to be firmly established as the test of proportionality in domestic law, at least in respect of Convention rights.[24] The three stages of this test are: (1) the legislative objective must be sufficiently important to justify limiting a fundamental right (often simply equated to the notion of 'legitimate aim'), (2) the measure designed to meet the objective must be rationally connected to it, and (3) the means used to impair the right must go no further than is necessary to accomplish the objective. The first stage is almost invariably satisfied. Its importance really lies in providing a structure and direction for the second and third stages. The second stage requires that the measure is rationally connected to the objective identified by the first stage. This is not the same as saying that the decision must be based on rational reasons. It requires that means chosen must advance the objective to an appreciable extent. It also provides a means of challenging measures which are over- or under-inclusive in their pursuit of a legitimate objective.[25] It is the third stage of the test which does most of the work in practice and which describes the balance that is

---

[21] *de Freitas v Permanent Secretary of Ministry of Agriculture* [1999] 1 AC 69.

[22] *Oakes* (n 6).

[23] *Daly* (n 1) [27]; *Huang* (n 5) [19]; *Shayler* (n 4) [61] (Lord Hope); *A v Secretary of State for the Home Department* [2005] 2 AC 68 [30] (Lord Bingham). It appears to have been common ground that this is the applicable test in respect of Convention rights in *Somerville* (n 4) [109] and [116].

[24] It has also been applied in the context of EC law; see, eg *Gough v Chief Constable of Derbyshire* [2002] QB 1213.

[25] See eg *Ghaidon v Godin-Mendoza* [2004] 2 AC 557.

required between individual rights and the public interest in attaining the legislative objective. In other cases and in other jurisdictions this aspect of the proportionality requirement is described as the 'least injurious means' or 'minimal impairment' test.[26] It is this aspect of the proportionality test which this chapter addresses.

The least injurious means test is problematic for a number of related reasons. Most obviously, it threatens to collapse the fundamental distinction between the role of judges and public officials. By specifying that public authorities must adopt the least intrusive course of action, the test appears to remove any element of choice or discretion from public authorities and legislatures as to what measure will best accomplish the public interest objective sought to be achieved. If, whenever a decision interferes with a protected right, the decision-maker is required to adopt a course that is 'least injurious' or 'minimal', and the court determines what that least injurious or minimal course of action is, then nothing is left over for the public official to decide in the public interest. Taken literally, the least injurious means test is therefore inconsistent with the proposition that the role of judges and public officials is distinct.

The problem is in fact more complicated than this, because in the overwhelming number of cases, any less injurious alternative will also be less effective in achieving the aim in question, to a greater or lesser extent. Adopting a less injurious alternative will almost always mean adopting a less effective alternative. It requires a trade-off between the attainment of the objective and the improvement in the position of those individuals whose protected rights are affected. But the least injurious means test does not contemplate the relevance of the respective efficacy of less intrusive measures. Taken at face value, at least, the third limb of the *de Freitas* test would require a public authority to adopt a less effective alternative measure wherever this reduces the interference with protected rights. It would appear to require a public authority to adopt a less injurious alternative, for instance, even where the improvement in the position of affective individuals is relatively slight or where the alternative is significantly less effective in attaining the objective in question, so long as it goes some way to attaining the objective. Certainly, the least injurious means test provides no criteria for gauging whether the extent of the improvement in the position of the person or persons whose rights are affected is sufficient to warrant a reduction in the effectiveness of the measure taken. It does not even suggest, on its face, that such a balancing exercise is required.

This difficulty was recognised by Maurice Kay LJ in *R (Clays Lane Housing Co-operative Ltd) v Housing Corp,* who remarked:

> If 'strict necessity' were to compel the 'least intrusive' alternative, decisions which were distinctly second best or worse when tested against the performance of a regulator's

---

[26] eg *Samaroo v Secretary of State for the Home Department* [2001] EWCA Civ 1139, [2001] UKHRR 1150; *R v Edwards Books and Art Ltd* [1986] 2 SCR 713; *RJR-MacDonald v Attorney-General (Canada)* [1995] 3 SCR 199 esp [160] (McLachlin J) (Canada); *Beit Sourik Village Council* (n 17) [41] (Israel).

statutory functions would become mandatory. A decision which was fraught with adverse consequences, would have to prevail because it was, perhaps quite marginally, the least intrusive. Whilst one can readily see why that should be so in some Convention contexts, it would be a recipe for poor public administration in the context of cases such as . . . the present case.[27]

Poor public administration may be something of an understatement, as the proportionality test, applied in this way, would extinguish the discretion of a public authority as to how best to achieve policy goals.

It will be suggested that there are solutions to these difficulties. But before explaining these solutions it is illuminating to address the way that courts have dealt with this issue. A helpful starting point is the judgment of the Supreme Court of Israel in the *Security Fence* case, which is the leading authority on the doctrine of proportionality in Israeli administrative law and under the Basic Law. In that case the Supreme Court articulated the 'least injurious means' test as follows: '[T]he means used by the administrative body must injure the individual to the least extent possible. In the spectrum of means which can be used to achieve the objective, the least injurious means must be used.'[28]

This is an emphatic statement that 'least injurious' means that which requires the most minimal interference with individual interests. However, the court went on to confine the application of the least injurious means test to narrow circumstances. The judgment makes clear that less injurious alternatives only need to be taken when such measures would be equally as effective, or more effective in attaining the desired objective. Essentially, less effective alternatives are not regarded as genuine, or comparable, alternatives.[29] This is perhaps the most obvious way that the least injurious means test can be reconciled with the need to maintain the different functions of judges and public official decision-makers because it only prescribes a particular course of conduct where that would not affect the attainment of the objective. The approach taken by the Supreme Court of Israel is however problematic.[30] It is sufficient to observe here that it is only very rarely the case in practice that a claimant will be able to point to a less injurious alternative that would be just as effective (or more effective) in attaining the objective. In the great majority of cases, less injurious alternatives will be less effective. If the test was confined in the manner contemplated by the Supreme Court of Israel, it would be rendered largely redundant. This is inconsistent with the prominence given to the least injurious means test as an aspect of the proportionality test. The *de Freitas* test would be shorn of its horns.

---

[27] *R (Clays Lane Housing Co-operative Ltd) v Housing Corp* [2005] 1 WLR 2229 [25].

[28] *Beit Sourik Village Council* (n 17) [41]. For discussion of the doctrine of proportionality articulated in Israeli law, see Hickman, 'Proportionality: Comparative Law Lessons' (n 6), 47–54.

[29] *Beit Sourik Village Council* (n 17) [58]. Although the Canadian case law is not so limited, McLachlin J stated in *RJR-MacDonald* (n 26), 'if the government fails to explain why a significantly less intrusive and equally effective measure was not chosen, the law may fail' ([160]).

[30] For an examination of the problems, see Hickman, 'Proportionality: Comparative Law Lessons' (n 6), 50–52.

Furthermore, the approach taken by the Israeli Supreme Court is not reflected in the approach of the Privy Council in *de Freitas* or in other, domestic, cases, which have implicitly accepted that adopting less intrusive alternatives may involve some reduction in the effectiveness of the measure taken. In *de Freitas* itself the Privy Counsel held that the Government of Antigua and Barbuda had to permit some classes of civil servants to express political views and this would undoubtedly be less effective in attaining the objective of maintaining the appearance of loyalty and impartiality of the civil service. A further example is also provided by *R (Laporte) v Chief Constable of Gloucester Constabulary*,[31] in which the House of Lords held that a chief constable had failed to show that there were not less drastic ways to prevent a breach of the peace at an anti-war demonstration at the Fairford RAF base other than escorting a coach full of protesters, which contained only a handful of known trouble-makers, back to London. In so holding, it was recognised that allowing the coach to proceed would undoubtedly have increased the risk of a breach of a peace, but this increased risk was considered to be insufficient to justify the drastic action that the police had taken.[32]

Domestic courts have, however, adopted an equally ingenious and not dissimilar solution to the problem presented by the least injurious means test to that taken by the Supreme Court of Israel. In a number of cases, the courts have defined the objective sought to be achieved very specifically, by close reference to the actual effects of the measure in question. This enables courts to say that the objective could not have been achieved by any other measures and, therefore, that no less injurious alternative means were available. This approach was explicitly taken by Wyn Williams J in *Smith v Secretary of State for Trade and Industry*. The claimants were Romany Gypsies and travellers who challenged an approval of a compulsory purchase order for land that they occupied which was needed for the Olympics redevelopment. It was claimed that the purchase should have been delayed until alternative accommodation had been identified for the claimants. Wyn Williams J recognised that, taken at face value, applying the least injurious means test would require a delay, hampering the redevelopment. He avoided this result by defining the objective of the purchase very narrowly. The objective of the compulsory purchase was, he held, to ensure that the site was in the possession of the London Development Agency by mid-June 2007. Since delaying the purchase could not have achieved this objective, it was held not to be a genuine alternative.[33] It was not therefore necessary to consider whether the impact of delay on the redevelopment was proportionate to the benefit that would accrue to the claimants.

---

[31] *R (Laporte) v Chief Constable of Gloucestershire* [2007] 2 AC 105.

[32] Lord Rodger mentioned that action could have been taken at RAF Fairford which would have materially reduced the risk of a breach of the peace, but it would not have avoided it altogether as turning back the coach had done ([69]). Lord Carswell stated that removing the known trouble-makers would have 'reduced the risk' of a breach of the peace ([105]).

[33] *Smith v Secretary of State for Trade and Industry* [2008] 1 WLR 394 [50].

Such an approach is also to be found in the *Countryside Alliance* case. The House of Lords, upholding the Court of Appeal, held that the Hunting Act 2004, which prohibits hunting foxes and other mammals with dogs, does not interfere with the right to respect for private life under Article 8 of the European Convention. Both courts (Lord Brown dissenting in the House of Lords) also held that had Article 8 been engaged, the ban was in any event proportionate. In so holding, Lord Bingham and Lord Hope in common with the Court of Appeal reasoned that since a principal objective of the legislation was to prevent suffering inflicted for recreation, which was judged by Parliament to be a cruel activity, rather than a reduction in suffering to animals overall, only an outright ban could have achieved this aim. Alternatives, such as a scheme promoted by the Government,[34] that would have allowed some hunting to continue, might not have been significantly less effective at reducing the suffering of foxes, but they would not have achieved the aim of prohibiting a practice that was judged to be unethical: only a ban could achieve that. The courts therefore avoided addressing the relative suffering caused by differing forms of control of foxes (including hunting itself).[35] There was no 'close and penetrating analysis of the factual justification' for the Hunting Act 2004, as has been held to be required:[36] it was simply held that since the aim (narrowly defined) was legitimate, an outright ban had to be proportionate since only such a ban was capable of achieving that aim.

As these cases illustrate, this approach relieves the proportionality principle of any effective role. If a very specific and legitimate aim can be identified, particularly where it is derived from or closely tied to the actual effect of the measure in question, then the issue of proportionality is largely redundant. It will almost

---

[34] The Hunting Bill 2002 (known as 'the Michael Bill') would have prohibited hunting of deer and hare coursing, but permitted hunting of foxes and mink with a dog if the hunting was exempt or registered. Registration could be obtained if it would significantly contribute to a reduction in damage caused by the animal sought to be hunted and this could not reasonably be achieved by means that caused significantly less pain and suffering to the animal.

[35] *R (Countryside Alliance) v Attorney-General* [2007] QB 305 [119]–[120], [2008] 1 AC 719. Lord Bingham stated that: 'If, as has been held, the object of the Act was to eliminate (subject to the specified exceptions) the hunting and killing of wild animals by way of sport, no less far-reaching measure could have achieved that end' ([46]). Lord Hope stated that since a reduction in the suffering of animals had not been a determinative objective, it was not necessary for those who promoted the legislation to have made a comparison with alternatives to a total ban of hunting for recreation ([78]). Baroness Hale considered that if Convention rights were engaged, the legislation fell within the margin of appreciation open to Parliament ([127]–[129]). Lord Brown held that had Art 8 been engaged, which to his regret it was not, he would have held then that the legislation was disproportionate in so far as it was based on moral indignation about hunting for sport lacking a legitimate aim ([153]–[154], [159]). Lord Rodger expressed no view on the point. Contrast the approach of the Divisional Court at [342], where the Court concluded that there was a reasonable basis for the conclusion that the legislation would reduce suffering. It went on to state that the Michael Bill was in any event not an appropriate measure to give effect to a judgment that hunting for recreation is cruel: [345]. For a further example, consider *R (Williamson) v Secretary of State for Education and Employment* [2005] 2 AC 246, esp [50] (Lord Bingham) and [86] (Baroness Hale): blanket prohibition on corporal punishment in schools was necessary to eliminate institutional violence.

[36] *Shayler* (n 4) [61] (Lord Hope).

inevitably be the case that the only measure that can achieve such an objective completely is the measure actually taken. The least injurious means test will not be applied, and there will be no assessment of the justification for choosing one measure in preference to another. The fact that the objective identified is regarded as legitimate will essentially resolve the issue of proportionality because the objective is to achieve precisely the result that has been attained.

The importance of this should not be underestimated. The argument is likely to be transposed to other contexts. For example, it would not be surprising to find the Government arguing that the objective of the next anti-terrorism measure is the *elimination of risk to the public* and therefore that only a measure that entirely removes a suspected person from society can meet this objective, and is therefore, ipso facto proportionate. It is not hard to see that the sidestep employed in *Smith v Secretary of State for Trade and Industry* and the *Countryside Alliance* case has the potential to rob the proportionality test of its function as a means for ensuring that there is a fair balance between individual rights and the desires of the general community, at least in many cases. This largely mirrors the shortcoming of the approach taken by Supreme Court of Israel.

It is in fact perfectly coherent to test even very specific objectives against alternatives that would not fully achieve the aim. As explained above, the least injurious means test anticipates a trade-off between the effectiveness of the measure in question and the degree of interference with individual rights. In the *Countryside Alliance* case, for instance, the alternatives to an outright ban should have been assessed as imperfect alternatives to the Hunting Act 2004. It may sometimes be necessary for imperfect solutions to be adopted, but the least injurious means test should not be regarded as requiring that they be adopted in every case. It is the misconception that the least injurious means test always requires a less effective measure to be adopted that lies behind the refusal of the courts to apply it in the cases considered above. If the court had assessed the less effective alternatives open to Parliament in the *Countryside Alliance* case, it is likely that it would not have regarded their rejection by Parliament as disproportionate, in particular because in practice a large amount of hunting would have continued and the alternatives would therefore have been very substantially less effective at achieving one of the aims, namely curtailing a practice regarded as cruel. Although it is unlikely to have made a difference on the facts of the *Countryside Alliance* case, it is crucial to effective protection of human rights under the Human Rights Act that courts do not avoid balancing the competing interests, which is an exercise that is integral to the proportionality assessment, and to requiring that imperfect measures are taken where this is required to protect fundamental rights.

A further problem with the approach taken in the *Countryside Alliance* case and *Smith v Secretary of State for Trade and Industry* is that it is doubtful whether it is often possible accurately to distil the objectives of a measure to the level of specificity relied upon in those cases where the measure is not accompanied by an explicit statement of its aims. The exercise of deducing implied objectives is particularly tortuous where the measure in question is primary legislation because it is the product of a vote and not supported by reasons.[37] A further difficulty in identifying specific objectives of legislation derives from the nature of proceedings under the Human Rights Act. Challenges to primary legislation are brought not against Parliament or any individual members, but against the sponsoring department and the Attorney-General. The *Countryside Alliance* case is a good example of these difficulties.[38] The Hunting Act 2004 was the product of a free vote in Parliament on a highly controversial issue, about which a plethora of different views are held. The objectives of those who voted for the measure are likely to have been diverse and not necessarily consistent. Moreover, the Bill that was originally introduced by the Government was very substantially amended—indeed fundamentally changed—during its passage through Parliament. In the Human Rights Act challenge, the Attorney-General and the Secretary of State for the Environment, Food and Rural Affairs (who were jointly represented) contended that the objective of the Hunting Act 2004 was not the ethical objective of prohibiting hunting for recreation, which ironically was ultimately the point on which the proportionality analysis turned in the Government's favour, but was the objective of the Bill that the Government originally introduced to Parliament, namely, reducing suffering and cruelty to animals per se. Whilst the claimants supported this view, the Divisional Court rejected both submissions and found (apparently of its own volition) that the position was more complex. It held that the objective of the Hunting Act 2004 was a 'composite one' of preventing or reducing unnecessary suffering to animals 'overlaid by a moral viewpoint that causing suffering to animals for sport is unethical and should, so far as is practical and proportionate, be stopped'.[39] The Court of Appeal and House of Lords both purported to accept this finding, although, as we have seen, it was the 'moral viewpoint' which it regarded as the predominant purpose and which justified sidestepping the least injurious means test. Given the important role played by the objective attributed to the legislation in resolving the issue of justification, the foundations of identifying this objective were remarkably infirm. Moreover, their Lordships also conveniently ignored the fact that the Divisional Court's finding was, in fact, that the 'ethical' dimension of the legislation was that causing suffering for sport should be stopped *so far as proportionate*. Attention to these words pulls the rug from beneath the reasoning in the Court of Appeal and House of Lords, because the ethical objective was stated to be qualified by the requirement of proportionality: it makes no sense to say that a total ban was proportionate because a less injurious measure would not meet the ethical objective when that objective was itself qualified by the requirement of proportionality. Yet the application of the

---

[37] See the discussion of Ronald Dworkin in *Law's Empire* (London, Fontana Press, 1991) 317–27.

[38] *Countryside Alliance* (n 35) Lord Hope remarked that: 'The findings of the courts below as to the legislative object of the 2004 Act which invited such detailed questions were, for the purpose of deciding this issue, unnecessarily elaborate' ([83]).

[39] *R (Countryside Alliance) v Attorney-General* [2006] Eu LR 178 [287]–[289] (defendant's submissions), [314] (claimants' submissions), [339] (court's conclusions).

proportionality test turned on these infirm nuances of Parliament's objective and led, essentially, to it being bypassed.

Thankfully, it will not always be open to the courts sensibly to define the objective of a measure in a manner that sidelines the least injurious means test. In many cases the aim of a measure is obviously more general and cannot be attributed such a specific objective as that attributed to the measures at issue in *Smith v Secretary of State for Trade and Industry* and the *Countryside Alliance* case. This is not however either a reassuring or a satisfactory answer. There are many cases in which this sidestep could be employed.

A further way that the courts have avoided the apparently undesirable implications of applying the least injurious means test is simply to ignore it. The House of Lords has taken this approach in cases involving 'broad social policy', in which the *de Freitas* test has not been cited. In these cases, on the issue of proportionality the speeches amount to little more than assertions that Parliament is entitled to choose as it sees fit between competing alternatives (possibly constrained by considerations of rationality). In *Wilson v First County Trust (No 2) Ltd,* for instance, Lord Nicholls stated that, in the context of consumer credit legislation, the court should not look at alternatives but should look only at the provision in question and its policy objective, 'and consider whether the provision bears so unfairly on the applicant that it was not open to Parliament to adopt this provision, even as part of an overall package . . .'.[40] In *R (Williamson) v Secretary of State for Education,* his Lordship stated in the context of a challenge to a ban on corporal punishment in all schools that, '[t]he legislature is to be accorded a considerable degree of latitude in deciding which course should be selected as the best course in the interests of school children as a whole'.[41] Similar approaches are to be found in cases concerning national policy on housing and welfare benefits.[42]

In yet another line of cases, the courts have found that a measure is proportionate on the basis that some accommodation has been made for individual rights, although the measure is not the most 'minimal' or 'least' injurious measure that was available. The *de Freitas* test has been cited in several of these cases, but the courts have not attempted to develop it or explain how the overall findings of

---

[40] *Wilson v First County Trust (No 2) Ltd* [2004] 1 AC 816 [79]. It was claimed that s 127(3) of the Consumer Credit Act 1974 was disproportionate in entirely excluding, by contrast with other provisions, a power of the court to enforce otherwise unenforceable money lending contracts in order to avoid hardship or unfairness to one of the parties. Lord Nicholls stated that the 'possible existence of alternative solutions does not in itself render the contested legislation unjustified' ([70]; see also [138] (Lord Hobhouse)). The case cannot be explained away as concerning Art 1 of the First Protocol, which requires a more relaxed approach to proportionality, since this did not form part of their Lordships' reasoning.

[41] *Williamson* (n 35) [51].

[42] See *R (Kay) v Lambeth LBC* [2006] 2 AC 465; *R (Carson) v Secretary of State for Work and Pensions* [2006] 1 AC 173; *R (Hooper) v Secretary of State for Work and Pensions* [2003] 1 WLR 2623 (CA), [2005] 1 WLR 1681. See further the exercise of the discretion by the Crown Prosecution Service: *R v G* [2008] 1 WLR 1379.

proportionality in these cases are to be rationalised with it.[43] For instance, in *R v Shayler* the House of Lords upheld a criminal prohibition on publication of information obtained by members of the security services in the course of their employment, under Article 10(2), although there was no public interest defence to prosecution and there were various ways that confidentiality and national security could have been protected by measures that were less intrusive of freedom of expression. Their Lordships held that sufficient accommodation had been made for those with public interest concerns.[44]

One way to make sense of these cases is suggested by the case law of the Supreme Court of Canada under the Canadian Charter of Rights and Freedoms 1982. The proportionality test applied under the Charter was articulated by Dickson CJ in his judgment in *R v Oakes*.[45] It includes the requirement that, 'the means, even if rationally connected to the objective . . . should impair "as little as possible" the right or freedom in question . . .'.[46] This requirement, referred to as the 'minimal impairment' test, divided the Supreme Court shortly afterwards in *R v Edwards Books and Art Ltd*, following criticism that it would paralyse the government's ability to regulate private activity.[47] In issue was an Ontario law prohibiting trading on Sundays. There was an exemption in the law for small businesses that wanted to observe a different Sabbath. It was argued that it was arbitrary for the exception to apply only to small businesses and the law could have exempted any person who demonstrated a sincere belief that they should observe a different Sabbath. This argument was accepted by Wilson J, who held that the minimal impairment test obliged the Ontario legislature to protect the freedom of religion of all those who wanted to observe a different Sabbath, not just a sub-group of them.[48] The

---

[43] *Shayler* (n 4); *R (Pretty) v DPP* [2002] 1 AC 800 (upholding blanket criminalisation of assisted suicide although criminalisation was not necessary in the claimant's case); *R (Rottman) v Commissioner of Police of the Metropolis* [2002] 2 AC 692 (common law power to search home when executing warrant for extradition proportionate although judicial search warrant could have been required); *Lichniak* [2003] 1 AC 903 (imposing mandatory life sentence where there was no risk of danger to the public); *Attorney-General v Punch Ltd* [2003] 1 AC 1046 (injunction prohibiting disclosure of information could have been more carefully tailored); *R (Animal Defenders International) v Secretary of State for Culture, Media and Sport* [2008] 2 WLR 781 (blanket ban on advertising on television by a body with mainly political objects upheld (Lord Scott at [44] suggested there may be contexts where it would go too far)).

[44] *Shayler* (n 4).

[45] *Oakes* (n 6).

[46] *Oakes* (n 6) [70].

[47] For an illuminating and incisive discussion of this case, including the memoranda passing between the Justices, see RJ Sharpe and K Roach, *Brian Dickson: a Judge's Journey* (Toronto, University of Toronto Press, 2004) 353–57. For criticism of *Oakes* see A Petter, 'The Politics of the Charter' (1986) 8 *Supreme Court Law Review* 473; P Monahan and A Petter, 'Developments in Constitutional Law: The 1985–86 Term' (1987) 9 *Supreme Court Law Review* 69.

[48] '[The legislature] cannot decide to subordinate the freedom of religion of some members of the group to the objective of a common pause day and subordinate the common pause day to the freedom of religion of other members of the same group. Yet this is the effect of the distinction between the large and small retailer adopted by the legislature in this legislation. It is, in my view, "a compromised scheme of justice" . . . The fault with s 3(4) [the small business exception] is, I believe, that it does not go far enough. It does not protect the freedom of religion of all those who close on Saturdays for religious reasons' ([208]).

Proportionality

majority upheld the law. Dickson CJ, Chouinard and Le Dain JJ, took the opportunity to make clear that minimal impairment does not always require that legislation impairs rights and freedoms to the smallest possible extent. Dickson CJ
stated that if the legislature had attempted 'very seriously to alleviate the effects of
those laws on Saturday observers' then the law would be justified. The small business exception, he held, represented a 'satisfactory effort'.[49] Although reaching the
same result, La Forest J regarded even this approach as too prohibitive. He urged
a departure from the test established in *R v Oakes* so that it would not be necessary
for any accommodation to be made where it might interfere with the objective
sought to be attained.[50] Instead, the majority led by Dickson CJ rearticulated the
minimal impairment test to make clear that so long as some accommodation is
made for individual rights, what is strictly the 'least intrusive' means does not have
to be taken. Legislatures are afforded some latitude to choose between ways of
achieving an objective. This approach was confirmed in *RJR-MacDonald Inc v
Attorney-General of Canada*, where McLachlin J (as she then was) stated that:

> If the law falls within a range of reasonable alternatives, the courts will not find it
> overbroad merely because they can conceive of an alternative which might better tailor
> objective to infringement.[51]

This approach has been followed by the Supreme Court,[52] and other invitations to
depart from the minimal impairment test to afford legislatures a freer hand in
matters of social policy have been rejected.[53]

It is therefore possible to view the domestic cases cited above as taking a similar
approach to the Canadian Supreme Court: as long as some accommodation has
been made to the rights of affected persons, and the legislation is reasonable overall, then it is regarded as proportionate. Such an analysis should not however be
accepted too readily. The Canadian jurisprudence is very far from a model of
clarity. In particular, it is difficult to predict when the presence of alternatives
will render a measure disproportionate.[54] Furthermore, the reintroduction of a
reasonableness test as articulated in *RJR-MacDonald Inc* would be difficult to rec-

---

[49] *R v Edwards Books and Art Ltd* [1986] 2 SCR 713 [148].

[50] 'In seeking to achieve a goal that is demonstrably justified in a free and democratic society, therefore, a legislature must be given reasonable room to manoeuvre to meet these conflicting pressures. Of
course, what is reasonable will vary with the context . . . In a case like the present, it seems to me, the
Legislature is caught between having to let the legislation place a burden on people who observe a day
of worship other than Sunday or create exemptions which in their practical workings may substantially
interfere with the goal the Legislature seeks to advance and which themselves result in imposing burdens on Sunday observers and possibly on others as well' ([183]). Beetz and McIntyre JJ also appreciated the potential effect of the *Oakes* test in limiting legislative freedom. For this reason, they held there
was no interference with religious freedom at all. They reasoned that if Jewish traders closed on
Saturdays as well as Sundays this was properly attributable to their religion and not to the Sunday
closing laws, although the *effect* was to restrict their religious freedom. This approach has not been
followed.

[51] *RJR-MacDonald* (n 26).

[52] These comments were approved in *Libman v Quebec (Attorney-General)* [1997] 3 SCR 569 [58].

[53] See *RJR-MacDonald* (n 26); *Newfoundland (Treasury Board) v NAPE* [2004] 3 SCR 381.

[54] Hickman, 'Proportionality: Comparative Law Lessons' (n 6), 44–45.

oncile with the fact that domestic courts, following Lord Steyn in *Daly,* have come to accept that a reasonableness test differs from the structured balancing exercise required by a proportionality assessment.[55] It would therefore represent a backwards step for our courts to follow the Canadian case law too closely on this point. The flexibility that has been built into the minimal impairment test in Canada has also rendered the third limb of the *R v Oakes* test of little practical significance.[56] The third limb states that even if there are no less injurious alternatives that ought to have been taken, nonetheless the measure may still be disproportionate if the *overall* impact of the measure on individual rights is disproportionate to the purposes it serves.[57] It will be suggested below that it is helpful to maintain a separation between these issues.

The relationship between the third limb of the proportionality test articulated in *R v Oakes* and the minimal impairment test articulated in *de Freitas* was considered by the House of Lords in *Huang.* It was submitted that the *de Freitas* formulation was deficient in omitting reference to the question of overall impact, which is the third limb of the proportionality test articulated in *R v Oakes.* The *de Freitas* test was, in other words, missing a limb. In a joint opinion, the House of Lords stated that this aspect 'should never be overlooked or discounted'.[58] These terse remarks failed to make clear whether their Lordships accepted that the requirement of overall fairness is an additional aspect of the proportionality test, so that a measure must be both least injurious and also proportionate overall[59] which is how it is treated in Canada; or whether the test of overall proportionality qualifies the *de Freitas* test so that, even where less intrusive measures could have been taken, if the measure viewed overall is proportionate there will be no breach of a protected right. There is more than a suggestion in *Huang* that the House of Lords viewed the least intrusive means test as subservient to the more general, less structured, question of whether overall the measure has struck a 'fair balance' between competing interests. This is an unfortunate aspect of *Huang,* since it has added to the already murky case law relating to the structure of the proportionality test.

[55] *Daly* (n 1) [24].

[56] Hickman, 'Proportionality: Comparative Law Lessons' (n 6), 45–47; See also PW Hogg, *Constitutional Law of Canada,* 5th edn supplemented, vol 2 (Toronto, Thomson, Carswell, 2007): 'So far as I can tell . . . this step has never had any influence on the outcome of any case. And I think that the reason for that is that it is redundant'; para 38.12, see also para 38.8.

[57] 'Even if an objective is of sufficient importance, and the first two elements of the proportionality test are satisfied, it is still possible that, because of the severity of the deleterious effects of a measure on individuals or groups, the measure will not be justified by the purposes it is intended to serve. The more severe the deleterious effects of a measure, the more important the objective must be if the measure is to be reasonable and demonstrably justified in a free and democratic society.' *Oakes* (n 6) [71].

[58] *Huang* (n 5) [19].

[59] This was also the approach of the Court of Appeal in *Samaroo* (n 26), a case preceding *Huang,* in which the Court of Appeal held that the question of proportionality should be approached in two stages. At the first stage, the court asks, 'can the objective of the measure be achieved by means which are less interfering of an individual's rights? . . . At the second stage, it is assumed that the means employed to achieve the legitimate aim are necessary in the sense that they are the least intrusive of Convention rights that can be devised in order to achieve the aim. The question at this stage of consideration is: does the measure have an excessive or disproportionate effect on the interests of affected persons?' ([19]–[20]).

A Proposed Solution: Relative and Overall Proportionality

It is now possible to turn to the way out of this muddle. The starting point is appreciating that there are two structural elements of the proportionality test. These can be described as 'relative' and 'overall' proportionality. Overall proportionality is the more straightforward. Overall proportionality compares the impact of the measure on individual rights together with the value in maintaining adherence to fundamental rights more generally (its costs) with the benefits of the measure in terms of the value of the objective that is actually achieved (its benefits). In very broad terms, what the court is doing when it evaluates overall proportionality is weighing the costs and benefits of the measure. That is not to say that the measure would be regarded as disproportionate if the court judges that the costs outweigh the benefits (even if it were possible to do so). That would essentially represent a correctness or public interest standard.[60] Furthermore, since the competing interests in play in human rights cases can be evaluated only in broad terms, both because of the inherent difficulty of placing a value on an interference with human rights and the difficulty in assessing the benefit of a measure to society generally, a precisely calibrated approach to competing costs and benefits is not possible.[61] The court is rather looking in broad terms at whether the costs of the measure stand in fair proportion to the benefits. This is reflected in the language of 'fair balance' employed by the Strasbourg Court and domestic courts. Possibly a more helpful way of expressing this is to say that a measure is disproportionate where there is a significant imbalance between the costs of a measure interfering with individual rights and its benefits to society.

In contrast, relative proportionality refers to the proportionality of choosing one measure *in preference to* another. This issue requires consideration of the relative costs and benefits of the available alternatives to the measure actually taken, if any, and a comparison between these and the costs and benefits of the chosen measure. In other words, the court's attention is directed to the *marginal utility* of the measure taken over the alternative(s). Again, the question of proportionality

---

[60] Although somewhat oddly it is more commonly expressed in legal analysis as a standard of reasonableness, see especially *United States v Carroll Towing Co* 159 F 2d 169, 173 (2d Cir 1947) in which Judge Learned Hand expressed the negligence test in terms of a utilitarian calculus. However, this approach does not take into account the possibility of a correctness standard. There are a number of other well-known problems with the so-called Hand Formula. For some discussion see DG Owen (ed), *Philosophical Foundations of Tort* (Oxford, OUP, 1995) 250–75, 474–75.

[61] Learned Hand himself recognised that his formula involves a judgment between incommensurables, and is therefore a jury question because it rests on 'commonly accepted standards, real or fancied': *Conway v O'Brian*, 111 F 2d 611, 612 (2d Cir 1940). However, we should not accept that the pros and cons are truly and completely incommensurable. The notion of fair balance implicitly accepts that they are capable of being compared in broad terms, which was also accepted by Learned Hand as the quotation makes clear. See also J Rivers, 'Proportionality and Variable Intensity of Review' (2006) 65 CLJ 174, 201.

should not be equated to the outcome of a cost benefit analysis. The question will usually be whether it is fair for individuals to bear a more significant interference with their rights where a less intrusive alternative measure could be taken, having regard to the added costs that would be entailed in taking that alternative measure (if any). Where there is a significant imbalance between the additional impact of the chosen measure and the saving to society in not taking the alternative, the state action can be regarded as disproportionate.[62] Another way to put this is to say that where the saving to society does not stand in proper proportion to the added impact on the individual, the measure will not be proportionate.

The crucial point being made here is that the precise way the balancing exercise is phrased is less important than that the exercise is carried out, and that it is recognised as different both from the question of overall proportionality and also from identifying whether a measure is the 'least injurious'.

There is no necessary connection between overall and relative proportionality. A measure may be proportionate overall because of its very great benefits, but may lack relative proportionality because an alternative measure is available which offers a significantly reduced impact on individuals without anything approaching a corresponding reduction in the ability of the state to attain the aim sought to be achieved. Equally, there may be no alternative measures available, or those that are available may be vastly less effective in meeting the objective, yet the measure may lack overall proportionality because the overall benefit of the measure does not stand in proper proportion to the impact on protected rights.

The next step is to recognise that these two aspects of the proportionality test are reflected, albeit imperfectly, in the case law on proportionality. The general question of overall proportionality is found in the third limb of the test set out in *R v Oakes* and in the notion of fair balance recognised by domestic courts, most significantly in *Huang*. On any view, this should now be an accepted part of the domestic test of proportionality.

The least injurious means test or the minimal impairment test found in the third stage of the *de Freitas* test is directed, albeit imperfectly, at relative proportionality because it requires a comparison between the measure taken and the alternatives. Although neither the Canadian nor UK courts have explicitly referred to relative proportionality, or articulated a criterion of proportionality for judging when one measure should be preferred to another, it helps to explain why the courts rarely require that governments adopt measures that represent the most minimal interference with protected rights and require only that some accommodation is made

---

[62] It follows from the text in this section that I cannot agree with Julian Rivers' suggestion that the test of proportionality or necessity reflects a Pareto optimal result, in the sense that, 'no alternative act could make the victim better off in terms of rights-enjoyment without reducing the level of realisation of some other constitutional interest' (J Rivers, 'Proportionality and Variable Intensity of Review' (2006) 65 *CLJ* 174, 198). Proportionality clearly does require a trade-off between the attainment of an end and rights-enjoyment. The relevant test of efficiency is Kaldor-Hicks efficiency, which says that a redistribution (ie alternative measure) is more efficient where those that benefit gain more overall than those who lose out (it is usually expressed in terms of the winners being theoretically able to compensate the losers).

for them. Governments will only be required to adopt alternatives that would be much less effective in attaining the objective where there was an even more significant reduction its deleterious effects. In cases such as *R v Shayler,* the court was influenced by the significant difficulties that would have been entailed in enforcing the Official Secrets Act and maintaining official secrecy if individuals could raise a defence of public interest in criminal proceedings or if they were at liberty to divulge information without prior authorisation. Therefore requiring a more tailored, less intrusive, legislative scheme, although possible, would, in the view of the House of Lords, have risked significantly reducing the effectiveness of the law on official secrets. It is also noticeable that in cases where significantly less intrusive measures are required, such as those anticipated in *de Freitas* and *Laporte,* these would have greatly reduced the impact on individual rights, indeed would have avoided any infringement altogether in respect of the junior civil servants who had to be exempted from the legislation considered in *de Freitas* and the protesters who had no intentions of breaching the peace in *Laporte.* Moreover, the courts in these cases appear to have accepted that such less intrusive measures, although entailing some reduction in the degree to which the objective could be attained, would not have been significantly or markedly less effective. The notion of relative proportionality is therefore close to the surface of the case law, although it has not yet been explicitly articulated by domestic courts.[63]

We are now in a position to draw some conclusions and make some suggestions as to how the structure of the proportionality test should be clarified in domestic law.

First, the minimal impairment or least injurious means test should be understood as a test of relative proportionality. It requires attention to the relative costs and benefits of the measure actually taken compared to the costs and benefits of any alternatives. Whether or not a public authority or legislature is required to take a less intrusive measure will depend on whether it is unfair for affected individuals to bear the additional impact of the measure actually taken, having regard to the degree to which that measure better achieves the stated aim and so represents an additional benefit to society generally.

Secondly, it would be preferable to abandon the language of minimal impairment and least injurious means altogether because it is misleading in suggesting that wherever there is a less intrusive alternative this must be taken. It does not provide a clear signal to courts and public authorities as to what is required by the proportionality principle and, as we have seen, has led to confusion and circumvention in domestic and foreign cases. It would be preferable to speak in terms of relative proportionality between the measure taken and possible alternatives.

[63] These two aspects of the proportionality test, namely, relative and overall proportionality, have however been expressly articulated by the Supreme Court of Israel as its third 'subtest' of proportionality (rational connection and least injurious means being the first and second subtests). The third subtest requires, first, a direct comparison between the advantages of the administrative act and the damage that results from it. The measure must bear a 'proper proportion' to the benefits gained from the interference. Secondly, the court must examine in a 'relative manner' how the measure compares with possible alternatives (*Beit Sourik Village Council* (n 17) [41]).

Thirdly, the test of overall fair balance should be understood as additional to the least injurious means test: a failure to satisfy either test should render a measure disproportionate. The test of overall proportionality refers to the overall impact of a measure (that is, not the relative impact) as compared with the overall benefits to society.

The Future of Proportionality

The reception of the principle of proportionality into domestic law has been a great advance, but it must be accompanied by a well-thought-out, clear, consistent and principled approach to its content and structure. This has not so far occurred. The law on proportionality presently fails to meet up to Lord Steyn's expectation that the proportionality test would provide courts with a more intrusive, precise and sophisticated test to apply to administrative decisions and policies. There is a real danger that proportionality will become no more than a label attached to the outcome of a judge's consideration of the facts of case. Although there is, of course, often an element of backwards-reasoning in judicial decision-making, the principle of proportionality can provide courts with a reasonably precise template for assessing whether an interference with a protected right is justified, whilst also providing practitioners with a reasonably accurate way of predicting the outcome of judicial decisions and providing public authorities with a reasonably clear understanding of what sort of decisions will be held to represent an unjustified interference with a protected right.

For the same reason that the internal structure of proportionality needs to be carefully and clearly structured, its relationship with other substantive standards in public law must also reflect a broader principled structure.[64] But establishing such a structure must follow the more immediately important exercise of establishing a clear and principled approach to the doctrine of proportionality itself. There is little prospect of establishing a satisfactory relationship between proportionality and other principles of public law until proportionality is itself properly understood and applied. We are at a crossroads, and there is a choice: proportionality can either become the fig leaf for unstructured judicial decision-making, or it can become a powerful normative and predictive tool in public law. This chapter has suggested some next steps down the latter path.

---

[64] This is the subject of ch 9.

7

Reasonableness

N O PRINCIPLE IN public law is as conceptually muddled as the principle of reasonableness. The principle is also much maligned and apparently threatened by continental competitors; most directly, it is claimed, the principle of proportionality. It is thus in double-trouble—a potential victim of both fragmentation and usurpation. For many, the enactment of the Human Rights Act sounded the death knell for the reasonableness principle, and as the Court of Appeal indicated in one case, following the reception of proportionality into domestic law, all that remained was for the House of Lords to 'perform the burial rites' for the reasonableness principle.[1] This chapter explains that on the contrary, the reasonableness principle is alive and well and it has a central place in public law after the Human Rights Act.

The discussion in this chapter also goes further. It contends that the Human Rights Act provides an opportunity for a review and rationalisation of the muddled and fragmented law on the principle of reasonableness. Engaging in that task, this chapter looks back to uncover the origins of the principle of reasonableness, an exercise that reveals both how the law has become confused, and a clear path back to a more principled position. It is argued that the Human Rights Act can and should forge a reunion of tort and administrative law and give rise to a single standard applicable to public decision-making in cases where reasonableness is the appropriate test.

Review and Rationalisation

There are two main reasons why the Human Rights Act provides the impetus for a review and rationalisation of the principle of reasonableness in modern public law. In the first place, the Human Rights Act introduces a new standard of reasonableness alongside the principle of proportionality. This is a bold claim, that will have to be made good in the discussion that follows. Secondly, the Human Rights Act applies to all decisions of public officials. It does not treat 'discretionary' decisions

---

[1] R (Association of British Civilian Internees: Far East Region) v Secretary of State for Defence [2003] QB 473 [35].

or 'policy' decisions as a separate category, subject to different standards. Nor does the Human Rights Act provide for different standards depending on whether a claim is proceeding by way of an ordinary civil claim or by way of judicial review: the standards of the European Convention apply however the claim is proceeding and whatever the nature of the decision in question. Put shortly, all decisions and conduct by public authorities must be compatible with Convention rights. By contrast, modern public law has created two separate (albeit overlapping) domains of public law: administrative law and tort law. Different tests and standards are applied, depending on the nature of decision that is made and the procedural route that the claim takes. The Human Rights Act requires joined-up thinking between these two domains of law and will increasingly challenge their very existence. Taken together, these two factors—the introduction of a new standard of reasonableness and the unitary nature of the obligations under the Human Rights Act—give rise to a compelling case for a review and rationalisation of the reasonableness principle. These points will become clearer as the discussion progresses.

Origins

Before we can re-evaluate meaningfully the principle of reasonableness in modern law, it is necessary to examine how the conceptual quagmire came about. It will be seen that the separation of tort law and administrative law principles is of recent and dubious pedigree, and that the approach taken by the courts until the second half of the twentieth century was more principled and straightforward.

If we trace the principle of reasonableness back through the volumes of the law reports, we find that the trail leads not to cases on the availability of the prerogative writs of certiorari, prohibition and mandamus, but to damages cases. Thus, the principle of reasonableness can be traced back to at least *Leader v Moxon,*[2] decided in 1773. In that case, the plaintiff complained that Paving Commissioners had raised the street adjacent to his property by six feet, blocking doors and windows, and leading to his tenants giving up the premises and refusing to pay rents. It is to be noted that there was never a question of the Commissioners having acted in bad faith; their design had been to create a 'regular descent' in the road from one end to the other. The Commissioners had, moreover, acted under statute that granted them power to direct alterations or repairs to streets, 'in such manner as the Commissioners shall think fit'. The issue before the King's Bench Division was whether an action could lie against the Commissioners. It was first submitted on the Commissioners' behalf that the legislation provided for an appeal to the Justices of the Peace at Quarter Sessions and this ousted any action in the King's Bench Division. It was also argued that if the Commissioners had power to alter the road they must have power to raise it, and if they had power to raise it an inch then 'they may lawfully raise it a foot, or six feet, as hath been done in the present

---

[2] *Leader v Moxon* (1773) 2 Bl 929, 96 ER 546, 3 Wils KB 461, 95 ER 1157 (Gould, Blackstone, and Nares, JJ, absent De Grey, CJ).

case'.[3] By such inexorable logic, which over the succeeding centuries has been pressed upon courts countless times by counsel for public authorities, it was said that if the court allowed the action, it would be cutting down authority conferred by statute. The statutory power to raise was said to be limitless, at least, it must be assumed, until such time as an alteration became something else entirely.

The Court's outrage at the Commissioners' misguided act of street improvement is palpable from report. The judges declined to grant mandamus to compel the Quarter Sessions to hear an appeal on the basis that the justices would have no power to give just satisfaction in damages. Then, without troubling the plaintiff's counsel, the Court held that the Commissioners had 'grossly exceeded their powers', since their discretion was limited 'by reason and law'. Their Lordships reasoned that, 'the Act could never intend that any of the householders should pay a rate of 1s. 6d. in the pound in order to have their houses buried under ground . . . .'.[4] The judges were notably unconcerned by any lack of expertise in street improvements (on their part or a jury's) and opined that, rather than a regular descent, a variety of descents might have been made, as the situation of the ground required.[5]

Leader v Moxon demonstrates a number of points very clearly. First, even in the eighteenth century, the position was established that apparently unfettered discretionary power could properly be read subject to a principle of reasonableness. Secondly, whilst the judges would no doubt have been slow to examine the minutiae of street repairs,[6] they felt no compunctions about second-guessing public officials employing special expertise. And, thirdly, there was no concern to apply a special or different standard of reasonableness because the Commissioners were exercising a statutory discretion than if they had been private landowners causing a nuisance to their neighbours. Yet even at this early stage in the case law, we find the seeds of conceptual confusion. In one report of *Leader v Moxon* (although, notably not Blackstone's report), Blackstone J is recorded as having remarked: 'I think the Commissioners have acted arbitrarily and tyrannically, and the damages are too small.'[7] The comment was later relied upon to suggest that it was necessary for a plaintiff to show that discretionary power had been exercised tyrannically or oppressively to establish that the statutory discretion had been exceeded and damages could be awarded.[8] This led to some muddle in the case law, which may well also have reflected increasing uncertainty about how to treat the growing number

---

[3] *Leader v Moxon* (n 2), 466.

[4] This comment seems to have been made by Blackstone J: 3 Wils KB 461, 468. Interestingly, Blackstone's own report of the case records the judgment as rather more measured, and less agitated, than the independent report.

[5] 2 Bl 924, 926. The outcome was therefore that the court found an action could lie against the Commissioners. The question of liability would ultimately have had to be settled by a jury if the defence was pursued.

[6] Blackstone J records the court as having decided that the justices at Quarter Sessions would be appropriate to 'adjust little disputes': 2 Bl 924, 926.

[7] 3 Wils KB 461, 468.

[8] *Sutton v Clarke* (1815) 6 Taunt 29, 42–43 (Gibbs CJ) (although on the facts the defendant had acted reasonably).

of statutory offices and statutory authorities created by Parliament in the nineteenth century. It is commonly found in the reports that the judges simply ran together the various standards that were referred to in earlier cases, without any sustained attempt to reconcile them. Thus, we find in one case a statement that an action would lie if a discretion had been exercised 'arbitrarily, carelessly or oppressively' or 'arbitrarily, wantonly, or oppressively'.[9]

Towards the end of nineteenth century some judges had begun the search for the wood in the trees. In one fascinating case in the Chancery Division decided in 1879 the reasonableness principle and its application to the exercise of discretionary powers was articulated with commendable clarity by the Vice Chancellor. The case concerned a decision by the Vestry of St James, Westminster (exercising statutory powers under the Metropolis Local Management Act 1855) to site a public urinal in a tiny cul-de-sac accessed from Regent Street. Malins VC accepted that there was 'a great want of a public urinal in Regent Street', but rejected the submission that the vestry had 'been made the supreme judge of the place, and cannot be controlled unless they are acting in bad faith'. The reasoning, logic, and articulation of respective roles of courts and administrators by Malins VC, has resonance even today:[10]

> . . . if the question before me were simply whether they were right in selecting the place, and whether one place or another was better, I should be bound to decide that the vestry are the sole judges as to what the situation should be. But great as the powers of vestries under the Act are, they are not absolute, and vestries are, like all other public bodies, liable to be controlled by this Court if they proceed to exercise their powers in an unreasonable manner, whether they are induced to do so by improper motives or from error of judgment.

In the previous year the House of Lords had applied the same principle to private persons incorporated by a local Act of Parliament for the purpose of constructing a reservoir and regulating water flow on the Upper Bann. In the course of his judgment (not referred to in the *Regent Street Urinal* case), Lord Blackburn famously stated:

> I take it, without citing cases, that it is now thoroughly well established that no action will lie for doing that which the legislature has authorised, if it be done without negligence, although it does occasion damage to anyone; but an action does lie for doing that which the legislature has authorised, if it be done negligently. And I think that if by a reasonable exercise of the powers, either given by statute to the promoters, or which they have

---

[9] *Boulton v Crowther* (1824) 2 B & C 703, 707 (Abbott CJ) and 707 (Bayley J). For other examples: *Goldberg & Sons Ltd v Mayor of Liverpool* (1900) 82 LT 362, 363 (Hall VC); *Whitehouse v Fellowes* (1861) 10 CB (NS) 765, 780 (Williams J); cf *Southwark and Vauxhall Water Co v Wandsworth Local Board* [1898] 2 Ch 603, 611 ('reasonably': Collins LJ).
[10] *Vernon v Vestry of St James, Westminster* (1880–81) LR 16 Ch D. 449, 459 (Malins VC) (the *Regent Street Urinal* case). The case was heard over seven days, and many witnesses were examined, although the reasonableness of the decision was not the only factual matter in issue. The Vice Chancellor's judgment was upheld by the Court of Appeal a year later (same report).

at common law, the damage could be prevented it is, within this rule, 'negligence' not to make such reasonable exercise of their powers.[11]

It is clear from this passage that Lord Blackburn considered that the unreasonable exercise of powers, coupled with actionable harm, could found an action in negligence. There is in both these cases the same simplicity and rationality that was displayed by the court a hundred years before in *Leader v Moxon*. There remained, nonetheless, the line of authority to which attention has already been drawn, where the law was not expressed in such straightforward terms. In *Howard-Flanders v Maldon Corporation*, decided in 1926, Scrutton LJ finally disproved the formula which he said had appeared in the cases for about a hundred years, 'which strings together . . . a series of adjectives or adverbs'.[12] In that case—another road improvement case—an action was brought against a highway authority which had, in perfectly good faith and for the public good, widened a road up to the plaintiff's front door. The plaintiff alleged that it was dangerous, inconvenient, and that water-flow was liable to cause damage to his property. The Court of Appeal upheld the finding of a county court judge that the powers had been exercised unreasonably. Scrutton LJ considered that it was 'much more intelligible and satisfactory' simply to ask whether the statutory powers had been exercised 'with reasonable regard to the rights of others'.[13]

Then, in 1940 in *East Suffolk Rivers Catchment Board v Kent*, which for many years was the governing authority on public authority liability in tort, Lord Atkin considered many of the cases again and, like Scutton LJ had done before him, cut through the verbiage. He stated that he regarded it as established in law that, 'a public authority whether doing an act which it is its duty to do, or doing an act which it is merely empowered to do, must in doing the act do it without negligence, or as it is put in some of the cases must not do it carelessly or improperly.'[14] Whilst the word 'reasonableness' was not used here, the reference to 'improperly' contemplated that a public authority making a careful but unreasonable decision could not claim to be acting properly with the authority of Parliament. In these cases references to reasonableness and carefulness were not expressions of deference or restraint to the judgment of the public authority. They reflected the principle established in *Mersey Docks v Gibbs* that public bodies were subject to the same duties and liabilities as those applying to public individuals, unless they had

---

[11] *Geddis v Proprietors of the Bann Reservoir* (1877–78) LR 3 App Cas 430, 455–56 (Lord Blackburn). The case is consistently supported by later authority, eg: *Lagan Navigation Co v Lambeg Bleaching, Dyeing and Fishing Co* [1927] AC 226.

[12] *Howard-Flanders v Maldon Corporation*(1926) 135 LT 6, 11–12; approving the formulation in *Southwark & Vauxhall Water Company v Wandsworth Local Board* 79 LT Rep 132, (1898) 2 Ch 603; and *Roberts v The Charing Cross Electric Railway Company* 87 LT Rep 732.

[13] Lord Hanworth MR held that it was not sufficient for the authority to show it had acted bona fide, but he did not distil any particular test from the authorities (*Howard-Flanders* (n 12), 11), Sargant LJ held that the obligation of the authority was to use reasonable care not to do any unnecessary damage (ibid, 12).

[14] *East Suffolk Rivers Catchment Board v Kent* [1941] AC 74, 90.

been excluded by statute.[15] Where a private person is duty-bound to act reasonably, so is a public authority or private person acting under statutory power. The exception was if the statute authorised the particular act or decision in question.[16] In such a case, the standard was over-ridden by the statutory mandate. Whilst there were other important exceptions where no action would lie in tort, in particular actions against the Crown or, in the absence of malice or bad faith, against those undertaking judicial functions, the exceptions were limited and do not detract from the straightforward application of a general reasonableness standard when tort liability was not excluded.[17]

The straightforward approach found in the early authorities has much to commend it, and does not detract from the diversity of situations to which the principle could be applied, ranging from simply careless to coldly considered but unreasonable decisions. Moreover, there was no difficulty in applying a reasonableness test to an authority's express consideration of its statutory powers. This is shown by a later case in which the plaintiff, who had been detained against his will under the Mental Deficiency Act 1913, argued that he had not been 'found neglected' within the meaning of the statute. The Court of Appeal considered that damages might follow if there had been a lack of reasonable care by the authority in considering and exercising its statutory powers.[18] The principle of reasonableness was not, of course, free-standing. It could only be invoked where the authority had caused harm, such as to found an action in tort.[19] But it was true to say that where the exercise of statutory powers caused injury or invaded a right, subject to contrary intention, the discretion had to be exercised reasonably.

There is one other question arising from these cases, which did not seem to be of much concern to the courts before the middle of the twentieth century, but which became of increasing importance as that century progressed, and ended up, as we shall see, quite unnecessarily driving the law into the conceptual quagmire from which it has not yet extracted itself. The question is whether, when a public authority acted unreasonably, and was found liable, it had acted intra or ultra vires. The better interpretation of the old cases is certainly that unreasonable conduct took an authority outside its powers, and in that sense it acted ultra vires.[20] It

---

[15] In *Mersey Docks & Harbour Board Trustees v Gibbs* (1866) LR 1 HL 93, 110–13, Lord Blackburn stated that a statutory body is subject to the same duties as the law would impose on a private individual doing the same thing.

[16] This is the consistent principle to emerge from the cases. It is probably best expressed by the House of Lords in *Geddis* (n 11) and the Court of Appeal in the *Regent Street Urinal* case (n 10).

[17] See *Everett v Griffiths* [1921] 1 AC 631.

[18] *Richardson v London County Council* [1957] 1 WLR 751 (approved by Hale LJ in *Wilkinson's* case); cf *De Freville v Dill* [1927] All ER Rep 205; *Harnett v Bond* [1925] AC 669.

[19] Two great judges of the time, Lord Atkin and Scrutton LJ, understood the law in this way: compare *Everett v Griffiths* [1920] 3 KB 163 (CA) 211–12 (Atkin LJ); *R v Roberts* [1924] 2 KB 695 (CA) 719 (Scrutton LJ), 727 (Atkin LJ); *East Suffolk Rivers Catchment Board* (n 14) 89–90 (Lord Atkin).

[20] *Mayor and Councillors of East Fremantle v Annois* [1902] AC 213; *Roberts v Charing Cross Railway Co* (1903) 87 LT 732; *Whitehouse v Fellows* (1861) 10 CB (NS) 765; *British Cast Plate Manufacturers v Meredith* (1792) 4 TR 794. For a sustained analysis supporting this view, see CB Bourne, 'Discretionary Powers of Public Authorities: Their Control by the Courts' (1948) *Toronto Law Journal* 395.

is clear from *Leader v Moxon* itself that the Paving Commissioners were held to have exceeded their powers. The central issue in most of the cases was whether the particular decision was or was not authorised by the governing statute. It follows logically that in those cases where liability was found to exist, the authority was considered to have acted outside its statutory authority, which is to say, ultra vires. It is true that some of the cases suggest that an unreasonable decision was an abuse, but not an excess, of power;[21] but from a modern perspective at least this is a distinction without a difference. Even an abuse of power takes a public authority outside its powers. In any event, the distinction has been recognised as faulty: in a judgment delivered in 1901 Lord MacNaughten, after reviewing many of the authorities, reached the sound and prophetic conclusion that, 'the only question is, Has the power been exceeded? Abuse is only one form of excess.'[22]

Fragmentation

In the twentieth century, courts were, increasingly, prepared to find implied duties in statutory powers that the powers be exercised reasonably, even where the exercise of the power did not cause harm capable of giving rise to an action in tort.[23] An important line of authority held that if the terms of a statutory power could not reasonably bear the conclusion reached by the decision-maker on the facts before them, jurisdiction would be have been exceeded.[24] However, the rapid expansion in the amount of general discretionary power in the twentieth century and the fact that proportionately fewer decisions touched the tortiously-protected interests of individuals meant that firmer and broader assertion of the reasonableness principle was required.[25] The concept of unreasonableness described by Lord Greene MR in *Associated Provincial Picture Houses v Wednesbury Corporation*, decided in 1947, was eventually adopted as a generally applicable standard in the administrative context.[26]

This standard differed from the principle of reasonableness that had been applied in the tort cases in two main respects. In the first place, Lord Greene was

---

[21] *Sutton v Clarke* (1815) 6 Taunt 29; *Boulton v Crowther* (1824) 2 B & C 703.

[22] *Mayor and Councillors of East Fremantle v Annois* [1902] AC 213 (PC) 218.

[23] eg *Roberts v Hopwood* [1925] AC 578; *Harman v Butt* [1944] KB 491. For some very early cases see HWR Wade and CF Forsyth, *Administrative Law*, 8th edn (Oxford, OUP, 2000) 353 and EG Henderson, *Foundations of English Administrative Law* (Cambridge Massachusetts, Harvard UP, 1963) 40–41.

[24] *Allison v General Council of Medical Education and Registration* [1894] 1 QB 750; *Lee v Showmen's Guild of Great Britain* [1952] 1 All ER. 1175; *R v Medical Appeal Tribunal, ex p Gilmore* [1957] 1 QB 575.

[25] SA de Smith, *Judicial Review of Administrative Action* (London, Stevens, 1959) 214: 'English law has not adopted a general principle that the validation of administrative action is conditional upon its reasonableness'; G Ganz, 'The Limits of Judicial Control over the Exercise of Discretion' [1964] *PL* 367.

[26] *Associated Provincial Picture Houses v Wednesbury Corporation* [1948] 1 KB 223. In the *GCHQ* case Lord Diplock referred to 'irrationality' as standing on its own feet across the entire field of administrative law. *Wednesbury* unreasonableness and irrationality are treated as synonymous, so much so that the standard is sometimes expressed in terms of '*Wednesbury* irrationality': *Council for Civil Service Unions v Minister for the Civil Service* [1985] AC 374, 410.

concerned with articulating the power of the courts to intervene rather than articulating a standard that the local authority had to abide by.[27] It is principally a case about the level of intrusiveness of the court's supervision of government, not about the duties that government officials owe to private individuals. Furthermore, Lord Greene articulated the standard in an extremely deferential way such that it disclaimed any power of the courts to intervene to quash a decision on grounds of simple unreasonableness; instead it required 'something overwhelming'. His Lordship had regard not only to the respective institutional responsibility of the courts and the authority but also, and importantly, considerations which in modern parlance would be called deference or restraint ('the local authority are entrusted by Parliament with the decision on a matter which the knowledge and experience of that authority can best be trusted to deal with'). In other words, not only is the court not the primary decision-maker, but the court is not able to make the decision as well as the authority. This led Lord Greene to set the 'four corners' of the applicable legal principles governing when a court can intervene a long way back.

The *Wednesbury* case was not, however, regarded as of any great significance at the time; not in any event by Lord Greene himself, who reserved giving judgment, if at all, only over the weekend and then said that the law was so 'well-known' and 'understood' that it was unnecessary to cite authority for the propositions that he set out.[28] The case was initially regarded as a case about local government powers, but de Smith at least recognised that it had potentially wider implications because it followed logically that if the courts could not legitimately scrutinise the exercise of statutory powers on grounds of simple unreasonableness, they should and could not properly do so in contexts such as tort claims where this was the applicable standard.[29] This is, in the event, precisely what happened. The principle became a generally applicable standard applicable to administrative decisions and it came to replace the principle of reasonableness even where private rights were in issue, thus reversing authorities of the highest authority all the way back to *Leader v Moxon*.

Lord Diplock's speech in *Home Office v Dorset Yacht* is the primary source of the disjuncture between the administrative and tortious conceptions of reasonableness. We have seen that this case was also the first occasion that the term 'public law' was used in its modern form in a reported domestic case (by Lord Diplock).[30]

---

[27] See ch 4, pp 102–103.

[28] [1948] 1 KB 223, 231.

[29] de Smith (n 25) 219, noting that this had implications for review of central government powers since the jurisdiction of the courts 'cannot, of course, be any wider'. The case also had no application to statutory tribunals and no direct application outside the local government context. In *Anisminic v Foreign Compensation Commission* [1969] 2 AC 163 several members of the House of Lords summarised the grounds on which a statutory tribunal might exceed its powers, but they did not mention the *Wednesbury* case, see eg Lord Reid at 171 and Lord Pearce at 195. The principle in *Edwards v Bairstow* [1956] AC 14 did, however, provide the basis for a similar jurisdiction to imply an error of law from irrational conduct.

[30] *Home Office v Dorset Yacht Co Ltd* [1970] AC 1004. His Lordship first employed the term in two opinions of the Privy Counsel given on 11 December 1969: *Ranaweera v Ramachandran* [1970] AC 962

These developments went hand-in-hand. Lord Diplock expressly rejected the straightforward approach embodied in *Geddis v Proprietors of the Bann Reservoir*, the essence of which was that private law rights and principles were applicable without modification to statutory authorities unless excluded by statute. Lord Diplock saw this approach as inapplicable in the modern age. He said that the courts' function 'is confined in the first instance to deciding whether the act or omission complained of fell within the statutory limits imposed upon the department's or authority's discretion'.[31] Whereas previously, as we have seen, this was achieved by assessing the reasonableness of the decision, Lord Diplock considered that:

> ... public law concept of *ultra vires* has replaced the civil law concept of negligence as the test of legality, and consequently of the actionability, of acts or omissions of government departments or public authorities in the exercise of discretion conferred on them by Parliament as to the means by which they are to achieve a particular public purpose.[32]

This was because he considered that the courts only had 'jurisdiction' to impose limitations on discretionary power derived from the 'public law concept of *ultra vires*'.[33] This jurisdictional premise was central because in Lord Diplock's view it was the foundation for the development of modern administrative law. It is what united the supervisory jurisdiction of the courts over inferior courts and tribunals with that over executive exercise of statutory discretion.[34] In the exercise of this jurisdiction, according to Lord Diplock, Parliament could only intend that the courts intervene if 'no reasonable person could have reached [the conclusion] *bona fide*' (ie the *Wednesbury* principle).[35] This public law jurisdiction therefore logically, as de Smith had foreseen, ousted and replaced the private law approach and the *Wednesbury* principle replaced the reasonableness principle in all actions against public officials exercising statutory powers. Henceforth, *Wednesbury* was the touchstone of the reasonableness principle and the historical legacy was marginalised. The approach became orthodoxy.[36]

(PC); *Kodeeswaran v Attorney-General Ceylon* [1970] AC 1111 (PC). *Dorset Yacht* was decided in May of the following year. Lord Wilberforce spoke of 'administrative law' in *Malloch v Aberdeen Corporation* [1971] 2 All ER 1278 but, perhaps significantly, preferred 'public law' in *Anns v Merton LBC* [1978] AC 728, 754, 756 and 757. For an earlier use of the term 'public law' in a different sense see *Burmah Oil v Lord Advocate* [1965] AC 75, 129 and 135 (Viscount Radcliffe).

[31] *Dorset Yacht* (n 30), 1068.

[32] *Dorset Yacht* ibid, 1067. Lord Diplock had suggested (1066) that the 'public law' approach only applies when interests otherwise protected by tort were not affected, but this was swallowed by his overriding test based on statutory discretion. See generally, C Harlow, *Compensation and Government Torts* (London, Sweet & Maxwell, 1982) 51–57; SH Bailey and MJ Bowman, 'The Policy/Operational Dichotomy—A Cuckoo in the Nest' (1986) 45 *CLJ* 430, 430–41.

[33] *Dorset Yacht* (n 30), 1065.

[34] In *Re Racal Communications Ltd* [1981] AC 374, 382 Lord Diplock described the *Anisminic* case as 'a legal landmark; it has made possible the rapid development in England of a rational and comprehensive system of administrative law on the foundation of the concept of ultra vires.'

[35] *Dorset Yacht* (n 30), 1068.

[36] In Professor Wade's *Administrative Law*, tort was initially treated in the chapter on 'Judicial Control of Administrative Powers: Acting in the Wrong Manner' (Oxford, Clarendon Press, 1961), but in the 1977 4th edition it was shifted to the rear of the book, where it has remained. Although referring

The concepts of *Wednesbury* unreasonableness and ultra vires were thus complementary. They concealed the development of administrative law in a cloak of moral neutrality and veiled common law principle behind a largely fictional attachment to the enforcement of Parliamentary intentions. This cloak of neutrality was described in *Anisminic Ltd v Foreign Compensation Commission* by Lord Wilberforce: '. . . the tribunal has a derived authority, derived, that is, from statute: at some point, and *to be found from a consideration of the legislation*, the field within which it operates is marked out and limited'.[37] Lord Wilberforce echoed these comments in his leading speech in *Anns v Merton LBC*, a negligence case following *Home Office v Dorset Yacht*, in which he held that the principle in *Geddis* could not automatically be applied to the exercise of statutory discretions because 'there must be acts or omissions taken outside the limits of the delegated discretion' before the common law could be applied.[38] His Lordship (in a speech with which Lord Diplock agreed) expressly invoked Lord Diplock's views in *Dorset Yacht* and even his terminology of 'public law'. This confirmed that the House of Lords was seeking to create two domains of law—public law and private law—in which the courts were exercising different jurisdictions and applying different normative concepts.

Lord Diplock's motives were, however, undoubtedly more radical than those of Lord Wilberforce; for he also sought a procedurally discrete public law.[39] His Lordship had signalled his desire for a 'single and comprehensive mode for applying for judicial review' in the de Smith Memorial Lecture delivered to the Cambridge Faculty of Law four years after the decision in *Dorset Yacht*.[40] He appeared finally to achieve this in *O'Reilly v Mackman* in 1982, which required that all 'public law' actions proceed by Order 53 procedure. This included negligence actions raising issues of 'public law'.[41] Lord Diplock followed this up in 1985 in the *GCHQ* case, with his re-articulation and simplification of the normative principles applicable in 'public law'.[42] The decision in *Dorset Yacht* laid the foundations for Lord Diplock's radical attempt formally to separate public law procedurally, theoretically, and conceptually. The formal procedural divide has, however, now largely been abandoned.[43] At the theoretical level, even adherents to the ultra vires

most extensively to Lord Reid's speech (p 628) Wade essentially adopted the approach taken by Lord Diplock. This is confirmed by later editions (e.g. 5th edn, 1982, pp 660–61). Tort law's marginalisation is apparent in all the leading textbooks on administrative and public law, and the seminal importance of *Dorset Yacht* in the history of the reasonableness principle goes unrecognised.

[37] *Anisminic* (n 29) 207 (emphasis added).

[38] *Anns* (n 30) 757, also 758.

[39] Contrast Lord Wilberforce's speech in *Davy v Spelthorne BC* [1984] 1 AC 262. For more general comparison of the philosophies of these two judges, see R Stevens, *Law and Politics—The House of Lords as a Judicial Body 1800–1976* (London, Weidenfeld & Nicolson, 1979) 555–69.

[40] Lord Diplock, 'Administrative Law: Judicial Review Revisited' (1974) 33 *CLJ* 233, 245, also 'Judicial Control of the Administrative Process' (1971) 24 *Current Legal Problems* 1.

[41] *Guevara v Hounslow LBC*, The Times 17 April 1987. The new division between public and private was boldly put by Denning MR in *O'Reilly v Mackman* [1983] 2 AC 237 (CA) 255–56.

[42] *GCHQ* (n 26) pp 407–09.

[43] *Clark v University of Lincolnshire and Humberside* [2000] 1 WLR 1988.

doctrine have thrown off the veil of neutrality and embrace normative review rooted in the common law.[44] However, the conceptual disjunction remains. It is time that it too is questioned.

It has been necessary to re-traverse some well-known cases in order to illustrate why two separate concepts of unreasonableness have been applied in actions against public authorities, to show that both must be addressed in any consideration of the reasonableness principle, and to question the justifiability of the continued disjunction between them. The approach which became orthodoxy following *Dorset Yacht* and the creation of modern 'public law', and the assumptions about the courts' jurisdiction and the limits on the capacity of courts to scrutinise the reasonableness of decisions taken pursuant to statutory powers, upon which it is premised, have dogged courts across the Commonwealth ever since *Dorset Yacht*.[45] Hayne J in the High Court of Australia has pithily summed up the orthodox position in the following terms:[46]

> In public law, decisions may be examined for error of law but, statute apart, there is no review of the merits of decisions made by such bodies. The closest the courts come to such a review is what is usually called *Wednesbury* unreasonableness . . . What the *Wednesbury* test reflects is that the courts are not well placed to review decisions made by such bodies when, as is often the case, the decisions are made in the light of conflicting pressures including political and financial pressures. The *Wednesbury* test is very different from the test which must be applied in an action for negligence.

Furthermore, Hayne J stated that because administrative law review is premised on the notion of error of law, the question of *Wednesbury* reasonableness is a question that goes to the duty of care, it is 'not a factual and evidentiary question about breach'.[47]

Abandonment

Two decisions of the House of Lords, *Barrett v Enfield LBC*[48] and *Phelps v Hillingdon LBC*[49] affirmed the view of Lord Browne-Wilkinson in *X (Minors) v Bedfordshire CC*[50] that it is no longer a precondition for an action in negligence to show that decisions taken in the exercise of a statutory discretion were ultra vires, and they emphasised Lord Browne-Wilkinson's statement that it is not 'helpful or

---

[44] See M Elliott, *The Constitutional Foundations of Judicial Review* (Oxford, Hart, 2001).

[45] eg *Sutherland Shire Council v Heyman* (1985) 157 CLR 424, 442 and 447–48 (Gibbs CJ), *cf* 458 and 468–69 (Mason J); *Just v British Columbia* (1990) 1 WWR 385, 390 and 395 (Sopinka J).

[46] *Brodie v Singleton Shire Council* (2001) 180 ALR 145 [310].

[47] *Brodie* ibid. *Cf Anns* (n 30), 758; *Dorset Yacht* (n 30), 1068–70.

[48] *Barrett v Enfield LBC* [2001] 2 AC 550.

[49] *Phelps v Hillingdon LBC* [2001] 2 AC 619. The approach taken in *Barrett* and *Phelps* has been followed: *Gorringe v Calderdale MBC* [2004] 1 AC 1057. For ambiguities in the speeches in *Barrett* and *Phelps*, see TR Hickman, 'The Reasonableness Principle: Reassessing its Place in the Public Sphere' (2004) *CLJ* 166, 174–75.

[50] *X (Minors) v Bedfordshire CC* [1995] 2 AC 633.

necessary' to 'introduce public law concepts as to the validity of a decision into the question of liability at common law for negligence'.[51] But, as we shall see, Lord Browne-Wilkinson in *X (Minors)* retained the idea that decisions made pursuant to statutory discretions would have to be shown to be unreasonable in the *Wednesbury* sense thus setting something of a puzzle, to which we shall return. In *Barrett* and *Phelps*, the House of Lords went further and rejected the need to show that a decision was *Wednesbury* unreasonable when taken in pursuance of a statutory discretion. The cases recognised that duties of care can be owed in relation to the placement of children in care and the mitigation of dyslexia by schools and local education authorities. Although the duties of care owed by public authorities were thereby broadened, their Lordships were at pains to emphasise that the standard of reasonableness required will be a high one, and that the professionals in question will be judged according to the private law standard expressed in *Bolam v Friern Hospital Management Committee*.[52] Significantly, however, *Geddis* was not referred to by their Lordships in either case. The connection between tort and the reasonableness principle in administrative law seemed to have been completely abandoned. These cases did not relate to public authority liability for omissions, which remained governed by the majority speech of Lord Hoffmann's in *Stovin v Wise*. In that speech Lord Hoffmann had, following the same logic as Lord Diplock, reasoned that it would have to be shown that a failure to exercise a statutory power was irrational before a private law claim in negligence could succeed.[53] But the courts have backed away from this stance also, and the law is now that the question of duty of care must be examined by reference to the statutory context but without reference to the rationality or vires of any decisions.[54]

The new approach has much in common with that long advocated by Bowman and Bailey. Their primary aim has been to persuade the courts to extricate 'public law' concepts from negligence and apply uncontaminated private law principles. They have argued, for example, that there has been insufficient attention to the level of deference accorded to professionals under the *Bolam* test and that private law can happily accommodate considerations that the peculiarly public law concepts were developed to address.[55] But this approach has disadvantages. It entails accepting that decisions may be the subject of a successful negligence claim although they have in fact been made intra vires and would not have been impugnable had an action been brought otherwise than for damages. In other words, conduct can apparently now amount to a wrong, although nothing has ever

---

[51] *X (Minors)* ibid 736.

[52] *Bolam v Friern Hospital Management Committee* [1957] 1 WLR 582.

[53] *Stovin v Wise* [1996] AC 923; also see *Kent v Griffiths* [2001] QB 36.

[54] *Gorringe v Calderdale MBC* (n 49) and *X, Y (Protected Parties represented by their litigation friend) v London Borough of Hounslow* [2009] EWCA Civ 286. Lord Hoffmann himself stated that his comments on this score were controversial and 'may have been ill-advised' ([26]).

[55] MJ Bowman and SH Bailey, 'Negligence in the Realms of Public Law: A Positive Obligation to Rescue?' [1984] *PL* 277, 306–7; (n 32), and SH Bailey and MJ Bowman, 'Public Authority Negligence Revisited' (2000) 59 *CLJ* 85, 114, 125–31. See also J Bell, 'Governmental Liability in Tort' (1996) 6 *National Journal of Constitutional Law* 97.

been done wrong. Furthermore, it is hardly satisfactory from the perspective of public officials whose decisions are subjected to different standards of reasonableness in respect of the same conduct, depending on the form that the claim eventually takes. Complexity in the hinterland between public and private cannot of course be avoided, but the apparent simplicity in separation comes at the expense of coherence. The domains of public and private law cannot be hermetically sealed. Bowman and Bailey have themselves suggested that although the differences between the administrative law concept of reasonableness and the tortious concept are generally thought to differ radically, they are sometimes actually extremely similar.[56] But if true, this requires a fundamental reassessment of the architecture of public law and the relationship between administrative law and tort and throws into doubt the continued separation between them.

There are two main reasons why the *Wednesbury* principle and the principle of reasonableness in tort law can be said to have reached a stage in their development such that they are actually essentially analogous when applied to the same decision. The first is that the principle of reasonableness in tort law has been developed in the context of professional negligence to accommodate the courts' lack of knowledge and expertise in those areas. The seminal judgment is that of McNair J in *Bolam v Friern Hospital Management Committee*. As with the *Wednesbury* case, this was not at the time a leading case. It was a direction to a jury and was only confirmed by the House of Lords some time later.[57] McNair J stated:[58]

> . . . negligence in law means a failure to do some act which a reasonable man in the circumstances would do, or the doing of some act which a reasonable man in the circumstances would not do[59] . . . But where you get a situation which involves the use of some special skill or competence, then the test . . . is the standard of the ordinary skilled man exercising and professing to have that special skill.

The question, then, that a judge has to address is whether a professionally skilled person acting reasonably could have done what the defendant did in the circumstances. McNair J in *Bolam* also added a famous qualification to the general proposition set out above. He said: '[a doctor] is not guilty of negligence if he has acted in accordance with a practice accepted as proper by a responsible body of medical men skilled in that particular art'.[60] Although this is a normative assessment that requires the courts to engage in a process of balancing values and policies to some degree, the court will not demand or prescribe the outcome it prefers: 'At common law and in common sense a defendant is not negligent if he has adopted one of two courses, when the man on the Clapham omnibus would say

---

[56] Bailey and Bowman 'Revisited' (n 55), 114 and 'Realms' (n 55), 306–7. Also P Craig and D Fairgrieve ('*Barrett*, Negligence and Discretionary Powers' [1999] *PL* 626), have suggested it is arguable that 'the meaning of reasonableness is in reality not very different in the two contexts because of "movement" from both sides' (647; generally 647–49).

[57] In *Whitehouse v Jordan* [1981] 1 WLR 246.

[58] *Bolam* (n 52), 586.

[59] See *Blyth v Birmingham Waterworks Co* (1856) 11 Exch 781, 784 (Alderson B).

[60] *Bolam* (n 52), 587.

that neither was negligent although in his opinion the other was to be preferred'.[61] The House of Lords in *Barrett* made clear that issues which are relevant to the question of justiciability, such as the political nature of the decision or the fact that it involves complex questions not suitable for resolution by the courts, can now also be factored in to the *Bolam* assessment so that appropriate latitude is afforded to the decision-maker in determining whether a decision is reasonable.[62] Indeed, the *Bolam* test has always absorbed such considerations. As Lord Woolf has acknowledged extra-judicially, the *Bolam* test was for many years applied in an overly protectionist way, with 'excessive deference' to public professionals (particularly doctors) for fear of inducing defensive practices,[63] and because judges were 'understandably reluctant to second-guess the conduct and opinions of respected professionals . . .'.[64] Breaking the mould of this protectionist era, in *Bolitho v City and Hackney Health Authority* the House of Lords established that if a professional practice, although accepted, can be shown to be illogical (a test with a glaring resemblance to Lord Diplock's 'irrationality' test[65]), the courts should uphold a claim in negligence.[66]

The second reason why the administrative law concept and the tortious concept have become analogous is that the *Wednesbury* concept has been modified at common law. Before the Human Rights Act, the *Wednesbury* standard was adjusted in cases in which in human rights were in issue. The courts gave such decisions 'anxious scrutiny'.[67] The more substantial the interference with human rights, the more that the court required by way of justification before it was satisfied that a decision was reasonable.[68] The overriding question remained one of reasonable-

[61] *Adams v Rhymney Valley DC* (2001) 3 LGLR 9, 141 (Sir Christopher Staughton). In *A v Tameside and Glossop HA*, The Times 27 November 1996, the Court of Appeal held that, although the best method of informing patients about a remote risk of infection with HIV was face-to-face, this was not the test to be applied and the (less desirable) method chosen was reasonable.

[62] *Barrett* (n 48), 591 (Lord Hutton) *cf* 572 (Lord Slynn). There is authority for courts taking into *account* limited resources and distributive dilemmas in negligence claims when determining what is reasonable: *Sussex Ambulance NHS Trust v King* (2002) 68 BMLR 177; *Walker v Northumberland CC* [1995] 1 All ER 737; *Knight v Home Office* [1990] 3 All ER 237; *East Suffolk Rivers Catchment Board* (n 14) 97 (Lord Thankerton).

[63] *Sidaway v Board of Governors of the Bethlam Royal Hospital* [1985] AC 871 (HL) 887 (Lord Scarman), 893 (Lord Diplock); *Whitehouse v Jordan* [1980] 1 All ER 650 (CA), [1981] 1 WLR 246 (HL).

[64] Lord Woolf, 'Are the Courts Excessively Deferential to the Medical Profession?' (2001) 9 Med LR 1, 1–2. For examples see, *Blyth v Bloomsbury HA* [1993] 4 Med LR 151; *Sidaway* (n 63) (disclosure of risks); *Hughes v Waltham Forest HA* [1991] 2 Med LR 155 ('one off' decisions rather than a practice); *Maynard v West Midlands Regional HA* [1984] 1 WLR 634.

[65] The origin of irrationality may be found in Lord Diplock's de Smith Memorial Lecture (n 40), 243 before it became part of the law in *GCHQ*. In the Court of Appeal in *Bolitho* (n 66), Dillon LJ drew a direct analogy between *Wednesbury* and *Bolam* [1993] PIQR P 334 (CA) 354. It has been rejected in other cases: *Joyce v Merton, Sutton and Wandsworth HA* [1996] PIQR P 121, 153 (Hobhouse LJ) (criticising Dillon LJ); *R v North West Lancashire HA, ex p A* [2000] 1 WLR 977, 998 (apparently in the mistaken belief that if a body of medical opinion supported funding of gender reassignment surgery, the health authority would be compelled to provide it); *Thompson v Home Office* [2001] EWCA Civ 331 [6] (without reasons).

[66] *Bolitho v City and Hackney HA* [1998] AC 232.

[67] *Bugdaycay v Secretary of State for the Home Department* [1987] AC 514, 531 (Lord Bridge).

[68] *R v Ministry of Defence, ex p Smith* [1996] QB 517, 514 (Bingham MR) and 539 (Simon Brown LJ).

ness, the justification required only went to the question whether a reasonable decision-maker could have justified the decision.[69] This became known as 'super-*Wednesbury*' review and it involved a more rigorous examination, including in appropriate cases finding facts based on the underlying documents, and the application of a less-deferential standard to the decision. But the modification of the *Wednesbury* principle has not been limited to human rights cases. There are other cases where the high threshold of unreasonableness has been lowered. The most important case is the *ITF* case, in which a claim was brought against a Chief Constable's decision to reduce the days on which protection would be given to animal livestock exporters whose trade was the target of angry and sometimes violent protests from welfare activists.[70] The traders had vowed to continue trading 'at whatever cost', but they weren't in fact prepared to bear these costs themselves, and brought proceedings against the cash-strapped police authority. The House of Lords dismissed the claim. Lord Slynn stated:

> If this matter is looked at *ex post facto*, it may be that some more money could have been squeezed from elsewhere to provide extra policing . . . But that is the wrong approach on this application. The question is what the Chief Constable reasonably believed at the time . . .[71]

This approach clearly envisages a role for the courts in weighing the value of actual and potential courses of conduct. It is evident from Lord Slynn's speech that the courts can in appropriate cases assess the weight given to relevant factors: he spoke for example of the adverse effect on ITF's trade as 'an important consideration' for the Chief Constable.[72] Lord Cooke in his speech preferred the 'unexaggerated' standard of simple unreasonableness.[73] The *ITF* case is all the more significant because the decision was complex and involved a subject matter—relating to public order and safety—which courts have traditionally been reluctant to scrutinise.

Therefore, although the *Wednesbury* test may still be applied in its traditional form in many contexts, in cases where decisions directly and seriously harm individuals or organisations, there is authority for a much more robust reasonableness test being applied. It may be thought that even if human rights are not engaged, where a public authority owes a duty to take care not to cause harm to a person or persons, its decision would be suitably scrutinised on the basis of a robust reasonableness test in administrative law. Any attempt to distinguish this from the

[69] *R v Home Secretary, ex p Brind* [1991] 1 AC 696, 748–49 (Lord Bridge).
[70] *R v Chief Constable of Sussex, ex p ITF Ltd* [1999] 2 AC 418.
[71] ibid, 433.
[72] ibid, 433. Cf *R v North West Lancashire HA, ex p A* [2000] 1 WLR 977, especially 995.
[73] Lord Cooke took these comments a stage further in *R (Daly) v Home Secretary* [2001] 2 AC 532 [32], stating that, 'the day will come when it will be more widely recognised that *Wednesbury* was an unfortunately retrogressive decision in English administrative law, insofar as it suggested that there are degrees of unreasonableness and that only a very extreme degree can bring an administrative decision within the legitimate scope of judicial invalidation'. These views were in turn a development of those set out in 'The Struggle for Simplicity in Administrative Law' in M Taggart (ed), *Judicial Review of Administrative Action in the 1980s—Problems and Perspectives* (Auckland, OUP, 1986), discussed in ch 9, p 268.

principle applicable to such a decision in an action in negligence founders on the rocks of the fact that, as we have seen, the limits of the courts' expertise and knowledge are accommodated within the test of reasonableness applied in professional negligence claims. It is difficult to see why any different approach should have been taken to the decision of the Chief Constable in the *ITF* case, for example, if the claim had been commenced as a negligence claim because of economic losses caused by the decision to reduce the protection given to exporters. Assuming, for the purposes of argument, that the traders could overcome the hurdle of establishing that the Chief Constable owed them a duty of care in tort, the court would have been faced with determining whether the decision was a reasonable one. That inquiry would have been essentially the same as the one that the court engaged in the administrative law challenge.

But if this is so, the suggestion that the courts are doing different things in private law negligence cases and in public law challenges based on unreasonableness is a fiction. This fiction sustains the approach taken by the House of Lords in *Barrett* and *Phelps* and in subsequent cases, which establishes a clear separation of private law from administrative law.

Unity

There is, however, a different way of looking at this difficult area where public and private law converge. This approach is different from both the orthodox approach based on the reasoning and logic of Lord Diplock in the *Dorset Yacht* case and also from the new approach based on *Barrett* and *Phelps*. It is reflected in a stream of authority and judicial opinion which has rejected the rigid disjunction of the administrative and tortious concepts, which is characteristic of both the orthodox and the new approaches to this issue. The hallmarks of this stream of authority and opinion are that the administrative law test of reasonableness is viewed as going not to duty but to breach, and it is postulated as part of a continuum with negligence. It thus maintains the connection between administrative law and tort. Lord Reid's speech in *Dorset Yacht* is the source of this approach in the modern case law. Lord Reid accepted that the *Geddis* principle applies where 'Parliament cannot reasonably be supposed to have licensed' conduct in disregard of the interests of others or without due care. However, '[w]here Parliament confers a discretion the position is not the same'. Even so, he recognised that:[74]

> ... there must come a stage when the discretion is exercised so carelessly or unreasonably that there has been no real exercise of the discretion which Parliament has conferred. ... In my view there can be no liability if the discretion is exercised with due care. There could only be liability if the person entrusted with the discretion either unreasonably failed to carry out his duty to consider the matter or reached a conclusion so unreasonable as again to show a failure to do his duty.

---

[74] *Dorset Yacht* (n 30), 1031.

Lord Reid recognised that an added degree of latitude was demanded when decisions were made in pursuance of a statutory discretion, however there was no disjunction between public and private: the distinction between the approach described in *Geddis* and cases of modern discretionary power was one of context not jurisdiction, and unreasonableness in either context exceeded the intentions of Parliament. His Lordship can be seen as developing, rather than rejecting, the unified approach established in the early case law. His approach had a great deal in common with the pre-*Mersey Docks* cases which established that where discretionary powers were exercised in an unreasonable manner, so as to exceed the permitted area of discretion, those responsible could be liable in tort.

In *X (Minors)* Lord Browne-Wilkinson, giving the leading speech, applied Lord Reid's speech in preference to that of Lord Diplock.[75] He rejected the orthodox contention that ultra vires was a condition precedent to finding a common law duty or had 'replaced' negligence. But as we have already observed, his Lordship also maintained that the plaintiffs would have to establish in appropriate cases that the impugned decisions were *Wednesbury* unreasonable in order to succeed in a claim in negligence. His Lordship thus set something of a puzzle. But the puzzle is not hard to resolve on a careful reading of his speech in the context in which it was given. His Lordship was not objecting to the cross-fertilisation of administrative law and tortious concepts in general, he was simply concerned about the precondition of ultra vires.[76] There were two reasons for this concern. In the first place, Lord Browne-Wilkinson wanted to distance himself from Lord Diplock's attempt to create a procedurally discrete administrative law. He affirmed his earlier view in *Lonrho plc v Tebbit* that a tortious action in negligence could proceed outside judicial review procedure and Order 53 of the Rules of the Supreme Court;[77] whereas the logic of Lord Diplock's approach, as had been held,[78] required negligence actions challenging the exercise of statutory discretions to be brought by judicial review procedure in order to establish the pre-condition that the discretion had been exercised ultra vires. Secondly, and connectedly, Lord Browne-Wilkinson recognised that if the pre-condition was that a discretion had been exercised ultra vires, that could be established by showing a breach of some public law duty, such as the principles of natural justice 'which', his Lordship said, 'have no relevance to the question of negligence'. Lord Browne-Wilkinson therefore wanted to get rid of the ultra vires principle as a precondition of finding tortious liability. But this logic did not necessitate the jettisoning also of the *Wednesbury* concept, because it was the standard of reasonableness that was applicable to the exercise of statutory discretion. His Lordship recognised that this must be the standard applicable in both administrative law claims and negligence claims. He said if a decision is not shown to be *Wednesbury* unreasonable, 'a local authority *cannot itself be in breach* of any

---

[75] *X (Minors)* (n 50), 736.
[76] *X (Minors)* ibid, 736.
[77] *Lonrho plc v Tebbit* [1991] 4 All ER 973, 987; [1992] 4 All ER 280 (CA).
[78] *Guevara v Hounslow LBC* (n 41).

duty . . .'.[79] Whereas, in relation to the professional decisions of the teachers and social workers 'on the ground' (that is, not relating to the exercise of statutory discretion) the applicable standard was *Bolam*.[80] The distinction between decisions taken pursuant to statutory discretion and those that were professional operational decisions was not itself stable,[81] but the basic reasoning was sound. In relation to discretionary decisions in relation to distribution of resources and other political matters there is no standard practice or professional benchmark to apply in order to determine what is reasonable. As such, the *Bolam* test is inapposite. Instead the *Wednesbury* formulation is better suited to the task and has been developed by the courts to judge whether such a decision is wrongful.

It is suggested that Lord Nicholls' important dissenting speech in *Stovin v Wise* can be located within this stream of opinion and authority.[82] His approach was not only reflective of the same unity in the standard applying in administrative law and tort claims, but does so on the basis of a modified administrative law standard of reasonableness. The case involved an authority's failure to remove a bank of earth from land adjoining the highway. Lord Nicholls stated:[83]

> . . . the council's existing public law obligations required the council to attain the standards expected of any reasonable highway authority in the circumstances. A statutory discretion cannot be exercised in an unreasonable manner, that is, in a way no sensible authority with a proper appreciation of its responsibilities would act.

His Lordship went on to assert that the extent of any private law obligation would 'march hand in hand with the authority's public law obligations', since this 'was to act as a reasonable authority' and the common law obligation was 'to the same effect'.[84] Lord Nicholls sliced through the verbal formulae and equated the two tests of unreasonableness, at least in the context of the case before him.[85] Far from resting 'on thin ice'[86] Lord Nicholls' speech in *Stovin v Wise* represents the maturity of an established stream of authority and reasoning that is prepared to countenance the transplantation or unification of the tests of reasonableness between tort and administrative law, with the standard applied dependent on

---

[79] *X (Minors)* (n 50), 737 (emphasis added). Admittedly when Lord Browne-Wilkinson applied his general analysis to the actual facts he occasionally appears to adopt a different approach. For example, at 761. Commentators have had difficulty making sense of all of his comments: P Cane, 'Suing Public Authorities in Tort' (1996) 112 *LQR* 13, 13; D Brodie, 'Public authorities-negligence actions-control devices' (1988) 8 LS 1, 5.

[80] See also the comments of Cane (n 79) at 17. His Lordship gave the example of running a school as a non-discretionary activity (*X (Minors)* (n 50), 739), whereas decisions of LEAs made more directly under statutory provisions would be (eg *X (Minors)* (n 50), 760–61).

[81] It is said that even the hammering in of a nail involves discretion: *Barrett* (n 48) 571 (Lord Slynn); the arrest of a suspected criminal has been held to involve the exercise of discretion: *Holgate-Mohammed v Duke* [1984] AC 437.

[82] *Stovin v Wise* [1996] AC 923 (Lord Slynn agreed).

[83] ibid, 936.

[84] ibid.

[85] By contrast, the majority speech of Lord Hoffmann follows the orthodox approach, and views irrationality and the tortious standard of unreasonableness as entirely separate.

[86] J Convery, 'Public or Private? Duty of Care in a Statutory Framework: *Stovin v Wise* in the House of Lords' (1997) 60 *MLR* 559, 567, 569.

context rather than on whether the claim is classified as an 'administrative law' or 'private law' claim. Thus identified, this approach forges a middle path between the orthodox approach and the new approach and provides a basis for a more coherent approach to the application of the reasonableness principle.

A clear example of how on this approach the courts should engage with the question of reasonableness is provided by Dyson LJ's speech in *Carty v Croydon London Borough Council*. His Lordship referred to statements in the authorities to the effect that where the act of which the complaint is made involves the exercise of a statutory discretion, it must be shown that the decision 'was so unreasonable that it fell outside the ambit of the discretion'. Reflecting puzzlement at Lord Browne-Wilkinson's speech in *X (minors)*, Dyson LJ (with whom Mummery LJ and Butler-Sloss P agreed) then said that such language is 'strikingly reminiscent' of the language of *Wednesbury* but was hesitant in drawing the conclusion that the *Wednesbury* test was intended because of Lord Browne-Wilkinson's comments that the ultra vires doctrine has no role to play. His Lordship then stated that *Barrett* and *Phelps* had removed the requirement that a different approach should be taken when a decision is made pursuant to a statutory discretion and those cases where it is not. He concluded, it is submitted rightly, that the sensible approach is simply to adjust the standard of reasonableness depending on the context, and not to distinguish between administrative and private law tests, or between discretionary and non-discretionary decisions:[87]

> It seems to me that, rather than focus on the elusive question of whether the decision at issue involved the exercise of discretion, it is preferable to consider the substance of the decision. In the field of special education, there is a spectrum at one end of which lie decisions which are heavily influenced by policy and which come close to being non-justiciable. In relation to such decisions, the court is unlikely to find negligence proved unless they are ones which no reasonable education authority could have made. At the other end of the spectrum are decisions involving pure professional judgment and expertise in relation to individual children such as, for example, whether a child is dyslexic or suffering from some other learning difficulty. In relation to these decisions, the court will only find negligence on the part of the person who made the decision (for which the authority may be vicariously liable) if he or she failed to act in accordance with a practice accepted at the time as proper by a responsible body of persons of the same profession or skill: see *Bolam v Friern Hospital Management Committee*.

His Lordship went on to recall Lord Slynn's comments in *Phelps*[88] that even in relation to decisions made at the operational level, the tasks involved and the circumstances in which people have to work in this area are difficult and sensitive, and unreasonableness should not be found too readily.

---

[87] *Carty v Croydon LBC* [2005] 1 WLR 2312 [26] and [27].
[88] *Phelps* n (49), 655.

Reasonableness under the ECHR: Strasbourg

In this section we examine the reasonableness test that has been developed by the ECtHR. It is perhaps significant that this standard was developed in tort-like situations of operational failings, rather than in relation to macro-administrative decisions. This standard was first articulated in *Osman v United Kingdom* in relation to the 'positive obligation on the authorities to take preventative operational measures to protect an individual whose life is at risk'.[89] In that case it was alleged that the police had violated the applicants' Article 2 rights, by failing to prevent a deranged school teacher from seriously injuring a student with whom he was obsessed and murdering the student's father. The parties accepted that Article 2 imposed positive obligations that went beyond having in place effective criminal law sanctions against murder and manslaughter and other conduct leading to a loss of life. But the scope of the obligation was in dispute and had not previously been defined by the ECtHR. The Court began by having regard to the need for such an obligation not to be too stringent, or, as it said, such that it would impose an impossible or 'disproportionate' burden on the domestic public authorities. It had regard to 'the difficulties involved in policing modern societies, the unpredictability of human conduct and the operational choices which must be made in terms of priorities and resources'.[90] Moreover, the Court considered that the scope of the positive obligation had to recognise that the police owe due process and other obligations to suspected criminals. Notably, none of the considerations to which the Court had regard related to the difficulty of *the Court* assessing whether conduct in question breached Article 2. The policy considerations to which the Court referred were intended to inform its delimitation of the fair and just standard of conduct that should apply to domestic authorities under Article 2. The Court formulated the standard of conduct required of domestic authorities without reference to its ability to enforce it. This is unsurprising, since it is the 'margin of appreciation' doctrine that the Court employs to give effect to such considerations.[91] The passage of the Court's judgments that articulates the standard illustrates these points, and is worth citing:

> . . . it must be established to its satisfaction that the authorities knew or ought to have known at the time of the existence of a real and immediate risk to the life of an identified individual or individuals from the criminal acts of a third party and that they failed to take measures within the scope of their powers which, judged reasonably, might have been expected to avoid that risk. The Court does not accept the Government's view that the failure to perceive the risk to life in the circumstances known at the time or to take preventive measures to avoid that risk must be tantamount to gross negligence or wilful disregard of the duty to protect life. Such a rigid standard must be considered to be

---

[89] *Osman v United Kingdom* (2000) 29 EHRR 245 [115].
[90] ibid.
[91] See the discussion in ch 4, pp 123–25.

incompatible with the requirements of Article 1 of the Convention and the obligations of Contracting States under that Article to secure the practical and effective protection of the rights and freedoms laid down therein, including Article 2. For the Court, and having regard to the nature of the right protected by Article 2, a right fundamental in the scheme of the Convention, it is sufficient for an applicant to show that the authorities did not do all that could be reasonably expected of them to avoid a real and immediate risk to life of which they have or ought to have knowledge.[92]

There is both a duty and breach aspect to the *Osman* test. The obligation to take reasonable steps to prevent harm—the breach aspect—only arises when a public authority has a duty to take protection measures, and this duty only arises where the authority knows or ought to have known of an imminent risk to life. This differs from the circumstances in which a duty of care to act reasonably will arise at common law.[93] Our focus here is on the breach aspect of the *Osman* test: the reasonableness standard. It is important to note, however, that subsequent cases have made clear that the duty established in *Osman* is not confined to the protection of life or to the conduct of law enforcement agencies. It has been applied in cases where it has been found that social services departments have breached Article 3 by failing to protect children from serious neglect and physical and sexual abuse.[94] It also applies to deaths occurring whilst individuals are detained by hospitals and prisons.[95] In several of these cases, including *Osman* itself, the ECtHR had regard to its findings under Articles 2 and 3 in holding that no separate issue arose under Article 8, thus suggesting that the principle might be extended to breach of Article 8; an extension confirmed in *Hatton v United Kingdom*, discussed below.[96] The *Osman* standard therefore has a potentially very broad field of application across the activities of government and public authorities.

Let us turn then to the standard of reasonableness itself. By contrast to positive infringements of rights, the burden is on the applicant to show that the authorities 'did not do all that can be reasonably expected of them'.[97] This is plainly not a proportionality test. The only reference to 'proportionality' in *Osman* is found in the court's remark that in framing the obligation on public authorities it is important not to impose a disproportionate burden on them. But the ECtHR also expressly rejected the analogy with gross negligence and extreme forms of unreasonableness.

---

[92] *Osman* (n 89) [116] (references omitted).
[93] *Van Colle v Chief Constable of Hertfordshire Police* [2009] 1 AC 225, in which the majority of the House of Lords refused to follow Lord Bingham in aligning the duty of care in tort with the duty component of the *Osman* test (articulated at [44]). On the facts, the *Osman* duty, but not a tortious duty, was held to be owed by the police in investigating crime where they were or ought to have been aware of an imminent risk to life. In the later case of *Savage v South Essex Partnership NHS Foundation Trust* [2009] 1 AC 681 the House of Lords accepted that unlike the duty of care, the *Osman* duty did not extend to clinical decisions of doctors.
[94] *E v UK* [2003] 1 FLR 348, esp [88] and [92]; *Z v UK* (2001) 34 EHRR 97.
[95] *Keenan v United Kingdom* (2001) 33 EHRR 913; *Savage* (n 93).
[96] *E v UK* (n 94) [105], *Z v UK* (n 94) [77]. An analogous positive duty may arise to protect property under Art 1 of the First Protocol, see *Öneryildiz v Turkey* (2004) 34 EHRR 869 [135]–[137].
[97] *cf Edwards v UK* (2002) 35 EHRR 19 [55] and [61]–[64].

In cases of alleged operational failings, the standard applies in much the same way as a standard of reasonable care. In *Edwards v United Kingdom*, for instance, a breach of Article 2 was found because information about the dangerousness of a prisoner was not passed on to the prison authorities, which resulted in the prisoner brutally murdering his cell mate. As the Court found: 'There was a series of shortcomings in the transmission of information, from the failure of the registrar to consult Richard Linford's notes in order to obtain the full picture, the failure of the police to fill in a Form CID2 (exceptional risk) and the failure of the police, prosecution or magistrates' court to take steps to inform the prison authorities in any other way of Richard Linford's suspected dangerousness and instability.'[98] Of course, the Strasbourg Court, unlike domestic courts, does not need to distinguish between the negligence of different public authorities. It is for this reason that in the passage cited, the ECtHR conducts something of a holistic appraisal of the State's failings. But it is clear that even acts of carelessness and oversight can breach the *Osman* standard in appropriate cases.

At the other end of the spectrum, the reasonableness standard applies also to 'policy' decisions.[99] In *Hatton v United Kingdom* the Grand Chamber considered a policy introduced by the Government in 1993 regulating night flights at Heathrow Airport, which affected the private and home lives of those who lived nearby. The Court acknowledged that the noise disturbances were caused by private enterprise and not by any activity on the part of the state, and suggested that the case could be analysed in terms of the state's failure to 'take reasonable and appropriate measures to secure the applicants' rights'.[100] This is surely right, but the Court did not finally determine the issue because it considered that given the margin of appreciation afforded to the State on issues of social and environmental policy, the basic test would be the same if the case was analysed as a positive interference with Convention rights (the argument was that the policy brought about detrimental changes to flight times and quantities), given the margin of appreciation afforded to states in such contexts. The Grand Chamber defined in terms of whether the State had struck a 'fair balance' between economic considerations and the Article 8 rights of those affected. The Grand Chamber's examination under the label 'fair balance' was in fact a classic review of the decision-making process. The Court stated:

> Whilst the State is required to give due consideration to the particular interests the respect for which it is obliged to secure by virtue of Art.8, it must in principle be left a choice between different ways and means of meeting this obligation. The Court's supervisory function being of a subsidiary nature, it is limited to reviewing whether or not the particular solution adopted can be regarded as striking a fair balance.[101]

This is not the language of *Wednesbury*. It was clear that the Court intended to apply a more rigorous standard from its finding in relation to Article 13, that the

---

[98] ibid [61].
[99] On the distinction between policy and operational decisions, see *Anns v Merton LBC* [1978] AC 728. It is no longer the case that policy decisions cannot attract tort liability. See eg *Barratt v Enfield LBC*.
[100] *Hatton v United Kingdom* (2003) 37 EHRR 28 [98] and [119.]
[101] ibid [123].

'patent unreasonableness' and 'irrationality' review which had been carried out by the High Court had not provided an effective remedy to the applicants.[102] The ECtHR nonetheless emphasised that in complex areas of policy, the Court's function is to review the decision made and it must leave a considerable area of latitude to state authorities. The requirement that due consideration be given to the particular rights and interest at stake (which was also a facet of the reasoning in *Osman*), and the need for the Court to assess the balance struck is reminiscent of the enhanced, super-*Wednesbury* test of review applicable at common law.

Applying this test, the Grand Chamber held that the Government had been entitled to have regard to statistical data on sleep disturbance, economic considerations and the possibility of people affected leaving the affected areas. Since the Government had given consideration to the effect of the noise pollution on individuals living in the flight paths and had taken steps to ameliorate the noise, the Court concluded that a fair balance had been struck.[103]

Three points need to be made about *Hatton*. First, we find (in contrast to *Osman*) that the Court's articulation of the applicable standard is influenced by considerations about its own limited capacity and its lack of democratic legitimacy.[104] Secondly, the Court's direct appeal to the notion of 'fair balance' was lazy. The whole of the Convention is said to manifest a fair balance between rights and the public interest and all of the standards articulated in the text of the Convention and by the ECtHR are supposed to reflect the fair balance of competing interest in a particular context or in relation to a particular right. By invoking directly the concept of fair balance, the Court provided no guidance on how that balance is to be assessed on the facts of individual cases. Thirdly, insofar as an actual standard emerges from the analysis of the Court in *Hatton*, it is the standard of reasonableness. The term is used several times by the Court in its analysis, and encapsulates the standard of review it applied.[105] There is no mention of 'proportionality' anywhere in the Court's judgment.

---

[102] ibid [141]. It is to be inferred that the Court considered that its scrutiny was more intense. It should also be noted that the Grand Chamber overturned the decision of the Chamber, which had found a breach of Art 8 on the basis that the Government ought to have adopted the 'least onerous' solution in terms of its impact with human rights (*Hatton v United Kingdom* (2002) 34 EHRR 1 [97]). This had attracted fierce criticism, see 'Unbalanced Judgment' *The Times* (London, 3 October 2001) editorial. Such proportionality-type reasoning found no favour with the Grand Chamber, but has crept back into the law in *Öneryildiz v Turkey* (2004) 34 EHRR 869.

[103] *Hatton* (n 100) [121]–[127]. At [128] the Court held that the process of consultation had also been conducted adequately.

[104] '. . . national authorities have direct democratic legitimation and are, as the Court has held on many occasions, in principle better placed than an international court to evaluate local needs and conditions. In matters of general policy, on which opinions within a democratic society may reasonably differ widely, the role of the domestic policy maker should be given special weight.' (*Hatton* (n 100) [97] (footnote omitted)).

[105] '. . . the Court considers it reasonable to assume that those flights contribute at least to a certain extent to the general economy' (*Hatton* (n 100) [126]). 'The Court considers it reasonable, in determining the impact of a general policy on individuals in a particular area, to take into account the individuals' ability to leave the area. . . . the fact that they can, if they choose, move elsewhere without financial loss must be significant to the overall reasonableness of the general measure.' (*Hatton* (n 100) [127]).

Reasonableness under the ECHR: Domestic Courts

The *Osman* test has now been considered in a number of cases in domestic courts. Things started off well, with the emphatic statement of Lord Carswell on behalf of the House of Lords in *Re Officer L* that the ECtHR had made clear in *Osman* that, 'the standard . . . is based on reasonableness, which brings in consideration of the circumstances of the case, the ease or difficulty of taking precautions and the resources available.'[106] Welcome comments were also made in *NHS Trust A v M*, which concerned the legality of the withdrawal of treatment to a person in a persistent vegetative state. Butler-Sloss P stated that the *Osman* test 'bears a close resemblance to the standard adopted in domestic law of negligence and approximates to the obligation recognised by the English courts in the *Bolam* test . . .'.[107] It was recognised that the approach in *Osman* does not require the public authority to justify its failure to act by reference to necessity, nor does it require action in the 'best interests' of the person whose right is at issue, it simply requires the decision of the doctors to be reasonable.[108]

Savage's case concerned the suicide of a person who had absconded from detention under the Mental Health Act 1983.[109] It was alleged that the responsible NHS Trust had failed to take reasonable measures to prevent the risk of suicide and properly assess the risk of absconding. The judge gave summary judgment for the defendant NHS Trust on the basis that no claim could succeed under Article 2 unless gross negligence could be shown. As we have seen, the ECtHR in *Osman* had explicitly ruled that the applicable reasonableness test was not to be equated with 'gross negligence',[110] however, in two other cases the Strasbourg Court had ruled that the *Osman* principle does not apply to cases of medical negligence leading to a patient's death. The Strasbourg Court has held that states comply with Article 2 where they have made adequate provision for securing standards and providing remedies in the sphere of medical negligence.[111] Although the case was

---

[106] *Re Officer L* [2007] 1 WLR 2135 [21].

[107] *NHS Trust A v M* [2001] Fam 348, 360. In the absence of consent to medical treatment (rather than withdrawal of treatment), the relevant test under the Convention is necessity: 'a measure which is a therapeutic necessity cannot be regarded as inhuman or degrading': *Herczegfalvy v Austria* (1993) 15 EHRR 437 [82] (detention of person of unsound mind); and in relation to Art 8 *Acmanne v Belgium* (1984) 40 D & R 241 (compulsory screening for tuberculosis).

[108] Butler-Sloss P explained that domestic law had moved beyond the *Bolam* test in this context and was prepared to analyse the legality of withdrawal on the basis of the patient's best interests. She also stated: 'In our use of the declaratory jurisdiction of the High Court in PVS cases we impose in our domestic law a higher test than the standard set by the European Court of Human Rights, since the High Court reviews the medical conclusion on best interests' (*NHS Trust A* (n 107) 360).

[109] *Savage* (n 93).

[110] *Osman* (n 89) [116].

[111] 'Where a contracting state has made adequate provision for securing high professional standards among health professionals and the protection of the lives of patients, it cannot be accepted that matters such as error of judgment on the part of a health professional or negligent co-ordination among health professionals in the treatment of a particular patient are sufficient of themselves to call a contracting state to account from the standpoint of its positive obligations under Art 2 of the Convention

initially about the *standard* of conduct and competence required of the NHS Trusts, by the time it reached the House of Lords the question had correctly emerged as one of duty: did the duty to take reasonable steps arise?[112] The House of Lords held that the duty did arise, preferring the analogy of suicides in custody to the analogy of medical negligence. In the course of her speech, Baroness Hale gave some helpful guidance on how reasonableness is to be assessed under the Convention, noting that in judging what the authority can reasonably be expected to do the court has shown itself aware of the need to take account of competing values under the Convention, such as liberty and autonomy; the court has also to take into account the problem of scarce resources.[113] Such considerations will, of course, be equally apposite to the negligence/*Bolam* test as well as in administrative law. Lord Rodger seemed to accept that where a duty arises under tort and under Article 2, the question of reasonableness will be the same:[114]

> The operational obligation arises only if members of staff know or ought to know that a particular patient presents a 'real and immediate' risk of suicide. In these circumstances article 2 requires them to do all that can reasonably be expected to prevent the patient from committing suicide. If they fail to do this, not only will they and the health authorities be liable in negligence, but there will also be a violation of the operational obligation under article 2 to protect the patient's life.

Unfortunately the case law is not all of a piece. The House of Lords in *E v Chief Constable of the Royal Ulster Constabulary* ('the *Holy Cross* case') muddied the waters considerably.[115] That case concerned the decision of the Ulster Constabulary to permit an intimidating and humiliating protest by 'loyalist' protesters along the road through a Protestant area leading to the Holy Cross Catholic Primary School for Girls. The protest was allowed to continue throughout a school term and had a marked effect on the physical and emotional health of the children, who were daily forced to walk past rows of abusive protesters, police in riot gear and lines of armoured vehicles. It was conceded by the RUC that the conduct of the protesters had been inhuman and degrading to the children and that it was not a legitimate exercise of the right to protest. The applicant and the Northern Ireland Human Rights Commission (NIHRC) (intervening) submitted that since the police could have taken action that would have put a stop to the protest, the obligation on them to do so was absolute, at least insofar as they did not make matters worse. Notably the NIHRC framed its submission as follows: 'To express the stan-

---

to protect life': *Dodov v Bulgaria* (2008) 47 EHRR 41 [82]; *Powell v United Kingdom* (2000) 30 EHRR CD 326. The ECtHR may have been concerned about the implications of transforming Art 2 into a general tort-type obligation in a sphere such as medical practice, which generates a very considerable number of claims, but medical provision is also not a core state function, such as policing or detention.

[112] This was clearly articulated by Baroness Hale, who said that the trigger is a 'real and immediate risk to life' about which the authorities knew or ought to have known at the time. She continued: 'If the duty is triggered, it is, as it was put in *Keenan's* case, to do "all that reasonably could have been expected of them to prevent that risk".' (*Savage* (n 93) [100]).

[113] *Savage* (n 93) [100].

[114] ibid [72].

[115] *E v Chief Constable of the Royal Ulster Constabulary* [2009] 1 AC 536.

dard of the state's responsibility in terms of "reasonableness" therefore fails to reflect the categorical imperative created by Article 3.' The submission was expressly rejected by a unanimous House of Lords.

The judgment itself was not surprising, since the positive obligation under *Osman v United Kingdom*, whilst more demanding than a *Wednesbury* approach, does not require risks to be eliminated or reduced as far as possible. It is a reasonableness test. But the reasoning of their Lordships was muddled. Lord Carswell, giving the leading speech, applied his judgment in *Re Officer L* and held that the obligation placed on the police was to take steps that could reasonably be expected of them.[116] However, his Lordship then went on to examine the reasoning of the courts below and in doing so he went astray. The Court of Appeal had applied the super-*Wednesbury* test and had held that the police had done all that was *reasonably* open to them to protect the rights of the child. That was plainly an acceptable thing for the Court to have held. But Lord Carswell held not. His Lordship reasoned that the Court of Appeal had been in error because in *Daly* the House of Lords had accepted the applicability of proportionality under the Convention, and that it differs materially from a *Wednesbury* test in whatever guise; his Lordship reasoned that therefore, 'the *Smith* test is insufficiently intense and that the actions of the police in the present case have to pass the test of proportionality, which must be decided by the court'.[117] One cannot help thinking that Lord Carswell here took the injunction of commentators to apply proportionality to Convention issues rather too literally. His reasoning is essentially based on the following equation: Human Rights Act challenge = proportionality principle. But this is a false equation. It fails to recognise, as Lord Steyn did in *Daly*, that due allowance must be made for 'important structural differences' between Convention rights.[118] It takes no account of the distinction between positive and negative obligations which is central in the Strasbourg case law. In fairness to Lord Carswell, the academic commentaries on proportionality have also failed to recognise this distinction and have no doubt encouraged judges to think in this simplistic, monistic, way.

The decision is difficult to square with *Osman*, *Savage* and *Hatton*. One possibility is that Lord Carswell had in mind that proportionality had to be applied because the decision was of an 'administrative character', which he said had been the case in *Daly*, *Denbigh High School* and *Huang*. But this is not a satisfactory explanation, because there is no reason why a higher standard (proportionality) should be applied just because the decision taken is classified as 'administrative'. In any event, the decision in *Hatton* was plainly of an administrative character, by contrast to the tactical judgments made on the ground.[119] *Hatton* was not cited to their Lordships and it may have provoked a different response. The distinction between administrative decisions and operational decisions is also a recipe for

---

[116] ibid [48]–[49]; *Re Officer L* [2007] 3 WLR 2135.
[117] ibid [54].
[118] (n 73) *Daly* [27].
[119] In summarising the facts, Lord Carswell refers to the police's decisions as 'strategy', 'expedient' and 'tactic' (*E* (n 115) [36]–[37]).

disaster. The law has tried and failed to draw distinctions between policy and operational decisions, discretionary and non-discretionary decisions and between
public and private law challenges. All of these distinctions have proved to be elusive and unworkable. The introduction of a new distinction between administrative decisions (= proportionality) and operational decisions (= reasonableness)
would be doomed to the same fate.

In order to understand Lord Carswell's judgment in *E* it is necessary to have
regard to the judgments of the Northern Ireland High Court and Court of Appeal
in the case, which go some way to explaining what lies behind the judgment.
Despite setting out the facts at length, the lower courts had not analysed the facts
in any detail. Both courts had dismissed the claimants' arguments in extraordinarily brief, general, terms.[120] Kerr LCJ dismissed the appeals on the basis that:

> It is precisely because the Police Service is better equipped to appreciate and evaluate the
> dangers of such secondary protests and disturbances that an area of discretionary judgment
> must be allowed them, particularly in the realm of operational decisions.... I cannot accept
> that it has been established that the measures taken by the police were unreasonable. I have
> concluded that no breach of article 3 has been demonstrated, therefore.

The Court of Appeal wasted even fewer words on the argument, simply stating
that, 'taking account of the nature and size of the operation that was mounted over
a considerable period of time and the perceived risk if other measures were
adopted the police did all that was reasonably open to them to protect the rights
of the child.'[121] Lord Carswell quite rightly thought this reasoning was inadequate.
His Lordship associated the lack of rigour and analysis with the fact that the Court
had not applied a proportionality test. He went on himself to analyse the facts in
greater detail than either of the lower courts had done, albeit he reached the same
conclusion as they had reached. But nothing in his Lordship's analysis remotely
resembles proportionality reasoning, and the term does not figure again in his
speech after it is employed to justify the finding that the Court of Appeal had
applied the wrong test. Indeed, his Lordship's ultimate conclusion was that, 'The
assertions made by the appellant and NIHRC that they might possibly have
adopted a more robust course are in my view quite insufficient to establish that the
course adopted was misguided, let alone unreasonable.'[122] Not only was Lord
Carswell using the language, and the standard, of reasonableness, but this passage
makes clear that he regarded the burden as having been on the applicant to establish illegality, rather than on the police to refute it: this is classic indicia of a reasonableness test. Lord Carswell was not therefore adopting proportionality as a
standard of legality, but as a standard of review: he was criticising the level of
scrutiny given to the facts, not the standard of conduct or legality that was applied
to them.[123] Talk of proportionality is really a red herring when it is employed in

---

[120] *Re Application for Judicial Review* [2004] NIQB 35 [46]
[121] *E, Re Application for Judicial Review* [2006] NICA 37 [89].
[122] *E* (n 115) [59].
[123] On this distinction see ch 4.

such a way, and it is extremely confusing. A proportionality test was not applied at all. Moreover, the *Osman* test requires the court to engage with the facts and give anxious scrutiny to decisions where there is a positive duty to protect individual rights. Therefore, the High Court and Court of Appeal judgments were wrong because they misapplied the right test, not because they applied the wrong one.

It must also be noted that the standard of scrutiny given to the police's conduct was no more than a product of the form that the case took, namely, a judicial review. Had the claim been litigated by way of ordinary civil claim there would have been far greater scrutiny of the facts. There were 'voluminous'[124] affidavits before the court and 'numerous factual disputes',[125] but none of these were resolved. An illuminating contrast can be drawn between the *Holy Cross* case and *Austin & Saxby v The Commissioner of Police for the Metropolis*[126] challenging the so-called 'kettling' of May Day protesters by police for over seven hours in Oxford Circus in 2001. The case was brought by way of ordinary civil claim and the court considered evidence from 11 witness (10 gave oral evidence), examined footage from helicopter TV cameras and photographers, read thousands of pages of contemporaneous police records, and that was just the claimants' evidence. The Commissioner of Police relied on evidence from 145 witnesses (eight were cross-examined). The judge himself found the facts and scrutinised them in considerable detail, in a judgment that runs to 608 paragraphs.

Lord Carswell's reference to the 'administrative character' of the decision would have been more appropriate to describe the nature of the proceedings rather than the nature of the decision.[127] Even so, it makes no sense to apply a proportionality test in judicial review proceedings and a reasonableness test in ordinary civil claims, and that is certainly not what the European Convention requires.[128]

Rationalisation

Few judges have yet had cause to compare the various standards of reasonableness in tort, administrative law and under the Convention. But where they have done so, they have often stated that they can see no practical difference between them. We have seen comments of Butler-Sloss P and Lord Rodger to this effect.[129] All of the standards are sensitive to context and apply flexibly (although the standard of

---

[124] [2009] 1 AC 564 [18].

[125] [2006] NICA 37 (CA) [64].

[126] *Austin & Saxby v The Commissioner of Police for the Metropolis* [2005] EWHC 480 (QB).

[127] *Huang* was, of course, only administrative proceedings in a broad sense. It was an appeal from a tribunal on a point of law.

[128] See also G Anthony, 'Positive obligations and policing in the House of Lords' (2009) EHRR 538, suggesting that the judgment is based on the reasoning that proportionality has displaced reasonableness in judicial review proceedings but that the distinction between claims under the Human Rights Act and outside it is now 'unsatisfactory'.

[129] Above p 217–18.

reasonableness is unvarying).[130] There is certainly no reason to think that the *Osman* standard is any less exacting than either the tort standard or the administrative law standard of reasonableness. Nor should we accept that the administrative law standard is any less exacting than the tortious standard applied to the same decision. If anything, there may be circumstances in which the negligence test needs to be applied with greater scrutiny than it currently is. In *Bolitho* the House of Lords upheld a medical practice that risked the lives of young children because it was capable of withstanding logical analysis, despite the fact that the trial judge had not been particularly persuaded by it and Lord Slynn expressed 'anxiety' about the result.[131] If this test were to be applied outside the medical sphere it might well be less demanding and intrusive than the *Osman* standard[132] (as noted above, the *Osman* principle does not apply to medical negligence). But whether or not the standards of reasonableness *are* currently aligned, it is submitted that they *should* be. Not only for the sake of simplicity but also for the sake of coherence.

In the pre-Human Rights Act case of *Thompson v Home Office*,[133] a prisoner who had been viciously attacked by a fellow inmate with a razor blade brought an action against the Home Office challenging the decision of the prison governor to adopt a policy allowing inmates to use razors. As it happened, since the harm had occurred, the claim brought was a negligence claim for damages, but the decision could just as easily have been the subject of a judicial review challenge, had the prisoner been motivated to litigate the issue before any harm had been caused. It would now be open to challenge for a breach of Articles 2 and 8 under the Human Rights Act. What good reason is there for applying a different test depending on the form that the proceedings take? The normative imperatives in tort law, administrative law and under the Convention all point, in such a scenario, to the appositeness of testing the governor's decision by reference to a standard of reasonableness. But given this, there is no obvious or convincing reason for applying different tests of reasonableness, particularly given the flexibility of the reasonableness test in each field of law. From the perspective of the public authority concerned it makes no sense. There is a compelling case for making reasonableness the standard governing such decisions, and for describing the standard in a simple, straightforward, way. *Thompson v Home Office* makes clear that whether a claim is framed under the Human Rights Act, in tort law or in administrative law, will often be the result of chance or circumstances, and not for any reason related to the properly applicable law.

The convergence of the three principles of reasonableness also means that it can no longer convincingly be maintained that a breach of the principle of reason-

---

[130] Lord Scott: 'The standard of care required by our domestic law to be shown in order to discharge the common law duty of care is a flexible one dependent upon the circumstances of each individual case. The same must be true of the standard of protection required by article 2.1 . . .' (*Savage* [2009] 2 WLR 2 115 [9] (Lord Scott)).

[131] *Bolitho* (n 66), 244.

[132] See for example, its application to child care decisions pre-dating the Human Rights Act: *Pierce v Doncaster MBC* [2007] EWHC 2968 (QB); [2008] EWCA Civ 1416.

[133] *Thompson v Home Office* [2001] LTL C0100889.

ableness in tort law is not ultra vires. A breach of the *Osman* duty constitutes an unlawful ultra vires act by virtue of section 6(1) of the Human Rights Act.[134] Actions under the Human Rights Act can be, and frequently are, brought alongside tort actions (as in *Austin & Saxby*, which included a false imprisonment claim). It would make no sense whatsoever to hold that a breach of a tortious duty is not unlawful in the public law sense but that a breach of an analogous Convention right is. The Human Rights Act, by establishing obligations that run the length of the policy-operations hierarchy, has exploded the heresy of *X (Minors)* that negligent conduct is not and cannot be treated as ultra vires. It has provided the impetus for a return to the straightforward and logical approach taken in the early cases back to *Leader v Moxon* whereby the unreasonable exercise of statutory power is an excess of power potentially giving rise to liability in tort (or today also under the Human Rights Act) if the requisite duty is owed. There is no longer any need to fear that this will require negligence claims to be commenced by way of judicial review, since the rigid procedural dichotomy is a thing of the past.[135]

Conclusion

It is perhaps a surprising and unexpected consequence of the Human Rights Act that it has given new life to the principle of reasonableness in public law, but the argument advanced in this chapter is that it has. Even if *Wednesbury* is in the twilight of its career as a juridical concept, the reasonableness principle is more pervasive, multi-faceted and deep-rooted. More than this, the Human Rights Act has given rise to a compelling case for a rationalisation of the law. There is no obvious justification for maintaining a distinction between the reasonableness principle as applicable in tort law, administrative law and under the Human Rights Act, although the criteria for the applicability of the reasonableness principle in each jurisdiction differ. It has shown that a path towards rationalisation already exists in a line of opinion and authority that unites the principle of reasonableness in private law and administrative law which can traced back through Lord Nicholl's speech in *Stovin v Wise* and Lord Browne-Wilkinson's speech in *X (Minors)*, all the way back to *Leader v Moxon* itself.

---

[134] Although see the comments of Lord Hope in *Somerville v Scottish Ministers* [2007] 1 WLR 2734 [13] suggesting that unlawfulness under the Human Rights Act has limited consequences.
[135] See *Clark* (n 43).

8

The Forbidden Process Element in Human Rights Review

THE RELATIONSHIP BETWEEN the Human Rights Act and administrative law is an uneasy one. On the one hand, the Human Rights Act can be viewed as an administrative law add-on, as adding to the grounds of illegality on which a decision made by a public authority will be held to be ultra vires (s 6), as enacting the principle of legality as a rule of domestic law with added bite (s 3), and as providing new damages and declaratory remedies not previously available in judicial review proceedings, without interfering with the doctrine of parliamentary sovereignty (ss 4, 8). The Act has, moreover, mainly been used in administrative law claims, as a means of challenging the discretionary decisions of public officials. Direct challenges to primary legislation are relatively few and far between.[1] In these respects, the Human Rights Act has been contrasted with the New Zealand Bill of Rights 1990 and the Canadian Charter of Rights and Freedoms 1982, which have been viewed in those countries as constitutional measures with only indirect, and until recently marginal, effect on administrative law.[2] But on the other hand, if the Human Rights Act is viewed as establishing the boundaries of a rights-based democracy in a constitutional document, and establishing standards of legality rather than standards of review, it seems to inhabit the world of constitutional, rather than administrative law.[3]

One area where this tension has come to the fore is in relation to process review. Process review is judicial review of a decision on the basis that the decision has been reached in the wrong way, rather than that the outcome is contrary to some right, or is unreasonable, perverse or disproportionate. Process review is usually based on the doctrines of relevant and irrelevant considerations, retention and fettering of discretion, and the duty to supply adequate reasons. What is required of decision-makers varies with context, and challenges to administrative decisions

---

[1] This is unsurprising, since usually both the claimant and the Government will prefer a s 3 solution to a s 4 declaration: claimants seek to avoid s 4 because it does not affect their legal entitlements and does not provide an effective remedy in their case, and the Government seeks to avoid s 4 because it can lead to a confrontation with Parliament.

[2] See generally, ch 2, pp 28–29. On the principle of legality see ch 4, pp 105–108.

[3] See *A and others v Secretary of State for the Home Department (No 1)* [2005] 2 AC 68 [42] (Lord Bingham) citing J Jowell. On standards of legality and standards of review, see ch 4, pp 99–108. This distinction is of less utility in the present context, since process standards generally operate both as procedural standards of legality and are part of the applicable standard of review.

have succeeded on other process grounds in addition to these, such as that public officials have failed to make sufficient inquiries or have failed to give a matter conscientious consideration.[4] This chapter considers the availability of such review under the Human Rights Act and whether the enactment of the Human Rights Act should have implications for the application of the common law grounds of procedural judicial review.

Process Review: The Forbidden Method

The teeth of public law are in process review. Most successful judicial review claims succeed on the basis that the decision-maker has done something in the wrong way, rather than that the decision-maker has made a decision that is, all things considered, unjustifiable. Process review has two principal advantages over substantive review. First, since the court does not have to address the substance or outcome of the decision, it is less controversial and easier to establish a process failing than a substantive one. Judges prefer to quash decisions on this basis, not only because it avoids the most difficult questions but also because it is more delicate and less confrontational than finding that a public official has acted irrationally, has breached a fundamental right or has gone against the terms of the empowering statute. Secondly, process review has the advantage that the decision can be remade on a proper basis by the person or body responsible for making it, often with a more or less firm judicial steer as to how the court would look on any renewed application for judicial review, but without any options as to which decision the public official is entitled to reach having been taken off the table. It therefore promotes good decision-making without cutting down the scope of discretion.

By way of example, *R v Camden LBC, ex p H* concerned the decision of a committee of school governors to reverse a decision of a head teacher to exclude two pupils for bringing to school a pellet gun and with it injuring a third pupil, the plaintiff.[5] The Court of Appeal held that the school governors had failed to investigate inculpatory accounts of the incident and had failed to consider what the effect of reversing the head teacher's decision would have on the plaintiff and on school discipline more generally. In this way the Court never had to turn its mind to the question of whether redeeming the pair of ruffians was itself reasonable, and the Court directed that the matter should be re-determined by a differently constituted committee of governors in the light of their judgment identifying the matters of importance.

---

[4] See M Fordham, *Judicial Review Handbook*, 5th edn (Oxford, Hart Publishing, 2008) ch 51, 483–93 (duty of sufficient inquiry). Oddly, given that it is the engine of judicial review, process review found no place in Lord Diplock's trichotomy of grounds of judicial review in *GCHQ* [1985] AC 374, 410–11.

[5] *R v Camden LBC, ex p H* [1996] ELR 360.

It is therefore only natural that, looked at from the perspective of administrative law, the Human Rights Act would be understood as imposing similar process requirements when a decision interferes with a Convention right. But more than this, there is a natural and understandable—indeed justifiable—tendency for judges to prefer to impose process requirements and fix upon process failings where possible. This is a characteristic feature of public law adjudication. It is also an example of the exercise of the passive virtues, because it avoids the courts having to determine the most controversial issues.[6] There is nothing in the Human Rights Act itself which precludes process review. Section 6(1) states that it is unlawful for a public authority to act incompatibly with a Convention right, but it leaves open what constitutes a breach of such a right and whether Convention rights may impose *procedural obligations.*

Before moving on, it is worth being absolutely clear about the nature of procedural obligations with which we are here concerned. Both the common law and Convention rights impose obligations of fairness on public authorities, such as rights to be heard, rights to make an effective challenge to a decision and rights to disclosure of information. We are not here concerned with these obligations. Such obligations are procedural obligations, in the sense that they impose obligations on public officials to ensure that individuals affected by their decisions are able to participate in (or at least know about) the decision being taken. Such obligations are imposed by the requirements of fairness both at common law and under Article 6 of the European Convention, and the ECtHR has also recognised that they can arise under certain substantive articles of the Convention.[7] There is no doubt that such procedural obligations arise under the Human Rights Act, where the Convention rights demand. But we are here concerned with whether the Convention rights and the Human Rights Act impose other types of procedural obligation relating to the way decisions affecting Convention rights are taken, even where all affected individuals have been treated fairly.

Just as the Convention rights have been interpreted so as to impose positive operational obligations on contracting states to take steps to protect Convention rights,[8] so Convention rights could be interpreted so as to impose positive duties on States in respect of their decision-making when this affects Convention rights. Article 8, at least, is termed in a way that would be conducive to the recognition of such duties, since it is a right to 'respect' for private and family life, a right that seems to demand that public authorities have due regard to the impact of their actions on the family relations and private lives of affected individuals.

However the House of Lords has ruled out such an approach. In three cases— *R (SB) v Governors of Denbigh High School, Belfast City Council v Miss Behavin' Ltd*

---

[6] On which see ch 3, pp 72–76.

[7] For example, deportation decisions are 'public law' decisions and so do not give rise to any rights under Art 6, but Art 8 has been recognised as imposing certain obligations to provide a means of challenge to such a decision and a right to be heard: eg *Lupsa v Romania* (2008) 46 EHRR 36; *CG v Bulgaria* (2008) 47 EHRR 51.

[8] For instance in the Art 2 context, see *Osman v United Kingdom* (2000) 29 EHRR 245.

and *Nasseri v Secretary of State for the Home Department*[9]—the House of Lords has overturned decisions of lower courts that have upheld Human Rights Act complaints on the basis that the public officials have made some error in reaching their decisions, irrespective of whether or not the outcome of the decision could have been found to be compatible with a Convention right. In *Miss Behavin' Ltd* Baroness Hale made explicit that a departure from the traditional approach to administrative law was envisaged:

> The role of the court in human rights adjudication is quite different from the role of the court in an ordinary judicial review of administrative action. In human rights adjudication, the court is concerned with whether the human rights of the claimant have in fact been infringed, not with whether the administrative decision-maker properly took them into account.[10]

Lord Hoffmann said that Article 9 confers no right to 'have a decision made in any particular way'; what matters is the 'result' of its decision-making process.[11]

Miss Behavin' Ltd and *Denbigh High School* involved qualified rights, which require the court to undertake a balancing of respective interests.[12] The cases held that the Human Rights Act does not require public authorities to carry out such a balancing exercise or to weigh the respective interests in any particular way, or have regard to any particular considerations, as long as the outcome of the decision is itself consistent with a fair balance between respective interests. But the logic of the reasoning of the House of Lords in both cases was clearly broader and applied even where the Convention does not require a balance to be struck between competing interests but also where it imposes absolute obligations on state agencies. The logic of the cases was that public authorities cannot be found to have acted incompatibly with absolute Convention rights under section 6 of the Human Rights Act just because they have failed to recognise that their decisions might affect such rights or because they have failed to consider what such rights require.[13] This was confirmed by *Nasseri*, in which the House of Lords rejected a challenge under Article 3 of the European Convention to a decision to deport an asylum-seeker to Greece. The Judicial Committee held that if the deportation gave rise to a real risk of the individual suffering inhuman or degrading treatment or torture, then it would violate Article 3, but it did not matter that the immigration

---

[9] *R (SB) v Governors of Denbigh High School* [2007] 1 AC 100; *Belfast City Council v Miss Behavin' Ltd* [2007] 1 WLR 1420 R *(Nasseri) v Secretary of State for the Home Department* [2010] 1 ACI 23. The approach has been applied by the House of Lords in other cases: *DA v Her Majesty's Advocate (the High Court of Justiciary Scotland)* [2007] UKPC D1 (PC) [82] (Lord Rodger); and *Down Liburn and Social Services Trust v H (AP)* [2006] UKHL 36 [64] (Lord Carswell).

[10] *Miss Behavin' Ltd* (n 9) [31].

[11] ibid [68].

[12] In *Miss Behavin' Ltd* ibid, the qualified right was Art 10 (right to freedom of expression); in *Denbigh High School* (n 9) the right was Art 9 (right to manifest religion).

[13] As we have seen, both qualified and unqualified rights establish standards of legality that public authorities must comply with: the injunction that 'no one shall be deprived of his life intentionally' no more demarcates the scope of Art 2 than the stipulation that, 'no one's freedom of expression shall be denied unnecessarily' demarcates the scope of Art 10. See ch 4, pp 108–109.

authorities had not enquired—and indeed were precluded from enquiring—into whether or not a real risk arose on the particular facts of the case, because Greece was included on a statutory list of safe countries. Lord Hoffmann, giving the leading speech, expressed some sympathy with the trial judge who had found to the contrary in a belief that the Human Rights Act was administrative law-*plus*:

> It is understandable that a judge hearing an application for judicial review should think that he is undertaking a review of the Secretary of State's decision in accordance with normal principles of administrative law, that is to say, that he is reviewing the decision-making process rather than the merits of the decision. . . . But that is not the correct approach when a challenge is based on an alleged infringement of a Convention right.[14]

The effect of the House of Lords' judgments in these three cases is that even where a decision-maker decides a case by an irrational process of reasoning, or even without any consideration at all, it will be compatible with Convention rights and it will be consistent with the decision-maker's responsibilities under the Human Rights Act, as long as the *outcome* is compatible with Convention rights. The three decisions of the House of Lords are particularly powerful not only because the reasoning led to the overturning of lower court judgments in each case but also because this approach did not provoke a single dissenting voice in any of these cases. The approach without doubt has become Human Rights Act orthodoxy. But it has not yet caught on, and there are so many problems with it that it must be doubted whether the breadth of the principle established by the House of Lords is sustainable in the long term.

Take for example the comments made obiter by Lord Walker in *Doherty*, a case decided before *Nasseri* but after the other two judgments had been delivered. His Lordship said that, 'Public authorities are bound to take account of human rights. As our domestic human rights jurisprudence develops and becomes bedded down, this should be seen as a normal part of their functions, not an exotic introduction.' His Lordship went to on state that the purpose of the Human Rights Act is to domesticate Convention rights and that must be 'woven into the fabric of public law'.[15] On the face of it, these comments are starkly at odds with the decisions of the House of Lords in *Denbigh High School*, *Miss Behavin' Ltd* and *Nasseri*, given that the House of Lords in those cases disclaimed any requirement for public authorities to have regard to Convention rights and distinguished Human Rights Act review from the approach taken by the common law. And there are numerous examples where the courts, including the House of Lords, seem to have assumed that the Human Rights Act does in fact impose procedural requirements on decision-makers that absent the Human Rights Act would not have arisen. In *R (Laporte) v Chief Constable of Gloucestershire Constabulary*[16] a challenge was made to a decision of the Gloucestershire Constabulary to prevent a coach con-

---

[14] *Nasseri* (n 9) [12].

[15] *Doherty v Birmingham City Council* [2009] 1 AC 367 [109]. Citing A Lester and D Pannick, 'The Impact of the Human Rights Act on Private Law: The Knights Move' (2000) 116 *LQR* 380 at 383.

[16] *R (Laporte) v Chief Constable of Gloucestershire Constabulary* [2007] 2 AC 105.

taining anti-war protesters from attending a demonstration at RAF Fairford in Gloucestershire because some of the passengers were known trouble-makers. In finding that escorting the coach back to London was disproportionate, Lord Rodger reasoned that, 'under the Human Rights Act 1998 the police must have regard to the rights to freedom of expression and freedom of assembly which protesters, such as the claimant, are entitled to assert.'[17] And Lord Carswell held that the police should have 'given consideration' to removing identified troublemakers and dangerous items from the coach and the possibility of allowing the rest of the protesters to proceed to the site of the demonstration and to any necessary further action there, which would have been a less intrusive course of action.[18] *Laporte* is a decision of the House of Lords itself which was premised on reasoning that must be regarded as wrong in law.

There are other examples to be found in speeches given in House of Lords in other cases, such as Lord Hope's statement in *A (No 1)* that Article 15 requires contracting states 'to consider with the greatest care whether an alternative course of action can be taken to deal with the exigencies of the situation . . .'; or Lord Nicholls' statement in *Re S (Care Plan)* that, 'Although Article 8 contains no explicit procedural requirements, the decision-making process leading to a care order must be fair and such as to afford due respect to the interests safeguarded by Article 8'; or Lord Bingham's statement in *R v Shayler* that when senior officers of the Intelligence Services decide whether to authorise disclosure of information they must consider the documentation 'with care' and 'weigh the merits' whilst 'bearing in mind the importance attached to the right of free expression and the need for any restriction to be necessary, responsive to a pressing social need and proportionate'.[19] If one looks to decisions of lower courts, the examples could be multiplied many times over.[20]

---

[17] *Laporte* ibid [85].

[18] *Laporte* ibid [105].

[19] *A and others v Secretary of State for the Home Department (No 1)* 56, [2005] 2 AC 68 [121]; *Re S (Children) (Care Order: Implementation of Care Plan)* [2002] 2 AC 291 [99]; *R v Shayler* [2003] 1 AC 247 [30]. In *R (Razgar) v Secretary of State for the Home Department* [2004] 2 AC 368 [17] Lord Bingham stated that the reviewing court must 'ask itself essentially the questions which would have to be answered by the adjudicator', and then listed specific questions relating to Art 8 to be taken into account (also Baroness Hale at [60]). In *E v Chief Constable of the Royal Ulster Constabulary* [2009] 1 AC 536 [60] Lord Carswell stated that whether police had had regard to rights of the child is 'a matter which may be relevant in determining whether the actions of the police satisfied the obligation placed on them by Article 3'.

[20] See eg *R (Hafner) v City of Westminster Magistrates' Court* [2009] 1 WLR 1005 [25] (a magistrates' court nominated under s 15 of the Crime (International Co-operation) Act 2003 must have regard to Art 8 rights) (Phillips CJ); *Pascoe v First Secretary of State* [2007] 1 WLR 885 [66], [84]–[85] (in making a compulsory purchase order inspector and Secretary of State must have carried out necessary balancing exercise); *R (X) v Chief Constable of the West Midland Police* [2005] 1 All ER 610 [47] (courts will not interfere with chief constable's decision taken properly on the basis of the evidence then available); *Shala v SSHD* [2003] EWCA Civ 233 (decision fell outside margin of discretion where Secretary of State had not reflected on consequences); *R (D) v SSHD* [2003] 1 FLR 979 [20]–[23]; *R (Goldsmith) v Wandsworth LBC* [2003] EWHC 1720 (Admin); *AB (Jamaica) v SSHD* [2008] 1 WLR 1893. For an example from the employment law context (age discrimination), see *Bloxham v Freshfields Bruckaus Deringer* [2007] Pens LR 375.

The implications of the anti-process rule now established are potentially far reaching and as yet not fully appreciated. For instance, cases that have held that Convention rights preclude the application of blanket policies and require, in some contexts at least, public officials to give individual consideration to the facts and circumstances of individual cases, seemed to be uncontroversial but now appear to be wrong.[21] Let us consider just one final example here, the decision of the Court of Appeal in *Rafferty and Jones v Secretary of State for Communities and Local Government.* The decision is of interest not only because it post-dates *Nasseri* but also because it shows just how ingrained into public law adjudication process review under the Human Rights Act has become. The question for the Court of Appeal was whether a planning inspector had acted contrary to Article 8 in refusing an application for a change of use of land to permit it to be used as a Gypsy caravan site. The Court of Appeal, consistently with the House of Lords cases, rejected the suggestion that the planning inspector's decision was unlawful because he had (wrongly) considered that Article 8 was not engaged (because the Gypsies were not yet on-site), but then, inconsistently with those cases, held that the process by which the planning inspector had reached his conclusion had complied with the requirements of Article 8:

> There is no doubt that the inspector had in mind and took into account the particular needs of the appellants, albeit he did not do so under the Article 8 label. . . . It seems to me therefore that even if the inspector had concluded Article 8(1) was applicable he would inevitably have reached the same conclusion on the appeal. In this case he weighed all the factors as planning considerations that would have to be weighed under Article 8(1).[22]

As is clear from the last few words of this quote, the entire premise of the Court of Appeal's reasoning, and indeed of the arguments in the case, was mistaken.

These cases are reflective of underlying tensions in the terms and purpose of the Human Rights Act, which were introduced in chapter 2. If the Human Rights Act is understood as protecting domestic law rights, it is a small step to recognising that these impose procedural as well as substantive obligations on domestic authorities. This is precisely the reasoning of Lord Walker in *Doherty* suggesting that human rights principles must be taken into account by public authorities and woven into the fabric of domestic public law. Whereas the approach that was taken by the House of Lords in *Denbigh High School, Miss Behavin' Ltd* and *Nasseri* was closely linked to the influential idea that the Human Rights Act is intended simply to provide a remedy in domestic courts for violations of the UK's international

---

[21] See in particular *R (P) v Secretary of State for the Home Department* [2001] 1 WLR 2002 (a prison policy requiring children to be removed from female prisoners at six months old was contrary to Art 8 insofar as it excluded consideration of individual circumstances) and *R v Shayler* [2003] 1 AC 247 (above: Lord Bingham held that a rubber-stamping approach to disclosure requests would not be consistent with Art 10); also see *R (Baiai) v Secretary of State for the Home Department* [2008] QB 143 (CA) (blanket application of criteria for determining when individuals subject to immigration control can marry is contrary to Art 9), affirmed on slightly different grounds [2009] 1 AC 287 (HL).

[22] *Rafferty and Jones v Secretary of State for Communities and Local Government* [2009] EWCA Civ 809 [38]–[39] (Scott-Baker LJ giving judgment of the court).

obligations. Relying on this idea, their Lordships reasoned that since in their view the ECtHR does not find violations of the Convention on the basis of a defective decision-making process, but only where the substance of a decision is incompatible with Convention rights, recognising procedural obligations (beyond those relating to fairness) would go beyond Parliament's intention in enacting the Human Rights Act and would provide additional rights of action not available to a litigant in Strasbourg.[23]

It will be suggested that the approach of the House of Lords has gone too far. The Human Rights Act is capable of being understood as imposing process requirements as well as requirements of outcome; in precluding this, the House of Lords has greatly reduced the impact that the Human Rights Act will have on administrative decision-making. The decisions also greatly reduce the potency of the Human Rights Act as a means of protecting human rights. These points will be developed below.

Despite this, it is not contended that the decisions in *Denbigh High School, Miss Behavin' Ltd* or *Nasseri* were actually wrong. It is simply that the reasoning on which the Committee based its conclusions was too broad and went too far. If it is now impossible to reverse the approach taken by the House of Lords, then it is submitted that the common law must be pressed into service. The new statutory ground of illegality under the Human Rights Act should be recognised as having implications for the common law grounds of process review. The common law and the Human Rights Act must be viewed symbiotically. Common law doctrines can be applied sensitively to the statutory context to mitigate the worst effects of the House of Lords' decisions. This will not be to reverse the effects of those decisions by the back door. The procedural rights would be located in the common law and not developed out of Convention rights. Moreover the common law is applied in a context-specific way and would not go as far as the lower courts' judgments that were overruled in *Denbigh High School, Miss Behavin' Ltd* and *Nasseri*.

---

[23] The first reason for forbidding process review under the Human Rights Act given by Lord Bingham in *Denbigh High School* (n 9) was that, 'the purpose of the Human Rights Act 1998 was not to enlarge the rights or remedies of those in the United Kingdom whose Convention rights have been violated but to enable those rights and remedies to be asserted and enforced by the domestic courts of this country and not only by recourse to Strasbourg. . . . But the focus at Strasbourg is not and has never been on whether a challenged decision or action is the product of a defective decision-making process, but on whether, in the case under consideration, the applicant's Convention rights have been violated' ([29]). See also at [68] (Lord Hoffmann). It is notable that the approach of the House of Lords, by adhering to a standard of legality, as opposed to a standard of review, approach can combine a remedial or pragmatic view of the Human Rights Act. On this, see especially Lord Bingham in *Denbigh High School* at [30]. This approach exhibits a further dimension of the tensions embedded in the Act as discussed in ch 2, pp 25–49.

Throwing the Baby out with the Bathwater

In both *Denbigh High School* and *Miss Behavin' Ltd* the House of Lords was faced with decisions made by lower courts that imposed unjustifiably extensive procedural obligations on public bodies. In *Denbigh High School* the Court of Appeal, reversing the first instance judge, held that a decision by the defendant school's governing body to refuse to allow a female Muslim student to attend school wearing a jilbab was incompatible with Convention rights because the school had not properly addressed itself to the interference with the claimant's right to manifest religious belief protected by Article 9 of the Convention. The school had, however, undertaken extensive consultations with parents, students and local mosques in drawing up its uniform policy, had gone to some lengths to explain its dress code to prospective pupils and parents, and had consulted religious authorities again after the claimant had refused to comply with the policy.[24] Brooke LJ, giving the leading judgment, held that the school authorities should have structured their decision-making process by reference to six questions directed at considering whether the interference was proportionate.[25] The House of Lords held that this was not necessary and that the action of the governors was proportionate because they were entitled to implement a uniform policy that permitted wearing other forms of Muslim dress but did not permit the wearing of the jilbab (which is full body length).

The rejection of Brooke LJ's structured approach was unsurprising and surely right. It is unrealistic to require public officials, such as teachers, nurses, policemen and other professionals to structure their decisions in such a manner when performing their day-to-day functions. As Lord Hoffmann put it, head teachers and school governors 'cannot be expected to make such decisions with textbooks on human rights law at their elbows'.[26] However, the reasoning of their Lordships on which this finding was premised was much wider, and, as we have seen, was to the effect that no shortcomings in the process by which a decision is reached are capable of rendering the decision disproportionate, because proportionality relates only to the outcome of a decision and its effect on the individual or individuals

---

[24] *R (Begum (Shabana)) v Headteacher and Governors of Denbigh High School* [2005] EWCA Civ 199 [7]–[8], [13]–[15].

[25] *Denbigh High School* ibid [75]: 'The decision-making structure should therefore go along the following lines. (1) Has the claimant established that she has a relevant Convention right which qualifies for protection under article 9(1)? (2) Subject to any justification that is established under article 9(2), has that Convention right been violated? (3) Was the interference with her Convention right prescribed by law in the Convention sense of that expression? (4) Did the interference have a legitimate aim? (5) What are the considerations that need to be balanced against each other when determining whether the interference was necessary in a democratic society for the purpose of achieving that aim? (6) Was the interference justified under article 9(2)?'

[26] *Miss Behavin' Limited* (n 9) [68]. Lord Bingham stated in the *Denbigh High School* case (n 9) that the 'Court of Appeal's decision-making prescription would be admirable guidance to a lower court or legal tribunal, but cannot be required of a head teacher and governors, even with a solicitor to help them' ([31]).

concerned. The House of Lords did not need to go this far. Their Lordships could have said that although Article 9 does not require a legalistic, highly structured decision-making process, it may nonetheless impose procedural obligations on public authorities, in appropriate cases, such as requiring that public authorities weigh the competing interests and consider adopting less injurious measures.

The House of Lords confirmed the breadth of its reasoning in the *Miss Behavin' Ltd* case, in which the claimant, Miss Behavin' Ltd, had been refused a licence to run a sex shop in premises in Gresham Street in Belfast by the council's Health and Environment Services Committee. The Committee had decided that the particular locality was not suitable for any sex shops and after considering the merits of Miss Behavin's application decided that no exception to this policy was warranted in its case. In so deciding the Committee did not expressly address Miss Behavin' Ltd's right to freedom of expression under Article 10 of the Convention or its right to enjoyment of its possessions under Article 1 of the First Protocol. The Court of Appeal in Northern Ireland held that the Committee's failure to address these rights rendered the decision contrary to the Human Rights Act.[27] The House of Lords found that it was not necessary for the Convention rights of Miss Behavin' Ltd to have been addressed by the Committee in reaching its decision. Lord Hoffmann stated that the decision of the Court of Appeal was 'contrary to the reasoning' in the *Denbigh High School* case, as well as being 'quite impractical'.[28] Baroness Hale made explicit that a departure from the traditional approach to judicial review was envisaged, as we have previously seen.[29]

Again, the House of Lords was surely right to have held that the Committee did not need to have explicit regard to Article 10 or Article 1 of the First Protocol, in the circumstances of the case. This was not a case where there was a serious infringement with human rights, Article 10 was engaged at only a 'low level',[30] and Article 1 of the First Protocol probably not at all (the point was never decided). The decision, like that of the school governors in *Denbigh High School*, was firmly at the administrative rather than judicial end of the spectrum and, most importantly of all, it was clear

---

[27] *In the matter of an application by Misbehavin Limited for judicial review* [2005] NICA 35 [58], [63] and [64].

[28] *Miss Behavin'* (n 9) [13]. Lord Rodger stated: '. . . if the refusal did not interfere disproportionately with the applicant's right to freedom of expression, then it was lawful for purposes of section 6(1)—whether or not the Council had deliberated on that right before refusing. . . . This is just to apply what was said by Lord Bingham of Cornhill and Lord Hoffmann in *R (SB) v Governors of Denbigh High School*' ([23]–[24]). See also Baroness Hale at [71], Lord Mance at [44]–[45] and Lord Neuberger at [90], indicating that the sole issue is whether the court considers there was violation of Art 10 and it is only where the Convention itself confers procedural rights that the process of decision-making can constitute a breach of a Convention right.

[29] *Miss Behavin'* (n 9) [31]. In the *Denbigh High School Ltd* case (n 9), Lord Hoffmann likewise stated: 'In domestic judicial review, the court is usually concerned with whether the decision-maker reached his decision in the right way rather than whether he got what the court might think to be the right answer. But article 9 is concerned with substance, not procedure. It confers no right to have a decision made in any particular way. What matters is the result: was the right to manifest a religious belief restricted in a way which is not justified under article 9(2)?' ([68]).

[30] *Miss Behavin'* (n 9) [16] (Lord Hoffmann), [94]–[95] (Lord Neuberger) also [39] (Baroness Hale).

from the way the Committee had in fact approached its decision that it had appreciated what was at stake for the applicant, taken this into account and advanced cogent reasons for refusing the licence.[31] But by resting its decision on the broad, anti-process reasoning that also underpinned the *Denbigh High School* case, the House of Lords went much further and ruled out a role for the Human Rights Act irrespective of how badly and inconsiderately the decision might have been made.

This brings us to *Nasseri*, the third case in the trilogy. Two issues that remained outstanding, at least theoretically, after *Denbigh High School* and *Miss Behavin' Ltd*, were, first, whether the application of the reasoning applied to cases where a decision interferes with an absolute right and, secondly, whether it applies where the decision is made by a judicial body. For instance, Gillen J in the High Court of Northern Ireland had distinguished *Denbigh High School* in holding that the Billy Wright Inquiry Panel had erred by not addressing Article 2 correctly when determining whether to grant witness anonymity, in part on the basis that the panel had not been addressing proportionality but an unqualified right, and in part because the decision made by the Panel was a judicial one.[32] *Nasseri* confirmed that the reasoning in *Denbigh High School* applies to all challenges to decisions where it is said that a Convention right has been infringed.

The appellant in *Nasseri* was an Afghan national who was claiming asylum in the UK but who had first claimed asylum in Greece. The relevant law provides that asylum-seekers who first claim asylum in another EU state must be returned to that state to have their application processed there. The appellant objected that there was a real risk that if returned to Greece he would be sent back to Afghanistan where he would suffer mistreatment, contrary to Article 3 of the Convention. Schedule 3 to the Asylum and Immigration (Treatment of Claimants, etc) Act 2004 lists certain countries in relation to which return is deemed not to violate Article 3 of the Convention. The Secretary of State accepted that this would breach Article 3 in cases where return to such a country would in fact give rise to a real risk of a person suffering ill-treatment contrary to Article 3, but the judge held that a failure to conduct an investigation of the risks of loss of life or torture in every case *itself* constituted a breach of Article 3. The Court of Appeal rejected this contention. Since the judge had not actually considered the risk of being returned to Afghanistan, the Court of Appeal then examined the factual material on this question for itself and concluded that whilst Greece had a 'shaky' history of compliance with its non-refoulement obligations, there were no removals

---

[31] The Committee stated that it had given consideration to the character of the locality, including the type of retail premises located there, the proximity of public buildings such as the Belfast Public Library, the proximity of ships that would attract children and families, and the proximity of places of worship. Indeed, it appears that the Committee also appreciated that freedom of speech was engaged: 'solicitor representing the respondent told the Committee that the right to free speech under the Convention was engaged by the Application, and the minutes of the meeting record that what had been said on behalf of the respondent had been taken into account. While that cannot be said to suggest any sort of careful consideration of Article 10, it does indicate that some regard was had to it.' ([96] (Lord Neuberger)).

[32] *A & Ors, Re Application for Judicial Review* [2007] NIQB 30 [36].

taking place to Afghanistan.[33] The House of Lords upheld the Court of Appeal on the basis of the *Denbigh High School* and *Miss Behavin' Ltd* line of authority. It held that there had been no need for the immigration authorities themselves to consider whether there was a risk of the appellant suffering mistreatment on return; Lord Hoffmann, giving the leading speech, made the remarks already cited.

But yet again, the House of Lords went further than it needed to have done, and failed to consider the implications of such a broad rule for other cases. What was at issue in *Nasseri* was Greece's history of compliance (or non-compliance) with its international obligations. Mr Nasseri did not allege that there were any factors specific to him that gave rise to a real risk in his case. It must be right that the government does not have to consider general country conditions in every case, just as the Immigration Appeals Tribunal itself relies on previous country conditions cases in later cases so that the exercise of assessing country conditions does not have to be undertaken in every case. The government is entitled to have a deeming list, whether that is established in primary or delegated legislation, or whether it is in some other published form. But the question is quite different where an individual raises factors specific to themselves that give rise to a real risk on removal. Here the common law certainly requires that such factors are at least considered by the immigration authorities (and the House of Lords has previously suggested that this is also required by Article 8[34]). The ratio of the House of Lords' ruling is that such specific factors do not need to be considered in order for immigration officials or the IAT to comply with the Human Rights Act. Moreover they do not have to consider Convention law on, for example, the circumstances in which deportation will constitute an unjustified infringement with a family's Article 8 right.

The prudent course would have been to avoid articulating such a general rule which forbids process requirements being developed out of Convention rights in domestic law in any context. It is unfortunate that the first two cases directly on this point that came before the House of Lord concerned decisions made by authorities that, in the respective contexts, reached and reasoned the decisions in a perfectly adequate way, giving due weight to the effect on the claimants, but had been condemned on appeal in judgments that imposed artificial and highly juridified procedural requirements on the public authorities in question.[35] This led their Lordships

---

[33] *R Nasseri v Secretary of State for the Home Department* [2008] 3 WLR 1386 [41].

[34] *Razgar* (n 19) in which Lord Bingham ([17]) and Baroness Hale ([60]) suggested that an immigration adjudicator ought to ask themselves a series of questions directed at determining whether deportation would breach Art 8. Baroness Hale stated: 'the adjudicator is an integral part of the decision-making process and thus would have to consider the issue of proportionality on the evidence before him.'

[35] David Dyzenhaus considers that, whilst the Court of Appeal was wrong to impose such a formalistic set of requirements, the Court of Appeal was right to regard the process of decision-making as defective because the school ought to have at least started from the premise that the claimant had a right recognised by English law: 'Militant Democracy in the House of Lords?' (unpublished paper, on file with author, cited here with permission). But even this is probably too formalistic. The school and its governors are not lawyers; the House of Lords itself found that the decision did *not* amount to an interference with Art 9; and the school was acutely aware of the impact of the policy on religious freedom in the more general sense (which accounted for the extensive consultation including with religious authorities).

into error. There are contexts, such as immigration decisions, where a structured form of decision-making process—with explicit regard to applicable Convention rights—should be required, but it is surely right that it should not be required of school governors or licensing committees. Unfortunately, in reversing the appellate courts in these cases, the House of Lords threw the baby out with the bathwater, and then in *Nasseri* threw the tub out as well.

Muzzling the Human Rights Act

The approach taken by the House of Lords in rejecting the notion that the Human Rights Act imposes process obligations on public authorities has greatly reduced the potency of the Human Rights Act. The effect of the decisions is not only that public authorities do not need to turn up the most recent human rights law learning before making their decisions, but they are not required by the Act to consider the impact of their decisions on individuals concerned at all, they are not required to make inquiries, they are not required to weigh competing interests and they are not required to consider whether other less intrusive alternatives exist. There are a number of specific reasons for questioning the desirability of this approach. We will consider these in turn.

Good Decision-Making and a Culture of Human Rights

We have seen that one of the purposes of the Human Rights Act was to create a 'culture of human rights'.[36] The Joint Committee on Human Rights has examined the idea of a culture of human rights and has suggested that it has two dimensions: a 'moral or personal' dimension and an 'institutional dimension'.[37] The institutional dimension requires that 'human rights should shape the goals, structures, and practices of our public bodies. In their decision-making and their service delivery, schools, hospitals, workplaces and other organs and agencies of the state should ensure full respect for the rights of those involved.' As the Constitution Unit at University College London has put it, the culture of human rights requires that human rights become 'part of the process (rules of the game) of government

---

[36] See ch 2, pp 23–24

[37] JCHR, 'The Case for a Human Rights Commission', Sixth Report 2002–03 (HL 67-I, HC 489-I), paras 1–9. 'The moral or personal dimension refers to the feelings of individuals in society that they have an entitlement to the affirmation of their fundamental rights together with a sense of social responsibility and social obligation towards others' (para 7). See further the submission paper to the JCHR on behalf of the Constitution Unit, University College London, 2 March 2001, describing the steps made by public authorities and the Government's Human Rights Task Force up to that date, available at: www.ucl.ac.uk/constitution-unit/files/HR.pdf.

and political life . . .'.[38] The courts have an important role in developing the institutional dimension of human rights by insisting that these emerging principles of public decision-making are observed as a matter of law.[39] That is not to say that the courts should enforce best practice or ideal forms of decision-making. The courts can however set minimum requirements for decision-making in human rights cases that require basic procedural steps to be taken and, where reasons for a decision are appropriate, that ensure that the decision-maker has given consideration to the impact of the decision on the affected person. The approach of the House of Lords effectively precludes such an approach.

This point is very well illustrated if we dig a little deeper into the history of the *Miss Behavin' Ltd* case. A point which does not appear to have been raised before the House of Lords was that in the years following the introduction of the Human Rights Act the Northern Ireland courts had developed a jurisprudence under the Act in which they required public authorities to give 'explicit recognition' to individual rights affected by their decisions, and that unless recognition of such impact would have made no difference to the outcome, the decision would be held unlawful.[40] This approach was a direct response to systemic failures by many public authorities in Northern Ireland to appreciate the need to respect human rights and to adjust their practices to conform to the Human Rights Act. The 'explicit recognition' doctrine was developed by the Northern Irish courts in an attempt to inculcate a culture of human rights in public authorities in Northern Ireland. Community Health and Social Services Trusts came in for particular criticism for failing to review their decision-making procedures in order to comply with Convention rights.[41] The approach taken by the Northern Ireland courts has now

---

[38] Submissions to JCHR, 1 March 2001: www.ucl.ac.uk/constitution-unit/files/HR.pdf, para 2.2. This is reflected in the training given to public officials and numerous booklets and guidance published by the Government to assist public officials in public authorities in identifying when a decision will affect Convention rights and how to approach such a decision. See eg two publications by the Department for Constitutional Affairs: *Making Sense of Human Rights, A short introduction*, 30 October 2006 and *Human Rights: Human Lives: A handbook for public authorities*, 10 October 2006.

[39] 'The differences which the Act has made in the approach to the issues in asylum appeals such as those before the House, in the material put before the courts and in the content and reasoning of decisions are profound, as may be seen from the opinions given by your Lordships': *R (Ullah) v Special Adjudicator* [2004] 2 AC 323 [54] (Lord Bingham).

[40] This was essentially the approach taken by the Court of Appeal in *Rafferty* (n 22). See *AR v Homefirst Community Trust* [2005] NICA 8; *Re Jennifer Connor's application* [2004] NICA 45; *In the matter of an Application by the Landlords Association for Northern Ireland* [2005] NIQB 22; *In the Matter of J (Care Order: Adoption Agencies)* [2002] NIFam 26; *W and M's application* [2005] NI Fam 2. *AR v Homefirst Community Trust* was considered by the House of Lords in *Down Lisburn Health and Social Services Trust v H (AP)* n 9. Lord Nicholls stated that the case should not be understood to mean that where a trust has considered a Convention right, 'that failure *ipso facto* invalidated its decision' (at [64]). His Lordship said that where the court is properly satisfied that the acts and decisions of the body concerned have been proportionate, 'then it may correctly conclude that no breach of article 8 has occurred, even if that body did not realise that article 8 was engaged and explicitly address the question of compliance' (ibid). In stating that the court 'may' conclude a decision was proportionate, his Lordship was not as emphatic as the Committee in *Denbigh High School* (n 9) and *Miss Behavin' Ltd* (n 9).

[41] See the staunch criticism expressed in *W and M* (n 40).

had to be abandoned.[42] Although the problems in Northern Ireland were acute, they are illustrative of the importance of procedural obligations in creating a culture of human rights. Thus, a study on behalf of the Scottish Executive in 2004 advocated the development of procedural obligations in order to achieve the 'internalisation' of human rights norms and 'improve the standards of the initial decision-making' across a wide spectrum of public authority functions in Scotland.[43] But such an approach has now been ruled out.

It might be argued that the House of Lords has retained an incentive for public officials to make decisions well. The Committee in *Denbigh High School* and *Miss Behavin' Ltd* emphasised that the decision-maker will be given credit if they do consider the impact on Convention rights, in the sense that the Court will give weight to a decision that has been fully informed and taken in a considered way.[44] However, there are several reasons why this does not provide a strong incentive for public officials to adopt good processes of decision-making. Most significantly, it does not alter the fact that there is no *requirement* for decision-makers to make decisions well. They can take their chances. A sloppy, ill-reasoned or hasty decision might be perfectly consistent with the public authorities' obligations under the Human Rights Act if it *happens* to be the case that the outcome of the decision does not infringe a Convention right.

Furthermore, the mere fact that a decision-maker has engaged in an impeccable decision-making process logically does not itself entitle the decision to any particular weight or respect. The court should only give weight to an assessment made by a public official where that official has superior knowledge or expertise in relation to one or more consideration relevant to the decision. It may be, of course, the case that in carrying out an impeccable decision-making process the public official acquires knowledge not shared by the court. This can be seen from the *Denbigh High School* case, in which the governors of the school had consulted widely on the impact of their school uniform policy on its Muslim students and had thus acquired considerable knowledge and local understanding not shared by

---

[42] *Denbigh High School* (n 9) was followed by the Northern Ireland High Court in *Northern Ireland Commissioner for Children and Young People v Secretary of State* [2007] NIQB 52, [38]–[40] and *Re Application for Judicial Review by William Mullen* [2006] NIQB 30.

[43] P Greenhill, T Mullen, J Murdoch, S Craig and A Miller, *The Use of Human Rights Legislation in the Scottish Courts* (Edinburgh, Scottish Executive Social Research, 2004) [6.26]. In the introduction to a book on the Equality and Human Rights Commission, the author notes: 'There is little or no understanding of the Human Rights Act 1998 as a means of balancing the rights of one individual against another ... Applying human rights may well assist public service providers in making difficult decisions where there are competing interests and needs. Greater engagement with the Act could lead to more confident decision-making.': S Makkan, *The Equality Act 2006: A Guide to the Constitution and Functions of the Commission for Equality and Human Rights* (Callow Publishing, London, 2008) 19.

[44] In *Denbigh High School* (n 9), Lord Bingham said that if 'it appears that such a body has conscientiously paid attention to all human rights considerations, no doubt the challenger's task will be harder' ([31]). In *Miss Behavin'* (n 9), Lord Mance said, 'where a council has properly considered the issue in relation to a particular application, the court is inherently less likely to conclude that the decision ultimately reached infringes the applicant's rights.' ([91]).

the court.[45] But in such a case it is the acquisition of knowledge to which respect is paid, not the process of decision-making as such.[46]

It follows that decision-makers are not given credit simply for engaging in a good decision-making process: it will depend on whether they have some superior expertise or experience that the court does not share. Thus, an immigration official's assessment of the impact of deportation on a family might be A+ standard, but the Immigration Appeal Tribunal ought not to afford it any weight because it will be better appraised of the facts relating to the impact of the decision on the family than the immigration official was.[47] As Lord Hoffmann stated in the *Denbigh High School* case, the 'most that can be said' is that the way in which a public authority approaches a problem 'may help to persuade a judge that its answer fell within the area of judgment accorded to it by the law', but there is no reason why the fact that a public authority has engaged in an impeccable decision-making process *as such* should be given any weight.[48] In other words, the decisions given by a public authority are themselves of no more value than counsel's skeleton argument.

There is a further reason why giving credit to well-reasoned decisions is, on close inspection, far from a strong incentive for public officials to engage in a good process of reasoning. The more detailed reasons provided by public officials, and the more explicitly that they invoke Convention rights or principles such as proportionality, the greater the likelihood that they will commit an actionable error of law. Faced with the option of potentially being given some credit for engaging in a comprehensively reasoned decision or running the risk of tripping up on some recent Strasbourg authority, public authorities would be well advised in most cases (absent a team of lawyers to review their decision in draft) to say less rather than more and to steer away from referring to the Convention requirements.

Disadvantages to Aggrieved Individuals and Difficulties for Human Rights Adjudication

As we have seen, the effect of the decisions of the House of Lords is that even where a decision-maker has paid no regard at all to the impact of a decision on an affected individual, the decision will survive a Human Rights Act challenge if sufficient evidence and arguments can be marshalled to justify it. An important implication of this is that public authorities are not tied to the decisions that they have made, the way the decision has been arrived at, or the evidence that was considered at the time, when defending Human Rights Act claims. They can legitimately alter the justification for the decision, introduce further evidence and invent new arguments.

---

[45] It was also the case that the head teacher and governors had existing expertise not shared by the court: see ch 5, p 150.

[46] These points are developed in ch 5, pp 150–53 in the discussion of weight.

[47] See the discussion of *Huang v Secretary of State for the Home Department* [2007] 2 AC 167 [15], discussed in ch 5, pp 132–35.

[48] *Denbigh High School* (n 9) [68].

This will seriously disadvantage affected individuals and is a further muzzling effect of the decisions of the House of Lords.

Claimants in judicial review cases invariably object to attempts by public authorities to rationalise their decisions on an ex post facto basis, and the courts have been relatively firm in preventing public bodies from doing so.[49] It is not difficult to see why allowing public authorities to advance ex post facto justifications disadvantages claimants. It permits public authorities a second bite at the cherry, and the introduction of witness statements and other evidence (which might include empirical studies, reports, or even expert evidence, depending on the nature of the decision under challenge) is extremely difficult and costly for claimants to respond to. Furthermore, where reliance can be placed on ex post facto justifications it is also much more difficult for claimants to predict in advance their chances of success. This is, in practice, a critical point. An individual who is aggrieved by a decision made by a public authority that interferes with his or her Convention rights is able to take advice on the likelihood of that decision being quashed. But if the authority is able to advance unlimited further reasons and evidence to justify that decision, even though these were not taken into account at the time, it becomes a great deal more difficult to predict whether the decision will be found unlawful under section 6 of the Human Rights Act.[50]

Of course, even if the courts recognised that failings of process could constitute breaches of Conventions rights, that would not mean that the focus would shift entirely to the process of decision-making. Claimants would still be able to say *in addition* that the outcome of the decision made contravened their Convention rights.[51] And ex post facto reasons and evidence would be admissible in relation to that issue. But allowing claimants to bring process challenges would at least mean that claimants with strong process grounds for complaint could assess their chances of success with greater certainty because it would be no defence for a public authority to show that the substance of the decision was compatible with Convention rights. On well-established judicial review principles, unless the defendant public authority could show that the decision would inevitably have been the same had it been properly made, the decision would be sent back to the primary decision-maker to be made on a proper basis.

---

[49] See for instance *R v Westminster City Council, ex p Ermakov* [1996] 2 All ER 302, 311–12; *R (Sporting Options plc) v Horserace Betting Levy Board* [2003] EWHC 1943 (Admin) [197]. In practice, public authorities usually seek to supplement their decisions with additional supporting reasons and evidence. In some circumstances this is expressly permitted; often the court acquiesces in the evidence being submitted even if it is not ultimately relied upon by the court.

[50] For the same reasons, the focus on substance can also be expected to increase the length and complexity of judicial review proceedings. Whilst it is true that public authorities could still advance this material if they could be held to have acted disproportionately in respect of *both* procedural failings and the outcome of their decisions, there would be much less incentive for public authorities to throw the kitchen sink at proving a measure is, in substance, proportionate if they are at risk of having failed properly to weigh the respective interests or investigate the matter properly in the first place (and it would not be a proportionate way to conduct litigation). Indeed, in many cases where a public authority is vulnerable on points of procedure, the proceedings will not be defended at all.

[51] Contrast Lord Bingham in *Denbigh High School* (n 9) [30].

Claimants will also be disadvantaged in an even more straightforward way: they will be forced to challenge administrative decisions for breach of human rights on the far more difficult substantive terrain. Judges are better suited to assessing matters of procedure and, as we saw at the outset of this chapter, are more inclined to invalidate decisions on process grounds. Being forced to address human rights complaints to the substance of the decision made is particularly disadvantageous to affected individuals because it is so difficult for courts, particularly in relation to decisions involving specialist knowledge or decisions that are made in areas of social and economic policy, to second-guess the decisions that have been made. In such cases courts are likely to give very considerable weight to the assessment made by the primary decision-maker relevant to whether in substance the decision is consistent with Convention rights. The individual then risks falling between two stools: the court refuses to engage with the decision-making process because that cannot affect the legality of the decision, whilst at the same time the court confers considerable weight to the decision-maker on the substance because it is better able to make the decision than the court.

A particular problem arises in cases where the primary decision-maker has not carried out an assessment of the respective interests at all, or has done so in a misconceived way, and where that decision-maker's assessment would ordinarily be afforded considerable weight by the court because of its superior knowledge and expertise. The court will not be able to find that the decision is vitiated under the Human Rights Act by a procedural defect. It will have to attempt to ascertain whether the measure is justified but without the benefit of any contemporary assessments made by the primary decision-maker. It is difficult to see how such an assessment made by the court could be sound.[52] Take for example a situation where a public authority has failed to consider the possibility of an alterative less injurious alternative, or its potential effectiveness, in a complex policy area. If an affected individual then claims that the failure to take this less injurious course was disproportionate, the court will have to attempt to determine for itself whether that alternative—which had not even been adverted to by the primary decision-maker—should have been taken. No doubt the public authority will produce ex post evidence and arguments to the effect that it was not necessary to take the alternative measure. Ordinarily such self-serving ex post material would have to be treated with extreme caution by the courts, but is difficult to see what option the court would have other than to accept it where it is self-confessedly unable to weigh properly the respective interests itself.[53]

The position is likely to cause injustice and it is out of step with the idea—central to traditional public law—that an individual is entitled to have a decision affecting him or her properly made by the decision-maker with primary responsibility for

---

[52] See, for example, the regulation of tobacco advertising in *R (British American Tobacco) v Secretary of State for Health* [2004] EWHC 2493 (Admin): '. . . the Court is in no position on a judicial review application to weigh up the pro's and con's of particular levels of this type of advertising.'([52] (McCombe J)).

[53] This problem is not limited to assessments of competing alternatives. The court would be faced with the same difficulty in many other situations, for instance, where a prisoner suffers harm and the prison authorities have failed to carry out a risk assessment (or a thorough risk assessment).

making it unless it can be shown that the procedural defect would have made no difference and the decision would inevitably have been the same had it not been made. The exclusive focus on substance denies courts the opportunity to protect human rights by insisting that the public authority with principal responsibility for making the decision, in accordance with Convention rights, makes the decision on a proper basis with due regard to such rights. And it ties the courts' hands because the court is often not in a position to assess the substantive issues itself where there has been a significant procedural failing. There was no need for such difficulties to have arisen. They have only arisen because of the House of Lords' dogmatic attachment to substantive illegality.

Several of the points just made can be illustrated by reference to *Chapman v United Kingdom*. The case concerned a failed application by a Gypsy for planning permission to develop land that she owned and on which she lived in a caravan with her family.[54] In the course of its judgment rejecting the application under Article 8 the ECtHR stated that it simply could not weigh the 'multitude of local factors' in such a case to determine whether planning permission should have been granted. But it went on to state:

> In these circumstances, the procedural safeguards available to the individual will be especially material in determining whether the respondent State has, when fixing the regulatory framework, remained within its margin of appreciation. In particular, the Court must examine whether the decision-making process leading to measures of interference was fair and such as to afford due respect to the interests safeguarded to the individual by Article 8.[55]

The ECtHR considered the process of decision-making in some detail and concluded that,

> In the circumstances, the Court considers that proper regard was had to the applicant's predicament both under the terms of the regulatory framework, which contained adequate procedural safeguards protecting her interest under Article 8 and by the responsible planning authorities when exercising their discretion in relation to the particular circumstances of her case. The decisions were reached by those authorities after weighing in the balance the various competing interests. It is not for this Court to sit in appeal on the merits of those decisions, which were based on reasons which were relevant and sufficient, for the purposes of Article 8, to justify the interferences with the exercise of the applicant's rights.[56]

The Court has therefore recognised that, in contexts where it cannot weigh the respective interests for itself, the only way it can effectively protect the right to respect for family life is to examine the process of decision-making. It is moreover clear from *Chapman* that had the proper process of decision-making not been gone through, a violation of Article 8 would have been found. This takes us to the third problem with the House of Lords' approach, which is that it is in fact out of step with the Strasbourg jurisprudence.

---

[54] *Chapman v United Kingdom* (2001) 33 EHRR 399 [92].
[55] ibid [92].
[56] ibid [114].

Out of Step with Strasbourg

We have seen that the decisions of the House of Lords in *Denbigh High School, Miss Behavin' Ltd* and *Nasseri* were premised on what the House of Lords regarded as the outcome-orientated approach of the ECtHR and that this was connected to the idea that the purpose of the Human Rights Act is simply to provide individuals with the same remedy they could obtain in Strasbourg. But the approach fails to appreciate the nuances in the approach taken by the Strasbourg Court. In *Chapman v United Kingdom*, for instance, we have seen that the ECtHR did in effect engage in process review because it was unable to assess whether or not planning permission ought to have been granted in order to comply with Article 8. In other cases the ECtHR has said that where a proper process is not gone through, the ultimate decision falls outside the margin of appreciation.[57] Since a state will have breached the Convention where it has exceeded this margin, inadequacies in the process are capable of amounting to a breach of the Convention. This is what occurred in *Dickson v United Kingdom*, a decision of the Grand Chamber which post-dates *Denbigh High School* and *Miss Behavin' Ltd* and which was not referred to the House of Lords in *Nasseri*. The Grand Chamber held that the Home Secretary's decision to refuse a life prisoner access to artificial insemination facilities breached Article 8. The breach of Article 8 was attributable to the fact that the Home Secretary's policy of only allowing access to artificial insemination facilities in 'exceptional circumstances' set too high a threshold, because it prevented the Home Secretary from considering specific considerations relevant to a person's Article 8 rights. The Grand Chamber stated, 'the policy as structured effectively excluded any real weighing of the competing individual and public interests, and prevented the required assessment of the proportionality of a restriction, in any individual case'.[58] Furthermore, there was no evidence that the competing interests had ever in fact been weighed by the Secretary of State or by Parliament. Therefore, 'in the absence of such an assessment' the decision was found to fall outside an acceptable margin of appreciation, 'so that a fair balance was not struck between the competing public and private interests involved'.[59] This is clearly in contrast with the approach that has been taken by the House of Lords. If it had applied such an approach, the Grand Chamber would have held that the failure to weigh the respective interests did not itself lead to a breach of Article 8, which would depend on whether the actual refusal of access to artificial insemination facilities was on the facts necessary. It would be artificial to seek to reconcile the cases on the basis that the Grand Chamber was simply affording weight to the

---

[57] In such cases the ECtHR is using the margin of appreciation doctrine in the second of the two ways described in ch 4, pp 123–25. The Strasbourg Court also places very significant weight on the process leading to the impugned measure and the degree to which competing interests are weighed and considered by domestic authorities: eg *Hirst v United Kingdom* (2006) 42 EHRR 41 [79].

[58] *Dickson v United Kingdom* (2008) 46 EHRR 41[82].

[59] ibid [83] and [85].

assessment made by national authorities: the Grand Chamber was undoubtedly engaged in process review.[60]

Another example is provided by the case of *Moser v Austria*, concerning a decision to take the first applicant's son into care. The case was in part about the implied rights of a parent to participate in such a decision, but the ECtHR considered separately the question of whether the process of decision-making had been adequate. It stated, 'a case like the present one called for a particularly careful examination of possible alternatives to taking the second applicant into public care'.[61] Although the Court rejected the applicant's contention that no consideration at all had been given to possible alternatives, it held that insufficient consideration to alternatives had been given. It reasoned:

> . . . no positive action was taken to explore possibilities which would have allowed the applicants to remain together, for instance by placing them in a mother-child centre. In this connection, the Court notes that according to the Government the fact that the applicants were foreigners did not exclude them from admission to a mother child centre under the Vienna Youth Welfare Act. However, this possibility was apparently not contemplated and no other measures such as clarifying the applicant's residence status were taken. . . .
>
> This failure to make a full assessment of all possible alternatives is aggravated by the fact that no measures were taken to establish and maintain the contact between the applicants while the proceedings were pending . . .[62]

Given the failure to have regard to these alternatives, together with additional failures to involve the applicant in the decision-making process, the Court found that the reasons supplied by the authorities for taking the child into care were not sufficient. The crucially important point is that the ECtHR in *Moser v Austria* did not decide that the child ought not to have been taken into care and that taking the child into care breached Article 8; it decided that the child ought not to have been taken into care *until a proper assessment had been carried out*. The Court made clear that there were minimum procedural pre-conditions that domestic authorities must satisfy which went beyond ensuring that the affected individuals were treated fairly.

It follows that even if the courts are right in their attachment to the idea that domestic courts can only provide claimants with a remedy where their claims would succeed in Strasbourg, the wholesale rejection of process review is contrary to that idea.

---

[60] A similar approach was taken by the Grand Chamber in *Hatton v United Kingdom* (2003) 37 EHRR 611 in which it held that the regulation of night-time flights at Heathrow Airport was within the UK's margin of appreciation under Art 8, relying in part on the detailed investigations and consultations that had been carried out by the Government. The Court treated this as a 'procedural aspect' (at [129]) of Art 8. This procedural aspect of Art 8 is distinct from the implied procedural right to fair procedures which arises under Art 8, since it was not suggested that these investigations were required in fairness to anyone (*cf McMichael v United Kingdom* (1995) 20 EHRR 205 [92]). In the *Denbigh High School* case (n 9), Lord Hoffmann attempted to distinguish *Hatton v United Kingdom*, by treating it as a case about implied procedural rights to fairness (at [51]); but the Grand Chamber's judgment went beyond fairness. For another case analogous to *Hatton*, see *Giacomelli v Italy* (2007) 45 EHRR 38 [83].
[61] *Moser v Austria* (App no 12643/02) 21 September 2006, [2007] 1 FLR 702, [69]
[62] ibid [70]–[71].

A New Formalism?

One of the reasons that led Lord Bingham in the *Denbigh High School* case to reject process review under the Human Rights Act was that the approach of the Court of Appeal would lead to a 'new formalism' and 'judicialisation on an unprecedented scale'.[63] This was the basis of criticism of the Court of Appeal's judgment by Thomas Poole, which was adopted by Lord Bingham.[64] Following the Court of Appeal decision, Poole had argued that requiring public authorities to adopt a highly structured proportionality analysis would impose a straight-jacketed approach that would have a 'stifling' effect on good administration.[65] In so arguing, Poole contended that the proper approach under the Human Rights Act must be entirely substantive and that no procedural obligations should be imposed as part of the test of justification at all. He stated, for example, that:

> striking down decisions of public authorities on 'pure' procedural grounds would amount, I suggest, not to the imposition of a higher standard of rights protection but rather to the erection of a new formalism which, in seeking to avoid coming to a conclusion about the substance of the decision or policy at issue, will threaten to make a fetish of procedure.[66]

He made clear that in his view, there is no legitimate basis for striking down a decision because it had not been made in the proper way if, in substance, it was found to be proportionate.[67]

It should now be clear that Poole, like the House of Lords, was over-reaching. His concern about the judicialisation of administrative decisions if public authorities were to be always required to adopt a highly structured rights-based reasoning process (as suggested by the Court of Appeal) does not support his argument for the rejection the imposition of *any* procedural requirements when judging whether interferences with qualified rights are justified. For example, the courts could require that public authorities have due regard to the fact that a deportation decision affected not only the individual concerned but also his or her family.[68] That would not require explicit consideration of Convention rights as such, nor would it require decision-makers to have books on human rights at their elbows.

---

[63] Note. Likewise, in the *Miss Behavin'* case, Lord Hoffmann stated: 'A construction of the 1998 Act which requires ordinary citizens in local government to produce such formulaic incantations would make it ridiculous': 9 [31] [13].

[64] T Poole, 'Of headscarves and heresies: the *Denbigh High School* Case and public authority decision making under the Human Rights Act' [2005] *PL* 685.

[65] For example at n 9, 695.

[66] Poole, 'Of headscarves and heresies' ibid, 691.

[67] Poole justified this approach in part on the basis, he claimed, that the focus of s 6 of the HRA is 'result-orientated' and that the test that the court ought to apply is therefore a 'substantive one'. For example ibid 690–91.

[68] In assessing whether there has been a breach of Art 8 rights, attention must be given to the effect of a decision on the family as a whole, and not just the impact on the individual member to whom the decision is addressed: *Beoku Betts v Secretary of State for the Home Department* [2009] 1 AC 115.

Thus, the Strasbourg Court in *Chapman v United Kingdom* referred to the domestic authority having had regard not to Article 8 itself, but to the 'interests safeguarded' by the Convention.[69] This does not require public authorities to employ the language of the Convention or even the language of rights. Nor would such obligations be unduly onerous. As we have seen, these were just the sort of procedural steps that were taken by Denbigh High School and Belfast City Council.

In a more recent paper, Poole has changed his tune. In this article Poole states that the basic issue in the *Denbigh High School* case will continue to arise because, 'there are some occasions when the imposition of an obligation to consider an issue in Convention rights-specific terms is justified'. It will, he now says, be entirely appropriate in some context for the decision-maker to 'bring its mind to bear directly on rights-related issues'.[70] The object of Poole's criticism in his more recent article is what he describes as 'a general duty on public authorities to approach decisions through an ECHR prism'. By this, Poole must be taken to mean a requirement that all decision-makers, in whatever context, expressly advert to applicable Convention rights and engage in a structured, staged, proportionality assessment. The problem with this argument is that, the overturned Court of Appeal judgment in the *Denbigh High School* case aside, Poole is unable to identify a single person who argues for such an approach.[71] And unsurprisingly: it would be palpable nonsense to argue, for example, that doctors, teachers and social workers making day-to-day decisions should explicitly identify relevant Convention rights, have a quick peek in Lester, Pannick & Herberg's *Human Rights Practice*, and then engage in a structured assessment of the competing interests reflecting the most recent case law. With the Court of Appeal's judgment

---

[69] *Chapman v United Kingdom* (n 54).

[70] T Poole, 'The Reformation of English Administrative law' (2009) 68 *CLJ* 142, 150, an earlier version of which is also published in the LSE Law, Society and Economy Working Papers Series 12/2007, LSE Law Department, www.lse.ac.uk/collections/law/wps/wps.htm. Poole gives the example of deportation decisions, but he does not refer to *Nasseri*, or explain how such an assertion is consistent with his previous views that were accepted by the House of Lords in *Denbigh High School* which led directly to *Nasseri*. Poole is right to recognise that procedural obligations are imposed in immigration decisions in relation to individual-specific factors. Of numerous examples that could be given, see eg *AB (Jamaica) v Secretary of State for the Home Department* [2007] EWCA Civ 1302 [18]–[22], [29]; *R (Razgar) v Secretary of State for the Home Department* [2003] Imm AR 529 (CA) [8] (Dyson LJ), and see the comments in *Ullah* (n 39) [41].

[71] Poole refers to work by TRS Allan, Jeffrey Jowell and David Beatty, and asserts, 'it is *plausible* to *assume* that they might favour the imposition of a general duty on public authorities to approach relevant decision-making through a Convention framework' ((2009) 68 *CLJ* 142, 153–54) (emphasis added). No such assumption is in fact warranted, and Poole gives no reasons for why he says such an assumption is plausible. He then goes on to refer to views of this author, as another 'hardliner' who 'share[s] the same root assumptions' as the rest (ibid). Although it is unclear what assumptions this author is assumed by Poole to hold, it can at least be said that in this book many of the views of the scholars referred to by Poole are in fact rejected. Poole then accurately summarises the position taken by the author in a draft paper (an early version of this chapter), and then, bizarrely, associates it with the approach taken by the Court of Appeal in *Denbigh High School* (n 9). His conclusion is that the approach is 'flawed because it is blind (or insensitive) to institutional context' (ibid). But it seems that Poole has come round to the same way of thinking as at least this author. It is actually the approach that Poole himself took in his earlier article that was formalistic and insensitive to context and which, regrettably, led the House of Lords astray.

in the Denbigh High School case having, rightly, been overturned, Poole is left shadow-boxing.

The approach argued for here is neither formalistic nor does it require a juridified approach to administrative decision-making. The considerations to which decision-makers would have to advert, the degree of investigation and inquiry that they ought to undertake, and the extent to which they ought to address Convention rights and legal tests explicitly (if at all) would depend on the type of decision and the context in which it was taken. What would be required of a school would not be the same as what would be required of a planning committee, and neither could be equated with decision-making by immigration officials. There is nothing novel in this. It is how administrative law has always worked. It is why education lawyers have books on education law at their elbows, whereas planning lawyers have books on planning law, and immigration lawyers have books on immigration law (and why generalist public lawyers have to buy a lot of books).

The point is that there is no one-size-fits-all formula. That is what is wrong with approach taken by Poole and endorsed by the House of Lords: it forbids process review under the Human Rights Act across the board, irrespective of the context. The effect is that the House of Lords has substituted one formalistic solution for another.

Re-enter the Common Law

If the House of Lords has now gone so far up the garden path that it cannot or will not be led back down, the most obvious potential solution is to fall back on the common law. The Human Rights Act has not of course displaced the existing requirements at common law that a decision-maker must have regard to all relevant considerations and the other process grounds considered at the beginning of this chapter. The question is whether the existence of the Human Rights Act can be relied upon as having changed the common law base-line and as requiring enhanced procedural requirements in cases where human rights issues are engaged. On one view the answer to this question seems obvious. The existence of the Human Rights Act alters the legal context in which decisions are made and establishes new, constitutionally significant, substantive obligations which public authorities must comply with. This must affect the considerations that are relevant to decisions taken by public authorities. For instance, the obligation on public authorities to act proportionately might well, and certainly in important contexts would, give rise to a requirement on decision-makers to have regard to less intrusive alternatives that are obviously open to them. It might even be argued that in appropriate cases the public authority ought to have express regard to the Convention right that will be affected by its decision, in the same way as it could be argued that a prison governor who wishes to inspect privileged legal correspondence must have regard to the privileged nature of that correspondence, a common law constitutional right.[72]

But this argument is not a sure-fire winner. In the first place it could be said to undermine the ground from under the feet of the House of Lords' decisions in *Denbigh High School, Miss Behavin' Ltd* and *Nasseri*. It might also be pointed out that the Human Rights Act has been treated as a reason for not advancing the common law in other contexts.[73] The counter-argument would be that Parliament has enacted new remedies to protect human rights, and the courts should not go beyond Parliament's intention.

The House of Lords considered the relationship between Convention rights and the relevant considerations doctrine in *R (Hurst) v London Northern District Coroner*.[74] The question was whether a decision by a coroner not to open an investigation into a violent death was unlawful. The Human Rights Act did not apply because the death occurred before the Act came into effect. It was nonetheless argued that when making the decision (which post-dated the Human Rights Act) the coroner should have had regard to Convention rights. The House of Lords rejected the view of Buxton LJ in the Court of Appeal that the coroner was 'bound to give full weight' to the Convention at common law. Their Lordships nonetheless unanimously accepted that a public official will be bound to give 'direct consideration' to the UK's obligations under the European Convention where it is 'obviously relevant'.[75] On the facts, however, the majority held that Article 2 is not 'obviously relevant' to the decision whether to reopen an investigation. This was a surprising conclusion given that inquests are the principal means that the investigatory obligation under Article 2 is satisfied in the UK.[76]

Hurst's case might therefore be taken to suggest that it will only be in rare cases that the courts will recognise that Convention obligations are a relevant consideration. However there are several reasons why this is probably not the case. What is 'obviously relevant' to a decision will depend on the facts and circumstances of each decision. The finding that Article 2 was not 'obviously relevant' is probably limited to pre-Human Rights Act inquests and need have no wider resonance. In other contexts it has been suggested that Convention rights *are* obviously relevant

---

[72] See *R v Secretary of State for the Home Department, ex p Leech (No 2)* [1994] QB 198; *R (Daly) v Secretary of State for the Home Department* [2001] 2 AC 532.

[73] See *Watkins v Secretary of State for the Home Department* [2006] 2 AC 395; *Savage v South Essex Partnership NHS Foundation Trust* [2009] 1 AC 681. See ch 2, pp 52–56.

[74] *R (Hurst) v London Northern District Coroner* [2007] 2 AC 189.

[75] *Hurst* ibid [18] (Baroness Hale), [57] (Lord Brown, with whom Lords Bingham and Rodger agreed) and [78] (Lord Mance), approving Cooke J in *CREEDNZ Inc v Governor General* [1981] 1 NZLR 172, 183. Lord Brown's speech is unfortunately apt to give rise to some confusion, because before citing Cooke J's comments, his Lordship referred to considerations which the 'decision maker may choose for himself whether or not to take into account' ([57]; see the concerns of Lord Mance at [78]). Since Lord Brown went on to consider whether Art 2 was 'obviously relevant' to the coroner's decision, he did not mean to contradict Cooke J, who he expressly approved. His remark appears to have been directed at matters which, while not obviously so, are nonetheless relevant. Cooke J's remarks were also approved by a unanimous House of Lords in *Re Findlay* [1985] AC 318, 334.

[76] See *R (Middleton) v West Somerset Coroner* [2004] 2 AC 182. This was the subject of strong, and it is respectfully submitted, persuasive, dissenting speeches by Baroness Hale and Lord Mance.

particularly after the enactment of the Human Rights Act. This indeed seems to be the best justification for comments made by the Court of Appeal in *Lough.*[77] In that case Pill LJ (with whom Keene LJ and Scott Baker LJ agreed) made the following comments in the context of a challenge to the decision of a planning inspector that planning permission should be refused:

> Recognition must be given to the fact that article 8 and article 1 of the First Protocol are part of the law of England and Wales. That being so, article 8 should in my view normally be considered as an integral part of the decision maker's approach to material considerations and not, as happened in this case, in effect as a footnote. The different approaches will often, as in my judgment in the present case, produce the same answer but if true integration is to be achieved, the provisions of the Convention should inform the decision maker's approach to the entire issue. There will be cases where the jurisprudence under article 8, and the standards it sets, will be an important factor in considering the legality of a planning decision or process.[78]

This statement is important for several reasons. First, it expressly recognises that the Human Rights Act has established new substantive principles and that this will have necessary effects on a decision-making process, including what should be regarded as 'relevant considerations'. Indeed, the Court was explicit in holding that the existence of the Human Rights Act led to enhanced procedural requirements at common law in the planning context.[79] Secondly, the Court of Appeal linked the approach to the need for 'integration' of human rights principles. We have seen that integration of human rights considerations into administrative decision-making is integral to creating a culture of human rights. This is consistent with the Court of Appeal's reasoning. Thirdly, the Court of Appeal went on to hold that the fact that the inspector had not expressly used the word 'proportionality' did not vitiate his decision. What was required was that in substance the decision had been made in a sound way with due regard to the affected interests and that competing consideration had been properly weighed. The approach taken by the Court of Appeal was therefore not akin to the approach taken by the Court of Appeal in the

---

[77] And also provides a source of justification for the later approach of the Court of Appeal in *Rafferty* (n 22); considered at the outset of this chapter.

[78] *Lough v The First Secretary of State* [2004] 1 WLR 2557 [48]. Also see on Convention rights as relevant considerations, *R v Secretary of State for the Environment, ex p National Administrative and Local Government Officers' Association* (1992) 5 Admin LR 785, 798 (Lord Templeman); *Rantzen v Mirror Group Newspapers (1986) Ltd* [1994] QB 670, 692 (Neil LJ giving the judgment of the Court of Appeal); *Diba v Chief Immigration Officer, Heathrow Airpor* (CA 19 October 1995) (Staughton LJ); *R v Lyons* [2003] 1 AC 976 [13] (Lord Bingham). See for discussion of the law up to 1997, M Hunt, *Using Human Rights Law in English Courts* (Oxford, Hart Publishing, 1997) 230–42, noting 'a growing judicial sympathy for the relevance of the ECHR to the exercise of administrative discretion' and 'an emerging judicial recognition of Art 8 as a relevant consideration in the immigration context'. Contrast H Woolf, J Jowell and A Le Sueur (eds), *De Smith's Judicial Review*, 6th edn (London, Sweet & Maxwell, 2007) 5-123: '. . . it still remains the case that a decision will not be held unlawful just because a public authority has failed to take into account an unincorporated treaty provision.'

[79] It stated that the issue on appeal was 'the impact of the 1998 Act, and in particular article 8 of the Convention which the Act incorporates into English law, upon the way that planning decisions . . . are taken'. It made clear that absent the Human Rights Act, the inspector had had regard to all relevant considerations and his decision could not have been impugned (*Lough* (n 78) [15]–[16]).

Denbigh High School case. It was sensitive to the institutional context and avoided requiring inspectors to adopt a formalistic approach to planning decisions.

Whilst in *Hurst* and *Lough* the issue was in part whether the public officer in question ought to have expressly considered the fact that Convention rights would be affected by the decision, other cases show how the relevant considerations doctrine can be used to impose process obligations on public authorities without requiring direct or explicit consideration of the Convention. It can require consideration of the underlying interests (such as injury to dignity or family life). This would be in line with the approach taken by the ECtHR in *Chapman v United Kingdom*, in which, as we have seen, the ECtHR referred to the need for domestic authorities to afford due respect to the 'interests safeguarded' by Article 8.[80] Such an approach can be seen in the Court of Appeal's judgment in *R v North and East Devon Health Authority, ex p Coughlan*, in holding that the defendant authority had unlawfully resiled from a promise that a care home would be the claimant's home for life. The Court criticised the authority in part because it was, 'clear from the health authority's evidence and submissions that it did not consider that it had a legal responsibility or commitment to provide *a home*, as distinct from care or funding of care, for the applicant and her fellow residents.'[81] The significance of the difference between responsibility for providing a home and funding care is attributable in large part to the substantive obligations imposed on public authorities by the Human Rights Act, but the court did not criticise the authority for failing to have regard to Article 8 itself (although it held it to be engaged). Thus, the process requirements imposed by the common law are capable of being applied sensitively without always requiring explicit regard to articles of the European Convention.

Additional support for enhanced common law process requirements in the human rights context can be found in recent cases requiring public officials to have regard to their international human rights obligations and fundamental rights. In *E v Chief Constable of the Royal Ulster Constabulary*, for example, Lord Carswell stated that the principle that all actions concerning children should be based on the best interests of the child, as required by the UN Convention on the Rights of the Child 1989, was 'a consideration which should properly be taken into account by the state and its emanations in determining upon their actions'.[82] A further example is provided by *R (Bancoult) v Secretary of State for Foreign and Commonwealth Affairs (No 2)*. A majority of their Lordships recognised a fundamental right of citizens to reside in their homeland.[83] Lord Hoffmann said it was an 'important right' and that the 'importance of the right to the individual is also something which must be taken into account by the Crown in exercising its

---

[80] See above at text to n 69, p 246.

[81] *R v North and East Devon Health Authority, ex p Coughlan* [2001] QB 213 [88] (emphasis supplied).

[82] *E v Chief Constable of the Royal Ulster Constabulary* [2009] 1 AC 536 [60].

[83] *R (Bancoult) v Secretary of State for Foreign and Commonwealth Affairs (No 2)* [2009] 1 AC 453 [110]–[111] (Lord Rodger), [131] (Lord Carswell), [151] Lord Mance. Lord Hoffmann did not consider that any fundamental right was in play.

legislative powers.'[84] This recognition of a minimum process requirement, even in the context of the exercise of legislative powers which were at issue in *Bancoult,* indicates that *Hurst* certainly does not close the lid on the development of common law process requirements in the human rights context. It does not follow, of course, that all emanations of the state must have regard to the rights of the child or the right of abode or of Convention rights in *everything* that they do or decide that affects such rights: it will depend upon context. But the cases do suggest that the human rights context can and should properly lead to enhanced process requirements notwithstanding the decisions of the House of Lords in *Denbigh High School, Miss Behavin' Ltd* and *Nasseri.*

Nonetheless, for the relevant considerations doctrine to be used effectively as a way of ensuring that public authorities observe an adequate process in reaching decisions affecting Convention rights, it would be necessary for the courts to give common law process requirements a new lease of life. The courts cannot be hamstrung by the traditional approach that prevents the court from examining the weight or priority given to relevant considerations[85] or the restrictive approach taken to the duty to make sufficient enquiries.[86] A more robust and dynamic approach is required in a context where public authorities are under a specific statutory duty to act compatibly with Convention rights and given the common law's recognition of the importance of human rights. Thus, in the context of the property rights, Laws J has stated:

> . . . reasonableness itself requires in such cases that in ordering the priorities which will drive his decision, the decision-maker must give a high place to the right in question. He cannot treat it merely as something to be taken into account, akin to any other relevant consideration; he must recognise it as a value to be kept, unless in his judgment there is a greater value that justifies its loss.[87]

Laws LJ's pre-Human Rights Act comments have until recently looked decidedly out of line with other more conservative cases on common law procedural requirements. But they now provide an important component in the development of enhanced common law process requirements in the human rights context.

---

[84] ibid [47]. *Laporte* (n 16) could also be interpreted as an example of process requirements being imposed by the common law.

[85] *Tesco Stores Ltd v Secretary of State for the Environment* [1995] 1 WLR 759, 763 (Lord Keith), 770 (Lord Hoffmann); *City of Edinburgh Council v Secretary of State for Scotland* [1997] 1 WLR 1447.

[86] eg *R (Khatun) v LB Newham* [2005] QB 37 [35] (Laws LJ): '. . . it is for the decision-maker and not the court, subject again to *Wednesbury* review, to decide upon the manner and intensity of inquiry'. The courts have traditionally been reluctant to find that a factor to which a decision-maker has not had regard is a mandatory consideration. Courts are much more inclined to find that irrelevant matters have been considered. See, for example, *R v Secretary of State for Transport, ex p Richmond LBC* [1994] 1 WLR 74, 94 (Laws LJ); *R (National Association of Health Stores) v Department of Health* [2005] EWCA Civ 154.

[87] *Chesterfield Properties Plc v Secretary of State for the Environment* (1998) 76 P & CR 117, 130. For another pre-Human Rights Act authority, see *R v Lord Saville of Newdigate, ex p A* [2000] 1 WLR 1855 [68], eg: 'the tribunal . . . does not seem to have paid sufficient attention' to the perception of fairness in denying anonymity, 'The tribunal may not have attached to the Widgery assurance the weight which we consider it should.'

The common law therefore provides a potentially powerful way of providing process protection for human rights. A revitalised common law would mitigate the worst effects of *Denbigh High School, Miss Behavin' Ltd* and *Nasseri* without requiring the introduction of a 'new formalism'. The development of the common law should not be stunted by the presence of the Human Rights Act. Since the House of Lords has held that section 6 does not impose process requirements, the development of common law process requirements would provide a *different* rather than overlapping remedy.[88] Moreover, the presence of the Human Rights Act (as well as the recognition of fundamental rights at common law) actually requires such an approach, because the common law works in harmony with primary legislation, and the requirements of the common law reflect the legal context in which administrative decisions are made.[89] The Human Rights Act was not enacted in a vacuum. It was enacted in the context of existing context-sensitive public law principles. Parliament can therefore be presumed to have intended that the Human Rights Act would have knock-on effects for process grounds of judicial of review.

Statutory Duties to have 'Due Regard'

In the context of race, sex and disability discrimination, Parliament has provided that public authorities must have 'due regard' to the need to eliminate discrimination and promote equality. For example, the relevant provisions relating to disability discrimination, contained in section 49A of the Disability Discrimination Act ('DDA') provide that public authorities must have due regard to, amongst other things, the need to eliminate disability discrimination, the need to promote 'positive attitudes towards disabled persons', and the need to 'promote equality of opportunity between disabled persons and other persons'. Moreover, regulations made pursuant to the statutory provisions require public authorities to publish race, disability and gender discrimination 'schemes' that demonstrate their proposals for assessing the likely impact of their policies and proposals on equality.

---

[88] By contrast with tort cases, such as *Watkins* (n 73), where the claimants were urging the court to develop overlapping tort remedies. One potential implication of a court finding that there is a procedural failing which renders a decision ultra vires in a context where there has been an interference with a protected right, is that such an interference will not be 'in accordance with law' and therefore, where there has been an interference with a protected right which must be in accordance with law, there will be a breach of the substantive article. See *R (Laporte) v Chief Constable of Gloucester Constabulary* [2007] 2 AC 105 [45], [56] (Lord Bingham, Lord Mance agreeing), [90] (Lord Rodger); *R v Governor of Brockhill Prison, ex p Evans* [2003] 3 WLR 843; *Pascoe v First Secretary of State* [2006] EWHC 2356 (Admin). Of course, in considering any remedy under s 8, where the process is one failing issues of causation of harm, and questions about whether the same decision would inevitably have been made in any event will arise.

[89] eg Lord Hoffmann stated in *Re McKerr* [2004] 1 WLR 807 [71], 'The common law develops from case to case in harmony with statute'.

In each case there is also a statutory code of practice.[90] These somewhat piecemeal provisions may well soon be superseded by a broader 'public sector equality duty' currently contained in section 143(1) of the Equality Bill, which will require public authorities to have due regard to the need to eliminate specified forms of discrimination, including in addition to the three presently covered, age, gender reassignment, pregnancy and maternity, sexual orientation and religion and belief, as well as to the need to advance equality of opportunity and the need to foster good relations in respect of those who have a relevant protected characteristic.[91]

The origin of the equality duties is to be found in the criticism made in 1999 by Sir William Macpherson in his inquiry into the police investigation of the racist murder of Stephen Lawrence. The Macpherson report criticised the Metropolitan Police for 'institutional racism' and also stated that it was incumbent on every institution to 'examine their policies and the outcome of their policies and practices to guard against disadvantaging any section of our communities.'[92] The equality duties are intended to improve public authority decision-making and assist in the development of a culture of equality and non-discrimination. The requirement to have *due* regard means that the nature and degree of consideration that needs to be given by public authorities to the need to eliminate discrimination (and the other specified matters) will vary depending upon the context. The terms of the duty also makes plain that this is not an obligation 'to achieve results or to refer in terms to the duty'.[93] The question is whether in substance the process has been sufficiently sensitive to discrimination issues and not whether any particular method of decision-making has been adopted. Summarising the case law on these provisions in *Domb*, Rix LJ stated that, 'the test of whether a decision maker has had due regard is a test of the substance of the matter, not of mere form or box-ticking, and that the duty must be performed with vigour and with an open mind; and that it is a non-delegable duty'.[94]

The courts have recognised that in interpreting the equality duties, they must balance the need to ensure sufficient regard is had by public officials to discrimination issues against the need not to hamper effective decision-making. In *Meany*, Davis J stated that local councils 'have a difficult enough task as it is without legalistic hurdles being set for them at every stage'.[95] The duties as framed

---

[90] s 49A of the Disability Discrimination Act 1995 (introduced by the Disability Discrimination Act 2005 s 3); s 71(1) of the Race Relations Act 1976 (introduced by the Race Relations (Amendment) Act 2000) provides: '(1) Every body or other person specified in Schedule 1A or of a description falling within that Schedule shall, in carrying out its functions, have due regard to the need—(a) to eliminate unlawful racial discrimination; and (b) to promote equality of opportunity and good relations between persons of different racial groups'; s 76A of the Sex Discrimination Act 1975 (as amended by the Equality Act 2006). For a discussion of these provisions, see the Court of Appeal's judgment in *Domb v London Borough of Hammersmith and Fulham* [2009] EWCA Civ 941.

[91] s 143(1), in drawing the disability equality duty into line with the other equality duties, the Bill as it currently stands would slightly weaken the discrimination equality duty.

[92] Sir W Macpherson, 'The Stephen Lawrence Inquiry' (Cm 4262-I) [46.27]. For the historical origins of the duty, see K Monaghan, *Equality Law* (Oxford, Oxford Univeristy Press, 2007) 48–49.

[93] *Domb* (n 90) [52].

[94] ibid [52].

[95] *R (Meany) v Harlow District Council* [2009] EWHC 559 (Admin) [85] (Davis J).

by Parliament and as interpreted by the courts are therefore applied with sensitivity to institutional context. In interpreting and applying the duties, the courts have trodden a careful path between the approach taken by the Courts of Appeal in *Denbigh High School* and *Miss Behavin' Ltd* and the approach taken by the House of Lords in those cases. Let us briefly consider a few examples.

Domb concerned a decision of a London borough council to charge for home care services provided to disabled residents of the borough. The court held that since the council had approved a budget that included a 3 per cent cut in council tax, the only option open to it was either to cut services or impose charges. The equality duty did not require the budget to be unravelled, and since the decision had been taken on the basis of a report which had highlighted the adverse impact of charging disabled persons for services (which was in any event obvious), the duty had been complied with.[96] *Domb* can be contrasted with *Chavda*, in which the High Court held that a decision of a borough council to restrict adult care services was unlawful for failure to have due regard to the matters referred to in section 49A of the Disability Discrimination Act.[97] The fact that the claimant failed to establish any other ground of illegality, including failure to conduct a proper consultation and breach of Convention rights, shows how significant such procedural obligations can be. The Court considered that, given the extent of the consultation and decision-making process, the relevant equality duties ought to have been *expressly* considered. The judge held that it was not enough for the relevant documents to have referred obliquely to the statutory duties of the council, because 'this would not give a busy councillor any idea of the serious duties imposed' on them. It was not enough that the council had a good disability discrimination record.

Finally, we should consider the important case of *Elias*, in which the Government's policy for compensating British citizens who had been imprisoned by the Japanese during the Second World War (the so-called 'debt of honour') was challenged on a number of grounds, including breach of the race equality duty.[98] The claimant was a British citizen who lived in Hong Kong and had been interned by the Japanese between 1941 and 1945. Neither she nor her parents or grandparents had been born in the UK. Given the 'bloodlink' requirement under the policy, the claimant did not qualify for compensation. The High Court held that the government departments responsible for the policy had failed to recognise the racial discrimination to which it gave rise. The Court also held that the civil servants responsible had failed properly to investigate the impact of the policy on those citizens with insufficient 'bloodlink' to the UK and had failed to determine whether the policy could be formulated in a less discriminatory way.[99] John

---

[96] *Meany* (n 95) [63]. Although the court did float the possibility that equality duties might have an impact on setting the budget, this issue was not before the court. See at [60]–[63] (Rix LJ) and [78]–[80] (Sedley LJ).

[97] *R (Chavda) v Harrow LBC* [2007] EWHC 3064 (Admin).

[98] *R (Elias) v Secretary of State for Defence* [2006] EWCA Civ 1293.

[99] 'The compensation scheme was not properly thought out in the first place, the issue of discrimination was not properly addressed at the relevant time and . . . poor standards of administration

Halford, a leading public law solicitor who represented Mrs Elias, has described the impact of section 71, as it was interpreted in that case, in the following terms:

> The complacent response of the civil servants who met to frame the bloodlink in March 2001 was to assert, in effect, 'that race equality was not considered at all because it was irrelevant'. That is indicative of a lack of self-awareness at an institutional level akin to the individual who protests 'but some of my friends are black!' when it is suggested that are making assumptions based on stereotype. It will simply not be good enough where there is discriminatory impact.[100]

These comments are borne out by the case law, in which the statutory equality duties have been successfully invoked by claimants even where public authorities have good records in relation to discrimination.[101] The rationale for these cases is that the need to eliminate discrimination must 'be integrated within the discharge of the public functions' of every public authority.[102] Thus, where decisions seriously impact on disadvantaged minorities, those decisions must be taken with a full appreciation of such impact and the responsibilities of the public authority with respect to equality.

The statutory equality duties underscore the importance of procedural obligations in internalising human rights considerations to government decision-making. They make clear the implications of *Denbigh High School, Miss Behavin' Ltd* and *Nasseri* in terms of frustrating Parliament's aim of inculcating a culture of human rights in public authorities through the mechanism of the Human Rights Act. The cases also demonstrate that the recognition of enhanced process obligations in the human rights context is not an all-or-nothing exercise. The courts can be trusted—as they have been trusted by Parliament under the equality legislation—to develop and apply process requirements in a manner that is sensitive to institutional context.

Whilst the Equality Bill, if enacted, will in general terms broaden the scope equality duties, it will have no application to decisions where no equality issues arise. The duties do however provide a model for a statutory reform that could

---

were evident. Consequently there was no proper attempt to achieve a proportionate solution by examining a range of criteria as a means of determining close links with the UK and by balancing the need for criteria to achieve the legitimate aim of close links with the UK with the seriousness of the detriment suffered by individuals who were discriminated against.' *Elias* ibid [176].

[100] J Halford, 'Statutory Equality Duties and the Public Law Courts' [2007] *Judicial Review* 89, 98.

[101] For instance in *R (Chavda) v London Borough of Harrow* [2007] EWHC 3064 (Admin) [40]. In *Meany* (n 95) the High Court held that although a local authority had a 'strong culture' with regard to disadvantaged person, by deciding to cut a welfare grant by 80% without having regard to those duties, the council had acted unlawfully, even though the decision was not irrational. In *R (Baker) v Secretary of State for Communities and Local Government* [2008] EWCA Civ 141 it was held that planning inspectors, in cases concerning relevant minorities, should refer explicitly to the equality duties as a matter of good practice, but on the facts the inspector had been well aware of the plight of Gypsies and there was no breach of s 71 RRA; see also *R (Brown) v Secretary of State for Work and Pensions* [2008] EWHC 3158 (Admin) [90]–[96] (Scott Baker LJ and Aikens LJ). At [91] the court stated: 'Attempts to justify a decision as being consistent with the exercise of the duty when it was not, in fact, considered before the decision, are not enough to discharge the duty' (at [91]).

[102] *R (Brown) v Secretary of State for Work and Pensions* [2008] EWHC 3158 (Admin) [92].

overturn the decisions of the House of Lords under the Human Rights Act. This is, moreover, something that could usefully be addressed in any new Bill of Rights. In this respect, the Victoria Charter of Human Rights is also informative. It provides that 'it is unlawful for a public authority to act in a way that is incompatible with a human right or, in making a decision, to fail to give proper consideration to a relevant human right'.[103] A domestic Bill of Rights could mirror this wording in an amended form of section 6 of the Human Rights Act (whilst preferably substituting the term 'due regard' to ensure consistency with the jurisprudence on the equality duties).

Conclusion

The Court of Appeal decision in the *Denbigh High School* case set in train a series of unwelcome decisions by the House of Lords which have had the effect of muzzling the Human Rights Act. It has led to one formalistic approach—the rigid and juridical reasoning process that the Court of Appeal had said was required of public officials—being substituted for a different but equally formalistic approach, namely, the rule that human rights protection under the Human Rights Act is exclusively concerned with outcomes. It has been suggested in this chapter that in order to mitigate the worst effects of these decisions, the common law process review should be pressed into service and that common law procedural requirements should be applied sensitively to the legislative context of the Human Rights Act. It may be, however, that statutory reform will be needed in order for process requirements to be developed and applied with sufficient robustness to ensure the achievement of a culture of human rights within public authorities. This is unfortunate. The enactment of a provision requiring public authorities to have 'due regard' to Convention rights (such as in a future Bill of Rights) would leave as much to case-by-case judicial development as would have been the case if procedural obligations had been developed under s.6 of the Human Rights Act.

---

[103] s 38.

9

The Substance and Structure of Public Law after the Human Rights Act

THIS CHAPTER ADDRESSES two connected issues which are central to the future shape and structure of public law: the role of the principle of proportionality in public law, and the question whether substantive judicial review should be structured on a 'sliding scale'. Those who support a sliding scale of review anticipate that a single standard of legality would apply across the entire field of judicial review, but the scrutiny given by the court would be inherently variable. The degree of scrutiny afforded would depend not on the category or type of decision in question, or on any single factor, such as whether it interferes with a protected right. Rather, the intrusiveness of the examination by the court would depend on the court's judgment in each individual case about the suitability of a particular decision for judicial scrutiny, having regard to the considerations which had been taken into account by the decision-maker, their nature and complexity, and the effect and impact of the decision on affected individuals and society generally.

The two issues are connected because those who argue for a sliding-scale approach have contended that proportionality should be the organising principle that should apply to all decisions across the entire field of public law, but which would be applied with varying intensity depending on factors specific to the decision under review. This chapter explains why this would be unjustified and undesirable. Moreover, it is contended that the adoption of proportionality outside the realm of protected fundamental rights must be clearly justified by reference to the particular task it is performing in each category of case in which it is applied.[1]

For the sake of the clarity of the argument advanced in this chapter, much of the discussion is premised on the generalisation that a test of proportionality applies when a decision interferes with fundamental rights. The discussions in chapters 4 and 7 have explained that the position is somewhat more complex than this, and that there is a range of standards of legality that apply under the European Convention in particular. This has important implications for the argument made in this chapter, and at important junctures the discussion departs from the generalisation and addresses this issue directly.

---

[1] The term 'fundamental rights' is used in this chapter as shorthand for Convention rights protected by the Human Rights Act, common law rights that are described as 'fundamental' or 'constitutional' and European Community rights.

Form and Substance in Public Law

The task of this chapter might be thought to be a rather easy one, because it makes a case for the maintenance of the status quo. Proportionality is not (yet) a general principle of administrative law, and a sliding-scale approach to substantive review is not (yet) reflected in the case law. But this would be to overlook the lessons of history. The history of administrative law in the United Kingdom is dominated by the progressive dismantling of formal distinctions. In the second half of the twentieth century the courts gradually ironed out certain distinctions that had previously had a central place in the law, including the criteria for the availability of the various prerogative writs, the distinction between errors within and without jurisdiction, the distinction between administrative and quasi-judicial decisions, and the distinction between prerogative and statutory power.[2] Without these developments it would not have been possible to develop a modern and effective regime of administrative law. The courts have continued along this trajectory: the rigid dichotomy between public and private law came and went,[3] and most recently the Court of Appeal has dismantled the categories of legitimate expectations that had been constructed by courts and commentators over the preceding quarter of a century, as the jurisdiction of the courts to enforce legitimate expectations advanced.[4] Any student of these developments who advances an argument for the maintenance of formal distinctions in public law does so with trepidation.[5]

The easier argument is in fact to characterise the recognition of substantive principles of public law as part of public law's steady progression towards a

[2] See *R v Board of Visitors of Hull Prison, ex p St Germain* [1979] QB 425 (relaxing the precondition that certiorari only lies when there has been a determination of rights); *Ridge v Baldwin* [1964] AC 40 (removing the requirement that duties of natural justice apply only to judicial decisions); *Anisminic Ltd v Foreign Compensation Commission* [1969] 2 AC 147 and *Re Racal Communications Ltd* [1981] AC 374 (the combined effect of which was to extinguish in most contexts the distinction between mistakes of law going to jurisdiction and those that do not); *R v Criminal Injuries Compensation Board, ex p Lain* [1967] 2 QB 864; *Council of Civil Service Unions v Minister for the Civil Service* [1985] AC 374 (*GCHQ* case) (permitting review of prerogative power).

[3] *O'Reilly v Mackman* [1983] 2 AC 237; *Roy v Kensington and Chelsea and Westminster Family Practitioner Committee* [1992] 1 AC 624; *Clarke v University of Lincolnshire and Humberside* [2000] 1 WLR 1988.

[4] *R (Nadarajah) v Secretary of State for the Home Department* [2005] EWCA Civ 1363 (collapsing different categories of legitimate expectations within a single principle). For discussion and categorisation of the developing jurisdiction protecting legitimate expectations see, CF Forsyth, 'The Provenance and Protection of Legitimate Expectations' (1988) 47 *CLJ* 238; PP Craig, 'Legitimate Expectations: a Conceptual Analysis' (1999) 108 *LQR* 79; S Schonberg and P Craig, 'Substantive legitimate expectations after *Coughlan*' [2000] *PL* 684.

[5] Moreover, with references to 'variable intensity', 'sliding scales' and 'heightened scrutiny' already deposited in the case law, it is not inconceivable that an activist Supreme Court could re-articulate the grounds of judicial review along such lines. Such steps are rare, but far from unheard of: consider eg Lord Diplock's remarkable reconcepualisation of the grounds of public law in *GCHQ* (considered at various places in this book) and the transformation of tort law in *Donaghue v Stevenson* [1932] AC 562 and *Hedley Byrne & Co Ltd v Heller & Partners Ltd* [1964] AC 465. See Sir Richard Buxton, 'How the Common Law Gets Made: *Hedley Byrne* and other cautionary tales' (2009) 128 *LQR* 60.

substantive underlying notion of justice. The argument would be that formal doctrines and categories are merely staging posts along the way. They may serve some useful purpose in moving the law forward, step-by-step, and in holding the distinction between review and appeal, but their usefulness will eventually wane. With their utility spent, the formal categories will be open to the charge that they are unjust, since the application of any formal distinction or category will, by its nature, limit or exclude arguments based on underlying moral and political considerations.[6] Their application can then be said to represent a deviation from the ultimate ideal, and they ought therefore to be managed out of the legal regime by the courts in the least disruptive way. Such an argument might even be portrayed as part of a more general process of freeing the law from the common law formalism of the nineteenth and early twentieth centuries. It has been said that legal development is characterised by the increasingly detailed consideration of facts by courts.[7] A fact-specific judicial review might thus be thought to represent the final destination in public law's development, since it would permit the courts to test all the facts directly against notions of justice and fairness, untrammelled by doctrinal restraints.

This argument has its attractions, and certainly has some explanatory force in relation to the developments in public law referred to above. But as a general argument it is too simplistic. It ignores the numerous functions that public law serves. It overlooks in particular three considerations that are of undoubted importance in public law: legal certainty, the need to demarcate the separate functions of the courts, the executive and Parliament, and the different, often overlapping, sources of the courts' jurisdiction.

Legal certainty is important not just to ensure the efficient administration of the country, but also to enable individuals, companies and other organisations to understand what rights they have. The need for legal certainty about when a decision is, or will be, unlawful and when it will not be, plays out in public law in numerous ways. Perhaps the most important and overlooked is that although the various grounds of judicial review run together (such as irrelevant considerations, improper purposes, unreasonableness and bad faith), nonetheless the different grounds are recognised, useful and indeed necessary for public law to function in any sort of predictable, regulated, way. No doubt the doctrines cannot be kept clearly apart, and are reflective of some underlying notion or notions of justice and fairness. But we would do well to remember that it is the doctrinal edifice, with all of its formal distinctions, which *is* public law. It is this edifice that prevents public law being sucked down the plughole of error of law or excess of power. This chapter seeks to explain how that edifice has been added to, and to resist attempts to pull it down.

---

[6] See PS Atiyah and RS Summers, *Form and Substance in Anglo-American Law* (Oxford, Clarendon Press, 1987).

[7] '... legal development consists in the increasingly detailed consideration of facts. If so, the limit at any time is the extent to which the legal process presents the facts for legal handling': SFC Milsom, 'Law and Fact in Legal Development' (1967) 17 *University of Toronto Law Journal* 1.

It is also necessary for public law to demarcate the respective roles of the courts, executive and Parliament. Some have argued that this ought to be done by means of recognising a formal doctrine of deference, part of the purpose of which would be to keep courts at arm's length from the executive and Parliament. The discussion in preceding chapters has rejected this idea on the basis that the proper approach is for public law properly to demarcate the scope of applicable standards so that courts are not required to stand in the shoes of public officials, and so that the ability of the administration to pursue legitimate goals is not unduly restricted. In this way the roles of the executive and the courts remain distinct.[8] But whatever view one takes, there needs to be some way of demarcating the different roles of the courts on the one hand, and of Parliament and the executive on the other, and this has to be done by formulating general principles which, when they apply, make explicit that the court is not able simply to determine whether an administrative decision was right or wrong, good or bad. If a doctrine of deference is invoked to perform this function it becomes necessary to articulate degrees and categories of deference with a level of precision that begins to look like the articulation of standards of review under another name.

Modern public law is also underpinned by different, often overlapping, sources of authority. The most important of these, for present purposes, is the distinction between claims that are justiciable in the courts by virtue of the Human Rights Act, and claims that are justiciable by reference to the High Court's supervisory jurisdiction over inferior tribunals and administrative decisions. The Human Rights Act has introduced a new and distinct head of illegality into public law. It has conferred jurisdiction on the courts to determine whether there has been a breach of Convention rights, and to provide a remedy for that breach, including the remedies of damages and declarations of incompatibility, both of which courts have no jurisdiction to award outside the Human Rights Act. Moreover, there is a different time limit for actions under the Human Rights Act and a different standing requirement.[9] Therefore despite the fact that the distinction between Human Rights Act challenges and common law claims cannot always be drawn clearly, the Human Rights Act jurisdiction is a limited one and the distinction can have very important implications. As long as the Human Rights Act or some equivalent statute remains in force, it is inescapable that there will be an important formal distinction in public law between judgments made under the jurisdiction conferred by that Act and those made under the ordinary judicial review jurisdiction. This is a significant consideration when considering how the doctrinal architecture of modern public law should be designed.

---

[8] The doctrine of deference would perform a dual task because it would also prescribe restraint where the court lacks knowledge and expertise. It has also been explained that courts already accommodate such considerations through the ordinary process of adjudication. See generally chs 4, 5 and 6.

[9] Damages can be awarded in judicial review proceedings but the claimant must establish an actionable tort or breach of contract. Under s 7 of the Human Rights Act, actions must be commenced within one year and only a 'victim' can bring proceedings.

A second important and also overlapping jurisdiction is the private law jurisdiction of the courts to protect individuals against wrongdoing, and provide damages for wrongs suffered (tort and contract). This gives courts a parallel jurisdiction to determine whether conduct of public officials is ultra vires (in trespass and false imprisonment claims, etc) and, significantly for present purposes, to determine whether the conduct is unreasonable where the public official in question, or the public body directly, owes an affected individual a duty of care.[10]

Formal distinctions cannot be justified by an abstract appeal to the need for formality in the law. The distinctions themselves have to be shown to be legitimate and important. These introductory comments are intended to set the background for that exercise. This chapter argues that having regard to the landscape of public law as it stands at the present time, a sliding-scale approach to judicial review cannot be justified. The recognition of a normative hierarchy in public law has been a great step forward in the protection of individual rights. Levelling out the law again would, it will be submitted, be a step back, rather than another step forward. Therefore not only should the law not take that step now, but it cannot at the present time even be regarded as a desirable future goal.[11] As will be apparent from what has already been said, the principle of proportionality is at the heart of the matter. The starting point is therefore to consider the different possible roles that have been proposed for the principle of proportionality in public law and the degree to which they have been accepted by the courts.

The First Argument for Proportionality: Effective Judicial Review

There have always been three types of argument in favour of recognising a principle of proportionality in domestic public law.

The first type of argument is essentially pragmatic. It is premised on the perceived usefulness of the doctrine of proportionality as a tool for judges to test the justification offered for executive decisions. This argument makes no claims about a constitutional imperative of recognising such a principle, and indeed it makes only weak appeals to principle. The core argument is that proportionality provides a more structured and rigorous template by which to review administrative decisions and, by extension, legislation. As Lord Steyn stated in *Daly*, proportionality offers 'criteria [that] are more precise and more sophisticated than the traditional grounds of review'.[12] One of the benefits of a proportionality analysis is that there

---

[10] On the overlapping action in negligence, see ch 2, pp 53–54 and ch 7.

[11] It is not disputed that future gradual or dramatic changes in the public law landscape might change the balance of arguments.

[12] *R (Daly) v Secretary of State for the Home Department* [2001] 2 AC 532 [27] (Lord Steyn). The structure and content of the proportionality principle was examined in detail in ch 6.

is a much tighter 'fit' between the reasons that are supplied for a decision and the objective that is sought to be achieved. The measure relates rationally to the particular objective sought to be achieved, and the court must make an assessment of the relative and overall costs and impact of the measure. If it finds against the public body, it must 'explain why it found that the action was not necessary'.[13] Given the pragmatic nature of this type of argument, it applies just as much to situations where individual rights have been infringed by an administrative decision as where they have not been. Equally, there is nothing in this type of argument for recognising a principle of proportionality that requires the replacement of other substantive tests of legality, such as unreasonableness review, with proportionality review. There is nothing that precludes the two concepts cohabiting within the conceptual space of public law. Proportionality is simply a useful tool that can be applied in appropriate cases.

There is a lot to commend this type of argument, despite the fact that it lacks the razzmatazz of arguments appealing to constitutional fundamentals. It is easy to forget that a developed system of administrative law is a very recent phenomenon in the UK. During the period of rejuvenation of administrative law in the 1960s there was not a great deal to hand in the way of tools. There were bits and pieces lying around in the law reports: a doctrine of error of law on the face of the record, a jurisdiction to prevent excess of jurisdiction, principles of natural justice of limited application, and a little-used principle of extreme unreasonableness in local government law.[14] This was the Stone Age of modern administrative law, and it continued until the transformation occurred in the conceptual and procedural landscape of judicial review in the 1970s. The ultra vires doctrine was adopted as the underlying justification for judicial intervention, and the principle of *Wednesbury* unreasonableness became the touchstone for judicial invalidation.[15] It was unsurprising that as the courts became ever more familiar with and adept at reviewing administrative decisions, they looked to expand their range of tools particularly when they were prevented from intervening to prevent injustice.[16] It is against this background that the principle of proportionality was recognised as a

---

[13] PP Craig, *Administrative Law*, 6th edn (London, Sweet & Maxwell, 2008) 637. Craig states that the three-prong proportionality test provides a 'structured form of inquiry' because of this discipline it brings to judicial decision-making and because it 'focuses the attention of both the agency being reviewed, and the court undertaking the review. The agency has to justify its behaviour in terms demanded by this inquiry. It has to explain that the challenged action really was necessary and suitable to reach the desired end, and why it felt that the action did not impose an excessive burden on the applicant'.

[14] In *R v Northumberland Compensation Appeal Tribunal* [1952] KB 338 the Court of Appeal accepted that the writ of certiorari could be used to correct an error on the face of the record of a statutory tribunal. The jurisdiction to prevent jurisdictional errors was asserted, in the face of an ouster clause, in *Anisminic v Foreign Compensation Commission* [1969] 2 AC 147. The principles of natural justice were rehabilitated in *Ridge v Baldwin* [1964] AC 40 and extended in *Re HK* [1967] 2 QB 617. The principle articulated in *Associated Provincial Picture Houses Ltd v Wednesbury Corp* [1948] 1 KB 223 was not recognised as having general application or applying to tribunals.

[15] See ch 2, pp 12–17 and ch 7, pp 200–204.

[16] A good example of how the courts strained to intervene is *Wheeler v Leicester City Council* [1985] 1 AC 1054 discussed below at and ch 4 at pp 103–104.

potential new tool. The point is illustrated most clearly by reference to Lord Diplock's speech in *GCHQ*, delivered in November 1984. Having held that a decision made pursuant to a prerogative power was not for that reason alone immune from judicial review, his Lordship famously embarked on a new rationalisation of the principles applicable to review of decisions made both by administrative tribunals and the government exercising public power:

> Judicial review has I think developed to a stage today when . . . one can conveniently classify under three heads the grounds upon which administrative action is subject to control by judicial review. The first ground I would call 'illegality,' the second 'irrationality' and the third 'procedural impropriety.' That is not to say that further development on a case by case basis may not in course of time add further grounds. I have in mind particularly the possible adoption in the future of the principle of 'proportionality' which is recognised in the administrative law of several of our fellow members of the European Economic Community.[17]

It is notable that in his speech, Lord Diplock referred to proportionality in the context of general principles of administrative law, and referred to the application of the doctrine by courts in other EC states. It is notable also that Lord Diplock had clearly in mind that proportionality would be a *supplementary* ground of review and would not displace reasonableness or illegality—a point made and endorsed by Lord Roskill in *Brind*.[18] Lord Diplock clearly envisaged that proportionality would provide an additional implement in the judicial tool-belt. He was not positing proportionality as an aspirational comprehensive doctrine for rationalising the grounds for judicial review of administrative and tribunal decisions.

Lord Diplock's suggestion was taken further by Professor Jeffrey Jowell and Anthony Lester QC in their influential article on substantive principles of administrative law, published not long after *GCHQ* was decided. They urged the courts to accept substantive principles of administrative law, which included but were not limited to proportionality. But their main argument was not based on high principle. Their argument was based on what they regarded as the vagueness and obscurity of the *Wednesbury* test, combined with the fact that, as they argued, substantive principles were *already* driving judicial decision-making, concealed from view beneath the expansive *Wednesbury* umbrella. They argued that the direct application of principles such as proportionality would promote openness and clarity in public law.[19] They also argued that recognising proportionality review did not necessarily involve the courts in expanding their power or becoming more activist. On the contrary, it would provide greater structure to judicial decision-making

[17] *GCHQ* (n 2), 410.
[18] *R v Secretary of State for the Home Department, ex p Brind* [1991] 1 AC 696, 750: '[Lord Diplock] clearly had in mind the likely increasing influence of Community law upon our domestic law which might in time lead to the further adoption of this principle as a separate category and not merely as a possible reinforcement of one or more of these three stated categories such as irrationality.'
[19] J Jowell and A Lester, 'Beyond *Wednesbury*: substantive principles of administrative law' [1987] *PL* 368.

than unhelpful vagaries of the *Wednesbury* test, and would ensure that judicial decisions were based on principle and not policy.[20]

Adherents to this view were given considerable encouragement by the obiter dictum of Lord Slynn in *Alconbury* when his Lordship stated that it was time to recognise that proportionality is part of the general administrative law as a separate principle to *Wednesbury* unreasonableness.[21] However, in a judgment handed down in October 2007, the House of Lords in *Somerville v Scottish Ministers* refused to decide whether or not proportionality constitutes an independent ground of judicial review in UK law. Lord Rodger said the matter could 'safely and prudently' be left until it was necessary to decide it.[22]

The Second Argument for Proportionality: The Protection of Fundamental Rights

The second type of argument for the reception of proportionality in domestic law reflects the liberal legalist idea that the function of public law is to protect individual rights against undue majoritarian interference. This translates into several connected requirements: (1) individual rights, such as freedom of expression and liberty, should be made resistant (albeit not generally immune) to executive intrusion, (2) they should thus be afforded an importance and weight which ensures that they are not overborne by a simple utilitarian calculus that pays no regard to their intrinsic importance as rights, and (3) any interference with such rights must be justified on substantive grounds by the executive.

A proportionality analysis gives effect to these requirements. Applying a proportionality test, the right or interest affected by an executive decision is attributed a priori importance. Interferences with it are prima facie unlawful. The executive must advance substantive reasons to justify interfering with the right or interest, and the courts must ensure that the utility of the measure in question, as expressed in the reasons and evidence advanced by the executive, stands in a proper proportion to the degree of interference with individual rights. It is not sufficient for a public official to point to a power to take the decision in question. Nor is it sufficient for an official to contend that the measure is useful, desirable or reasonable:

---

[20] Jowell and Lester, 'Beyond *Wednesbury*' (n 19), 381. As they put it in a later paper: '*Wednesbury* camouflage at best invites attack on the ground of inadequate justification and at worst invites suspicion on the ground of political motivation . . . [proportionality] focuses more clearly on the precise conduct it seeks to prevent. By concentrating on the specific it is more effective in excluding general considerations based on policy rather than principle': 'Proportionality: Neither Novel Nor Dangerous' in J Jowell and D Oliver (eds), *New Directions in Judicial Review* (London, Stevens, 1988) 68. The authors argued that proportionality is not novel because it has been applied in many cases in substance and is not dangerous because it reflects a basic notion of fairness.

[21] *R (Alconbury Developments Ltd and Others) v Secretary of State for the Environment, Transport and the Regions* [2003] 2 AC 295 [51]; also see the more ambiguous comment of Lord Clyde at [169].

[22] *Somerville v Scottish Ministers* [2007] 1 WLR 2734 [147]; also see Lord Hope at [53]–[56].

the courts must ensure that the measure in question is genuinely necessary and there are good reasons why alternative measures have not been taken.

This represents a significant departure from the theoretical and conceptual orientation of administrative law as it has traditionally been conceived. In the first place, the courts were, as we have seen, essentially concerned with articulating standards of review and not standards of legality or principles that the executive had to abide by in the conduct of administration. The courts did not articulate constitutional rights that constrained the power of government.[23] Judges operated against the backcloth of the Diceyan orthodoxy that the courts are concerned with providing remedies for particular wrongs, and not applying, still less articulating, general constitutional rights or principles.[24] Insofar as the new administrative law *had* identified standards of conduct, the focus was on the 'public duty' of officials rather than the rights of individuals. The focus was on whether anything had gone wrong with the decision. As Sedley LJ observed in *Ex p Dixon*, 'public law is not at base about rights; it is about wrongs—that is to say misuses of public power.'[25] Years before, Lord MacNaughten had said, 'a public body invested with statutory powers . . . must take care not to exceed or abuse its powers . . . it must act in good faith. And it must act reasonably.'[26]

The restrictions of this approach are shown by *Wheeler v Leicestershire County Council*, decided by the Court of Appeal only a few months after the House of Lords had given its judgment in *GCHQ*. The court was unanimously of the view that the local council, in withdrawing the licence of a rugby club to use a recreation ground because it refused to condemn a tour to apartheid South Africa, had not acted so unreasonably that no reasonable authority could have done the same. Ackner LJ stated that the council's policy had been, 'fully considered by the Council well before the events of 1984, and in view of the make-up of the population of the city it was a view which understandably was very strongly supported.'[27] Browne-Wilkinson LJ thought that the council held 'the entirely reasonable view that sporting links with South Africa were undesirable and that the proposed rugby tour of South Africa was wrong'.[28] Indeed, the decision was influenced by the council's duties under the Race Relations Act. Browne-Wilkinson LJ put his finger on why the decision was unjust and why the club and its players deserved protection from an entirely reasonable decision. This was because it interfered with freedom of expression. But he explained how in the absence of a written constitution which 'delimits what is within the ambit of the powers of the elected majority' there was no recognised basis for the courts to intervene.[29] However, as

---

[23] See the discussion in ch 2, pp 12–21 and ch 4, pp 98–108; the limited exception was the right of access to the courts, out of which other substantive constitutional rights eventually grew.

[24] AV Dicey, *An Introduction to the Study of the Law of the Constitution*, 8th edn (London, Macmillan, 1915) 191, 194–95.

[25] *R v Somerset County Council, ex p Dixon* [1998] Env LR 111, 121 (Sedley LJ).

[26] *Westminster Corporation v London and North Western Railway* [1905] AC 426, 430.

[27] *Wheeler v Leicestershire County Council* [1985] AC 1054, 1061.

[28] ibid, 1061–62.

[29] ibid, 1065.

we saw in chapter 4, his Lordship, dissenting, reasoned that it had become necessary for the courts to recognise a principle of freedom of expression at common law. This approach was not endorsed on appeal by the House of Lords. Their Lordships, restricted by the self-imposed confines of traditional duty-based doctrine but nonetheless sympathetic to the merits of the plaintiff's case, overturned the Court of Appeal by strained application of the principles of improper purposes and procedural fairness, which are not recorded as even having been argued by counsel before them.[30] The fact that efforts of judicial imagination in the House of Lords, with all the licence available to the highest court, ultimately managed to provide a remedy, does not detract from the illustration of how a rights-based orientation has direct substantive effects on the review of executive decision-making by courts.

Perhaps most importantly, a rights-orientated approach to public law is inconsistent with two connected ideas that underpin the traditional approach. It is inconsistent with the notion that particular exercises of public power do not need to be *substantively* justified: it is sufficient for the executive to identify a source of authority for the exercise of the power in question. And secondly, it is inconsistent with the presumption that public officials have exercised their power properly unless and until the converse is shown.[31]

The second argument for proportionality sought to overturn this orthodoxy and reorientate administrative law in cases where administrative decisions affect fundamental rights. The argument for recognising proportionality thus went hand in hand with the development of a catalogue of rights that are differentiated from other interests and given a constitutional significance as standards of legality in public law. Moreover the catalogue of rights is not only, and not principally, a set of norms regulating judicial review (that is, standards of review[32]): they were conceived as constitutional principles that speak directly to administrators and make clear that their decisions must comply with certain fundamental rights and principles. Since proportionality is a core component of those rights-based principles, proportionality takes its place in public law both as a standard of review and as a constitutional or quasi-constitutional standard of legality.

The House of Lords' judgment in *Daly* represents in large part an acceptance of this second argument for proportionality.[33] The question was whether a policy

---

[30] *Wheeler* (n 27). Two substantive speeches were given, by Lord Roskill and Lord Templeman. Lord Roskill said that if necessary he would have held the decision to be *Wednesbury* unreasonable, but he did not explain why. Adam Tomkins describes Lord Roskill's speech as 'curious and cryptic' and points out that Lord Templeman 'did not even condescend to articulate which ground of judicial review he thought he was relying on': A Tomkins, *Public Law* (Clarendon, Oxford, 2003) 180.

[31] See eg *R v Ministry of Agriculture, Fisheries and Food, ex p First City Trading* [1997] 1 *CMLR* 250, 279 in which Laws LJ stated that when applying a proportionality analysis it is not sufficient for the minister 'merely to set out the problem, and assert that within his jurisdiction the Minister chose this or that solution, constrained only by the requirement that his decision must have been one which a reasonable Minister might make'; rather the minister must put forward 'substantial factual considerations' to justify it.

[32] For the distinction between standards of review and standards of legality, see ch 4.

[33] *Daly* (n 12).

requiring prisoners to be absent whilst privileged correspondence was examined was ultra vires. The House of Lords held that the policy represented an interference with the common law right to confidentiality of privileged correspondence, a right that Lord Bingham described as having a 'solid base of recent authority'.[34] Since there was no good reason for excluding the prisoner in all cases, the policy was held to be unlawful because it went further than it needed to. The question whether the House of Lords accepted the proportionality test as applicable in respect of common law rights is not entirely free from doubt. Lord Bingham did not use the term 'proportionality', but he did approach the question in an analogous way. He expressed the issue as whether 'the policy can be justified as a necessary and proper response to the acknowledged need to maintain security, order and discipline in prisons and to prevent crime'.[35] Lord Steyn confined his remarks to Article 8 of the European Convention. The key lies in the speech of Lord Cooke, who stated that it was of great importance that the common law is 'recognised as a sufficient source of the fundamental right to confidential communication with a legal adviser . . .' and went on to equate the approach required by Article 8 with what he described as the approach required by 'the common law of human rights' (both of which he contrasted with *Wednesbury* review).[36] Lord Cooke appeared therefore to have accepted that the approach applied under Article 8, as articulated by Lord Steyn, is the same as that applied to fundamental common law rights. Lord Bingham, Lord Steyn and Lord Scott agreed with Lord Cooke.[37]

We therefore find in *Daly* the House of Lords recognising that a proportionality approach is necessary and appropriate to judge the legitimacy of interferences with common law fundamental rights. There is, however, nothing in that case to suggest that proportionality has any wider application as a general principle of administrative law. It is doubtful whether this was quite what Lord Diplock had in mind when he prophesied the reception of proportionality in *GCHQ*.

The Third Argument for Proportionality: Simplicity and Substance

The third type of argument in favour of proportionality is the most ambitious and the most significant for the overall structure of public law. According to this view, proportionality is a vehicle for structuring the court's review of administrative

---

[34] ibid [6].
[35] ibid [18].
[36] ibid [30] and [32].
[37] Lord Steyn in *McCarten Turkington Breen v Times Newspapers Ltd* [2001] 2 AC 277, 297 also stated that the constitutional right of freedom of expression is subject to justification on grounds of proportionality.

decision-making across the entire field of substantive judicial review. Adherents to this view are attracted by the fact that a proportionality test addresses the balance between the interests of the individual and those of the state. Since all governmental decisions represent a balance between competing interests, the proportionality analysis, it is said, provides a means for examining and testing the substantive balance struck in all cases. There is nothing about the proportionality analysis itself which limits its application to cases concerning fundamental rights, and it does not require any particular weight to be afforded to individual interests. Where the effect of a decision is relatively minor, the proportionality analysis will require comparatively less in the way of justification for the decision in question to be justified. Where it is grave it will require more. Proportionality is thus portrayed as an empty vessel: it is (according to this argument) a methodology rather than a principle. Viewed in this way, there appears to be no need to retain other substantive concepts in public law such as *Wednesbury* unreasonableness. Proportionality can act as a 'sliding scale' of substantive review across the entire field of public law.

We will examine the problems with this argument in detail in due course. It is worth observing at this point that, as we have seen, the adoption of a proportionality analysis *does* in fact represent a significant change in constitutional orthodoxy, not least because it requires a substantive justification to be advanced which is sufficiently compelling to permit individual interests to be overborne. It is not an empty vessel. This argument is therefore particularly ambitious because it requires the alteration of that constitutional orthodoxy outside the context of constitutional rights as well as in cases where the impact of an impugned decision is comparatively mild.

Two considerations that influence those who make this argument are particularly influential. The first of these is the value of simplicity in administrative law. The supporters of this view follow Sir Robin Cooke (later Lord Cooke), who in a famous speech in 1986 on the 'struggle for simplicity in administrative law' argued provocatively that the substantive principles of judicial review 'are simply that the decision-maker must act in accordance with law, fairly and reasonably'.[38] The modern simplifiers of judicial review would replace 'reasonably' in Sir Robin Cooke's sentence with 'proportionately'.

Indeed, they go further. They argue that substantive fairness is also to be measured by a test of proportionality. This latter argument finds some support in recent cases on substantive legitimate expectations, which need now to be introduced.

---

[38] The Rt Hon Robin Cooke, 'The Struggle for Simplicity in Administrative Law', in M Taggart (ed), *Judicial Review in the 1980s—Problems and Prospects* (Oxford, Oxford University Press, 1986) 5. If one traces the idea back a little further, observations of Lord Greene MR in *Wednesbury* (n 14) at 229 are of particular significance: 'I am not sure myself whether the permissible grounds of attack cannot be defined under a single head. It has been perhaps a little bit confusing to find a series of grounds set out. . . . If they cannot all be confined under one head, they at any rate, I think, overlap to a very great extent.'

The first step was taken in *Coughlan*, where the Court of Appeal rejected the view that a public authority can resile from an engendered expectation, unless to do so would be *Wednesbury* unreasonable,[39] and held that it was unfair for a local authority to resile from a promise that the care home in which the severely disabled claimant lived would be her 'home for life'. The authority needed to show that there were some overriding public interest reasons to justify resiling from the promise. Lord Woolf MR, giving the judgment of the Court, spoke in terms of the Court weighing fairness against the countervailing policy considerations to determine whether resiling from the expectation would constitute an abuse of power:

> ... authority now establishes that here too the court will in a proper case decide whether to frustrate the expectation is so unfair that to take a new and different course will amount to an abuse of power. Here, once the legitimacy of the expectation is established, the court will have the task of weighing the requirements of fairness against any overriding interest relied upon for the change of policy.[40]

The Court distinguished the case from two different types of legitimate expectation cases, namely, where the decision-maker must only take into account a previous representation and where it is required to grant some procedural benefit to satisfy the legitimate expectation.[41] On the particular facts of the case (which included the fact that the quality of alternative accommodation was not known), resiling from the promise was held not to be justified by the public interest reasons advanced by the defendant authority.

In *Coughlan* the Court did not use the language of necessity or proportionality, but it laid the ground for the application of a proportionality test by endorsing an approach that required the court to determine whether the legitimate reasons for resiling from the promise were adequate and sufficient. It was unclear however whether this case was limited to its particular facts, not least because the right to respect for one's home was squarely engaged and the proposed conduct—closing the care home—amounted to an interference with Article 8. A further step was nonetheless taken in *Nadarajah* by a differently constituted Court of Appeal. Laws LJ, giving the only reasoned judgment, stated (in what he acknowledged to be an obiter dictum) that the test of whether the public interest considerations are capable of overriding a promise or other engendered expectation is whether such a course would be proportionate:

---

[39] This was the approach taken by the Court of Appeal in *R v Secretary of State for the Home Department, ex p Hargreaves* [1997] 1 WLR 906.

[40] *R v North East Devon Health Authority, ex p Coughlan* [2001] QB 213 [57] (Woolf MR, Sedley and Mummary LJJ). The presence of Sedley LJ on the Court is significant, given his published views on the idea of abuse of power, which are similar to those of Laws LJ; see below n 47.

[41] ibid at para [57] of *Coughlan* these categories are not particularly helpful because they refer to what effect a representation has rather than different types of representations (policies, promises, practices, etc). For other more helpful taxonomies see C Forsyth, 'The Provenance and Protection of Legitimate Expectations' [1988] *CLJ* 238 and S Schonberg and P Craig, 'Substantive legitimate expectations after *Coughlan*' [2002] *PL* 683.

The principle that good administration requires public authorities to be held to their promises would be undermined if the law did not insist that any failure or refusal to comply is objectively justified as a proportionate measure in the circumstances.[42]

In this context at least, proportionality has therefore now been deployed as the measure of substantive fairness.

One also suspects that, given the chance, modern-day arch-simplifiers would argue that Sir Robin Cooke's reference to decisions being made in 'accordance to law' adds nothing of any substance, since what is done according to law will require reference to some substantive rule or principle. Thus it is by a process of reduction and substitution that Sir Robin Cooke's trinity can be reduced to a single principle: proportionality.

Those who hold this view of modern public law are not only simplifiers, they are also monists. They are monists in the sense that they consider that substantive public law should be governed by a single doctrinal principle (or methodology). But just as importantly, they are often monists in another, deeper, sense. The second influencing factor underlying the argument for recognising proportionality as the organising principle of substantive public law is the idea that public law itself reduces to some root concept or justificatory principle, irrespective of context or the particular statutory regime under which a decision is taken. Most commonly, this basic concept or principle is called 'abuse of power', but more recently the notion of public law as 'justification' has gained some currency and Sir John Laws has flirted with the idea of the 'rule of reason'.[43] These reductionist tendencies, when combined with an infatuation with the euro-principle of proportionality, result in an evangelical belief in the principle's rationalising potential in public law.

---

[42] *Nadarajah* (n 4) [68]; applied in *R (Highly Skilled Migrants Programme Forum Ltd) v Secretary of State for the Home Department* [2008] EWHC 664 (Admin).

[43] On abuse of power see Sir Stephen Sedley, *Freedom, Law and Justice* (50th Hamlyn Lectures, 1998), (London, Sweet & Maxwell, 1999) 33–38, and *Coughlan* (n 40) [57] and [61]. For the views of Sir John Laws, see 'Wednesbury' in C Forsyth and I Hare (eds), *The Golden Metwand and the Crooked Cord—Essays in Honour of Sir William Wade QC* (Oxford, Clarendon Press, 1998) (on the rule of reason); *Nadarajah* (n 4, and discussed below); and *R v Secretary of State for Education and Employment, ex p Begbie* [2001] 1 WLR 115. On justification see D Dyzenhaus, 'Law as Justification: Etienne Mureinik's Conception of Legal Culture' (1998) 14 *South African Journal on Human Rights*; M Hunt, 'Sovereignty's Blight: Why Contemporary Public Law Needs the Concept of "Due Deference"', in N Bamforth and P Leyland (eds), *Public Law in a Multi-Layered Constitution* (Oxford, Hart Publishing, 2003). In one sense those who claim that the legitimacy of judicial review derives from the ultra vires doctrine (described by Sir Stephen Sedley as 'perhaps the most fundamental of all public law concepts' (*Freedom, Law and Justice*, above, 26)) are also monists, in that they consider that the single justificatory principle for judicial review is the will of Parliament. Executive action is unlawful insofar and only insofar as it exceeds Parliament's general or specific intention. However, since the ultra vires doctrine is a formal doctrine with no substantive content, it does not point to any substantive (or procedural) principles for the courts to apply when reviewing administrative decisions. (Hence it is argued against those who subscribe to the ultra vires doctrine as the justification for judicial review that since the courts *have* established robust principles of public law these principles cannot owe their legitimacy to the will of Parliament.) The result is that adherents to the ultra vires doctrine are monists in only in a rather limited sense. On the ultra vires doctrine, attack and counter-attack, see C Forsyth (ed), *Judicial Review and the Constitution* (Oxford, Hart Publishing, 2000).

Let us consider the writing of three influential individuals who advance this radical, third argument for proportionality. The first is Sir John Laws. In an article published in 1992, Sir John Laws advocated a simplified approach to administrative law based on a sliding scale of justification. He wrote:

> What I have in mind is this: the greater the intrusion proposed by a body possessing public power over the citizen into an area where his fundamental rights are at stake, the greater must be the justification which the public authority must demonstrate.[44]

In the article Sir John Laws expressed a disinclination to deploy the *Wednesbury* principle as the medium for this flexible approach. Instead he stated that proportionality is a 'ready-made tool in our hands'.[45] In a paper published six years later, Sir John Laws returned to the theme, but rowed back on his advocacy of the proportionality principle as the means by which to achieve his goal. He advocated the recognition of a 'unitary or singular principle' to give effect to the underlying principle of public law, which he described as 'the rule of reason'. But he then said that it should be the *Wednesbury* principle which should give it effect:

> . . . we shall not, I think, make much progress towards acceptance of a concept such as proportionality as an engine of principle in judicial review until we cast it in the language of reasonableness, and also firmly leave behind us the misleading notion that *Wednesbury* can only represent a monolithic standard of review.[46]

It may be that Sir John Laws had come to accept that the adoption of proportionality was too radical a step, or it may be that he had come to regard the *Wednesbury* test as more flexible (indeed, the paper itself was a homage to Lord Greene's judgment in that case). One way or another, it certainly seems that Sir John Laws had come to regard *Wednesbury* as the appropriate vehicle for rationalising public law.

In the legitimate expectation case of *Begbie*, his Lordship adopted the notion of 'abuse of power' in preference to the rule of reason as the root concept of administrate law.[47] In a passage that represents one of the clearest articulations of a monistic approach to public law, Laws LJ stated that 'abuse of power' had become or was fast becoming the 'root concept which governs and conditions our general principles of public law'.[48] He said it was this principle which is the rationale of the

---

[44] J Laws, 'Is the High Court the guardian of fundamental constitutional rights?' [1993] *PL* 59, 69: 'This would represent a conceptual shift away from *Wednesbury* unreasonableness: or, if that is too startling a description, at any rate a significant refinement of it.' And later, 'We should apply differential standards in judicial review according to the subject-matter, and to do so deploy the tool of proportionality, not the bludgeon of *Wednesbury*.' (ibid, 78.)

[45] ibid, 74.

[46] ibid 201.

[47] Laws had stated in an earlier article that there is a 'single principle' of 'abuse of power' at the heart of the common law. He wrote: 'The principle is: the common law will not permit abuse of power. This is the basis of judicial review, and it is the basis of all those private law doctrines where public policy has been held to restrain one man's hold over another': J Laws, 'Public law and employment law' [1997] *PL* 455, 464. Laws traces the single principle into what he describes as the Kantian ideal of the sovereignty of every individual and the idea that any interference with individual freedom requires justification. Laws' constitutional theory is sketched more fully, and questioned, by Professor John Griffiths in JAG Griffiths, 'The Brave New World of Sir John Laws' (2000) 63 *MLR* 159.

[48] *R v Secretary of State for Education and Employment, ex p Begbie* [2001] 1 WLR 1115.

doctrines enshrined in the *Wednesbury* case, *Padfield v Minister of Agriculture, Fisheries and Food*,[49] illegality 'or the requirement of proportionality', procedural fairness, and 'all three categories of legitimate expectation cases as they have been expounded by this court in *Coughlan*'.[50] His Lordship also introduced the idea that fairness and reasonableness are each 'a spectrum', not a single point, which 'shade into one another'. The *Wednesbury* principle was described as providing 'a sliding scale of review, more or less intrusive according to the nature and gravity of what is at stake'.[51] These remarks were developed further in *Nadarajah*, the legitimate expectations case that has already been mentioned. In this case, as we have seen, it was the principle of proportionality which came to the fore as reflective of the underlying concept of abuse of power, and not the *Wednesbury* concept. Laws LJ stated that in order to 'move the law's development a little further down the road', it was necessary to recognise the principle of proportionality as the touchstone for judging when a departure from a legitimate expectation is justified.[52] It may be that Laws LJ considers that public law is finally reaching the end of the path down which he pointed in 1992.

Of the academic commentators who espouse views of this sort, two merit particular mention. They are Professor Paul Craig and Murray Hunt. Craig is markedly less evangelical and more measured (dare one say, proportionate) in his advocacy of the doctrine of proportionality than Sir John Laws,[53] but two features of his exposition of substantive public law have always stood out. First, he would willingly perform the burial rights for the reasonableness principle, even in the more straightforward and less deferential form. Craig would therefore like to see proportionality span the terrain of public law and apply to all justicible issues. Secondly, although Craig would locate proportionality alongside other substantive principles such as legitimate expectations, fundamental rights and equality, it would be the principle of proportionality that would apply to test whether those principles had been breached in any given case. In some cases these principles would require considerable latitude to be given to decision-makers, in other cases they might require a de novo decision by the courts, but the whole doctrinal ensemble would be controlled by the principle of proportionality.[54]

Hunt is more evangelical in his belief in the desirability of a monistic approach to public law and has argued strongly against the 'bifurcation' of public law

---

[49] *Padfield v Minister of Agriculture, Fisheries and Food* [1968] AC 997.

[50] *Ex p Begbie* (n 48) [76].

[51] ibid [78].

[52] *Nadarajah* (n 4) [67].

[53] Craig states, just a little unconvincingly, that, 'Proportionality should neither be regarded as a panacea that will cure all ills, real and imaginary, within our existing regime of review, nor should it be perceived as something dangerous or alien.' Craig, *Administrative Law* (n 13) p 637, para 19-026.

[54] Craig, *Administrative Law* (n 13), p 642, para 10-030. Craig discusses approvingly the application of a proportionality test in legitimate expectation cases (ibid, p 725, para 19-010) and of a variable scrutiny approach in discrimination cases (p 697, para 21-005 to p 707, para 21-013). In an article published in 1999 Craig stated unequivocally that he supported the replacement of reasonableness review: 'Unreasonableness and Proportionality in UK Law' in E Ellis (ed) *The Principle of Proportionality in the Laws of Europe* (Oxford, Hart Publishing, 1999) 105.

between human rights cases and other cases. He views proportionality and deference as complementary principles that together should structure judicial review of the substance of government decision-making and legislation.[55] Hunt argues that the concept of proportionality is not a standard ground of review but a 'methodology for ascertaining whether the impact of a decision, action or omission, on something we value has been demonstrated to be adequately justified'.[56] What he appears to envisage is that proportionality is a way of measuring whether a decision impacts disproportionately, and therefore in his view unjustifiably, on any protected interest. Since, he says, all decisions made by government affect 'something we value', the proportionality analysis can be anchored to all decisions as a means to determine whether a fair balance between the general interests of society and the 'something we value' has been struck. We will have to examine the specific arguments of Craig and Hunt later in this chapter.

Proportionality and the Structure of Public Law

The three arguments for proportionality can shortly be summarised.

The first type of argument for proportionality is essentially an argument about enabling and controlling effective judicial scrutiny of executive action. The driving concern is *effectiveness*, and proportionality is advocated as a means to improve the judicial involvement in governance. In one sense this is an argument for an increase in judicial power, by arguing for a more invasive judicial process, but in another sense it restricts judicial power by limiting and structuring judicial discretion. It is not suggested that proportionality will always be the appropriate test: the argument is premised on a principled co-existence with other substantive standards of review.

The second type of argument for proportionality is driven by a belief in the normative *distinctiveness* of questions of fundamental rights, and by the need to afford priority and weight to such rights, not only in the way courts go about the business of judicial review but in government generally, by establishing rights-based principles of legality that speak directly to public officials.

The third type of argument is more ambitious than the first two. It claims that proportionality is the appropriate tool for judging the substantive justification and therefore legality of *all* legislation and governmental decisions. This argument is driven by a belief that substantive doctrines serve only to distort an underlying

---

[55] M Hunt, 'Against Bifurcation' in D Dyzenhaus, M Hunt and G Huscroft (eds), *A Simple Common Lawyer—Essays in Honour of Michael Taggart* (Oxford, Hart Publishing, 2009). Hunt's essay responds to an essay by Michael Taggart in favour of a bifurcated public law: M Taggart 'Proportionality, Deference, *Wednesbury*' [2008] *New Zealand Law Review* 423. Taggart's views in this article are themselves a departure from his views expressed in M Taggart, 'The Tub of Public Law' in D Dyzenhaus (ed), *The Unity of Public Law* (Oxford, Hart, 2004).

[56] Hunt, 'Against Bifurcation' (n 55) 111.

question of principle. Proportionality is considered to be the doctrinal tool that best expresses the underlying question of principle and which best presents it for judicial consideration. The retention of different standards is no longer justified because such formal distinctions distort the underlying substantive question of principle and add only unnecessary complexity to public law.

These arguments have been set out as a way of approaching the wider issue of how modern substantive public law should be structured. Neither the first or second arguments directly address that issue. The first argument does not address whether other standards, in addition to *Wednesbury* unreasonableness and proportionality, might promote the effectiveness of public law. The second argument only relates directly to the distinction between fundamental rights cases and other cases. The third argument by contrast *is* comprehensive: it refers to the structure of substantive public law as a whole. The first two types of argument are, nonetheless, highly relevant to the wider question of how public law should be structured. Proportionality must, after all, have a central place in post-Human Rights Act public law. And the first two arguments speak indirectly to the wider issue in the sense that those who subscribe to either or both of the first two arguments for proportionality must of necessity reject the third. They cannot accept the third argument because the third argument (1) rejects the possibility of co-existence and (2) rejects the normative distinctiveness of fundamental rights.

The remainder of this chapter will suggest that the third argument is flawed and has undesirable consequences; in so doing, the chapter will seek to develop the first two arguments in more complete and comprehensive form, and begin to sketch a structure of modern public law that is faithful to both the principle of co-existence and the principle of distinctiveness.

Structured Public Law

This section sets out the case for a structured or tiered approach to substantive principles of public law. Having done so, the objections to this approach are then considered.

Legal Certainty

The starting point is that there are a range of different substantive standards to be found in modern public law, a number of which are built in to the European Convention and the jurisprudence of the ECtHR. Some of the European Convention standards are absolute standards, such as that the state must not engage in torture. However, even absolute rights often impose less than absolute conditions for determining whether or not they have been breached. With some qualifications, a person can be subjected to forced labour where this is 'ordinary' or 'normal' and does not impose an excessive burden on particular individuals,[57] and the criterion for removal of persons from the UK being unlawful where such persons might face torture or inhuman or degrading treatment on return is that there is a 'real risk' of such ill-treatment at the time of removal (the *Soering* principle).[58] Other rights, including those which are usually regarded as 'absolute', such as Article 2 and Article 6, impose other standards: proportionality/necessity is one; strict proportionality/indispensability/strict necessity is another; reasonableness is another.[59] In addition to these, common law rights have introduced common law standards of legality which supplement the traditional and modified principles of *Wednesbury* review.

As standards of legality, these standards determine whether a particular decision will be lawful. The normative justification for requiring decision-makers to satisfy these standards varies. Some of these standards are relatively clear and are set out in terms in the text of the European Convention, others are less clear, still others are still emerging or have not yet achieved a settled sphere of application. But the fact that the landscape is somewhat muddy does not mean that areas of firm ground are not present.

Given then that a range of standards are present in the normative building blocks of public law, openness and legal certainty dictate that these should be patent rather than latent in the judicially elaborated architecture of public law. The adoption of a single, entirely flexible, meta-principle of substantive review would obscure and submerge these different standards.

Indeed, adopting a meta-principle of proportionality may even throw doubt on the standards that demarcate the boundaries of absolute rights. Thus, the UK Government has argued in several cases before the ECtHR that the *Soering* real risk test should be qualified by a proportionality test that allows the risk of ill-treatment to be balanced against the national security risk posed by the individual whose deportation is desired. The ECtHR has robustly rejected these submissions to date.[60] But if proportionality becomes a generally applicable methodology for reviewing administrative decision-making, one can expect the submission to be renewed before the domestic courts in some form, such as that the decision of the Secretary of State that the deportation of suspected terrorist *X* to country *Y* would not expose him to a risk of torture was, given his danger to the public, sufficiently and adequately justified.[61] In other words, proportionality could be used as a standard of review that in effect qualifies the applicable standard of legality. One might respond by saying that those who favour the general application of the proportionality principle do not envisage its application in the context of absolute rights, where no balancing of interests is involved. But this is not a satisfactory

---

[57] Art 4, see ch 4, p 118; *Van der Mussele v Belgium* (1983) 6 EHRR 163.

[58] See *Soering v United Kingdom* (1989) 11 EHRR 439.

[59] See ch 4 pp 116–23. On Art 2 see *McCann v United Kingdom* (1996) 21 EHRR 97; in relation to Art 6 see *Ashingdane v United Kingdom* (1985) 7 EHRR 528.

[60] See eg *Chahal v United Kingdom* (1997) 23 EHRR 413 and *Saadi v Italy* (2009) 48 EHRR 30.

[61] This was essentially the approach taken by the common law in *Bugdaycay v Secretary of State for the Home Department* [1987] AC 514.

answer. And we have seen that the boundaries of many 'absolute' rights impose a balancing of interests of some sort. Logic would dictate that a proportionality methodology would be applicable in such cases.

It is therefore submitted that unless there is good reason not to do so, legal certainty demands that the various standards of substantive legality present in modern public law should be articulated, refined and exposed, rather then 'rationalised' into a flexible meta-principle. The need for legal certainty is important whether the standard in question is operating as a standard of legality or a standard of review, but the arguments for legal certainty are not identical. This is an important point because those commentators who have argued for the adoption of a single meta-principle of substantive review—and a sliding-scale approach— assume that the principle of proportionality and *Wednesbury* reasonableness are no more than standards of review.

Let us first consider the matter from this perspective. Let us assume that the substantive principles of reasonableness, proportionality etc simply regulate the intensity of judicial scrutiny of an impugned decision. Although the *Wednesbury* standard of review is flexible and applies with variable intensity, it remains a relatively light-touch approach. Public bodies and their legal advisers know that it will not require a full merits review and that there will have to be something clearly wrong before the court will intervene to quash a decision. Likewise, where a proportionality test applies, public bodies and their legal advisers know more or less what to expect if the decision is reviewed by a court. Therefore, when one knows what standard applies to a particular decision, one can tell with a reasonable degree of confidence what approach a court will take on review.

However, if an inherently flexible standard of review is adopted, this degree of certainty will, inevitably, greatly diminish. The fact that a proportionality analysis was applicable would in itself tell the public body and its advisers nothing about the standard or intensity of review that the court would adopt when reviewing the decision: it could be a robust merits review or something akin to an irrationality review. The context and subject matter of the decision would, of course, indicate the sort of intensity of review that can be expected. But, to borrow a phrase from realpolitik, 'everything remains on the table'. The range of possibilities is significantly expanded. This will lead to particular uncertainty where there are some aspects of the decision that call for intense scrutiny and other aspects that indicate that a light-touch approach is warranted. A decision may, for instance, be made in the field of economic policy but may gravely impact on individual rights. In cases such as these the opposing sides will no doubt stake out positions further apart than they would otherwise be able to do: government counsel will argue for irrationality review and the claimant will argue for something approaching a full merits review.

It is no answer to say that over time, the courts could give guidance on what degree of scrutiny would be applied in particular contexts, because that would concede the desirability of formal categories in order to provide a sufficient degree of stability and certainty in the law. Nor is it any answer to point to the fact that in some cases there would be uncertainty as to whether reasonableness or proportionality review, or some other substantive standard, applies. In the first place, the criteria for which standard is applicable will generally be more straightforward and formal than simply asking whether the relevant considerations in the case warranted a strict or relaxed scrutiny.[62] A condition that proportionality review applies where there is an interference with a fundamental right leaves much less room for argument than criteria that are entirely fact-specific. Secondly, there will be many cases when there will be no uncertainty as to what standard of review applies. Where a museum challenges a grant decision made by the Arts Council, the museum's legal counsel is unlikely to risk his credibility before the court in arguing that a proportionality standard should apply because there has been an interference with a protected right.

The argument is even more compelling when one looks at public law through constitutional law spectacles rather than administrative law spectacles, and recognises that many of the standards, particularly those applicable under the European Convention, are standards of legality that define the circumstances in which executive conduct is lawful, and not just the degree of scrutiny that courts apply to review government decisions. It is of great importance that public officers know that they can *only* take action that is proportionate, or strictly necessary; or that they have an obligation to take reasonable steps rather than every possible step; or that they cannot deport a person to face a flagrant breach of their family life or right to a fair trial.[63] The adoption of a single over-arching standard of proportionality obscures these differences and therefore obscures the grounds on which governmental decisions can legitimately be taken.

A parallel can be drawn between this argument for legal certainty and that advanced by Jowell and Lester in their article on the substantive grounds of judicial review. It will be recalled that they argued that substantive principles of judicial review were wrongly concealed within the *Wednesbury* umbrella and should be separately identified and articulated. It has taken many years for substantive principles to be recognised in domestic public law: it would be a retrograde step for them now to be concealed under a sliding-scale proportionality principle.

We have also seen that one of the implicit premises of the first argument for recognising proportionality as a supplementary ground of review is that such a principle would help to structure the exercise of judicial discretion. However if the proportionality principle is regarded as inherently flexible, ranging from irrationality to a full merits review, the structure and discipline that it would bring to

---

[62] Andrew Le Sueur has also expressed doubts about such an approach: A Le Sueur, 'The Rise and Ruin of Unreasonableness?' [2005] *Judicial Review* 32, 40: 'Of course, we all know that in judicial review "context is everything". I have some doubts, however, whether a sliding scale approach is the best one. Arguably, recognising categories may make it easier for there to be a principled and more certain approach to the court's role: if situation A then intensity B, rather than slithering around in grey areas . . . .'.

[63] On flagrant breaches of Convention rights see *RB (Algeria) v Secretary of State for the Home Department* [2009] 2 WLR 512.

judicial decision-making would be lost, or at least greatly reduced. Professor Michael Taggart has been particularly influenced by this concern in a paper in which he argues for public law to continue to distinguish between human rights cases (proportionality) and other cases (unreasonableness). His view is that unless we undertake a mapping project of the substantive principles of modern public law, 'the law will continue to be rather chaotic, unprincipled, and result-orientated. In other words, it will partially negate the rule of law that judicial review is meant to instantiate.' Implicit in this argument, he says, 'is a desire to constrain judicial discretion'.[64] Taggart's view on this point is entirely in accord with the argument advanced in this chapter.

This concern is well illustrated by the case of *Nadarajah*, which repays close examination. The claimant in that case was a Tamil asylum-seeker who had travelled from Sri Lanka to the UK via Germany, where he had first applied for asylum. In accordance with European asylum policy, the Secretary of State sought to return him to Germany. Before this occurred the claimant's wife had also entered the UK and had also applied for asylum. Her claim was rejected but she appealed. Under a policy known as the Family Links Policy, the Government had undertaken to consider asylum claims substantively when a person's wife was present in the UK. The Secretary of State had never intended that the policy would apply when a spouse's asylum application had been refused, and had consistently applied it in the way he had understood it. The policy was revised to make this clear, but not before the Secretary of State had refused to consider the claimant's asylum application. The claimant and his solicitors were not aware of the Family Links Policy before it was revised, although his solicitors had raised the presence of his wife in the UK and the status of her own asylum application with the Secretary of State in correspondence and relied on this in general terms in contending that the claimant's asylum claim should be considered. At first instance, Stanley Burnton J held that the policy applied even when an applicant's spouse had been refused asylum and was appealing the refusal; it ought therefore to have been applied to the claimant. However, he held that if the claim was reconsidered, the Secretary of State would be entitled to apply his new policy, so the claim was dismissed.

The claimant appealed on the basis that he had a legitimate expectation that the Family Links Policy would be applied to him. Laws LJ, giving the only reasoned judgment stated:

> . . . there is no abuse of power here, and therefore nothing, in terms of legitimate expectation, to entitle the appellant to a judgment compelling the Secretary of State to apply the unrevised Family Links Policy in his case. I would so conclude on the simple ground that the merits of the Secretary of State's case press harder than the appellant's, given the

[64] Taggart, 'Proportionality, Deference, *Wednesbury*' (n 55) 452. Mike Taggart's article makes several other points in common with those made here, in the context of New Zealand law. In particular Taggart argues that there is no compelling normative justification for applying a proportionality test outside the realm of fundamental rights, and considers the application of a proportionality test 'rather awkward' when dislocated from the context of rights (477).

way the points on either side were respectively developed by counsel. If my Lords agree, that disposes of the appeal. But I find it very unsatisfactory to leave the case there. The conclusion is not merely simple, but simplistic. It is little distance from a purely subjective adjudication.[65]

His Lordship then said that the notion of 'abuse of power', although it 'catches the moral impetus of the rule of law', was not sufficient to supply the principle which justified his finding. He turned therefore to the notion of proportionality and, in comments that have been cited already, held that the principle of proportionality applies to test the justification for resiling from legitimate expectations. He concluded by saying that the label of proportionality could be applied to his conclusion, stating, '[t]here is nothing disproportionate, or unfair' in the claimant being refused the benefit of the policy.[66]

Whilst there is no doubt an element of backward reasoning in many judicial decisions, this is a remarkably explicit example. Employed in this way, proportionality has no content and no structure. It does no work. Indeed, although Laws LJ went on to say that his conclusion was an expression of the proportionality principle, he never actually analysed the respective arguments in proportionality terms. Had he done so, he could not properly have reached the conclusion that he did.

By the time the case reached the Court of Appeal, the Secretary of State accepted that he had always misinterpreted his own policy and he did not appeal the finding of Stanley Burnton J that it had applied to the claimant's case. Moreover, there was an obvious and direct detriment to the claimant in the policy not having been applied to him, and although his solicitors were unaware of the policy they had, as noted above, raised all material facts relating to his wife's presence in the UK with the Home Office. The submission made on behalf of the Secretary of State in the Court of Appeal was that the Secretary of State had acted honestly and consistently and that his conduct could not be characterised as an abuse of power. This was the submission that Laws LJ accepted in the above quoted paragraph.[67] But this submission was not sufficient to establish that there was some pressing social need for the policy not to be applied to the claimant's case, as was his prima facie right. Nor was it contended that the Secretary of State would have had good reason to make an exception to the policy had it been recognised as applying to the claimant's case. Nor was it submitted by the Secretary of State that there was any substantive reason for not applying the policy on reconsideration. All that was said was that the Secretary of State had never intended to have such a policy. Where was the overriding public interest? There was none, or at least none was advanced. The most that could be said for the Secretary of State was that he had acted bona fide and reasonably in reliance on an erroneous interpretation of the law. But the essence of a proportionality approach is that it is focused on the right of the individual not the culpability of the public official: it is rights-based, not

---

[65] *Nadarajah* (n 4) [68].
[66] *Nadarajah* (n 4) [71].
[67] Counsel's arguments that were accepted by Laws LJ are summarised at [63]–[65].

duty-based, and the right cannot be overridden without some substantive reasons of public interest that render this necessary.[68]

An analogy can be drawn with *R v Governor of Brockhill Prison, ex p Evans* in which a prison governor claimed that he had a defence to a false imprisonment claim, because in detaining a prisoner for 59 days longer than she should have been he had been acting in accordance with the law as he had understood it to be. The House of Lords rejected this argument, holding that acting honestly and reasonably is not a defence to a tort of strict liability.[69] Although in a legitimate expectations case the public official *does* have a defence of proportionality, acting on an honest and reasonable interpretation of the law is still not sufficient.

Evans also points to another basis for doubting *Nadarajah*, although the point does not appear to have been argued. When applying a proportionality test under the European Convention jurisprudence, before one reaches the stage of substantive justification it is necessary to establish that the conduct is according to law. In *Evans*, although the Human Rights Act was not then in effect, the House of Lords drew support from the requirement under the European Convention that interferences with protected rights must be according to law, in holding that the prison governor's reasonable mistake as to what the law required could not render the detention lawful at common law. Since the Secretary of State had accepted that the policy applied to the applicant, the fact that the failure to apply the policy was bona fide and consistent is not capable, as *Evans* shows, of rendering the failure to apply it in accordance with the law.[70]

Nadarajah is an unsatisfactory case for a number of reasons. If the courts are not prepared to apply a proper proportionality approach in the absence of knowledge or detrimental reliance, then it may be better that such cases are not treated as legitimate expectation cases at all, since there is in effect no public law right being protected but only the requirement of reasonable and consistent treatment.[71]

---

[68] In fact the Secretary of State's position does not seem *even* to be put as high as contending that the Secretary of State had acted on a *reasonable* misinterpretation of the law, although this must be implicit in the submissions. Laws LJ also placed some weight on the fact that the claimant had not changed his position in reliance on the policy. This does not affect the points made in respect of the application of a proportionality test: detrimental reliance would simply make the argument for unfairness even more powerful. Moreover, detrimental reliance is not generally required where there is a departure from an established policy (see *R (Rashid) v Secretary of State for the Home Department* [2005] EWCA Civ 744 and Craig, *Administrative Law* (n 13), 660, who criticises the case on this basis at 665). Detrimental reliance is at best a factor tending to reduce the degree of public interest in a public authority departing from expectation necessary to establish that the departure was justified. However on the facts of *Nadarajah*, the public interest reasons advanced by the government were negligible.

[69] *R v Governor of Brockhill Prison, ex p Evans* [2001] 2 AC 19.

[70] Unless that concept is improperly collapsed in to the question of substantive proportionality.

[71] Without at least knowledge of a representation, it is difficult to see how there is a legitimate expectation, properly understood. The only expectation is that the law will be applied and administrative decisions made properly, which is what the law requires in any event without the need to invoke the doctrine of legitimate expectations. The claimant may have had a right to the application of the policy (absent an exception being made), but that does not flow from any legitimate expectation. The position is analogous to cases where fairness requires a person to be given a hearing irrespective of any undertaking or practice to this effect. In such cases there is no need to frame the issue as one of legitimate expectations.

Nadarajah vividly illustrates the danger of applying the proportionality test as an inherently flexible principle. It demonstrates how, unless the rigour of the proportionality test is maintained, it will provide no discipline or structure to the business of judging. Judges will be able to decide whether they consider a claim is justified on some unarticulated basis and then simply apply the stamp of proportionality as a disingenuous way to vouch for the pedigree of the judge's conclusions. The virtue of Laws LJ's judgment in *Nadarajah* is that he was frank and open that this was what he was doing. The unintended consequence is that his Lordship has provided a powerful warning of the dangers that can result from a sliding-scale approach to judicial review with proportionality as the organising principle. The obvious irony is that this is an approach which Laws LJ has done more than anyone else to champion, including in *Nadarajah* itself.

The Distinctiveness of Fundamental Rights

The adoption of a single meta-principle would also inevitably remove the distinction between fundamental rights cases and other cases. There are two principal objections to this; the first is normative and the second is consequential.

The normative objection is that the reasons for applying a proportionality or strict proportionality standard do not generally apply to non-rights cases. The nature of a fundamental right is that it is afforded priority and importance that is not afforded to other interests. As Sedley LJ has stated, 'the legal standards by which the decisions of public bodies are supervised can and should differentiate between those rights which are recognised as fundamental and those which, though known to the law, do not enjoy such a pre-eminent status.'[72] The justification for applying a proportionality analysis in fundamental rights cases is that such an analysis places a burden on the executive to advance substantive justifications that demonstrate that there is a pressing need for the public interest to displace the right in question.[73] It follows that where an affected interest does not have the status of a fundamental right, this reason for applying a proportionality analysis does not exist. Until interests which are affected by government decisions are recognised as fundamental, either by the common law or by Parliament, there is, without more, no justification for affording them the priority and importance that currently attaches to such rights. Whilst the borderline between fundamental rights and non-fundamental interests is not always clear-cut and is in a state of development, the distinction itself is well established[74] and identifying

---

[72] *R v Secretary of State for the Home Department, ex p McQuillan* [1995] 4 All ER 400, 422.
[73] '... there is a presumption that any inroad should interfere with the right as little as possible, and no more than is merited by the occasion. ... the recognition of proportionality is a natural and necessary adjunct to the recognition of fundamental rights.' Craig, *Administrative Law* (n 13), 629.
[74] The Convention rights are defined by s 2 of the Human Rights Act. The distinction between fundamental or constitutional rights at common law is now reflected in a considerable number of authorities and is less broad and uncertain in scope than Convention rights: J Beatson, S Grosz, T Hickman, R Singh, *Human Rights: Judicial Protection in the UK* (London, Sweet & Maxwell, 2008) 6–18, paras 1-11 to 1-34.

the scope of both Convention rights and common law rights is not unduly problematic.[75]

The other objection is that applying proportionality to all non-rights cases simply because an individual interest has been affected threatens to undermine the protections currently afforded to fundamental rights. Those commentators who argue for a sliding-scale approach to substantive review seem to regard this as having the salient effect of bolstering judicial protection in non-rights cases, but it is just as likely to weaken the protection that should be afforded to fundamental rights. In the first place, the special and distinctive nature of fundamental rights will be removed. The fact that a measure affects a fundamental right will simply be one factor to weigh in the scales when judging the fairness of a particular measure: it will not call for any different analysis as such. The difference will be purely one of degree and not one of kind. Secondly, and of more concern, is the potential for the test of justification applicable in rights cases to become watered-down as the more relaxed standards applied in non-rights cases are applied by analogy in cases where rights are engaged. Such cross-fertilisation will be fuelled by the fact that courts will be encouraged to leave open the question of whether a fundamental right is engaged on the facts and go straight to the question of justification, since the question of whether a right is in fact engaged will often be of little significance in the case.[76]

The *Nadarajah* case also provides an example of how watering-down could easily occur. In that case, Laws LJ described the principle that the promises and practices of public authorities should not be departed from as a 'constitutional principle' which sits alongside rights recognised by the European Convention. But as has been explained, his Lordship's approach to the proportionality test was different and less rigorous than that which should be applied when there is an interference with Convention rights. Nor can it be said that Laws LJ was justified in this because the Secretary of State had particular expertise or knowledge and he was conferring weight in the particular context to his judgment. No reason for affording weight to the Secretary of State's judgment was present. The Secretary of State had simply made a mistake. He had not made a carefully calculated decision on a complex matter. What Laws LJ did was to regard proportionality as meaning something different from that which it is understood to mean in the Convention context. The focus was on the degree of culpability of the Secretary of State and not the right of the individual. But it is not hard to see how such an approach could be applied in future cases, not only in cases such as *Coughlan* in which the decision of

---

[75] In the context of common law rights, see *Watkins v Secretary of State for the Home Department* [2006] 2 AC 395 [26] (Lord Bingham), [62] (Lord Rodger) and [73(3)] (Lord Walker), who held that the distinction is workable in the context of applying the principle of legality, by which only express words or necessary implication can override a fundamental or constitutional right. See also the discussion below, p 291.

[76] It will be of significance if, for example, there is a declaration of incompatibility, or damages are claimed. Such cases, although important, remain in the minority of cases in which fundamental rights are engaged.

the public authority also engages Convention rights, but beyond the legitimate expectation cases altogether, into the realm of fundamental rights.

Specific Contexts in which a Proportionality Test is Justified

This is not to say that there are no contexts in which a proportionality test of some sort can properly be applied outside the area of fundamental rights. There is some authority, as we have seen, for its application in legitimate expectations and penalties cases. There are particular justifications for the application of (a properly rigorous) proportionality test in specific contexts such as these. The key point is that the fact that proportionality can be applied outside the context of fundamental rights does not justify its application in preference to a reasonableness standard in all cases. It is worth saying something more about the particular justification for applying the proportionality standard in the legitimate expectation and penalties cases.

In the context of legitimate expectations, proportionality has only been applied in relation to one sub-category of cases (despite the potentially wider dicta of Laws LJ in *Nadarajah*). These are cases where a public authority has created a clear and unequivocal expectation that it will do or refrain from doing a certain thing and it later changes its mind. In these cases, the conduct of the authority must have created an expectation that is broadly akin to a contractual promise or entitlement and would have been actionable in contract had there been consideration and an intention to contract. The expectation must be sufficiently clear, precise and devoid of relevant qualification.[77] There is therefore essentially a specific public law right that has been created by the authority itself. If the authority's decision deviating from that right is tested on only *Wednesbury* grounds, the law would give no recognition or content to the right. The expectation or promise would be no more than a relevant consideration which the authority had to take into account. It would stand alongside numerous other relevant considerations, including previous dealings between the authority and the individual concerned, that did not give rise to a legitimate expectation. As such, what the public authority had previously said or done would exert no particular control on the subsequent decision. The law would fail to reflect the unfairness in an authority departing from an engendered expectation.[78]

The Court of Appeal explained the special nature of such a situation in *Coughlan* in slightly different, albeit consistent terms. It stated that in the ordinary

---

[77] See *R v North and East Devon Health Authority, ex p Coughlan* [2001] QB 213 [59], [69], [86]. For a recent example of how strictly this requirement is applied, see *R (Bancoult) v Secretary of State for Foreign and Commonwealth Affairs* [2009] 1 AC 453.

[78] In *Nadarajah* (n 4), Laws LJ made essentially this point more shortly: 'the principle that good administration requires public authorities to be held to their promises would be undermined if the law did not insist that any failure or refusal to comply is objectively justified as a proportionate measure in the circumstances.' ([68]).

case there is 'no space for intervention on grounds of abuse of power once a rational decision directed to a proper purpose has been reached by lawful process'. But it was 'visibly different' where a legitimate expectation had been engendered. It involves 'not one but two lawful exercises of power (the promise and the policy change) by the same public authority, with consequences for individuals trapped between the two'.[79] The court went on to say that a rationality test does not address the specific issue of unfairness where a public authority seeks to resile from the promise that it has previously made. The new decision to resile from a promise may well be a rational one to take, but that does not address whether the treatment of the individual concerned by the combined effect of the two decisions has been fair.

A second area where proportionality has a legitimate place is in relation to the imposition of excessive penalties, although the authority for applying proportionality in this context is, like the context of legitimate expectations, somewhat infirm. In what is still the leading case of *Hook*,[80] Lord Denning MR said that the courts can quash a punishment that is 'out of proportion to the occasion', but the only authority identified was a case in which a fine had been found to be unreasonable.[81] Be that as it may, Lord Denning MR's judgment has been accepted by the leading textbooks,[82] and with justification. The decision of a public authority to punish an individual requires specific statutory authority and calls for the imposition of high standards of fairness and natural justice: it is a judicial function. The courts are also extremely well placed to assess the impact and nature of penalties, since levying of punishment is one of the core responsibilities of the courts. *Hook* itself well illustrates this, because in finding the penalty imposed on a market trader who had been seen after hours urinating up a side street was disproportionate, Lord Denning MR relied on the fact that the plaintiff could have been taken before the magistrate for his misdemeanour, and that the punishment inflicted by the council far exceeded anything that the magistrate had the power to impose.[83] It must also be emphasised that the nature of the penalty imposed is only one aspect of a decision taken by a public authority when it decides to exact a punishment; the decision will be likely to include findings of fact and must, of

[79] *R v North and East Devon Health Authority, ex p Coughlan* [2001] QB 213 [66].

[80] *R v Barnsley MBC, ex p Hook* [1976] 1 WLR 1052, 1057.

[81] Lord Denning referred to his own judgment in *R v Northumberland Compensation Appeal Tribunal, ex p Shaw* [1952] 1 KB 338, 350 where he had referred, without citation, to what he described as a 'striking instance' of the King's Bench Division intervening to quash a decision of the Commissioners of Sewers imposing an excessive fine, 'on the ground that in law their fines ought to be reasonable'. Moreover it is not clear whether Lord Denning's comments were supported by the court. Lord Scarman found for the plaintiff on the basis of a breach of natural justice, not the excessive nature of the penalty. Sir John Pennycuick appeared to regard his reasoning as different from both his brethren. He held that there was not 'good cause' for the penalty imposed, albeit because the penalty imposed was the 'disproportionately drastic step of depriving Mr. Hook of his [market trader's] licence'.

[82] Craig, *Administrative Law* (n 13), 629; Lord Woolf, J Jowell and A Le Sueur (eds), *De Smith's Judicial Review*, 6th edn (London, Sweet & Maxwell, 2007) 586 para 11-076; W Wade and C Forsyth, *Administrative Law*, 10th edn (Oxford, Oxford University Press, 2009) 312.

[83] *Ex p Hook* (n 80), 1058.

course, include a decision to levy a penalty. These matters are not encompassed within the principle that penalties cases are subject to proportionality review: it is only the extent of the penalty that must be assessed in proportionality terms.[84]

The Limitations of Proportionality

This last observation brings us to another objection to the argument for an all-encompassing proportionality principle. There are numerous decisions made by public officials which it is conceptually unsatisfactory to examine through the template of proportionality. When one reflects on the numerous decisions that are challenged as unlawful, a vast number of them can only sensibly be analysed in terms of their reasonableness. It is undoubtedly the case that most of these never get close to trial even if proceedings are ever issued; but public lawyers are constantly reviewing decisions that are illogical, bizarre or unreasonable, but which cannot sensibly be said to be *disproportionate*. Even if a proportionality analysis could be applied to some aspect of the decision, other aspects of the decision can only be shoehorned into a proportionality review by distorting the nature of that review and by a wilful abuse of language. Consider the following examples:

1. a finding that a person is not a fit and proper person, challenged by the person concerned;
2. a decision to hold a private rather than public inquiry, challenged by an interested person;
3. a decision by a council to close one of its waste disposal facilities, challenged by a local resident;
4. a decision by a planning inspector to grant planning permission, challenged by a local resident.

The first scenario involves a public authority (or inferior court or tribunal) making a finding of fact, or at least drawing an evaluative conclusion from primary factual findings based on evidence. Such conclusions constitute decisions that are susceptible to judicial review on grounds of irrationality.[85] Public authorities make comparable findings of fact in many different contexts, such as regulation, planning, licensing and health and safety. The example of a finding that a person is not a fit and proper person is just one such possibility. Just such a finding could be made by a statutory regulator or by a licensing committee. It is not unusual to see findings of fact that, in the cold light of day, are irrational, but it is difficult to see how they could be regarded as disproportionate, or how such decisions could

---

[84] A further point is whether the same proportionality test applies outside the context of fundamental rights. In neither legitimate expectation cases nor penalties cases have the criteria in *De Freitas* been applied. The approach that has been applied is less structured. See *De Freitas v Permanent Secretary of Ministry of Agriculture, Fisheries, Lands and Housing* [1999] 1 AC 69. See also, *De Smith's Judicial Review*, (n 82), 585–86, paras 11-075 to 11-076.

[85] For instance see *Secretary of State for Transport, Local Government and the Regions v Snowdon* [2002] EWHC 2394 (Admin).

be analysed through the template of proportionality. Even if the finding leads to a second decision to take some action that can be analysed in proportionality terms, to regard the irrational finding of fact as rendering the action disproportionate obscures the true basis of the decision. Proportionality adds nothing whatsoever to the analysis.

Another example is a decision where an individual is interested in a decision but not directly affected by it. Take the example of a Secretary of State refusing to hold a public inquiry. That is a decision which is reviewed on *Wednesbury* grounds. Save in relatively rare cases, no human rights principles are engaged[86] and the decision will not interfere with a protected right. Whilst the courts will probe with care the reasons given for holding an inquiry in private in the particular context, it is difficult to see how they could sensibly ask whether the decision to hold a public inquiry was disproportionate.[87] That would raise the question, disproportionate to what? One might suggest openness, or the wishes of concerned individuals; but it is artificial and unwarranted to stand up such matters as protected interests to which a proportionality analysis can be applied because those matters, as important as they are, should not be regarded as having a priority and importance over countervailing considerations, such as the need for inquiries to conclude quickly so that changes can be implemented. Thus, it has been held that there is no general presumption that inquiries will be held in public (from which a departure would have to be justified).[88] And as to the wishes of interested individuals, their right is to have their views heard and considered, there is no basis for regarding their views as prima facie determinative, subject to the sufficiency of any countervailing considerations that the Secretary of State advances to displace them.

Essentially the same points could be made in relation to the third and fourth examples: a decision to close a waste disposal facility and a decision to grant planning permission which is objected to by a concerned local resident. These are decisions that would be reviewed by reference to *Wednesbury* unreasonableness (or irrationality), and it is difficult to see how they could sensibly be analysed in proportionality terms.[89]

An example of a type of decision that is generally unsuited to analysis in proportionality terms is a decision of a public authority not to act. Consider the case of a public authority that decides not to remove a bank of earth from land

[86] Where there is alleged to be a breach of Art 2 or 3 of the European Convention by a public authority, for instance in death in custody cases, then victims have a right to an independent investigation. Such cases raise special issues and can be left aside for present purposes.

[87] See *R (Howard) and R (Wright-Hogeland) v Secretary of State for Health* [2003] QB 830 in which two applications for judicial review of decisions of the Secretary of State for Health to hold private inquiries rather than public inquiries were dismissed. Both cases concerned serious and systematic misconduct by doctors who had been struck off the medical register and in one case convicted on numerous counts of sexual assault. The judge held that there was no presumption that inquiries would be held in public, and Art 10 was not engaged. He applied a *Wednesbury* test and held that the reasons for holding a private inquiry were reasonable and sufficiently based on evidence.

[88] ibid.

[89] For example see *R (Morris) v Secretary of State for Communities and Local Government* [2009] EWHC 1656 (Admin).

adjoining a road, which impairs the visibility of motorists.[90] It would be artificial to seek to challenge such a decision on grounds of proportionality, and even if the facts could be twisted and the issues distorted in order to fit within a proportionality template, a court would look askance at submissions to this effect.

Numerous other examples could be given of where a *Wednesbury* analysis is currently applied and where it is difficult to see how a proportionality analysis could sensibly be applied or how it would add anything at all to the matter. Recent cases in which an irrationality test has been applied and which it is difficult to see how they could properly have been analysed in proportionality terms include: the calculation of an award of compensation for miscarriage of justice,[91] a decision by a local authority not to amend a statement of special educational needs,[92] the decision of the Office of Fair Trading to discontinue an investigation into alleged infringements of competition law,[93] and the decision of a licensing committee to grant a casino licence to a competitor of the applicant.[94]

Of course, just as there are contexts in which it is appropriate to apply a proportionality test, so there are contexts in which it is appropriate to apply a test that differs from *Wednesbury*. One example is a decision by a Secretary of State not to accept findings of maladministration made by the Parliamentary Ombudsman.[95] It has been held that these can only be rejected for cogent reasons; that is to say, a more exacting test will be applied than *Wednesbury* unreasonableness. This is justified in this context because the Ombudsman is charged by Parliament with responsibility for making such findings, is independent, and will have conducted a detailed investigation into the matter.[96] Ensuring that the findings cannot be rejected too easily, and without the government carefully explaining its reasons why the Ombudsman's findings cannot be accepted, helps to ensure that Parliament's intention in establishing the Ombudsman regime is not undermined by hasty or routine refusals to accept her findings. There are myriad examples from across government where particular local considerations affect the precise nature of the substantive test that should be applied. Again, it is difficult to see how a decision to reject factual findings made by an Ombudsman can sensibly be analysed in terms of proportionality.[97] Therefore, even if there are situations in

---

[90] See *Stovin v Wise* [1996] AC 923.

[91] For example see *R (Millar) v Independent Assessor* [2009] EWCA Civ 609.

[92] *R (D (A Child)) v Birmingham City Council* [2009] EWHC 1319 (Admin).

[93] *R (Cityhook) v OFT* [2009] EWHC 57 (Admin).

[94] *R (Gala Casinos) v Gaming Licensing Committee for the Petty Sessional Division of Northampton* [2007] EWHC 2185 (Admin).

[95] Another example is a decision to make an exception to a policy, which requires cogent reasons, see eg *Nadarajah* (n 4) [38]; *Gransden & Co Ltd v Secretary of State for the Environment* (1987) 54 P & CR 86, 94. See further M Fordham, *Judicial Review Handbook*, 5th edn (Oxford, Hart Publishing, 2008) 610, para 62.2.9.

[96] *R (Bradley) v Secretary of State for Work and Pensions* [2009] QB 114 [72]; *R (Equitable Members Action Group) v HM Treasury* [2009] EWHC 2495 (Admin).

[97] The same can be said for a decision not to accept recommendations for redress made by the Ombudsman as a consequence of adverse findings, although in such a case there is a direct impact on complainants (the refusal of redress), which gives more scope for a proportionality analysis. Nonetheless, it is not clear that a proportionality analysis would be warranted, not least because decisions to refuse to

which departure from a reasonableness test is justified, it is a step too far to make generalised claims about the suitability of a proportionality test.

Procedural Consequences

The distinction between cases in which proportionality is applied and those in which it is not also has significant implications for the court's management of the procedure applicable to a claim. In *Tweed v Parades Commission* it was accepted by the House of Lords that where a proportionality test is applicable, the need for disclosure is greater than in run-of-the-mill judicial review applications.[98] The same must also be true of the availability of cross-examination. If proportionality were to be accepted as applying across the board of judicial review, the effect on the nature of judicial review could be quite dramatic. Insofar as the test on review would be enhanced, such that it required anxious scrutiny of the underlying facts and circumstances, claimants would legitimately be able to apply for disclosure and cross-examination in many more cases. If, however, the proportionality test which applied outside the field of fundamental rights was in fact akin to an irrationality test, then the utility of distinguishing between proportionality cases and non-proportionality cases for the purposes of granting disclosure would be undermined.

The Existence of Tort Law

A further argument against a blanket application of a proportionality principle is that it overlooks the application of a reasonableness test where damages are claimed in negligence (and sometimes in nuisance). This has been the subject of detailed analysis in chapter 7, and it has been shown how incoherence results when administrative law develops without regard to tort law. One cannot recover in damages for disproportionate conduct even where harm results. That seems unlikely to change, given that it would involve departing from the principle that, save in relation to trespassory torts, liability arises from culpable wrongdoing by an individual.[99] The House of Lords has rejected the argument that breach of fundamental rights is tortious, on the basis that it is contrary to authority and would be too uncertain.[100] That judgment rules out recovery for other disproportionate

---

accept recommendations are usually based on some objection to the Ombudsman's analysis (eg of factual findings, approach to causation etc), and not because any countervailing public interest is being pursued by the government department or (in the case of the Local Government Ombudsman) by the local authority in question.

[98] *Tweed v Parades Commission* [2007] 1 AC 650 [3] (Lord Bingham) and [39] (Lord Carswell).

[99] Contrast with C Knight, 'Proportionality and Public Authority Liability: Spanner in the Works or Cog in the Machine?' [2007] *JR* 165. Knight argues for proportionality to be applied to determine tort liability. Such a move towards no-fault liability of public servants in cases where there is no trespass or imprisonment, whilst theoretically possible, departs fundamentally from the normative foundations of tort law and, even if it were justified, would probably not be appropriate for judicial development, not least because of the knock-on implications for cases not brought against public authorities.

[100] *Watkins v Secretary of State for the Home Department* [2006] 2 AC 395

conduct. If then, unreasonableness will continue to have to be shown in tort cases, a complete rationalisation of standards across public law cannot be achieved and a reasonableness principle will remain.[101]

Authority

There is also a question, which certainly cannot be marginalised, as to whether a sliding-scale approach to judicial review would be contrary to House of Lords authority. A majority of the House of Lords in *Brind* left open the reception of proportionality into domestic law on a case-by-case basis.[102] However, the House of Lords also made clear in that case, as well as in *Daly*, that *Wednesbury* review is not to be equated with proportionality review.[103] If this rules out developing proportionality review under cover of *Wednesbury* review, as it does, then it must also be doubtful whether it is appropriate to development of a *Wednesbury*-type review out of a proportionality test where fundamental rights are not engaged. At the very least, the courts, which have accepted the submission that there are 'concrete differences' between proportionality review and reasonableness review, are likely to look sceptically on a submission that proportionality review is, in certain contexts, rationality review by all but name.[104]

Conclusions

The argument which has been advanced in this chapter can be concluded with a few propositions distilled from the preceding discussion:

1. The adoption of the principle of proportionality as an organising principle to test the substantive justification of all executive decisions and legislation, with the nature of the test varying on a 'sliding scale', would be undesirable, unjustified and difficult to reconcile with authority.
2. A test of unreasonableness or irrationality will remain necessary and desirable.
3. A proportionality approach is legitimate outside the field of fundamental rights in certain contexts, but the application of such a test needs to be clearly justified in each category of case in which it is adopted.

[101] There will, of course, inevitably be cases where an unjustified interference with a fundamental right also potentially gives rise to liability in negligence—a disproportionate decision to place a child in care is one such example. In this case both a reasonableness test and a proportionality test will have to be applied. But these cases will be relatively rare. Most negligence cases do not engage Convention rights. It is suggested however that there will be a great deal more uncertainty and incoherence created by applying a sliding scale approach in all cases to determine unlawfulness in public law whilst applying a reasonableness test to the question of liability.

[102] *R v Secretary of State for the Home Department, ex p Brind* [1991] 1 AC 696, 750.

[103] *Ex p Brind* (n 102), 722 and *Daly* (n 12) [27].

[104] ibid (Lord Steyn). The undoubted fact that in many cases a reasonableness analysis and a proportionality analysis will produce the same result is not a satisfactory answer to this point. All this shows is that in many cases a decision will be *both* reasonable *and* proportionate (or both unreasonable and disproportionate), it does not establish that the *same test* is applied under each head of review.

4. The fact that it may be *possible* to apply a proportionality analysis is not sufficient to justify its application.
5. The courts must proceed with great care in order to ensure that the protection afforded to fundamental rights is not eroded.

The Objections

Having set out a case for a structured, hierarchical, public law, we can now turn to consider specifically the arguments that have been advanced in favour of a sliding-scale approach to public law, most recently by Murray Hunt and also by Paul Craig.

Murray Hunt has argued against a distinction between fundamental rights cases and non-fundamental rights cases.[105] The first argument made by Hunt is that since many judicial review claims will involve decisions that affect important interests of individuals the law is not 'easily' divided between fundamental rights cases and other cases.[106] In making this argument, Hunt does not contend that there is any reason of principle or policy for giving additional protection to cases not involving fundamental rights, and yet dismantling the distinction between fundamental rights cases and non-fundamental rights cases would either increase the protection afforded to the latter or decrease the protection afforded to the former. For this reason, this argument must be regarded as at best a make-weight argument for some other argument which explains why the distinction between fundamental rights and other interests is not justified.

Hunt's argument is limited in another respect also. He does not contend that it is impossible to draw a line between fundamental rights and other interests. It is certainly true that the line between fundamental rights and other interests is not *always* clear, but in most instances the scope of such rights can be identified with reasonable precision. As Baroness Hale has observed, the right to respect for private life, the home and correspondence is, 'the right most capable of being expanded to cover everything that anyone might want to do.'[107] But even in respect of that right, the courts have been able to identify when it does and does not apply. In the first 10 years of the Human Rights Act, few cases on the scope of Article 8 have reached the House of Lords, and the case in which the House of Lords was urged to give Article 8 the broadest interpretation—the *Countryside Alliance* case, in which hunting with hounds was said to be an exercise of private

---

[105] Dyzenhaus and Hunt (eds), *A Simple Common Lawyer* (n 55), 105–8. Hunt's arguments are developed in response to Mike Taggart's article (Taggart, 'Proportionality, Deference, *Wednesbury*' (n 55)).

[106] Craig makes the point that many cases to which a *Wednesbury* test was formerly applicable could now be brought under the Human Rights Act: See Craig, *Administrative Law* (n 13), 621.

[107] *R (Countryside Alliance) v Attorney General* [2008] 1 AC 719 [115].

life—their Lordships concluded unanimously and without evident difficulty that Article 8 was not engaged.[108]

The distinction between Convention rights and other interests is in any event one that has been drawn by Parliament and not by the courts; and it will continue to be necessary to identify the scope of Convention rights because more turns on it than the applicable standard of review. It is only when there is a breach of a Convention right that there is a power to award damages under section 8 of the Human Rights Act or issue a declaration of incompatibility under section 4. Claims for breach of Convention rights under section 7 of the Human Rights Act also have a different time limit from ordinary claims. Furthermore, the scope of Convention rights also defines the jurisdiction of the ECtHR. Where there is no interference with such a right, the court generally has no jurisdiction over a dispute. If the distinction between Convention rights and other protected interests can be made to work for all these purposes, then it must equally be capable of being made to work for the purposes of selecting the appropriate standard of review.

There is no reason to think that the scope of common law rights should be any less certain than the scope of Convention rights, and there is no right yet recognised as fundamental which is as broadly framed as Article 8 of the Convention. In *Watkins v Secretary of State for the Home Department,* Lord Rodger observed that the distinction between such rights and other cases 'works well enough' in the context of statutory interpretation when determining whether express words or necessary implication are required to effect a change in the law.[109] It is true that their Lordships did consider that the scope of such rights was not sufficiently certain to delimit cases in which there would be an actionable right to damages in tort. But it is not difficult to see that there is a need for a high degree of certainty in such a context as to when a right to damages arises, not least because uncertainty would breed litigation against public authorities.[110]

Hunt's second argument is as follows:

human rights are not the only substantive fundamental values that public law has increasingly come to be seen as protecting in recent years. Those values include, but are not confined to, human rights. They include other substantive principles such as consistency of treatment, non-retrospectivity and access to court to question the legality of a decision.[111]

Hunt then gives the example of legitimate expectation cases as an example of the courts applying a 'proportionality-type' methodology and suggests that such

---

[108] *Countryside Alliance* ibid. Lord Rodger gave a speech in which he argued for a broad interpretation of Art 8, but even he did not think it stretched to protecting those going on the hunt.
[109] *Watkins v Secretary of State for the Home Department* [2006] 2 AC 395 [62].
[110] It is also worth recalling the words of Lord Reid in *Ridge v Baldwin* [1964] AC 40, 64 when he referred, in the context of the scope of principles of natural justice, to the 'perennial fallacy that because something cannot be cut and dried or nicely weighed or measured therefore it does not exist'.
[111] Dyzenhaus and Hunt (eds), *A Simple Common Lawyer* (n 55), p 106.

methodology is therefore capable of being applied to these various substantive principles. As the preceding discussion makes clear, this point can be accepted, as far as it goes. Hunt's argument does not establish that all impugned decisions are capable of anchoring a proportionality methodology, and in fact the argument seems implicitly to accept that this will not be the case. More significantly, whilst no doubt many non-fundamental rights cases could be analysed in proportionality terms, the fact that a proportionality analysis is *capable* of being applied does not mean that it *ought* to be applied. As explained above, there are circumstances in which it *is* both possible and legitimate to apply a proportionality analysis outside the realm of fundamental rights, but this has to be determined in each particular context or category of case. Hunt's second argument does not engage with this exercise.[112]

Hunt's third argument is that it is wrong to suppose that a more intense scrutiny is justified in fundamental rights cases. He points out that a variable intensity of review is applied even in fundamental rights cases: some cases are scrutinised intensely, while in other cases, such as involving social policy, courts adopt a 'deferential' approach. He also argues that some non-rights cases may call for stricter scrutiny than some cases where fundamental rights are engaged. There is therefore, Hunt contends, a spectrum of review which does not necessarily correspond to the distinction between rights cases and non-rights cases.

The first point to note about this argument is that it does not advert to the fact that proportionality is not only a standard of review: it is principally a standard of legality. The fact that the court might apply an intense review in some cases in which it applies a reasonableness test, and a less intense approach in some cases where a fundamental right is engaged, does not alter the fact that, where different substantive standards apply, the standard of legality applicable in each context is different. To illustrate with an over-simplification: a decision of the public authority which does not amount to an interference with a Convention right *must be reasonable*, whereas if the decision interferes with a Convention right *it must be proportionate*. Leaving aside how the court approaches its determination of whether such standards have been breached and the standard of scrutiny the court applies, the standards applicable to the executive are plainly different. The fact that both contexts might warrant anxious scrutiny, assuming that to be true, does not alter that fact. It may seem superficially attractive for the courts to 'upgrade' the standard applicable to a particular decision from a standard of reasonableness to a standard of proportionality; but it is rather less attractive to argue that standards of strict necessity should be 'downgraded' to standards of proportionality.

---

[112] It is also notable that of the examples given by Hunt, one (the right of access to the court) is an example of a well-established constitutional right (see Ch 2 p 19), another (the right of non-retrospectivity) is arguably a fundamental right (see *R v Secretary of State for the Home Department, ex p Pierson* [1998] AC 539) and the third (consistency) Hunt himself acknowledges is the basis for the application of proportionality in legitimate expectation cases.

The second response to Hunt's argument is that, at least as a general matter, a more intense scrutiny *is* warranted in fundamental rights cases.[113] Not only that but, perhaps even more importantly, where a decision interferes with a fundamental right, it is appropriate to impose a burden of substantive justification and a high standard of justification on the executive. This is part and parcel of the approach required by the European Convention under the Human Rights Act, as well as by the common law in fundamental rights cases. Whilst there are contexts outside the context of fundamental rights which call for an analogous approach, such an approach is generally not justified outside the realm of fundamental rights.

The examples referred to by Hunt in advancing this argument are also instructive. He refers to a public authority's departure from a substantive legitimate expectation causing grave unfairness as an example of a context calling for strict scrutiny, and an interference with a property right as an example calling for less anxious scrutiny. But we have seen that the application of a proportionality test can be justified in the particular context of substantive legitimate expectations and the particular justification for it has been articulated by the courts. That justification does not extend beyond that context. As to property rights, the standard applied by the courts under Article 1 of the First Protocol is not an ordinary proportionality test. The text of the Convention itself refers to limitations being 'in the public interest' and the 'general interest', which is not a test of necessity.[114] Hunt also refers to the deferential approach of the courts when applying the European Convention in social policy cases. The deferential approach of the courts in such contexts has been criticised,[115] and insofar as such criticism is valid, reliance on these cases is itself misplaced. It has been suggested that the courts will be justified in conferring weight on assessments made by the primary decision-maker in relation to certain issues in the context of social policy, but that is because the court is less well placed to determine the issue and is handicapped (in relation to at least one aspect of its determination) in determining whether a right has been breached. That is not the same as adjusting the scope of the right or the applicable standard, which is what Hunt envisages.

There is also a danger in Hunt's argument that there are interests which fall short of being fundamental rights which call for enhanced protection, and that this provides further justification for a sliding-scale approach. The danger is not hard to see. The argument is essentially one for levelling-up, that is, providing enhanced protection outside the parameters of fundamental rights cases. This gives rise to a risk that applying a sliding-scale approach will also lead to levelling-down in cases where fundamental rights *are* in play, even in cases where this could not be justified. Of course, that risk might be one worth taking. We might put our faith in judges to apply a sliding-scale approach in a manner that was perfectly reflective

---

[113] In *Daly* (n 12) [27], Lord Steyn stated that *as a generalisation*, 'the intensity of review is somewhat greater under the proportionality approach'.

[114] See ch 4, pp 118–20.

[115] See ch 6, p 186.

of the underlying normative considerations. In assessing whether we should be prepared to take that risk, we have to set it against the up-side, which is posited by Hunt, namely that some interests which are not recognised as fundamental are currently not receiving sufficient protection. The choice therefore boils down to this. Are we prepared to risk watering down protections afforded to the most important rights in order to attempt to give increased protection to less important ones? Put in such terms, the answer must be a clear 'no': it is more important to protect the most fundamental rights than to provide added protection to less important ones.

This answer is reinforced by the consideration that if an interest is regarded as of comparable importance to one that is recognised as fundamental, it can be given equivalent enhanced protection by embracing it within the range of recognised fundamental rights, or expanding the scope of such rights. In other words, the argument that some interests are not given sufficient protection in a system that distinguishes between fundamental rights and non-fundamental rights and interests is not an argument for a sliding-scale approach, but an argument to broaden—or at least adjust—the scope of recognised fundamental rights. The desired result should be achieved by advancing arguments of principle and policy for the recognition of such interests as fundamental, and not by seeking to afford them equivalent force by the back door by applying proportionality to every governmental decision and raising the bar of justification when the effect of a decision is particularly grave. It is notable in this respect that Laws LJ in *Nadarajah* stated that he regarded the principle of consistent dealing with the public as a 'constitutional principle' of good administration.[116] His Lordship's approach, for all it has been criticised above, at least had the merit of raising the question of whether a substantive legitimate expectation ought to be regarded as akin to a fundamental right.[117]

In his treatment of proportionality in his influential textbook on administrative law, Paul Craig advances two main arguments in favour of proportionality. Let us first consider Craig's argument that, 'the nature of the test should not differ radically depending upon which side of the borderline a case is said to fall'.[118] The difficulty for this argument is that the purpose of the law, insofar as it lays down any rules, is to draw distinctions between categories of case. Wherever distinctions are drawn there is a degree of unfairness, even arbitrariness, on either side of the line. The law, both at common law and under the Human Rights Act, has reached the stage of recognising that enhanced protection should be afforded to certain

---

[116] *Nadarajah* (n 4) [68].

[117] Hunt makes a fourth point (at p 107) which is not developed. He says that the case for decision-makers to provide 'transparent justification' for their decisions and the case for courts deferring to judgments made by the executive apply both in rights cases and in non-rights cases. As to transparent justification, it is not clear why this is an argument for applying a proportionality test rather than an argument for a decision-maker supplying reasons for his or her decision. As to deference considerations, it is certainly the case that these apply across the field of public law (see ch 5), but it is not clear how this justifies the application of a proportionality test outside the arena of fundamental rights.

[118] Craig, *Administrative Law* (n 13), 637.

rights. The inevitable effect is that situations in which a claimant narrowly fails to establish that there is an interference with such a right will not qualify for enhanced protection. The fact that these cases have only narrowly failed to satisfy the criteria is not in itself any reason for applying enhanced protection. If the affected interests ought to qualify for enhanced protection, then the line should be re-drawn to include such cases.[119]

The more substantial argument advanced by Craig is as follows:

> [It is] difficult to see that the factors which would be taken into account [applying a straightforward test of reasonableness] would be very different from those used in the proportionality calculus. The courts would in some manner, shape or form want to know how necessary the measure was, and how suitable it was, for attaining the desired end.[120]

Craig concludes that since these matters are taken into account, then 'it will be difficult to persist with the idea that this is really separate from a proportionality test.'[121]

The first thing to note about this argument is that it is difficult to reconcile with Craig's recognition that in some cases a 'radically different' approach will be taken in human rights cases from others. In making these comments, Craig is focusing on cases where a reasonableness test is applied robustly, and not where it is applied in its 'irrationality' form. His argument is expressly premised on the desirability of the courts rejecting irrationality review in favour of a more robust and straight-forward reasonableness review. Once irrationality review is dispensed with, Craig's view is that there is insufficient clear blue water between the tests of rea-sonableness and proportionality to justify maintaining the distinction. But it is important to recognise that Craig's argument depends on these two stages. Even if we address only the second stage of the argument, a large part of the discussion in this chapter and elsewhere in this book has been directed at explicating the differ-ence between reasonableness review (even in its more robust form) and propor-tionality review, and in so doing it seeks to meet not only the nub of Craig's argument, which he articulates in the passage cited above, but of the sustained discussion of the two concepts that precedes it. Those points will not be repeated, and it will have to be left to the reader to decide whether the elucidation of those differences is sufficiently persuasive to meet Craig's argument.

But let us pause to note a telling feature of the comments made by Craig which are cited above. Craig refers to the courts having to take into account the necessity and suitability of a measure 'in some manner, shape or form' when conducting a

---

[119] See also Taggart, 'Proportionality, Deference, *Wednesbury*' (n 55), 470, who has made a similar point: 'This sort of line drawing has gone out of fashion. It will always produce borderline cases and in close cases those that fall just short of the desired side can appear formalistic and possibly arbitrary. Yet it can be a strength if it encourages the identification and articulation of factors that pull each way and a careful balancing of those factors before reaching a decision. Thus, it should assist in making admin-istrative law and practice more predictable.'

[120] Craig, *Administrative Law* (n 13), 636.

[121] ibid.

reasonableness review. This begs the question, because it is precisely the fact that courts take account of such considerations in a different manner, and apply a differently shaped and formed test, when conducting a reasonableness review that distinguishes it from cases where a proportionality test is applied in human rights cases. The different features of a proportionality analysis, including the burden placed on public officials and the need for substantial justification that stands in proper proportion to the degree of interference with protected rights, has been explained.[122] It is submitted that they are important and are not merely semantic. Properly applied, they lead to concrete differences in analysis and outcome.[123] The example that was used in *Daly* was *Ex p Smith*. The Court of Appeal, applying a super-*Wednesbury* approach, held that a policy on banning homosexuals from the military was reasonable. The ECtHR held that reasonable it may have been, but the reasons were not sufficiently powerful to justify such a blatant interference with private life.[124] The discussion in this chapter has sought to explain how and why the difference between reasonableness review and a rights-based methodology matters by reference to other cases, in particular *Wheeler* and *Nadarajah*.

Conclusion

It has been argued that proportionality should not become the single organising principle applicable across the field of substantive public law. This chapter has defended the distinctiveness of cases involving human rights; and it has defended formal distinctions between substantive standards in public law.

If this defence is successful, then the shape and structure of modern public law begins to come into focus. It is made up of a cascade of standards, flowing from bad faith at the highest point, through irrationality, super-*Wednesbury*/intense scrutiny, proportionality, strict necessity, and lastly the rarest of cases where a judge has to remake a decision previously made by a public official.[125] To this

---

[122] See chapters 4, 6 and 7.

[123] This was recognised by Lord Steyn in *Daly* (n 12) [27]–[28].

[124] *Smith v United Kingdom* (2000) 29 EHRR 493 [102]–[105]. Craig, *Administrative Law* (n 13), also argues that proportionality provides a more structured form of inquiry than reasonableness review and requires a reasoned and sound justification to be advanced. Three brief points can be made in response to this. First, this is not an argument for applying a proportionality test as such, but for requiring cogent justification or something more robust than a *Wednesbury* test. Secondly, the argument does not take account of the many contexts in which the methodology of proportionality seems to be inapposite. Thirdly, the argument does not address the issue of whether applying a proportionality approach in all contexts is *legitimate*. After all, an appellate approach would be yet more robust and structured and yet that would be illegitimate.

[125] The only context in which the court is required to step into the shoes of a public body and re-make the decision rather than apply a standard of legality is where the decision must be made by an independent and impartial tribunal, which the decision-maker is not, and a more restricted judicial review will not suffice. Such cases are extremely rare, since judicial review will generally suffice. For an example see, *R (Wilkinson) v Broadmoor Hospital Authority* [2002] 1 WLR 419; and generally, see Beatson, Grosz, Hickman and Singh, *Human Rights* (n 74) paras 6–83 to 6–115.

range of standards must be added the range of protected rights, both under the Convention and at common law. Together they create a complex but coherent scheme of substantive public law. Importantly, they are distinct standards, and not simply points on a sliding scale.

Even this is inevitably an over-simplification. It is like a map of London with only the main tourist attractions shown on it. Local considerations will require the tailoring of standards to fit the context of the dispute. Consider for example a challenge to a decision of a Chief Constable relating to some aspect of a police operation that has gone wrong. The lawyers and the judge in deciding the case will be less concerned with the trend of recent cases on substantive judicial review than they will be with the last most similar challenge to a decision of a Chief Constable. In this sense, context *is* everything in public law:[126] public law is less about general principles than one might think. Although an appeal to context is characteristically pressed into service by the simplifiers and the monists, reference to context in fact requires the maintenance, and even the development, of formal distinctions.

The structure of public law cannot be settled at the level of principle. It must be settled by a process of working backwards and forwards between the general and the specific, between principles and the detail of decided cases and legislative requirements. This chapter and previous chapters have embarked on this exercise, but they come nowhere near to completing it. The final two chapters of this book address particular contexts—albeit still at a relatively general level—namely, decisions deviating from the right of access to court, and decisions made in derogation from the European Convention. In doing so, these chapters carry forward the general arguments developed in this and previous chapters.

---

[126] 'In law context is everything'. Lord Steyn in *Daly* (n 12) [28].

10

The Right of Access to Court

THE RIGHT OF access to the court is at the heart of the common law constitution and is, as we have seen, the wellspring for the modern jurisprudence on fundamental common law rights.[1] Lord Diplock once stated that:

> Every civilised system of government requires that the state should make available to all its citizens a means for the just and peaceful settlement of disputes between them as to their respective legal rights. The means provided are the courts of justice to which every citizen has a constitutional right of access in the role of plaintiff to obtain the remedy to which he claims to be entitled in consequence of an alleged breach of his legal or equitable rights by some other citizen, the defendant.[2]

In addition to this right of access to court, there is a general principle in domestic law that everyone, 'whatever be his rank or condition', is subject to the same law and amenable to the jurisdiction of the ordinary courts.[3] On the one hand, public officials are not immune from the law, and on the other, no person is outlawed or otherwise denied its protection. This is the principle of legal equality. Unlike the right of access to a court, the principle of legal equality has a substantive dimension. It does not require the state to recognise any *particular* legal rights, but it does prevent individuals or classes of individuals being denied (or exempted from) legal rights that are generally recognised. In English law both these principles have been limited in their application by the principle of Parliamentary sovereignty. Thus, although legislation which limits these rights can be read strictly, ultimately it prevails. As products of the common law, these principles have, furthermore, not themselves been applied to curb established common law doctrines where they are at variance with them. Most obviously, the common law continued to recognise Crown immunity from suit, and it was left to Parliament to remove it by the Crown Proceedings Act 1947, although, as we shall see, remnants of the immunity

---

[1] See ch 2, p 19.

[2] *Bremer Vulkan Schiffbau und Maschinenfabrik v South India Shipping Co Ltd* [1981] AC 909, 977.

[3] AV Dicey, *Introduction to the Study of the Law of the Constitution*, 8th edn (London, Macmillan, 1915) 189. Lord Scarmen stated in *Khawaja v Secretary of State for the Home Department* [1984] AC 74, 111 that 'Every person within the jurisdiction enjoys the equal protection of our laws'; in *Kruse v Johnson* [1898] 2 QB 91, 99 Lord Russell of Killowen CJ stated that a law would be unlawful if it was partial or unequal between different classes. In *R v Immigration Appeal Tribunal, ex p Jeyeanthan* [1998] Im AR 369, 374 Sedley J stated that the principle of equality before the law would be jeopardised if the state is treated differently from other litigants.

remained.[4] It is also the case that both the right of access to the courts and the right of legal equality are, in part because of the limits in their applicability just described, relatively underdeveloped, at least by comparison with the equivalent Strasbourg jurisprudence. This is despite the fact that they are at the very heart of public law and at the very heart of the law's protection of human rights.

It is the Strasbourg jurisprudence with which this chapter is concerned. The relationship between this jurisprudence and domestic law remains unsettled, and it has been the area where domestic law has clashed most spectacularly with that developed by the ECtHR.

Conspectus

In one of its first cases, the ECtHR in *Golder v UK*[5] held that Article 6(1) of the European Convention impliedly protects the right to a court. What constitutes a limitation on this right is, however, a question that has evoked mixed and often inconsistent responses in both the ECtHR and the English courts. Take the cases of *Hill v Chief Constable of West Yorkshire*[6] and *Osman v Ferguson*.[7] These cases denied that the police owe a duty of care when conducting criminal investigations. The ECtHR in *Osman v UK*[8] thought the combined effect of these decisions was to establish an immunity that unjustifiably limited the right of access to court. This led Lord Browne-Wilkinson to give a judgment in *Barrett v Enfield LBC* in which he explained that the *Osman* decision gave rise to 'many and various' problems for the English law of negligence, and that it was a decision which he found 'extremely difficult to understand'. He explained that, properly understood, where a claim is struck out because no duty of care is owed on the basis that it would not be fair, just and reasonable to recognise such a duty, this is not the application of an immunity properly so-called, it is a pre-requisite of liability. It does not therefore amount to the denial of access to court, but the substantive determination of civil rights.[9] Three years later the ECtHR declared, in an unprecedented statement, that it had been persuaded by *Barrett v Enfield LBC* that denying a duty of care on grounds of policy was not actually an immunity at all, and it effectively overruled *Osman v UK* on this point.[10]

---

[4] The Act followed the House of Lords' criticism of the practice of naming nominal public officers to stand as defendants in claims, in *Adams v Naylor* [1946] AC 543. To be sure, the courts did strictly confine Crown immunity and, in contrast to courts in the United States, refused to apply it to statutory authorities and municipal corporations: *Mersey Docks Trustees v Cameron* (1864) 11 HLC 443; *Birkenhead Dock Trustees v Birkenhead Overseers* (1852) 2 El Bl 148; *Mersey Docks v Gibbs* (1866) LR 1 HL 93. The courts strictly construed statutory provisions restricting claims against government, such as the Public Authorities Protection Act 1893, see *Bradford Corporation v Myers* [1916] 1 AC 242.

[5] *Golder v UK* (1975) 1 EHRR 524.

[6] *Hill v Chief Constable of West Yorkshire* [1989] AC 53 [118].

[7] *Osman v Ferguson* [1993] 4 All ER 344.

[8] *Osman v UK* (1998) 29 EHRR 245.

[9] *Barrett v Enfield LBC* [2001] 2 AC 550 [130] (Lord Nolan and Lord Steyn agreed).

[10] *Z v UK* (2002) 34 EHRR 3 [96] and [100].

However, in between these two pronouncements the House of Lords had itself decided *Arthur J.S. Hall & Co (a firm) v Simons*, in which it held that advocates do owe a duty of care in relation to the conduct of court-related work.[11] In so deciding, their Lordships treated the earlier case of *Rondel v Worsley*[12] as upholding 'an ancient immunity'[13] from liability on grounds of public policy that could no longer be justified.[14] The inconsistency is brought home by the fact that the decision in *Hill* was expressly premised on the ground that the police were 'immune from an action of this kind on grounds similar to those which in *Rondel v Worsley* were held to render a barrister immune from actions for negligence in his conduct of proceedings in court'.[15]

Much of the problem stems from the fact that the concept of an immunity is inherently normative. Whether or not we categorise a rule as an immunity should depend on the reason for inquiring whether an immunity exists in the first place. Thus, a rule might properly be considered to be an immunity for some purposes, but not for others. When addressing compatibility with Article 6, it is therefore necessary to ask what this article is intended to protect individuals from. The ECtHR jurisprudence is blighted by a frequent failure to recognise, or at least observe, this crucial point. This problem has been aggravated by the ECtHR's tendency (which is thankfully becoming less common) to combine discussion of related submissions under the head of a single article or address a submission hypothetically without deciding whether the article is actually engaged. This has proved a particular obfuscation in this context, because it has tended to eclipse and elide substantive articles with Article 6.

The House of Lords in *Matthews v Ministry of Defence*[16] and *Wilson v First County Trust Ltd (No 2)*[17] addressed this issue directly. The first instance judge in *Matthews* and the Court of Appeal in *Wilson* had found violations of Article 6, however the House of Lords held it inapplicable in both cases. Their Lordships recognised that in applying the right to a court, it is necessary to have regard to the fundamental principles underlying Article 6. In *Matthews*, Lord Hoffmann proposed that, 'instead of arguing over labels, it would be more helpful to go back to the fundamental principles deriving from *Golder*'.[18] This is in stark contrast to the approach of the Court of Appeal, which had not referred to *Golder* in either *Matthews* or *Wilson*.[19] Lord Hope explicitly acknowledged that many of the

---

[11] *Arthur J.S. Hall & Co (a firm) v Simons* [2002] 1 AC 615.
[12] *Rondel v Worsley* [1967] 1 QB 443.
[13] *Arthur J.S. Hall* (n 11) 676 (Lord Steyn).
[14] ibid, 683 (Lord Steyn); 684–85 (Lord Browne-Wilkinson); 707 (Lord Hoffmann); 753 (Lord Millett); and in respect of civil proceedings only, 710–11, 726 (Lord Hope); 728,734–35 (Lord Hutton); 736, 745 (Lord Hobhouse). All of their Lordships, with the exception of Lord Hoffmann, who expressly declined to consider the matter, considered that advocate immunity required justification to be compatible with Art 6(1).
[15] *Rondel v Worsley* (n 12), 64 (Lord Keith).
[16] *Matthews v Ministry of Defence* [2003] 1 AC 1163.
[17] *Wilson v First County Trust Ltd (No 2)* [2004] 1 AC 816.
[18] *Matthews* (n 16) [43].
[19] Although it was cited by counsel in both cases.

Strasbourg decisions have no clear ratio, and it was therefore 'better to have regard instead to the underlying principles'.[20] Such an approach recognises that Article 6 does not provide a panacea for the ill-effects of formalistic distinctions and surviving immunities. Its application must be limited to its underlying rationale. This methodological approach is extremely welcome and may pave the way for a stable and consistent approach to the right to a court in the future; at least in UK courts. Having regard to underlying principle, the House of Lords emphasised in both cases that Article 6 is a procedural guarantee and endorsed the view that the right to a court is engaged in respect of immunities or bars that can be characterised as procedural. Nevertheless, the path ahead is far from settled. In *Matthews,* Lord Walker recognised that the 'uncertain shadow of *Osman* still lies over this area of the law'.[21]

This chapter takes up Lord Hoffmann's prompt and returns to the wellspring of the jurisprudence on the right to a court in order to propose an interpretation of the jurisprudence that dovetails with the underlying fundamental principles. This provides a foundation from which to examine critically the interpretations given to the right in the *Wilson* and *Matthews* cases and the Strasbourg cases which have followed them. The chapter argues that the remaining uncertainty results from the failure to recognise that Article 6 has always had both procedural and substantive components, reflecting the right of access and the principle of legal equality, and from the insistence that Article 6 must be interpreted monistically, in the sense that there must be identified a single implied right with a single test of justification. But whether or not this analysis of Article 6 is preferred, it will be possible, by carefully unpicking the case law, to throw some light on the uncertain shadow which continues to obscure this important area of public law.[22]

The Right to a Court Founded and the *Golder* Dual-Limb Test

The various approaches to the right to a court apparent in the Strasbourg case law present domestic courts with a degree of choice as to which to endorse or follow. The historical approaches can usefully be divided into three: (1) the dual-limb approach, (2) the maximalist approach, and (3) the minimalist approach. It is argued that the dual-limb approach is most faithful to underlying principle and that the important case of *Fayed v UK*,[23] as well as subsequent cases, can be best interpreted as developing this approach.

---

[20] *Matthews* (n 16) [53].
[21] ibid [140].
[22] For a different dissection of the case law see CA Gearty, 'Unravelling *Osman*' (2001) 64 *MRL* 159. Professor Gearty's thesis is discussed below.
[23] *Fayed v UK* (1994) 18 EHRR 393.

It is necessary to begin with an analysis of *Golder,* which has been somewhat resurrected by the House of Lords. Golder was a prisoner who wished to instigate libel proceedings against a prison officer who had accused him of being involved in a prison disturbance. Although the accusations of wrongdoing were later dropped, the comments remained on the prison record and were, Golder alleged, preventing his parole. The libel action was an attempt to clear his name. However, under the Prison Rules, Golder required the consent of the Home Secretary to write to a solicitor in order to initiate proceedings. Consent was not forthcoming and Golder alleged that his Article 6 rights had been violated. So far as relevant, Article 6(1) ECHR states:

> In the determination of his civil rights and obligations . . . everyone is entitled to a fair and public hearing within a reasonable time by an independent and impartial tribunal established by law.

The ECtHR remarked in *Golder* that the 'fair, public and expeditious characteristics of judicial proceedings are of no value at all if there are no judicial proceedings'.[24] The right to a court therefore arises by necessary implication. Article 6 presupposes civil rights and obligations adjudicated upon by a system of courts and tribunals, and to be effective it must protect the ability of these institutions to engage in such adjudications. It protects the rule of law by denying arbitrary or executive rule. Therefore, reading Article 6(1) in the light of the requirements of the rule of law, the ECtHR held that it 'embodies the "right to a court", of which the right of access, that is the right to institute proceedings before courts in civil matters, constitutes one aspect only'.[25] From the first then, the right of access was but one aspect of a broader protection of the ordinary courts (the right to a court) enshrined in Article 6. At its very roots the right to a court is not one-dimensional.

Golder's complaint related to the denial of access to court, not the absence of a court with jurisdiction to determine his grievance. The ECtHR clearly pointed out that the right of access is 'not an extensive interpretation forcing new obligations on the Contracting states . . .'.[26] It was also accepted that limitations could be placed on this right in both fact and law.[27] The impediment faced by Golder was that his access to court was entirely in the hands of the minister and this, the Court held, was sufficient to violate Article 6. However, in an important passage, the ECtHR explained the broader protection afforded to a court under Article 6(1):[28]

> Were Art.6 para.1 to be understood as concerning exclusively the conduct of an action which had already been initiated before a court, a Contracting State could, without acting in breach of that text, do away with its courts, or take away their jurisdiction to determine certain classes of civil actions and entrust it to organs dependent on the Government. Such assumptions, indissociable from a danger of arbitrary power, would

---

[24] *Golder* (n 5) [36].
[25] ibid.
[26] ibid.
[27] ibid [26] and [37].
[28] ibid [35].

have serious consequences which are repugnant to the [fundamental principles of law] . . . and which the Court cannot overlook.

We can describe this aspect of the right to a court as a constitutional safeguard. It protects the existence of independent courts with jurisdiction to determine the law. Just as the right to a fair trial would be meaningless if access to courts could be prevented, so access to courts would be meaningless if they had no jurisdiction to exercise.

This 'second limb' complements the right of access to courts and the explicit protection under Article 6 that civil rights and obligations will be determined by an independent tribunal. However, many questions remained unanswered by *Golder*. For example, the constitutional protection might be thought otiose: if civil rights were removed from courts and determined by organs dependent on government, the express guarantee of independence would seemingly be violated. We find explanations and refinements in subsequent cases.

The 'first limb' right of access was soon explained as a right of effective access. It was not enough that an individual could get in the courtroom door if she was denied the means of effectively presenting her case to the court.[29] Thus, it seemingly extends beyond the separation of powers to ensure that procedural or practical impediments do not undermine the existence of substantive rights and the express guarantee of their independent, impartial and fair determination in Article 6. In *Ashingdane v UK*, consideration was given to both limbs. The applicant complained about the effect of section 141 of the Mental Health Act 1959. This provision, which has since been repealed, required leave to be granted by the High Court before any detained patient could bring a claim. Furthermore, it ruled out any possible claim based on strict liability for breach of the Act. The Commission in *Ashingdane* cited *Golder* at length and recognised that it established a dual-limb approach to the right to a court. It stated that there was no violation of the right of access to court to have a determination of a (domestic) civil right. It is 'for the national courts to decide disputes as to whether the plaintiff can invoke such a [domestic civil] right', and the court would do so in the exercise of its jurisdiction to grant leave.[30] Since such proceedings were fair, there was no violation of Article 6. Moreover, the Commission held that, although the concept of 'civil right' under Article 6 was to a certain degree autonomous of domestic law,[31] section 141 served to 'extinguish certain of the possible civil claims of mental health patients'.

Rather than disposing of the matter, this finding brought the second limb constitutional safeguard into play.[32] Clarifying the meaning of this constitutional protection, the Commission stated that the jurisdiction of the courts could not be removed altogether or limited beyond a certain point. Unlike in *Golder*, no

---

[29] *Airey v Ireland* (1979) 2 EHRR 305.
[30] *Ashingdane v UK* (1984) 6 EHRR CD 69 [91]. On the facts, the applicant failed to apply for leave but the Court of Appeal indicated that it would not have granted it because no fault was alleged. See *Ashingdane v Secretary of State for Social Services* 18 February 1980.
[31] See further *Sporrong and Lönnroth v Sweden* 8 October 1980 (Com).
[32] *Ashingdane* (n 30) [92].

mention was made of the need for civil claims to be transferred to tribunals that were not independent; it was sufficient that certain civil claims were taken away or extinguished. This requirement was satisfied on the facts, since the restriction of the applicant's civil rights was 'not arbitrary or unreasonable'[33] and the statute had not 'unduly restricted' the applicant's civil rights, it had merely limited them to claims for bad faith or fault.[34] The inability to sue for breach of statutory duty did not place the authorities above the law or deny the applicant the law's protection. Thus, in *Ashingdane* the dual-limb approach was clearly developed by the Commission and closely linked to the statements of principle in *Golder*.

The principle stated in *Golder* can therefore be seen to reflect the principle of legal equality, in that it requires everybody to be subject to the ordinary law and the jurisdiction of the ordinary courts. Public servants cannot claim the benefit of special process, and marginalised sections of the community cannot be denied the protection of independent courts. This aspect of the protection afforded by Article 6 clearly makes no distinction between procedural and substantive abrogations of rights. It makes no difference whether a person or a class is placed above the law, or put below it, by a procedural rule or a substantive rule of law. But it is a macro- rather than micro-protection. It is a constitutional safeguard.

Dyer v UK[35] and the associated cases of *Ketterick v UK*[36] and *Pinder v UK*[37] added further refinements. It is worth setting out the background to these cases in some detail, since the same issue was revisited in *Matthews*. It is trite law that the Crown's immunity from suit in tort actions was removed by the Crown Proceedings Act 1947, but the statute contained many exceptions. Section 10(1) stated that nothing done by a member of the armed forces while on duty shall sub-ject either him or the Crown to liability for causing death or personal injury to another person in so far as the injury is due to anything suffered by a serviceman on duty at the time or on land, premises, ship, aircraft or vehicle used by the armed forces. To benefit from this immunity the Secretary of State had also to certify that the injury was attributable to service for the purposes of entitlement to a disability award. The effect of section 10(1) was to 'exempt'[38] the Crown from tort liability where it applied. It also introduced a limited immunity for individual servicemen that had not previously existed. The section was repealed in 1987, but Parliament reserved to the executive power to revive the effect of section 10(1) in specified circumstances, such as imminent national danger.[39] It was clearly neither the intention nor the effect of section 10(1) that injured servicemen would be left without compensation. There was substituted a disablement pension with a strict liability entitlement to compensation. Such compensation was undoubtedly far

---

[33] ibid.
[34] ibid.
[35] *Dyer v UK* (1984) 39 D & R 246.
[36] *Ketterick v UK* (1983) 5 EHRR 465.
[37] *Pinder v UK* (1984) 7 EHRR 464.
[38] s 10(1)(b).
[39] Crown Proceedings (Armed Forces) Act 1987 s 2(2).

lower than tortious damages, but the breadth of recipients was also far greater and the difficulties and repercussions of litigation (which were particularly acute when the practice was to claim Crown privilege for a wide range of service documents) were avoided.

In 1981 Dyer suffered serious injuries in a motor accident in the course of a training exercise. After a certificate was issued in respect of both the driver of the vehicle and the Ministry of Defence, Dyer commenced an action alleging that his right to a court had been infringed. The Commission held that section 10(1) served to remove the civil right to sue in tort and established a substantive 'immunity'. Echoing its approach in *Ashingdane,* the Commission stated that it was not competent to review the substantive content of the civil law that ought to obtain in contracting states, and for this reason states do 'not bear the burden of justifying an immunity from liability which forms part of its civil law by reference to a pressing social need . . .'.[40] It was made perfectly clear that it was impermissible under Article 6 to demand state justification for rules of substantive law, such as was required for interferences with substantive Convention articles. On this basis, section 10(1) escaped anxious scrutiny. However, the Commission *was* competent to ensure that such substantive rules did not infringe the constitutional safeguard. Turning to this second limb, the Commission stated: 'These principles apply not only in respect of procedural limitations such as the removal of the jurisdiction of the court, but also in respect of a substantive immunity from liability as in the present case.' Indeed, it follows from *Golder* that Article 6 must prevent states simply removing whole tracts of civil rights. In *Dyer* the Commission clarified this point by adding that states could not consistently with Article 6, 'confer immunities from liability on certain groups'.[41] This does not create any requirements for the *particular content* of substantive rights, however, it does have the effect of conferring a measure of constitutional protection on the institution of private law. It ensures that civil claims are not abrogated unlawfully or without reason, or that any person is denied legal rights beyond such a point as would be incompatible with the rule of law. It ensures that no one is denied the law's protection and that no one is not answerable to the law. On the facts of *Dyer,* the Commission denied that section 10(1) violated Article 6:

> The creation of a pension entitlement to provide certain coverage of the needs of injured servicemen without enquiry as to fault, in recognition of [the heightened] professional risks, cannot be regarded as either arbitrary or unreasonable . . . such a system is common to many State parties to the Convention in the field of workmen's compensation.[42]

The Commission noted the costly and time-consuming nature of the tort system, as contrasted with a system providing an immediate payment linked to inflation and degree of disablement.

---

[40] *Dyer* (n 35) [5].
[41] ibid [6].
[42] ibid [9].

Seeking Simplicity: a Maximalist Approach

When *Ashingdane* was decided by the ECtHR, the Court essentially adopted an approach that maximised the potential intrusiveness of the right to a court, by conflating the two limbs of the *Golder* test.[43] The Court's first step was to refuse to consider the Government's contention that the applicant had no civil claim at all and therefore that his claim fell outside the ambit of Article 6. It treated the case as if Article 6 were hypothetically applicable. Secondly, it clarified that there is a right of access to a court where one has an 'arguable' case that a limitation on a civil right is unlawful, or where the existence of the civil right is unclear, as well, presumably, as when it is.[44] It then stated that the fact that the applicant had been to court to have his claim determined meant that he had had 'access to the remedies that existed within the domestic system'.[45] This was not necessarily the end of the matter, even on conventional reasoning, because a substantive legal prohibition must still not violate the constitutional second limb. Sure enough, the Court referred to comments made in *Golder* and in the Opinion of the Commission for the proposition:

> This of itself does not exhaust the requirements of Article 6. It must still be established that the degree of access afforded under the national legislation was sufficient to secure the individual's 'right to a court', having regard to the rule of law in a democratic society.

However, it went on to state that any limitation on access must satisfy the twin requirements of legitimacy of aim and reasonable proportionality of means and must not impair the 'very essence' of the right.[46] But this was a wrong step. The comments of the Commission and the Court relied upon clearly referred to the second limb constitutional safeguard, to which the intrusive test of justification had explicitly been held to be inapplicable. The Court ran together these two limbs so that, irrespective of the form of the restriction on court remedies, the intrusive test of justification would be universally applicable.[47] Yet significantly it failed to provide any justification in principle for this radical step.

The effect of this apparent rationalisation and simplification was to open the possibility of *any* denial of a civil claim being deemed a bar on access and subject to rigorous justification. The Court attempted to downplay the radical potential of its judgment, stating that 'it is no part of the Court's function to substitute for the assessment of the national authorities any other assessment of what might be the

---

[43] The roots of such an approach were, however, apparent in several of the Court's earlier judgments in which it notably failed to distinguish Art 6 from substantive articles: *Holy Monasteries v Greece* (1994) 20 EHRR 1; *Sporrong and Lönnroth v Sweden* (1982) 5 EHRR 35; *James v UK* (1986) 8 EHRR 123, in which Judge Thór Vilhjálmsson's dissent recognised the flaw in the Court's approach.

[44] *Ashingdane v United Kingdom* (1985) 7 EHRR 528 [55].

[45] ibid [56].

[46] ibid [57] and [59].

[47] ibid [57]. It might be explained, but not justified, by the fact that *Ashingdane* can be interpreted as raising both a procedural (leave—first limb) and substantive (limited substantive immunity—second limb) issue (see Lord Walker in *Matthews* (n 16) [113]). The ECtHR simply ran the issues together.

best policy in this field'.[48] And it held on the facts that the limitation was justified. However, we shall see that in *Osman* the full implications of this approach came to the fore.

Reaction: a Minimalist Approach

In a surprising about-turn the ECtHR in following cases accepted submissions by the respondent governments that there was simply no civil right at issue and, unlike in *Ashingdane*, thereby refused to apply a test of legitimacy and proportionality at all. For example, in *Powell and Raynor v UK* a statutory bar abrogated the right to sue in nuisance for aircraft noise. The ECtHR held that the provision had 'the result that the applicants cannot claim to have a substantive right under English law . . .'.[49] Perhaps recognising the implications of its judgment in *Ashingdane*, the ECtHR emphasised that Article 6 'does not in itself guarantee any particular content for [civil] 'rights and obligations' in the substantive law of [the] Contracting state'.[50] These cases reveal that the *Golder* test had been transformed from a sensitive dual-limb test into an all-or-nothing test of legitimacy and proportionality applicable to any limitation on a civil right. The reaction of the Court was to deny its application at all where civil rights had been extinguished, as well as when they were simply non-existent. In so doing, the Court was renouncing a great deal of the constitutional protection recognised as underpinning the right to a court in *Golder*.

Reviving the Two Limbs and the Distinction Between Procedure and Substance

In *Fayed v UK* the ECtHR was faced with an argument primarily directed to Article 6, and this presented an opportunity to rationalise and clarify the competing case law.[51] The facts, briefly, were these. An investigation of the Al Fayeds' conduct of their takeover of House of Fraser concluded that they had dishonestly misrepresented their wealth, origins and resources, as well as misleading inspectors who had been appointed by the Government to investigate the takeover. The applicants

---

[48] ibid [57]. Judge Pettiti dissenting made plain the direction in which some judges were pushing the law on the right to a court. He stated that while a state may lawfully grant immunities to certain categories of public servants, such immunities should be rigorously justified. Where they are wider than necessary, they will infringe the principle of proportionality. Since Ashingdane was not a vexatious litigant, the provisions went, he considered, too far in excluding his claim.

[49] *Powell and Raynor v UK* (1990) 12 EHRR 355 [36]; *James v UK* (1986) 8 EHRR 123.

[50] ibid [81].

[51] *Fayed v UK* (1994) 18 EHRR 393.

argued that, because the common law privileged the reports of the inspectors, they were denied effective access to court to sue for defamation. The justification for the privilege is broadly similar to that underpinning the limited immunity of advocates and the police; namely, concern for the inhibiting effect of potential exposure to civil liability. Applying the ECtHR's judgment in *Ashingdane,* the Commission thought that the defence of privilege did limit access to court, albeit that it was justified. However, the Court was more circumspect. In a passage which has been recited in subsequent cases, it stated:[52]

> Whether a person has an actionable domestic claim may depend not only on the sub-stantive content, properly speaking, of the relevant civil right as defined under national law but also on the existence of procedural bars preventing or limiting the possibilities of bringing potential claims to court. In the latter kind of case Art.6 para.1 (Art.6-1) may have a degree of applicability. Certainly the Convention enforcement bodies may not create by way of interpretation of Art.6 para.1 (Art.6-1) a substantive civil right which has no legal basis in the State concerned. However, it would not be consistent with the rule of law in a democratic society or with the basic principle underlying Art.6 para.1 (Art.6-1)—namely that civil claims must be capable of being submitted to a judge for adjudication—if, for example, a State could, without restraint or control by the Convention enforcement bodies, remove from the jurisdiction of the courts a whole range of civil claims or confer immunities from civil liability on large groups or categor-ies of persons (see the Commission's admissibility decision . . . *Dyer v. the United Kingdom*, Decisions and Reports 39, pp. 246–66 at pp. 251–52).

This may be termed the composite paragraph. It represents an attempt to recon-cile the conflicting jurisprudence up to this point. The Court explained the notion that Article 6 has a degree of applicability in relation to 'procedural bars'. We shall return to this distinction between procedure and substance very shortly. It is important first to address the last sentence of the composite paragraph, in which the Court appears to introduce a caveat. This sentence has caused much confu-sion, but properly located against the background jurisprudence we can see that it represents the retention of the second limb constitutional safeguard, which is traceable all the way back to *Golder.* This is made clear by the express endorsement of the approach taken by the Commission in *Dyer.*

We have seen that this safeguard confers a degree of substantive protection on domestic rights. However, as was held in *Dyer,* this second limb differs from the test of legitimacy and proportionality applicable in relation to the first limb, and to what the Court now terms 'procedural bars' on access. This was confirmed by the Court in *Fayed.* The Court refused to determine a separate argument that the defence of privilege amounted to a limitation on the right to respect for private life, but it considered that the point was 'devoid of significance'[53] because, '[i]f the Court were to treat the facts underlying the complaints declared inadmissible by

---

[52] ibid [65].

[53] ibid [67]; also in extracts distilled from *Ashingdane* set out after the composite paragraph the Court endorsed the approach to the test of justification adopted, but it seems it limited the test to procedural bars on access, rather than the constitutional protection of the jurisdiction of the courts.

the Commission as raising a substantive, rather than a procedural complaint going to the right to respect for private life under Article 8 of the Convention—as it has jurisdiction to do—the same central issues of legitimate aim and proportionality as under Art.6(1) would be posed'. The sum of this reasoning is as follows. The test of legitimacy and proportionality under Article 6(1) is the same as that applied under Article 8(2) to scrutinise substantive rules of law; however, *only* procedural bars fall to be justified in this manner. This express rejection of the maximalist position is coupled with retention of the constitutional safeguard so clearly set out in *Dyer* and, thus, *Fayed* represents a modern reading of the *Golder* dual-limb test.

The most important aspect of *Fayed* is, however, undoubtedly the promotion of the distinction between procedure and substance. The Court recognised that it 'is not always an easy matter to trace the dividing line between procedural and substantive limitations of a given entitlement under domestic law'.[54] This honest acknowledgment of the difficulty of the distinction was coupled with a welcome determination to defer to the categorisation arrived at by domestic authorities. However, this should not obscure the fact that the concept of a 'procedural bar' should be given an autonomous Convention meaning reflecting the underlying concerns to which Article 6(1) is addressed. So construed, the express recognition of this distinction in this context is a beneficial and welcome one for a number of reasons. First, the notion of a 'procedural bar' complements the autonomous nature of 'civil rights' under the Convention. This enables protection to be afforded to individuals even though they have no 'right' in domestic law. In traditional English law terms, the presence of a right flows from the availability of a remedy. However, the effect of a procedural bar on domestic rights might be to render them unarguable in domestic law, but it does not serve to extinguish the underlying 'civil right' and so avoid Article 6's protections. To this extent Article 6 may create an actionable domestic right where none previously existed, but only if, of course, such procedural bars cannot be justified.

The second benefit is that the distinction allows states substantively to limit, remove, or abrogate civil rights, subject only to the constitutional guarantee. Additionally, Article 6 cannot create a completely new civil right that has no legal basis in the state concerned. The effect of requiring substantive limitations of civil rights to be subject to the tests of legitimacy and proportionality would be to tip the delicate balance of policy underlying such rights in favour of their presence, which, while welcome to the litigating party, is equally detrimental to the person against whom the right is exerted. Moreover, it would be productive of a bias in favour of generality and against legal certainty.[55] This would have destabilising repercussions, as many central doctrines of private law would be open to challenge, from the doctrine of consideration to the duty of care.[56] It must be correct that where a claim is ruled out on the substantive merits the only question, subject to any constitutional inquiry, is whether in denying the claim the proceedings

---

[54] ibid [67].
[55] See eg Judge Pettiti, above n 48.
[56] For a similar point see Lord Hoffmann in *Matthews* (n 16) [32].

were fair and satisfied the express requirements of Article 6.[57] The court should not have additionally to be satisfied that the law pursues a legitimate aim and is proportionate, this would not only lead to uncertainty and instability in the law, but it would upset the balance of principle and policy that underpins the rule of law in question and would establish a bias in favour of liability. The distinction therefore maintains the connection between the intrusive scrutiny demanded by the test of justification and the central orientation of Article 6, which is procedural. It rightly consigns anxious scrutiny of the substantive law to the protection afforded to substantive fundamental rights in other articles.

Thirdly, we can welcome the explicit recognition of the distinction because it is familiar to the common law. The law does distinguish between different reasons for the denial of a remedy. For example, certain statutory provisions and common law doctrines that immunise individuals from suit in tort have been held to be merely procedural bars so that the individual's employer remains vicariously liable for the tort.[58] The distinction is also central to the law on choice of law.[59] Given that these cases rest on different normative pressures,[60] the notion of a procedural bar is likely to be differently defined when applying Article 6. However, it shows that the inquiry is not alien or troubling for the common law. It is also necessary to emphasise a final point. It was unfortunate that the decision to treat Article 6 as hypothetically engaged avoided a critical issue; namely whether a judge-made rule of the common law could ever infringe the right to a court as either a procedural bar or as a substantive limitation engaging the constitutional limb of the *Golder* test. There appears to be an assumption that it could. If so, it might only attract Article 6 in so far as the courts impose procedural bars which might engage a wider concern than strictly with the separation of powers.[61]

Professor Gearty's Thesis

Professor Gearty has offered an important interpretation and analysis of the case law. He has also argued for recognition of a two-part test to determine alleged infringements of the right to a court. However, Professor Gearty offers a very different interpretation of the parts of this test. In his view, the court first applies a 'threshold test'. This is met if the interference with the exercise of the applicant's rights was arguably unlawful. If met, the court then asks whether the determination was fair, independent and impartial. Where there is clearly no domestic cause of action, as in *Ashingdane,* it is not arguable that the interference is unlawful and the threshold will not be met. In such cases the Court, so Gearty argues, applies a

---

[57] See *Clunis v UK* (App no 45049/98) 11 September 2001.
[58] *Broom v Morgan* [1953] 1 QB 597, especially 609 (Denning LJ); *Dyer v Munday* [1895] 1 QB 742.
[59] As recognised in *Matthews* (n 16), eg at [34] (Lord Hoffmann) [127] (Lord Walker)
[60] Those relating to the circumvention of immunities in tort may have been lessened by the development of direct liability of employers.
[61] See further Gearty, 'Unravelling *Osman*', (n 22), 175.

second test, which he terms 'the European fallback test'. It is only at this stage that the Court considers whether the restriction is justified according to the familiar concepts of legitimacy and proportionality.[62]

Clearly no interpretation can hope to be fully consistent with all of the Strasbourg jurisprudence.[63] However, Gearty's analysis of the application of a two-stage approach is unappealing and does not fit happily with the cases. It is clear from the analysis presented above that it is precisely where the claim meets with a substantive bar, which would rule out achievement of Gearty's threshold condition, that the Court has been and should be *less* inclined to require the exclusion to be justified. The 'fallback' position should be a far less intrusive constitutional guarantee that provides a background protection for Article 6. Gearty's interpretation seems to get this the wrong way around. His analysis hangs largely on the approach taken by the Court in *Ashingdane*, which we have seen to be both out of line with previous and later cases and also representing a departure from underlying principle.[64] Furthermore, by stressing instead the notion of arguability, Gearty's approach eschews a distinction at the Convention level between procedure and substance. He considers that the introduction of this distinction in *Fayed* was 'arid nonsense'.[65] Since this distinction is now central to the right of access to court, and, as we shall see, has been accepted as such by the House of Lords, acceptance of the Gearty approach would, it is suggested, require a significant change of direction.

Prelude to *Matthews v Ministry of Defence* and *Wilson v First County Trust Ltd (No 2)*

Matthews and *Wilson* can only be understood against the background of four cases that followed *Fayed*. The cases are *Osman v UK*,[66] *Z v UK*,[67] *Tinnelly & Sons Ltd v UK*[68] and *Fogarty v UK*.[69]

---

[62] Gearty, 'Unravelling *Osman*' (n 22), 168–69.

[63] Professor Gearty does not make such a claim for his thesis. For example, although approving the decision of the ECtHR in *Ashingdane*, Gearty states: 'one would have wanted the Court to have been more explicit than it was' ('Unravelling *Osman*' (n 22) 169). And he says of his own interpretation of *Fayed*: '. . . although the Court was never explicit about any of this . . .' ('Unravelling *Osman*' (n 22), 178); similarly in *Tinnelly & Sons Ltd v UK* (1999) 27 EHRR 249 182. For Gearty's interpretation of *Z v UK*, see CA Gearty, '*Osman* unravels' (2002) 65 MLR 87. He there states that his fallback test would apply to limitations that would seem to fall under the concept of a procedural bar (97). On this approach, his thesis appears to be akin to the maximalist position.

[64] For different criticisms of Gearty's analysis, but in support of an approach similarly reliant on the court in *Ashingdane*, see J Wright, *Tort Law and Human Rights* (Oxford, Hart Publishing, 2001) ii–iii.

[65] *Fayed* (n 51), 17.

[66] *Osman* (n 8).

[67] *Z v UK* (n 10).

[68] *Tinnelly* (n 63).

[69] *Fogarty v UK* (2001) 34 EHRR 302.

The decision in *Osman* has been the subject of much criticism and analysis. The renowned tort scholar Tony Weir wrote critically of the decision that, 'Nations should decide for themselves whether public funds should be directed to victims of past malfunction in public services or used to reduce the number of such malfunctions in the future.'[70] Lord Hoffmann in extra-judicial comments in a similar vein stated that the decision challenged the autonomy of the state and indeed Parliament to deal with social welfare questions concerning allocation of resources.[71] The few who were favourably disposed to the judgment saw it as curing ills largely unconnected with the right of access to court.[72] It is necessary to deal briefly with the judgment. The first step in the reasoning of the ECtHR in *Osman* was that it considered the applicants had a right to seek an adjudication on the merits of an arguable claim in negligence.[73] Instead of then examining whether the adjudication afforded had been fair and, perhaps, whether the substantive rule of law by reference to which the claim was struck out violated the constitutional guarantee, it proceeded to consider whether what it characterised as the 'exclusionary rule' applied was justifiable, and found that it was not. The Court did not mention the substantive/procedural distinction promoted in *Fayed*, yet it is difficult to see that the rule was anything other than pertaining to the substance of the right. It was no more of an immunity than other no-liability precedents. And whilst some commentators prefer to describe the duty of care as laying down areas of 'immunity' from liability in negligence,[74] the concept of immunity is here invoked for a different purpose, as a way of describing the internal dynamics of negligence law. Indeed, it has never been the case that unreasonably caused harm is tortious, even presumptively.

There was, however, a motivation for the Court's decision to scrutinise the substantive law in *Osman* which requires emphasis. One of the applicants' submissions

---

[70] T Weir, 'Down Hill—All the Way?' (1999) 58 *CLJ* 4. AWB Simpson, *Human Rights and the End of Empire: Britain and the Genesis of the European Convention* (Oxford, Oxford University Press, 2001) 7 refers to email correspondence with Weir 'under the heading "End of Civilised Life As We Know It"'. For other criticism see M Lunney, 'A Tort Lawyer's View of *Osman v United Kingdom*' (1999) *King's College Law Journal* 238, G Monti, '*Osman v UK*: Transforming English Negligence Law into Frency Administrative Law' (1999) *International and Comparative Law Quarterly* 757.

[71] 'Human Rights and the House of Lords' (1999) 62 *MLR* 159, 164. Sir Richard Buxton also criticised the decision extra-judicially: 'The Human Rights Act and Private Law' (2000) 116 *LQR* 48, 62–64.

[72] See Simpson, *Human Rights and the End of Empire* (n 70) 7–8, who sought to explain the decision on the basis that it reflected the need to ensure police accountability in European countries where the history of policing 'is not happy'. BS Markesinis, J-B Auby, D Coester-Waltjen and S Deakin, *Tortious Liability of Statutory Bodies: A Comparative and Economic Analysis of Five English Cases* (Oxford, Hart Publishing, 1999) 96–104 welcomed the decision on the basis that the new 'human rights environment' and 'human rights values' should affect the existence and content of national rights, and viewed it as a step towards the concept of 'duty' in negligence law entirely. In his lecture to the British Academy in 2002 entitled 'Human Rights: Have the Public Benefited?', Lord Woolf stated that 'I have also to acknowledge that, while my original reaction was sceptical, after reflection I came to appreciate that [*Osman*] had substantial merits' (available at www.britac.ac.uk, p 6). For a sustained defence of *Osman* on its own terms, see Wright, *Tort Law and Human Rights* (n 64).

[73] *Osman* (n 8) [139].

[74] eg D Howarth, *Textbook on Tort* (London, Butterworths, 1995).

was that the absence of an investigation into failings of the police authority infringed their right to life as protected by Article 2. In a crucial passage the Court considered that 'the essence of the applicants' complaint under this head concerns their inability to secure access to a court or other remedy to have an independent assessment of the police response to the threat posed . . . to the lives of the Osman family'.[75] The Court considered, therefore, that it was appropriate to consider this complaint under Article 6. Only in later cases did the Court develop a freestanding procedural obligation to investigate deaths under Article 2, which properly reflects this concern.[76] *Osman* thus represents yet another example of the confusion of Article 6 with substantive articles; but the foundations were laid by the erroneous judgment of the Court in *Ashingdane* and the maximalist approach there adopted.

The error was not repeated in *Z*, which evinced a return to *Fayed* and the dual-limb approach. In *Z* the ECtHR resiled from its earlier judgment in *Osman*, stating that it,

> considers that its reasoning in the *Osman* judgment was based on an understanding of the law of, heavily influenced by the decision of the House of Lords in *Barrett and Enfield LBC*, negligence which has to be reviewed in the light of the clarification subsequently made in the domestic courts and notably in the House of Lords [in *Barrett v Enfield LBC*].[77]

It held that by denying the existence of a duty of care on grounds of public policy the House of Lords had neither invoked a procedural bar,[78] nor, since it refused to recognise a novel category of claim, had it established a substantive immunity by removing a civil obligation from a state authority.[79] It also made clear that although the decision was allegedly sweeping and blanket in nature, denying recognition of particular alleged wrongs, or failing to extend liability, it did not infringe the constitutional safeguard despite the fact that the non-existence of a cause of action under domestic law may be described as having the same effect as an immunity.[80] The reasoning clearly suggests that decisions denying a common law right of action, which are declaratory and apply retrospectively, may never be able to infringe this limb.[81] The ECtHR in *Z* therefore affirmed the distinction between procedure and substance, whilst not discarding the constitutional

---

[75] *Osman* (n 8) [123].

[76] The source of confusion derives from *McCann v UK* (1995) 21 EHRR 97 [160] where the ECtHR left open the possibility of requiring civil proceedings in connection with deprivation of life under Art 2, mentioning that it was a question going to Arts 6 and 13. However, at [161] it recognised the need for 'some form of official investigation', which has since been developed under Art 2, eg *McKerr v UK* (2001) 34 EHRR 20, *Jordan v United Kingdom* (2003) 37 EHRR 2. The absence of a remedy is now correctly addressed only under Art 13: *E v UK* (2002) 36 EHRR 519.

[77] *Z v UK* (2002) 34 EHRR 3 [100].

[78] ibid [95].

[79] ibid [96].

[80] ibid [98].

[81] It is therefore odd that the ECtHR found Art 6(1) applicable at all. Perhaps it felt it needed to deal substantively with these issues after *Osman*. For another example see *Clunis* (n 57).

safeguard. It also affirmed that Article 6 does not guarantee any particular content for 'civil rights and obligations' in the substantive law of contracting states.[82]

In contrast to *Osman* and *Z*, *Tinnelly* and *Fogarty* are important more for their circumstances, which bear close resemblance to those in *Dyer* and *Matthews*, than their reasoning.[83] In *Tinnelly* the ECtHR considered the Fair Employment (Northern Ireland) Act 1976. Section 17(1) made it unlawful for employers to discriminate between persons seeking employment, but by section 42, the Act 'shall not apply to an act done for the purposes of safeguarding national security' and a certificate issued by the Secretary of State is conclusive evidence of this. A certificate was issued against the applicants, causing them to withdraw a claim for discrimination and (unsuccessfully) challenge the issue by judicial review. The ECtHR held that section 42 was a procedural bar because it barred access to the Fair Employment Tribunal and the county court, which could not consider the correctness of the issue although the Court considered them capable of doing so. Further, it held that the bar was disproportionate. In *Fogarty* the ECtHR held that state immunity, which had been claimed by the US Government in respect of a claim under the Sex Discrimination Act 1975, constituted a procedural bar on access to court. It reasoned that an action was not barred *in limine* because the respondent state had an option whether to assert it. In this respect the applicants' case that the bar was procedural appeared stronger than in *Tinnelly*.[84]

Revisiting *Dyer*: *Matthews v Ministry of Defence*

The peculiarities of asbestos-related illnesses have forced radical modifications to established doctrines of the common law.[85] However, in *Matthews* the House of Lords refused the opportunity presented by the extensive latent periods of such conditions to rule that the preservation of Crown immunity in tort under section 10(1) of the Crown Proceedings Act 1947, although prospectively abolished in

---

[82] *Z v UK* (2003) 34 EHRR 3 [87]. Judge Thomassen, joined by Judges Casadevall and Kovle, and Judge Rozakis joined by Judge Palm gave dissenting opinions. Lady Arden, the UK judge, gave a concurring opinion in which she emphasised that she attached 'particular importance' to the principle that 'Article 6 does not guarantee any particular content for civil rights and obligations' (O-14).

[83] Attention should also be drawn to *A v UK* (2002) 36 EHRR 917 in which the ECtHR considered that the prohibition in s 9 of the Bill of Rights 1689, prohibiting the impeachment or questioning of parliamentary speech in any court, was probably a procedural bar, but declined actually to decide the matter.

[84] In another it was much weaker. Lord Millet in *Matthews* took exception to the decision. He pointed out that the immunity was not imposed by UK courts, Parliament or the Government. The immunity was a limitation on UK sovereignty enjoyed by the US which was not a party to the Convention. It had nothing to do with the separation of powers. Art 6(1) could not attack or remove this immunity because it could not create an adjudicative jurisdiction that did not exist, nor could the UK be answerable for its absence ([101]–[106], applying the reasoning in *Holland v Lampen-Wolfe* [2000] 1 WLR 1573, not cited to the ECtHR).

[85] eg *Fairchild v Glenhaven Funeral Services Ltd* [2003] 1 AC 32.

1987, violated Article 6.[86] To do so would have thrown into question the remaining areas in which Crown and similar immunities continue to apply.

Matthews served as an electrical mechanic aboard asbestos-riddled ships in the 1950s and 1960s. As a consequence, he claimed to have developed pleural plaques and bilateral diffuse pleural fibrosis. These conditions are not life-threatening and were described as having almost no symptoms, such that Matthews suffered no disability sufficient for compensation. He instigated a claim in tort in March 2001 which was defended on the basis that the Ministry of Defence intended to apply for a certificate from the Secretary of State. As a preliminary issue Keith J held that section 10(1) only preserved an immunity from being sued, not 'a primary right not to be exposed to asbestos in circumstances amounting to negligence or breach of statutory duty'.[87] Moreover, relying strongly on *Tinnelly* and *Fogarty* he held that the issue of the certificate would constitute a bar engaging and violating Article 6. A certificate was subsequently issued, but the Court of Appeal reversed Keith J.[88] Its view was that Article 6 is exclusively concerned with procedure and Matthews' complaint related to the substance of his rights (or rather the lack thereof). Permission to appeal to the House of Lords was nonetheless granted.

The state of the authorities cannot have been conducive to formulating clear submissions, and counsel for Matthews before the House of Lords concentrated on what seemed the best point: the close analogy with *Fogarty* and *Tinnelly*. However, this required important concessions. First, it was conceded that Article 6 only bites on procedural bars. We have seen that this does not in fact follow from the case law. Hence, from the outset the claimant's arguments were limited. Secondly, it was conceded that had section 10(1) been drafted so as to preserve Crown immunity without the requirement of executive certification of any material component, then Article 6 could not have applied. This concession followed largely from the first. Nonetheless, it is certainly arguable that Crown immunity is a procedural bar in itself. It flows at root from the inability to sue the Monarch in their own courts.[89] In fact, counsel's second concession limited the claimant's case in a more practical manner. Since it was a condition for the award of disability pension that an injury was attributable to service, certifying the satisfaction of this condition prevented the serviceman from falling between the strict liability regime and tort law.[90] The procedure *safeguarded* the position of servicemen by acting as a kind of estoppel. It was intended to *limit* executive power, not confer it.

[86] The MoD conceded points relating to retrospectivity of the HRA and application of Art 6 to state service.

[87] *Matthews* (n 16) [21].

[88] *Matthews* (n 16). Despite submissions from Professor Gearty on behalf of the post-traumatic stress disorder group.

[89] Moreover the King was originally under an unenforceable duty not to do wrong. Admittedly, this was later misunderstood to mean the King was immune from wrongdoing, and Crown immunity is the mongrel descent of these two ideas: PW Hogg and PJ Monahan, *Liability of the Crown*, 3rd edn (Toronto, Carswell, 2000) 4. See also the cases cited at n 58 above which would have supported an argument attacking Crown immunity.

[90] This relationship was analysed in some detail by Lords Hope and Millett, *Matthews* (n 88) [64]–[69] and [94]–[99].

Furthermore, counsel also laid much stress on the argument that Matthews had a cause of action subsisting up until the issue of such a certificate. The effect of this emphasis was perhaps to detract from the fact that procedural bars can operate to deny a cause of action from subsisting in the first place.

The discussion here will focus on the speeches of Lord Bingham, Lord Walker and Lord Hoffmann. Lord Bingham, leading the House, had the agreement of Lords Millett and Walker. Lord Walker had the express agreement of Lords Hoffmann, Hope and Millett and his speech represents most closely the grounds of the decision. Lord Hoffmann, with whom Lords Millett and Walker agreed, made some particularly important wider observations on Article 6 and the Convention.

Lord Bingham denied that there was any civil right in domestic law for the purposes of Article 6 and, since Article 6 cannot create a civil right that is not recognised in domestic law, this disposed of the matter. In so deciding, Lord Bingham reasoned that '[f]ew common law rules were better established or more unqualified than that which precluded any claim in tort against the Crown',[91] it was 'absolute'[92] in nature and any practitioner asked to advise Matthews would have considered that there was 'no claim with any prospect of success'.[93] Whilst undoubtedly correct, such observations are, with respect, beside the point. If there is no civil right in domestic law there will certainly be no cause of action, but the absence of a cause of action might be because of either a substantive or procedural bar on a civil right as well as because the civil right has never been recognised.[94] At least in the former two situations Article 6 will be engaged, albeit to considerably different degrees. The kernel of Lord Bingham's reasoning, however, actually appears to go to the point that there was no substantive right to be barred either procedurally or substantively, because it had never been recognised. He held that '[h]istorically, no such right existed'[95] and section 10(1) simply preserved this state of affairs.[96]

Dyer and *Pinder* were relied upon by counsel to support the applicability of Article 6 to section 10(1). We have seen that the Commission only applied the constitutional safeguard in those cases. Since counsel had conceded that Article 6 only applied to procedural bars. Lord Bingham understandably had some trouble with this submission. He questioned, '. . . whether the Commission was right to ask "whether s.10 of the 1947 Act constitutes an arbitrary limitation of the applicant's substantive civil claims" when in truth the applicant had no civil claim'.[97] However, he later recognised that these cases established a 'third class of case' within the Strasbourg jurisprudence, 'in which there was some legal basis for a

---

[91] ibid [4].
[92] ibid [15](7).
[93] ibid [15](8).
[94] It is difficult to reconcile his grounds for distinguishing *Fayed*, ibid [17].
[95] ibid [15](1) and [19] 'the right which Mr Matthews seeks to assert has never, at any time relevant to his claim, existed in national law'.
[96] Particularly ibid [16].
[97] ibid.

right in domestic law which was subject to a substantive immunity'.[98] Relying on
Z, he considered it unnecessary to explore this authority because there was 'strictly
speaking' no immunity introduced by section 10(1), simply an historical absence
of any right at all.[99] He was also unimpressed by the argument that the certificate
created a procedural dimension such as to engage Article 6. His own researches
turned up a line of argument not advanced by counsel for the Government.
Tracing the origins and preparation of the Crown Proceedings Act 1947, he noted
that in earlier drafts the certification procedure was absent and it had been conceded (as we have seen) that the case for Matthews hinged on this procedure. Lord
Bingham noted that the introduction of the procedure was intended to protect
servicemen, by making it straightforward for them to assert an entitlement to disablement pension, and not alter the substance of the provision. He considered that
it would have altered the substance of his rights only had it been framed in discretionary terms.[100] The implications of Lord Bingham's reasoning would seem to be
three-fold. Where the law has never recognised a substantive cause of action there
would never be, in his Lordship's opinion, a substantive immunity from liability,
still less a procedural bar. A discretionary power over a cause of action would,
however, constitute a procedural bar. He also expressly left open the possibility of
recognising the existence of the constitutional guarantee (a 'third class of case')
should the matter arise.

Lord Walker's judgment hinged on his endorsement of the distinction between
procedure and substance, and he accepted that counsel's concession on this point
had been correctly made.[101] As a matter of principle, he considered that Article 6
is 'concerned with procedural fairness and integrity of a state's judicial system, not
with the substantive content of its national law'.[102] His Lordship considered that
the 'most obvious examples of purely procedural bars are those which have no
connection with the substance of a would-be litigant's claim'.[103] These include any
need to provide security for costs or to obtain the court's permission to commence
or continue proceedings, such as might be the case where the claimant is a
vexatious litigant or is in contempt of court. This seems to accept that procedural
bars may be imposed by courts at common law. Statutes of limitation would also
usually be regarded as procedural.[104] Lord Walker explained that such restrictions
have 'nothing to do with the material facts which together constitute the

---

[98] ibid [19].
[99] Quite obviously this distinction is as troublesome as the distinction between procedure and substance. In practice it might be avoided by simply asking the question: 'Is there here an unreasonable or
arbitrary immunity from liability or extinction of civil rights beyond such a point as to infringe the rule
of law?'
[100] *Matthews* (n 16) [15] (3)–(5).
[101] ibid [142].
[102] ibid.
[103] ibid [128].
[104] *Stubbings v UK* (1996) 23 EHRR 213. For rules of evidence protecting criminal acquittals, see
Ringvold v Norway (App no 34964/97) 11 February 2003 [38]; T Hickman and F Saifee [2003] *EHRLR*
539, 545.

claimant's cause of action'.[105] He also recognised some addition to this principle such as where immunity is waivable, which accounted for state immunity.[106] Furthermore, he emphasised that it was inappropriate to rely on the right of access to denounce substantive rules of law that might be objectionable because they confer an immunity on a particular class, such as, he considered, the ECtHR had done in *Osman*.[107]

In Lord Walker's view, the nub of Matthews' case was whether the certification procedure amounted to a procedural bar, by analogy with *Fogarty*. He considered *Fogarty* not to be in point because there is a wide executive discretion on foreign states whether or not to submit to the jurisdiction of the court.[108] In contrast, '[i]n practice, the Secretary of State issues a certificate under section 10 in any case in which he is satisfied that the statutory conditions are met, and in which a certificate would serve a useful purpose'.[109] This reasoning seems sound, as the issue of the certificate concerned a matter of judgment, not discretion; and this consideration seems to have formed at least part of the reasoning of all of their Lordships.[110] It is submitted that *Tinnelly*, which was not discussed by Lord Walker, can be distinguished in much the same way. The assertion of national security could not be questioned at all by the tribunals in the proceedings in which it is asserted. The High Court itself did not consider the factual basis for the certificates and essentially deferred to the executive. Basically therefore the executive was able to exempt public officers from the general law without being subject to effective judicial scrutiny and without having to establish the justification for doing so. Lord Hoffmann distinguished *Tinnelly* on a slightly different basis, namely, that section 10 of the Crown Proceedings Act did not create an executive power to conclusively determine a right of action but a decision by Parliament to substitute a right for a compensation scheme. In *Tinnelly* there was an 'encroach[ment] upon the functions of the judicial branch of government'.[111] This ground of distinction is a fine one, since it raises the question whether the result in *Tinnelly* should have been different if provision had been made in the statutory scheme for applicants unable to bring discrimination claims to be compensated. It is submitted that this cannot be determinative.

It is important to emphasise that, despite his endorsement of the procedural/substantive distinction, Lord Walker, like Lord Bingham, also left the door ajar to future recognition of a substantive dimension to Article 6. He identified 'contrast-

---

[105] *Matthews* (n 16) [128].

[106] Relying on AV Dicey, CGJ Morse et al (eds) *Dicey & Morris on the Conflict of Laws*, 13th edn (London, Sweet & Maxwell, 2000) para.7-040.

[107] *Matthews* (n 16) [129].

[108] ibid [147]. Lord Bingham said *Fogarty* was 'categorically different', without clearly explaining why ([18]). Lord Millett thought *Fogarty* was wrong on other grounds (n 84 above). Lord Hoffmann stressed that there was a discretion, but also that the reason for this was to protect a different value from the merits of the tort action, namely international relations ([41]).

[109] *Matthews* (n 16) [118].

[110] ibid [15] (Lord Bingham); [28], [39], (Lord Hoffmann); [71] (Lord Hope); [96]–[98] (Lord Millett).

[111] ibid [38] and [39].

ing themes' in the Strasbourg cases: some in which a test of legitimacy and proportionality was unaskingly applied and others where its application was limited to procedural bars.[112] His Lordship cited *Pinder* and *Dyer* as examples of the former. Moreover, referring to the composite paragraph in *Fayed* he commented that it 'is hard to tell how far the last sentence . . . goes'.[113] Recognition of the tension in the case law is most welcome, but it is less pervasive than the picture painted by Lord Walker suggests, once the difference between the two limbs is fully recognised. For example, the last sentence of the composite paragraph, as has been shown, represents the survival of the second limb constitutional safeguard. Ironically, but perfectly in keeping with his recognition that Article 6 protects the 'integrity of the State's judicial system', Lord Walker seemingly reintroduced the constitutional limb, stating in his conclusions: 'The notion that a state should decide to substitute a no-fault system of compensation for some injuries which might otherwise lead to claims in tort is not inimical to article 6(1), as the Commission said in *Dyer* . . . [when addressing the constitutional guarantee[114].'[115] Such a statement is wholly irrelevant in the absence of recognition of the protection afforded by the constitutional safeguard. Moreover, it suggests that, contrary to the view of Lord Bingham, Crown immunity, as preserved by section 10(1), would engage Article 6.[116] There is a great deal of merit in such a view. Crown immunity is a peculiar immunity that operates to immunise the agents and agencies of the Crown from accountability to the law.[117] It works against the separation of powers.[118] The constitutional safeguard potentially provides a method for ensuring that such an immunity is not legislatively endorsed and perpetuated without reason or without retaining a sufficient degree of legal supervision.

Lord Hoffmann was more forthright and sweeping in holding that Article 6 made no contribution to the questions before the court.[119] In Lord Hoffmann's view, tort law is simply an imperfect medium for affording compensation to victims of injury. It is open to countries to adopt different systems for achieving this goal, such as the no-fault system of personal injury compensation that now applies in New Zealand. He considered that since 'Art.6 is concerned with standards of justice, the separation of powers and the rule of law' it would seem to have 'little to do with whether or not one should have an action in tort'. That, said Lord Hoffmann, 'is a matter of national policy'.[120] This point has a great deal of force.

---

[112] ibid [130].
[113] ibid [136].
[114] See text to n 42 above.
[115] *Matthews* (n 16) [142].
[116] This is supported by Lord Hoffmann: ibid [32].
[117] See the criticism of Lord Salvesen, *Macgregor v Lord Advocate* 1921 SC 847, 852–53.
[118] Contrast police immunity in *Hill* which, as Lord Hoffmann explained, does not offend the separation of powers: *Matthews* (n 16) [43].
[119] Also ibid [53] (Lord Hope).
[120] ibid [25]. Lord Hoffmann's views on tort law cannot be explored here. He was resistant to the civilian notion that liability exists wherever loss has been caused by negligence; the default position is that losses negligently caused lie where they fall, *Matthews* (n 16) [43]; *Stovin v Wise* [1996] AC 923, 949 and see also Lord Hoffmann, 'Human Rights and the House of Lords' (1999) 62 MLR 159, 162. Tort law is thus a mechanism of distributive justce not corrective justice.

However, even if tort law is to be viewed from such an instrumental perspective, it does not follow that Article 6 should not ensure that states do not leave certain groups without the protection of the law or confer blanket immunities without reason. Lord Hoffmann also suggested that Article 6 would only be engaged where the *executive* was transferred power to determine a domestic cause of action.[121] He preferred such an approach to a 'formalistic' distinction between substance and procedure.[122] Whilst underlining that executive discretion will require justification is clearly welcome, it by no means follows that Article 6 has no wider application. Statutory limitations might be equally perilous to the separation of powers.

In an even more sweeping remark, Lord Hoffmann said, alluding to *Osman*, that a rule that people should not be compensated out of public funds for the failure of the police to take reasonable care in conducting investigations 'may or may not be fair as between victims of negligent police investigations and victims of road accidents but that . . . is not a question of human rights'.[123] He considered that this followed from his earlier comment, no less sweeping but more justifiable,[124] that human rights 'certainly do not include the right to a fair distribution of resources or fair treatment in economic terms . . .'.[125] To be sure, whether there should be a right to compensation for bungled police investigations is not a question to be determined by Article 6, but it might become a question of human rights if the failure of the police service infringes Articles 2 or 3 ECHR.[126] Recall that *Osman* was principally concerned with whether the police's failures constituted a violation of Article 2. Despite these pronouncements, Lord Hoffmann was prepared to dismiss the claim on the narrow ground that the issue of the certificate extinguished any cause of action and went to the substance of the right defined by Parliament.[127] His wider remarks were therefore unnecessary to decide the case. It would be unfortunate if the sweeping and reactionary nature of some of Lord Hoffmann's comments was to obscure the fact that the House of Lords has taken a step forward from *Osman* and not a step back.

Visiting the Law of Contract:
Wilson v First County Trust Ltd (No 2)

Osman sent not so much a ripple, as a tidal wave, through the backwaters of commercial law, when in May 2001 the Court of Appeal declared section 127(3) of the Consumer Credit Act 1974 incompatible with Article 6. The relevant

---

[121] *Matthews* (n 16) [29].
[122] ibid [30].
[123] ibid [43].
[124] But *cf* R Dworkin, *Sovereign Virtue* (Cambridge, Harvard University Press, 2000).
[125] *Matthews* (n 16) [26].
[126] See *Van Colle v Chief Constable of Hertfordshire Constabulary* [2009] 1 AC 225.
[127] *Fayed v United Kingdom* (1994) 18 EHRR 393. *Matthews* (n 16) [32] and [39].

provisions of the Act regulate agreements between individual debtors and creditors for a loan not exceeding £25,000. In order to protect these small-time borrowers, such agreements must be in a prescribed form, containing prescribed terms, to be treated as properly executed.[128] Where the agreement fails these formalities, it is not enforceable against the debtor except by order of the court,[129] although it remains enforceable by the debtor against the creditor, and against the debtor with consent. A court must enforce such an agreement, unless it would be unjust to do so, and it must have regard to its powers to impose conditions or make consequential changes to the terms.[130] The troublesome provision is section 127(3), which denies the courts this power to enforce agreements if they are not signed containing all the prescribed terms. First County Trust Ltd, a two-man outfit, lent £5,000 on the security of a BMW car. By adding a document fee of £250 it was held to have misrepresented the amount of credit. The agreement was therefore unenforceable because it had not been signed on the correct terms. The effect was that First County could neither keep the car nor demand repayment of the loan or interest thereon. The Court of Appeal was so concerned at this outcome that it adjourned the hearing and indicated in an interim judgment that it would consider making a declaration of incompatibility with Article 6 because section 127(3) denied First County its right to court to enforce the agreement.[131] In a subsequent judgment it held that the agreement and delivery of the pawn conferred rights on the creditor which were subject to restriction on enforcement.[132] Article 6 was therefore engaged. It further held that by excluding the courts from any meaningful consideration of the creditor's rights, section 127(3) employed disproportionate means in relation to the aim of ensuring the inclusion of prescribed terms in the signed document. Since it was not possible to read the section in a way that would have given the courts an analogous power to that enjoyed where section 127(3) does not apply, it made a declaration of incompatibility. The judgment opened the door for widespread challenges to the contours of commercial rights (and beyond) and the possibility that a great many would be held to be disproportionately sweeping or rigid.

With the exception of Lord Hope, the Judicial Committee was differently constituted from that which decided *Matthews*; but the result was the same. Lord Nicholls, giving the leading speech on the Article 6 argument, identified *Golder* and *Matthews* as the dominant sources of the relevant guiding principles.[133] On the principles derived from these cases their Lordships were unanimous in emphasising that Article 6 is concerned with 'procedural fairness' and does not 'guarantee that a person's substantive civil rights are of any particular character'.[134] Lord

---

[128] *Matthews* (n 16) [36]; s 61(1)(a).
[129] s 65(1).
[130] ss 127(1)(2), 135, 136.
[131] *Wilson v First County Trust Ltd* [2001] QB 407.
[132] *Wilson and others v Secretary of State for Trade and Industry* [2002] QB 74.
[133] *Wilson (No 2)* (n 17) [32] and [35].
[134] ibid [104] (Lord Hope). See [33]–[34] (Lord Nicholls); [132] (Lord Hobhouse); [165] (Lord Scott); [209] and [215] (Lord Rodger).

Nicholls stated that: 'The content of substantive national law may call for scrutiny under other articles of the Convention or its Protocols, but that is not the target of article 6(1)'.[135] He considered that a procedural bar was a restriction preventing a court from making a determination on the merits.[136] It was held that the Court of Appeal had gone astray by failing to recognise as a matter of principle that Article 6 is concerned with procedure. In mitigation, it is worth noting (although the House of Lords did not) that the Court of Appeal's judgment, which had itself been followed by Keith J in *Matthews*, was decided on the basis of *Osman* before judgment in *Z*.

Applying these principles, it was held that section 127(3) restricts the scope of the rights acquired by a creditor and does not bar access to court to decide whether the case is caught by the restriction. It was therefore not a procedural bar, despite the fact that the right was circumscribed by limiting the availability of a remedy. Lord Nicholls stated:

> in taking that power away from a court the legislature was not encroaching on territory which ought properly to be the province of the courts in a democratic society . . . it no more offends the rule of law and the separation of powers than would be the case if parliament had said that such an agreement is void.[137]

This reasoning is a little opaque, but the essence is clear enough. The restriction was closely tied to the merits of the legal relations between creditor and debtor and did not involve transferring any part of the determination to the executive, or otherwise barring a determination of the merits of any claim.

The House of Lords in *Wilson*, then, built on the determination evinced in *Matthews* to disentangle the procedural and substantive protections under the Convention, which, as we have seen, has been the bane of this area of the law. Although section 127(3) was not procedural and therefore did not give rise to requirements of justification under Article 6, a majority held that the legislation extinguished a lender's property rights and required justification under Article 1 of Protocol 1.[138] Lord Nicholls noted:

> I do not think there is any inconsistency between this conclusion and the conclusion stated above regarding article 6(1). A statutory provision may be characterised at one and the same time as a [substantive] limitation on the scope of a creditor's rights for the purposes of article 6(1) and as a law depriving a person of his possessions for the (different) purposes of article 1 of the First Protocol.[139]

---

[135] ibid [33]; also [165] (Lord Scott).

[136] ibid [34]. Unfortunately, other comments appear to drift towards equating a substantive bar with the traditional domestic approach whereby the unavailability of a remedy denies any right (especially Lord Scott at [165]). Clearly, the unavailability of a remedy is just as likely to be a procedural bar and it is not possible to avoid normative inquiry in this manner.

[137] ibid [36] and [37].

[138] It was held that in order to protect small-time borrowers, Parliament was entitled to deprive a lender of their contractual rights where they failed to comply with strict statutory requirements. Since s 127(3) pursued a legitimate aim and was proportionate, there was no question of it infringing the constitutional guarantee under Art 6(1).

[139] ibid [45].

Wilson thus confirms that the substantive rights do not call for anxious scrutiny under Article 6 that might be required by substantive articles. There was no need to recognise any background constitutional safeguard, but unlike in *Matthews*, there was no hint of it in the speeches. The passage cited nonetheless evinces a welcome recognition of the fact that the various Convention articles are expressions of different normative concerns. They should not be treated as interchangeable, nor separate questions of breach conflated.

Matthews in Strasbourg

The decision of the House of Lords in *Matthews* subsequently received the endorsement of a narrow majority of the Grand Chamber of the ECtHR in *Roche v United Kingdom* in a judgment adopted in September 2005.[140] The application had been made by a former serviceman who had been subjected to chemical weapons testing at Porton Down in the 1960s, which had caused him significant adverse health in later life. The Secretary of State had issued a certificate under section 10 of the Crown Proceedings Act to prevent an action being brought in tort. The Grand Chamber reviewed the speeches in *Matthews* in detail. It rejected the applicant's submission that, contrary to the reasoning of the House of Lords, a proportionality test ought to be applied whether or not the immunity or bar in question is characterised as procedural or substantive.[141] It expressly reconsidered and re-affirmed the necessity for there to be a distinction between procedure and substance. It said, 'fine as it may be in a particular case, this distinction remains determinative of the applicability and, as appropriate, the scope of the guarantees of Article 6 of the Convention'.[142] The Court also stated that the Commission decisions in *Ketterick*, *Pinder* and *Dyer* must be read 'in the light' of the Court's later jurisprudence emphasising the distinction between procedural and substantive limitations; and reiterated that Article 6 does not guarantee the particular content of substantive law, which it described as a 'fundamental principle'.

It also rejected that applicant's alternative submission that Article 10 in fact imposed a procedural bar. It said that where the superior national courts have analysed the law in a comprehensive and convincing manner and the restriction, on the basis of Convention case law, the Strasbourg Court would need 'strong reasons to differ from the conclusion reached'.[143] The Court also pointed out that it is necessary to 'look beyond appearances' and to 'concentrate on the realities of the situation'.[144] The Court must not be unduly influenced, it stated, by the use of terms such as 'immunity'. This represents a welcome, albeit belated, recognition

---

[140] *Roche v United Kingdom* (2006) 42 EHRR 30.
[141] ibid [105], [118]–[119].
[142] ibid [119].
[143] ibid [120].
[144] ibid [121].

of the normative and context dependent nature of rules that are described as immunities. The reasons for describing rules as immunities are not always the same and the effect is not always to restrict access to the courts properly understood.

The ECtHR distinguished *Fogarty* on the same basis as Lord Walker had done in *Matthews*, stating that it involved a wide executive discretion and, following remarks of Lord Hoffmann, said that *Tinnelly* was not in point because that case involved an executive act conclusively determining a civil right, which was an 'encroachment by the executive in to the judicial realm' and not the choice by Parliament as to the means by which persons should be compensated. The Grand Chamber concluded that there was no reason to differ from the judgment of the House of Lords.[145]

However, of the 17-judge court, seven judges[146] joined a dissenting opinion of Judge Louciades. Judge Louciades's opinion accepted the distinction between procedure and substance but considered that the facts of the case were on the wrong side of the line. The judge reasoned that the Secretary of State was at liberty not to issue a certificate under section 10, and this was sufficient. It was not, however, explained how this was to be reconciled with the analysis of domestic law by the House of Lords. The judge also relied on belatedly discovered legal advice dating from 1953 in which the Treasury Solicitor had stated that section 10 certificates could not be issued in relation to the testing at Porton Down, since it was not covered by the wording of section 10. However the advice did not illustrate that the Secretary of State had any greater, or significant, discretion, but simply demonstrated that the Government had previously considered that there was no power under section 10 to issue a certificate in respect of the tests. Judge Zupančič, who subscribed to Judge Louciades's dissent, also gave a separate opinion attacking the distinction between procedure and substance. He considered that the UK cases which had come before the Court had highlighted the artificial nature of the distinction between procedural and substantive restrictions on the right of access to court.

Strasbourg Divided

The cases considered above provide a case study of the influence of the House of Lords on the interpretation of the European Convention by the Strasbourg Court. It was the shot across the bows by the House of Lords, in *Barrett v Enfield LBC,* that led the Strasbourg Court to reverse the maximalist approach that it had been developing, which found its most radical and expansive expression in *Osman v United Kingdom.* The ECtHR's apologetic and more balanced decision in *Z* was

---

[145] ibid [123] and [124].
[146] Judges Rozakis, Zupančič, Strážnická, Casadevall, Thomassen, Maruste and Traja.

followed by the House of Lords' detailed examination of the Strasbourg case law and its pronouncement on the scope of Article 6 in *Matthews*. This was accepted, albeit by the narrowest of majorities, by the Grand Chamber in *Roche*. It is true that the distinction between procedure and substance was developed by the ECtHR and not by the House of Lords, but its importance and meaning has undoubtedly been shaped by the House of Lords' judgments. Following *Roche* it was possible to say that the interplay between the two courts had resulted in a clearer and more principled approach to Article 6, which would ensure that that article is confined primarily to questions of procedure and does not upset the apple cart of domestic substantive law. Such a conclusion would, however, have been too hasty. Subsequent cases have not been entirely consistent with the approach taken by the majority in *Roche*. A degree of inconsistency is regrettably a common feature of Strasbourg law, but what has proved particularly surprising is how deeply the Court is divided on this subject and how quickly even more fundamental tensions have emerged than those on which the Grand Chamber divided in *Roche*. These cases suggest that uncertainty in the case law on the right of access to a court, at least in Strasbourg, has not been eradicated.

In June 2006 the ECtHR decided *Wos v Poland*[147] in which it found a violation of the right of access to a court because a decision made by the Polish-German Reconciliation Foundation, refusing the applicant compensation for a period of forced labour in occupied Poland during the Second World War, could not be challenged in the administrative or civil courts. The Court held that the independence of the Foundation was open to serious doubt, and it lacked basic procedural guarantees. The ECtHR did not address the distinction between substance and procedure at all. Instead it invoked *Golder* directly and applied a proportionality analysis to the law that prevented any legal challenge to the Foundation's decision, apparently without recognising the controversial nature of doing so, if (as seems to have been the case) the applicant simply had no legal rights that could be asserted in the ordinary courts. Whilst *Wos* might be thought to concern a classic *Anisminic*-type situation, which domestic law would regard as an infringement on the right of access to the courts, under Convention case law it would probably have been more coherent to have found a straightforward violation of the requirements of fairness and independents guaranteed by Article 6. According to established case law, a lack of independence and fairness can only be cured by a sufficiently full judicial review or judicial appeal.[148] Absent that, there is a breach of the independence and fair trial guarantee, not the right of access to court.

The issue was considered again by a (differently constituted) Grand Chamber in *Markovic v Italy*, just over a year after *Roche*.[149] The Court was again divided by the narrowest of margins, with a one-judge majority adhering to *Z v United Kingdom* and *Roche v United Kingdom*. The majority held that judgments of the Italian

---

[147] *Wos v Poland* (2007) 45 EHRR 28. Court's reasoning.
[148] *Albert and Le Compte v Belgium* (1983) 5 EHRR 533 [86] and *Bryan v United Kingdom* (1995) 21 EHRR 342.
[149] *Markovic v Italy* (2007) 44 EHRR 52.

courts holding that claims brought against the Italian Government, relating to civilian deaths caused by the NATO bombing of a radio station building in Belgrade in 1999, were non-justiciable political questions, represented a substantive not procedural bar on the applicants' access to the Italian courts, and were thus not to be subject to a test of legitimacy and proportionality. The UK Government intervened in the case in an attempt to keep the ECtHR 'on-message', which it succeeded in doing as it had in *Roche*. The majority accepted the UK Government's submissions that following *Z*,

> it is a principle of Convention case law that Art.6 does not in itself guarantee any particular content for civil rights and obligations in national law. It is not enough to bring Art.6(1) into play that the non-existence of a cause of action under domestic law may be described as having the same effect as an immunity, in the sense of not enabling the applicant to sue for a given category of harm.[150]

The Court also said that it agreed with the British Government that the case was analogous to *Z*: 'As in *Z*, the applicants in the present case were afforded access to a court; however, it was limited in scope, as it did not enable them to secure a decision on the merits.'[151] The Court also reserved the possibility of applying the constitutional safeguard if the immunity from liability for the state authorities was 'absolute or general nature'.[152]

Seven of the 17 judges dissented, with Judge Costa dissenting in part. They held that Article 6 applied to the no-liability rule of Italian law. The reasoning of the dissenting judges in *Markovic* revealed that the Court is deeply divided at a level of principle and that the division of the Court in *Roche* cannot simply be attributed to a difference of opinion over the classification of a particular restriction as procedural or substantive.[153] The dissenting judges sought to distinguish *Z* from the facts of *Markovic* on the basis that, in ruling out negligence claims on grounds of public policy, the English courts had nevertheless carefully balanced the respective interests, and had not simply applied a rule of non-justiciability.[154] Such a basis for distinction is unsatisfactory, since the rule of no-liability, once established, will be applied by lower courts in the same way as a rule of non-justiciability. It would be a waste of time and money for them to do otherwise. Whilst the judgments of the Italian courts may have been poorly reasoned, undesirable as a matter of principle or policy, or even wrong as a matter of Italian law, that, as the majority judgment reflected, is no reason to hold that the applicants did not have access to the courts.

---

[150] ibid [113].
[151] ibid [115].
[152] ibid [113].
[153] Dissenting Opinion of Judge Zagrebelsky joined by Judges Zupanāiā, Jungwiert, Tsatsa-Nikolovska, Ugrekhelidze, Kovler and David Thór Björgvinsso. Judge Costa also dissented from the reasoning of the majority although not the result. His reasoning seemingly aligns with that of the minority. Thus, he identified what he regarded as the true questions to be determined by Art 6 as these, which manifestly address the substance of the law: 'Does this exemption from liability in domestic law constitute a disproportionate interference with the right of access to a court afforded by the Convention? Does it amount to a denial of justice that is incompatible with the Convention?' O-117.
[154] ibid O-116.

The minority view is motivated by an understandable concern to ensure that politicians are not shielded from the law and it therefore appeals to the idea of legal equality. But this principle, reflected in the constitutional safeguard, cannot be applied under the Article 6 jurisprudence to create *particular* substantive rights that do not otherwise exist. That would be inconsistent with the fundamental principle that Article 6 does not guarantee the particular content of national law. Thus, if the substantive Italian law on non-justiciability was subjected to a test of necessity and proportionality then, to the extent that it failed that test on the facts of particular cases, Article 6 would be creating civil rights; moreover it would be determining substantive law by altering the balance of principle and policy that underlie substantive doctrines. It is a more general protection which must look at the legal liability of such individuals as a whole to asses the equality of treatment with other persons.

In a concurring Opinion, Judge Bratza (joined by Judge Rozakis) attempted to explain that the decision to decline jurisdiction had to be regarded as a substantive bar, as it was:

> a self-imposed limitation, the Court of Cassation concluding not only that such jurisdiction was not conferred by the instruments relied on by the applicants, but that the nature of the applicant's claim gave rise to issues which were not capable of being determined in the national courts.[155]

It was pointed out that the non-justiciability of international relations, foreign policy and the conduct of hostilities, is a familiar feature of legal systems.

Given the deeply divided nature of the Court, it is unsurprising that there are other problematic decisions. In *Mizzi v Malta*[156] for example, the ECtHR held that Maltese law which prevented the applicant from establishing that his wife's child was not his own, because he could not show concealment on the part of his wife, constituted an unjustifiable breach of the right of access to a court. Since the applicant had been time-barred from bringing an action in which he could deny paternity without having to show concealment, the case can be understood as a straightforward challenge to a limitation period—plainly a procedural bar. However, the reasoning of the court paid no regard to the distinction between procedural and substantive restrictions and effectively required Malta to establish a right to deny paternity.[157] Other difficult cases, albeit of little authority, are *Mond*

---

[155] O-117. In addition Judge Bratza provided some guidance on the distinction between procedure and substance at O-113 and O-114.

[156] *Mizzi v Malta* (2006) 46 EHRR 27. The President was Judge Rozakis, who was in the majority in the (subsequent) case *Markovic* and who dissented in *Roche*, although accepting the procedure/substance distinction. Judge Louciades, whose dissenting judgment in *Roche* Judge Rozakis joined, was also a member of the Court. The other judges were in neither *Roche* nor *Markovic*. This lends support to the procedural analysis offered in the text.

[157] See also *Lawyer Partners AS v Slovakia* (App no 54252/07) 16 June 2009. The applicant company had submitted a number of claims on DVDs. The claims were declared time-barred after the Slovakian courts refused to register them. The case concerned a straightforward procedural bar, but as in *Mizzi v Malta* the Court did not reason by reference to the distinction between procedure and substance. It referred only to *Ashingdane* and paragraphs in *Markovic* that did not advert to the distinction ([52]).

v United Kingdom, an admissibility decision in which witness immunity from suit in England was considered to be a procedural bar (or was at least subjected to a proportionality test), and *Patel v United Kingdom*, another admissibility decision, in which it was implicit that had advocate's immunity not been abolished by the House of Lords in *Arthur JS Hall v Simons*, it would have been held to constitute a restriction on the right of access to court.[158] Following *Barret v Enfield LBC* and *Matthews*, however, such immunities should be regarded as substantive rules of law, albeit underpinned by public policy considerations.[159]

Conclusions

The House of Lords has firmly rejected the notion that Article 6 can prescribe the substantive content of domestic rights, and has accepted that the test of legitimacy and proportionality is only applicable to procedural bars. It has held that Article 6 is only applicable to limitations and immunities that are not part of the substantive merits of the cause of action. It has gone firmly down the right of access route, rather than the legal equality route. It has thereby sought to head off the discovery of substantive equal protection and due process protection within Article 6. Nonetheless, as Lord Walker recognised in *Matthews*, *Osman* still casts its uncertain shadow over the law. The reason for this, it has been suggested, is that there is and always has been a substantive component to Article 6 that derives from the need to prevent matters being taken out of the hands of the courts, and to prevent persons or classes of persons being placed above the law or, on the other hand, being denied the law's protection. Just as the common law recognises principles of access to the courts and a right of equal protection of the law, Article 6 goes further than merely protecting the right of access to court. The idea of legal equality, and protection for the rule of law and the separation of powers is also found in Article 6. It has been suggested that it is expressed in the constitutional safeguard that ensures that blanket immunities are not tolerated by national legal systems, and states do not remove individual rights from persons or classes of persons arbitrarily and unreasonably such as to deny them the protection of the law. But this constitutional safeguard is very much a background protection which does not apply to specific no-liability decisions in isolation from the application of the law as a whole to a person or class of persons. If one is still unsure about the existence of such a protection, the point can be tested in the following way. Imagine a situation in which Parliament sought to extinguish or greatly diminish the rights of asylum-seekers, or of children, or of convicted criminals. Surely, at a certain point,

---

[158] *Mond v United Kingdom* (2003) 37 EHRR CD129; *Patel v UK* (App no 38199/97) (the Court included Judge Costa (President), Judge Rozakis, and Judge Louciades).

[159] See *JD v East Berkshire Community NHS Trust* [2004] QB 558 [22] in holding that where no duty of care is owed because it would not be fair, just and reasonable to recognise such a duty there is a substantive not procedural bar.

Article 6 would bite to protect the rule of law. But it would be wrong to claim that Article 6 would in such a case be protecting any right of *access* to the courts to have arguable legal rights determined. The protection would be different and altogether more fundamental; and the applicable criteria need not be packaged-up in the box marked 'right of access'.

Concerns about legal equality continue to distort the case law of the ECtHR under Article 6. It can now be seen that the reason for this is not that the judges are wrong in recognising that there is more to Article 6 than a protection against procedural limitations on access to courts, but because of the tendency to search for monistic interpretations of Convention rights with single criteria of engagement and single tests of justification (legitimacy and proportionality). It leads to the application of the test of legitimacy and proportionality to particular substantive rules of law. This approach has, for the time being at least, been ruled out both by the Grand Chamber and by the House of Lords. But unless some conceptually separate test for protecting legal equality comes clearly to be recognised, the tensions and inconsistencies in the law are unlikely to go away.

The speeches of Lord Bingham and Lord Walker in *Matthews* are particularly welcome for the willingness to grapple with the multi-dimensionality of the right to a court and have left open, if only just, the possibility of recognising the constitutional safeguard.

One reason why courts might have been be reluctant to recognise a wider macro-constitutional protection under Article 6 is that it could then be argued that whenever a claim is prevented by a substantive rule of law, the claimant is nonetheless within the 'ambit' of Article 6 and could then invoke Article 14, which would, in many cases at least, introduce a test of legitimacy and proportionality.[160] For example, having dismissed the claim under Article 6, the Commission in *Dyer* held that since the constitutional limb had been engaged, it could consider whether the Crown's immunity was discriminatory. However, Article 14 should remain inapplicable where a claim is prevented because of a substantive rule of law rules it out. The constitutional safeguard is a safety-net; it is not engaged just because a claim fails. The constitutional guarantee is in many ways a background protection that does not necessarily bring substantive immunities within the ambit of Article 6.[161] This is supported by the Grand Chamber decision in *Roche*, which held that where a claim is barred by a rule of substantive law there is no 'civil right' and therefore Article 6 was not applicable such as to engage Article 14.[162] This is a further welcome aspect of that judgment, but one suspects that it also may not be the last word on the matter.

---

[160] See *Matthews* (n 16) [50].

[161] *Pinder v United Kingdom* (1984) 7 EHRR 464. A procedural bar will have this effect: *Rasmussen v Denmark* A/87: (1984) 7 EHRR 371. Art 14 would also only have effect if the substantive rule of law applied on the basis of the claimant's 'status': see *R (Clift) v Secretary of State for the Home Department* [2007] 1 AC 484.

[162] *Roche* (n 140) [133].

11

Derogation and Emergency

Defensive Democracy

THE ATTACKS ON America on 11 September 2001 heralded an era of what has been described as defensive democracy.[1] Governments across the democratic world have acted to concentrate power into their own hands whilst shutting their outer gates. But although strength is undoubtedly the first necessity of any constitution, the line between strength and unbridled power is dangerously fine. Moreover, the first casualties of defensive measures are inevitably the civil liberties and human rights that individuals normally enjoy. It is therefore imperative that in order to maintain the very democratic systems that defensive postures are intended to protect, state constitutions operate to defend the threatened bridgeheads of legality and human rights. This issue is raised in no more stark form than in relation to the UK's derogation from the European Convention on Human Rights, which followed the September 11 attacks, and the resistance to derogation that has been provided by the non-governmental institutions of the UK's constitutional regime.

The extent of the *judicial* resistance to derogation was authoritatively established by the House of Lords' decision in *A v Secretary of State for the Home Department ('A (No 1)')*.[2] This chapter examines the decision against the background of three differing constitutional models relating to the nature of derogation. Each model represents a very different approach to the defence of the twin bridgeheads of legality and human rights. These models offer a perspective from which to evaluate the House of Lords' decision and, to some degree, we find each reflected in the decision. But before turning to these models and to the critical analysis of the decision, it is useful to begin by setting out the ruling and its immediate context.

---

[1] A Barak, 'Foreword: A Judge on Judging: The Role of a Supreme Court in a Democracy' (2002) 116 *Harvard Law Review* 16, 21.

[2] *A v Secretary of State for the Home Department* [2005] 2 AC 68.

The Challenge to the UK's Derogation

The government has well-established powers to deport non-nationals on grounds of national security and, so long as steps are being taken toward deportation, even detaining such individuals for several years may not violate the Convention.[3] However, the attacks of 11 September 2001 prompted the Government to enact powers in section 23 of the Anti-Terrorism, Crime and Security Act 2001 (ATCSA) to detain non-nationals indefinitely in circumstances where deportation was prevented either by some practical consideration or because to do so would subject individuals to a risk of torture.[4] On 11 November 2001, the day before the Bill was laid before Parliament, the Home Secretary notified the Secretary General of the Council of Europe of the Government's intention to take measures derogating from Article 5 of the Convention, under the provision for derogation contained in Article 15, in order to meet the threat posed by Al-Qaeda. On the same day, the Government made the Human Rights Act 1998 (Designated Derogation) Order 2001, which designated the proposed detention powers under Article 14(6) of the Human Rights Act.

The detainees, eight of whom were detained as early as December 2001, brought proceedings challenging both the measures themselves and the Designated Derogation Order.[5] They claimed that there was no 'public emergency threatening the life of the nation' and that indefinite detention was not 'strictly required by the exigencies of the situation', as required by Article 15 of the Convention. The detainees also argued that the detention powers were discriminatory in contravention of Article 14 of the Convention, which article had not been notified for derogation. The Special Immigration Appeals Commission (SIAC) partially upheld these complaints, but the Court of Appeal upheld the Home Secretary's appeal.[6] On 16 December 2005 a specially constituted panel of nine Law Lords, by a majority of eight to one, quashed the Designated Derogation Order and declared the detention power in section 23 ATCSA to be incompatible with Article 5 of the Convention.

---

[3] *Chahal v United Kingdom* (1996) 23 EHRR 413 [122]. The immigration detention powers contained in Sch 3 to the Immigration Act 1971 permit detention in certain circumstances 'pending' deportation. The requirement was authoritatively analysed in *R v Governor of Durham Prison, ex p Hardial Singh* [1984] 1 WLR 704 and *Tan Te Lam v Superintendent of Tai A Chau Detention Centre* [1997] AC 97 and helpfully summarised in *R (I) v Secretary of State for the Home Department* [2002] EWCA Civ 888 [46] (Dyson LJ). As established in those cases, the Secretary of State must not only intend to deport a person who is detained, and act with diligence and expedition in effecting deportation, but the detention must not exceed a period that is reasonable in all the circumstances. If it becomes apparent that deportation cannot be effected within a reasonable period, the Secretary of State 'should not seek to exercise the power of detention'. Art 5(1)(f) of the Convention uses the language of action being taken with 'a view to deportation'.

[4] On which see *Chahal v United Kingdom* (1996) 23 EHRR 413 [80], [86], [107].

[5] ATCSA s 30 provided that challenges to derogation or designation had to be heard by SIAC.

[6] *A v Secretary of State for the Home Department* [2004] QB 335 (CA).

Lord Bingham gave the leading speech, which had the agreement of six of their Lordships (not Lord Hoffmann or Lord Walker), and this speech most closely reflects the decision of the Judicial Committee. Although Lord Bingham was not prepared to hold that there was no public emergency that threatened the life of the nation, he nonetheless upheld the appeal on the grounds that the detention powers were disproportionate and discriminatory. On proportionality, Lord Bingham reasoned that the powers were not rationally connected to the objective of tackling the imminent Al-Qaeda threat because they did not correspond to that objective in important respects: the powers applied to non-Al-Qaeda terrorists; they applied to Al-Qaeda supporters who posed no direct threat to national security;[7] they did not apply to the threat from Al-Qaeda operatives who were UK nationals (which SIAC had held to be just as grave as that posed by nationals) and, furthermore, they allowed any detained Al-Qaeda operative 'to leave our shores and depart to another [safe third-]country, perhaps a country as close of France, there to pursue his criminal designs'.[8] His Lordship went on to hold that the measures were also excessively burdensome. He considered that it was 'reasonable to assume' from the different treatment of UK nationals, as well as from the fact that one former detainee had been released on bail subject to bail conditions, that the 'severe penalty of indefinite detention' exceeded what was necessary to meet the Al-Qaeda threat. Lord Bingham considered that the Attorney-General 'could give no persuasive answer' to this prima facie case.[9]

Finally, Lord Bingham held that addressing the terrorist threat by means of immigration control was discriminatory. With respect, Lord Bingham quite rightly considered that whilst status as a non-national justifiably leaves a person vulnerable to deportation, as well as to detention 'pending' deportation, it cannot justify the person's indefinite detention without trial, or render that person's rights under Article 5 any less secure where action is not being taken pending deportation.[10] The Government's central submission in the case was that it was

---

[7] The House of Lords previously had held that deportation on national security grounds does not require any direct threat to the UK and can be for foreign policy reasons where the threat is indirect: *Secretary of State for the Home Department v Rehman* [2003] 1 AC 153.

[8] *A (No 1)* (n 2) [33].

[9] ibid [35] and [43]. In accord: [76]–[78] (Lord Nicholls); [126]–[132] (Lord Hope); [155] (Lord Scott); [168], [181]–[186] and [189] (Lord Rodger); [228] and [231] (Baroness Hale).

[10] ibid [43] and [68]. In accord: [84] (Lord Nicholls); [103], [105], [132] and [138] (Lord Hope); [157]–[158] (Lord Scott); [171] (Lord Rodger); [229] and [236] (Lady Hale). A different view has been taken by Professor Finnis (J Finnis, 'Nationality, Alienage and Constitutional Principle' (2007) 123 LQR 417 in accord, D Campbell, 'The threat of terror and the plausibility of positivism' [2009] PL 510). Finnis argues that there is a 'constitutional principle' that 'the political community, while it cannot shift to other communities the risks presented by one of its own nationals, need not unconditionally accept the *risk presented by aliens*.' (422). From this premise, Finnis argues that this principle justifies the power to detain non-nationals who present a risk to security indefinitely, even where their deportation is prevented, and that failing to treat nationals in like fashion is not therefore unjustified or discriminatory. However, there are at least two problems with this argument. The first is that it is very doubtful that any power to deport or detain aliens exists, other than the expressly limited statutory power to detain persons pending deportation. Finnis suggests the possibility of a common law or prerogative power, but Dicey was clear that there was no such power, and even dangerous aliens could not be detained beyond the ordinary criminal process: AV Dicey, *Introduction to the Study of the*

entitled to put less weight on the rights of non-nationals *generally* when formulating its response to national security threats. Upholding the detainees' claim that the powers were discriminatory is therefore at the heart of the decision of the House of Lords. However, the other aspects of the decision shed more light on the Court's approach to derogation, and it is therefore upon these aspects that the critical examination of the speeches will focus. But first the nature of derogation itself must be explained.

The Derogation Model

The inclusion of derogation clauses in international human rights treaties represents a concession to the belief that when governments perceive threats to the nation, they will inevitably take action seriously impinging upon civil liberties, and more often than not the action taken is to introduce detention without trial.[11] Unlike schemes of international obligations that do not allow for derogation,[12] by accepting at the outset the inevitability of exceptional measures, instruments that

Law of the Constitution, 8th edn (London, Macmillan, 1915) 220–23. More fundamentally, even if some power to detain pending deportation might be found which is not an expressly limited statutory power, Finnis's constitutional principle is either banal or unjustifiable. As initially expressed in the quotation just given, the principle is presented as a right to shift or pass risks to other political communities. Such a principle would be banal since it would represent no more than a moral-political generalisation of the law, and it would not speak to the situation where risks are presented by foreign nationals but where these cannot be shifted to other communities. Such a principle has no justificatory force in relation to detention of non-nationals where deportation of such individuals is not possible. As Finnis's argument progresses, the principle takes on a broader form, so that it becomes a principle that the 'nation does not have to accept from foreigners the same degree of risk as it accepts from its nationals' (eg 439). Such a principle would indeed provide a prima facie justification for depriving foreign nationals of their liberty if they posed a risk to security, but it would also provide a prima facie justification for much else besides, namely, all other conduct reducing the risk emanating from foreign nationals, which could include such things as banishment, harassment or destitution. This would be surprising, to say the least. The breadth of the justificatory principle is a reflection of the fact that the principle is over-broad. A principle to the effect that the nation does not have to accept risks to the community from foreign nationals cannot be inferred from a power to deport or a power to detain pending deportation. It is invalidated by all the situations in which such risks have to be tolerated, including where action cannot be taken to deport the person concerned. The principle would be more correctly expressed as a principle that security risks emanating from foreign nationals do not have to be borne where another country accepts responsibility for bearing such risks (subject to the rider in the modern law that the other country must also be sufficiently safe to permit return). Even this, however, fails to reflect the fact that the deportation and detention power over foreign nationals is not directed at national security risks, and there are many circumstances in which individuals can be deported and detained pending deportation, although they present no such risk. Indeed, non-nationals can be deported for no other reason than that they are non-nationals. Finnis's principle just doesn't fit with the shape of immigration law powers and cannot therefore be invoked as a justification for indefinite detention (or other interferences with human rights) of non-nationals who pose risks to security.

[11] See International Commission of Jurists, *States of Emergency—Their Impact on Human Rights* (Geneva, The Commission, 1983). Moreover, the action is usually directed at non-citizens, see: D Cole, *Enemy Aliens: Double Standards and Constitutional Freedoms in the War on Terrorism* (New York, The New Press, 2003); C Sunstein, 'The Laws of Fear' (2002) 115 *Harv L Rev* 1110.

[12] See the Universal Declaration of Human Rights, which has no derogation clause.

allow for derogation seek to extend the scope of the legal regime to allow for and embrace such exceptional cases. The intention is to ensure that even exceptional state action remains governed by independent norms, which in turn allows for supervision by independent tribunals.

There are, however, strong objections to attempts to extend legal regimes to accommodate emergency action. It is argued that fundamental rights and the integrity of the law are better defended by constitutional systems that allow for extra-legal emergency action. This can be termed the 'extra-legal measures model'.[13] The arguments in favour of the extra-legal measures model boil down to arguments that attempts to accommodate emergencies within legal regimes are both futile and counterproductive. The argument from futility asserts that it is never possible to expunge the need and scope for uncontrolled executive action within a legal constitutional system. The argument that seeking to do so is counterproductive asserts that accommodating exceptional measures within a normative frame hampers the exercise of executive powers when it is most important not to do so, and, what is more, that embracing situations of emergency within the legal regime contaminates the fundamental principles of the regime itself by merging the exceptional and the normal.[14] The extra-legal measures model invokes the views of John Locke, who insisted that the good of society requires that the executive retain the 'Power of doing publick good without a Rule'.[15] In more concrete terms, it is therefore argued that a constitutional regime should allow for exceptional measures to be taken outside the legal regime in times of public emergency and that such measures should be subject to political and not judicial accountability.

The arguments in favour of the extra-legal measures model provide a useful foil for the distinction which will now be drawn between two understandings of derogations. The first approach can be called the 'limitation model'. According to the limitation model, derogation provisions should be understood merely as part of the network of limitations and qualifications upon the rights guaranteed in human rights instruments.[16] On this view, derogations are of the same order as qualifications on rights on such familiar grounds as protection of health, morals and national security, and derogation therefore requires no special justification. Admittedly, the arguments of the supporters of the extra-legal measures model do apply with some force to this understanding of derogations, since no special licence is afforded to government in times of public emergency and no special insulation is provided to the fundamental rights and principles of the legal system

---

[13] See especially, O Gross in 'Chaos and Rules: Should Responses to Violent Crises Always be Constitutional' (2003) 112 *Yale Law Journal* 1011; and also M Loughlin, *The Idea of Public Law* (Oxford, Oxford University Press, 2003) chs 3, 7 and 8.

[14] A version of this latter argument was famously put by Jackson J (dissenting) in *Korematsu v US*, 232 US 214 (1944), 244–46.

[15] P Laslett (ed), J Locke, *Two Treatises of Government* (Cambridge, Cambridge University Press, 1988), Second Treatise, para 166. Another influence is G Schwab (tr), Carl Schmitt, *Political Theology: Four Chapters on the Concept of Sovereignty.* (Cambridge, Mass, MIT Press, 1988).

[16] R Higgins, 'Derogation Under Human Rights Treaties' (1976–77) 48 *British Yearbook of International Law* 281; MS McDougal, HD Lasswell and Lung-chu Chen, *Human Rights and World Public Order* (New Haven, Yale University Press, 1980) 802–15.

at such times. But there is an alternative and more persuasive understanding of derogations that is considerably resistant to the arguments in favour of the extra-legal measures model. This can be called the 'derogation model'.

The derogation model recognises an important distinction between derogation and limitations on rights. Derogation is understood as a mechanism to provide for governmental freedom of action by releasing States from their obligation to observe protected rights. It provides governments with an 'emergency exit' from treaty obligations, which has the effect of placing rights in abeyance. Where States have validly derogated from a human rights treaty, they are absolved from the obligation to refrain from violating rights protected by it as well as from their obligation to advance legitimate justification for any interference with such rights. It is for precisely this reason that derogation from the most fundamental rights is not allowed. Derogation is therefore of a different order to qualifications and limitations on rights found for instance in Articles 8(2) and 10(2) of the Convention.[17] A state of emergency is not advanced as a justification for interferences with rights, but in relation to a question that is logically prior, namely, whether such a justification is required at all. This has concrete practical effects. Whilst the application of a measure that is validly in derogation is subject to legal supervision, it is not subject to supervision on human rights grounds: if detention on reasonable suspicion is strictly required then it is unnecessary (and it would be inconsistent) to require detention itself to be subject to the standards of justification required by the human rights norms set out in the treaty.[18]

The point to stress is that the derogation model creates a space between fundamental human rights and the rule of law. Whilst governments are permitted to step outside the human rights regime, their action remains within the law and subject to judicial supervision. Understood in this way, derogation creates a double-layered constitutional system: both layers exist within a regime of legality, but only one exists within the human rights regime. Such a model is much more resistant to the critique of the advocates of the extra-legal measures model, because fundamental human rights principles are insulated from contamination, whilst

---

[17] In support of this view: JE Hartman, 'Derogation from Human Rights Treaties in Public Emergencies' (1981) 22 *Harv Int LJ* 1; AC Kiss, 'Permissible Limitations on Rights' in L Henkin (ed) *The International Bill of Rights* (New York, Columbia University Press, 1981) 290. The UN Human Rights Committee has stated in relation to the International Covenant on Civil and Political Rights, Art 4, that 'Derogation from some Covenant obligations in emergency situations is clearly distinct from restrictions or limitations allowed even in normal times under several provisions of the Covenant', although it also stated that the strictly required standard reflects the proportionality principle which is common to both: 'General Comment 29—States of Emergency (article 4)' (2001) UN Doc CPR/C.21.Rev.l/Add.11 [4].

[18] See *A v United Kingdom* (App no 3455/05) 19 February 2009 [185]. The Grand Chamber rejected the submission that it is particular detentions that must be strictly required, rather than the detention power itself. By contrast, the UN Human Rights Committee 'General Comment' 29' (n 17) has suggested that where measures are strictly required, specific measures in pursuance of them must still be shown to be strictly required. This envisages a distinction between general measures (eg detention without trial) and specific measures (eg actual detention on certain grounds). But if detention on grounds of *reasonable suspicion* is held to be *strictly required* it would be unnecessary (as well as inconsistent) to seek to limit the meaning of reasonable suspicion so that the power could only be exercised when strictly required. It should be sufficient that detention pursuant to such powers is lawful.

governmental freedom from human rights norms is permitted.[19] Fundamentally, the derogation model has the critical benefit that scope for arbitrary governmental action that is beyond judicial scrutiny remains excluded. The derogation model therefore provides a principled and practical solution to the criticisms of constitutional systems that seek to provide for and control emergency action: the arguments of futility and counter-productivity are considerably reduced. However, creating a space between legality and human rights has important implications. Derogation clauses 'reflect a certain tentativeness about the individual as a subject of international law and grave fears by governments about the consequences of a binding commitment to the international protection of human rights.'[20] They test the degree to which governments are committed to human rights and the degree to which they are merely fair-weather supporters. Since derogation (unlike limitation) constitutes a departure from the fundamental commitment of governments to observe and respect human rights norms, the conditions on the exercise of derogation powers must be narrowly construed and strictly enforced.[21]

Now comes the crucial step. Since the Human Rights Act gives effect to Convention rights in domestic law 'subject to any designated derogation',[22] it has translated the derogation model from the international to the domestic plane. If, as I contend, the derogation model exhibits a double-layered structure on the international plane, then the nature of constitutionalism in the UK under the Human Rights Act should now be understood in the same way. Designated derogation therefore represents a departure from the UK's domestic commitment to human rights, and of a different order from interference with Convention rights. Where measures are validly in derogation, they are removed from the human rights regime and their application is not subject to either the derogated-from Convention norms (including, where appropriate, the requirement of proportionality) or the requirement that what would otherwise amount to an interference with a right is itself strictly required. Yet the state action remains subject to general requirements of legality and is properly subject to judicial supervision.[23]

[19] Of course, providing for exceptional cases at all will always have some unsettling effects on a legal system (see International Commission of Jurists, *States of Emergency* (n 11), 244, 245, 417), but the defenders of the extra-legal measures model greatly underestimate the versatility of legal constitutional regimes in relation to their day-to-day operation and bundle the derogation model together with the limitation model. For a similar point see, D Dyzenhaus, 'The State of Emergency in Legal Theory' in VV Ramraj, M Hor and K Roach (eds), *Global Anti-terrorism Law and Policy* (Cambridge, CUP, 2005).

[20] Hartman, 'Derogation from Human Rights Treaties' (n 17), 11.

[21] See further T Buergenthal, 'To Respect and to Ensure: State Obligations and Permissible Derogations' in Henkin, *The International Bill of Rights* (n 17), who argues that the interpretation of Art 4 of the ICCPR should be guided by the nature of the Covenant as an instrument of (international) constitutional dimension and therefore derogations should be allowed only in rare and exceptional circumstances.

[22] Human Rights Act s 1(2).

[23] See *A v Secretary of State for the Home Department (No 2)* [2005] 1 WLR 414 [234] (Laws LJ) (the common law may make up the difference) and *Secretary of State for the Home Department v M* [2004] EWCA Civ 324. But for conflicting views, see SIAC's obscure comments that s 25 powers allow a detainee to argue that, 'even if what is said against him were true, recourse to so draconian a power was disproportionate in the light of other circumstances' *(Ajouau and A, B, C and D* [2003] (App nos SC/1/2002, SC/6/2002, SC/7/2002, SC/10/2002) 29 October 2003 [14] (the 'generic judgment')). The

Therefore, since designated derogation cuts across the commitment embodied in the Human Rights Act to observe fundamental constitutional rights—the very reason why the Human Rights Act is treated as a constitutional statute—it is incumbent on domestic authorities to put up a rigorous and robust defence against unnecessary derogation. And the derogation model thus provides criteria against which the action and inaction of domestic institutions (both judicial and non-judicial) can be measured. But equally, if either the extra-legal measures model or the derogation model is preferred, then that will have corresponding normative implications for domestic authorities.

In practical terms, courts that are persuaded (to a greater or lesser degree) by the extra-legal measures model would, for example, establish zones of immunity from judicial standards and scrutiny. By contrast, courts that are persuaded by the limitation model will treat claims to derogation as they do limitations on rights. Such claims are claims to limit rights that are respected, rather than—as it has been suggested actually represents the nature of derogation—claims to step beyond the observance and respect of rights altogether.

The various models also starkly illuminate the difference between the UK Government's policy toward derogation before and after September 11. Before the September 11 attacks the Government's policy tracked the derogation model. The importance of withdrawing the UK's outstanding derogation relating to executive detention in Northern Ireland was clearly expressed in the White Paper on the Human Rights Bill[24] and was central to the enactment of the Terrorism Act 2000, which allowed the derogation to be withdrawn.[25] Introducing the Terrorism Bill, the then Home Secretary stated that: 'we will have handed the terrorists the victory that they seek if, in combating their threats and violence, we descend to their level and undermine the essential freedoms and rule of law that are the bedrock of our democracy.'[26] Although the Government apparently appreciated the fundamental tension between bringing rights home and suspending them, immediately following the September 11 attacks the Government, a mere nine months after the outstanding derogation was withdrawn,[27] sought once again to derogate from the Convention. Indeed, this was accompanied by a sea-change in the Government's

Joint Committee on Human Rights appears to view derogation from the perspective of the limitation model, eg 'Fifth Report 2002–2003', HL 59/HC 462 [23], [28].

[24] 'Rights Brought Home: The Human Rights Bill' (Cm 3782, 1997) [4.3]–[4.4]. See also the important limitations on the period for which derogations subsist embodied within the Human Rights Act (s 16).

[25] On the extent to which the importance of avoiding derogation completely overshadowed other ways that the 2000 Act might not be Convention compliant, see C Gearty, Terrorism and Human Rights' (1999) 19 *Legal Studies* 366; H Fenwick, *Civil Rights—New Labour, Freedom and the Human Rights Act* (Harlow, Longman, 2000).

[26] Jack Straw, MP, Hansard HC col 152 (14 December 1999). See also 'Legislation Against Terrorism—A Consultation Paper' (Cm 4178, 1998) eg [0.8] and [1.4]. See further Hansard HC vol 341 col 162 (14 December 1999) (Jack Straw). Admittedly, the derogation issue attracted a great deal more interest and discussion in the Lords. See eg Hansard HL cols 691–694 (24 May 2000) (Lord Bassam of Brighton) and col 690 (Lord Dubs), to similar effect.

[27] It was withdrawn in the UK in February 2001, but not in relation to the Isle of Man or the Channel Islands, see C Walker, *Blackstone's Guide to the Anti-Terrorism Legislation* (Oxford, Oxford University Press, 2002) 287–88.

attitude towards derogation. After September 11 the Government portrayed derogation as if it were a mere limitation on rights. Thus, incredibly, it saw fit to issue a statement of *compatibility* with Convention rights under section 19(1)(a) Human Rights Act in relation to ATCSA, apparently in the belief that laying the Designated Derogation Order before Parliament the day before the Bill was introduced rendered the proposed powers compatible with Convention rights (and although derogation did not actually occur until ATCSA came into force).[28] At the same time, the Home Secretary was reported as stating that derogation was a legal technicality[29] and, subsequently, the measures have been said not to require denial of traditional liberties but are merely about 'achieving a balance which maintains those rights'.[30]

Derogation in the House of Lords

We are now in a position to return to the decision of the House of Lords. The first aspect of the decision that bears on the nature and status of derogation in domestic law is the fact that the courts accepted the invitation to consider the validity of the UK's derogation at all. As Lord Scott pointed out, it is something of a 'puzzle' from the terms of the Human Rights Act why a derogation order should be thought to be unlawfully made if the legislative measure to which it refers deviates from the requirements of Article 15, since Article 15 itself is not given effect in domestic law by the Human Rights Act.[31] Lord Scott expressed 'doubts' that authority to designate a derogation under the Human Rights Act was 'limited by the terms of article 15'.[32] But such an approach would remove any substantive check on designation orders: it would be enough to disable the courts from testing legislation covered by a derogation order for conformity with the Convention rights that a derogation order had been formally made.[33] There would be no independent scrutiny of whether a national emergency existed or whether the

---

[28] In contrast to a statement of incompatibility under s 19(1)(b). See letter from David Blunkett to Chairman of the JCHR, 31 January 2003: 'Fifth Report 2002–2003' (n 23), Appendix 2. The Committee considered the Government's approach to be 'unacceptable' ([31]).

[29] In comments to *The Guardian* in November 2001 (reported and criticised in Human Rights Watch, 'United Kingdom—Human Rights Developments', *World Report 2002*, available at www.hrw.org).

[30] David Blunkett MP, 'Defending the Democratic State and Maintaining Liberty—Two Sides of the Same Coin?' speech to Harvard Law School, 8 March 2004. See further Lord Falconer, 'Human Rights and Constitutional Reform', lecture delivered to the Law Society and Human Rights Lawyers' Association, 17 February 2004 (the lectures are available at www.dca.gov.uk).

[31] *A (No 1)* (n 2) [151]. Moreover, s 30 of ATCSA purports to restrict the courts' jurisdiction to consider derogation issues, not to confer it. *Cf* [164] (Lord Walker).

[32] *A (No 1)* (n 2) [152] and [160].

[33] Human Rights Act s 1(2) qualifies 'Convention rights', to which legislation must conform, as the listed Articles 'subject to any designated derogation . . .'. Lord Scott appears to have overlooked this provision, since he also expresses puzzlement at what legal effect designated derogation has ibid [150]. The answer is that it disables the courts from invoking ss 3, 4 or 6 of the Human Rights Act.

derogation is strictly required and non-discriminatory. It truly would be the government 'who decides on the state of exception', and which would therefore enjoy uncontrolled sovereignty over the observance of Convention rights.[34] That would not be consistent with the idea that the Human Rights Act is a constitutional statute. Both the limitation model and the derogation model require that the reference in section 14(1) of the Human Rights Act to designated derogation as being 'derogation by the United Kingdom from an Article of the Convention' is interpreted to mean a derogation *valid* under Article 15 of the Convention.[35] The implicit requirement that any derogation referred to in a derogation order is itself valid is necessary to prevent the possibility of unreviewable executive opt-out of the human rights protection created by the Human Rights Act.

From the perspective of the derogation model of constitutionalism it is also crucial that the conditions for valid derogation are narrowly construed and strictly enforced. From this perspective, the rejection of the detainees' submissions on 'public emergency'—albeit both reluctant[36] and unsurprising—is disappointing. In particular, Lord Bingham's approach essentially absolves the Government from advancing clear and convincing evidence to Parliament and (if subsequently required by litigation) the courts to show that a public emergency threatening the life of the nation actually exists. There are three steps in Lord Bingham's reasoning on this point, and each is questionable. First, his Lordship reasoned that SIAC (which had concluded that there was a public emergency) had not misdirected itself in law, and since it had considered the closed material which the Attorney-General declined to ask the House of Lords to read, its decision should not be disturbed.[37] Bizarrely, by his own tactical decision not to show his hand, the Attorney-General was thus relieved from justifying his decision to the standard required by SIAC. Secondly, Lord Bingham approved and applied the extremely deferential Strasbourg case law on Article 15. His Lordship considered that to hold that there was no public emergency in such cases, where 'a response beyond that provided by the ordinary course of law was required, would have been perverse'.[38] With respect, this is backwards reasoning.[39] If one is to infer from the fact that exceptional measures have been taken that such measures are legitimate, then the criterion of legitimacy (ie public emergency) is relieved of substance. Moreover, the Strasbourg cases are expressly premised on the Court's especially restrained supervisory role in relation to Article 15, and have very little relevance to the approach to be taken by a national authority.

Then, thirdly, Lord Bingham stated that the Government's decision had to be shown to be 'wrong and unreasonable', and concluded that 'the appellants have

---

[34] Schmitt, *Political Theology* (n 15), 5.
[35] *A (No 1)* (n 2) [164] (Lord Walker) and [225] (Baroness Hale).
[36] Lord Bingham admitted to 'misgivings' (*A (No 1)* (n 2) [26]); Lord Scott expressed 'very great doubt' ([154]) and Lord Rodger had 'some hesitation' ([165]).
[37] *A (No 1)* (n 2) [27]. In accord: [166] (Lord Rodger); [226] (Lady Hale).
[38] ibid [28]. See also Lord Rodger at [165].
[39] Although the error is actually the Strasbourg Court's; see *Lawless* v *Ireland* (1961) 1 EHRR 15 [36]–[37].

shown no ground strong enough to warrant displacing the Secretary of State's decision on this important threshold question.'[40] Apparently, this burden fell on the applicants merely by the Government identifying an organisation with the capacity and will to commit an atrocity in the UK. This represents an extraordinarily light burden—indeed, one struggles to think of a recent period of history when it could not have been shown—and it seriously dilutes the threshold requirement that a public emergency exists.[41] Moreover, it is wrong in principle for a burden to be imposed on individuals to show that derogation from their human rights is unlawful. The Government should be required to advance convincing evidence for derogating from its obligation to observe our human rights. And as a practical matter, it is difficult to envisage circumstances in which individuals will ever be able to disprove the Government's view that an emergency exists, not least because the relevant evidence will be in the hands of the Government.

It was Lord Hoffmann's dissenting decision on this issue that grabbed the headlines. Like Lord Bingham, Lord Hoffmann did not suggest that the Government has a heavy burden of proof. But he did hold, with respect rightly, that it is insufficient merely to produce evidence of a credible plot to commit terrorist outrages, since that does not meet the need to show that terrorism was 'threatening the life of the nation'. Moreover, in Lord Hoffmann's view the threshold for the exercise of the UK's emergency exit from Convention rights should refer only to exceptional threats to the fabric of the state itself:

> Of course the Government has a duty to protect the lives and property of its citizens. But that is a duty which it owes all the time and which it must discharge without destroying our constitutional freedoms. There may be some nations too fragile or fissiparous to withstand a serious act of violence. But that is not the case in the United Kingdom. When Milton urged the government of his day not to censor the press even in time of civil war, he said: 'Lords and Commons of England, consider what nation is whereof ye are, and whereof ye are the governors.[42]

In so holding, Lord Hoffmann demanded that the Government not be merely fair-weather supporters of human rights. 'The real threat to the life of the nation', he claimed, is laws derogating from human rights.[43] However, we must not be under any illusions that Lord Hoffmann is actually supportive of the derogation model of constitutionalism. Lord Hoffmann's speech must be read together with his speech in *Rehman*, which some commentators have thought to be inconsistent with his speech in *A (No 1)*. There is in fact no inconsistency. In *Rehman*, his

---

[40] *A (No 1)* (n 2) [29].
[41] ibid [25]. Likewise Lord Hope seriously diluted the 'emergency' threshold. His Lordship held that the 'picture which emerges' from the broad brushstrokes of the Government's evidence on the question was that there is a current state of emergency, and this despite the fact that Lord Hope held that there was no threat of imminent attack and therefore that the level of emergency was 'of a different kind, or on a different level' than if the threat were ever to materialise ([119]). Lord Scott also gave the Home Secretary 'the benefit of the doubt' ([154]).
[42] ibid [95].
[43] ibid [97].

Lordship held that although the meaning of the word 'national security' is a matter for the courts, the question of whether measures were needed 'in the interests of' national security was 'not a matter for judicial decision' and was 'entrusted to the executive'.[44] This reasoning is in accord with the extra-legal measures model, based as it is on there being zones of judicial immunity, free from rule or scrutiny, subject to accountability, if at all, only through the political process. Applying the logic of his remarks in *Rehman*, the condition of 'public emergency' was the only condition for derogation that could be enforced by the courts with any rigour, since its meaning, like that of 'national security', is a question of law for the courts. By contrast, what measures are 'strictly required' to meet an emergency (like what is 'in the interests of' national security) is, in Lord Hoffmann's view, a matter that is for the executives and not the courts. This explains why his Lordship was conspicuously reticent on the question of whether the powers were discriminatory and, moreover, why on the question of whether they were 'strictly required' he suggested that the court should only ask whether the Government's view was 'irrational'.[45] Had Lord Hoffmann considered that the evidence established the existence of national emergency, he would have recognised few legal restraints on executive discretion. Enthusiasm for the rhetorical exuberance of Lord Hoffmann's speech is therefore misplaced.[46]

As we have seen, Lord Bingham, unlike Lord Hoffmann, found against the Government on the question whether indefinite detention was 'strictly required'. In so holding, his Lordship rejected a submission of the Attorney-General closely resembling Lord Hoffmann's approach in *Rehman* that it was for Parliament and the executive, and not the courts, to judge the response necessary to protect the public. Lord Bingham pointed out that it is 'a cardinal feature of the modern democratic state' that the independent judiciary interpret and apply the law. The courts should not therefore relinquish their responsibility to fulfil this role on the basis that they are not elected or answerable to Parliament.[47] This elucidation of the separation of powers in terms of a separation of functions represents a welcome and important statement of constitutional principle that properly affirms a commitment to the rule of law as understood in modern liberal democracies.[48]

Nonetheless, Lord Bingham's approach to the question of whether the measures were 'strictly required' cannot be said to represent an endorsement of the derogation model. His Lordship treated the question of derogation as if it were an

---

[44] *Home Secretary v Rehman* [2003] 1 AC 153 [50]. Lord Hoffmann concluded: 'Accordingly it seems to me that the Commission is not entitled to differ from the opinion of the Secretary of State on the question of whether, for example, the promotion of terrorism in a foreign country by a United Kingdom resident would be contrary to the interests of national security' ([53]).

[45] *A (No 1)* (n 2) [97].

[46] Indeed, Lord Hoffmann relied as much on rhetoric as reasoning. In fact, one can easily become disorientated reading through the speech: whilst he repeatedly speaks of the traditions of 'this country' his references oscillate dizzyingly between the historic rights of English, British and UK citizens.

[47] *A (No 1)* (n 2) [42].

[48] On which see further, TR Hickman, 'In Defence of the Legal Constitution' [2005] 55 *University of Toronto Law Journal* 981.

ordinary limitation on rights by applying the pervasive (but by no means universal) standard applicable to test such limitations, namely, proportionality. Lord Bingham stated that the Convention 'imposes a test of strict necessity or, in Convention terminology, proportionality'.[49] This is unfortunate. We have previously considered the statement of principle in *Handyside v United Kingdom* in which the Strasbourg Court expressly differentiated the 'strictly required' standard in Article 15 from the ordinary standard of necessity which the Court (but, *contra* Lord Bingham, not the *Convention)* translates into the principle of proportionality. The Court articulated three tiers of standards found in the Convention: reasonableness (found in Articles 5(3) and 6(1)), necessity (found eg in Article 10(2)) and indispensability.[50] Indispensability was associated with the phrase 'strictly required' in Article 15 and the phrase 'absolutely necessary' in Article 2(2).[51] Subsequently the Court has stated:

> . . . the use of the term 'absolutely necessary' in Article 2(2) indicates that a stricter and more compelling test of necessity must be employed from that normally applicable when determining whether state action is 'necessary in a democratic society' under paragraph 2 of Articles 8 to 11 of the Convention. In particular, the force used must be strictly proportionate to the achievement of the aims set out in sub-paragraphs 2(a), (b) and (c) of Article 2.[52]

By contrast to Article 2, the stricter standard of necessity is justified in the context of Article 15 not by the importance of the right at stake, but by the nature of the measure, which is to take a state outside the human rights regime. In failing to observe the difference between the strictly required standard and the ordinary proportionality standard, Lord Bingham failed to appreciate that derogation is of a different order from ordinary limitations on rights, and the need for the judiciary to guard even more jealously against political attempts at derogation. More generally, Lord Bingham's approach represents a manifestation of the desire of some judges and academics to adopt a monistic approach to legal justification based on a context-specific application of the proportionality standard to all questions under the Convention and even in public law as a whole.[53] Such an approach obscures fundamental structural differences in the Convention scheme that forms part of the UK's own constitutional architecture.

It is therefore welcome that Lords Hope, Scott and Rodger and Lady Hale all stressed the significance of the 'strictly required' standard and by so doing their speeches are more closely aligned with the derogation model.[54] Lord Hope held

---

[49] *A (No 1)* (n 2) [30].
[50] *Handyside v United Kingdom* (1976) 1 EHRR 737 [48]. See further *Silver v United Kingdom* (1983) 5 EHRR 439 [97].
[51] See ch 4.
[52] *McCann and Others v United Kingdom* (1995) 21 EHRR. 97 [149]. Although the court famously split 9–10 in the case, on this point it was unanimous.
[53] See ch 9.
[54] *McCann* (n 52) [155] (Lord Scott); [172] (Lord Rodger); [227] and [231] (Lady Hale). This is also the approach of the Joint Committee on Human Rights, eg 'Sixth Report, 2003–2004' [34].

that the ordinary proportionality approach, encapsulated in the Charter jurisprudence of the Canadian Supreme Court, 'does not fit the precise wording of article 15(1) as to the standard that must be achieved by the derogation'. His Lordship considered that it was therefore inappropriate to give any leeway to the legislator on whether less intrusive measures were available.[55] He held that whilst disrupting the activities of non-nationals suspected of being terrorists had been obviously desirable, it had not been shown that indefinite detention was strictly required.[56] Of course, in the circumstances of the case Lord Bingham's approach led to precisely the same result; but it may not always do so. The 'strictly required' test invites the Government to show, without any initial evidence from which the contrary is to be inferred, that it has considered the alternatives and that no less intrusive possibility exists. It demands the most anxious scrutiny by the courts and insists upon convincing evidence that even carefully tailored measures are indispensable. Where measures are more widely framed than they need to be, it will be extremely difficult—if not impossible—to show that they are strictly required.

The Constitutional Context

Whilst the House of Lords' decision in *A (No 1)* represents a welcome defence of the rule of law, in several key respects it also represents a disappointing defence of the UK's newly established human rights regime. When measured against the derogation model of constitutionalism, weaknesses and inadequacies in the decision are exposed.

A full appreciation of the decision requires, however, a wider appraisal of the constitutional context and its place within the complex and complementary arrangement of checks and balances under the UK's peculiar constitutional arrangements. Even in this regard, a sobering comparison can be drawn with the uncompromising conclusions of the Newton Committee which, in its review of ATCSA in December 2003, identified the need to derogate from the Convention as a problem of principle with the detention powers and recommended new legislation that did not require derogation. It more fully embraced the derogation model than the House of Lords has done. The consequences of the Newton Committee's report also appear to be more significant than the consequences of the House of Lords' decision. Whereas the declaration of incompatibility granted by the House of Lords had no effect whatsoever on the continued enforceability and validity of the detention powers, the Newton Committee exercised its authority to specify that ATCSA would cease to have effect in the absence of confirmation by Parliamentary motion within six months of the date its report was laid.[57]

---

[55] *A (No 1)* (n 2) [131].

[56] ibid [124]–[132].

[57] Privy Council Review Committee, *ATCSA Review: Report* (London: The Stationary Office, 2003) pursuant to s 123 ATCSA.

However, although undoubtedly important, the seemingly more robust consti-tutional check provided by the Newton Committee masks a more subtle and important constitutional reality. The Newton Committee provided a very partial institutional mechanism for protecting against unnecessary derogation. It was not a standing committee. Its powers were ad hoc, the result of governmental conces-sion, and it was far from free from the potential for governmental influence.[58] It was, moreover, only the Law Lords' decision that provoked a full—albeit rushed—Parliamentary re-consideration and which led to new legislation in the form of the Prevention of Terrorism Act 2005, which established a regime of 'control orders' which can be imposed on persons suspected of involvement in terrorism-related activity, whether they are nationals or non-nationals. The control order regime was designed so that it did not require derogation from Article 5. The most signif-icant impact of the Newton Committee report may in fact have been in fortifying their Lordships in holding that the detention powers breached the Convention, which is what led directly to the control order regime.[59]

The nature of the political debate that the Law Lords' ruling provoked is also of considerable importance. The political debate did not question the *correctness* of the decision. Rather, the Government took the view that it would be constitutionally inappropriate to renew the detention powers in the face of it. The Government's view was that before the powers came up for renewal, the law should be made *com-patible* with the House of Lords' ruling. Introducing the Prevention of Terrorism Bill for its second reading, the Home Secretary explained that a 'motivating prin-ciple' behind it was 'the need to meet the Law Lords' judgment'. He stated that, 'we should not ignore the judgment or flout it, but act on it and try to put in place a regime that is both proportionate and not discriminatory'.[60] The only question was how best this was to be achieved. It was not therefore a political debate such as that envisaged by Lord Scott, who suggested that the judicial task in relation to declara-tions of incompatibility under the Human Rights Act is merely to provide 'ammu-nition to those who disapprove of the Act and desire to agitate for its amendment or repeal'.[61] It was not a political debate *with* the Law Lords or about their interpreta-tion of fundamental principles. Their Lordships were not taken to have proposed

---

[58] Notably, the Government held the Committee's purse-strings (although there was in fact no question of Governmental influence).
[59] See for example the lengthy extract cited by Lord Bingham, *A (No 1)* (n 2) [34].
[60] Charles Clarke MP, Hansard HC vol 431 cols 345–46 (23 February 2005). Another, and over-lapping, motivating principle for the Bill was the fact that the Government anticipated a (successful) challenge in the ECtHR on the basis that the detainees would not have been afforded an effective rem-edy in domestic law, as guaranteed by Art 13, if the powers had simply been renewed (see ibid col 347).
[61] *A (No 1)* (n 2) [145] (Lord Scott). Lord Scott stated that a court's function in granting a declara-tion of incompatibility is 'political not legal' ([142]). His comments reflect what has been described as 'principle-proposing dialogue' (see ch 3). It is crucial that, whatever approach is actually adopted by Parliamentarians, the courts fulfil their function under the Human Rights Act on the basis that they are the ultimate bastions of the rule of law and human rights, not that they can merely propose arguments of principle to the other branches. Whilst Parliament undoubtedly retains power to deviate from judi-cial decisions, it must do so, as Lord Hoffmann stated, 'in full knowledge that the law does not accord with our constitutional traditions' ([90]).

their considered view on the requirements of constitutional justice for consideration and resolution by politicians. They were taken to have resolved the question of
what the Convention requires. The political debate was informed by, but ultimately
took place within, the parameters of principle as expounded in their Lordships'
speeches.[62] Whilst Lord Scott's comments are therefore of some concern, the treatment of the status of the decision by the Government and Parliament is greatly to be
welcomed. It is entirely in accordance with the form of constitutionalism at the
heart of the Human Rights Act and the respective constitutional functions that it
envisages.[63] It is of cardinal importance that under the Human Rights Act the courts
are understood to retain their function of determining questions of rights and set-
tling disputes of principle. The Human Rights Act has enhanced this role, as well as
enhancing the exchange and dialogue with the other branches of the state.

Despite the apparently limited nature of the relief granted by the House of
Lords, both the constitutional significance and impact of the decision are therefore
of the highest order. The decision is of central importance to an understanding of
our constitution and of constitutionalism in the Human Rights Act era.

The Strasbourg Postscript

On 19 February 2009 the ECtHR handed down its judgment in *A v United
Kingdom*, a petition brought by 11 individuals detained under section 23 of
ATCSA, including the claimants in *A (No 1)*. The ECtHR permitted the
Government to run a new argument,[64] that the detentions had been justified
under Article 5(1)(f) because the individuals were being detained whilst action
was being taken with a view to their deportation. The Court rejected this submission, noting that it had been a principal assumption in the derogation notice, the
detention powers in ATCSA and the decision to detain the applicants (and one
might add, in the argument before the House of Lords) that the individuals could
not be deported for the time being. Indeed, the Court held that there was no real-
istic prospect of deporting the individuals, given the UK's obligations not to
deport individuals to face torture, and in the case of one applicants, the fact that
he was stateless. The men had not therefore been detained in order to deport them,
as no deportation was possible, and the detention was not therefore properly to be
regarded as immigration detention.[65]

---

[62] Interestingly, Charles Clarke admitted that behind-the-scenes 'informal discussions' were taking
place with senior members of the judiciary as to the Bill's compatibility with Convention rights: see
Hansard HC vol 431 col 346 (23 February 2005).

[63] This is developed as the notion of strong form constitutional dialogue, in ch 3.

[64] Suggested by Finnis, 'Nationality, Alienage and Constitutional Principle' (n 10), 423–29.

[65] *A v United Kingdom* (2009) 49 EHRR 29, [171]. The Court held that keeping the possibility
of deportation under review was not sufficient, and the UK had not sought to secure diplomatic
assurances from the governments of the home states until much later. The ECtHR did reach a different conclusion in the case of two of the applicants, one of whom had been detained for three days and

The ECtHR went on to uphold the House of Lords' judgment on the question of national emergency, without any great scrutiny of the issue. The applicants had mainly pinned their colours to Lord Hoffmann's mast, which provided a relatively clear point of law on the meaning of national emergency with which to attempt to circumnavigate the margin of appreciation doctrine. Rejecting Lord Hoffmann's approach, the ECtHR said that it was unnecessary to show that 'the institutions of the State' are 'imperiled' by a threat, at least 'to the extent envisaged by Lord Hoffmann'. It then observed that domestic authorities have a wide margin of appreciation and that domestic authorities, including the courts, are better placed to assess the actual situation in the UK, and their views were to be given 'significant weight'. The Court concluded without reasoning that it shared the view of the majority of the House of Lords that there was a public emergency threatening the life of the nation.[66] The Court also gave considerable weight to the views of the majority of the House of Lords on the question of whether the measures were 'strictly required'. Rejecting the Government's submissions, it stated only that, 'having regard to the careful way in which the House of Lords approached the issues, it cannot be said that inadequate weight was given to the views of the executive of Parliament'. As to discrimination, the Court stated that the House of Lords had been correct to reject the submission that the powers were immigration measures and therefore the power was discriminatory.[67]

On all of these points the judgment of the ECtHR added very little to the UK case law. By far the most significant part of the judgment was the ECtHR's consideration of Articles 5(4) and 6, and its finding that persons detained on suspicion of involvement in terrorism must at a minimum be told sufficient of the material relied upon against them to enable them to challenge their detention effectively. Disclosure of material to 'special advocates' appointed to represent the interests of the detainees, but who could not take instructions on closed material, was not sufficient to provide the detainees with a fair hearing.[68] This was a point which the claimants had lost in the Court of Appeal in *A (No 1)*, and the issue had not been pursued on appeal to the House of Lords.

The principle of fairness articulated in *A v United Kingdom* was applied by the House of Lords to the control order regime under the Prevention of Terrorism Act 2005 in *AF (No 3) v Secretary of State for the Home Department*, a case argued less then two weeks after the judgment in *A v United Kingdom* had been handed down. Their Lordships held that although persons subjected to non-derogating control orders are not deprived of their liberty, and so Article 5(4) is not in play, the right

---

the other for three months. Both had left the UK voluntarily. The Court held that during these periods, the UK Government was still in the process of investigating their nationalities and other details, and therefore action was being taken with a view to deportation ([166]–[170]).

[66] *A v UK* (n 65) [181]–[182].

[67] ibid [184] and [186]. The Court also rejected the Government's argument that it was entitled to target non-nationals because they were the 'most serious source' of the threat. The ECtHR noted that this was contrary to the findings of SIAC, which had held that the threat emanated just as much from UK citizens.

[68] ibid [220].

to a fair trial under Article 6 of the European Convention requires that they be told sufficient information about the case against them to enable them to provide a defence and to effectively challenge the Government's case. The ECtHR's judgment nonetheless had a mixed reception in the Judicial Committee. On the one hand, Lord Phillips, giving the leading speech, reasoned that the approach taken by the ECtHR was supported by principle and policy, Lord Hope thought that it was integral to the rule of law, Lord Scott said that the common law would have reached the same result and Baroness Hale indicated that it accorded with her own views. But on the other hand, Lord Carswell, Lord Brown and Lord Hoffmann applied *A v United Kingdom* with barely disguised hostility, and Lord Rodger and Lord Walker applied it without endorsement (although agreeing with the reasoning of Lord Phillips). At the time of writing, the meaning and breadth of application of the principle of fairness articulated in *A v United Kingdom* and *AF (No 3)* remain uncertain and are still being worked out in the courts.[69] However, the Government appears to have decided not to attempt to derogate from Article 6, and is therefore continuing with its attempt to pursue a counter-terrorism strategy that is within the human rights regime and not outside it. This is greatly to be welcomed and is a direct result of the robustness of the House of Lords' decision in *A (No 1)* in defending human rights.

---

[69] See, eg *R (BB) v Secretary of State for the Home Department* [2009] EWHC 2927 (Admin) (application to 'light touch' control orders); *R (U) v Secretary of State for the Home Department* [2009] EWHC 3052 (application to SIAC bail).

INDEX

Introductory Note

References such as '178–9' indicate (not necessarily continuous) discussion of a topic across a range of pages. Wherever possible in the case of topics with many references, these have either been divided into sub-topics or only the most significant discussions of the topic are listed. Because the entire volume is about the 'Human Rights Act' and 'public law', the use of these terms (and certain others which occur constantly throughout the book) as entry points has been minimised. Information will be found under the corresponding detailed topics.

Index

indefinite, 9, 35, 331–3, 341, 343
  pending deportation, 331–3
  powers, 331–3, 335, 343–5
dialogic constitutional theories, 69–81, 97
  principle-proposing dialogue, 60, 69–72, 81,
    87–8, 90, 344
  strong form dialogue, 71–89
  weak form dialogue, 69–71
dialogue, 4, 59–60, 63–4, 66–8, 72–4, 82–3,
    96–7
  constitutional, 57–60, 62–4, 66, 69–82, 84,
    86–8
  principle-proposing, 60, 69–72, 81, 87–8, 90,
    344
  strong form, 71–89
  weak form, 69–71
Dicey, Albert Venn, 12–16, 65, 71–2, 76–82,
    94–5, 108, 332
disability discrimination, 252–4
disclosure, 88, 138, 141, 153, 207, 226, 288
discretion, 111–12, 180–1, 196–7, 199–200,
    209–12, 224–5, 318
  statutory, 13, 102, 196, 202–5, 210–12
discretionary area of judgment, 98, 123–5, 129,
    131, 139
discretionary decisions, 23, 194, 211, 224
discretionary powers, 196–7, 202, 206, 210,
    317
discrimination, 40, 46, 85–6, 163–4, 252–5,
    331–3, 346
  disability, 252–4
disproportionate interference, 112, 131, 146,
    170, 178, 326
distinctions, formal, 258–9, 261, 297
doctrinal approach, 129, 137–9, 141–2, 168–9,
    172
domestic authorities, 112, 114, 124–5, 213,
    243–4, 337, 346
domestic constitutional rights, 30, 36, 41, 48
domestic law, 15–19, 21–3, 25–7, 31, 41–4,
    316–17, 324–6
domestic public law, 17, 27, 101, 103, 128, 132,
    230
domestic rights, 27, 42, 45, 308–9, 328
  constitutional, 30, 36, 41, 48
  new, 26–7, 31, 44
dual-limb approach, 301, 303–4
dual-limb test, 301–10, 313
  revival, 307–10
  and right of access to court, 301–5
due deference, 124, 131, 137, 153, 270
due regard, 252–6
duty of care, 53–4, 204–5, 209, 214, 222,
    299–300, 312–13
Dworkin, Ronald, 16–17, 67–9, 73, 75–6, 78, 87,
    109
Dyzenhaus, David, 25, 130–1, 153, 270, 273,
    290–1, 336

ECtHR *see* European Court of Human Rights
effective remedy, 7, 23, 29, 31, 50, 62, 95
effectiveness, 73, 180, 182, 184, 192, 273–4
emergencies, 86, 170, 330–47
  see also derogation
equality, 17, 24, 75, 238, 252–3, 255, 272
  equality duties, 253–6
  legal equality, 8, 299, 327–9
error of law, 100, 201, 204, 259, 262
European Convention on Human Rights and
    Fundamental Freedoms *see Table of
    Legislation*
European Court of Human Rights (ECtHR),
    especially, 29–34, 36–46, 115–25,
    213–19, 242–4, 299–302, 323–8
  derogation postscript, 345–7
  and domestic courts, 243–4
  internal divisions, 324–8
  Matthews case, 323–4
  and reasonableness, 213–16
eviction, 178
evidence, 131–2, 146, 153–5, 171–2, 221,
    239–40, 339–41
Ewing, Keith, 16, 22, 60
executive decisions, 67, 98, 160, 170, 261, 264,
    289
expectations, legitimate expectations, 258, 269,
    272, 278–80, 283–4
expediency, 2, 60, 71–2, 74–5, 80, 84, 97
experience, 135–8, 141–2, 145–50, 153, 201, 239
expertise, 137–9, 141–50, 152–3, 167, 176, 238–9
expression, freedom of, 19–21, 30, 51, 151, 227,
    233, 264–7
extra-legal measures model, 334–7, 341

fair balance, 117, 121, 157, 172, 179–93, 215–16
fair trial, 88, 94, 277, 303, 347
fairness, 4, 16, 65, 128, 244, 259, 346–7
  procedural, 141, 266, 272, 317, 321
false imprisonment, 14–15, 19
fault, 120, 303–5
Finnis, John, 332–3, 345
forced labour, 116–18, 274, 325
foreign nationals *see* non-nationals
formal distinctions, 258–9, 261, 297
formal legality, 64–6
formalism,
  in process review, 244–52
  and structure of public law, 261
Forsyth, Christopher, 200, 258, 269–70, 284
France, 12, 36, 44, 79, 120, 122, 124
freedom of expression, 19–21, 30, 51, 151, 227,
    233, 264–7
freedom of religion, 187
fundamental common law rights, 51, 105, 107,
    173, 267, 298
fundamental principles, 2, 7, 66–7, 71–4, 79–80,
    106–7, 300

Index